Special Edition: GAAP Financial Statement Disclosures Manual

by George Georgiades, CPA

Highlights

CCH's *Special Edition: GAAP Financial Statement Disclosures Manual* provides a complete, quick, and valuable reference source for financial statement disclosures and key presentation requirements.

Specifically, the Manual contains over 750 examples of realistic sample footnote disclosures to assist in the preparation of financial statements for an audit, a review, or a compilation engagement; facilitates compliance with U.S. generally accepted accounting principles (GAAP) by integrating the specific disclosure requirements with the sample footnotes; and incorporates all currently effective accounting standards, including those that cover areas of unusual difficulty, such as financial instruments, fair value, business combinations, consolidation, income taxes, pensions, accounting changes, and variable interest entities. In addition, as further discussed below, this edition has been completely reorganized consistent with the broad structure of the *FASB Accounting Standards Codification*™.

The Manual also includes a financial statement disclosures checklist that provides a centralized resource of the required and recommended GAAP disclosures and key presentation items currently in effect, using the style referencing under the *FASB Accounting Standards Codification*™ as well as references to pre-Codification FASB literature.

All of the sample disclosures in this Manual, along with the financial statement disclosures checklist, are included on the CD-ROM that accompanies this book.

Special Edition

On July 1, 2009, the Financial Accounting Standards Board (FASB) officially launched the *FASB Accounting Standards Codification*™

(FASB ASC or Codification), which has become the single official source of authoritative, nongovernmental U.S. GAAP, in addition to guidance issued by the Securities and Exchange Commission (SEC). FASB ASC supersedes all prior FASB, AICPA, EITF, and related literature. Essentially, the GAAP hierarchy is now comprised of two levels: one that is authoritative (in the Codification) and one that is nonauthoritative (not in the Codification). The Codification, which is effective for interim and annual periods ending after September 15, 2009, is organized into approximately 90 accounting topics. The FASB no longer issues new standards in the form of Statements, FASB Staff Positions, or Emerging Issues Task Force Abstracts. Instead, amendments to the Codification are made by issuing "Accounting Standards Updates" that will display an issue date expressed as the year with a sequential number for each update (e.g., 2009-02 is the second update in the year 2009).

The Codification content is arranged within (*a*) Topics, (*b*) Subtopics, (*c*) Sections, and (*d*) Subsections, as follows:

- Topics. Topics represent a collection of related guidance and reside in five main areas: (1) *general principles* (e.g., generally accepted accounting principles); (2) *presentation* (e.g., income statement, balance sheet); (3) *financial statement accounts* (e.g., assets, liabilities, equity); (4) *broad transactions* (e.g., business combinations, derivatives and hedging); and (5) *industry* (e.g., airlines, real estate).

- Subtopics. Subtopics represent subsets of a "Topic" and are generally distinguished by type or by scope. For example, "Operating Leases" and "Capital Leases" are two Subtopics of the "Leases" Topic.

- Sections. Sections represent the nature of the content in a "Subtopic" (e.g., recognition, measurement, disclosure).

- Subsections. Sections are further broken down into subsections, paragraphs, and subparagraphs.

The following is the structure of the Codification classification system: XXX-YY-ZZ-PP, where:

XXX	=	Topic
YY	=	Subtopic
ZZ	=	Section
PP	=	Paragraph

Thus, for example, the following is a sample reference for receivables:

ASC 310 = Receivables (Topic)
ASC 310-10 = Overall (Subtopic)
ASC 310-10-50 = Disclosure (Section)

Each chapter of this Manual includes references to the Codification using this classification system and is preceded by the acronym "ASC."

The *Special Edition* is intended to be used as a guide for determining whether the financial statements of for-profit type entities include the disclosures and key presentation requirements as required by U.S. GAAP. The guidance in this Manual has been conformed to reflect reference to FASB ASC using the style referencing under the Codification. In addition, to facilitate an effective and efficient transition, the disclosure and key presentation requirements reference pre-Codification FASB literature as well. However, users should be cautioned that financial statements issued for interim and annual periods ending after September 15, 2009, should use FASB ASC style referencing.

This Manual is arranged into the following major parts, consistent with the Codification's broad structure:

- Part 1—General Principles (Topic Codes 100s)
- Part 2—Presentation (Topic Codes 200s)
- Part 3—Assets (Topic Codes 300s)
- Part 4—Liabilities (Topic Codes 400s)
- Part 5—Equity (Topic Codes 500s)
- Part 6—Revenue (Topic Codes 600s)
- Part 7—Expenses (Topic Codes 700s)
- Part 8—Broad Transactions (Topic Codes 800s)
- Part 9—Other

Special Edition: GAAP Financial Statement Disclosures Manual is current through FASB Accounting Standards Update No. 2009-13, *Revenue Recognition (Topic 605)—Multiple-Deliverable Revenue Arrangements*.

Unless specifically indicated, the examples provided assume that the most recent financial statements presented are for the year ended December 31, 20X2.

CCH Learning Center

CCH's goal is to provide you with the clearest, most concise, and up-to-date accounting and auditing information to help further your professional development, as well as a convenient method to help you satisfy your continuing professional education requirements. The CCH Learning Center* offers a complete line of self-study courses covering complex and constantly evolving accounting and auditing issues. We are continually adding new courses to the library to help you stay current on all the latest developments. The CCH Learning Center courses are available 24 hours a day, seven days a week. You'll get immediate exam results and certification. To view our complete accounting and auditing course catalog, go to: **http://cch.learningcenter.com.**

Accounting Research Manager™

Accounting Research Manager is the most comprehensive, up-to-date, and objective online database of financial reporting literature. It includes all authoritative and proposed accounting, auditing, and SEC literature, plus independent, expert-written interpretive guidance.

Our Weekly Summary e-mail newsletter highlights the key developments of the week, giving you the assurance that you have the most current information. It provides links to new FASB, AICPA, SEC, PCAOB, EITF, and IASB authoritative and proposal-stage literature, plus insightful guidance from financial reporting experts.

Our outstanding team of content experts takes pride in updating the system on a daily basis, so you stay as current as possible. You'll learn of newly released literature and deliberations of current financial reporting projects as soon as they occur! Plus, you'll benefit from their easy-to-understand technical translations.

----

* CCH is registered with the National Association of State Boards of Accountancy (NASBA) as a sponsor of continuing professional education on the National Registry of CPE Sponsors. State boards of accountancy have final authority on the acceptance of individual courses for CPE credit. Complaints regarding registered sponsors may be addressed to the National Registry of CPE Sponsors, 150 Fourth Avenue North, Nashville, TN 37219-2417. Telephone: 615-880-4200.

* CCH is registered with the National Association of State Boards of Accountancy as a Quality Assurance Service (QAS) sponsor of continuing professional education. Participating state boards of accountancy have final authority on the acceptance of individual courses for CPE credit. Complaints regarding QAS program sponsors may be addressed to NASBA, 150 Fourth Avenue North, Suite 700, Nashville, TN37219-2417. Telephone: 615-880-4200.

With **Accounting Research Manager**, you maximize the efficiency of your research time while enhancing your results. Learn more about our content, our experts, and how you can request a FREE trial by visiting us at **http://www.accountingresearchmanager.com.**

12/09

For questions concerning this shipment, billing or other customer service matters, call 1 800 248 3248.

SPECIAL EDITION

GAAP

FINANCIAL STATEMENT DISCLOSURES MANUAL

GEORGE GEORGIADES, CPA

CCH
a Wolters Kluwer business

ISBN: 978-0-8080-2283-1

© 2009 CCH. All Rights Reserved.
4025 W. Peterson Ave.
Chicago, IL 60646-6085
1 800 248 3248
http://CCHGroup.com

Portions of this work were published in a previous edition.

Printed in the United States of America

Our Peer Review Policy

Thank you for ordering the *Special Edition: GAAP Financial Statement Disclosures Manual*. Each year we bring you the best accounting and auditing reference guides available. To confirm the technical accuracy and quality control of our materials, CCH voluntarily submitted to a peer review of our publishing system and our publications (see the Peer Review Statement on the following page).

In addition to peer review, our publications undergo strict technical and content reviews by qualified practitioners. This ensures that our books and electronic workpapers meet "real-world" standards and applicability.

Our publications are reviewed every step of the way—from conception to production—to ensure that we bring you the finest guides on the market.

Updated annually, peer reviewed, technically accurate, convenient, and practical—the *Special Edition: GAAP Financial Statement Disclosures Manual* shows our commitment to creating books and electronic workpapers you can trust.

Note that the most recent Peer Review Statement will be included in our next edition and is available upon request by emailing: sandra.lim@wolterskluwer.com.

Caldwell, Becker, Dervin, Petrick & Co., L.L.P.
CERTIFIED PUBLIC ACCOUNTANTS

April 25, 2006

Executive Board
CCH, a Wolters Kluwer business

We have reviewed the system of quality control for the development and maintenance of GAAP Financial Statement Disclosures Manual (2006–2007 Edition), of CCH, a Wolters Kluwer business (the company), applicable to non-SEC issuers in effect for the year ended March 31, 2006, and the resultant materials in effect at March 31, 2006. The design of the system, and compliance with it, are the responsibilities of the company. Our responsibility is to express an opinion on the design of the system, and the company's compliance with that system based on our review.

Our review was conducted in accordance with the standards for reviews of quality control materials promulgated by the Peer Review Committee of the Center for Public Company Audit Firms of the American Institute of Certified Public Accountants. In performing our review, we have given consideration to the following general characteristics of a system of quality control. A company's system for the development and maintenance of quality control materials encompasses its organizational structure and the policies and procedures established to provide the users of its materials with reasonable assurance that the quality control materials are reliable aids to assist them in conforming with professional standards in conducting their accounting and auditing practices. The extent of a company's quality control policies and procedures for the development and maintenance of quality control materials and the manner in which they are implemented will depend upon a variety of factors, such as the size and organizational structure of the company and the nature of the materials provided to users. Variance in individual performance and professional interpretation affects the degree of compliance with prescribed quality control policies and procedures. Therefore, adherence to all policies and procedures in every case may not be possible.

Our review and tests were limited to the system of quality control for the development and maintenance of the aforementioned quality control materials of CCH and to the materials themselves and did not extend to the application of these materials by users of the materials nor to the policies and procedures of individual users.

In our opinion, the system of quality control for the development and maintenance of the quality control materials of CCH was suitably designed and was being complied with during the year ended March 31, 2006, to provide users of the materials with reasonable assurance that the materials are reliable aids to assist them in conforming with those professional standards in the United States of America applicable to non-SEC issuers. Also, in our opinion, the quality control materials referred to above are reliable aids at March 31, 2006.

CALDWELL, BECKER, DERVIN, PETRICK & CO., LLP.
CALDWELL, BECKER, DERVIN, PETRICK & CO., L.L.P.

20750 Ventura Boulevard, Suite 140 • Woodland Hills, CA 91364
(818) 704-1040 • FAX (818) 704-5536

Contents

Part 4—Liabilities

Part 5—Equity

Part 6—Revenue

Part 7—Expenses

Part 8—Broad Transactions

Preface

The *Special Edition: GAAP Financial Statement Disclosures Manual* provides a complete, quick, and valuable reference source for financial statement disclosures and key presentation requirements. Specifically, the Manual:

- Provides over 750 examples of realistic sample footnote disclosures to assist in the preparation of financial statements for an audit, a review, or a compilation engagement.
- Facilitates compliance with U.S. GAAP by integrating, in each chapter, the specific disclosure and key presentation requirements with the sample footnotes.
- Provides sample disclosures that are technically sound, understandable, and comprehensive and that cover a variety of scenarios, from the most common to the most unusual.
- Incorporates all currently effective accounting standards, including those that cover areas of unusual difficulty, such as financial instruments, fair value, business combinations, consolidation, income taxes, pensions, accounting changes, and variable interest entities.

All of the sample disclosures in the *Special Edition: GAAP Financial Statement Disclosures Manual* are included on the accompanying CD-ROM. Therefore, once you've identified the disclosure suited to your specific needs, you can simply select it from the CD-ROM, place it into your financial statements, then modify it as necessary.

This Manual is arranged into the following major parts, consistent with the Codification's broad structure:

- Part 1—General Principles (Topic Codes 100s)
- Part 2—Presentation (Topic Codes 200s)
- Part 3—Assets (Topic Codes 300s)
- Part 4—Liabilities (Topic Codes 400s)
- Part 5—Equity (Topic Codes 500s)
- Part 6—Revenue (Topic Codes 600s)
- Part 7—Expenses (Topic Codes 700s)
- Part 8—Broad Transactions (Topic Codes 800s)
- Part 9—Other

The Manual is designed for ease of use. Accordingly, each chapter is structured as a stand-alone chapter, providing you with all the information you'll need on a specific topic. The majority of chapters consist of the following parts:

1. **Executive Summary.** This summary provides a clear and concise discussion of the specific financial statement topic.

2. **Accounting Literature.** This section provides reference to the relevant FASB ASC Topic, as well as reference to pre-Codification accounting literature so that you can access the information quickly and easily.

3. **Disclosure and Key Presentation Requirements.** This section provides a detailed listing of (a) the disclosure requirements (FASB ASC Section 50) and (b) those key presentation requirements (FASB ASC Section 45) that are relevant to enhance compliance with and better understand the disclosure requirements. This section also provides specific references to the FASB ASC paragraphs and the related pre-Codification literature that prescribe the specific disclosure or key presentation requirement.

4. **Examples of Financial Statement Disclosures.** This section contains specific examples of disclosures that cover different situations, circumstances, assumptions, and so on. Unless specifically indicated, the examples provided assume that the most recent financial statements presented are for the year ended December 31, 20X2. It should be noted that references to authoritative literature in financial statements and related footnotes should be conformed to FASB ASC rather than to pre-Codification standards, effective for interim and annual periods ending after September 15, 2009.

The Manual also includes a financial statement disclosures checklist that provides a centralized resource of the required and recommended GAAP disclosures and key presentation items currently in effect, using the style referencing under the *FASB Accounting Standards Codification*™ as well as references to pre-Codification FASB literature. It is designed to assist the user in determining whether the required financial statement disclosures and key presentation matters have been addressed. The *Special Edition: GAAP Financial Statement Disclosures Manual* is current through FASB Accounting Standards Update No. 2009-13, *Revenue Recognition (Topic 605)—Multiple-Deliverable Revenue Arrangements*.

The author and publisher welcome comments, suggestions, and recommendations to improve this Manual. These will be considered for incorporation in future revisions of the Manual. Please send your comments to Sandra Lim, sandra.lim@wolterskluwer.com.

Acknowledgments

Thanks are due to the staff of CCH, especially to Sandra Lim, Developmental Editor, for her efforts in overseeing the production of the manual and to Curt Berkowitz, Senior Manuscript Editor, for bringing this edition to press. The author and publisher also thank Vincent J. Love, CPA, for his thorough review and comments on the Manual as this year's special edition got under way. Also, I thank my dear wife, Caroline, for her continuous patience and encouragement. She has spent many late hours meticulously verifying references to authoritative literature, and this special edition would not have been possible without her generous contribution of time, talent, and support. We are both grateful to our wonderful sons, Alex and Dmitri, for their inspiration and constant source of energy and joy.

George Georgiades
Laguna Niguel, California

About the Author

George Georgiades, CPA, has more than 29 years of experience in public accounting, including seven years as an audit senior manager with a major international accounting firm. He currently has his own firm and consults exclusively with CPA firms on technical accounting, auditing, and financial statement disclosure issues. In writing this Manual, Mr. Georgiades has capitalized on the extensive experience he has gained from association with clients and with international, national, regional, and local accounting firms. He has been personally involved in more than 600 audit engagements and related financial statements of both small, closely held companies and large, publicly held enterprises. He has personally conducted more than 75 peer reviews, consulting reviews, and inspections. He also brings to the Manual extensive hands-on experience in performing independent technical reviews of financial statements.

Mr. Georgiades is also the author of the *GAAS Practice Manual* and the *GAAS Update Service*. He is a member of the American Institute of Certified Public Accountants and the California Society of Certified Public Accountants, and served on the California Society of CPAs' Peer Review Committee.

PART 1—
GENERAL PRINCIPLES

CHAPTER 1
ASC TOPIC 105: GENERALLY ACCEPTED ACCOUNTING PRINCIPLES

CONTENTS

EXECUTIVE SUMMARY

Generally Accepted Accounting Principles

ASC Topic 105 establishes the FASB Accounting Standards Codification™ (Codification) as the source of authoritative generally accepted accounting principles (GAAP) recognized by the FASB to be applied by nongovernmental entities. Rules and interpretive releases of the Securities and Exchange Commission (SEC) under authority of federal securities laws are also sources of authoritative GAAP for SEC registrants.

All guidance contained in the Codification carries an equal level of authority. Accounting and financial reporting practices not included in the Codification are nonauthoritative (e.g., FASB Concepts Statements; AICPA Issues Papers; and accounting textbooks, handbooks, and articles).

The FASB no longer issues new standards in the form of Statements, FASB Staff Positions, or Emerging Issues Task Force Abstracts. Instead, amendments to the Codification are made by issuing "Accounting Standards Updates" that will display an issue date expressed as the year with a sequential number for each update (e.g., 2009-03 is the third update in the year 2009). Accounting Standards Updates are not considered authoritative in their own right; rather, they serve only to update the Codification, provide background information about the guidance, and provide the bases for conclusions on changes in the Codification.

Accounting Literature

FASB Accounting Standards Codification Topic	*Pre-Codification Accounting Literature*
105, *Generally Accepted Accounting Principles*	FAS-168, *The "FASB Accounting Standards Codification™" and the Hierarchy of Generally Accepted Accounting Principles*

DISCLOSURE AND KEY PRESENTATION REQUIREMENTS

1. For nonpublic nongovernmental entities that have not previously followed the guidance included in the AICPA Technical Inquiry Service (TIS) Section 5100, "Revenue Recognition," paragraphs 38–76:

   a. Those entities should account for the adoption of that guidance as a change in accounting principle on a prospective basis for revenue arrangements entered into or materially modified in those fiscal years beginning on or after December 15, 2009, and interim periods within those years (ASC 105-10-65-1) (FAS -168, par. 14).

   b. If an accounting change results from the application of that guidance, the entity should disclose the nature and reason for the change in accounting principle (ASC 105-10-65-1) (FAS-168, par. 14).

2. The effect, if any, of applying the provisions of the Codification should be accounted for as a change in accounting principle or correction of an error, as applicable, in accordance with ASC Section 250-10-50, *Accounting Changes and Error Corrections—Overall—Disclosure*. In addition, the entity should disclose the accounting principles that were used before and after the application of the provisions of the Codification and the reason that applying the Codification resulted in a change in accounting principle or correction of an error (ASC 105-10-65-1) (FAS-168, par. 16). See Chapter 9, "ASC Topic 250: Accounting Changes and Error Corrections."

EXAMPLES OF FINANCIAL STATEMENT DISCLOSURES

For sample disclosures relating to accounting changes and error corrections, see Chapter 9, "ASC Topic 250: Accounting Changes and Error Corrections."

PART 2—
PRESENTATION

CHAPTER 2
ASC TOPIC 205: PRESENTATION OF FINANCIAL STATEMENTS

CONTENTS

EXECUTIVE SUMMARY

Overall

The presentation of comparative financial statements enhances the usefulness of annual and interim reports. Although not required, ordinarily it is desirable that financial statements of two or more periods be presented. Footnotes and explanations that appeared on the statements for the preceding years should be repeated, or at least referred to, in the comparative statements to the extent that they continue to be of significance.

It is necessary that prior-year figures shown for comparative purposes be comparable with those shown for the most recent period, or that any exceptions to comparability be clearly identified and described.

Discontinued Operations

The results of discontinued operations, less applicable income taxes, should be reported as a separate component of income before extraordinary items. A gain or loss recognized on the disposal should be disclosed either on the face of the income statement or in the notes to the financial statements.

Adjustments to amounts previously reported in discontinued operations that are directly related to the disposal of a component of an entity in a prior period should be classified separately in the current period in discontinued operations. In addition, the nature and amount of such adjustments should be disclosed.

The assets and liabilities of discontinued operations should be presented separately in the asset and liability sections, respectively, of the balance sheet. Those assets and liabilities should not be offset and presented as a single amount.

Accounting Literature

FASB Accounting Standards Codification Topic	*Pre-Codification Accounting Literature*
205, *Presentation of Financial Statements*	FAS-144, *Accounting for the Impairment or Disposal of Long-Lived Assets*
	EITF 87-24, *Allocation of Interest to Discontinued Operations*
	EITF 03-13, *Applying the Conditions in Paragraph 42 of FASB Statement No. 144 in Determining Whether to Report Discontinued Operations*
	ARB-43, Chapter 2A, *Comparative Financial Statements*

DISCLOSURE AND KEY PRESENTATION REQUIREMENTS

Overall

1. If comparative financial statements are presented, the prior-year figures should be shown for comparative purposes comparable with those shown for the most recent period, and any exceptions to comparability should be adequately considered and addressed. (ASC 205-10-45-3) (ARB-43, Ch. 2A, par. 3) (*Note:* Although not required, the presentation of comparative financial statements is ordinarily desirable.)

2. The notes to financial statements, explanations, and accountants' reports containing qualifications that appeared on the statements for the preceding years should be repeated, or at least referred to, in the comparative statements to the extent that they continue to be of significance. (ASC 205-10-45-4) (ARB-43, Ch. 2A, par. 2)

3. If, because of reclassifications or for other reasons, changes have occurred in the manner of or basis for presenting corresponding items for two or more periods, information should be disclosed that will explain the change. (ASC 205-10-50-1) (ARB-43, Ch. 2A, par. 2)

Discontinued Operations

1. The results of operations of a component of an entity that either has been disposed of or is classified as held for sale

should be reported in discontinued operations if (a) the operations and cash flows of the component have been, or will be, eliminated from the ongoing operations of the entity, and (b) the entity will not have any significant continuing involvement in the operations of the component after the disposal transaction. (ASC 205-20-45-1) (FAS-144, par. 42)

2. The following presentation and disclosure matters should be addressed for each period in which a component of an entity has been disposed of or is classified as held for sale:

   a. Results of operations of the component, including any gain or loss on disposal and less applicable income taxes (benefit), reported as a separate component of income before extraordinary items (if applicable). (ASC 205-20-45-3) (FAS-144, par. 43)

   b. Adjustments made to amounts previously reported in discontinued operations (that are directly related to the disposal of a component of an entity in a prior period) classified separately in the current period in discontinued operations, and disclosure of the nature and amount of such adjustments. (ASC 205-20-45-4; 205-20-50-5) (FAS-144, par. 44)

   c. A description of the facts and circumstances leading to the expected disposal, the expected manner and timing of that disposal, and if not separately presented on the face of the balance sheet, the carrying amounts of the major classes of assets and liabilities included as part of the disposal group. (ASC 205-20-50-1) (FAS-144, par. 47)

   d. Gain or loss recognized on the disposal disclosed either (a) on the face of the income statement or (b) in the notes to financial statements (including the caption in the income statement that includes that gain or loss). (ASC 205-20-45-3; 205-20-50-1) (FAS-144, pars. 43 and 47)

   e. The amounts of revenue and pretax profit or loss reported in discontinued operations. (ASC 205-20-50-1) (FAS-144, par. 47)

   f. If applicable, the segment in which the long-lived asset (disposal group) is reported. (ASC 205-20-50-1) (FAS-144, par. 47)

   g. The assets and liabilities held for sale presented separately in the asset and liability sections of the balance sheet, with the major classes of such assets and liabilities separately disclosed either on the face of the balance sheet or in the notes. (ASC 205-20-45-10; 205-20-50-2) (FAS-144, par. 46) (*Note:* The assets and liabilities held for sale should *not* be offset and presented as a single amount in the balance sheet.)

3. Interest on debt that is to be assumed by the buyer and interest on debt that is required to be repaid as a result of a disposal transaction should be allocated to discontinued operations. (ASC 205-20-45-6 through 45-8) (EITF 87-24)

4. General corporate overhead should *not* be allocated to discontinued operations. (ASC 205-20-45-9) (EITF 87-24)

5. If an entity decides not to sell a long-lived asset (disposal group) previously classified as held for sale, or removes an individual asset or liability from a disposal group previously classified as held for sale, the following disclosures should be made in the financial statements that include the period of that decision (ASC 205-20-50-3) (FAS-144, par. 48):

   a. A description of the facts and circumstances leading to the decision to change the plan to sell the long-lived asset (disposal group).

   b. The effect on the results of operations for all periods presented.

6. For each discontinued operation that generates continuing cash flows, the following disclosures should be made (ASC 205-20-50-4) (EITF 03-13):

   a. The nature of the activities that give rise to continuing cash flows.

   b. The period of time continuing cash flows are expected to be generated.

   c. The principal factors used to conclude that the expected continuing cash flows are not direct cash flows of the disposed component.

7. If there is a continuation of activities between the ongoing entity and the disposed component after the disposal transaction (ASC 205-20-50-6) (EITF 03-13):

   a. If the ongoing entity's activities include continuation of revenues and expenses that were previously eliminated intercompany transactions (for purposes of the consolidated financial statements) before the disposal transaction, disclosures should be made of the intercompany amounts before the disposal transaction for all periods presented.

   b. In the period in which operations are initially classified as discontinued, disclosures should be made of the types of continuing involvement with the component, if any, that the entity will have after the disposal transaction.

8. If the criteria for classification as held for sale for a long-lived asset (disposal group) are met after the balance sheet date, but before the financial statements are issued or are available to be issued, the long-lived asset (disposal group) should continue to be classified as held and used in those financial statements, and the following information should be disclosed (ASC 360-10-45-13; 205-20-50-1(a)) (FAS-144, par. 33):

   a. A description of the facts and circumstances leading to the expected disposal.

   b. The expected manner and timing of the disposal.

   c. The carrying amount(s) of the major classes of assets and liabilities included as part of a disposal group, if not separately presented on the face of the balance sheet.

EXAMPLES OF FINANCIAL STATEMENT DISCLOSURES

 The following sample disclosures are available on the accompanying disc.

Overall

Example 1: Reclassifications of a General Nature

Certain amounts in the prior periods presented have been reclassified to conform to the current period financial statement presentation. These reclassifications have no effect on previously reported net income.

Example 2: Reclassifications Are Described in Detail

In 20X2, the Company's presentation of certain expenses within its income statements was changed, as follows:

- Depreciation expense recorded in connection with the manufacture of the Company's products sold during each reporting period is now included in the caption "Cost of sales." Depreciation expense not associated with the manufacture of the Company's products and amortization expense are now included in the caption "Selling and administrative expenses." Depreciation and amortization expense were previously combined and reported in the caption "Depreciation and amortization."

- Certain operating income and expense items previously included in the caption "Other income, net" have been reclassified to "Selling and administrative expenses."

In connection with these reclassifications, the Company added the captions "Gross profit" and "Operating income" to its income statements. The Company believes that this change in presentation provides a more meaningful measure of its cost of sales and selling and administrative expenses and that gross profit and operating income are useful, widely accepted measures of profitability and operating performance. These reclassifications had no effect on previously reported income before income taxes and net income.

Amounts presented for the year ended December 31, 20X1, have been reclassified to conform to the current presentation. The following table provides the amounts reclassified for the year ended December 31, 20X1:

Amounts reclassified:	
Cost of sales	$ 3,700,000
Selling and administrative expenses	1,000,000
Depreciation and amortization	(4,500,000)
Other income, net	(200,000)

Discontinued Operations

Example 3: Presentation of Discontinued Operations in an Income Statement That Does Not Include Extraordinary Items

	20X2	20X1
Income from continuing operations before income taxes	$ 3,117,000	$2,018,000
Provision for income taxes	(1,311,000)	(827,000)
Income from continuing operations	1,806,000	1,191,000
Discontinued operations:		
Loss from operations of discontinued Minimed Component (including loss on disposal of $322,000 in 20X2)	(925,000)	(790,000)
Income tax benefit	375,000	280,000
Loss on discontinued operations	(550,000)	(510,000)
Net income	$ 1,256,000	$ 681,000

Example 4: Presentation of Discontinued Operations in an Income Statement That Includes Extraordinary Item

	20X2	20X1
Income from continuing operations before income taxes	$ 3,117,000	$2,018,000
Provision for income taxes	(1,311,000)	(827,000)
Income from continuing operations	1,806,000	1,191,000
Discontinued operations:		
Loss from operations of discontinued Minimed Component (including loss on disposal of $322,000 in 20X2)	(925,000)	(790,000)
Income tax benefit	375,000	280,000
Loss on discontinued operations	(550,000)	(510,000)
Income before extraordinary item	1,256,000	681,000
Extraordinary item, net of income tax expense of $682,000 (Note X)	1,100,000	-0-
Net income	$ 2,356,000	$ 681,000

Example 5: Disclosure of Discontinued Operations in the Period in Which a Component of an Entity Is Classified as Held for Sale

On September 1, 20X2, the Company determined to discontinue operations at its Paramount division, a manufacturer of electronic power systems, and put the assets and business up for sale. The Company decided to sell this division primarily because it has incurred significant operating losses in each of the last four years and because the division has lost significant market share in the last two years. The expected disposal date is June 1, 20X3. Paramount's sales, reported in discontinued operations, for the years ended December 31, 20X2, and December 31, 20X1, were $7,359,000 and $6,986,000, respectively. Paramount's pretax loss, reported in discontinued operations, for the years ended December 31, 20X2, and December 31, 20X1, were $603,000 and $790,000, respectively. Prior year financial statements for 20X1 have been restated to present the operations of the Paramount division as a discontinued operation.

In conjunction with the discontinuance of operations, the Company recognized a loss of $322,000 in 20X2 to write down the related carrying amounts to their fair values less cost to sell. The assets and liabilities of the discontinued operations are presented separately under the captions "Assets of discontinued division" and "Liabilities of discontinued division," respectively, in the accompanying Balance Sheets at December 31, 20X2 and December 31, 20X1, and consist of the following:

	20X2	20X1
Assets of discontinued division:		
Accounts receivable	$ 403,000	$3,488,000
Inventories	622,000	723,000
Property and equipment, net	1,954,000	1,995,000
Other assets	123,000	100,000
Total assets	$3,102,000	$6,306,000
Liabilities of discontinued division:		
Accounts payable	$ 862,000	$1,156,000
Accrued liabilities	134,000	221,000
Total liabilities	$ 996,000	$1,377,000

Note: The following table illustrates the reporting of the discontinued operations on the face of the Statements of Operations for the years ended December 31, 20X2, and December 31, 20X1.

	20X2	20X1
Income from continuing operations before income taxes	$ 3,117,000	$2,018,000
Provision for income taxes	(1,311,000)	(827,000)
Income from continuing operations	1,806,000	1,191,000
Discontinued operations:		
Loss from operations of discontinued Minimed Component (including loss on disposal of $322,000 in 20X2)	(925,000)	(790,000)
Income tax benefit	375,000	280,000
Loss on discontinued operations	(550,000)	(510,000)
Net income	$ 1,256,000	$ 681,000

Example 6: Disclosure of Discontinued Operations in the Period in Which a Component of an Entity Has Been Sold

Note: For this example, assume the same background information as in Example 3, but the financial statements presented are for the years ended December 31, 20X3 (the year of disposal), and December 31, 20X2.

On September 1, 20X2, the Company determined to discontinue operations at its Paramount division, a manufacturer of electronic power systems, and put the assets and business up for sale. The Company decided to sell this division primarily because it has incurred significant operating losses in each of the last four years and because the division has lost significant market share in the last two years. On June 1, 20X3, the Company completed the sale of this division for total cash proceeds of $1,730,000. The assets sold consisted primarily of accounts receivable, inventories, property and equipment, and other assets. The buyer also assumed certain accounts payable and accrued liabilities.

In 20X2, the Company recognized a loss on disposal of $322,000 for the initial write-down of the division's carrying amounts to fair value less cost to sell. In 20X3, the actual loss on the sale of net assets totaled $380,000. Accordingly, the accompanying Statement of Operations for 20X3 includes an additional loss of $58,000.

Paramount's sales, reported in discontinued operations, for the five months ended May 31, 20X3, and for the year ended December 31, 20X2, were $2,863,000 and $7,359,000, respectively. Paramount's pretax loss, reported in discontinued operations, for the five months ended May 31, 20X3, and for the year ended December 31, 20X2, were $275,000 and $603,000, respectively.

The following is a summary of the net assets sold as initially determined at December 31, 20X2 and as finally reported on the closing date of June 1, 20X3:

	June 1, 20X3	December 31, 20X2
Accounts receivable	$ 387,000	$ 403,000
Inventories	602,000	622,000
Property and equipment, net	1,904,000	1,954,000
Other assets	100,000	123,000
Total assets	2,993,000	3,102,000
Accounts payable	858,000	862,000
Accrued liabilities	125,000	134,000
Total liabilities	983,000	996,000
Net assets of discontinued operations	$2,010,000	$2,106,000

> **Note:** The following table illustrates the reporting of the discontinued operations on the face of the Statements of Operations for the years ended December 31, 20X3, and December 31, 20X2.

	20X3	20X2
Income from continuing operations before income taxes	$ 3,692,000	$ 3,117,000
Provision for income taxes	(1,552,000)	(1,311,000)
Income from continuing operations	2,140,000	1,806,000
Discontinued operations:		
Loss from operations of discontinued Minimed Component (including loss on disposal of $58,000 in 20X3 and $322,000 in 20X2)	(333,000)	(925,000)
Income tax benefit	135,000	375,000
Loss on discontinued operations	(198,000)	(550,000)
Net income	$ 1,942,000	$ 1,256,000

Example 7: Adjustment of Loss Reported in a Prior Period on Discontinued Operations

In 20X1, the Company sold all of the assets, net of certain liabilities, associated with its Stretchflex product line. The loss on disposal of this segment recognized in 20X1 was $940,000. In 20X2, the Company revised its loss on disposal of the segment by $200,000 for the estimated loss on a note received in connection with the sale. A tax benefit was not recorded on this loss in 20X2 due to limitations on current tax recognition.

> **Note:** The following table illustrates the reporting of the adjustment of loss on the face of the Statements of Operations.

	20X2	20X1
Income from continuing operations before income taxes	$1,563,000	$1,832,000
Provision for income taxes	(601,000)	(658,000)
Income from continuing operations	962,000	1,174,000
Discontinued operations:		
Income from operations of discontinued segment, net of income tax expense of $382,000	-0-	609,000

	20X2	20X1
Loss on disposal of business segment, net of income tax benefit of $576,000 in 20X1	(200,000)	(940,000)
Loss on discontinued operations	(200,000)	(331,000)
Net income	$ 762,000	$ 843,000

Example 8: Subsequent Event—Long-Lived Assets to Be Disposed of by Sale

On January 24, 20X3, the Company signed a definitive agreement to sell its Aquatech retail and wholesale distribution business unit. The Company anticipates the sale to be completed by June 30, 20X3. The asset group involved was tested for recoverability as of the balance sheet date; accordingly, an impairment loss of $500,000 was recognized which represents the amount by which the carrying amount of the asset group exceeded its fair value at the balance-sheet date.

The assets and liabilities of Aquatech are comprised of the following at December 31, 20X2, and December 31, 20X1:

	20X2	20X1
Assets:		
Accounts receivable	$ 637,000	$ 418,000
Inventories	3,570,000	2,913,000
Other current assets	37,000	22,000
Property, plant and equipment, net	1,322,000	1,174,000
Other assets	62,000	65,000
Total assets	$5,628,000	$4,592,000
Liabilities:		
Accounts payable	$1,698,000	$1,996,000
Accrued liabilities	211,000	678,000
Other noncurrent liabilities	35,000	47,000
Total liabilities	$1,944,000	$2,721,000

CHAPTER 3
ASC TOPIC 210: BALANCE SHEET

CONTENTS

EXECUTIVE SUMMARY

Overall

The distinction between current and noncurrent assets and liabilities in a classified balance sheet is an important feature of financial reporting because considerable interest in the liquidity of the reporting enterprise exists. One way to measure a company's liquidity is to have separate classification of current assets and liabilities. Therefore, classified balance sheets should present current assets and current liabilities separately from other assets and liabilities. Resources that are expected to be realized in cash, sold, or consumed during the next year (or operating cycle, if longer) are classified as *current assets*. Assets not expected to be realized within one year (or operating cycle, if longer) should be included as *noncurrent*. Asset valuation allowances (e.g., uncollectible accounts) should be deducted from the assets to which they relate.

The major assets are generally presented in the following order:

- Cash
- Short-term investments (including marketable securities)
- Trade accounts receivable

- Inventories
- Long-term investments (including marketable securities)
- Property, plant, and equipment
- Intangible assets
- Other noncurrent assets (e.g., deferred charges, deposits)

Current liabilities are obligations that are reasonably expected to be settled by either liquidating current assets or creating other current liabilities. Current liabilities include obligations that, by their terms, are due and payable on demand. Current liabilities may be listed on the balance sheet in order of maturity, according to amount (largest to smallest), or in order of liquidation preference. However, generally, trade accounts payable or short-term debt is listed first and a catchall caption such as "Other liabilities" or "Accrued expenses" is typically listed last. Current liabilities typically include the following:

- Trade accounts payable
- Short-term debt (e.g., notes and loans, including borrowings under line of credit arrangements)
- Current maturities of long-term debt
- Current maturities of capital lease obligations
- Employee-related liabilities (e.g., salaries, wages, bonuses, commissions, and related benefits)
- Taxes (e.g., income taxes payable, deferred income taxes, and sales taxes)
- Dividends payable
- Accrued interest
- Customer deposits and advances
- Deferred income
- Accrued expenses (e.g., product warranties, royalties)

Long-term liabilities primarily consist of debt obligations (e.g., bonds, mortgages, notes, and capital leases), deferred income taxes, and a catchall caption such as "Other long-term liabilities."

If several "Other liabilities" type items (current or noncurrent) are included as a single line item in the balance sheet, and the amount is material, it is generally informative to include the details of such items in a note to the financial statements.

Offsetting

Offsetting assets and liabilities (i.e., the display of a recognized asset and a recognized liability as one net amount in a financial statement) is improper except where a right of setoff exists. The following four criteria must be met for the right to offset assets and liabilities to exist:

1. Each party owes the other party specific amounts.

2. The reporting party has the right to set off the amount payable, by contract or other agreement, with the amount receivable from the other party.

3. The reporting party intends to set off.

4. The right of setoff is enforceable by law.

Accounting Literature

FASB Accounting Standards Codification Topic	*Pre-Codification Accounting Literature*
210, *Balance Sheet*	FAS-6, *Classification of Short-Term Obligations Expected to Be Refinanced*
	FIN-39, *Offsetting of Amounts Related to Certain Contracts*
	APB-10, *Omnibus Opinion—1966*
	ARB-43, Chapter 3A, *Current Assets and Current Liabilities*

DISCLOSURE AND KEY PRESENTATION REQUIREMENTS

Overall

1. A one-year time period should be used as a basis for the segregation of current assets in cases where there are several operating cycles occurring within a year. (ASC 210-10-45-3) (ARB-43, Ch. 3A, par. 5) (*Note*: If the period of the operating cycle is more than 12 months, the longer period should be used. If a particular entity has no clearly defined operating cycle, the one-year rule should govern.)

2. If a classified balance sheet is used:

    a. A total of current assets should be presented. (Generally accepted practice)

    b.   A total of current liabilities should be presented. (ASC 210-10-45-5) (FAS-6, par. 15)

3.   If the amounts of the periodic payments of an obligation are, by contract, measured by current transactions (e.g., by rents or revenues received in the case of equipment trust certificates), the portion of the total obligation to be included as a current liability should represent the amount accrued at the balance sheet date. (ASC 210-10-45-11) (ARB-43, Ch. 3A, par. 8)

4.   The amounts at which current assets are stated should be supplemented by information that discloses, for the various classifications of inventory items, the basis upon which their amounts are stated and, where practicable, indication of the method of determining the cost (e.g., average cost, FIFO, LIFO). (ASC 210-10-50-1) (ARB-43, Ch. 3A, par. 9)

Offsetting

1.   If an entity decides to offset a related asset and a liability, the required setoff criteria should be met. (ASC 210-20-45-1) (FIN-39, par. 5)

2.   If an entity does not intend to offset a related asset and a liability, even though the ability to offset exists, the related amounts should *not* be offset in the balance sheet. (ASC 210-20-45-4) (FIN-39, par. 45)

3.   Cash or other assets should *not* be offset against the tax liability or other amounts owing to governmental bodies (except when governments issue securities that are specifically designated as being acceptable for the payment of taxes of those governments). (ASC 210-20-45-6 and 45-7; 740-10-45-13) (APB-10, par. 7)

EXAMPLES OF FINANCIAL STATEMENT DISCLOSURES

See individual chapters relating to specific balance sheet accounts for examples of financial statement disclosures.

CHAPTER 4
ASC TOPIC 215: STATEMENT OF SHAREHOLDER EQUITY

The disclosure and key presentation requirements for items that comprise shareholders' equity are discussed in detail in ASC Topic 505, *Equity*. For further guidance, see Chapter 34, "ASC Topic 505: Equity."

CHAPTER 5
ASC TOPIC 220: COMPREHENSIVE INCOME

CONTENTS

EXECUTIVE SUMMARY

Comprehensive Income

Generally accepted accounting principles (GAAP) require comprehensive income and its components to be reported when a company presents a full set of financial statements that report financial position, results of operations, and cash flows. The term *comprehensive income* refers to net income plus other comprehensive income, that is, certain revenues, expenses, gains, and losses that are reported as separate components of stockholders' equity instead of net income. Examples of other comprehensive income include the following:

1. Unrealized gains and losses on certain investments in debt and equity securities
2. Foreign currency translation adjustments
3. Gains and losses, prior service costs or credits, and transition assets or obligations associated with pension or other postretirement benefits

An entity is required to (1) present items of other comprehensive income by their nature in a financial statement *and* (2) display the accumulated balance of other comprehensive income separately from retained earnings and additional paid-in capital in the equity section of a balance sheet.

In addition, if an entity has an outstanding noncontrolling interest: (1) amounts for both comprehensive income attributable to the parent and comprehensive income attributable to the noncontrolling interest in a less-than-wholly-owned subsidiary should be reported on the face of the financial statement in which comprehensive income is presented in addition to presenting consolidated comprehensive income; and (2) components of other comprehensive income attributable to the parent and noncontrolling interest in a less-than-wholly-owned subsidiary should be disclosed as part of the entity's equity reconciliation.

Accounting Literature

FASB Accounting Standards Codification Topic	*Pre-Codification Accounting Literature*
220, *Comprehensive Income*	FAS-130, *Reporting Comprehensive Income*
815, *Derivatives and Hedging*	FAS-133, *Accounting for Derivative Instruments and Hedging Activities*
	FAS-160, *Noncontrolling Interests in Consolidated Financial Statements*

DISCLOSURE AND KEY PRESENTATION REQUIREMENTS

1. Components of comprehensive income and total comprehensive income should be displayed in one of the following three alternative presentation formats (ASC 220-10-45-1 through 45-14) (FAS-130, pars. 14 and 22):

    a. In a single statement of income and comprehensive income that extends a traditional income statement to include (following net income) the components of other comprehensive income and the total of comprehensive income.

    b. In a separate statement of comprehensive income that begins with net income and includes the components of other comprehensive incomeand then a total of comprehensive income.

    c. In the statement of changes in equity.

    Note: The presentation and disclosure requirements in item 2 below are prescribed by ASC Topic 810, *Consolidation*, based on FAS-160, *Noncontrolling Interests in Consolidated Financial Statements,* and should be applied retrospectively for all periods presented. These requirements are effective for fiscal years, and interim periods within those fiscal years, beginning on or after December 15, 2008. Early adoption is not permitted.

2. If an entity has an outstanding noncontrolling interest (minority interest):

    a. Amounts for both comprehensive income attributable to the parent and comprehensive income attributable to the noncontrolling interest in a less-than-wholly-owned subsidiary should be reported on the face of the financial statement in which comprehensive income is presented in addition to presenting consolidated comprehensive income. (ASC 220-10-45-5; 810-10-50-1A(a)) (FAS-160, Appendix C, par. C9)

    b. The components of other comprehensive income attributable to the parent and noncontrolling interest in a less-than-wholly-owned subsidiary should be disclosed as part of the entity's equity reconciliation. (ASC 220-10-45-8; 810-10-50-1A(c)) (FAS-160, Appendix C, par. C9)

3. Components of other comprehensive income should be shown either: (a) net of related tax effects or (b) before related tax effects with one amount shown for the aggregate income tax expense or benefit related to the total of other comprehensive income items. (ASC 220-10-45-11) (FAS-130, par. 24)

4. The amount of income tax expense or benefit allocated to each component of other comprehensive income, including reclassification adjustments, should be disclosed either: (a) on the face of the financial statement in which the components are displayed or (b) in the notes to the financial statements. (ASC 220-10-45-12) (FAS-130, par. 25)

5. The accumulated balance of other comprehensive income should be reported separately from retained earnings and additional paid-in capital in the equity section of the balance sheet. (ASC 220-10-45-14) (FAS-130, par. 26)

6. The ending accumulated balances for each item in accumulated other comprehensive income should be disclosed either: (a) on the face of the balance sheet, (b) in a statement of changes in equity, or (c) in the notes to the financial statements. (ASC 220-10-45-14) (FAS-130, par. 26)

7. Reclassification adjustments for each classification of other comprehensive income should be disclosed either: (a) on the face of the financial statement in which comprehensive income is reported or (b) in the notes to the financial statements. (ASC 220-10-45-17) (FAS-130, par. 20)

8. For interim-period reporting, a total for comprehensive income should be reported in condensed financial statements. (ASC 220-10-45-18) (FAS-130, par. 27)

9. For derivative instruments and hedging activities, the following disclosures should be made (ASC 815-30-45-1; 815-30-50-2) (FAS-133, pars. 46–47):

   a. The net gain or loss on derivative instruments designated and qualifying as cash flow hedging instruments reported as a separate classification within other comprehensive income.

   b. As part of the disclosures of accumulated other comprehensive income:

      (1) The beginning and ending accumulated derivative instrument gain or loss.

      (2) The related net change associated with current period hedging transactions.

      (3) The net amount of any reclassification into earnings.

EXAMPLES OF FINANCIAL STATEMENT DISCLOSURES

The following sample disclosures are available on the accompanying disc.

Example 1: Comprehensive Income Reported in a Single Statement of Income and Comprehensive Income

ABC Company
Statement of Income and Comprehensive Income
Years Ended December 31, 20X2, and December 31, 20X1

	20X2	20X1
Revenues	$ 12,760,000	$ 11,312,000
Costs and expenses	(12,663,000)	(11,226,000)
Other income and expenses, net	10,000	5,000
Income from operations before tax	107,000	91,000
Income tax expense	(44,000)	(37,000)
Net income	63,000	54,000
Other comprehensive income, net of tax:		
Unrealized gains on securities:		
Unrealized holding gains arising during the period	13,000	18,000
Less: reclassification adjustment for gains included in net income	(2,000)	(4,000)
	11,000	14,000
Defined benefit pension plans:		
Prior service cost arising during the period	(1,100)	(3,200)
Net loss arising during the period	(1,000)	(2,000)
Less: amortization of prior service cost included in net periodic pension cost	100	200
	(2,000)	(5,000)
Foreign currency translation adjustment	8,000	3,000
Other comprehensive income, net of tax	17,000	12,000
Comprehensive income	$ 80,000	$ 66,000

Note: Components of other comprehensive income also could be displayed on a before tax basis, with one amount shown for the aggregate income tax effect as follows:

	20X2	20X1
Net income	$ 63,000	$ 54,000
Other comprehensive income, before tax:		
Unrealized gains on securities:		
Unrealized holding gains arising during the period	18,000	26,000
Less: reclassification adjustment for gains included in net income	(3,000)	(6,000)
	15,000	20,000
Defined benefit pension plans:		
Prior service cost arising during the period	(2,650)	(6,350)
Net loss arising during the period	(1,500)	(3,000)
Less: amortization of prior service cost included in net periodic pension cost	150	350
	(4,000)	(9,000)
Foreign currency translation adjustment	11,000	4,000
Other comprehensive income, before tax	22,000	15,000
Income tax expense related to items of other comprehensive income	(5,000)	(3,000)
Other comprehensive income, net of tax	17,000	12,000
Comprehensive income	$ 80,000	$ 66,000

Example 2: Comprehensive Income Reported in a Separate Statement of Comprehensive Income

ABC Company
Statement of Income and Comprehensive Income
Years Ended December 31, 20X2, and December 31, 20X1

	20X2	20X1
Net income	$63,000	$54,000
Other comprehensive income, net of tax:		
Unrealized gains on securities:		
Unrealized holding gains arising during the period	13,000	18,000

	20X2	20X1
Less: reclassification adjustment for gains included in net income	(2,000)	(4,000)
	11,000	14,000
Defined benefit pension plans:		
Prior service cost arising during the period	(1,100)	(3,200)
Net loss arising during the period	(1,000)	(2,000)
Less: amortization of prior service cost included in net periodic pension cost	100	200
	(2,000)	(5,000)
Foreign currency translation adjustment	8,000	3,000
Other comprehensive income, net of tax	17,000	12,000
Comprehensive income	$ 80,000	$ 66,000

Note: Components of other comprehensive income also could be displayed on a before tax basis, with one amount shown for the aggregate income tax effect, as illustrated in Example 1 above.

Example 3: Comprehensive Income Reported in a Statement of Changes in Equity

ABC Company
Statement of Changes in Stockholders' Equity
Years Ended December 31, 20X2, and December 31, 20X1

	Common Stock Shares	Common Stock Amount	Additional Paid-in Capital	Retained Earnings	Accumulated Other Com- prehensive Income	Total
Balance at December 31, 20X0	$1,250,000	$125,000	$250,000	$49,000	$ 13,000	$437,000
Comprehensive income:						
Net income				54,000		54,000
Unrealized gains on securities, net of reclassification adjustment					14,000	14,000
Defined benefit pension plans (net prior service cost and net loss)					(5,000)	(5,000)

	Common Stock Shares	Common Stock Amount	Additional Paid-in Capital	Retained Earnings	Accumulated Other Comprehensive Income	Total
Foreign currency translation adjustment					3,000	3,000
Total comprehensive income						66,000
Common stock issued	250,000	25,000	50,000			75,000
Dividends				(15,000)		(15,000)
Balance at December 31, 20X1	1,500,000	150,000	300,000	88,000	25,000	563,000
Comprehensive income:						
Net income				63,000		63,000
Unrealized gains on securities, net of reclassification adjustment					11,000	11,000
Defined benefit pension plans (net prior service cost and net loss)					(2,000)	(2,000)
Foreign currency translation adjustment					8,000	8,000
Total comprehensive income						80,000
Common stock issued	500,000	50,000	100,000			150,000
Dividends				(10,000)		(10,000)
Balance at December 31, 20X2	$2,000,000	$200,000	$400,000	$141,000	$ 42,000	$783,000

Example 4: Income Tax Expense or Benefit Allocated to Each Component of Other Comprehensive Income, Including Reclassification Adjustments

The pretax, tax, and after-tax effects of the components of other comprehensive income (loss) for 20X2 and 20X1 are as follows:

	Pre-Tax Amount	Tax (Expense) Benefit	After-Tax Amount
20X2			
Unrealized gains on securities:			
Unrealized holding gains arising during the period	$ 18,000	$ (5,000)	$ 13,000
Less: reclassification adjustment for gains included in net income	(3,000)	1,000	(2,000)
Net unrealized gains	15,000	(4,000)	11,000
Defined benefit pension plans:			
Prior service cost from plan amendment during the period	(2,650)	1,550	(1,100)
Less: amortization of prior service cost included in net periodic pension cost	150	(50)	100
Net prior service cost arising during the period	(2,500)	1,500	(1,000)
Net loss arising during the period	(1,500)	500	(1,000)
Defined benefit pension plans, net	(4,000)	2,000	(2,000)
Foreign currency translation adjustment	11,000	(3,000)	8,000
Other comprehensive income	$ 22,000	$ (5,000)	$ 17,000
20X1			
Unrealized gains on securities:			
Unrealized holding gains arising during the period	$ 26,000	$ (8,000)	$ 18,000
Less: reclassification adjustment for gains included in net income	(6,000)	2,000	(4,000)
Net unrealized gains	20,000	(6,000)	14,000

	Pre-Tax Amount	Tax (Expense) Benefit	After-Tax Amount
Defined benefit pension plans:			
Prior service cost from plan amendment during the period	(6,350)	3,150	(3,200)
Less: amortization of prior service cost included in net periodic pension cost	350	(150)	200
Net prior service cost arising during the period	(6,000)	3,000	(3,000)
Net loss arising during the period	(3,000)	1,000	(2,000)
Defined benefit pension plans, net	(9,000)	4,000	(5,000)
Foreign currency translation adjustment	4,000	(1,000)	3,000
Other comprehensive income	$15,000	$(3,000)	$12,000

Note: Alternatively, the tax amounts for each component of other comprehensive income can be displayed parenthetically on the face of the financial statement in which comprehensive income is reported.

Example 5: Display of Accumulated Other Comprehensive Income Separately as a Component of Equity in a Balance Sheet

	20X2	20X1
Stockholders' Equity:		
Common stock; par value $.10; authorized 10,000,000 shares; issued and outstanding 2,000,000 shares in 20X2 and 1,500,000 shares in 20X1	$200,000	$150,000
Additional paid-in capital	400,000	300,000
Retained earnings	141,000	88,000
Accumulated other comprehensive income	42,000	25,000
Total stockholders' equity	$783,000	$563,000

Example 6: Details of the Accumulated Balances for Each Component Comprising Accumulated Other Comprehensive Income

Balances of related after-tax components comprising accumulated other comprehensive income (loss), included in stockholders' equity, at December 31, 20X2, and December 31, 20X1, are as follows:

	Unrealized Gains on Securities	Defined Benefit Pension Plans	Foreign Currency Translation Adjustment	Accumulated Other Comprehensive Income
Balance at December 31, 20X0	$12,000	$ 5,000	$(4,000)	$13,000
Change for 20X1	14,000	(5,000)	3,000	12,000
Balance at December 31, 20X1	26,000	-0-	(1,000)	25,000
Change for 20X2	11,000	(2,000)	8,000	17,000
Balance at December 31, 20X2	$37,000	$(2,000)	$ 7,000	$42,000

> **Note:** Alternatively, the balances of each classification within accumulated other comprehensive income can be displayed in a statement of changes in equity or in a balance sheet.

Example 7: Presentation of Comprehensive Income Attributable to the Parent and the Noncontrolling Interest on the Face of the Consolidated Statement in Which Comprehensive Income Is Presented

	20X2	20X1
Net income	$ 39,000	$ 26,000
Other comprehensive income, net of tax:		
Unrealized holding gain on available-for-sale securities, net of tax	5,000	15,000
Total other comprehensive income, net of tax	5,000	15,000
Comprehensive income	44,000	41,000

	20X2	20X1
Comprehensive income attributable to the noncontrolling interest	(2,000)	(7,000)
Comprehensive income attributable to XYZ Company	$ 42,000	$ 34,000

Example 8: Presentation in the Consolidated Statement of Changes in Equity of a Reconciliation at the Beginning and End of the Period of the Carrying Amount of Consolidated Equity, Equity Attributable to the Parent, and Equity Attributable to the Noncontrolling Interest

				XYZ Company Shareholders			
	Total	*Com-prehensive Income*	*Retained Earnings*	*Accumu-lated Other Compre-hensive Income*	*Common Stock*	*Paid-in Capital*	*Non-controlling Interest*
Beginning balance, 01/01/20X2	$ 481,000	$ -0-	$ 167,000	$16,000	$200,000	$ 50,000	$ 48,000
Purchase of subsidiary shares from noncontrolling interest	(30,000)			2,000		(8,000)	(24,000)
Comprehensive income:							
Net income	39,000	39,000	37,500				1,500
Other comprehensive income, net of tax:							
Unrealized gain on securities	5,000	5,000		4,500			500
Other comprehensive income	5,000	5,000					
Comprehensive income	44,000	$44,000					
Dividends paid on common stock	(10,000)		(10,000)				
Ending balance, 12/31/20X2	$ 485,000		$ 194,500	$22,500	$200,000	$ 42,000	$ 26,000

CHAPTER 6
ASC TOPIC 225: INCOME STATEMENT

CONTENTS

EXECUTIVE SUMMARY

Extraordinary, Unusual, or Infrequently Recurring Items

Extraordinary items are events and transactions that are distinguished by their unusual nature *and* by the infrequency of their occurrence. Therefore, *both* of the following criteria should be met to classify an event or transaction as an extraordinary item:

1. *Unusual nature*—The underlying event or transaction possesses a high degree of abnormality and is of a type clearly unrelated to, or only incidentally related to, the ordinary and typical activities of the enterprise, taking into account the environment in which the entity operates.

2. *Infrequency of occurrence*—The underlying event or transaction is of a type that would not reasonably be expected to recur in the foreseeable future, taking into account the environment in which the entity operates.

Extraordinary items should be presented separately in the income statement, net of any related income tax effect. If the income statement includes discontinued operations, extraordinary items should be presented following discontinued operations.

Events or transactions that are *either* unusual or infrequent, but not both (and therefore do not meet the criteria for extraordinary items), should be classified and reported as separate components of income from continuing operations. However, the income statement presentation should *not* imply that the event is an extraordinary item. Therefore, the separately identified item should *not* be reported net of its related tax effect as a separate line item following income from continuing operations. Instead, it should be classified separately as a component of ordinary income or loss.

Business Interruption Insurance

The types of costs and losses covered by business interruption insurance generally include:

- Gross margin that was lost or not earned due to the suspension of normal operations.

- A portion of fixed charges and expenses related to that lost gross margin.

- Other expenses incurred to reduce the loss from business interruption (e.g., rent of temporary facilities and equipment, use of subcontractors).

Accounting Literature

FASB Accounting Standards Codification Topic	*Pre-Codification Accounting Literature*
225, *Income Statement*	EITF 01-13, *Income Statement Display of Business Interruption Insurance Recoveries*
	APB-9, *Reporting the Results of Operations*
	APB-30, *Reporting the Results of Operations—Reporting the Effects of Disposal of a Segment of a Business, and Extraordinary, Unusual, and Infrequently Occurring Events and Transactions*

DISCLOSURE AND KEY PRESENTATION REQUIREMENTS

Overall

1. Net income should reflect all items of profit and loss recognized during the period except for error corrections. (ASC 225-10-45-1) (APB-9, par. 6)

2. The income statement is generally classified into appropriate functional areas such as sales, cost of goods sold, operating expenses, and other items. (Generally accepted practice)

Extraordinary Items

1. Items unusual in nature *and* infrequent in occurrence should be classified as extraordinary items. (ASC 225-20-45-2) (APB-30, par. 20)

2. All extraordinary items should be segregated from the results of ordinary operations and the following captions should be used in the income statement when extraordinary items are reported (and there are no discontinued operations) (ASC 225-20-45-9 through 45-12) (APB-30, pars. 10–12):

   a. Income before extraordinary items.

   b. Extraordinary items (less applicable income taxes).

   c. Net income.

   d. Earnings per share data for extraordinary items, where applicable (either on the face of the income statement or in the related notes).

3. The following items should be presented or disclosed when extraordinary items are reported:

   a. Descriptive captions and the amounts (including applicable income taxes) for individual extraordinary events or transactions presented on the face of the income statement (preferably, if practicable), or disclosed in related notes. (ASC 225-20-45-11) (APB-30, par. 11)

   b. A description of the nature of an extraordinary event or transaction and the principal items entering into the determination of an extraordinary gain or loss. (ASC 225-20-45-11) (APB-30, par. 11)

4. The following transactions or events should *not* be reported as extraordinary items (ASC 225-20-45-4) (APB-30, par. 23):

   a. Write-down or write-off of receivables, inventories, equipment leased to others, deferred research and development costs, or other intangible assets.

   b. Gains or losses from exchange or translation of foreign currencies, including those relating to major devaluations and revaluations.

   c. Gains or losses on disposal of a component of an entity.

   d. Other gains or losses from sale or abandonment of property, plant, or equipment used in the business.

   e. Effects of a strike, including those against competitors and major suppliers.

   f. Adjustments of accruals on long-term contracts.

5. Each adjustment in the current period of an element of an extraordinary item that was reported in a prior period should be presented and disclosed in the following manner (ASC 225-20-45-13; 225-20-50-2) (APB-30, par. 25; FAS-16, par. 16):

   a. Separately disclosed as to year of origin, nature, and amount.

    b. Classified separately in the current period in the same manner as the original item.

Unusual or Infrequently Recurring Items

1. Material transactions that are either unusual in nature *or* infrequent in occurrence (but not both and, therefore, not meeting the criteria for extraordinary items) should not be classified as extraordinary items. (ASC 225-20-45-16) (APB-30, par. 26)

2. Material transactions that are either unusual in nature or infrequent in occurrence (but not both) should be presented and/or disclosed in the following manner (ASC 225-20-45-16; 225-20-50-3) (APB-30, par. 26):

    a. Reported as a separate component of income from continuing operations.

    b. Nature and financial effects of each event or transaction disclosed either on the face of the income statement or in a note to the financial statements. (*Note:* Gains or losses of a similar nature that are not individually material should be aggregated.)

    c. Not reported on the face of the income statement, net of income taxes, or in any other manner that may imply that the item is extraordinary.

    d. Not reported on an earnings-per-share basis.

Business Interruption Insurance

1. Business interruption insurance recoveries should be classified in the income statement consistent with existing GAAP. (ASC 225-30-45-1) (EITF 01-13) (*Note:* For example, in order to classify business interruption insurance recoveries as an extraordinary item, the requirements of ASC Subtopic 225-20, *Income Statement—Extraordinary and Unusual Items*, with respect to extraordinary item classification must be met.)

2. The following disclosures should be made in the notes to the financial statements in the period in which business interruption insurance recoveries are recognized (ASC 225-30-50-1) (EITF 01-13):

    a. The nature of the event resulting in business interruption losses.

    b. The aggregate amount of business interruption insurance recoveries recognized during the period and the line item(s) in the income statement in which those recoveries are classified (including amounts reported as an extraordinary item pursuant to ASC Subtopic 225-20, *Income Statement—Extraordinary and Unusual Items*).

EXAMPLES OF FINANCIAL STATEMENT DISCLOSURES

 The following sample disclosures are available on the accompanying disc.

Extraordinary Items

Example 1: Presentation of Extraordinary Items in an Income Statement That Does Not Include Discontinued Operations

	20X2	20X1
Income before income taxes and extraordinary items	$2,078,000	$ 2,774,000
Provision for income taxes	(874,000)	(1,138,000)
Income before extraordinary items	1,204,000	1,636,000
Extraordinary items:		
Gain on litigation settlement, less income tax of $233,000	-0-	417,000
Insurance settlement for earthquake damage, less income tax expense of $310,000	624,000	-0-
Net income	$1,828,000	$ 2,053,000

Example 2: Presentation of Extraordinary Items in an Income Statement That Includes Discontinued Operations

	20X2	20X1
Income (loss) from continuing operations before income taxes	$ 4,914,000	$(1,811,000)
Income taxes	(2,113,000)	652,000
Income (loss) from continuing operations	2,801,000	(1,159,000)
Discontinued operations:		

	20X2	20X1
Loss from operations of discontinued component, net of income tax benefit of $617,000 in 20X2 and $1,515,000 in 20X1	(1,568,000)	(3,726,000)
Gain on disposal of component, net of income tax expense of $986,000	1,347,000	-0-
Loss on discontinued operations	(221,000)	(3,726,000)
Income (loss) before extraordinary item	2,580,000	(4,885,000)
Extraordinary item—Loss on litigation settlement, net of income tax benefit of $165,000	(452,000)	-0-
Net income (loss)	$ 2,128,000	$(4,885,000)

Example 3: Extraordinary Gain Related to Insurance Settlement for Earthquake Damage

In September 20X2, the Company's headquarters building in Apple Valley, Florida, was severely damaged by an earthquake. After the settlement with the insurer in December 20X2, the Company retired the building and recognized an extraordinary gain of $624,000, net of income taxes of $310,000, during 20X2.

Example 4: Adjustment of a Prior-Period Extraordinary Item

In September 20X1, the Company's warehouse in Los Angeles, California, was substantially damaged by fire. As a result, the Company recorded in 20X1 an extraordinary loss of $918,000 (net of income tax benefit of $491,000 and net of insurance proceeds of $1,836,000). Included in the 20X1 extraordinary loss was a provision for estimated inventory damage. During 20X2, the Company determined that actual inventory damage exceeded its original estimate. Therefore, an extraordinary loss of $386,000, net of income tax benefit of $211,000, has been included in the Statement of Operations for 20X2.

The following table illustrates the reporting of the adjustment of loss on the face of the Statements of Operations.

	20X2	20X1
Income before income taxes and extraordinary items	$1,563,000	$1,832,000
Provision for income taxes	(601,000)	(658,000)
Income before extraordinary items	962,000	1,174,000
Extraordinary item:		
Fire loss, net of income tax benefit of $211,000 in 20X2 and $491,000 in 20X1	(386,000)	(918,000)
Net income	$ 576,000	$ 256,000

Example 5: Investor's Proportionate Share of Investee's Extraordinary Gain

The extraordinary item of $320,000 represents the Company's proportionate share of a gain realized on the extinguishment of debt by Kametz, Ltd., a manufacturer of electronic parts in which the Company has a 40% interest that is accounted for on the equity method. The Company has not provided any income tax related to its share of the extraordinary gain because it is the Company's intention to reinvest all undistributed earnings of Kametz, Ltd. indefinitely.

> **Note:** The following table illustrates the portion of the income statement reflecting the Company's proportionate share of extraordinary item reported by Kametz, Ltd.

	20X2	20X1
Income before income taxes	$ 8,941,000	$ 7,916,000
Provision for income taxes	(3,576,000)	(3,287,000)
Income before equity in net income of affiliate and extraordinary item	5,365,000	4,629,000
Equity in net income of affiliate, excluding extraordinary gain of $320,000 in 20X2	554,000	716,000
Income before extraordinary item	5,919,000	5,345,000
Extraordinary item—Equity in undistributed extraordinary gain of affiliate	320,000	-0-
Net income	$ 6,239,000	$ 5,345,000

Unusual or Infrequently Recurring Items

Example 6: Unusual/Infrequent Items—Pre-Opening Store Costs and Charges Related to Hiring and Litigation

In September 20X2, the Company recorded unusual expenses of $1,044,000 before taxes. This is presented separately as a component of income from operations in the Statement of Operations. The unusual expenses relate to (1) $712,000 incurred in pre-opening costs for two new company-owned stores opened in Los Angeles, California, and Chicago, Illinois; (2) $217,000 incurred in the hiring of the new chief executive officer; and (3) $115,000 of cost of litigation associated with such hiring.

> **Note:** The following table illustrates the portion of the income statement reflecting an unusual or infrequent item.

	20X2	20X1
Net sales	$82,174,000	$74,311,000
Costs and expenses:		
Cost of sales	50,947,000	46,816,000
Selling expenses	4,142,000	3,268,000
General and administrative expenses	23,743,000	19,492,000
Unusual expenses	1,044,000	-0-
	79,876,000	69,576,000
Income before income taxes	$ 2,298,000	$ 4,735,000

Example 7: Unusual/Infrequent Items—Write-Off of Receivables and Inventories of a Former Affiliate

In 20X2, the Company recorded a special charge of $425,000 relating to the write-off of receivables due from a former affiliate, Biznetics Corp., and for inventories that were dedicated to the market, which this former affiliate served. The write-off was necessary because the former affiliate did not, and is not expected to, meet its financial obligations to the Company.

Example 8: Unusual/Infrequent Items—Hiring of a New Company President

In 20X2, the Company recorded unusual expenses of $250,000, before taxes, which was incurred in the hiring of the new Company president in June 20X2. This is presented separately as a component of income (loss) from operations in the Statement of Operations.

Business Interruption Insurance

Example 9: Business Interruption Insurance—Hurricane

The Company maintains insurance for both property damage and business interruption relating to catastrophic events. Business interruption coverage covers lost profits and other costs incurred. Non-refundable insurance recoveries received in excess of the net book value of damaged assets, clean-up and demolition costs, and post-event costs are recognized as income in the period received.

In 20X2, the Company reached final settlement agreements with its insurance carrier related to losses from a hurricane in Florida. In total, the Company received insurance recoveries of $2 million, which exceeded the $1.2 million net book value of damaged assets and post-storm costs incurred. The Company recognized the $800,000 of excess insurance recoveries in "Other income" in 20X2.

Example 10: Business Interruption Insurance—Fire

The Company maintains insurance for both property damage and business interruption relating to catastrophic events. Business interruption coverage covers lost profits and other costs incurred. Non-refundable insurance recoveries received in excess of the net book value of damaged assets, clean-up and demolition costs, and post-event costs are recognized as income in the period received.

In 20X2, the Company received $1 million of proceeds from its insurance carriers related to the Edmington fire. The damaged assets have been fully depreciated. Accordingly, the Company recognized the business interruption insurance recoveries of $1 million in "Other income" in 20X2.

CHAPTER 7
ASC TOPIC 230: STATEMENT OF CASH FLOWS

CONTENTS

EXECUTIVE SUMMARY

Statement of Cash Flows

A statement of cash flows is required as part of a complete set of financial statements prepared in conformity with generally accepted accounting principles (GAAP) for all business enterprises. A statement of cash flows specifies the amount of net cash provided by or used by an enterprise during a period from (1) operating activities, (2) investing activities, and (3) financing activities. The statement of cash flows indicates the net effect of these cash flows on the enterprise's cash and cash equivalents. A reconciliation of beginning and ending cash and cash equivalents is included in the statement of cash flows. Also, a statement of cash flows should contain separate related disclosures about all investing and financing activities of an enterprise that affect its financial position but do not directly affect its cash flows during the period. Descriptive terms such as "Cash" or "Cash and cash equivalents" are required in the statement of cash flows, whereas ambiguous terms such as "Funds" are inappropriate.

Cash equivalents are short-term, highly liquid investments that are (1) readily convertible to known amounts of cash and (2) so near their maturities that they present insignificant risk of changes in value because of changes in interest rates. As a general rule, only investments with original maturities of three months or less qualify as cash equivalents. Examples of items commonly considered to be cash equivalents include Treasury bills, commercial paper, and money market funds.

GAAP specifically prohibit reporting cash flow per share.

Accounting Literature

FASB Accounting Standards Codification Topic	*Pre-Codification Accounting Literature*
230, *Statement of Cash Flows*	FAS-95, *Statement of Cash Flows*
830, *Foreign Currency Matters*	FAS-102, *Statement of Cash Flows—Exemption of Certain Enterprises and Classification of Cash Flows from Certain Securities Acquired for Resale*

FASB Accounting Standards Codification Topic	*Pre-Codification Accounting Literature*
	FAS-149, *Amendment of Statement 133 on Derivative Instruments and Hedging Activities*
	EITF 95-13, *Classification of Debt Issue Costs in the Statement of Cash Flows*
	EITF 02-6, *Classification in the Statement of Cash Flows of Payments Made to Settle an Asset Retirement Obligation within the Scope of FASB Statement No. 143*

DISCLOSURE AND KEY PRESENTATION REQUIREMENTS

1. The beginning and ending balances of cash and cash equivalents as shown in the statement of cash flows should be the same amounts as similarly titled line items or subtotals shown in the balance sheet. (ASC 230-10-45-4) (FAS-95, par. 7) (*Note:* The statement of cash flows should use descriptive terms such as cash or cash and cash equivalents, rather than ambiguous terms such as funds.)

2. The statement of cash flows should report net cash provided or used by operating, investing, and financing activities and the net effect of those cash flows on cash and cash equivalents during the period in a manner that reconciles beginning and ending cash and cash equivalents. (ASC 230-10-45-1; 230-10-45-10; 230-10-45-24) (FAS-95, pars. 6, 14, 26) (*Note:* Separate disclosure of cash flows pertaining to extraordinary items or discontinued operations reflected in those categories is not required.)

3. Gross amounts of cash receipts and cash payments should be presented in the statement of cash flows, except for certain items that have a quick turnover, large amounts, or short maturities, which may be presented on a net basis. (ASC 230-10-45-7 through 45-9) (FAS-95, pars. 11–13)

4. The statement of cash flows should properly classify cash receipts and cash payments as resulting from operating, investing, and financing activities. (ASC 230-10-45-10 through 45-27) (FAS-95, pars. 14–31; FAS-102, pars. 8-9; EITF 95-13; EITF 02-6)

5. If the direct method of reporting cash flows from operating activities is used:

    a. A reconciliation of net income and net cash flows from operating activities should be provided in a separate schedule. (ASC 230-10-45-2; 230-10-45-28 through 45-30) (FAS-95, pars. 6, 28, 29, 30)

    b. At a minimum, the following classes of operating cash receipts and payments should be separately reported (ASC 230-10-45-25) (FAS-95, par. 27):

       (1) Cash collected from customers, including, for example, lessees or licensees.

       (2) Interest and dividends received.

       (3) Other operating cash receipts, if any.

       (4) Cash paid to employees and other suppliers of goods or services, including, for example, suppliers of insurance or advertising.

       (5) Interest paid.

       (6) Income taxes paid and, separately, the cash that would have been paid for income taxes if increases in the value of equity instruments issued under share-based payment arrangements that are not included as a cost of goods or services recognizable for accounting purposes also had not been deductible in determining taxable income.

       (7) Other operating cash payments, if any.

6. If the indirect method of reporting cash flows from operating activities is used:

    a. A reconciliation of net income to operating cash flows should be presented in the statement of cash flows or in a separate schedule. (ASC 230-10-45-2; 230-10-45-28 through 45-32) (FAS-95, pars. 6, 28, 29, 30) (*Note:* If the reconciliation is presented in the statement of cash flows, all adjustments to net income to determine net cash flow from operating activities should be clearly identified as reconciling items.)

    b. Amounts of interest paid (net of amounts capitalized) and income taxes paid during the period should be disclosed. (ASC 230-10-50-2) (FAS-95, par. 29)

7. The accounting policy for determining which items are treated as cash equivalents should be disclosed. (ASC 230-10-45-6; 230-10-50-1) (FAS-95, par. 10) (*Note:* Any change to that policy is a change in accounting principle that should be effected by restating financial statements for earlier years presented for comparative purposes.)

8. Information about noncash investing and financing activities should be disclosed (either narrative or summarized in a schedule) and the disclosures should clearly relate the cash and noncash aspects of transactions involving similar items. (ASC 230-10-50-3 through 50-6) (FAS-95, pars. 32, 74)

9. If cash flows from derivative instruments that are accounted for as fair value hedges or cash flow hedges are classified in the same category as the cash flows from the items being hedged, that accounting policy should be disclosed. (ASC 230-10-45-27) (FAS-149, par. 37)

10. The effect of exchange rate changes on cash balances held in foreign currencies should be reported as a separate part of the reconciliation of the change in cash and cash equivalents. (ASC 830-230-45-1) (FAS-95, par. 25)

EXAMPLES OF FINANCIAL STATEMENT DISCLOSURES

 The following sample disclosures are available on the accompanying disc.

Example 1: Statement of Cash Flows—Indirect Method

	Year Ended December 31	
	20X2	20X1
Operating activities:		
Net income (loss)	$ 36,000,000	$ 19,000,000
Adjustments to reconcile net income (loss) to net cash provided by (used in) operating activities:		
Depreciation and amortization	7,500,000	3,700,000
Amortization of deferred compensation	1,300,000	800,000
Deferred taxes	(1,500,000)	(500,000)
Changes in operating assets and liabilities, net of effects from acquired companies:		
Accounts receivable	(20,000,000)	(8,000,000)
Inventory	(4,500,000)	(1,200,000)
Income taxes receivable	(3,500,000)	(2,400,000)

	Year Ended December 31	
	20X2	20X1
Prepaid expenses and other assets	(2,000,000)	(500,000)
Accounts payable	14,000,000	7,000,000
Other accrued liabilities	5,500,000	3,500,000
Net cash provided by (used in) operating activities	32,800,000	21,400,000
Investing activities:		
Net assets of acquired companies, net of cash acquired	(16,000,000)	(10,000,000)
Purchases of property and equipment	(11,000,000)	(12,000,000)
Purchases of investments	(2,000,000)	(1,000,000)
Net cash used in investing activities	(29,000,000)	(23,000,000)
Financing activities:		
Proceeds from bank term loan	1,000,000	5,700,000
Payments on bank term loan	(500,000)	(7,000,000)
Payments on capital lease obligations	(700,000)	(800,000)
Proceeds from issuance of common stock	2,000,000	3,000,000
Payments on repurchase of preferred stock	(200,000)	(300,000)
Net cash provided by financing activities	1,600,000	600,000
Effect of exchange rate changes on cash and cash equivalents	(100,000)	200,000
Increase (decrease) in cash and cash equivalents	5,300,000	(800,000)
Cash and cash equivalents at beginning of year	2,300,000	3,100,000
Cash and cash equivalents at end of year	$ 7,600,000	$ 2,300,000

Example 2: Statement of Cash Flows—Direct Method, Including Reconciliation of Net Income to Net Cash from Operating Activities

	Year Ended December 31	
	20X2	*20X1*
Cash flows from operating activities:		
Cash received from customers	28,000,000	22,000,000
Cash paid to suppliers and employees	(25,500,000)	(21,700,000)
Interest received	200,000	100,000
Interest paid	(1,000,000)	(1,500,000)
Income tax refunds received	400,000	100,000
Income taxes paid	(1,500,000)	(2,000,000)
Other cash received (paid)	(200,000)	100,000
Net cash provided by (used in) operating activities	400,000	(2,900,000)
Cash flows from investing activities:		
Payments for business acquisitions, net of cash acquired	(1,500,000)	(1,000,000)
Purchases of property and equipment	(500,000)	(500,000)
Proceeds from disposition of capital equipment	400,000	1,700,000
Purchases of short-term investments	(300,000)	(100,000)
Proceeds from short-term investments	200,000	400,000
Net cash provided by (used in) investing activities	(1,700,000)	500,000
Cash flows from financing activities:		
Proceeds from short-term borrowings	3,000,000	100,000
Repayment of long-term debt	(700,000)	(200,000)
Proceeds from issuance of long-term debt	800,000	1,500,000
Proceeds from issuance of common stock	200,000	400,000

	Year Ended December 31	
	20X2	20X1
Net cash provided by financing activities	3,300,000	1,800,000
Effect of exchange rate changes on cash and cash equivalents	(400,000)	(100,000)
Increase (decrease) in cash and cash equivalents	1,600,000	(700,000)
Cash and cash equivalents at beginning of year	1,200,000	1,900,000
Cash and cash equivalents at end of year	$ 2,800,000	$ 1,200,000

Reconciliation of Net Income (Loss) to Net Cash Provided by (Used in) Operating Activities

	Year Ended December 31	
	20X2	20X1
Net income (loss)	$(3,500,000)	$ 4,700,000
Adjustments to reconcile net income (loss) to net cash provided by (used in) operating activities:		
Depreciation and amortization	1,800,000	1,400,000
Deferred income taxes	(500,000)	200,000
Foreign exchange (gains) losses	(150,000)	100,000
Loss (gain) on sale of equipment	(100,000)	250,000
Inventory write-off	400,000	300,000
Equity in losses of affiliates	(100,000)	100,000
Changes in operating assets and liabilities, net of effects of business acquisitions:		
Accounts receivable	2,000,000	(3,850,000)
Inventory	(4,000,000)	(2,000,000)
Income taxes receivable	300,000	100,000
Prepaid expenses and other assets	700,000	(600,000)
Accounts payable	1,650,000	(2,500,000)

	Year Ended December 31	
	20X2	*20X1*
Other accrued liabilities	1,900,000	(1,100,000)
Net cash provided by (used in) operating activities	$ 400,000	$(2,900,000)

Example 3: Statement of Cash Flows—Discontinued Operations

> **Note:** ASC Topic 230 (FAS-95) does not require discontinued operations to be separately disclosed in the statement of cash flows. This example is provided for entities that nevertheless choose to report such category. It should be noted that, although separate disclosure of cash flows related to discontinued operations is not required, separate disclosure is permitted so long as those separate cash flows are presented in conformity with the basic requirements of ASC Topic 230 (FAS-95) and are presented consistently for all periods. If a company chooses to separately present cash flows from discontinued operations, the presentation should discretely report the operating, investing and financing cash flows from discontinued operations by category. It would not be appropriate to aggregate all cash flows from discontinued operations within a single line item, either as a separate category or within an existing category, such as operating cash flows.

	Year Ended December 31	
	20X2	*20X1*
Cash flows from operating activities:		
Net income	$ 6,000,000	$ 9,000,000
Adjustments to reconcile net income to net cash provided by operating activities:		
Depreciation and amortization	2,500,000	1,700,000
Estimated loss on disposal of discontinued operations	2,400,000	-0-
Increase in accounts receivable	(2,000,000)	(6,000,000)
Increase in accounts payable	3,000,000	4,000,000
Net cash provided by operating activities	11,900,000	8,700,000
Cash flows from investing activities:		
Purchases of property and equipment	(7,000,000)	(2,000,000)

	Year Ended December 31	
	20X2	20X1
Net investing activities of discontinued operations	(3,000,000)	(1,200,000)
Net cash used in investing activities	(10,000,000)	(3,200,000)
Cash flows from financing activities:		
Payments on capital lease obligations	(700,000)	(800,000)
Net financing activities of discontinued operations	(500,000)	(400,000)
Net cash used in financing activities	(1,200,000)	(1,200,000)
Increase in cash and cash equivalents	700,000	4,300,000
Cash and cash equivalents at beginning of year	6,500,000	2,200,000
Cash and cash equivalents at end of year	$ 7,200,000	$ 6,500,000

Example 4: Statement of Cash Flows—Extraordinary Items

Note: ASC Topic 230 (FAS-95) does not require extraordinary items to be separately disclosed in the statement of cash flows. This example is provided for entities that nevertheless choose to report such category.

	Year Ended December 31	
	20X2	20X1
Cash flows from operating activities:		
Net income	$36,000,000	$19,000,000
Adjustments to reconcile net income to net cash provided by operating activities:		
Depreciation and amortization	7,500,000	3,700,000
Extraordinary loss on fire damage	2,300,000	-0-
Net cash provided by operating activities	45,800,000	22,700,000

(Remaining details omitted.)

Example 5: Foreign Currency Cash Flows

ASC Topic 230 (FAS-95) specifies that the effect of exchange rate changes on cash balances held in foreign currencies be reported as a separate part of the reconciliation of the change in cash and cash equivalents in the Statement of Cash Flows.

> **Note:** For examples of reporting foreign currency cash flows, see Examples 1 and 2 above.

Example 6: Cash Overdraft Reported as a Financing Activity

	Year Ended December 31	
	20X2	*20X1*
Cash flows from financing activities:		
Proceeds of long-term borrowings	1,000,000	500,000
Payments on capital lease obligations	(700,000)	(800,000)
Net increase (decrease) in bank overdrafts	500,000	(400,000)
Net cash provided by (used in) financing activities	800,000	(700,000)

(Remaining details omitted.)

Example 7: Other Adjustments to Arrive at Net Cash Flows from Operating Activities

> **Note:** This example is a comprehensive illustration of adjustments to arrive at net cash flows from operating activities, other than changes in operating assets and liabilities. The objective of these adjustments is to account for noncash operating activities, by adding noncash expenses to net income and subtracting noncash revenues from net income. For complete examples of statements of cash flows under the direct and indirect methods, see Examples 1 and 2 above.

	Year Ended December 31	
	20X2	*20X1*
Cash flows from operating activities:		
Net income	$4,000,000	$5,000,000
Adjustments to reconcile net income to net cash provided by operating activities:		

	Year Ended December 31	
	20X2	20X1
Cash value of life insurance	(100,000)	(200,000)
Common stock issued to employees	500,000	100,000
Depreciation and amortization	1,500,000	1,700,000
Foreign currency translation loss (gain)	100,000	(300,000)
Gain on litigation settlement	(600,000)	(100,000)
Imputed interest on debt	300,000	100,000
Inventory write-down	200,000	300,000
LIFO effect	200,000	(250,000)
Loss (gain) on sale of property and equipment	(300,000)	100,000
Provision for environmental remediation	200,000	700,000
Provision for losses on accounts receivable	700,000	500,000
Provision related to early retirement program	1,100,000	900,000
Restructuring charges	900,000	600,000
Undistributed (earnings) losses of affiliate	300,000	(400,000)
Write-down of certain long-lived assets	150,000	200,000
Write-off of advances to affiliates	500,000	200,000
Changes in operating assets and liabilities:		
Accounts receivable	600,000	(400,000)

(Remaining details omitted.)

Net cash provided by operating activities	10,250,000	8,750,000

(Remaining details omitted.)

Example 8: Cash Flows from Investing Activities

Note: This example is a comprehensive illustration of cash flows provided by and used in investing activities. For complete examples of statements of cash flows under the direct and indirect methods, see Examples 1 and 2 above.

	Year Ended December 31	
	20X2	*20X1*
Cash flows from investing activities:		
Additions to long-term notes receivable	(600,000)	(900,000)
Collections of loans to officers	250,000	150,000
Deconsolidation of joint ventures	(200,000)	(500,000)
Increase in intangibles	(400,000)	(200,000)
Increase in restricted cash equivalents	(1,000,000)	-0-
Investment in and advances to affiliates	(500,000)	(700,000)
Payment for business acquisitions, net of cash acquired	(1,000,000)	(2,000,000)
Payments on long-term notes receivable	200,000	300,000
Proceeds from property insurance settlement	200,000	300,000
Proceeds from sale of assets held for resale	450,000	150,000
Proceeds from sale of marketable securities and investments	6,000,000	2,000,000
Proceeds from sale of property and equipment	1,000,000	3,000,000
Purchase of marketable securities and investments	(3,000,000)	(6,000,000)
Purchases of property and equipment	(1,000,000)	(2,000,000)
Release of restricted cash equivalents and investments	(1,000,000)	-0-
Repayments from (loans to) employees	100,000	(50,000)

	Year Ended December 31	
	20X2	20X1
Restricted funds held in escrow	(1,200,000)	(1,500,000)
Sale (purchase) of available-for-sale securities	1,800,000	(400,000)
Sale (purchase) of investments held-to-maturity	(600,000)	500,000
Net cash provided by (used in) investing activities	1,500,000	(7,850,000)

(Remaining details omitted.)

Example 9: Cash Flows from Financing Activities

Note: This example is a comprehensive illustration of cash flows provided by and used in financing activities. For complete examples of statements of cash flows under the direct and indirect methods, see Examples 1 and 2 above.

	Year Ended December 31	
	20X2	20X1
Cash flows from financing activities:		
Debt issue costs	(300,000)	(100,000)
Decrease (increase) in funds restricted for payment of long-term debt	600,000	(400,000)
Loans to ESOP	(400,000)	(300,000)
Net borrowings under line-of-credit agreement	1,000,000	2,000,000
Net increase (decrease) in bank overdrafts	200,000	(450,000)
Payment of debt and capital lease obligations	(3,500,000)	(800,000)
Payment of dividends	(100,000)	(200,000)
Premiums paid on early retirement of debt	(500,000)	(300,000)
Proceeds from issuance of common stock	700,000	600,000

	Year Ended December 31	
	20X2	20X1
Proceeds from issuance of long-term debt	2,000,000	3,000,000
Proceeds from notes receivable—stock	100,000	200,000
Proceeds from stock options exercised	200,000	300,000
Proceeds of preferred stock issued to ESOP	250,000	150,000
Reduction of loan to ESOP	150,000	100,000
Repurchase of common stock	(1,500,000)	(1,300,000)
Treasury stock issued	400,000	500,000
Treasury stock purchased	(600,000)	(700,000)
Net cash provided by (used in) financing activities	(1,300,000)	2,300,000

(Remaining details omitted.)

Noncash Investing and Financing Activities

Example 10: Note Receivable Received in Connection with Sale of Business

In 20X2, the Company sold certain assets of its frozen food distribution business. The selling price was $2,800,000, which included a cash payment of $1,000,000 and a note receivable of $1,800,000 payable in three equal annual installments.

Example 11: Casualty Results in an Insurance Claim Receivable

On August 13, 20X2, the Company experienced a major fire, which destroyed a significant part of the manufacturing facility. The total amount of the insurance claim was for $8,500,000, which is presented as "Business interruption insurance" in the 20X2 Income Statement. The Company has received $7,000,000 in cash in 20X2 and the balance of $1,500,000 is recorded as an insurance claim receivable due from the insurance company. The receivable was received in January 20X3.

Example 12: Forgiveness of Note Receivable

During the year ended December 31, 20X2, the Company forgave a note receivable, including interest, totaling $210,000, in connection with its sales quota agreement with Sarak, Inc.

Example 13: Conversion of Accounts Receivable to Notes Receivable

During the year ended December 31, 20X2, the Company converted $350,000 of accounts receivable to notes receivable.

Example 14: Note Receivable Balance Reduced for Expenses Incurred

During the year ended December 31, 20X2, the Company reduced its note receivable balance from its affiliate, Sisak Corp., by $125,000 for a management fee charged by the affiliate.

Example 15: Property Acquired under Capital Lease Obligations

The Company acquired equipment of $430,000 and $310,000 in 20X2 and 20X1, respectively, under capital lease obligations.

Example 16: Note Payable Issued in Connection with Property Acquisition

During the years ended December 31, 20X2, and December 31, 20X1, the Company issued notes payable for $450,000 and $375,000, respectively, in connection with the acquisition of certain property and equipment.

Example 17: Property Distributed to Shareholder as Salary

In 20X2, the Company distributed an automobile with a book value of $17,900 to a 5% shareholder as salary.

Example 18: Property Acquired in Exchange for Services Rendered

In 20X2, the Company acquired furniture and equipment with a value of $38,500 in exchange for consulting services rendered.

Example 19: Issuance of Preferred Stock and Warrants as Payment of Accrued Interest

In 20X2, the Company issued 30,000 shares of Amended Series A Preferred Stock and 150,000 warrants to acquire shares of Common Stock, in respect of approximately $750,000 of accrued interest payable to certain institutional holders of secured subordinated debt.

Example 20: Issuance of Warrants Recorded as Stock Dividends

In 20X2, the Company issued warrants to holders of its Series B Preferred Stock at $0.15 per share, which was recorded as a preferred stock dividend of approximately $400,000.

Example 21: Issuance of Warrants as Finder's Fee

During May 20X2, the Company issued to a finder 20,000 warrants to purchase 20,000 shares of common stock, as compensation for the placement with its clients of 200,000 units, comprising shares of common stock and warrants to purchase common stock.

Example 22: Conversion of Preferred Stock into Common Stock

In April 20X2, the 4,000 shares of 5% redeemable convertible preferred stock with a total stockholders' equity value of $4,800,000 were converted into an aggregate of 100,000 shares of the Company's common stock.

Example 23: Common Stock Issued Pursuant to Conversion of Bridge Financing Notes

500,000 shares of common stock were issued in 20X2 pursuant to the conversion of bridge financing promissory notes, which provided net proceeds of $2,000,000.

Example 24: Issuance of Stock Dividends

In 20X2, the Company declared and issued a stock dividend of 2,545,000 common shares resulting in a transfer from retained earnings to additional paid-in capital of $725,000.

Example 25: Business Combinations

Supplemental cash flow information regarding the Company's acquisitions in 20X2 and 20X1 are as follows:

	20X2	20X1
Fair value of assets acquired	$ 3,100,000	$ 2,900,000
Less liabilities assumed	(900,000)	(200,000)
Net assets acquired	2,200,000	2,700,000
Less shares issued	(300,000)	(400,000)
Less cash acquired	(100,000)	(200,000)
Business acquisitions, net of cash acquired	$ 1,800,000	$ 2,100,000

Example 26: Assets and Liabilities Contributed to Newly Formed Joint Venture

In April 20X2, the Company contributed its medical diagnostics business to a newly formed, equally owned joint venture with Sabak, Inc. This transaction had the following noncash effect on the Company's 20X2 balance sheet:

Current assets	$(300,000)
Property and equipment	(900,000)
Long-term receivables	500,000
Current liabilities	600,000

Example 27: Transfer of Inventory to Property and Equipment

During the years ended December 31, 20X2, and December 31, 20X1, the Company transferred $80,000 and $95,000 of inventory to property and equipment, respectively.

Example 28: Refinance of Term Loan

During the year ended December 31, 20X2, the Company refinanced a term loan of $3,500,000 for the same amount.

Example 29: Insurance Premiums Financed

During 20X2 and 20X1, the Company financed $75,000 and $63,000, respectively, of insurance premiums relating to general liability and workers' compensation. The liability is recorded as a note payable.

Accounting Policy for Cash Equivalents

Example 30: Cash Equivalents Include Money Market Accounts and Short-Term Investments

Cash and cash equivalents include cash on hand, money market accounts, and short-term investments with original maturities of three months or less.

Example 31: Cash Equivalents Include Marketable Securities

For purposes of the Statements of Cash Flows, marketable securities purchased with an original maturity of three months or less are considered cash equivalents.

Example 32: Cash Equivalents Exclude Securities Held in Trust

The Company considers all short-term debt securities purchased with an initial maturity of three months or less and not held in trust to be cash equivalents.

Example 33: Cash Equivalents Include Repurchase Agreements

At December 31, 20X2, cash equivalents include overnight repurchase agreements.

Example 34: Negative Book Cash Balances Are Included in Accounts Payable

Cash equivalents consist of all highly liquid investments with an original maturity of three months or less. As a result of the Company's cash management system, checks issued but not presented to the banks for payment may create negative book cash balances. Such negative balances are included in trade accounts payable and totaled $175,000 and $150,000 as of December 31, 20X2, and December 31, 20X1, respectively.

Disclosure of Interest and Income Taxes Paid (When the Indirect Method Is Used)

Example 35: Interest and Income Taxes Paid

Cash paid for interest and income taxes for 20X2 and 20X1 were as follows:

	20X2	20X1
Interest, net of amount capitalized of $113,000 in 20X2	$166,000	$244,000
Income taxes	$100,000	$125,000

CHAPTER 8
ASC TOPIC 235: NOTES TO FINANCIAL STATEMENTS

CONTENTS

EXECUTIVE SUMMARY

Notes to Financial Statements

An entity's accounting policies are important to understanding the content of its financial statements. The disclosure of significant accounting policies is an integral part of financial statements when the statements are intended to present financial position, cash flows, or results of operations in conformity with generally accepted accounting principles (GAAP). An accounting policy is significant if it materially affects the determination of financial position, cash flows, or results of operations.

The preferable presentation of disclosing an entity's accounting policies is as part of the first note of the financial statements, under the caption "Summary of Significant Accounting Policies" or "Significant Accounting Policies." However, the accounting literature does recognize the need for flexibility in the matter of formats. Disclosures of accounting policies need not duplicate information presented elsewhere in the financial statements. Therefore, in some instances the accounting-policies note may refer to information that will be found in another note.

Generally, the "Summary of Significant Accounting Policies" note deals with policies and not with numbers (unless the related amounts are not addressed elsewhere in the notes). For example, a company may disclose in its summary note the inventory cost method used (e.g., FIFO) and indicate in a separate note the dollar breakdown of raw materials, work-in-process, and finished goods.

Accounting standards often require an entity to disclose a specific accounting policy. Following are examples of areas of accounting for which policies are specifically required to be disclosed:

- Basis of consolidation
- Depreciation methods
- Inventory methods
- Retirement plans
- Cash and cash equivalents

Accounting Literature

FASB Accounting Standards Codification Topic	*Pre-Codification Accounting Literature*
235, *Notes to Financial Statements*	APB-22, *Disclosure of Accounting Policies*

DISCLOSURE AND KEY PRESENTATION REQUIREMENTS

1. A description of all of the entity's significant accounting policies should be included as an integral part of the financial statements. (ASC 235-10-50-1) (APB-22, par. 8) (*Note:* This is not applicable to unaudited interim financial statements issued between annual reporting dates if the entity has not changed its accounting policies since the end of its preceding fiscal year. [ASC 235-10-50-2] [APB-22, par. 10])

2. The accounting policies disclosure should (ASC 235-10-50-3 and 50-6) (APB-22, pars. 12 and 15):

   a. Identify and describe the accounting principles followed by the entity and the methods of applying those principles that materially affect the determination of financial position, results of operations, or cash flows.

   b. Encompass important judgments as to appropriateness of principles relating to recognition of revenue and allocation of asset costs to current and future periods.

   c. Encompass those accounting principles and methods that involve any of the following:

      (1) A selection from existing acceptable alternatives.

      (2) Principles and methods peculiar to the industry in which the entity operates (even if such principles and methods are predominantly followed in that industry).

      (3) Unusual or innovative applications of GAAP.

   d. Appear in a separate summary of significant accounting policies preceding the notes to financial statements, or as the initial note, under the same or a similar title. (*Note:* This is the preferred format, although the need for flexibility is recognized.)

3. The financial statement disclosure of accounting policies should avoid duplicate details (e.g., composition of inventories or of property and equipment) presented elsewhere as part of the financial statements and, in some cases, should refer to related details presented elsewhere as part of the financial statements. (ASC 235-10-50-5) (APB-22, par. 14)

EXAMPLES OF FINANCIAL STATEMENT DISCLOSURES

 The following are examples of the nature of information frequently disclosed in the "Summary of Significant Accounting Policies," the first note to the financial statements. The following sample disclosures are available on the accompanying disc.

Accounting Period

Example 1: Calendar Year—Saturday Nearest December 31

The Company's accounting period ends on the Saturday nearest December 31. The 20X2 and 20X1 years ended on December 28, 20X2, and December 29, 20X1, respectively.

Example 2: Fiscal Year—52- or 53-Week Period

The Company's fiscal year is the 52 or 53 weeks ending on the last Saturday in July. The fiscal year ended July 28, 20X2, comprised a 52-week year, and the fiscal year ended July 29, 20X1, comprised a 53-week year.

Example 3: Change in Fiscal Year

During 20X2, the Company changed its fiscal year from one ending on the last Sunday in April to one ending on the last Sunday in December. Accordingly, the Company's transition period that ended on December 30, 20X2, includes the 34 weeks from April 29, 20X2, to December 30, 20X2, (Transition 20X2). The Company's full fiscal years include either 52 or 53 weeks. Fiscal 20X2 and 20X1 each include 52 weeks.

The following are selected financial data for Transition 20X2 and for the comparable 34-week period of the prior year:

	December 30, 20X2 (34 weeks)	December 31, 20X1 (34 weeks)
Net sales	$45,000,000	$40,000,000
Cost of goods sold	30,000,000	27,000,000
Gross profit	15,000,000	13,000,000
Selling and administrative expenses	10,000,000	9,000,000
Interest expense	1,000,000	1,000,000

	December 30, 20X2 (34 weeks)	December 31, 20X1 (34 weeks)
Other income, net	500,000	800,000
Income before income taxes	4,500,000	3,800,000
Income tax expense	2,000,000	1,500,000
Net income	$2,500,000	$2,300,000

Accounts Receivable

Example 4: Allowance Method Used to Record Bad Debts—General Description

The Company uses the allowance method to account for uncollectible accounts receivable. Accounts receivable are presented net of an allowance for doubtful accounts of $425,000 and $365,000 at December 31, 20X2, and December 31, 20X1, respectively.

Example 5: Allowance Method Used to Record Bad Debts—Detailed Description

The Company provides an allowance for doubtful accounts equal to the estimated uncollectible amounts. The Company's estimate is based on historical collection experience and a review of the current status of trade accounts receivable. It is reasonably possible that the Company's estimate of the allowance for doubtful accounts will change. Accounts receivable are presented net of an allowance for doubtful accounts of $940,000 and $790,000 at December 31, 20X2, and December 31, 20X1, respectively.

Example 6: Unbilled Receivables

Unbilled receivables represent revenue earned in the current period but not billed to the customer until future dates, usually within one month.

Example 7: Classification of Accounts Receivable with Credit Balances

Accounts receivable with credit balances have been included as a current liability in "Accounts payable" in the accompanying balance sheet.

Advertising Costs

Example 8: Advertising Costs Are Expensed as Incurred

Advertising costs are expensed as incurred. Advertising expense totaled $295,000 for 20X2 and $270,000 for 20X1.

Example 9: Advertising Costs Are Expensed the First Time the Advertising Takes Place

Production costs of future media advertising are expensed the first time the advertising takes place. Advertising expense totaled $457,000 for 20X2 and $393,000 for 20X1.

Example 10: Direct-Response Advertising Costs Are Capitalized and Amortized

Direct-response advertising costs, consisting primarily of catalog book production, printing, and postage costs, are capitalized and amortized over the expected life of the catalog, not to exceed six months. Direct response advertising costs reported as prepaid assets are $275,000 and $350,000 at December 31, 20X2, and December 31, 20X1, respectively. Total advertising expenses were $1,900,000 in 20X2 and $1,600,000 in 20X1.

Example 11: Certain Advertising Costs Are Expensed the First Time the Advertising Takes Place and Direct-Response Advertising Costs Are Capitalized

The Company expenses the production costs of advertising the first time the advertising takes place, except for direct-response advertising, which is capitalized and amortized over its expected period of future benefits. Direct-response advertising consists primarily of magazine advertisements that include order coupons for the Company's products. The capitalized costs of the advertising are amortized over the six-month period following the publication of the magazine in which it appears.

> **Note:** This example assumes that the details of advertising costs expensed and capitalized are disclosed in a separate note to the financial statements. See Chapter 22, "ASC Topic 340: Other Assets and Deferred Costs," for an illustration.

Capitalization of Interest

Example 12: Capitalization of Interest Costs on Borrowings

The Company capitalizes interest cost on borrowings incurred during the new construction or upgrade of qualifying assets.

Capitalized interest is added to the cost of the underlying assets and is amortized over the useful lives of the assets. For 20X2 and 20X1, the Company capitalized $450,000 and $525,000 of interest, respectively, in connection with various capital expansion projects.

Cash Equivalents

Example 13: Types of Cash Equivalents Specifically Identified

Cash and cash equivalents consist primarily of cash on deposit, certificates of deposit, money market accounts, and investment grade commercial paper that are readily convertible into cash and purchased with original maturities of three months or less.

Example 14: Types of Cash Equivalents Described in General Terms

The Company considers deposits that can be redeemed on demand and investments that have original maturities of less than three months, when purchased, to be cash equivalents. As of December 31, 20X2, the Company's cash and cash equivalents were deposited primarily in three financial institutions.

Comprehensive Income

Example 15: Components of Other Comprehensive Income Described

Comprehensive income consists of net income and other gains and losses affecting shareholders' equity that, under generally accepted accounting principles, are excluded from net income. For the Company, such items consist primarily of unrealized gains and losses on marketable securities and foreign currency translation gains and losses.

Example 16: No Items of Other Comprehensive Income

The Company has no items of other comprehensive income in any period presented. Therefore, net income as presented in the Company's Statement of Operations equals comprehensive income.

Concentrations of Credit and Other Risks

For examples of financial statement disclosures, see Chapter 14, "ASC Topic 275: Risks and Uncertainties," and Chapter 49, "ASC Topic 825: Financial Instruments."

Consolidation Policy

Example 17: Consolidation Policy Specifically Described

The accompanying consolidated financial statements include the accounts of the Company and its majority-owned subsidiary partnerships and corporations, after elimination of all material intercompany accounts, transactions, and profits. Investments in unconsolidated subsidiaries representing ownership of at least 20%, but less than 50%, are accounted for under the equity method. Nonmarketable investments in which the Company has less than 20% ownership and in which it does not have the ability to exercise significant influence over the investee are initially recorded at cost and periodically reviewed for impairment.

Example 18: Combined Financial Statements

The financial statements of ABC, Inc. and XYZ Corp. are combined because each company is owned beneficially by identical shareholders. All significant intercompany accounts and transactions have been eliminated in the combination.

Contingencies

Example 19: General Accounting Policy for Contingencies

Certain conditions may exist which may result in a loss to the Company, but which will only be resolved when one or more future events occur or fail to occur. The Company's management and its legal counsel assess such contingent liabilities, and such assessment inherently involves an exercise of judgment. In assessing loss contingencies related to legal proceedings that are pending against the Company, or unasserted claims that may result in such proceedings, the Company's legal counsel evaluates the perceived merits of any legal proceedings or unasserted claims as well as the perceived merits of the amount of relief sought or expected to be sought therein.

If the assessment of a contingency indicates that it is probable that a material loss has been incurred and the amount of the liability can be estimated, the estimated liability would be accrued in the Company's financial statements. If the assessment indicates that a potentially material loss contingency is not probable but is reasonably possible, or is probable but cannot be estimated, the nature of the contingent liability, together with an estimate of the range of possible loss if determinable and material, would be disclosed.

Loss contingencies considered remote are generally not disclosed unless they arise from guarantees, in which case the guarantees would be disclosed.

Deferred Revenue

Example 20: Amounts Billed in Advance

The Company recognizes revenues as earned. Amounts billed in advance of the period in which service is rendered are recorded as a liability under "Deferred revenue."

Earnings per Share

Example 21: Basic and Diluted Net Earnings per Share

Basic net earnings (loss) per common share is computed by dividing net earnings (loss) applicable to common shareholders by the weighted-average number of common shares outstanding during the period. Diluted net earnings (loss) per common share is determined using the weighted-average number of common shares outstanding during the period, adjusted for the dilutive effect of common stock equivalents, consisting of shares that might be issued upon exercise of common stock options. In periods where losses are reported, the weighted-average number of common shares outstanding excludes common stock equivalents, because their inclusion would be anti-dilutive.

Environmental Costs

Example 22: Environmental Expenditures Expensed or Capitalized

Costs related to environmental remediation are charged to expense. Other environmental costs are also charged to expense unless they increase the value of the property and/or provide future economic benefits, in which event they are capitalized. Liabilities are recognized when the expenditures are considered probable and can be reasonably estimated. Measurement of liabilities is based on currently enacted laws and regulations, existing technology, and undiscounted site-specific costs. Generally, such recognition coincides with the Company's commitment to a formal plan of action.

Example 23: Accruals for Environmental Matters Exclude Claims for Recoveries

Accruals for environmental matters are recorded when it is probable that a liability has been incurred and the amount of the liability can be reasonably estimated, or if an amount is likely to fall within a range and no amount within that range can be determined to be the better estimate, the minimum amount of the range is recorded. Accruals for environmental matters exclude claims for recoveries from insurance carriers and other third parties until it is probable that such recoveries will be realized.

Estimates

Example 24: General Note Regarding Estimates Inherent in the Financial Statements

Preparing the Company's financial statements in conformity with accounting principles generally accepted in the United States of America ("GAAP") requires management to make estimates and assumptions that affect reported amounts of assets and liabilities and disclosure of contingent assets and liabilities at the date of the financial statements and the reported amounts of revenues and expenses during the reporting period. Actual results could differ from those estimates.

Example 25: Significant Estimates Relating to Specific Financial Statement Accounts and Transactions Are Identified

The financial statements include some amounts that are based on management's best estimates and judgments. The most significant estimates relate to allowance for uncollectible accounts receivable, inventory obsolescence, depreciation, intangible asset valuations and useful lives, goodwill impairments, retirement benefits, environmental obligations, warranty costs, taxes, contingencies, and costs to complete long-term contracts. These estimates may be adjusted as more current information becomes available, and any adjustment could be significant.

Financial Instruments

Example 26: Fair Value of Financial Instruments Approximates Carrying Amount

The Company's financial instruments are cash and cash equivalents, accounts receivable, accounts payable, notes payable, and long-term debt. The recorded values of cash and cash equivalents, accounts receivable, and accounts payable approximate their fair values based on their short-term nature. The recorded values of notes payable and long-term debt approximate their fair values, as interest approximates market rates.

Example 27: Fair Value of Financial Instruments Is Based on Quoted Market Prices or Pricing Models

Fair values of long-term investments, long-term debt, interest rate derivatives, currency forward contracts, and currency options are based on quoted market prices or pricing models using prevailing financial market information as of December 31, 20X2.

Example 28: Fair Value of Financial Instruments Is Based on Management's Estimates

The fair value of current assets and liabilities approximate carrying value because of the short-term nature of these items. There is no quoted market value for the Senior Secured Notes; however, management estimates that, based on current market conditions, such Notes have a fair value of approximately 45% to 55% of the face value of such Notes. Fair value of such financial instruments is not necessarily representative of the amount that could be realized or settled.

Example 29: Fair Value of Long-Term Debt Is Estimated Based on Current Rates and Terms Offered to the Company

The fair value of the Company's long-term debt is estimated based on the current rates offered to the Company for debt of similar terms and maturities. Under this method, the Company's fair value of long-term debt was not significantly different from the carrying value at December 31, 20X2.

Example 30: Fair Value of Notes Receivable Is Based on Discounted Cash Flows

The fair value of notes receivable, which is based on discounted cash flows using current interest rates, approximates the carrying value at December 31, 20X2.

Foreign Operations

Example 31: Company's Future Operations Are Dependent on Foreign Operations

The Company's future operations and earnings will depend on the results of the Company's operations in [*name of foreign country*]. There can be no assurance that the Company will be able to successfully conduct such operations, and a failure to do so would have a material adverse effect on the Company's financial position, results of operations, and cash flows. In addition, the success of the Company's operations will be subject to numerous contingencies, some of which are beyond management's control. These contingencies include general and regional economic conditions, prices for the Company's products, competition, and changes in regulation. Because the Company is dependent on international operations, specifically those in [*name of foreign country*], the Company will be subject to various additional political, economic, and other uncertainties. Among other risks, the Company's operations will be subject to the risks of restrictions on transfer of funds; export duties, quotas and embargoes; domestic and international customs and tariffs; changing taxation policies; foreign exchange restrictions; and political conditions and governmental regulations.

Example 32: Foreign Currency Adjustments—Functional Currency Is the Foreign Country's Local Currency

The financial position and operating results of substantially all foreign operations are consolidated using the local currencies of the countries in which the Company operates as the functional currency. Local currency assets and liabilities are translated at the rates of exchange on the balance sheet date, and local currency revenues and expenses are translated at average rates of exchange during the period. The resulting translation adjustments are recorded directly into a separate component of shareholders' equity.

Example 33: Foreign Currency Adjustments—Functional Currency Is the U.S. Dollar

The Company's functional currency for all operations worldwide is the U.S. dollar. Nonmonetary assets and liabilities are translated at historical rates and monetary assets and liabilities are translated at exchange rates in effect at the end of the year. Income statement accounts are translated at average rates for the year. Gains and losses from translation of foreign currency financial statements into U.S. dollars are included in current results of operations. Gains and losses resulting from foreign currency transactions are also included in current results of operations.

Example 34: Foreign Currency Adjustments—Certain Assets and Liabilities Are Remeasured at Current Exchange Rates and Others Are Remeasured at Historical Rates

The U.S. dollar is the "functional currency" of the Company's worldwide continuing operations. All foreign currency asset and liability amounts are remeasured into U.S. dollars at end-of-period exchange rates, except for inventories, prepaid expenses and property, plant and equipment, which are remeasured at historical rates. Foreign currency income and expenses are remeasured at average exchange rates in effect during the year, except for expenses related to balance sheet amounts remeasured at historical exchange rates. Exchange gains and losses arising from remeasurement of foreign currency denominated monetary assets and liabilities are included in income in the period in which they occur.

Going Concern Issues

Example 35: Company's Successful Operations Are Dependent on Those of Its Parent

The Company has historically relied on its parent company to meet its cash flow requirements. The parent has cash available in the amount of approximately $83,000 as of December 31, 20X2, and a working capital deficit of $80 million. The Senior Secured Notes in the amount of $65 million have been reclassified because the Company's parent company does not currently have sufficient funds to make the next interest payment (in the approximate amount of $6 million) due in May 20X3. Failure by the parent to make such payment could allow the holders of the Notes to declare all amounts outstanding immediately due and payable. The Company and its parent will need additional funds to meet the development and exploratory obligations until sufficient cash flows are generated from anticipated production to sustain operations and to fund future development and exploration obligations.

The parent plans to generate the additional cash needed through the sale or financing of its domestic assets held for sale and the completion of additional equity, debt, or joint venture transactions. There is no assurance, however, that the parent will be able to sell or finance its assets held for sale or to complete other transactions in the future at commercially reasonable terms, if at all, or that the Company will be able to meet its future contractual obligations.

Income Taxes

Example 36: Election to Defer Application of ASC Topic 740, Income Taxes, Based on FSP FIN 48-3, Effective Date of FASB Interpretation No. 48 for Certain Nonpublic Enterprises

In June 2006, the Financial Accounting Standards Board issued FASB Interpretation No. 48 (FIN-48), *Accounting for Uncertainty in Income Taxes—An Interpretation of FASB Statement No. 109.* FIN-48 clarifies the accounting for uncertainty in income taxes recognized in an entity's financial statements in accordance with Statement of Financial Accounting Standards No. 109, *Accounting for Income Taxes.* This Interpretation prescribes a recognition threshold and measurement attribute for the financial statement recognition and measurement of a tax position taken or expected to be taken in a tax return. In addition, FIN-48 provides guidance on derecognition, classification, interest and penalties, accounting in interim periods, disclosure, and transition.

FASB Staff Position (FSP) FIN 48-3, *Effective Date of FASB Interpretation No. 48 for Certain Nonpublic Enterprises,* which was issued in

December 2008, defers the effective date of FIN-48 for nonpublic entities to annual financial statements for fiscal years beginning after December 15, 2008. This guidance was codified into ASC Topic 740, *Income Taxes*, effective July 1, 2009.

The Company has elected to defer the application of this guidance, as permitted under generally accepted accounting principles. The Company presently recognizes income tax positions based on management's estimate of whether it is reasonably possible that a liability has been incurred for unrecognized income tax benefits by applying ASC Topic 450, *Contingencies*. The Company will be required to adopt the new requirements in its 2009 annual financial statements. Management is currently assessing the impact of these requirements on its financial statements.

Example 37: C Corporation

Deferred tax assets and liabilities are recognized for the future tax consequences attributable to differences between the financial statement carrying amounts of existing assets and liabilities and their respective tax bases. Deferred tax assets, including tax loss and credit carryforwards, and liabilities are measured using enacted tax rates expected to apply to taxable income in the years in which those temporary differences are expected to be recovered or settled. The effect on deferred tax assets and liabilities of a change in tax rates is recognized in income in the period that includes the enactment date. Deferred income tax expense represents the change during the period in the deferred tax assets and deferred tax liabilities. The components of the deferred tax assets and liabilities are individually classified as current and non-current based on their characteristics. Deferred tax assets are reduced by a valuation allowance when, in the opinion of management, it is more likely than not that some portion or all of the deferred tax assets will not be realized.

Example 38: S Corporation

The Company, with the consent of its stockholders, has elected under the Internal Revenue Code to be taxed as an S Corporation. The stockholders of an S Corporation are taxed on their proportionate share of the Company's taxable income. Therefore, no provision or liability for federal income taxes has been included in the financial statements. Certain specific deductions and credits flow through the Company to its stockholders.

This election is valid for [State]; however, [State] law requires a minimum tax of [amount]% on State taxable income. Therefore, a provision and a related liability have been included in the financial statements for [State] income taxes.

Example 39: Limited Liability Company

As a limited liability company, the Company's taxable income or loss is allocated to members in accordance with their respective percentage ownership. Therefore, no provision or liability for income taxes has been included in the financial statements.

Example 40: Partnership

The Partnership is not a taxpaying entity for federal or state income tax purposes; accordingly, a provision for income taxes has not been recorded in the accompanying financial statements. Partnership income or losses are reflected in the partners' individual or corporate income tax returns in accordance with their ownership percentages.

Example 41: Proprietorship

The Proprietorship is not a taxpaying entity for federal or state income tax purposes; accordingly, a provision for income taxes has not been recorded in the accompanying financial statements. Federal and state income taxes of the proprietor are computed on [his/her] total income from all sources.

Example 42: Realization of the Deferred Income Tax Asset Is Dependent on Generating Future Taxable Income

Deferred tax assets are reduced by a valuation allowance when, in the opinion of management, it is more likely than not that some portion or all of the deferred tax assets will not be realized. Realization of the deferred income tax asset is dependent on generating sufficient taxable income in future years. Although realization is not assured, management believes it is more likely than not that all of the deferred income tax asset will be realized. The amount of the deferred income tax asset considered realizable, however, could be reduced in the near term if estimates of future taxable income are reduced.

Example 43: Company Has Substantial Net Operating Loss Carryforwards and a Valuation Allowance Is Recorded

The Company recognizes the amount of taxes payable or refundable for the current year and recognizes deferred tax liabilities and assets for the expected future tax consequences of events and transactions that have been recognized in the Company's financial statements or tax returns. The Company currently has substantial net operating loss carryforwards. The Company has recorded a 100% valuation allowance against net deferred tax assets due to uncertainty of their ultimate realization.

Example 44: Subchapter S Status Terminated

Before January 1, 20X2, the Company had operated as a C corporation. Effective January 1, 20X2, the stockholders of the Company elected to be taxed under Subchapter S of the Internal Revenue Code. During such period, federal income taxes were the responsibility of the Company's stockholders as were certain state income taxes. As of the effective date of the election, the Company was responsible for Federal built-in-gain taxes to the extent applicable. Accordingly, the consolidated statement of operations for the year ended December 31, 20X2, provides for such taxes. The S corporation election terminated in connection with the consummation of the initial public offering of the Company's common stock on October 10, 20X2.

Example 45: Conversion from an LLC to a C Corporation

From the Company's inception in March 19X7 to February 20X2, the Company was not subject to federal and state income taxes since it was operating as a Limited Liability Company (LLC). On February 2, 20X2, the Company converted from an LLC to a C corporation and, as a result, became subject to corporate federal and state income taxes. The Company's accumulated deficit of $4.3 million at that date was reclassified to additional paid-in capital.

Example 46: Conversion from Cash Basis to Accrual Basis for Tax Purposes Results in a Deferred Tax Liability

In the current year, the Company converted from a cash basis to an accrual basis for tax purposes in conjunction with its conversion to a C corporation. Due to temporary differences in recognition of revenue and expenses, income for financial reporting purposes exceeded income for income tax purposes. The conversion to an accrual basis along with these temporary differences resulted in the recognition of a net deferred tax liability, and a corresponding one-time charge to expense, of $3.5 million as of December 31, 20X2.

Example 47: Subsidiary Files a Consolidated Federal Income Tax Return with Its Parent

The Company files a consolidated federal income tax return with its parent company, but files a separate state income tax return. In accordance with the intercorporate tax allocation policy, the Company pays to or receives from the parent company amounts equivalent to federal income tax charges or credits based on separate company taxable income or loss using the statutory rates.

Inventory

Example 48: Inventories Accounted for under FIFO

Inventories are stated at the lower of cost (first-in, first-out basis) or market (net realizable value).

Example 49: Inventories Accounted for under LIFO

Inventories are stated at the lower of cost or market. Cost is determined by the last-in, first-out (LIFO) method for all inventories. Market value for raw materials is based on replacement cost and for work-in-process and finished goods on net realizable value.

Example 50: Inventory Stated at Standard Cost—Due Consideration Given to Obsolescence and Inventory Levels in Evaluating Net Realizable Value

Inventories are stated at the lower of cost or market. Cost is determined on a standard cost basis that approximates the first-in, first-out (FIFO) method. Market is determined based on net realizable value. Appropriate consideration is given to obsolescence, excessive levels, deterioration, and other factors in evaluating net realizable value.

Example 51: Inventories Accounted for under LIFO and FIFO

Inventories, consisting of manufactured products and merchandise for resale, are stated at the lower of cost or market. Manufactured products include the costs of materials, labor, and manufacturing overhead. Inventories accounted for using the last-in, first-out (LIFO) method approximated 60% and 65% of total inventory as of year-end 20X2 and 20X1, respectively. Remaining inventories are generally determined using the first-in, first-out (FIFO) cost method. For detailed inventory information, see Note [X].

Example 52: Inventory Valuation Includes Provision for Obsolescence

Inventories are stated at the lower of cost (FIFO) or market, including provisions for obsolescence commensurate with known or estimated exposures. Inventories are shown net of a valuation reserve of $450,000 at December 31, 20X2, and $300,000 at December 31, 20X1.

Example 53: Inventory Note Describes Accounting Policy for New Products

Inventories are stated at the lower of cost (determined by the first-in, first-out method) or market (net realizable value). Costs associated with the manufacture of a new product are charged to engineering, research and development expense as incurred until the product is proven through testing and acceptance by the customer.

Example 54: Inventory Note Addresses Risk Exposure to Technological Change

Inventories are stated at the lower of cost (FIFO) or market. Inventories consist primarily of components and subassemblies and finished products held for sale. Rapid technological change and new product introductions and enhancements could result in excess or obsolete inventory. To minimize this risk, the Company evaluates inventory levels and expected usage on a periodic basis and records adjustments as required.

Investments

Example 55: Short-Term Investments

As part of its cash management program, the Company from time to time maintains a portfolio of marketable investment securities. The securities have an investment grade and a term to earliest maturity generally of less than one year and include tax exempt securities and certificates of deposit. These securities are carried at cost, which approximates market.

Example 56: Held-to-Maturity, Trading, and Available-for-Sale Marketable Securities

The Company classifies its debt and marketable equity securities into held-to-maturity, trading, or available-for-sale categories. Debt securities are classified as held-to-maturity when the Company has the positive intent and ability to hold the securities to maturity. Debt securities for which the Company does not have the intent or ability to hold to maturity are classified as available for sale. Held-to-maturity securities are recorded as either short-term or long-term on the balance sheet based on contractual maturity date and are stated at amortized cost. Marketable securities that are bought and held principally for the purpose of selling them in the near term are classified as trading securities and are reported at fair value, with unrealized gains and losses recognized in earnings. Debt and marketable equity securities not classified as held-to-maturity or as trading are classified as available-for-sale and are carried at fair market value, with the unrealized gains and losses, net of tax, included in the determination of comprehensive income and reported in shareholders' equity.

Example 57: Reverse Repurchase Agreements

Securities purchased under agreements to resell (reverse repurchase agreements) result from transactions that are collateralized by negotiable securities and are carried at the amounts at which the securities will subsequently be resold. It is the policy of the Company not to take possession of securities purchased under agreements to resell. At December 31, 20X2, and December 31, 20X1, agreements to resell securities in the amount of $1,300,000 with a three-day maturity and $3,200,000 with a 14-day maturity were outstanding, respectively.

Example 58: Accounting Policy Describes the Method of Accounting for Unconsolidated Subsidiaries

The equity method of accounting is used when the Company has a 20% to 50% interest in other entities. Under the equity method, original investments are recorded at cost and adjusted by the Company's share of undistributed earnings or losses of these entities. Nonmarketable investments in which the Company has less than a 20% interest and in which it does not have the ability to exercise significant influence over the investee are initially recorded at cost, and periodically reviewed for impairment.

Nature of Operations

Example 59: Company Describes Its Primary Products

The Company designs, manufactures, markets, and services test systems and related software, and backplanes and associated connectors. The Company's top five products are (1) semiconductor test systems, (2) backplane connection systems, (3) circuit-board test systems, (4) telecommunications test systems, and (5) software test systems.

Example 60: Company Describes the Types of Customers It Has

The Company is a leading global developer, manufacturer, and distributor of hand tools, power tools, tool storage products, shop equipment, under-hood diagnostics equipment, under-car equipment, emissions and safety equipment, collision repair equipment, vehicle service information, and business management systems and services. The Corporation's customers include professional automotive technicians, shop owners, franchised service centers, national accounts, original equipment manufacturers, and industrial tool and equipment users worldwide.

Example 61: Company Describes U.S. Geographic Locations Where It Operates

The Company is a leading designer and manufacturer of open-architecture, standard embedded computer components that system designers can easily use to create a custom solution specific to the user's unique application. The Company has operations in New York, New Mexico, Minnesota, North Carolina, and California. The Company's product lines include CPU boards, general purpose input/output modules, avionics interface modules and analyzers, interconnection and expansion units, telemetry boards, data acquisition software, and industrial computer systems and enclosures.

Example 62: Company Indicates That Its Operations Are Vulnerable to Changes in Trends and Customer Demand

The Company is a nationwide specialty retailer of fashionable and contemporary apparel and accessory items designed for consumers with a young, active lifestyle. The Company's success is largely dependent on its ability to gauge the fashion tastes of its customers and to provide merchandise that satisfies customer demand. The Company's failure to anticipate, identify, or react to changes in fashion trends could adversely affect its results of operations.

Example 63: Company's Operations Are Substantially in Foreign Countries

Substantially all of the Company's products are manufactured in the Dominican Republic, Mexico (under the Maquiladora program), Switzerland, Ireland, and Slovakia. These foreign operations represent captive manufacturing facilities of the Company. The Company's operations are subject to various political, economic, and other risks and uncertainties inherent in the countries in which the Company operates. Among other risks, the Company's operations are subject to the risks of restrictions on transfer of funds; export duties, quotas, and embargoes; domestic and international customs and tariffs; changing taxation policies; foreign exchange restrictions; and political conditions and governmental regulations.

Example 64: Company Specifies Percentage of Net Sales Relating to Foreign Operations

Sales to customers outside the United States approximated 35% of net sales in 20X2 and 25% of net sales in 20X1.

New Accounting Pronouncements

Example 65: Adoption of New FASB Accounting Standard in the Current Year—Prior-Year Financial Statements Restated

In 20X2, the Company adopted FASB ASC [*number*] [(*title*)], which requires [*describe briefly the requirements of the new standard*]. The effect of this change was to [*increase/decrease*] 20X2 income before extraordinary items and 20X2 net income by $[*amount*]. The financial statements for 20X1 have been retroactively restated for the change, which resulted in an [*increase/decrease*] in income before extraordinary items and net income for 20X1 of $[*amount*]. Retained earnings as of January 1, 20X1, has been adjusted for the effect of retroactive application of the new standard.

Example 66: Adoption of New FASB Accounting Standard in the Current Year—No Material Effect on the Financial Statements

In 20X2, the Company adopted FASB ASC [*number*] [(*title*)], which requires [*describe briefly the requirements of the new standard*]. There was no material impact on the Company's results of operations or financial condition upon adoption of the new standard.

Example 67: New FASB Accounting Standard to Be Adopted in the Future

In December 20X2, the Financial Accounting Standards Board issued [*number*] [(*title*)], which requires [*describe briefly the requirements of the new standard*]. The new standard is effective for the year ending December 31, 20X3. The adoption of the new standard is not expected to have a material effect on the Company's financial position, results of operations, or cash flows.
   Or:
   The Company is currently evaluating the effect that implementation of the new standard will have on its financial position, results of operations, and cash flows.

Pension and Other Employee Benefit Plans

Example 68: Defined Benefit Pension Plans

The Company has two defined benefit retirement plans that cover substantially all of its employees. Defined benefit plans for salaried employees provide benefits based on employees' years of service and five-year final overall base compensation. Defined benefit plans for hourly paid employees, including those covered by multi-employer pension plans under collective bargaining agreements, generally provide benefits of stated amounts for specified periods of service. The Company's policy is to fund, at a minimum, amounts as are necessary on an actuarial basis to provide assets sufficient to meet the benefits to be paid to plan members in accordance with the requirements of the Employee Retirement Income Security Act of 1974 (ERISA). Assets of the plans are administered by an independent trustee and are invested principally in fixed income securities, equity securities, and real estate.

Example 69: Defined Contribution Plan

Certain employees are covered by defined contribution plans. The Corporation's contributions to these plans are based on a percentage of employee compensation or employee contributions. These plans are funded on a current basis.

Example 70: Profit-Sharing Plan

The Company has a profit-sharing plan covering most employees with more than two years of service. The Company contributes 5% of earnings before income taxes to the Plan. The Company's contributions to the Plan were $325,000 for 20X2 and $215,000 for 20X1.

Example 71: Salary Reduction Plan

The Company has a defined contribution, salary-reduction plan that covers all its employees after one year of service. Employees may contribute up to 15% of their salary to the plan and the Company makes a matching contribution of 50%, up to 3% of compensation.

Property and Equipment and Depreciation Methods

Example 72: Basis for Recording Fixed Assets, Lives, and Depreciation Methods

Property and equipment are recorded at cost. Expenditures for major additions and improvements are capitalized, and minor replacements, maintenance, and repairs are charged to expense as incurred. When property and equipment are retired or otherwise disposed of, the cost and accumulated depreciation are removed from the accounts and any resulting gain or loss is included in the results of operations for the respective period. Depreciation is provided over the estimated useful lives of the related assets using the straight-line method for financial statement purposes. The Company uses other depreciation methods (generally accelerated) for tax purposes where appropriate. The estimated useful lives for significant property and equipment categories are as follows:

Vehicles	3 to 10 years
Machinery and equipment	3 to 20 years
Commercial containers	8 to 12 years
Buildings and improvements	10 to 40 years

Example 73: Amortization of Leasehold Improvements

Amortization of leasehold improvements is computed using the straight-line method over the shorter of the remaining lease term or the estimated useful lives of the improvements.

Example 74: Assets Held under Capital Leases

Assets held under capital leases are recorded at the lower of the net present value of the minimum lease payments or the fair value of the leased asset at the inception of the lease. Amortization expense is computed using the straight-line method over the shorter of the estimated useful lives of the assets or the period of the related lease.

Example 75: Construction in Progress and Estimated Cost to Complete Construction of New Facility

The Company is constructing a new facility scheduled to be completed in 20X4, at which time depreciation will commence. As of December 31, 20X2, the Company incurred and capitalized in Construction in Progress $1,600,000. The estimated cost to be incurred in 20X3 and 20X4 to complete construction of the facility is approximately $12 million.

Example 76: Review of Carrying Value of Property and Equipment for Impairment

The Company reviews the carrying value of property, plant, and equipment for impairment whenever events and circumstances indicate that the carrying value of an asset may not be recoverable from the estimated future cash flows expected to result from its use and eventual disposition. In cases where undiscounted expected future cash flows are less than the carrying value, an impairment loss is recognized equal to an amount by which the carrying value exceeds the fair value of assets. The factors considered by management in performing this assessment include current operating results, trends and prospects, the manner in which the property is used, and the effects of obsolescence, demand, competition, and other economic factors. Based on this assessment there was no impairment at December 31, 20X2.

Reclassifications

Example 77: Items Reclassified Not Specifically Identified

Certain reclassifications have been made to the prior years' financial statements to conform to the current year presentation. These reclassifications had no effect on previously reported results of operations or retained earnings.

Example 78: Items Reclassified Specifically Identified

In the current year, the Company separately classified trademarks and copyrights in the Balance Sheets and has included stock-based compensation as selling, general, and administrative expense in the Statements of Operations. For comparative purposes, amounts in the prior years have been reclassified to conform to current year presentations.

Rent Obligation

Example 79: Operating Lease Contains Provisions for Future Rent Increases

The Company has entered into operating lease agreements for its corporate office and warehouses, some of which contain provisions for future rent increases or periods in which rent payments are reduced (abated). In accordance with generally accepted accounting principles, the Company records monthly rent expense equal to the total of the payments due over the lease term, divided by the number of months of the lease term. The difference between rent expense recorded and the amount paid is credited or charged to "Deferred rent obligation," which is reflected as a separate line item in the accompanying Balance Sheet.

Reincorporation

Example 80: Reincorporation in a New State

The Company originally was organized under the laws of the state of New York on June 1, 19X9 and was subsequently reincorporated under the laws of the state of Georgia on November 12, 20X1. The name of the company was changed to DEF, Inc. from ABC Corp. on October 15, 20X2. In connection with the re-incorporation of the Company in November 20X1, as approved by the stockholders, the number of authorized shares of the Company's common stock was increased to one hundred million (100,000,000) and each share of common stock was assigned a par value of $.01. The shares outstanding and all other references to shares of common stock reported have been restated to give effect to the re-incorporation.

Research and Development Costs

Example 81: Research and Development Costs Expensed

Research, development, and engineering costs are expensed in the year incurred. For 20X2 these costs were $2,050,000 and for 20X1 they were $1,100,000.

Example 82: Product Development Costs Deferred

The Company defers certain costs related to the preliminary activities associated with the manufacture of its products, which the Company has determined have future economic benefit. These costs are then expensed in the period in which the initial shipment of the related product is made. Management periodically reviews and revises, when necessary, its estimate of the future benefit of these costs and expenses them if it is deemed there no longer is a future benefit. At December 31, 20X2, and December 31, 20X1, capitalized product development costs totaled $611,000 and $523,000, respectively.

Restricted Funds

Example 83: Restricted Funds Held by Trustees

Restricted funds held by trustees of $1,300,000 and $900,000 at December 31, 20X2 and 20X1, respectively, are included in other non-current assets and consist principally of funds deposited in connection with plant closure obligations, insurance escrow deposits, and amounts held for new plant and other construction arising from industrial revenue financing. These amounts are principally invested in fixed income securities of federal, state, and local governmental entities and financial institutions. The Company considers such trustee-restricted investments to be held to maturity. At December 31, 20X2, and December 31, 20X1, the aggregate fair value of these investments approximates their amortized costs, and substantially all of these investments mature within one year.

Example 84: Investments Restricted for Construction Financing

Restricted investments consist of U.S. governmental obligations with maturities of more than one year. These investments are carried at fair value and are restricted as to withdrawal for construction financing. Restricted investments are held in the Company's name and custodied with two major financial institutions.

Example 85: Restricted Cash Included in Other Non-Current Assets

At December 31, 20X2, other non-current assets included restricted cash of $1,200,000 pledged to support a bank credit facility. At December 31, 20X1, restricted cash balances of $2,450,000 represented amounts pledged to support bank guarantees issued on several large construction contracts.

Revenue Recognition

For examples of financial statement disclosures, see Chapter 35, "ASC Topic 605: Revenue Recognition."

Self-Insurance

Example 86: Self-Insured Claims Liability

The Company is primarily self-insured, up to certain limits, for automobile and general liability, workers' compensation, and employee group health claims. Operations are charged with the cost of claims reported and an estimate of claims incurred but not reported. A liability for unpaid claims and the associated claim expenses, including incurred but not reported losses, is actuarially determined and reflected in the balance sheet as an accrued liability. The self-insured claims liability includes incurred but not reported losses of $1,500,000 and $1,745,000 at December 31, 20X2, and December 31, 20X1, respectively. The determination of such claims and expenses and the appropriateness of the related liability is continually reviewed and updated.

Example 87: Self-Insured Health Plan Supplemented by Stop-Loss Insurance

The Company has a self-insured health plan for all its employees. The Company has purchased stop-loss insurance in order to limit its exposure, which will reimburse the Company for individual claims in excess of $50,000 annually or aggregate claims exceeding $1,000,000 annually. Self-insurance losses are accrued based on the Company's estimates of the aggregate liability for uninsured claims incurred using certain actuarial assumptions followed in the insurance industry. At December 31, 20X2 and December 31, 20X1, the accrued liability for self-insured losses is included in accrued expenses and approximates $1,300,000 and $900,000, respectively.

Shipping and Handling Activities

Example 88: Shipping and Handling Fees Charged to Customers and Reported as Revenue

Shipping and handling fees billed to customers are classified on the Statement of Operations as "Net sales" and were $2 million and $1.8 million for 20X2 and 20X1, respectively. The associated shipping and handling costs are classified in "Cost of sales" and were $2.3 million and $2.1 million for 20X2 and 20X1, respectively.

Example 89: Shipping and Handling Costs Are Included in Cost of Sales

The Company's shipping and handling costs are included in cost of sales for all periods presented.

> **Note:** If shipping and handling costs are significant and are not included in costs of sales, then disclosure is required of the amount of such costs and the line item in which they are included on the income statement. See Example below for appropriate disclosure when shipping and handling costs are not included in cost of sales.

Example 90: Shipping and Handling Costs Are Included in Selling, General and Administrative Expenses

> **Note:** If shipping and handling costs are significant and are *not* included in costs of sales, then disclosure is required of the amount of such costs and the line item in which they are included on the income statement.

Shipping and handling costs of $785,000 in 20X2 and $692,000 in 20X1 are included in selling, general, and administrative expenses.

Warranty Costs

Example 91: Accrual for Warranty Costs Is Made in the Period in Which the Revenue Is Recognized

The Company provides product warranties for specific product lines and accrues for estimated future warranty costs in the period in which the revenue is recognized.

Example 92: Accrual for Warranty Costs Is Made When Such Costs Become Probable

Provision for estimated warranty costs is made in the period in which such costs become probable and is periodically adjusted to reflect actual experience.

Example 93: Product Warranty Policy and Period Described

The Company warrants its products against defects in design, materials, and workmanship generally for three to five years. A provision for estimated future costs related to warranty expense is recorded when products are shipped.

Example 94: Warranty Costs Are Subject to Significant Estimates

The Company's warranty accruals are based on the Company's best estimates of product failure rates and unit costs to repair. However, the Company is continually releasing new and more complex and technologically advanced products. As a result, it is at least reasonably possible that products could be released with certain unknown quality and/or design problems. Such an occurrence could result in materially higher than expected warranty and related costs, which could have a materially adverse effect on the Company's results of operations and financial condition in the near term.

CHAPTER 9
ASC TOPIC 250: ACCOUNTING CHANGES AND ERROR CORRECTIONS

CONTENTS

EXECUTIVE SUMMARY

Accounting changes are broadly classified into three categories:

1. Changes in accounting estimates

2.   Changes in accounting principles

3.   Changes in the reporting entity

Corrections of errors in previously issued financial statements are not accounting changes, but they are covered in the same accounting literature because of their similarity.

Changes in Accounting Estimates

A change in an accounting estimate usually is the result of new events, changing conditions, more experience, or additional information, any of which requires previous estimates to be revised. Estimates are necessary in determining depreciation and amortization of long-lived assets, uncollectible receivables, provisions for warranty, and a multitude of other items involved in preparing financial statements.

A change in accounting estimate is accounted for in the period of change if the change affects only that period, or in the period of change and future periods if the change affects both. A change in accounting estimate is not accounted for by restating or retrospectively adjusting amounts reported in financial statements of prior periods or by reporting pro forma amounts for prior periods.

Distinguishing between a change in accounting principle and a change in accounting estimate may be difficult. In some cases, a change in estimate is effected by a change in accounting principle, such as when a depreciation method is changed to reflect a change in the estimated future benefits of the asset or the pattern of consumption of those benefits. Changes in accounting estimates that are inseparable from changes in accounting principles should be accounted for as changes in accounting estimates. Similar to other changes in accounting principle, a change in accounting estimate that is effected by a change in accounting principle is appropriate only if the new principle is justifiable on the basis that it is preferable.

> **Note:** A change in depreciation, amortization, or depletion method for long-lived assets should be accounted for as a change in accounting estimate, effected by a change in accounting principle. Therefore, the change may only be made if the new depreciation method is preferable. A change in depreciation method (e.g., from the double declining balance method to the straight-line method) should not be accounted for by retrospective application to prior periods because it constitutes a change in estimate.

Changes in Accounting Principles

An entity may change an accounting principle only if the change is required by a newly issued accounting pronouncement or the entity can justify the use of a different allowable accounting principle on the basis that it is preferable. Common changes in accounting principles include the following:

- Changing the method of pricing inventory (e.g., changing from LIFO to FIFO or from FIFO to LIFO)
- Changing the method of accounting for long-term construction-type contracts
- Adopting a new accounting principle

An entity making a change in accounting principle should report that change by retrospective application of the new principle to all periods presented unless it is impracticable to do so or unless the new accounting pronouncement requires alternative transition requirements. Retrospective application requires the following steps:

1. The cumulative effect of the change to the new principle on periods prior to those presented should be reflected in the carrying amount of assets and liabilities as of the beginning of the first period presented;

2. An offsetting adjustment, if any, should be made to the opening balance of retained earnings for that period; and

3. Financial statements for each individual prior period presented should be adjusted to reflect the period-specific effects of applying the new principle.

If the cumulative effect of applying a change in accounting principle to all prior periods can be determined, but it is impracticable to determine the period-specific effects of that change on all prior periods presented, the cumulative effect of the change should be applied to the carrying amounts of assets and liabilities as of the beginning of the earliest period to which the new accounting principle can be applied. The offsetting adjustment, if any, should be made to the opening balance of retained earnings for that period.

If it is impracticable to determine the cumulative effect of applying a change in accounting principle to any prior period, the new principle should be applied prospectively as of the earliest date practicable. A change from the first-in, first-out (FIFO) inventory method to the last-in, first-out (LIFO) inventory method when the effects of having been on LIFO in the past cannot be determined is an example of this situation.

Changes in the Reporting Entity

A change in the reporting entity takes place when the following occurs:

- Presenting consolidated or combined financial statements in place of statements of individual companies
- Changing specific subsidiaries that make up the group of companies for which consolidated financial statements are presented
- Changing the companies included in combined financial statements

An accounting change that results in financial statements that are, in effect, those of a different reporting entity should be retrospectively applied to the financial statements for the new reporting entity.

Correction of Errors

Errors that are discovered in financial statements subsequent to their issuance are reported as prior-period adjustments. Errors result from mistakes in mathematics and in the application of an accounting principle or from misjudgment in the use of facts. Although correcting an error and changing an estimate are similar and are sometimes confused, they differ in that a change in estimate is based on new (revised) information that was previously unavailable. A change from an unacceptable accounting principle to a generally accepted one is considered an error correction for financial reporting purposes.

An error in financial statements of prior periods that is discovered after those statements are issued is reported as a prior-period adjustment by restating the prior-period financial statements. This requires the following three steps:

1. The cumulative effect of the error on periods prior to those presented (i.e., the period in which the error is discovered and corrected) is reflected in the carrying amounts of assets and liabilities as of the beginning of the first period presented;

2. An offsetting adjustment, if any, is made to the opening balance of retained earnings (or other component of equity or net assets in the statement of financial position) for that period; and

3. Financial statements for each individual prior period presented are adjusted to reflect correction of the period-specific effects of the error.

Accounting Literature

FASB Accounting Standards Codification Topic	*Pre-Codification Accounting Literature*
250, *Accounting Changes and Error Corrections*	FAS-16, *Prior Period Adjustments*
270, *Interim Reporting*	FAS-154, *Accounting Changes and Error Corrections*
	APB-9, *Reporting the Results of Operations*
	APB-28, *Interim Financial Reporting*
	AU 9410, *Adherence to Generally Accepted Accounting Principles—Auditing Interpretations of Section 410, Adherence to Generally Accepted Accounting Principles*

DISCLOSURE AND KEY PRESENTATION REQUIREMENTS

Changes in Accounting Estimates

1. A change in accounting estimate should be accounted for in the period of change if the change affects that period only, or in the period of change and future periods if the change affects both. (ASC 250-10-45-17) (FAS-154, par. 19) (*Note:* A change in accounting estimate should *not* be accounted for by restating or retrospectively adjusting amounts reported in financial statements of prior periods or by reporting pro forma amounts for prior periods.)

2. For a change in accounting estimate that affects several future periods (e.g., change in service lives of depreciable assets), the effect of the change on the following for the current period should be disclosed (ASC 250-10-50-4) (FAS-154, par. 22): (*Note:* Disclosure of these effects is not necessary for estimates made each period in the ordinary course of accounting [e.g., uncollectible accounts, inventory obsolescence] unless the effect of the change in estimate is material.)

    a. Income from continuing operations.

    b. Net income.

    c. Related per-share amounts, if applicable.

3. For a change in accounting estimate that has no material effect in the period of change but is reasonably certain to have a material effect in later periods, a description of the change should be disclosed whenever the financial statements of the period of change are presented. (ASC 250-10-50-4) (FAS-154, par. 22)

4. If a change in accounting estimate is effected by a change in accounting principle, the change should be considered a change in estimate and the disclosures in item 4 under "Changes in Accounting Principles" below should be made. (ASC 250-10-45-18; 250-10-50-4) (FAS-154, pars. 20 and 22)

Changes in Accounting Principles

1. A reporting entity should change an accounting principle only if either of the following applies (ASC 250-10-45-2) (FAS-154, par. 5):

    a. The change is required by a newly issued Codification update.

    b. The entity can justify the use of an allowable alternative accounting principle on the basis that it is preferable.

2. In the unusual instance that there are no transition requirements specific to a particular Codification update, a change in accounting principle effected to adopt the requirements of that Codification update should be reported in accordance with item 3 below. (ASC 250-10-45-3) (FAS-154, par. 6) (*Note*: It is expected that Codification updates normally will provide specific transition requirements. Early adoption of a Codification update, when permitted, should be effected in a manner consistent with the transition requirements of that update.)

3. A change in accounting principle should be reported as follows:

    a. Through retrospective application of the new accounting principle to all prior periods presented (unless it is impracticable). (ASC 250-10-45-5) (FAS-154, par. 7)

    b. If the cumulative effect of applying a change in accounting principle to all prior periods can be determined, but it is impracticable to determine the period-specific effects of that change on all prior periods presented, the cumulative effect of the change to the new accounting principle should be applied to the carrying amounts of assets and liabilities as of the beginning of the earliest period to which the new accounting principle can be applied (with an offsetting adjustment, if any, made to the opening balance of retained earnings for that period). (ASC 250-10-45-6) (FAS-154, par. 8)

c. If it is impracticable to determine the cumulative effect of applying a change in accounting principle to any prior period, the new accounting principle should be applied as if the change was made prospectively as of the earliest date practicable. (ASC 250-10-45-7) (FAS-154, par. 9)

d. Retrospective application should include only the direct effects of a change in accounting principle (including any related income tax effects). (ASC 250-10-45-8) (FAS-154, par. 10)

4. The following should be disclosed in the fiscal period in which a change in accounting principle is made (ASC 250-10-50-1 and 50-2) (FAS-154, par. 17) (*Note:* An entity that issues interim financial statements should provide the required disclosures in the financial statements of both the interim period of the change and the annual period of the change):

a. The nature of and reason for the change in accounting principle, including an explanation of why the newly adopted accounting principle is preferable.

b. The method of applying the change.

c. A description of the prior-period information that has been retrospectively adjusted.

d. The effect of the change on the following for the current period and any prior periods retrospectively adjusted:

(1) Income from continuing operations.

(2) Net income.

(3) Any other affected financial statement line item.

(4) Any affected per-share amounts, if applicable.

e. The cumulative effect of the change on retained earnings (or other components of equity) as of the beginning of the earliest period presented.

f. If retrospective application to all prior periods is impracticable, the reasons why, and a description of the alternative method used to report the change.

g. If indirect effects of a change in accounting principle are recognized:

(1) A description of the indirect effects of a change in accounting principle, including the amounts that have been recognized in the current period, and the related per-share amounts, if applicable.

(2) Unless impracticable, the amount of the total recognized indirect effects of the accounting change and the related per-share amounts, if applicable, that are attributable to each prior period presented.

5. In the fiscal year in which a new accounting principle is adopted, financial information reported for interim periods after the date of adoption of a new accounting principle should disclose the effect of the change on income from continuing operations, net income, and related per-share amounts, if applicable, for those post-change interim periods. (ASC 250-10-50-3) (FAS-154, par. 18)

6. For a change in accounting principle that has no material effect in the period of change but is reasonably certain to have a material effect in later periods, disclosures should be made of the nature of and reason for the change in accounting principle, including an explanation of why the newly adopted accounting principle is preferable, whenever the financial statements of the period of change are presented. (ASC 250-10-50-1) (FAS-154, par. 17)

7. When an accounting pronouncement has been issued but is not yet effective as of the balance sheet date, consideration should be given to disclosing the following information (Generally accepted practice and AU 9410.13-.18):

a. Existence of the new accounting pronouncement.

b. Date the entity must adopt the new pronouncement or, if early adoption is permitted, the date that it plans to adopt it.

c. Method of adoption (e.g., retroactive application).

d. Impact of new pronouncement on reported financial position and results of operations. (If the impact has been quantified, indicate amount; if immaterial or not determined, so state.)

8. If a public entity that regularly reports interim information makes an accounting change during the fourth quarter of its fiscal year and does not report the data specified in item 4 above in a separate fourth-quarter report or in its annual report, the entity should include disclosure of the effects of the accounting change on interim-period results, as specified in item 4 above, in a note to the annual financial statements for the fiscal year in which the change is made. (ASC 250-10-45-15) (FAS-154, par. 16)

Changes in the Reporting Entity

1. When an accounting change results in financial statements that are, in effect, the statements of a different reporting entity, the change should be retrospectively applied to the financial statements of all prior periods presented to show financial information for the new reporting entity for those periods. (ASC 250-10-45-21) (FAS-154, par. 23) (*Note:* Previously issued interim financial information should be presented on a retrospective basis.)

2. A description of the nature of the change in reporting entity and the reason for it should be disclosed in the period of the change. (ASC 250-10-50-6) (FAS-154, par. 24)

3. The effect of the change in reporting entity on the following should be disclosed for all periods presented (ASC 250-10-50-6) (FAS-154, par. 24):

   a. Income before extraordinary items.

   b. Net income.

   c. Other comprehensive income.

   d. Related per-share amounts, if applicable.

4. For a change in reporting entity that has no material effect in the period of change but is reasonably certain to have a material effect in later periods, disclosures should be made of the nature of and reason for the change, whenever the financial statements of the period of change are presented. (ASC 250-10-50-6) (FAS-154, par. 24)

Correction of Errors

1. Any errors in the financial statements of a prior period discovered after their issuance should be reported as an error correction, by restating the prior-period financial statements. (ASC 250-10-45-23) (FAS-154, par. 25)

2. Error corrections that are material to an interim period, but not material to the estimated income for the full fiscal year, or to the trend of earnings, should be disclosed separately in the interim period. (ASC 250-10-45-27) (APB-28, pars. 28-29) (*Note:* In determining materiality for the purpose of reporting the correction of an error, amounts should be related to the estimated income for the full fiscal year and also to the effect on the trend of earnings.)

3. If the financial statements have been restated to correct an error, the following should be disclosed in the period (annual

or interim) in which the adjustments are made (ASC 250-10-50-7 through 50-10) (FAS-154, par. 26; APB-9, par. 26) (*Note:* Financial statements of subsequent periods are not required to repeat the disclosures.):

   a. The fact that previously issued financial statements have been restated.

   b. A description of the nature of the error.

   c. The effect of the correction on each financial statement line item and any per-share amounts, if applicable, affected for each prior period presented.

   d. The cumulative effect of the change on retained earnings (or other appropriate components of equity), as of the beginning of the earliest period presented.

   e. When single-period financial statements are presented, the effect (both gross and net of applicable income tax) of prior-period adjustments on beginning retained earnings and on net income (and on related per-share amounts when presented) of the immediately preceding period.

   f. When financial statements for more than one period are presented, the effect (both gross and net of applicable income tax) of prior- period adjustments on net income (and on related per-share amounts when presented) for each period presented.

4. The following disclosures should be made in interim financial statements about adjustments related to prior interim periods of the current fiscal year (ASC 250-10-50-11) (FAS-16, par. 15):

   a. The effect on income from continuing operations and net income (and related per-share amounts, if applicable) for each prior interim period of the current fiscal year.

   b. Restated income from continuing operations and net income (and related per-share amounts, if applicable) for each prior interim period restated in accordance with ASC paragraph 250-10-45-26 (FAS-16, par. 14).

5. If a restated historical, statistical-type summary of financial data for a number of periods (commonly 5 or 10 years) is presented and prior-period adjustments have been recorded during any of the periods included therein, disclosure should be made of the restatements in the first summary published after the adjustments. (ASC 250-10-45-28) (APB-9, par. 27)

EXAMPLES OF FINANCIAL STATEMENT DISCLOSURES

 The following sample disclosures are available on the accompanying disc.

Changes in Accounting Estimates

Example 1: Change in Depreciable Lives of Property and Equipment—General

The Company's policy is to periodically review the estimated useful lives of its fixed assets. This review during 20X2 indicated that actual lives for certain asset categories generally were longer than the useful lives used for depreciation purposes in the Company's financial statements. As a result, the Company revised the estimated useful lives of certain categories of property, principally machinery and equipment, effective January 1, 20X2. The effect of this change in estimate was to reduce 20X2 depreciation expense by $100,000, increase 20X2 income from continuing operations by $80,000, and increase 20X2 net income by $60,000.

Example 2: Change in Depreciable Lives of Property and Equipment—Specific Reference Made to Average Depreciation Lives

Effective January 1, 20X2, the Company changed its estimates of the useful lives of certain machinery and equipment at its manufacturing plant. The plant's asset depreciation lives that previously averaged ten years were increased to an average of 15 years, while those that previously averaged six to eight years were increased to an average of ten years. The Company made these changes to better reflect the estimated periods during which such assets will remain in service. This change had the effect of reducing 20X2 depreciation expense by $250,000, increasing 20X2 income from continuing operations by $170,000, and increasing 20X2 net income by $120,000.

Example 3: Change in Accounting Principle Inseparable from Change in Accounting Estimate—The Change Is Accounted for as a Change in Accounting Estimate

Prior to October 1, 20X2, production and tooling costs were charged to cost of sales based on the estimated average unit cost for Projects A, B, C, and D (the Projects) which, in the aggregate, consist of 100,000 lead-rubber bearings. Effective October 1, 20X2, the Company changed its accounting for cost of sales on the Projects from the average cost basis to the specific-unit cost basis. This change to the specific-unit costing method for the Projects was made in recognition of production rates, existing order base, and length of time required to achieve project deliveries, and, therefore, the resultant increased difficulty, which became apparent in the fourth quarter of 20X2, in making the estimates necessary under the average cost basis method. Because the effect of this change in accounting principle was inseparable from the effect of the change in accounting estimate, the change was accounted for as a change in estimate. As a result, the Company recorded a noncash pretax charge to operations of $500,000 in the fourth quarter of 20X2. The effect of the charge was to decrease 20X2 income from continuing operations by $350,000 and decrease 20X2 net income by $300,000.

Changes in Accounting Principles

Example 4: Retrospective Application of a Change in Accounting Principle—Effect on Prior Years Is Determinable and Financial Statements for Prior Periods Retroactively Restated

On January 1, 20X2, ABC Company elected to change its method of valuing its inventory to the first-in, first-out (FIFO) method, whereas in all prior years inventory was valued using the last-in, first-out (LIFO) method. The new method of accounting for inventory was adopted because management believes the FIFO method provides a more meaningful presentation of its financial position because it reflects more recent costs in the balance sheet. Under the current economic environment of low inflation and an expected reduction in inventories and lower production costs, the Company believes that the FIFO cost method also results in a better matching of current costs with current revenues. Comparative financial statements of prior years have been adjusted to apply the new method retrospectively. The following financial statement line items for fiscal years 20X2 and 20X1 were affected by the change in accounting principle.

Income Statement—20X2

	As Computed under LIFO	As Reported under FIFO	Effect of Change
Sales	$ 3,000,000	$ 3,000,000	$ -0-
Cost of goods sold	(1,130,000)	(1,100,000)	(30,000)
Selling, general, and administrative expenses	(1,000,000)	(1,000,000)	-0-
Income before profit sharing and income taxes	870,000	900,000	30,000
Profit sharing	(87,000)	(96,000)[*]	(9,000)

	As Computed under LIFO	As Reported under FIFO	Effect of Change
Income before income taxes	783,000	804,000	21,000
Income taxes	(313,000)	(322,000)	(9,000)
Net income	$ 470,000	$ 482,000	$ 12,000

* This amount includes a $90,000 profit-sharing payment attributable to 20X2 profits and $6,000 profit-sharing payment attributable to 20X1 profits, which is an indirect effect of the change in accounting principle. The incremental payment attributable to 20X1 would have been recognized in 20X1 if ABC Company's inventory had originally been accounted for using the FIFO method.

Income Statement—20X1

	As Originally Reported	As Adjusted	Effect of Change
Sales	$ 3,000,000	$ 3,000,000	$ -0-
Cost of goods sold	(1,000,000)	(940,000)	(60,000)
Selling, general, and administrative expenses	(1,000,000)	(1,000,000)	-0-
Income before profit sharing and income taxes	1,000,000	1,060,000	60,000
Profit sharing	(100,000)	(100,000)	-0-
Income before income taxes	900,000	960,000	60,000
Income taxes	(360,000)	(384,000)	(24,000)
Net income	$ 540,000	$ 576,000	$ 36,000

Balance Sheet—12/31/20X2

	As Computed under LIFO	As Reported under FIFO	Effect of Change
Cash	$2,738,000	$2,732,000	$(6,000)
Inventory	320,000	390,000	70,000
Total assets	$3,058,000	$3,122,000	$ 64,000

	As Computed under LIFO	As Reported under FIFO	Effect of Change
Accrued profit sharing	$ 87,000	$ 90,000	$ 3,000
Income tax liability	313,000	338,000	25,000
Total liabilities	400,000	428,000	28,000
Paid in capital	1,000,000	1,000,000	-0-
Retained earnings	1,658,000	1,694,000	36,000
Total stockholders' equity	2,658,000	2,694,000	36,000
Total liabilities and stockholders' equity	$3,058,000	$3,122,000	$64,000

Balance Sheet—12/31/20X1

	As Originally Reported	As Adjusted	Effect of Change
Cash	$2,448,000	$2,448,000	$ -0-
Inventory	200,000	240,000	40,000
Total assets	$2,648,000	$2,688,000	$40,000
Accrued profit sharing	$ 100,000	$ 100,000	$ -0-
Income tax liability	360,000	376,000	16,000
Total liabilities	460,000	476,000	16,000
Paid-in capital	1,000,000	1,000,000	-0-
Retained earnings	1,188,000	1,212,000	24,000
Total stockholders' equity	2,188,000	2,212,000	24,000
Total liabilities and stockholders' equity	$2,648,000	$2,688,000	$40,000

As a result of the accounting change, retained earnings as of January 1, 20X1 decreased from $648,000, as originally reported using the LIFO method, to $636,000 using the FIFO method.

Statement of Cash Flows—20X2

	As Computed under LIFO	As Reported under FIFO	Effect of Change
Net income	$ 470,000	$ 482,000	$ 12,000
Adjustments to reconcile net income to net cash provided by operating activities:			
Increase in inventory	(120,000)	(150,000)	(30,000)
Decrease in accrued profit sharing	(13,000)	(10,000)	3,000
Decrease in income tax liability	(47,000)	(38,000)	9,000
Net cash provided by operating activities	290,000	284,000	(6,000)
Net increase in cash	290,000	284,000	(6,000)
Cash, January 1, 20X2	2,448,000	2,448,000	-0-
Cash, December 31, 20X2	$ 2,738,000	$ 2,732,000	$ (6,000)

Statement of Cash Flows—20X1

	As Originally Reported	As Adjusted	Effect of Change
Net income	$ 540,000	$ 576,000	$ 36,000
Adjustments to reconcile net income to net cash provided by operating activities:			
Increase in inventory	(100,000)	(160,000)	(60,000)
Decrease in accrued profit sharing	(20,000)	(20,000)	-0-
Decrease in income tax liability	(72,000)	(48,000)	24,000
Net cash provided by operating activities	348,000	348,000	-0-

	As Originally Reported	As Adjusted	Effect of Change
Net increase in cash	348,000	348,000	-0-
Cash, January 1, 20X1	2,100,000	2,100,000	-0-
Cash, December 31, 20X1	$2,448,000	$2,448,000	$ -0-

Example 5: Retrospective Application of a Change in Accounting Principle Is Impracticable

Effective January 1, 20X2, the Company changed its method of valuing a significant component of its inventory from the first-in, first-out (FIFO) method to the last-in, first-out (LIFO) method. Management believes the LIFO method results in a better matching of current costs with current revenues and minimizes the effect of price-level changes on inventory valuations. It was impracticable to determine the cumulative effect of this accounting change and the retroactive application of the LIFO method to prior years, because the Company's accounting records do not provide sufficient information to apply the new method. As a result, the effect of the change has been applied prospectively in 20X2. The effect of the change in 20X2 was to increase cost of goods sold by $750,000, decrease income taxes by $300,000, and decrease net income by $450,000.

Example 6: Indirect Effects of Change in Accounting Principle Are Recognized

Effective January 1, 20X2, the Company changed its method of accounting for long-term contracts from the completed contract method to the percentage-of-completion method. The Company believes that the new method more accurately reflects periodic results of operations and conforms to revenue recognition practices predominant in the industry. The effect of this change was to increase 20X2 net income by $800,000. As a result of the change in accounting principle, pension expense for 20X2 has also increased by $145,000.

Example 7: Change from Cash Basis to Accrual Basis of Accounting

In previous years, the Company prepared its financial statements on a cash basis of accounting, which is a comprehensive basis of accounting other than GAAP. In 20X2, the financial statements have been prepared on the accrual basis of accounting, in conformity with generally accepted accounting principles. Management also believes that the accrual basis of accounting more accurately reflects the Company's financial position and results of operations. The effect of this change was to increase net income for 20X2 by $375,000. The financial statements for 20X1 have been retroactively restated for the change, which resulted in a decrease of net income for 20X1 of $125,000. Retained earnings has been increased by $150,000 as of January 1, 20X1, for the effect of retroactive application of the new basis of accounting, as follows:

	Increase (Decrease) in Retained Earnings as of January 1, 20X1
Adjustment to record accounts receivable	$500,000
Adjustment to record prepaid expenses and other assets	25,000
Adjustment to record accounts payable	(125,000)
Adjustment to record deferred revenue	(150,000)
Adjustment to record related deferred tax liability on items above	(100,000)
Net increase in retained earnings as of January 1, 20X1	$150,000

Example 8: Adoption of New Accounting Standard in the Current Year—Prior-Year Financial Statements Not Restated

In 20X2, the Company adopted FASB ASC [*number*] [(*title*)], which requires [*describe briefly the requirements of the new standard*]. The effect of this change was to [*increase/decrease*] 20X2 income before extraordinary items and 20X2 net income by $[*amount*]. Financial statements for 20X1 have not been restated, and the cumulative effect of the change, totaling $[*amount*], is shown as a one time [*credit/charge*] to income in the 20X2 income statement.

Example 9: Adoption of New FASB Accounting Standard in the Current Year—Prior-Year Financial Statements Restated

In 20X2, the Company adopted FASB ASC [*number*] [(*title*)], which requires [*describe briefly the requirements of the new standard*]. The effect of this change was to [*increase/decrease*] 20X2 income before extraordinary items and 20X2 net income by $[*amount*]. The financial statements for 20X1 have been retroactively restated for the change, which resulted in an [*increase/decrease*] in income before extraordinary items and net income for 20X1 of $[*amount*]. Retained earnings as of January 1, 20X1, has been adjusted for the effect of retroactive application of the new standard.

Example 10: Adoption of New FASB Accounting Standard in the Current Year—No Material Effect on the Financial Statements

In 20X2, the Company adopted FASB ASC [number] [(title)], which requires [describe briefly the requirements of the new standard]. There was no material impact on the Company's results of operations or financial condition upon adoption of the new standard.

Example 11: New FASB Accounting Standard to Be Adopted in the Future

In December 20X2, the Financial Accounting Standards Board issued FASB ASC [number] [(title)], which requires [describe briefly the requirements of the new standard]. The new standard is effective for the year ending December 31, 20X3. The adoption of the new standard is not expected to have a material effect on the Company's financial position, results of operations, or cash flows.

Or:

The Company is currently evaluating the effect that implementation of the new standard will have on its financial position, results of operations, and cash flows.

Changes in the Reporting Entity

Example 12: Financial Statements Currently Consolidated to Include the Accounts of a Previously Unconsolidated Affiliate

Effective January 1, 20X2, the Company began to consolidate into its financial statements the accounts of XYZ Corporation, formerly an unconsolidated affiliate. XYZ Corporation, which primarily manufactures medical equipment, is a venture between the Company and ABC Company of Ohio. The consolidation occurred as a result of revisions of the Stockholders' Agreement between the Company and ABC Company of Ohio. Financial data presented for previous years have not been restated to reflect the consolidation of XYZ Corporation. The consolidation is not material to financial position or results of operations for the periods presented and had no effect on previously reported net income, which included XYZ Corporation on an equity basis.

Example 13: Financial Statements Currently Include on the Equity Basis of Accounting the Accounts of a Previously Consolidated Business

On January 1, 20X2, the Company transferred its medical equipment business segment and contributed certain assets and liabilities, totaling $15 million and $4 million, respectively, to a joint venture named

Hope Enterprises (a partnership). The Company's equity interest in the joint venture is 35%. As a result, the 20X1 income statement, which included the accounts of the medical equipment business segment on a consolidated basis, has been retroactively restated to reflect adjustment of line items for revenue and costs applicable to the medical equipment business segment transferred to the joint venture and to reflect the losses of this business on the equity basis of accounting. The effect of this change was to increase income before extraordinary items, net income, and other comprehensive income for 20X1 by $489,000, $375,000, and $72,000, respectively.

Correction of Errors

Example 14: Correction of Error in Comparative Financial Statements—Error Relates to a Year Not Presented in the Comparative Financial Statements

Retained earnings as of January 1, 20X1, has been reduced by $125,000, net of income tax effect of $75,000, to correct an error made in 20X0 [*or a prior year*] by including in inventory certain costs totaling $200,000 that should have been expensed to conform with generally accepted accounting principles. The error had no effect on net income for 20X1.

> **Note:** The following table illustrates the correction of error as shown on the face of the Company's statement of retained earnings or statement of stockholders' equity (assume the Company's year-end is December 31 and the error relates to 20X0 or a prior year).

	20X2	20X1
Retained earnings at beginning of year, as previously reported	$3,125,000	$2,625,000
Prior-period adjustment—Error in capitalizing certain inventory costs that should have been expensed in 20X0 (or a prior year)	-0-	(125,000)
Retained earnings at beginning of year, as restated	3,125,000	2,500,000
Net income	700,000	625,000
Retained earnings at end of year	$3,825,000	$3,125,000

Example 15: Correction of Errors in Comparative Financial Statements—Errors Relate to First Year Presented in the Comparative Financial Statements and to Prior Year

The Company has restated its previously issued 20X1 consolidated financial statements for matters related to the following previously reported items: sales and accounts receivable; inventory costs and valuation reserves; revisions to the previous policy regarding the capitalization of costs associated with the bulk purchase of inventory; reserves for returns and allowances; unrecorded liabilities; additional bad debt expense; and the related income tax effects. The accompanying financial statements for 20X1 have been restated to reflect the corrections. Also, retained earnings at January 1, 20X1, was reduced by $499,000 as a result of adjustments to sales previously reported and previously unrecorded liabilities in 20X0.

The following is a summary of the restatements for 20X1:

Reduction of previously reported sales, net of related costs of sales	$ 788,000
Inventory cost adjustments and increase to inventory valuation reserves	310,000
Changes to accounting policy regarding the capitalization of costs associated with the bulk purchase of inventory	243,000
Increase in reserves for returns and allowances	116,000
Unrecorded liabilities	488,000
Additional bad debt expense	281,000
Subtotal	2,226,000
Income tax effect of restatement	(345,000)
Total reduction in 20X1 net earnings	$1,881,000

The effect on the Company's previously issued 20X1 financial statements is summarized as follows:

Balance Sheet as of December 31, 20X1

	Previously Reported	Increase (Decrease)	Restated
Current Assets	$12,298,000	$(2,414,000)	$9,884,000
Other Assets	247,000	(79,000)	(168,000)

	Previously Reported	Increase (Decrease)	Restated
Total Assets	17,108,000	(2,493,000)	14,615,000
Current Liabilities	12,569,000	(148,000)	12,421,000
Deferred Tax Liability	51,000	35,000	86,000
Total Liabilities	16,640,000	(113,000)	16,527,000
Stockholders' Deficit:			
Accumulated Deficit—December 31, 20X0	(254,000)	(499,000)	(753,000)
Net Income (Loss) for 20X1	315,000	(1,881,000)	(1,566,000)
Accumulated Deficit—December 31, 20X1	61,000	(2,380,000)	(2,319,000)
Total Liabilities and Stockholders' Deficit	17,108,000	(2,493,000)	(14,615,000)

Statement of Operations for the Year Ended December 31, 20X1

	Previously Reported	Increase (Decrease)	Restated
Net Sales	$24,871,000	$(1,016,000)	$23,855,000
Cost of Sales	18,162,000	267,000	18,429,000
Gross Profit	6,709,000	(1,283,000)	5,426,000
Selling and Administrative Expenses	5,861,000	838,000	6,699,000
Income (Loss) from Operations	848,000	(2,121,000)	(1,273,000)
Interest Expense	491,000	105,000	596,000
Income (Loss) before Taxes	357,000	(2,226,000)	(1,869,000)
Provision for Income Taxes	42,000	(345,000)	(303,000)
Net Income (Loss)	315,000	(1,881,000)	(1,566,000)

Note: The following table illustrates the correction of errors as shown on the face of the Company's statement of retained earnings or statement of stockholders' equity (assume the Company's year-end is December 31 and the errors relate to 20X1 and 20X0). Also, the balance sheet, the income statement, and the statement of cash flows should clearly indicate in the 20X1 column the word "Restated."

	Number of Shares	Common Stock	Accumulated Deficit	Total Stockholders' Equity (Deficit)
Balance at January 1, 20X1, as previously reported	1,800,000	$18,000	$(254,000)	$(236,000)
Prior period adjustment	—	—	(499,000)	(499,000)
Balance at January 1, 20X1, as restated	1,800,000	18,000	(753,000)	(735,000)
Net loss for 20X1, as restated	—	—	(1,566,000)	(1,566,000)
Balance at December 31, 20X1, as restated	1,800,000	18,000	(2,319,000)	(2,301,000)
Issuance of stock	1,400,000	14,000	—	14,000
Net income for 20X2	—	—	404,000	404,000
Balance at December 31, 20X2	3,200,000	$32,000	$(1,915,000)	$(1,883,000)

Example 16: Correction of Errors in Single-Year Financial Statements—Errors Relate to Immediately Preceding Year

The Company's financial statements as of December 31, 20X1, contained the following errors: (1) overstatement of accounts receivable by $150,000, (2) understatement of accounts payable by $200,000, and (3) understatement of accrued expenses by $50,000. Retained earnings as of January 1, 20X2, has been reduced by $275,000 to correct the aggregate effect of the errors of $400,000, net of their related income tax effect of $125,000. Had the errors not been made, net income for 20X1 would have been decreased by $200,000, net of income tax of $100,000.

Note: The following table illustrates the correction of error as shown on the face of the Company's statement of retained earnings or statement of stockholders' equity (assume the Company's year-end is December 31 and the error relates to 20X1).

	20X2
Retained earnings at beginning of year, as previously reported	$3,500,000
Prior period adjustment—See Note [X]	(275,000)
Retained earnings at beginning of year, as restated	3,225,000
Net income	500,000
Retained earnings at end of year	$3,725,000

CHAPTER 10
ASC TOPIC 255: CHANGING PRICES

CONTENTS

EXECUTIVE SUMMARY

Changing Prices

Financial statements prepared in conformity with generally accepted accounting principles (GAAP) are based on the assumption of a stable monetary unit. That is, the assumption is made that the monetary unit used to convert all financial statement items into a common denominator (i.e., dollars) does not vary sufficiently over time so that distortions in the financial statements are material. Also, financial statements prepared in conformity with GAAP are primarily historical-cost based (i.e., the characteristic of most financial statement items that is measured and presented is the historical cost of the item).

Over the years, two approaches have been proposed and procedures developed to compensate for changes in the monetary unit and in the value of assets and liabilities after their acquisition. The two approaches are current value accounting and general price-level accounting. Current value accounting substitutes a measure of current value for historical cost as the primary measurement upon which the elements of financial statements are based. General price-level accounting adheres to historical cost but substitutes a current value of the dollar for historical dollars through the use of price indexes. Neither current value accounting nor general price-level accounting is required at the present time. However, procedures are established in the accounting literature for enterprises that choose to develop either general price-level or current value financial statements.

Accounting Literature

FASB Accounting Standards Codification Topic	*Pre-Codification Accounting Literature*
255, *Changing Prices*	FAS-89, *Financial Reporting and Changing Prices*

DISCLOSURE AND KEY PRESENTATION REQUIREMENTS

The following are the disclosure and key presentation requirements for entities that elect to present supplementary information on the effects of changing prices (these items are currently voluntary, not required):

1. For each of the five most recent years, disclosures should include (ASC 255-10-50-3, 50-8, and 50-9) (FAS-89, pars. 7-9):

    a. Net sales and other operating revenues.

    b. Income from continuing operations on a current cost basis.

    c. Purchasing power gain or loss on net monetary items.

    d. Increase or decrease in the current cost or lower recoverable amount of inventory and property, plant, and equipment, net of inflation.

    e. The aggregate foreign currency translation adjustment on a current cost basis, if applicable.

    f. Net assets at year-end on a current cost basis.

    g. Income per common share from continuing operations on a current cost basis.

    h. Cash dividends declared per common share.

    i. Market price per common share at year-end.

    j. The Consumer Price Index—All Urban Consumers (CPI-U) used for each year's current cost/constant purchasing power calculations.

    k. If the entity has a significant foreign operation measured in a functional currency other than the U.S. dollar, disclosure should be made of whether adjustments to the current cost information to reflect the effects of

general inflation are based on the U.S. general price
level index or on a functional currency general price
level index.

2. In addition to the disclosures in item 1 above, if income from
continuing operations on a current cost/constant purchasing
power basis differs significantly from income from continuing
operations reported in the primary financial statements, the
following additional information should be disclosed (ASC
255-10-50-11 through 50-16) (FAS-89, pars. 11–13 and 25):

   a. Components of income from continuing operations for
   the current year on a current cost/constant purchasing
   power basis.

   b. Separate amounts for the current cost or lower recoverable amount at the end of the current year of inventory
   and property, plant, and equipment.

   c. The increase or decrease in current cost or lower recoverable amount before and after adjusting for the effects
   of inflation of inventory and property, plant, and equipment for the current year.

   d. The principal types of information used to calculate the
   current cost of (1) inventory; (2) property, plant, and
   equipment; (3) cost of goods sold; and (4) depreciation,
   depletion, and amortization expense.

   e. Any differences between (1) the depreciation methods,
   estimates of useful lives, and salvage values of assets
   used for calculations of current cost/constant purchasing
   power depreciation and (2) the methods and estimates
   used for calculations of depreciation in the primary
   financial statements.

   (*Note:* If an entity has assets [i.e., timberlands and growing
   timber, income-producing real estate, or motion picture
   films] that may raise doubts about the applicability of the
   current cost measurement methods required for other assets,
   it may disclose historical cost amounts adjusted by an exter-
   nally generated index of a broad-based measure of general
   purchasing power as substitutes for current cost amounts for
   such assets and their related expenses [see items 2(b) and
   2(d) above].) (ASC 255-10-50-32) ((FAS-89, par. 26)

3. For companies with mineral resource assets (other than
oil and gas), such as metal ores or coal, the following additional disclosures should be made (ASC 255-10-50-17) (FAS-
89, par. 14):

   a. Estimates of significant quantities of proved mineral
   reserves or proved and probable mineral reserves
   (whichever is used for cost amortization purposes) at the

end of the year or at the most recent date during the year for which estimates can be made.

b. If the mineral reserves include deposits containing one or more significant mineral products, the estimated quantity, expressed in physical units or in percentages of reserves, of each mineral product that is recoverable in significant commercial quantities.

c. Quantities of each significant mineral produced during the year.

d. Quantity of significant proved, or proved and probable, mineral reserves purchased or sold in place during the year.

e. The average market price of each significant mineral product or, for mineral products transferred within the enterprise, the equivalent market price prior to use in a manufacturing process.

4. When determining the quantities of mineral reserves to be reported in item 3 above, the following should be applied (ASC 255-10-50-18) (FAS-89, par.15):

a. If consolidated financial statements are issued, 100 percent of the quantities attributable to the parent company and 100 percent of the quantities attributable to its consolidated subsidiaries (whether or not wholly owned) should be included.

b. If the entity's financial statements include investments that are proportionately consolidated, the entity's quantities should include its proportionate share of the investee's quantities.

c. If the entity's financial statements include investments that are accounted for by the equity method, the investee's quantities should not be included in the disclosures of the entity's quantities. However, the entity's share of the investee's quantities of reserves should be reported separately, if significant.

EXAMPLE OF FINANCIAL STATEMENT DISCLOSURES

The following sample disclosure is available on the accompanying disc.

Example 1: Five-Year Comparison of Selected Financial Data Adjusted for the Effects of Changing Prices

The Company is voluntarily presenting certain historical cost/ constant dollar information to indicate the effect of changes in the general price level on certain items that are shown in the primary financial statements based on dollar values determined as of the varying historical dates when the transactions occurred.

Revenues for 20X2 are assumed to have occurred ratably in relation to the change in the Consumer Price Index during the year and are therefore already expressed in average 20X2 dollars. The presentation also shows the gain from decline in purchasing power as a result of net amounts owed. All information shown is in terms of average 20X2 dollars as measured by the Consumer Price Index for all Urban Consumers (CPI-U).

The preparation of these numbers requires the use of certain assumptions and estimates and these disclosures should, therefore, be viewed in that context and not necessarily as a precise indicator of the specific effect of changing prices on the Company's operating results or its financial position. Also, the Company's costs may not change in proportion to changes in the Consumer Price Index.

The following table presents a five year comparison of selected supplementary financial data adjusted for the effect of changes in the general price level.

	Year Ended December 31				
	20X2	20X1	20X0	19X9	19X8
Revenues:					
Historical	$500,000	$450,000	$400,000	$350,000	$300,000
Constant dollar basis	$500,000	$461,000	$411,000	$361,000	$318,000
Income (loss) from continuing operations	$ 21,800	$ 15,300	$ (5,100)	$ (7,200)	$ 11,700
Gain from decline in purchasing power of net amounts owed	$ 10,000	$ 8,000	$ 9,000	$ 6,000	$ 7,000
Excess of increase in specific prices of inventory and property, plant, and equipment over increase in the general price level	$ 27,500	$ 23,000	$ 18,000	$ 19,000	$ 8,000
Foreign currency translation adjustment	$ (1,400)	$ (800)	$ (500)	$ (400)	$ (600)
Net assets at end of year	$200,000	$160,000	$135,000	$120,000	$105,000
Per share information:					
Income (loss) from continuing operations	$ 2.75	$ 1.10	$ (.24)	$ (.70)	$ .65
Cash dividends declared	$ 1.10	$ 1.00	$ .95	$ .90	$ .87
Market price at year end	$ 51.50	$ 41.75	$ 33.20	$ 27.90	$ 25.70
Average consumer price index	314.7	306.9	298.4	289.1	272.4

CHAPTER 11
ASC TOPIC 260: EARNINGS PER SHARE

CONTENTS

EXECUTIVE SUMMARY

Earnings per Share

Earnings per share (EPS) is an important measure of corporate performance for investors and other users of financial statements. EPS figures are required to be presented in the income statement of a publicly held company and should be presented in a manner consistent with the captions included in the company's income statement. Certain securities, such as convertible bonds, preferred stock, and stock options, permit their holders to become common stockholders or add to the number of shares of common stock already held. When potential reduction, called *dilution*, of EPS figures is inherent in a company's capital structure, a dual presentation of EPS is required—basic EPS and diluted EPS.

For purposes of presenting earnings per share, a distinction is made between enterprises with a simple capital structure and those with a complex capital structure. *A simple capital structure* is one that consists of capital stock and includes no potential for dilution via conversions, exercise of options, or other arrangements that would increase the number of shares outstanding. For organizations with complex capital structures, two EPS figures are presented with equal prominence on the face of the income statement: basic EPS and diluted EPS. The difference between basic EPS and diluted EPS is that *basic EPS* considers only outstanding common stock, whereas *diluted EPS* incorporates the potential dilution from all potentially dilutive securities that would have reduced EPS.

Basic EPS excludes dilution and is computed by dividing income available to common stockholders by the weighted-average number of common shares outstanding for the period. Diluted EPS reflects the potential dilution that could occur if securities or other contracts to issue common stock were exercised or converted into common stock or resulted in the issuance of common stock that then shared in the earnings of the entity. The computation of diluted EPS should not assume conversion, exercise, or contingent issuance of securities that would have an anti-dilutive effect on earnings per share.

Accounting Literature

FASB Accounting Standards Codification Topic	*Pre-Codification Accounting Literature*
260, *Earnings per Share*	FAS-128, *Earnings per Share*
	FSP FAS 129-1, *Disclosure Requirements under FASB Statement No. 129, Disclosure of Information about Capital Structure, Relating to Contingently Convertible Securities*
	EITF 00-27, *Application of Issue No. 98-5 to Certain Convertible Instruments*

DISCLOSURE AND KEY PRESENTATION REQUIREMENTS

Note: Nonpublic companies are *not* required to present earnings per share (ASC 260-10-15-2) (FAS-128, par. 6). In addition, per-share amounts not required to be presented by ASC Subtopic 260-10 that an entity chooses to disclose should be computed in accordance with that Subtopic and disclosed only in the notes to financial statements, noting whether the per-share amounts are pretax or net of tax (ASC 260-10-45-5) (FAS-128, par. 37).

1. The following EPS presentation should be made on the face of the income statement (ASC 260-10-45-2) (FAS-128, par. 36):

   a. For entities with simple capital structures (i.e., those with only common stock outstanding), basic per-share amounts for income from continuing operations and for net income should be presented.

   b. For all other entities, basic and diluted per-share amounts for income from continuing operations and for net income should be presented with equal prominence.

2. For entities that report a discontinued operation or an extraordinary item in a period, basic and diluted per-share amounts for those line items should be presented either on the face of the income statement or in the notes to the financial statements. (ASC 260-10-45-3) (FAS-128, pars. 9 and 37) (*Note:* An entity that does not report a discontinued operation but reports an extraordinary item in the period should use that line item (e.g., income before extraordinary items) whenever the line item income from continuing operations is referenced by the guidance in this ASC Subtopic.)

3. EPS data should be presented for all periods for which an income statement or summary of earnings is presented. (ASC 260-10-45-7) (FAS-128, par. 38)

4. If diluted EPS data is reported for at least one period, they should be reported for all periods presented, even if they are the same amounts as basic EPS. (ASC 260-10-45-7) (FAS-128, par. 38) (*Note*: If basic and diluted EPS are the same amount, dual presentation can be accomplished in one line on the income statement.)

5. The following disclosures should be made for each period for which an income statement is presented:

   a. A reconciliation of the numerators and denominators of the basic and diluted EPS computations for income from continuing operations, including the individual income and share amount effects of all securities that affect EPS. (ASC 260-10-50-1) (FAS-128, par. 40)

b. The effect that has been given to preferred dividends in determining the income available to common stockholders in computing basic EPS. (ASC 260-10-50-1) (FAS-128, par. 40)

c. Securities (including those issuable pursuant to contingent stock agreements) that could potentially dilute EPS in the future, but which were not included in the calculation of diluted EPS because to do so would have been antidilutive for the periods presented. (ASC 260-10-50-1) (FAS-128, par. 40; EITF 00-27) (*Note:* Full disclosure of the terms and conditions of these securities is required even if a security is not included in diluted EPS in the current period.)

6. For the latest period for which an income statement is presented, disclosures should be made of any transaction that occurs after the end of the most recent period but before the financial statements are issued or are available to be issued that would have changed materially the number of common shares or potential common shares outstanding at the end of the period if the transaction had occurred before the end of the period. (ASC 260-10-50-2) (FAS-128, par. 41)

7. When prior EPS amounts have been restated in compliance with authoritative literature requiring restatement, disclosure should be made of the per-share effect of the restatement. (ASC 260-10-55-15) (FAS-128, par. 57)

8. When the number of common shares outstanding increases as a result of a stock dividend or stock split, or decreases as a result of a reverse stock split, the computations of basic and diluted EPS should be adjusted retroactively for all periods presented to reflect such changes in the number of shares, and that fact should be disclosed. (ASC 260-10-55-12) (FAS-128, par. 54)

9. If changes in common stock resulting from stock dividends, stock splits, or reverse stock splits occur after the close of the period but before the financial statements are issued or are available to be issued, the per-share computations for all periods presented should be based on the new number of shares, and that fact should be disclosed. (ASC 260-10-55-12) (FAS-128, par. 54)

10. For shares that would be issued if contingently convertible securities were converted, disclosure should be made about whether the shares are included in the calculation of diluted EPS, and the reasons why or why not. (ASC 505-10-50-9) (FSP FAS 129-1, par. 4)

EXAMPLES OF FINANCIAL STATEMENT DISCLOSURES

 The following sample disclosures are available on the accompanying disc.

Example 1: Earnings-per-Share Calculation Shows Reconciliation of Denominator

Basic net earnings per share is computed using the weighted-average number of common shares outstanding. The dilutive effect of potential common shares outstanding is included in diluted net earnings per share. The computations of basic net earnings per share and diluted net earnings per share for 20X2 and 20X1 are as follows:

	20X2	20X1
Net earnings from continuing operations	$10,174,000	$9,143,000
Basic weighted-average shares	6,119,000	6,625,000
Effect of dilutive securities:		
Common and convertible preferred stock options	90,200	55,400
Convertible preferred stock	70,800	42,600
Dilutive potential common shares	6,280,000	6,723,000
Net earnings per share from continuing operations:		
Basic	$ 1.66	$ 1.38
Diluted	$ 1.62	$ 1.36

Example 2: Dilutive Potential Common Shares Are Calculated in Accordance with the Treasury Stock Method That Is Described

Basic earnings per common share for the years ended December 31, 20X2, and December 31, 20X1, are calculated by dividing net income by weighted-average common shares outstanding during the period. Diluted earnings per common share for the years ended December 31, 20X2, and December 31, 20X1, are calculated by dividing net income by weighted-average common shares outstanding during the period plus dilutive potential common shares, which are determined as follows:

	20X2	*20X1*
Weighted-average common shares	20,745,000	21,881,000
Effect of dilutive securities:		
Warrants	5,550,000	4,734,000
Options to purchase common stock	219,000	241,000
Dilutive potential common shares	26,514,000	26,856,000

Dilutive potential common shares are calculated in accordance with the treasury stock method, which assumes that proceeds from the exercise of all warrants and options are used to repurchase common stock at market value. The amount of shares remaining after the proceeds are exhausted represents the potentially dilutive effect of the securities. The increasing number of warrants used in the calculation is a result of the increasing market value of the Company's common stock.

Example 3: Diluted Net Earnings per Share Excludes Securities with Antidilutive Effect

Basic earnings per share is computed by dividing net income by the weighted-average number of common shares outstanding during the period. Diluted earnings per share is computed by dividing net income by the weighted-average number of common shares and dilutive potential common shares outstanding during the period.

The following is a reconciliation of the number of shares used in the calculation of basic earnings per share and diluted earnings per share for the years ended December 31, 20X2, and December 31, 20X1:

	20X2	*20X1*
Net income	$5,323,000	$10,471,000
Weighted-average number of common shares outstanding	7,419,000	7,699,000
Incremental shares from the assumed exercise of dilutive stock options	198,000	174,000
Dilutive potential common shares	7,617,000	7,873,000
Net earnings per share:		
Basic	$ 0.72	$ 1.36
Diluted	$ 0.70	$ 1.33

The following securities were not included in the computation of diluted net earnings per share as their effect would have been anti-dilutive:

	20X2	20X1
Options to purchase common stock	1,140,000	1,173,000
Warrants to purchase common stock	227,000	282,000
Unvested shares of common stock subject to repurchase	55,000	-0-
Convertible preferred stock	125,000	110,000
Convertible subordinated notes	1,022,000	1,022,000
	2,569,000	2,587,000

Example 4: EPS Calculations Are Adjusted for Tax-Effected Interest Expense to Calculate Diluted Earnings per Share and for Stock Split

In December 20X2, the Company issued a two-for-one stock split effected in the form of a 100% stock dividend. Previously reported share and earnings per share amounts have been restated. Basic earnings per share is computed by dividing net earnings by the weighted-average number of common shares outstanding. Diluted earnings per share is computed by dividing net earnings by the sum of the weighted-average number of common shares outstanding and the weighted-average number of potential common shares outstanding. The calculations of basic and diluted earnings per share for 20X2 and 20X1 are as follows:

	20X2	20X1
Calculation of basic earnings per share:		
Net earnings	$1,614,000	$1,160,000
Weighted-average number of common shares outstanding	1,471,000	1,459,000
Basic earnings per share	$ 1.10	$ 0.80
Calculation of diluted earnings per share:		
Net earnings	$1,614,000	$1,160,000
Tax-effected interest expense attributable to 3% Notes	23,000	23,000
Net earnings assuming dilution	$1,637,000	$1,183,000
Weighted-average number of common shares outstanding	1,471,000	1,459,000

	20X2	20X1
Effect of potentially dilutive securities:		
3% Notes	48,000	48,000
Employee stock plans	28,000	17,000
Weighted-average number of common shares outstanding assuming dilution	1,547,000	1,524,000
Diluted earnings per share	$ 1.06	$ 0.78

Employee stock plans represent shares granted under the Company's employee stock purchase plan and stock option plans. For 20X2 and 20X1, shares issuable upon conversion of the Company's 3% Notes were included in weighted-average shares assuming dilution for purposes of calculating diluted earnings per share. To calculate diluted earnings per share, net earnings are adjusted for tax-effected net interest and issue costs on the 3% Notes and divided by weighted-average shares assuming dilution.

Example 5: EPS Calculations Include Discontinued Operations and Extraordinary Items

> **Note:** This example illustrates (1) the presentation of earnings per share on the face of the income statement and (2) the computation of basic earnings per share and diluted earnings per share for income from continuing operations in a note to the financial statements.

Income Statement

	20X2	20X1
Income from continuing operations	$ 8,750,000	$ 7,450,000
Discontinued operations:		
Income from discontinued operations, net of taxes	500,000	-0-
Gain on disposition of business, net of taxes	600,000	-0-
Extraordinary items, net of taxes	-0-	(700,000)
Net income	$ 9,850,000	$ 6,750,000
Earnings per share—Basic:		
Income from continuing operations	$ 0.51	$ 0.45
Discontinued operations	0.06	-0-
Extraordinary items	-0-	(0.04)
Net income	$ 0.57	$ 0.41

	20X2	20X1
Earnings per share—Diluted:		
Income from continuing operations	$ 0.50	$ 0.44
Discontinued operations	0.06	-0-
Extraordinary items	-0-	(0.04)
Net income	$ 0.56	$ 0.40
Weighted-average number of shares—Basic	17,160,000	16,600,000
Weighted-average number of shares assuming dilution	17,530,000	16,825,000

Note to the Financial Statements

Basic earnings per share is computed by dividing net income by the weighted-average number of common shares outstanding during the period. Diluted earnings per share is computed by dividing net income by the weighted-average number of common shares and dilutive potential common shares outstanding during the period. The computation of basic earnings per share and diluted earnings per share for "Income from continuing operations" is as follows:

	20X2	20X1
Income from continuing operations	$ 8,750,000	$ 7,450,000
Weighted-average number of common shares outstanding—Basic	17,160,000	16,600,000
Effect of dilutive securities—Stock options	370,000	225,000
Weighted-average number of common shares outstanding—Diluted	17,530,000	16,825,000
Net earnings per share from continuing operations:		
Basic	$ 0.51	$ 0.45
Diluted	$ 0.50	$ 0.44

Example 6: Earnings-per-Share Amounts for Prior Period Have Been Restated to Give Effect to the Adoption of a New Accounting Standard

In 20X2, the Company adopted FASB ASC [*number*] [*title*], which requires [*describe briefly the requirements of the new standard*]. The effect of this change was to [*increase/decrease*] 20X2 net income by

$[amount]$, basic earnings per share by $[amount]$, and diluted earnings per share by $[amount]$. The financial statements for 20X1 have been retroactively restated for the change, which resulted in an [*increase/decrease*] in net income for 20X1 of $[amount]$. Earnings per share amounts for 20X1 have been restated to give effect to the application of the new accounting standard. The effect of the restatement was to [*increase/decrease*] 20X1 basic earnings per share by $[amount]$ and diluted earnings per share by $[amount]$. Retained earnings as of January 1, 20X1, has been adjusted for the effect of retroactive application of the new standard.

Example 7: EPS Calculations Reflect Deemed Dividend Related to Beneficial Conversion Feature on Preferred Stock and Accretion of Preferred Stock to Redemption Value

> **Note:** This example illustrates the presentation of earnings per share on the face of the income statement giving effect to deemed dividend related to beneficial conversion feature on preferred stock and accretion of preferred stock to redemption value.

Income Statement

	20X2	20X1
Net loss before income taxes	$(6,015,800)	$(6,911,000)
(Benefit) Provision for income taxes	(238,800)	200,000
Net loss	(6,254,600)	(6,711,000)
Deemed dividend related to beneficial conversion feature on Series A Preferred Stock	(332,700)	-0-
Accretion of Series A Preferred Stock to redemption value	(589,500)	-0-
Series A Preferred Stock dividends	(40,000)	-0-
Net loss attributable to common stockholders	$(7,216,800)	$(6,711,000)
Basic and diluted net loss per share attributable to common stockholders	$ (1.25)	$ (1.29)
Weighted-average number of shares—Basic and diluted	5,760,000	5,202,325

CHAPTER 12
ASC TOPIC 270: INTERIM REPORTING

CONTENTS

EXECUTIVE SUMMARY

Interim Reporting

Interim financial reports may be issued quarterly, monthly, or at other intervals, and may include complete financial statements or summarized data. Each interim period should be viewed as an integral part of the annual period. The results for each interim period should be based on the accounting principles and reporting practices generally used by the entity to prepare its latest annual financial statements, with limited exceptions, such as a change in an accounting principle. Also, certain accounting principles may require modification at interim dates so that the interim period's results better relate to the annual results. For example, when interim physical inventory counts are not taken, inventories may be estimated at interim dates using the gross profit method. Similarly, income taxes may be estimated at interim periods to reflect the entity's best estimate of the effective tax rate expected to be applicable for the full year.

The following guidelines should be observed for recognizing revenues and expenses during interim periods:

1. Revenues should be recognized as earned on the same basis as followed for the full year.

2. Costs and expenses that are associated directly with revenue (e.g., material costs, wages and salaries, fringe benefits, manufacturing overhead, and warranties) should be reported in the same period that the related revenue is recognized.

3. All other costs and expenses should be charged against income in the interim period as incurred, or allocated among interim periods based on an estimate of time expired, benefit received, or other activity associated with the periods.

4. Certain costs and expenses are frequently subjected to yearend adjustments even though they can reasonably be approximated at interim dates. Examples of such items include allowances for uncollectible accounts, year-end bonuses, depreciation, and inventory shrinkage. Adjustments for such items should be estimated and assigned to the interim period so that the interim period bears a reasonable portion of the anticipated annual amount.

5. Material extraordinary items, unusual or infrequent transactions, and gains and losses on disposal of a business segment should be recognized in the interim period in which they occur and should not be prorated over the full year.

6. Income taxes should be determined by applying an estimated annual effective tax rate, based on the current year's estimated annual results, to income or loss from continuing operations.

Accounting Literature

FASB Accounting Standards Codification Topic	*Pre-Codification Accounting Literature*
270, *Interim Reporting*	FAS-154, *Accounting Changes and Error Corrections*
	APB-28, *Interim Financial Reporting*

DISCLOSURE AND KEY PRESENTATION REQUIREMENTS

Note: See appropriate other chapters in this Manual for applicability of disclosure and key presentation requirements related to specific topics (e.g., segment reporting, retirement benefits, fair value, business combinations) for interim periods. The incremental disclosure and key presentation requirements in this section apply only to interim financial statements.

1. If the company uses estimated gross profit rates to determine the cost of goods sold during interim periods or uses other methods different from those used at annual inventory dates, the following disclosures should be made (ASC 270-10-45-6) (APB-28, par. 14):

    a. The method used at the interim date.

    b. Any significant adjustments that result from reconciliations with the annual physical inventory.

2. When costs and expenses incurred in an interim period cannot be readily identified with the activities or benefits of other interim periods, disclosures should be made about the nature and amount of such costs. (ASC 270-10-45-7 and 45-8) (APB-28, par. 15) (*Note*: Disclosure is not required if items of a comparable nature are included in both the current interim period and the corresponding interim period of the preceding year.)

3. If revenues of the entity are subject to material seasonal variations, the following disclosures should be made to avoid the possibility that interim results may be taken as

fairly indicative of the estimated results for a full fiscal year (ASC 270-10-45-11) (APB-28, par. 18):

   a. The seasonal nature of the business activities.

   b. Information for 12-month periods ended at the interim date for the current and preceding years (*optional*).

4. Extraordinary items, gains or losses from the disposal of a component of an entity, unusual seasonal results, business combinations, unusual and infrequently occurring transactions, and events that are material to the operating results of the interim period should be reported separately and included in the determination of net income for the interim period in which they occur. (ASC 270-10-45-11A and 50-5) (APB-28, par. 21)

5. Disclosures should be made of any changes in accounting principles or practices from those applied in (ASC 270-10-45-12 and 45-13) (APB-28, par. 23):

   a. The comparable interim period of the prior year.

   b. The preceding interim periods in the current year.

   c. The prior annual financial statements.

6. Disclosures should be made about contingencies and other uncertainties that could be expected to affect the fairness of presentation of the interim financial information. (ASC 270-10-50-6) (APB-28, par. 22) (*Note*: Such disclosures should: (*a*) include, but not be limited to, those matters that form the basis of a qualification of an independent auditor's report and (*b*) be repeated in interim and annual reports until the contingencies have been removed or resolved or have become immaterial.)

Items 7 through 10 below are additional disclosures that are applicable only to public entities

7. For public entities that report summarized financial information to their security holders at interim dates (including reports on fourth quarters), the following items, at a minimum, should be reported (ASC 270-10-50-1 and 50-3) (APB-28, pars. 30 and 32) (*Note*: When summarized financial data are regularly reported on a quarterly basis, the information with respect to the current quarter and the current year-to-date or the last 12 months to date should be provided with comparable data for the preceding year.):

   a. Sales or gross revenues.

   b. Provision for income taxes.

   c. Extraordinary items (including related income tax effects).

   d. Net income.

   e. Comprehensive income.

   f. Basic and diluted earnings-per-share data for each period presented.

   g. Seasonal revenue, costs, or expenses.

   h. Significant changes in estimates or provisions for income taxes.

   i. Disposal of a component of an entity and extraordinary, unusual, or infrequently occurring items.

   j. Contingent items.

   k. Changes in accounting principles or estimates.

   l. Significant changes in financial position.

   m. The effects of significant events on the interim financial results. (*Note:* Entities are *encouraged*, but not required, to disclose this information.)

8. If interim financial data and disclosures are not separately reported for the fourth quarter, or that information is not presented in the annual report, the following information about the fourth quarter should be disclosed in the annual report in a note to the annual financial statements (ASC 270-10-45-10; 270-10-50-2) (APB-28, pars. 17 and 31):

   a. Disposals of components of an entity.

   b. Extraordinary, unusual, or infrequent items.

   c. The aggregate effect of year-end adjustments that are material to the operating results of the fourth quarter.

9. If a public entity that regularly reports interim information makes an accounting change during the fourth quarter of its fiscal year and does not report the data specified in item 7 above in a separate fourth-quarter report or in its annual report, the entity should include disclosure of the effects of the accounting change on interim-period results in a note to the annual financial statements for the fiscal year in which the change is made. (ASC 270-10-45-12 through 45-14; 270-10-50-2) (FAS-154, par. 16; APB-28, pars. 23, 24, 26, and 31)

10. If condensed interim balance sheet information or cash flow data are not presented at interim reporting dates, disclosure should be made of significant changes since the last reporting period with respect to liquid assets, net working capital, long-term liabilities, or stockholder's equity. (ASC 270-10-50-4) (APB-28, par. 33)

EXAMPLES OF FINANCIAL STATEMENT DISCLOSURES

Note: For examples of other disclosures pertaining to specific topics (e.g., segment reporting, retirement benefits, fair value, business combinations), see the applicable chapters in this Manual.

 The following sample disclosures are available on the accompanying disc.

Example 1: Quantities and Costs Used in Calculating Cost of Goods Sold on a Quarterly Basis Include Estimates of the Annual LIFO Effect

The quantities and costs used in calculating cost of goods sold for the three month and six month periods ended June 30, 20X2, include estimates of the annual LIFO effect. The actual effect cannot be known until the year-end physical inventory is completed and quantity and price indices developed.

Example 2: Seasonal Nature of Operations Due to Normal Maintenance

Although there is no pronounced seasonality in demand for the Company's products, typically the second quarter of the year is the Company's best in terms of profitability. Generally, in the third quarter of the year, plants are closed for the first week of July for scheduled normal maintenance.

Example 3: Nature of Operations Affected by Weather and Spending Patterns of Significant Customers

The Company has historically experienced variability in revenues, income before income taxes and net income on a quarterly basis. A significant amount of this variability is due to the fact that the Company's business is subject to seasonal fluctuations, with activity in its second and, occasionally, third fiscal quarters being adversely affected by weather. In addition, budgetary spending patterns of significant customers, which often run on a calendar year basis, have resulted in greater volatility of second fiscal quarter results. Therefore, the results of operations presented for the three months ended March 31, 20X2, are not necessarily indicative of results of operations for the full year.

Example 4: Seasonal Nature of Operations Quantified

The Company's business is highly seasonal with between 65% and 80% of sales occurring in the second and third fiscal quarters combined.

Example 5: Unusual or Nonrecurring Item

The results of operations for the third quarter of 20X2 include (1) a $798,000 ($483,000 after-tax) nonrecurring charge to address the impairment of existing manufacturing facilities in Carson City, Nevada, and to relocate certain contractual employees to the Company's new facility in Chandler, Arizona; (2) a gain of $1,500,000 ($908,000 after-tax) related to the termination of a license agreement, net of charges for related equipment write-offs and capacity adjustments; and (3) charges of $1,300,000 ($782,000 after-tax) for the settlement of certain environmental litigation.

Example 6: Extraordinary Item

In the second quarter of 20X2, the Company's manufacturing facility in Orange, Florida, was severely damaged by an earthquake. After the settlement with the insurer, the Company retired the building and recognized an extraordinary gain of $719,000, net of income taxes of $342,000.

Example 7: Significant Change in Income Tax Rate

The effective tax rate for the three-month period ended September 30, 20X2, was 48%, which was higher than the tax rate for the preceding quarters. The higher tax rate is primarily the result of a proposed tax adjustment of approximately $1,200,000 by the Internal Revenue Service.

Example 8: Significant Items Affecting Fourth-Quarter Results of Operations Disclosed—Financial Information Is Not Separately Reported for the Fourth Quarter

In the fourth quarter of 20X2 the Company recorded net pretax charges for inventory and related reserves of approximately $3,500,000 and a goodwill write-down of $1,000,000 primarily as a result of changes in customer demand for certain Company products. In addition, the credit for income taxes in the fourth quarter of 20X2 was favorably affected by approximately $1,000,000 as a result of the settlement of tax examinations for earlier years. These adjustments reduced fourth quarter net income per share by $0.10.

Example 9: Summarized Quarterly Data

The following sets forth certain unaudited quarterly statements of operations data for each of the Company's quarters for 20X2 and 20X1. In management's opinion, this quarterly information reflects all adjustments, consisting only of normal recurring adjustments, necessary for a fair presentation for the periods presented. Such quarterly results are not necessarily indicative of future results of operations and should be read in conjunction with the audited consolidated financial statements of the Company and the notes thereto.

	Dec. 31, 20X2	Sept. 30, 20X2	June 30, 20X2	March 31, 20X2
Net revenues	$7,014,000	$6,131,000	$5,227,000	$5,101,000
Cost of sales and expenses	3,176,000	3,192,000	3,027,000	2,749,000
Income before income taxes	3,838,000	2,939,000	2,200,000	2,352,000
Income tax expense	1,774,000	1,380,000	1,028,000	1,079,000
Net income	$2,064,000	$1,559,000	$1,172,000	$1,273,000
Basic earnings per share	$.62	$.46	$.35	$.39
Diluted earnings per share	$.59	$.44	$.33	$.36

	Dec. 31, 20X2	Sept. 30, 20X2	June 30, 20X2	March 31, 20X2
Net revenues	$5,914,000	$5,331,000	$5,460,000	$6,048,000
Cost of sales and expenses	3,116,000	2,804,000	2,343,000	2,307,000
Income before income taxes	2,798,000	2,527,000	3,117,000	3,741,000
Income tax expense	1,274,000	1,153,000	1,472,000	1,758,000
Net income	$1,524,000	$1,374,000	$1,645,000	$1,983,000
Basic earnings per share	$.53	$.48	$.50	$.61
Diluted earnings per share	$.49	$.44	$.46	$.55

Example 10: Pension and Other Postretirement Benefit Plans—Public Entities

Components of net periodic benefit cost for the Company's pension plan are as follows:

	Three Months Ended September 30		Nine Months Ended September 30	
	20X2	*20X1*	*20X2*	*20X1*
Service cost	$1,200,000	$1,100,000	$3,700,000	$3,400,000
Interest cost	1,400,000	1,156,000	3,900,000	3,250,000
Expected return on plan assets	(1,600,000)	(900,000)	(4,200,000)	(3,900,000)
Amortization of prior service cost	240,000	160,000	525,000	260,000
Amortization of net (gain) loss	70,000	(10,000)	90,000	115,000
Net periodic benefit cost	$1,310,000	$1,506,000	$4,015,000	$3,125,000

Components of net periodic benefit cost for the Company's post-retirement benefit plan are as follows:

	Three Months Ended September 30		Nine Months Ended September 30	
	20X2	*20X1*	*20X2*	*20X1*
Service cost	$200,000	$170,000	$700,000	$625,000
Interest cost	400,000	350,000	990,000	695,000
Expected return on plan assets	(150,000)	(190,000)	(315,000)	(420,000)
Amortization of prior service cost	(70,000)	(10,000)	(125,000)	(150,000)
Net periodic benefit cost	$380,000	$320,000	$1,250,000	$750,000

The Company previously disclosed in its financial statements for the year ended December 31, 20X1, that it expected to contribute $4,800,000 to its pension plan and $900,000 to its postretirement benefit plan in 20X2. As of September 30, 20X2, contributions of $3,700,000 and $650,000 have been made to the pension plan and postretirement benefit plan, respectively. The Company presently anticipates contributing an additional $1,500,000 to fund its pension plan in 20X2 for a total of $5,200,000. Also, the Company presently anticipates contributing an additional $450,000 to fund its postretirement benefit plan in 20X2 for a total of $1,100,000.

Example 11: Pension and Other Postretirement Benefit Plans—Nonpublic Entities

The Company previously disclosed in its financial statements for the year ended December 31, 20X1, that it expected to contribute $4,800,000 to its pension plan and $900,000 to its postretirement benefit plan in 20X2. As of September 30, 20X2, contributions of $3,700,000 and $650,000 have been made to the pension plan and postretirement benefit plan, respectively. The Company presently anticipates contributing an additional $1,500,000 to fund its pension plan in 20X2 for a total of $5,200,000. Also, the Company presently anticipates contributing an additional $450,000 to fund its postretirement benefit plan in 20X2 for a total of $1,100,000.

CHAPTER 13
ASC TOPIC 272: LIMITED LIABILITY ENTITIES

CONTENTS

EXECUTIVE SUMMARY

Limited Liability Entities

A limited liability company (LLC) generally has the following characteristics:

- It is an unincorporated association of two or more "persons";
- Its members have limited personal liability for the obligations or debts of the entity; and
- It is classified as a partnership for federal income tax purposes.

LLCs have characteristics of both corporations and partnerships but are dissimilar from both in certain respects. Like a corporation, the members (owners) of an LLC generally are not personally liable for the liabilities of the LLC. However, like a partnership, the members of an LLC (rather than the entity itself) are taxed on their respective shares of the LLC's earnings.

A complete set of LLC financial statements should include:

- A balance sheet as of the end of the reporting period;

- A statement of operations for the period;
- A statement of cash flows for the period; and
- Notes to financial statements.

In addition, information related to changes in members' equity for the period, should be (*a*) presented as a separate statement; (*b*) combined with the statement of operations, or (*c*) provided in the notes to the financial statements.

In addition, the headings of a LLC's financial statements should identify clearly the financial statements as those of a limited liability company.

Accounting Literature

FASB Accounting Standards Codification Topic	Pre-Codification Accounting Literature
272, *Limited Liability Entities*	PB-14, *Accounting and Reporting by Limited Liability Companies and Limited Liability Partnerships*

DISCLOSURE AND KEY PRESENTATION REQUIREMENTS

Note: In addition to all the presentation and disclosure requirements that typically apply to any other business entity, the following additional matters should be addressed in the financial statements of a limited liability entity.

1. The headings of the financial statements should clearly identify the financial statements as those of a limited liability entity. (ASC 272-10-45-2) (PB-14, par. 9)

2. If comparative financial statements are presented, the prior-year figures should be shown for comparative purposes comparable with those shown for the most recent period, and any exceptions to comparability should be adequately disclosed. (ASC 272-10-45-6, 45-7, and 50-2) (PB-14, par. 14) (*Note:* Although not required, the presentation of comparative financial statements is ordinarily desirable.)

3. If the entity records amounts due from members for capital contributions, such amounts should be presented as deductions from members' equity. (ASC 272-10-45-5) (PB-14, par. 13) (*Note:* Presenting such amounts as assets should be inappropriate, except in very limited circumstances when there is

substantial evidence of ability and intent to pay within a reasonably short period of time, or if the amounts have been collected in cash before issuance of the financial statements.)

4. The following additional disclosures should be made:

   a. A description of any limitation of members' liability. (ASC 272-10-50-3) (PB-14, par. 15)

   b. The different classes of members' interests and the respective rights, preferences, and privileges of each class. (ASC 272-10-50-3) (PB-14, par. 15)

   c. The amount of each class of members' equity (deficit) in the notes to the financial statements (if the entity does not report separately the amount of each class within the equity section of the balance sheet). (ASC 272-10-45-3, 45-4, 50-1, and 50-3) (PB-14, pars. 10, 11, and 15)

   d. Components of members' equity (e.g., undistributed earnings, earnings available for withdrawal, or unallocated capital) either on the face of the balance sheet or in the notes, if the entity maintains separate accounts for such components. (ASC 272-10-50-1) (PB-14, par. 12) (*Note:* This disclosure is optional.)

   e. The date the LLC or LLP will cease to exist, if the entity has a finite life. (ASC 272-10-50-3) (PB-14, par. 15)

   Note: The disclosure requirement in item (f) below is to be followed until the adoption of ASC Topic 805, *Business Combinations*, based on FAS-141R, *Business Combinations*, which is effective for business combinations for which the acquisition date is on or after the beginning of the first annual reporting period beginning on or after December 15, 2008. Thereafter, the disclosure requirement in item (f) below is eliminated. Early adoption is not permitted.

   f. In the year of formation for LLCs and LLPs formed by combining entities under common control or by conversion from another type of entity, the fact that the assets and liabilities were previously held by a predecessor entity or entities. (ASC 272-10-50-3) (PB-14, par. 15)

EXAMPLES OF FINANCIAL STATEMENT DISCLOSURES

The following sample disclosures are available on the accompanying disc.

Example 1: Description of Different Classes of Members' Interests

ABC, LLC (the Company) was formed on March 1, 20X2, as a Limited Liability Company under State of Delaware statutes, and began operations on April 1, 20X2. Under the terms of the LLC Operating Agreement, the term of the Company expires on December 31, 20Y9. At December 31, 20X2, a total of 100,000 units of membership were held by the members of the Company, with the Managing Member holding 80,000 units and the Special Member holding 20,000 units. Under the terms of the LLC Operating Agreement, allocations of profits, losses, capital gains, and distributions are in the following priorities:

- *Profits.* Profits are allocated in accordance with respective unit ownership percentages until the allocation to the Managing Member is equal to the 25% annual compounded return on the Managing Member's contributions, then 20% to the Special Member and 80% to the Managing member until cumulative allocation to the Managing Member is equal to 35% annual compounded return, and thereafter 25% to the Special Member and 75% to the Managing member.

- *Losses.* Losses are allocated in accordance with respective unit ownership percentages.

- *Gain from Capital Event.* Any gain from a capital event (as defined) is allocated $100,000 to the Special Member, then $200,000 to the Special Member (if the Company generates operating cash flows of more than $800,000 during the period from January 1 through December 31, 20X5), and thereafter in accordance with the requirements for the allocation of profits.

- *Distributions of Cash.* Cash distributions are allocated in accordance with the requirements for the allocation of profits.

Example 2: Income Taxes—LLC

As a limited liability company, the Company is not a taxpaying entity for federal income tax purposes. Accordingly, the Company's taxable income or loss is allocated to its members in accordance with their respective percentage ownership. Therefore, no provision or liability for income taxes has been included in the accompanying financial statements.

CHAPTER 14
ASC TOPIC 275: RISKS AND UNCERTAINTIES

CONTENTS

EXECUTIVE SUMMARY

Risks and Uncertainties

Volatility and uncertainty in the business and economic environment result in the need to disclose information about the risks and uncertainties confronted by reporting entities. GAAP requires entities to disclose significant risks and uncertainties in the following areas:

1. *Nature of operations.* Disclosures concerning the nature of operations do not have to be quantified, and relative importance may be described by terms such as *predominantly, about equally,* and *major.*

2. *Use of estimates in the preparation of financial statements.* Financial statements should include an explanation that their preparation in conformity with GAAP requires the application of management's estimates.

3. *Certain significant estimates.* Disclosure regarding an estimate is required when both of the following conditions are met: (a) it is at least reasonably possible that the effect on the financial statements of a condition, situation, or set of circumstances that existed at the date of the financial statements will change in the near term due to one or more future confirming events, and (b) the effect of the change would be material to the financial statements.

4. *Current vulnerability due to certain concentrations.* Financial statements should disclose concentrations if all of the following conditions are met: (a) the concentration existed at the date of the financial statements, (b) the concentration makes the enterprise vulnerable to the risk of a near-term severe impact, and (c) it is at least reasonably possible that the events that could cause the severe impact will occur in the near term.

Accounting Literature

FASB Accounting Standards Codification Topic	*Pre-Codification Accounting Literature*
275, *Risks and Uncertainties*	SOP 94-6, *Disclosure of Certain Significant Risks and Uncertainties*

DISCLOSURE AND KEY PRESENTATION REQUIREMENTS

1. Disclosures should be made about the nature of the entity's operations, including the following (ASC 275-10-50-2) (SOP 94-6, par. 10):

   a. A description of the entity's major products or services.

    b. The principal markets (e.g., industries and types of customers) for the entity's products or services.

    c. If the entity operates in more than one business, the relative importance of the entity's operations in each business and the basis for that determination (e.g., based on assets, revenues, or earnings). (*Note*: Relative importance need not be quantified and could be conveyed by use of terms, such as *predominately, about equally,* or *major.*)

2. Disclosure should be made that the preparation of financial statements in conformity with GAAP requires the use of management's estimates. (ASC 275-10-50-4) (SOP 94-6, par. 11)

3. The following disclosures should be made regarding significant estimates used in the determination of the carrying amounts of assets or liabilities or in disclosure of gain or loss contingencies, if: (1) it is at least reasonably possible that the effect on the financial statements of a condition, situation, or set of circumstances that existed at the date of the financial statements will change in the near term due to one or more future confirming events and (2) the effect of the change would be material to the financial statements (ASC 275-10-50-6 through 50-10) (SOP 94-6, pars. 13–15) (*Note:* In determining whether disclosures about an estimate are required, the criterion in item (2) is considered met in regard to intangible assets if the effect of a change in either: (*a*) the useful life or (*b*) the expected likelihood of renewal or extension of an intangible asset would be material to the financial statements, either individually or in aggregate by major intangible asset class.):

    a. The nature of the uncertainty.

    b. An indication that it is at least reasonably possible that a change in the estimate will occur in the near term.

    c. The factors that cause the estimate to be sensitive to change. (This disclosure is encouraged, but not required.)

    d. If the estimate involves a loss contingency covered by ASC Subtopic 450-20, *Contingencies—Loss Contingencies*, an estimate of the possible loss or range of loss, or a statement that such an estimate cannot be made.

    e. If the entity uses risk-reduction techniques to mitigate losses or the uncertainty that may result from future events and, as a result, determines that the criteria described above are not met, the disclosures in (a)–(d) and of the risk-reduction techniques. (This disclosure is encouraged, but not required.)

4. The following concentrations should be disclosed if: (1) the concentration exists at the date of the financial statements, (2)

the concentration makes the entity vulnerable to the risk of a near-term severe impact, and (3) it is at least reasonably possible that the events that could cause the severe effect will occur in the near term (ASC 275-10-50-16 through 50-22) (SOP 94-6, pars. 20–24):

a. Concentrations in the volume of business transacted with a particular customer, supplier, lender, grantor, or contributor. (For purposes of this disclosure, it is always considered at least reasonably possible that any customer, grantor, or contributor will be lost in the near term.)

b. Concentrations in revenue from particular products, services, or fund-raising events.

c. Concentrations in the available sources of supply of materials, labor, or services, or of licenses or other rights used in the entity's operations.

d. Concentrations in the market or geographic area in which the entity conducts its operations. (For purposes of this disclosure, it is always considered at least reasonably possible that operations located outside an entity's home country will be disrupted in the near term.)

e. For concentrations of labor subject to collective bargaining agreements, the percentage of the labor force covered by a collective bargaining agreement and the percentage of the labor force covered by a collective agreement that will expire within one year.

f. For concentrations of operations located outside the entity's home country, the carrying amounts of net assets and the geographic areas in which they are located.

EXAMPLES OF FINANCIAL STATEMENT DISCLOSURES

 The following sample disclosures are available on the accompanying disc.

Nature of Operations

Example 1: Company Describes Its Primary Products

The Company designs, manufactures, markets, and services test systems and related software, and backplanes and associated connectors. The Company's top five products are semiconductor test systems, backplane connection systems, circuit-board test systems, telecommunications test systems, and software test systems.

Example 2: Company Describes the Types of Customers It Has

The Company is a leading global developer, manufacturer, and distributor of hand tools, power tools, tool storage products, shop equipment, under-hood diagnostics equipment, under-car equipment, emissions and safety equipment, collision repair equipment, vehicle service information, and business management systems and services. The Corporation's customers include professional automotive technicians, shop owners, franchised service centers, national accounts, original equipment manufacturers, and industrial tool and equipment users worldwide.

Example 3: Company Describes U.S. Geographic Locations Where It Operates

The Company is a leading designer and manufacturer of open-architecture, standard embedded computer components that system designers can easily utilize to create a custom solution specific to the user's unique application. The Company has operations in New York, New Mexico, Minnesota, North Carolina, and California. The Company's product lines include CPU boards, general purpose input/output modules, avionics interface modules and analyzers, interconnection and expansion units, telemetry boards, data acquisition software, and industrial computer systems and enclosures.

Example 4: Company Indicates That Its Operations Are Vulnerable to Changes in Trends and Customer Demand

The Company is a nationwide specialty retailer of fashionable and contemporary apparel and accessory items designed for consumers with a young, active lifestyle. The Company's success is largely dependent on its ability to gauge the fashion tastes of its customers and to provide merchandise that satisfies customer demand. The Company's failure to anticipate, identify, or react to changes in fashion trends could adversely affect its results of operations.

Example 5: Company's Operations Are Substantially in Foreign Countries

Substantially all of the Company's products are manufactured in the Dominican Republic, Mexico (under the Maquiladora program), Switzerland, Ireland, and Slovakia. These foreign operations represent captive manufacturing facilities of the Company. The Company's operations are subject to various political, economic, and other risks and uncertainties inherent in the countries in which the Company operates. Among other risks, the Company's operations are subject to the risks of restrictions on transfer of funds; export duties, quotas and embargoes; domestic and international customs and tariffs; changing taxation policies; foreign exchange restrictions; and political conditions and governmental regulations.

Example 6: Company Specifies Percentage of Net Sales Relating to Foreign Operations

Sales to customers outside the United States approximated 35% of net sales in 20X2 and 25% of net sales in 20X1.

Estimates

Example 7: General Note Regarding Estimates Inherent in the Financial Statements

The preparation of the Company's financial statements in conformity with accounting principles generally accepted in the United States of America (GAAP) requires management to make estimates and assumptions that affect reported amounts of assets and liabilities and disclosure of contingent assets and liabilities at the date of the financial statements and the reported amounts of revenues and expenses during the reporting period. Actual results could differ from those estimates.

Example 8: Significant Estimates Relating to Specific Financial Statement Accounts and Transactions Are Identified

The financial statements include some amounts that are based on management's best estimates and judgments. The most significant estimates relate to allowance for uncollectible accounts receivable, inventory obsolescence, depreciation, intangible asset valuations and useful lives, employee benefit plans, environmental accruals, taxes, contingencies, and costs to complete long-term contracts. These estimates may be adjusted as more current information becomes available, and any adjustment could be significant.

Example 9: Significant Accounting Estimates—Inventory

The Company's provisions for inventory write-downs are based on the Company's best estimates of product sales prices and customer demand patterns, and its plans to transition its products. However, the Company operates in a highly competitive industry that is characterized by aggressive pricing practices, downward pressures on gross margins, and rapid technological advances. As a result of the industry's dynamic nature, it is at least reasonably possible that the estimates used by the Company to determine its provisions for inventory write-downs will be materially different from the actual amounts or results. These differences could result in materially higher than expected inventory provisions and related costs, which could have a materially adverse effect on the Company's results of operations and financial condition in the near term.

Example 10: Significant Accounting Estimates—Assets Held for Sale

In October 20X2, in connection with its strategy to reduce debt, the Company decided to sell land and buildings formerly used by a discontinued manufacturing unit. As a result, the Company recorded a non-cash write-down of $1,400,000 to reflect these assets at their estimated fair value of $4,200,000, which is shown as "Assets held for sale" at December 31, 20X2. The charge of $1,400,000 reflects the Company's best estimate of the amount anticipated to be realized on the disposition of the assets. This estimate is based on negotiations with potential buyers and independent parties familiar with valuations of this nature. The amount that the Company will ultimately realize could differ materially from the amount recorded in the financial statements.

Example 11: Significant Accounting Estimates—Deferred Tax Assets

Included in the accompanying Balance Sheets at December 31, 20X2, and December 31, 20X1, are deferred tax assets of $2,500,000 and $2,200,000, respectively, representing tax loss and credit carryforwards. Realization of that asset is dependent on the Company's ability to generate future taxable income. Management believes that it is more likely than not that forecasted taxable income will be sufficient to utilize the tax carryforwards before their expiration in 20X8 and 20X9 to fully recover the asset. However, there can be no assurance that the Company will meet its expectations of future income. As a result, the amount of the deferred tax assets considered realizable could be reduced in the near term if estimates of future taxable income are reduced. Such an occurrence could materially adversely affect the Company's results of operations and financial condition.

Example 12: Significant Accounting Estimates—Self-Insured Claims

The Company is primarily self-insured, up to certain limits, for automobile and general liability, workers' compensation, and employee group health claims. The Company has purchased stop-loss insurance, which will reimburse the Company for individual claims in excess of $50,000 annually or aggregate claims exceeding $1,000,000 annually. Operations are charged with the cost of claims reported and an estimate of claims incurred but not reported. A liability for unpaid claims and the associated claim expenses, including incurred but not reported losses, is actuarially determined and reflected in the Balance Sheet as an accrued liability. Total expense under the program was approximately $3,200,000 and $2,900,000 in 20X2 and 20X1, respectively. The self-insured claims liability includes incurred but not reported losses of $1,500,000 and $1,745,000 at December 31, 20X2, and December 31, 20X1, respectively.

The determination of such claims and expenses and the appropriateness of the related liability is continually reviewed and updated. It is reasonably possible that the accrued estimated liability for self-insured claims may need to be revised in the near term.

Other Risks, Uncertainties, and Concentrations

Example 13: Company Describes the Risks of the Industry in Which It Operates and Potential Effect on the Company's Operations

The Company participates in a highly volatile industry that is characterized by rapid technological change, intense competitive pressure, and cyclical market patterns. The Company's results of operations are affected by a wide variety of factors, including general economic conditions, decreases in average selling prices over the life of any particular product, the timing of new product introductions (by the Company, its competitors, and others), the ability to manufacture sufficient quantities of a given product in a timely manner, the timely implementation of new manufacturing process technologies, the ability to safeguard patents and intellectual property from competitors, and the effect of new technologies resulting in rapid escalation of demand for some products in the face of equally steep decline in demand for others. Based on the factors noted herein, the Company may experience substantial period-to-period fluctuations in future operating results.

Example 14: Company Has Geographic Exposure to Catastrophe Losses

The Company has a geographic exposure to catastrophe losses in certain areas of the country. These catastrophes can be caused by various events, including hurricanes, windstorms, earthquakes, hail, severe winter weather, and fires, and the incidence and severity of catastrophes are inherently unpredictable. The extent of losses from a catastrophe is a function of both the total amount of insured exposure in the area affected by the event and the severity of the event. Most catastrophes are restricted to small geographic areas; however, hurricanes and earthquakes may produce significant damage in large, heavily populated areas. The Company generally seeks to reduce its exposure to catastrophes through individual risk selection and the purchase of catastrophe reinsurance.

Example 15: Company Requires No Collateral and Concentrations of Credit Risk Virtually Limited

Financial instruments that potentially subject the Company to concentrations of credit risk consist primarily of cash and cash equivalents and accounts receivable. The Company places its cash and cash equivalents with high quality financial institutions and limits the amount of credit exposure with any one institution. Concentrations of credit risk with respect to accounts receivable are limited because a large number of geographically diverse customers make up the Company's customer base, thus spreading the trade credit risk. At December 31, 20X2, and December 31, 20X1, no single group or customer represents greater than 10% of total accounts receivable. The Company controls credit risk through credit approvals, credit limits, and monitoring procedures. The Company performs credit evaluations of its commercial and industrial customers but generally does not require collateral to support accounts receivable.

Example 16: Company Requires Collateral and Has Concentrations in Accounts Receivable

The Company sells its products to distributors and original equipment manufacturers throughout the world. The Company performs ongoing credit evaluations of its customers' financial condition and, generally, requires collateral, such as letters of credit, whenever deemed necessary. At December 31, 20X2, three customers, each of who accounted for more than 10% of the Company's accounts receivable, accounted for 58% of total accounts receivable in aggregate. At December 31, 20X1, four customers, each of who accounted for more than 10% of the Company's accounts receivable, accounted for 52% of total accounts receivable in aggregate.

Example 17: Concentrations in Sales to Few Customers

In 20X2, the two largest customers accounted for 30% and 21% of sales. In 20X1, the three largest customers accounted for 32%, 19%, and 18% of sales.

Example 18: Concentrations in Sales to Foreign Customers

During 20X2 and 20X1, approximately 38% and 35%, respectively, of the Company's net sales were made to foreign customers. An adverse change in either economic conditions abroad or the Company's relationship with significant foreign distributors could negatively affect the volume of the Company's international sales and the Company's results of operations.

Example 19: Company Has Accounts Receivable and Contract Concentrations in Specific Industries

The majority of accounts receivable and all contract work in progress are from engineering and construction clients primarily concentrated in the steel and utility industries throughout the United States. The Company generally does not require collateral, but in most cases can place liens against the property, plant, or equipment constructed or terminate the contract if a material default occurs. The Company maintains adequate reserves for potential credit losses and such losses have been minimal and within management's estimates.

Example 20: Company Is Dependent on Few Major Suppliers

The Company is dependent on third-party equipment manufacturers, distributors, and dealers for all of its supply of communications equipment. In 20X2 and 20X1, products purchased from the Company's three largest suppliers accounted for approximately 51% and 65% of product purchases, respectively. The Company is dependent on the ability of its suppliers to provide products on a timely basis and on favorable pricing terms. The loss of certain principal suppliers or a significant reduction in product availability from principal suppliers could have a material adverse effect on the Company. The Company believes that its relationships with its suppliers are satisfactory; however, the Company has periodically experienced inadequate supply from certain handset manufacturers.

Example 21: Risks Associated with Concentrations in the Available Sources of Supply of Materials

Certain components and products that meet the Company's requirements are available only from a single supplier or a limited number of suppliers. The rapid rate of technological change and the necessity of developing and manufacturing products with short life cycles may intensify these risks. The inability to obtain components and products as required, or to develop alternative sources, if and as required in the future, could result in delays or reductions in product shipments, which in turn could have a material adverse effect on the Company's business, financial condition, and results of operations.

Example 22: Company Uses Parts and Materials That Are Subject to Industry-Wide Shortages Which Has Forced Suppliers to Allocate Available Quantities

The Company uses numerous suppliers of electronic components and other materials for its operations. Some components used by the Company have been subject to industry-wide shortages, and suppliers have been forced to allocate available quantities among their customers. The Company's inability to obtain any needed components during periods of allocation could cause delays in manufacturing and could adversely affect results of operations.

Example 23: Concentrations of Labor Subject to Collective Bargaining Agreement

At December 31, 20X2, the Company had a total of approximately 1,200 employees. Of this total, approximately 1,000 are hourly workers and 200 are salaried. Approximately 98% of the Company's hourly employees and 37% of its salaried employees are represented by a union. The existing union agreement will expire in November 20X3.

Example 24: Company Limits the Amount of Credit Exposure Through Diversification

The Company places its short-term investments in a variety of financial instruments and, by policy, limits the amount of credit exposure through diversification and by restricting its investments to highly rated securities.

Example 25: Cash in Excess of FDIC Insured Limits

The Company maintains its cash in bank deposit accounts which, at times, may exceed federally insured limits. Accounts are guaranteed by the Federal Deposit Insurance Corporation (FDIC) up to certain limits. At December 31, 20X2, and December 31, 20X1, the Company had approximately $1,250,000 and $1,155,000, respectively, in excess of FDIC insured limits. The Company has not experienced any losses in such accounts.

CHAPTER 15
ASC TOPIC 280: SEGMENT REPORTING

CONTENTS

EXECUTIVE SUMMARY

Segment Reporting

Generally accepted accounting principles (GAAP) require that public entities report certain information (1) about operating segments in complete sets of financial statements and in condensed financial statements of interim periods and (2) about the segments' principal products and services, the geographic areas in which they operate, and their major customers. Although the disclosures about segments of an entity are not required for *nonpublic* business entities or for not-for-profit organizations, such entities are encouraged to provide the same information as public business entities.

Operating segments are components of an entity that meet all of the following criteria:

1. Engage in business activities from which revenues may be earned and in which expenses may be incurred

2. Operating results are regularly reviewed by the entity's chief operating decision maker (e.g., chief executive officer, chief operating officer, or a group of individuals) for purposes of making decisions about resource allocation and performance evaluation

3. Discrete financial information is available

An entity should report separately information about each operating segment that meets any of the following quantitative criteria:

1. The operating segment's total revenues (both external, such as sales to other entities, and intersegment, such as sales between operating segments) make up 10% or more of the combined revenue of all reported operating segments

2. The absolute amount of the reported profit or loss of the operating segment is 10% or more of the greater (in absolute amount) of (a) the combined reported profit of all operating segments that did not report a loss or (b) the combined reported loss of all operating segments that did report a loss

3. The operating segment's assets are 10% or more of the combined assets of all operating segments

For purposes of the above criteria, two or more operating segments may be aggregated into a single operating segment if the segments have similar economic characteristics and if the segments are similar in each of the following areas:

1. The nature of their products and services

2. The nature of their production processes

3. Their type or class of customers

4. Their distribution methods

5. The nature of their regulatory environment, if applicable, (e.g., banking, insurance)

The following are other situations in which separate information about an operating segment should be reported:

- If total external revenue reported by operating segments constitutes less than 75% of total consolidated revenue, then additional operating segments should be identified as reportable segments (even if they do not meet the quantitative criteria above) until at least 75% of the total consolidated revenue is included in reportable segments.

- Information about other business activities and operating segments that are not reportable should be combined and disclosed in an "all other" category.

- If a prior-year reportable segment fails to meet one of the quantitative criteria in the current reporting period, but management believes the segment to be of continuing significance, then information about that segment shall continue to be presented.

- If an operating segment meets the criteria as a reportable segment for the first time in the current period, prior-year segment information that is presented for comparative purposes should be restated to reflect the new reportable segment as a separate segment, unless it is impracticable.

There may be a practical limit to the number of reportable segments that an entity separately discloses so that segment information does not become extremely detailed. As a practical matter, authoritative literature indicates that as the number of reportable segments exceeds ten, an entity should consider whether a practical limit has been reached.

Accounting Literature

FASB Accounting Standards Codification Topic	*Pre-Codification Accounting Literature*
280, *Segment Reporting*	FAS-131, *Disclosures about Segments of an Enterprise and Related Information*
	FASB Implementation Guide (Q&A), *Segment Information: Guidance on Applying Statement 131*

DISCLOSURE AND KEY PRESENTATION REQUIREMENTS

Note: Nonpublic entities are *not* required to disclose segment information. For public entities, the disclosures are required for each period for which an income statement is presented.

However, reconciliations of balance sheet amounts for reportable segments to consolidated balance sheet amounts are required only for each year for which a balance sheet is presented. Previously reported information for prior periods should be restated. (ASC 280-10-50-20) (FAS-131, par. 25)

1. Disclosures should be made of the factors used to identify the entity's reportable segments, including the basis of organization, such as (ASC 280-10-50-21) (FAS-131, par. 26):

   a. Differences in products and services.

   b. Geographic areas.

   c. Regulatory environments.

   d. A combination of factors.

2. The types of products and services from which each reportable segment derives its revenues should be disclosed. (ASC 280-10-50-21) (FAS-131, par. 26)

3. The amount of profit or loss and total assets for each reportable segment should be disclosed. (ASC 280-10-50-22) (FAS-131, par. 27)

4. The following financial information should be disclosed about each reportable segment, if the specified amounts are included in the measure of segment profit or loss reviewed by the chief operating decision maker, or are otherwise regularly provided to the chief operating decision maker even if not included in that measure of segment profit or loss (ASC 280-10-50-22) (FAS-131, par. 27):

   a. Revenues from external customers.

   b. Revenues from transactions with other operating segments of the same entity.

   c. Interest revenue. (*Note:* This may be reported net of interest expense if a majority of the segment's revenues are from interest and the chief operating decision maker relies primarily on net interest revenue to assess performance of the segment and make decisions about resources to be allocated to the segment.)

   d. Interest expense.

   e. Depreciation, depletion, and amortization.

   f. Unusual items (as described in ASC paragraph 225-20-45-16 [APB-30, par. 26]).

   g. Equity in the net income of investees accounted for by the equity method.

   h. Income tax expense or benefit.

    i.   Extraordinary items.

    j.   Significant noncash items other than depreciation, depletion, and amortization.

5. The following financial information should be disclosed about each reportable segment, if the specified amounts are included in the determination of segment assets reviewed by the chief operating decision maker, or are otherwise regularly provided to the chief operating decision maker even if not included in the determination of segment assets (ASC 280-10-50-25) (FAS-131, par. 28) (*Note:* If no asset information is provided for a reportable segment, that fact and the reason for it should be disclosed [ASC 280-10-50-26] [Q&A-131, par. 4].):

    a.   The amount of investment in equity-method investees.

    b.   Total expenditures for additions to long-lived assets (other than financial instruments, long-term customer relationships of a financial institution, mortgage and other servicing rights, deferred policy acquisition costs, and deferred tax assets).

6. Disclosures should be made of the measurements used for segment profit or loss and segment assets for each reportable segment, including at a minimum the following information (ASC 280-10-50-29) (FAS-131, par. 31):

    a.   The basis of accounting for any transactions between reportable segments.

    b.   The nature of any differences between the measurements of the reportable segments' profit or loss and the entity's consolidated income before income taxes, extraordinary items, and discontinued operations (if not apparent from the reconciliations described in item 7 below). (*Note:* Those differences could include accounting policies and policies for allocation of centrally incurred costs that are necessary for an understanding of the reported segment information.)

    c.   The nature of any differences between the measurements of the reportable segments' assets and the entity's consolidated assets (if not apparent from the reconciliations described in item 7 below). (*Note:* Those differences could include accounting policies and policies for allocation of jointly used assets that are necessary for an understanding of the reported segment information.)

    d.   The nature of any changes from prior periods in the measurement methods used to determine reported segment profit or loss and the effect, if any, of those changes on the measure of segment profit or loss.

    e.   The nature and effect of any asymmetrical allocations to segments (e.g., an entity might allocate depreciation expense to a segment without allocating the related depreciable assets to that segment).

7.   Reconciliations of all of the following items should be disclosed (ASC 280-10-50-30 and 50-31) (FAS-131, par. 32):

    a.   The total of the reportable segments' revenues to the entity's consolidated revenues.

    b.   The total of the reportable segments' measures of profit or loss to the entity's consolidated income before income taxes, extraordinary items, and discontinued operations. (*Note:* However, if an entity allocates items such as income taxes and extraordinary items to segments, the entity may choose to reconcile the total of the segments' measures of profit or loss to consolidated income after those items.)

    c.   The total of the reportable segments' assets to the entity's consolidated assets.

    d.   The total of the reportable segments' amounts for every other significant item of information disclosed to the corresponding consolidated amount (e.g., an entity may choose to disclose liabilities for its reportable segments, in which case the entity would reconcile the total of reportable segments' liabilities for each segment to the entity's consolidated liabilities if the segment liabilities are significant).

8.   The following items should be disclosed on an "entity-wide" basis (for annual reporting only), unless they are disclosed as part of the information about reportable segments (ASC 280-10-50-38 through 50-42) (FAS-131, pars. 36–39) (*Note:* Entities that have a single reportable segment are also required to disclose this information.):

    a.   Revenues from external customers for each product and service or each group of similar products and services, based on the financial information used to produce the entity's general-purpose financial statements (unless it is impracticable to do so, in which case that fact should be disclosed).

    b.   The following information about geographic areas, based on the financial information used to produce the entity's general-purpose financial statements (unless it is impracticable to do so, in which case that fact should be disclosed):

        (1)   Revenues from external customers: (a) attributed to the entity's country of domicile and (b) attributed to

all foreign countries in total from which the entity derives revenues. (*Note:* If revenues from external customers attributed to an individual foreign country are material, those revenues should be disclosed separately; an entity should disclose the basis for attributing revenues from external customers to individual countries.)

    (2) Long-lived assets (other than financial instruments, long-term customer relationships of a financial institution, mortgage and other servicing rights, deferred policy acquisition costs, and deferred tax assets) located in: (a) the entity's country of domicile and (b) all foreign countries in total in which the entity holds assets. (*Note:* If assets in an individual foreign country are material, those assets should be disclosed separately.)

  c. The extent of the entity's reliance on a single external customer from which 10% or more of revenues are derived, the amount of revenues earned from each such single customer, and the operating segment reporting the revenue. (*Note:* The entity need not disclose the identity of a major customer or the amount of revenues that each segment reports from that customer. In addition, a group of entities known to the reporting entity to be under common control should be considered as a single customer, and the federal government, a state government, a local government (e.g., a county or municipality), or a foreign government each should be considered as a single customer.)

9. The following information should be disclosed about each reportable segment in condensed financial statements of interim periods (ASC 280-10-50-32; 270-10-50-1) (FAS-131, par. 33):

  a. Revenues from external customers.

  b. Intersegment revenues.

  c. A measure of segment profit or loss.

  d. Total assets for which there has been a material change from the amount disclosed in the last annual report.

  e. A description of differences from the last annual report in the basis of segmentation or in the basis of measurement of segment profit or loss.

  f. A reconciliation of the total of the reportable segments' measures of profit or loss to the entity's consolidated income before income taxes, extraordinary items, and discontinued operations. (*Note:* However, if an entity allocates items such as income taxes and extraordinary items to segments, the entity may choose to reconcile the total of the segments' measures of profit or loss to consolidated income after those items. Significant reconciling items should be separately identified and described in that reconciliation.)

10.   If an entity changes the structure of its internal organization in a manner that causes the composition of its reportable segments to change, the corresponding information for earlier periods, including interim periods, should be restated, unless it is impracticable to do so. (ASC 280-10-50-34 and 50-35) (FAS-131, pars. 34–35) (*Note:* The entity should also disclose that it has restated the segment information for earlier periods. If the segment information for earlier periods, including interim periods, is not restated to reflect the change, the entity should disclose in the year in which the change occurs segment information for the current period under both the old basis and the new basis of segmentation, unless it is impracticable to do so.)

EXAMPLES OF FINANCIAL STATEMENT DISCLOSURES

 The following sample disclosures are available on the accompanying disc.

Example 1: Company Operates in a Single Business Segment and Discloses Entity-Wide Geographic Data and Sales to Major Customers

The Company operates in a single business segment that includes the design, development, and manufacture of electronic surveillance equipment and products for the commercial electronics industry. The following table summarizes the Company's revenues and long-lived assets in different geographic locations:

	20X2	*20X1*
Revenues:		
United States	$59,820,000	$54,338,000
Singapore	11,341,000	9,102,000
Other foreign countries	20,145,000	17,010,000
Total	$91,306,000	$80,450,000
Long-lived assets:		
United States	$16,764,000	$15,430,000
Singapore	6,450,000	6,020,000

	20X2	20X1
Other foreign countries	1,230,000	1,113,000
Total	$24,444,000	$22,563,000

Geographic area data is based on product shipment destination. Export sales as a percentage of revenues were 40% for 20X2 and 35% for 20X1.

In 20X2 and 20X1, sales to a single customer were 13% and 11% of total sales, respectively.

The geographic summary of long-lived assets is based on physical location.

Example 2: Company's Operations Are Classified Into Two Principal Reportable Segments: Domestic and International Operations

The Company manages its operations through two business segments: domestic and international. Each unit sells railroad electronics and related products as well as services to railroads and transit authorities. The international business segment sells the Company's products and services outside the U.S.

The Company evaluates performance based on net operating profit. Administrative functions such as finance, treasury, and information systems are centralized. However, where applicable, portions of the administrative function expenses are allocated between the operating segments. The operating segments do not share manufacturing or distribution facilities. In the event any materials and/or services are provided to one operating segment by the other, the transaction is valued according to the company's transfer policy, which approximates market price. The costs of operating the manufacturing plants are captured discretely within each segment. The Company's property, plant and equipment, inventory, and accounts receivable are captured and reported discretely within each operating segment.

Summary financial information for the two reportable segments is as follows:

	20X2	20X1
United States Operations:		
Net sales	$25,200,000	$22,400,000
Operating income	2,150,000	2,410,000
Assets	15,600,000	14,400,000
Accounts receivable	5,070,000	4,510,000
Inventory	4,250,000	4,325,000

	20X2	*20X1*
International Operations:		
Net sales	$ 1,360,000	$ 1,310,000
Operating income	69,000	31,000
Assets	65,000	59,000
Accounts receivable	171,000	143,000
Inventory	56,000	42,000
Consolidated Operations:		
Net sales	$26,560,000	$23,710,000
Operating income	2,219,000	2,441,000
Assets	15,665,000	14,459,000
Accounts receivable	5,241,000	4,653,000
Inventory	4,306,000	4,367,000

Example 3: Company Has Five Operating Segments That Are Aggregated into Three Reportable Segments and Are Reconciled to the Company's Consolidated Amounts

The Company has five principal operating segments, which are the design, manufacturing and marketing of (1) semiconductor test systems, (2) backplane connection systems, (3) circuit-board test systems, (4) telecommunication test systems, and (5) software test systems. These operating segments were determined based on the nature of the products and services offered. Operating segments are defined as components of an enterprise about which separate financial information is available that is evaluated regularly by the chief operating decision-maker in deciding how to allocate resources and in assessing performance. The Company's chief executive officer and chief operating officer have been identified as the chief operating decision makers. The Company's chief operating decision makers direct the allocation of resources to operating segments based on the profitability and cash flows of each respective segment.

The Company has determined that there are three reportable segments: (1) semiconductor test systems segment, (2) backplane connection systems segment, and (3) other test systems segment. The other test systems segment comprises circuit-board test systems, telecommunication test systems, and software test systems; these operating segments were not separately reported as they do not meet any of the quantitative thresholds under applicable accounting literature.

The Company evaluates performance based on several factors, of which the primary financial measure is business segment income before taxes. The accounting policies of the business segments are the same as those described in "Note 1: Summary of Significant Accounting Policies." Intersegment sales are accounted for at fair value as if sales were to third parties. The following tables show the operations of the Company's reportable segments:

	Semiconductor Test Systems Segment	Backplane Connection Systems Segment	Other Test Systems Segment	Corporate and Eliminations	Consolidated
20X2					
Sales to unaffiliated customers	$19,670,000	$5,458,000	$4,975,000	$ -0-	$30,103,000
Intersegment sales	-0-	275,000	-0-	(275,000)	-0-
Net sales	19,670,000	5,733,000	4,975,000	(275,000)	30,103,000
Income before taxes (1)	2,125,000	692,000	531,000	(450,000)	2,898,000
Total assets (2)	10,391,000	3,850,000	2,700,000	6,200,000	23,141,000
Property additions (3)	1,400,000	640,000	150,000	700,000	2,890,000
Interest expense	120,000	74,000	53,000	-0-	247,000
Depreciation and amortization (3)	545,000	280,000	200,000	320,000	1,345,000
20X1					
Sales to unaffiliated customers	$17,840,000	$4,940,000	$4,310,000	$ -0-	$27,090,000
Intersegment sales	-0-	210,000	-0-	(210,000)	-0-
Net sales	17,840,000	5,150,000	4,310,000	(210,000)	27,090,000
Income before taxes (1)	1,930,000	584,000	487,000	(400,000)	2,601,000
Total assets (2)	10,110,000	3,725,000	2,574,000	5,900,000	22,309,000
Property additions (3)	1,050,000	420,000	170,000	400,000	2,040,000
Interest expense	113,000	67,000	48,000	-0-	228,000
Depreciation and amortization (3)	510,000	240,000	180,000	290,000	1,220,000

(1) Income before taxes of the principal businesses exclude the effects of employee profit sharing, management incentive compensation, other unallocated expenses, and net interest income.

(2) *Total business assets* are the owned or allocated assets used by each business. *Corporate assets* consist of cash and cash equivalents, marketable securities, unallocated fixed assets of support divisions and common facilities, and certain other assets.

(3) Corporate property additions and depreciation and amortization expense include items attributable to the unallocated fixed assets of support divisions and common facilities.

Information as to the Company's sales in different geographical areas is as follows:

	20X2	20X1
Sales to unaffiliated customers:		
United States	$16,112,000	$13,143,000
Asia Pacific region	5,477,000	6,374,000
Europe	4,993,000	4,065,000
Japan	2,300,000	2,439,000
Other	1,221,000	1,069,000
	$30,103,000	$27,090,000

Sales are attributable to geographic areas based on location of customer. Neither the Company nor any of its segments depends on any single customer, small group of customers, or government for more than 10% of its sales.

Also, because a substantial portion of the Company's sales are derived from the sales of product manufactured in the United States, long-lived assets located outside the United States are less than 10%.

Example 4: Company Discloses Sales to Major Customers and the Identity of the Segments Reporting the Sales

> **Note:** This example assumes the same facts as in Example 3 above, except that the Company has sales to major customers, for which disclosure is required of (1) the total amount of sales to the major customer and (2) the identity of the segment reporting the sales.

In 20X2 and 20X1, sales to a customer of the Company's Semiconductor Test Systems segment totaled approximately $4,214,000 (14%), and $3,522,000 (13%), respectively, of the Company's consolidated sales. In 20X2 and 20X1, sales to a different customer of the Company's Backplane Connection Systems segment totaled $3,913,000 (13%), and $3,251,000 (12%), respectively, of the Company's consolidated sales.

Example 5: Company Discloses Its Exposure to Economic Conditions in Foreign Countries

The Company has operations in Mexico, Russia, and Poland. These countries have experienced illiquidity, volatile currency exchange rates and interest rates, and reduced economic activity. The Company will be affected for the foreseeable future by economic conditions in these regions, although it is not possible to determine the extent of the effects.

PART 3—ASSETS

CHAPTER 16
ASC TOPIC 305: CASH AND CASH EQUIVALENTS

CONTENTS

EXECUTIVE SUMMARY

Cash and Cash Equivalents

Cash generally consists of cash on hand, available funds on deposit at a financial institution, and negotiable instruments (e.g., money orders, personal checks). Cash equivalents generally consist of highly liquid investments (e.g., certificates of deposit, money market accounts) with initial maturity of three months or less.

The following are common balance sheet captions used to describe cash and cash equivalents on the face of a balance sheet:

- Cash (this is used if there are no cash equivalents)
- Cash and cash equivalents
- Cash and equivalents
- Cash, including certificates of deposit
- Cash and short-term investments

Cash overdrafts not having free cash balances against which they may be offset should be classified as a current liability. The following are common balance sheet captions used to describe the overdraft as a current liability on the face of a balance sheet:

- Overdraft
- Cash overdraft
- Bank overdraft
- Checks drawn in excess of available bank balances

To be classified as a current asset, cash and cash equivalents must be readily available to pay current obligations and free from any contractual restrictions. Cash that is restricted or in escrow should be segregated from the general cash category; the restricted cash is either classified in the current asset or in the noncurrent asset section, depending on the date of availability or disbursement. If the cash is to be used for payment of existing or maturing obligations (within a year or within the operating cycle, whichever is longer), classification as a current asset is appropriate; otherwise, it should be shown as a noncurrent asset.

Accounting Literature

ASC Topic 305 does not prescribe any specific disclosure requirements relating to cash and cash equivalents. However, the matters discussed below are considered informative for users of the financial statements and are generally observed in practice.

DISCLOSURE AND KEY PRESENTATION REQUIREMENTS

ASC Topic 305 does not prescribe any specific disclosure requirements relating to cash and cash equivalents. However, the following matters are considered informative for users of the financial statements and are generally observed in practice:

- Cash overdrafts not subject to offset by other accounts in the same financial institution are classified as current liabilities.
- Checks from customers held as of the end of the period are accounted for as cash.
- Checks payable to vendors held as of the end of the period are accounted for as accounts payable.
- The following disclosures are generally made for legally restrictive compensating balance agreements:
  — The terms of the compensating balance agreement.
  — The amount of the compensating balance requirement.
  — The amount required to be maintained to assure future credit availability and the terms of that agreement.
  — The maintenance of compensating balances for the benefit of a related party.

EXAMPLES OF FINANCIAL STATEMENT DISCLOSURES

The following sample disclosures are available on the accompanying disc.

Example 1: Note Discloses the Components of Cash and Cash Equivalents

Cash and cash equivalents consist of the following:

	20X2	20X1
Cash	$1,102,000	$116,000
Certificates of deposit	200,000	250,000
Money market funds	300,000	125,000
Commercial paper	500,000	500,000
Total	$1,102,000	$991,000

Example 2: Restricted Cash from Industrial Revenue Bonds Is Shown as a Noncurrent Asset

	20X2	20X1
Noncurrent assets:		
Restricted cash from industrial revenue bonds	$1,200,000	$ -0-
Intangible assets	200,000	220,000
Deposits	125,000	100,000
Total noncurrent assets	$1,525,000	$320,000

At December 31, 20X2, the Company had borrowings under Industrial Revenue and Job Development Authority Bonds available for and restricted for the construction of a new facility and the purchase of certain equipment. The unexpended portion of such funds totaling $1,200,000 has been classified as "Restricted cash from industrial revenue bonds" in the accompanying Balance Sheet.

Example 3: Cash Not Available for Use in Operations and Restricted for Capital Expenditures Is Shown as a Noncurrent Asset

	20X2	20X1
Noncurrent assets:		
Cash restricted for capital expenditures	$3,200,000	$ -0-
Intangible assets	200,000	220,000
Deposits	125,000	100,000
Total noncurrent assets	$3,525,000	$320,000

The Company has classified as restricted certain cash and cash equivalents that are not available for use in its operations. At December 31, 20X2, the Company had commitments to construct additional warehouse facilities at an estimated cost of $8,600,000. At December 31, 20X2, the Company expended $5,400,000 on this capital program and had $3,200,000 in cash and cash equivalents on hand restricted for use in completing this project.

Example 4: Restricted Cash Has Both a Current and Noncurrent Portion

	20X2	20X1
Current assets:		
Cash	$ 723,000	$ 1,325,000
Restricted cash for litigation settlement	600,000	-0-
Accounts receivable	4,736,000	4,244,000
Inventory	4,317,000	3,978,000
Total current assets	10,376,000	9,547,000
Property and equipment, net	6,759,000	6,316,000
Noncurrent assets:		
Restricted cash for litigation settlement	900,000	-0-
Deposits	125,000	100,000
Total assets	$18,160,000	$15,963,000

At December 31, 20X2, the Company has $1,500,000 of restricted cash of which $900,000 is classified as a noncurrent asset. The restricted cash serves as collateral for an irrevocable standby letter of credit that provides financial assurance that the Company will fulfill its obligations with respect to certain litigation settlement discussed in Note [X]. The cash is held in custody by the issuing bank, is restricted as to withdrawal or use, and is currently invested in money market funds. Income from these investments is paid to the Company. The current portion of restricted cash of $600,000 represents the amount of current liability for amounts billed to the Company for certain repairs agreed to be made under the settlement agreement.

Example 5: Note Discloses Cash Equivalents That Include Securities Purchased under Agreement to Resell

The Company considers all investments purchased with initial maturity of three months or less to be cash equivalents. On December 31, 20X2, and December 31, 20X1, the Company purchased $2,500,000 and $2,000,000, respectively, of U.S. government securities under agreements to resell on January 4, 20X3, and January 5, 20X2, respectively, which are included in cash and cash equivalents in the accompanying Balance Sheets. Due to the short-term nature of the agreements, the Company did not take possession of the securities, which were instead held in the Company's safekeeping account at the bank.

Example 6: General Accounting Policy Describes the Components of Cash Equivalents and Indicates There Is No Exposure to Credit Risk

Cash equivalents include money market accounts, certificates of deposit, and commercial paper, all of which have maturities of three months or less. Cash equivalents are stated at cost plus accrued interest, which approximates market value. The maximum amount placed in any one financial institution is limited in order to reduce risk. The Company does not believe it is exposed to any significant credit risk on cash and cash equivalents.

Example 7: General Accounting Policy Describes Cash Equivalents and Indicates at Times They May Exceed the FDIC Insurance Limit

Cash and cash equivalents include all cash balances and highly liquid investments with an initial maturity of three months or less. The Company places its temporary cash investments with high credit quality financial institutions. At times such investments may be in excess of the Federal Deposit Insurance Corporation (FDIC) insurance limit.

Example 8: Concentration of Credit Risk for Cash Deposits at Banks

Financial instruments that potentially subject the Company to concentrations of credit risk consist principally of cash deposits. Accounts at each institution are insured by the Federal Deposit Insurance Corporation (FDIC) up to certain limits. At December 31, 20X2, and December 31, 20X1, the Company had approximately $2,317,000 and $1,945,000 in excess of FDIC insured limits, respectively.

Example 9: Concentration of Credit Risk for Cash Deposits at Brokerage Firms

Financial instruments that potentially subject the Company to concentrations of credit risk consist principally of cash deposits at a brokerage firm. The accounts at the brokerage firm contain cash and securities. Balances are insured up to $500,000, with a limit of $100,000 for cash, by the Securities Investor Protection Corporation (SIPC). At December 31, 20X2, and December 31, 20X1, the

Company had approximately $434,000 and $369,000 in excess of SIPC insured limits, respectively.

Example 10: Compensating Balance Requirement Is Based on a Percentage of the Available Line of Credit

As part of its line of credit agreement with a bank, the Company is expected to maintain average compensating cash balances that are based on a percentage of the available credit line. The amount of compensating balances required at December 31, 20X2, was $300,000. The compensating balances are held under agreements that do not legally restrict the use of such funds and, therefore, the funds are not segregated on the face of the balance sheet. The compensating cash balances are determined daily by the bank based on cash balances shown by the bank, adjusted for average uncollected funds and Federal Reserve requirements. During the year ended December 31, 20X2, the Company was in substantial compliance with the compensating balance requirements. Funds on deposit with the bank and considered in the compensating balances are subject to withdrawal; however, the availability of the line of credit is dependent on the maintenance of sufficient average compensating balances.

> **Note:** Alternatively, the disclosure of compensating balances may be included in the note disclosure of the related debt agreement.

Example 11: Compensating Balance Requirement Is a Fixed Amount

As part of its line of credit agreement with a bank, the Company has agreed to maintain average compensating balances of $150,000. The balances are not legally restricted as to withdrawal and serve as part of the Company's normal operating cash.

> **Note:** Alternatively, the disclosure of compensating balances may be included in the note disclosure of the related debt agreement.

Example 12: Change in Method of Classifying Cash Equivalents and Restatement of Prior-Year Balances

During the year ended December 31, 20X2, the Company changed the method of classifying cash equivalents and has restated prior-year balances to reflect the change. All highly liquid investments with original maturities of three months or less at date of purchase are carried at cost, which approximates fair value, and are considered to be cash equivalents. These investments were previously classified as marketable securities. All other investments not considered to be a cash equivalent now are categorized separately as investments.

CHAPTER 17
ASC TOPIC 310: RECEIVABLES

CONTENTS

EXECUTIVE SUMMARY

Overall

For financial statement purposes, accounts and notes receivable are generally classified into two categories: (1) trade receivables and (2) nontrade receivables. *Trade receivables* are amounts owed by customers for goods and services sold as part of the normal operations of the business and include open accounts, notes, and installment contracts. *Nontrade receivables*, or other receivables, include items such as advances to officers and employees, interest and dividend receivables, tax refund claims, and receivables from sales of assets. Technically, a great distinction does not exist between accounts and notes receivable, except that typically a note receivable (1) involves a formal promissory note, (2) carries interest, and (3) is of a longer duration.

Valuation allowances for losses on trade receivables should be recorded if a loss is probable and the amount of the loss can be reasonably estimated, and should be deducted from the related receivables. Similarly, a note receivable generally is considered impaired, and a valuation allowance should be recorded, when it is probable that a creditor will be unable to collect all amounts due, including principal and interest, according to the contractual terms and schedules of the loan agreement.

For transfers, sales, and securitizations of receivables, see Chapter 57, "ASC Topic 860: Transfers and Servicing."

Nonrefundable Fees and Other Costs

Loan origination fees are fees charged to a borrower in connection with the process of originating, refinancing, or restructuring a loan. These fees include, but are not limited to, points, management, arrangement, placement, application, underwriting, and other fees pursuant to a lending transaction. Commitment fees are charged for entering into an agreement that obligates an entity to make or acquire a loan. These fees include, but are not limited to, fees for letters of credit and obligations to purchase a loan or group of loans and pass-through certificates.

Loan origination fees and related direct loan origination costs for a given loan should be offset and the net amount deferred and amortized as a reduction of (addition to) interest income over the life of the loan, except for fees and costs related to certain restructurings. Generally, loan commitment fees should be deferred and, if the commitment is exercised, recognized over the life of the loan as an adjustment of interest income (yield). If the commitment expires unexercised, loan commitment fees should be recognized as service fee income upon expiration of the commitment.

Loans and Debt Securities Acquired with Deteriorated Credit Quality

The initial carrying amount of certain loans with credit quality deterioration that were acquired should not reflect a valuation allowance. The valuation allowance on such loans should only take into consideration those losses incurred after the loan was acquired. In addition, such loans give rise to an accretable yield (i.e., undiscounted cash flows expected as of the acquisition date less the initial investment in the loan) and nonaccretable difference (i.e., the payments contractually required by the loan less the undiscounted cash flows expected as of the acquisition date).

The accounting for certain loans with credit quality deterioration should be performed on a loan-by-loan basis unless each loan individually is subject to the specific accounting requirements and the loans being aggregated for accounting purposes have common risk characteristics. Once loans are aggregated into a pool, the results of one pool should not be used to offset the results of another pool.

Troubled Debt Restructurings by Creditors

A troubled debt restructuring occurs if, because of the debtor's financial difficulties, a creditor grants a concession to a debtor that it would not otherwise consider. Implicit in this definition is the expectation that the fair value of the modified terms or the assets or equity interest received are less than the recorded investment in the loan.

There are three common types of troubled debt restructurings: (*a*) a transfer of assets (or equity interest) from the debtor in full satisfaction of the loan; (*b*) a modification in terms of the loan; and (*c*) a transfer of assets in partial satisfaction of the loan in combination with a modification of the terms of the remaining loan. Loans subject to troubled debt restructurings are usually impaired before the date of restructure. However, a minor modification of terms, such as changes in covenants and other changes that tend to occur frequently and in the ordinary course of business, are not considered, and therefore not subject to, troubled debt restructurings.

Accounting Literature

FASB Accounting Standards Codification Topic	*Pre-Codification Accounting Literature*
310, *Receivables*	FAS-5, *Accounting for Contingencies*

FASB Accounting Standards Codification Topic	*Pre-Codification Accounting Literature*
	FAS-15, *Accounting by Debtors and Creditors for Troubled Debt Restructurings*
	FAS-91, *Accounting for Nonrefundable Fees and Costs Associated with Originating or Acquiring Loans and Initial Direct Costs of Leases*
	FAS-107, *Disclosure about Fair Value of Financial Instruments*
	FAS-114, *Accounting by Creditors for Impairment of a Loan*
	FAS-118, *Accounting by Creditors for Impairment of a Loan—Income Recognition and Disclosures*
	FAS-140, *Accounting for Transfers and Servicing of Financial Assets and Extinguishments of Liabilities*
	EITF 85-1, *Classifying Notes Received for Capital Stock*
	EITF 92-5, *Amortization Period for Net Deferred Credit Card Origination Costs*
	EITF 96-22, *Applicability of the Disclosures Required by FASB Statement No. 114 When a Loan Is Restructured in a Troubled Debt Restructuring into Two (or More) Loans*
	EITF Topic D-80, *Application of FASB Statements No. 5 and No. 114 to a Loan Portfolio*
	FASB Implementation Guide (Q&A), *A Guide to Implementation of Statement 91, "Accounting for Nonrefundable Fees and Costs Associated with Originating or Acquiring Loans and Initial Direct Costs of Leases"*

FASB Accounting Standards Codification Topic	*Pre-Codification Accounting Literature*
	APB-12, *Omnibus Opinion—1967*
	ARB-43, Chapter 1A, *Rules Adopted by Membership*
	ARB-43, Chapter 3A, *Current Assets and Current Liabilities*
	SOP 01-6, *Accounting by Certain Entities (Including Entities with Trade Receivables) That Lend to or Finance the Activities of Others*
	SOP 03-3, *Accounting for Certain Loans or Debt Securities Acquired in a Transfer*
	Practice Bulletin 1, *Purpose and Scope of AcSEC Practice Bulletins and Procedures for Their Issuance*

DISCLOSURE AND KEY PRESENTATION REQUIREMENTS

Overall

1. Major categories of loans or trade receivables should be presented separately either in the balance sheet or in the notes to the financial statements. (ASC 310-10-45-2 and 50-3) (SOP 01-6, par. 13)

2. Loans or trade receivables held for sale should be presented as a separate balance sheet category. (ASC 310-10-45-2) (SOP 01-6, par. 13) (*Note:* Loans or trade receivables other than those held for sale may be presented on the balance sheet as aggregate amounts.)

3. Foreclosed and repossessed assets should be classified as a separate balance sheet amount, or included in other assets on the balance sheet with separate disclosures in the notes to financial statements. (ASC 310-10-45-3 and 50-11) (SOP 01-6, par. 13) (*Note:* Certain returned or repossessed assets, such as inventory, should not be classified separately if the assets subsequently are to be utilized by the entity in operations.)

4. Valuation allowances for losses on receivables should be deducted from the receivables balance and the amount properly disclosed. (ASC 310-10-45-4 and 50-14) (APB-12, pars. 2 and 3)

5. Changes in the observable market price of an impaired loan or the fair value of the collateral of an impaired collateral-dependent loan should be reported as bad debt expense or a reduction in bad debt expense. (ASC 310-10-45-6) (FAS-114, par. 59)

6. Unearned discounts (other than cash or quantity discounts and similar items), finance charges, and interest included in the face amount of receivables should be shown as a deduction from the related receivables. (ASC 310-10-45-8) (ARB-43, Ch. 3A, par. 10)

7. Current assets should include the following types of receivables that are reasonably expected to be realized in cash or sold or consumed during the entity's normal operating cycle (ASC 310-10-45-9) (ARB-43, Ch. 3A, par. 4) (*Note:* ASC Section 210-10-45, *Balance Sheet—Overall—Other Presentation Matters,* [ARB-43, Ch. 3A, *Current Assets and Current Liabilities*], provides further guidance on the required presentation of current assets in the balance sheet.):

   a. Trade accounts, notes, and acceptances receivable.

   b. Receivables from officers, employees, affiliates, and others, if collectible in the ordinary course of business within a year.

   c. Installment or deferred accounts and notes receivable if they conform generally to normal trade practices and terms within the business.

8. Notes or accounts receivable due from officers, employees, or affiliated companies should be shown separately and not included under a general heading such as notes receivable or accounts receivable. (ASC 310-10-45-13) (ARB-43, Ch. 1A, par. 5)

9. Notes received as equity contributions should *not* be reported as an asset, except in very limited circumstances when there is substantial evidence of ability and intent to pay within a reasonably short period of time. (ASC 310-10-45-14) (EITF 85-1)

10. Acquisition, development, and construction arrangements accounted for as investments in real estate or joint ventures should be combined and reported in the balance sheet separately from those acquisition, development, and construction arrangements accounted for as loans. (ASC 310-10-45-15) (PB-1, par. 17)

11. For all loans and trade receivables, the summary of significant accounting policies should include the following disclosures (ASC 310-10-50-2) (SOP 01-6, par. 13):

    a. The basis for accounting for loans, trade receivables, and lease financings, including those classified as held for sale.

    b. The method used in determining the lower of cost or fair value of nonmortgage loans held for sale (i.e., aggregate or individual asset basis).

    c. The classification and method of accounting for interest-only strips, loans, other receivables, or retained interests in securitizations that can be contractually prepaid or otherwise settled in a way that the holder would not recover substantially all of its recorded investment.

    d. The method for recognizing interest income on loan and trade receivables, including a statement about the entity's policy for treatment of related fees and costs, including the method of amortizing net deferred fees or costs.

12. The following items should be disclosed in the financial statements (ASC 310-10-50-4) (SOP 01-6, par. 13):

    a. The allowance for credit losses.

    b. The allowance for doubtful accounts.

    c. Any unearned income.

    d. Any unamortized premiums and discounts.

    e. Any net unamortized deferred fees and costs.

13. The carrying amount of loans, trade receivables, securities, and financial instruments that serve as collateral for borrowings should be disclosed pursuant to ASC paragraph 860-30-50-1(b) (FAS-140, par. 17). (ASC 310-10-50-5) (SOP 01-6, par. 13) (See Chapter 57, "ASC Topic 860: Transfers and Servicing.")

14. For nonaccrual and past due loans and trade receivables:

    a. The summary of significant accounting policies should include the following disclosures (ASC 310-10-50-6) (SOP 01-6, par. 13):

        (1) The policy for placing loans and trade receivables, if applicable, on nonaccrual status (or discontinuing accrual of interest).

        (2) The policy for recording payments received on nonaccrual loans and trade receivables, if applicable.

        (3) The policy for resuming accrual of interest.

        (4) The policy for charging off uncollectible loans and trade receivables.

(5) The policy for determining past due or delinquency status (i.e., whether past due status is based on how recently payments have been received or contractual terms).

b. The following disclosures should be made for each period for which a balance sheet is presented (ASC 310-10-50-7) (SOP 01-6, par. 13):

(1) The recorded investment in loans and trade receivables on nonaccrual status.

(2) The recorded investment in loans and trade receivables past due 90 days or more and still accruing.

Note: For trade receivables that do not accrue interest until a specified period has elapsed, nonaccrual status would be the point when accrual is suspended after the receivable becomes past due. (ASC 310-10-50-8) (SOP 01-6, par. 13)

15. For credit losses and doubtful accounts:

a. The entity should disclose a description of the accounting policies and methodology used to estimate the following (ASC 310-10-50-9) (SOP 01-6, par. 13):

(1) Allowance for loan losses.

(2) Allowance for doubtful accounts.

(3) Any liability for off-balance-sheet credit losses and related charges for loan, trade receivable or other credit losses. (ASC 310-10-50-10) (SOP 01-6, par. 13) (*Note:* Off-balance-sheet credit losses refer to losses on off-balance-sheet loan commitments, standby letters of credit, financial guarantees, and other similar instruments, except for instruments within the scope of ASC Topic 815, *Derivatives and Hedging* [FAS-133, *Accounting for Derivative Instruments and Hedging Activities*].)

b. The description in item (a) above should identify the factors that influenced management's judgment, for example, historical losses and existing economic conditions. (ASC 310-10-50-9) (SOP 01-6, par. 13) (*Note:* Such description may also include discussion of risk elements relevant to particular categories of financial instruments.)

c. For each period for which results of operations are presented, disclosures should be made of the activity in the total allowance for credit losses related to loans, including the following (ASC 310-10-50-12) (FAS-114, par. 20A):

 (1) The balance in the allowance at the beginning and end of each period.

 (2) Additions charged to operations.

 (3) Direct write-downs charged against the allowance.

 (4) Recoveries of amounts previously charged off.

16. For impaired loans, as defined in ASC paragraphs 310-10-35-16 and 35-17, (FAS-114, par. 8), the following information should be disclosed in either the body of the financial statements or in the accompanying notes:

Note: The disclosures in this item should be provided only for impaired loans that have been charged off partially. Loans that have been charged off fully are excluded because both the recorded investment and the allowance for credit losses will equal zero. (ASC 310-10-50-16) (FAS-118, par. 19)

In addition, information about loans meeting the scope of ASC Subtopic 310-30, *Receivables—Loans and Debt Securities Acquired with Deteriorated Credit Quality*, (SOP 03-3, *Accounting for Certain Loans or Debt Securities Acquired in a Transfer*), should be included in the disclosures required by items (a) and (b) below if the condition in ASC paragraphs 320-10-35-18 through 35-34 (FSP FAS 115-1 and FAS 124-1) or ASC paragraph 450-20-25-2(a) (FAS-5, par. 8) is met. (ASC 310-10-50-18) (SOP 03-3, par. 15)

a. As of the date of each balance sheet presented (ASC 310-10-50-15) (FAS-114, par. 20):

 (1) The total recorded investment in the impaired loans.

 (2) The amount of that recorded investment for which there is a related allowance for credit losses (determined in accordance with ASC Section 310-10-35, *Receivables–Overall–Subsequent Measurement* [FAS-114, *Accounting by Creditors for Impairment of a Loan*]), and the amount of that allowance.

 (3) The amount of that recorded investment for which there is no related allowance for credit losses (determined in accordance with ASC Section 310-10-35, *Receivables–Overall–Subsequent Measurement* [FAS-114, *Accounting by Creditors for Impairment of a Loan*]).

b. The creditor's policy for recognizing interest income on impaired loans, including how cash receipts are recorded. (ASC 310-10-50-15) (FAS 114, par. 20)

c. For each period for which results of operations are presented (ASC 310-10-50-15) (FAS-114, par. 20):

(1) The average recorded investment in the impaired loans during each period.

(2) The related amount of interest income recognized during the time within that period that the loans were impaired.

(3) The amount of interest income recognized using a cash-basis method of accounting during the time within that period that the loans were impaired, unless not practicable.

d. The amount of interest income that represents the change in the present value of expected future cash flows attributable to the passage of time, if the entity chooses to report the change in present value as interest income rather than bad debt expense. (ASC 310-10-50-19) (FAS-114, par. 59) (*Note:* ASC paragraphs 310-10-45-5 and 45-6 (FAS-114, par. 58) explain that a creditor that measures impairment based on the present value of expected future cash flows is permitted to report the entire change in present value as bad debt expense, but may also report the change in present value attributable to the passage of time as interest income.)

17. If there is significant uncertainty as to collection of receivables and the entity is unable to make a reasonable estimate of the amount of loss from uncollectible receivables (ASC 310-10-50-23) (FAS-5, par. 23):

a. The installment method, the cost recovery method, or some other method of revenue recognition should be used.

b. The appropriate disclosures should be made as required by ASC paragraphs 450-20-50-3 through 50-6 (FAS-5, pars. 10 and 59). See Chapter 30, "ASC Topic 450: Contingencies."

18. If the carrying amount of trade receivables does *not* approximate fair value, the required disclosures of fair value under ASC Section 825-10-50, *Financial Instruments–Overall–Disclosure*, should be made. (ASC 310-10-50-26) (FAS-107, par. 13). See Chapter 49, "ASC Topic 825: Financial Instruments."

Nonrefundable Fees and Other Costs

1. The unamortized balance of loan origination, commitment, and other fees and costs, and purchase premiums and discounts that are being recognized as an adjustment of yield should be reported on the entity's balance sheet as part of the

loan balance to which it relates. (ASC 310-20-45-1 and 50-3) (FAS-91, par. 21; Q&A-91, par. 63) (*Note:* Additional disclosures, such as unamortized net fees and costs, *may* be included in the footnotes to the financial statements if the lender believes that such information is useful to the users of financial statements.)

2. Commitment fees that meet the criteria of ASC paragraph 310-20-35-3 (FAS-91, par. 8), should be classified as deferred income in the financial statements. (ASC 310-20-45-2) (Q&A-91, par. 59)

3. Amounts of loan origination, commitment, and other fees and costs recognized as an adjustment of yield should be reported as part of interest income. (ASC 310-20-45-3) (FAS-91, par. 22)

4. The amortization of other fees, such as commitment fees that are being amortized on a straight-line basis over the commitment period or included in income when the commitment expires, should be reported as service fee income. (ASC 310-20-45-3) (FAS-91, par. 22)

5. The summary of significant accounting policies should include the method for recognizing interest income on loan and trade receivables, including a statement about the entity's policy for treatment of related fees and costs and the method of amortizing net deferred fees or costs. (ASC 310-20-50-1) (SOP 01-6, par. 13)

6. If the entity anticipates prepayments of loan balances in applying the interest method, disclosures should be made of that policy and the significant assumptions underlying the prepayment estimates. (ASC 310-20-50-2) (FAS-91, par. 19)

7. For credit card fees and costs for both purchased and originated credit cards, the entity should disclose (a) its accounting policy, (b) the net amount capitalized at the balance sheet date, and (c) the amortization periods. (ASC 310-20-50-4) (EITF 92-5)

Loans and Debt Securities Acquired with Deteriorated Credit Quality

1. For loans and debt securities acquired with deteriorated credit quality (ASC 310-30-45-1) (SOP 03-3, par. 5):

   a. The amount of accretable yield should *not* be displayed in the balance sheet.

b. The loan's contractually required payments receivable in excess of the amount of its cash flows expected at acquisition (i.e., nonaccretable difference) should *not* be displayed in the balance sheet or recognized as an adjustment of yield, a loss accrual, or a valuation allowance for credit risk.

2. Disclosures should be made of how prepayments are considered in the determination of contractual cash flows and cash flows expected to be collected. (ASC 310-30-50-1) (SOP 03-3, par. 14)

3. For each balance sheet presented, the following disclosures should be made separately for both those loans that are accounted for as debt securities and those loans that are not accounted for as debt securities (ASC 310-30-50-2 and 50-3) (SOP 03-3, pars. 16 and 23):

   a. The outstanding balance and related carrying amount at the beginning and end of the period. (*Note:* For loans that have a net carrying amount, the outstanding balance is the undiscounted sum of all amounts, including amounts deemed principal, interest, fees, penalties, and other under the loan, owed to the investor at the reporting date, whether or not currently due and whether or not any such amounts have been written or charged off by the investor.)

   b. The amount of accretable yield at the beginning and end of the period, reconciled for additions, accretion, disposals of loans, and reclassifications to or from nonaccretable difference during the period.

   c. For loans acquired during the period, the contractually required payments receivable, cash flows expected to be collected, and fair value at the acquisition date.

   d. For those loans for which the income recognition model is not applied in accordance with ASC paragraph 310-30-35-3 (SOP 03-3, par. 6), the carrying amount at the acquisition date for loans acquired during the period and the carrying amount of all loans at the end of the period.

4. The following additional disclosures should be made for those loans that are not accounted for as debt securities (ASC 310-30-50-2) (SOP 03-3, par. 16):

   a. The amount of the allowance for uncollectible accounts at the beginning and end of the period.

   b. The amount of any expense recognized pursuant to paragraph ASC 310-30-35-10(a) (SOP 03-3, par. 8).

c.   The amount of any reductions of the allowance recognized pursuant to paragraph ASC 310-30-35-10(b)(1) (SOP 03-3, par. 8) for each period for which an income statement is presented.

Troubled Debt Restructurings by Creditors

1.   The amount of commitments, if any, to lend additional funds to debtors owing receivables whose terms have been modified in troubled debt restructurings should be disclosed, either in the body of the financial statements or in the accompanying notes, as of the date of each balance sheet presented. (ASC 310-40-50-1) (FAS-15, par. 40)

2.   The following disclosures should be made, either in the body of the financial statements or in the accompanying notes, about impaired loans that have been restructured in a troubled debt restructuring involving a modification of terms:

Note: The disclosures required by this item need not be made in years after the restructuring if both of the following conditions exist: (1) the restructuring agreement specifies an interest rate equal to or greater than the rate that the creditor was willing to accept at the time of the restructuring for a new loan with comparable risk, and (2) the loan is not impaired based on the terms specified by the restructuring agreement. (ASC 310-40-50-2) (FAS-114, par. 20)

Note: When a loan is restructured in a troubled debt restructuring into two or more loan agreements, the restructured loans should be considered separately when assessing the applicability of the disclosures in this item in years after the restructuring because they are legally distinct from the original loan. (ASC 310-40-50-5) (EITF 96-22)

a.   As of the date of each balance sheet presented (ASC 310-40-50-2; 310-10-50-15) (FAS-114, par. 20):

(1)   The total recorded investment in the impaired loans.

(2)   The amount of that recorded investment for which there is a related allowance for credit losses (determined in accordance with ASC Section 310-10-35, *Receivables–Overall–Subsequent Measurement* [FAS-114, *Accounting by Creditors for Impairment of a Loan*]) and the amount of that allowance.

(3)   The amount of that recorded investment for which there is no related allowance for credit losses (determined in accordance with ASC Section 310-10-35,

Receivables–Overall–Subsequent Measurement [FAS-114, *Accounting by Creditors for Impairment of a Loan*]).

b. For each period for which results of operations are presented (ASC 310-40-50-2; 310-10-50-15) (FAS-114, par. 20):

(1) The average recorded investment in the impaired loans during each period.

(2) The related amount of interest income recognized during the time within that period that the loans were impaired.

(3) The amount of interest income recognized using a cash-basis method of accounting during the time within that period that the loans were impaired, unless not practicable.

3. If the creditor has written down a loan and the measure of the restructured loan is equal to or greater than the recorded investment, the following disclosures should be made (ASC 310-40-50-4) (EITF D-80, par. 31):

a. In the year of the write-down, the amount of the write-down and the recorded investment in the loan.

b. In subsequent years, the recorded investment in the loan. (*Note:* This disclosure is not required if both of the following conditions exist: (1) the restructuring agreement specifies an interest rate equal to or greater than the rate that the creditor was willing to accept at the time of the restructuring for a new loan with comparable risk, and (2) the loan is not impaired based on the terms specified by the restructuring agreement.)

EXAMPLES OF FINANCIAL STATEMENT DISCLOSURES

The following sample disclosures are available on the accompanying disc. For additional examples, see:

- Chapter 8, "ASC Topic 235: Notes to Financial Statements," for examples of general accounting policy disclosures relating to accounts receivable.

- Chapter 35, "ASC Topic 605: Revenue Recognition," for sample disclosures of contract receivables and related concentrations in connection with long-term contracts.

- Chapter 49, "ASC Topic 825: Financial Instruments," for sample disclosures of fair value of financial instruments, including accounts and notes receivable, and concentrations of credit risk.

- Chapter 52, "ASC Topic 840: Leases," for sample disclosures of lease receivables.
- Chapter 54, "ASC Topic 850: Related Party Disclosures," for sample disclosures of accounts receivable due from related parties.
- Chapter 57, "ASC Topic 860: Transfers and Servicing," for additional sample disclosures of sales of receivables.

Overall

Example 1: Accounting Policy for Trade Accounts Receivable and Allowance for Doubtful Accounts

Trade accounts receivable are stated at the amount the Company expects to collect. The Company maintains allowances for doubtful accounts for estimated losses resulting from the inability of its customers to make required payments. Management considers the following factors when determining the collectibility of specific customer accounts: customer credit-worthiness, past transaction history with the customer, current economic industry trends, and changes in customer payment terms. Past due balances over 90 days and other higher risk amounts are reviewed individually for collectibility. If the financial condition of the Company's customers were to deteriorate, adversely affecting their ability to make payments, additional allowances would be required. Based on management's assessment, the Company provides for estimated uncollectible amounts through a charge to earnings and a credit to a valuation allowance. Balances that remain outstanding after the Company has used reasonable collection efforts are written off through a charge to the valuation allowance and a credit to accounts receivable.

[*If the changes in the valuation allowance for trade accounts receivable are material to the financial statements, disclosure of the changes in the valuation allowance might be appropriate, such as provided below.*]

Changes in the allowance for doubtful accounts are as follows:

	20X2	20X1
Beginning balance	$2,354,000	$1,941,000
Provision for doubtful accounts	456,000	785,000
Write-offs	(219,000)	(372,000)
Ending balance	$2,591,000	$2,354,000

Example 2: Accounting Policy for Loans and Trade Receivables

The allowance for loan losses on small-balance receivables reflects management's best estimate of probable losses determined principally on the basis of historical experience. For larger loans, the allowance for losses is determined primarily on the basis of management's best estimate of probable losses, including specific allowances for known troubled accounts. All accounts or portions thereof deemed to be uncollectible or to require an excessive collection cost are written off to the allowance for losses. Small-balance accounts generally are written off when 6 to 12 months delinquent, although any such balance judged to be uncollectible, such as an account in bankruptcy, is written down immediately to estimated realizable value. Large-balance accounts are reviewed at least quarterly, and those accounts with amounts that are judged to be uncollectible are written down to estimated realizable value.

When collateral is repossessed in satisfaction of a loan, the receivable is written down against the allowance for losses to the estimated fair value of the asset less costs to sell, transferred to other assets, and subsequently carried at the lower of cost or estimated fair value less costs to sell.

For trade receivables, the allowance for doubtful accounts is based on management's assessment of the collectibility of specific customer accounts, the aging of the accounts receivable, historical experience, and other currently available evidence. If there is a deterioration of a major customer's credit worthiness or actual defaults are higher than the historical experience, management's estimates of the recoverability of amounts due the Company could be adversely affected.

Example 3: Company Requires No Collateral and Concentrations of Credit Risk Virtually Limited

Concentrations of credit risk with respect to accounts receivable are limited because a large number of geographically diverse customers make up the Company's customer base, thus spreading the trade credit risk. At December 31, 20X2, and December 31, 20X1, no single group or customer represents greater than 10% of total accounts receivable. The Company controls credit risk through credit approvals, credit limits, and monitoring procedures. The Company performs ongoing credit evaluations of its customers but generally does not require collateral to support accounts receivable.

> **Note:** For disclosure requirements of concentrations of credit risk arising from financial instruments (including receivables), see Chapter 49, "ASC Topic 825: Financial Instruments."

Example 4: Company Requires Collateral and Has Concentrations in Accounts Receivable

The Company sells its products to distributors and original equipment manufacturers throughout the United States. The Company performs ongoing credit evaluations of its customers' financial condition and, generally, requires collateral, such as letters of credit, whenever deemed necessary. At December 31, 20X2, three customers, each of which accounted for more than 10% of the Company's accounts receivable, accounted for 58% of total accounts receivable in aggregate. At December 31, 20X1, four customers, each of which accounted for more than 10% of the Company's accounts receivable, accounted for 52% of total accounts receivable in aggregate.

> **Note:** For disclosure requirements of concentrations of credit risk arising from financial instruments (including receivables), see Chapter 49, "ASC Topic 825: Financial Instruments."

Example 5: Details of Current Accounts Receivable

Current accounts receivable consist of the following at December 31, 20X2, and December 31, 20X1:

	20X2	20X1
Trade receivables	$8,659,000	$9,054,000
Income taxes receivable	216,000	192,000
Due from officers and employees	200,000	100,000
Interest and dividend receivable	81,000	73,000
Receivable from affiliate	354,000	297,000
Insurance claim receivable	162,000	175,000
Litigation settlement (received in January 20X3)	314,000	-0-
	9,986,000	9,891,000
Allowance for doubtful accounts	(418,000)	(504,000)
Allowance for returns and discounts	(376,000)	(452,000)
	$9,192,000	$8,935,000

Example 6: Allowances for Commitments Regarding Price Concessions and Sales Returns Are Based on Historical Experience

The Company has agreements with distributor customers that, under certain conditions, allow for returns of overstocked inventory and provide protection against price reductions initiated by the Company. Allowances for these commitments are included in the

Balance Sheets as reductions in trade accounts receivable. The Company adjusts sales to distributors through the use of allowance accounts based on historical experience. During 20X2 and 20X1, provisions for these commitments were recorded in the amounts of $2,679,000 and $3,182,000, respectively.

Example 7: Write-Off of a Significant Account Receivable Balance

The "Special charge" of $513,000 in the 20X2 Statement of Operations relates to the write-off of receivables due from a customer who filed for protection under Chapter 11 of the U.S. Bankruptcy Code during the year. The write-off was necessary because the Company's receivable was unsecured and the amount that the Company may ultimately recover, if any, is not presently determinable.

Example 8: Receivable from Sale of Assets

In December 20X2, the Company sold substantially all of the assets of its electrical tools division for a gain of $716,000. The sales price of $4,825,000 consisted of $1,500,000 in cash and a term note of $3,325,000. The term note bears interest at 2% above the prime rate (9% at December 31, 20X2). Interest and principal payments on the note are due monthly until maturity at December 31, 20X6. Certain mandatory prepayments are required upon the occurrence of certain events. The note receivable is collateralized by the assets of the purchaser.

Principal contractual maturities on the note receivable are as follows:

Year	Maturities
20X3	$1,200,000
20X4	850,000
20X5	800,000
20X6	475,000
	$3,325,000

Example 9: Notes Receivable Requiring Imputation of Interest Are Received in Payment of Outstanding Trade Receivables from Major Customer Pursuant to a Bankruptcy Decree

In March 20X2, the Company received $50,000 in cash and $2,200,000 in notes in full payment of outstanding trade receivables resulting from the reorganization by a major customer, pursuant to a bankruptcy decree. The notes vary in maturity from six months to five years. They include non-interest bearing notes and notes bearing interest at rates of 4% to 6%. The notes are recorded at the present value of the future cash flows, utilizing an imputed interest of 10%, which equals $2,017,000. During 20X2, the Company received all scheduled payments on a timely basis. In management's opinion, the remaining balance is collectible. Notes receivable are due as follows: $418,000 in 20X3, $536,000 in 20X4, $374,000 in 20X5, $318,000 in 20X6, and $196,000 in 20X7.

The trade receivables balance due from the customer of $3,136,000 exceeded the fair value of the settlement amounts received by $1,069,000 and, accordingly, a loss in that amount has been charged to operations in 20X2.

Example 10: Installment Receivables and Disclosure of Changes in the Allowance Account

Installment receivables bear interest at rates ranging from 8% to 13% and have initial terms of three to seven years. Installment receivables were reduced for unearned finance charges of $1,284,000 and $918,000 at December 31, 20X2, and December 31, 20X1, respectively. Unearned finance charges are amortized to interest income using a method that approximates the interest method. The installment receivables are collateralized by security interests in the related machinery and equipment sold to customers.

Details of installment receivables at December 31, 20X2, and December 31, 20X1 are as follows:

	20X2	*20X1*
Due in:		
20X2	$ -0-	$1,637,000
20X3	1,961,000	1,176,000
20X4	1,381,000	833,000
20X5	1,006,000	522,000
20X6	675,000	420,000
20X7	385,000	382,000
Thereafter	719,000	200,000
Gross installment receivables	6,127,000	5,170,000
Less: unearned finance charges	(1,284,000)	(918,000)
Less: allowance for doubtful receivables	(566,000)	(419,000)
Installment receivables, net	$ 4,277,000	$3,833,000

	20X2	20X1
Current balance	$1,711,000	$1,039,000
Long-term balance	2,566,000	2,794,000
	$4,277,000	$3,833,000

An analysis of the allowance for doubtful installment receivables for 20X2 and 20X1 follows:

	20X2	20X1
Balance, beginning of the year	$ 419,000	$ 390,000
Provision charged to operations	322,000	317,000
Amounts written off	(225,000)	(363,000)
Recoveries	50,000	75,000
Balance, end of the year	$ 566,000	$ 419,000

Example 11: Impaired Loans and Disclosure of Changes in the Allowance Account

The Company's impaired notes receivable, including current portion, are as follows at December 31, 20X2, and December 31, 20X1:

	20X2	20X1
Impaired notes with related allowances	$ 3,589,000	$1,743,000
Credit loss allowance on impaired notes	(1,176,000)	(718,000)
	2,413,000	1,025,000
Impaired notes with no related allowances	211,000	763,000
Net impaired notes receivable	$ 2,624,000	$1,788,000

Average investments in impaired notes were $3,140,000 in 20X2 and $1,413,000 in 20X1.

Activity in the allowance for credit losses is as follows:

	20X2	20X1
Balance, beginning of the year	$ 718,000	$ 597,000
Provision charged to operations	617,000	269,000
Amounts written off	(224,000)	(241,000)

	20X2	20X1
Recoveries	65,000	93,000
Balance, end of the year	$1,176,000	$718,000

Interest income on impaired loans is recognized only when payments are received and totaled $289,000 in 20X2 and $173,000 in 20X1.

Example 12: Noncurrent Receivables from Related Parties

At December 31, 20X2, and December 31, 20X1, "Other noncurrent receivables" in the Balance Sheets consist of accounts and notes receivable from employees and officers that are due on demand and are uncollateralized. The notes receivable carry interest at rates ranging from 6% to 10% per annum. Accrued interest receivable included in these balances totaled $43,000 and $31,000 at December 31, 20X2, and December 31, 20X1, respectively. The aggregate receivable balances have been classified as noncurrent assets because they are not expected to be collected within one year from the Balance Sheet dates.

Example 13: Transfer of Accounts Receivable Does Not Qualify as a Sale

The Company has an asset securitization program with a large financial institution to sell, with recourse, certain eligible trade receivables up to a maximum of $12 million. As receivables transferred to the financial institution are collected, the Company may transfer additional receivables up to the predetermined facility limit. Gross receivables transferred to the financial institution amounted to $9,760,000 and $10,397,000 in 20X2 and 20X1, respectively. The Company has the right, and is obligated, to repurchase transferred receivables under the program and, therefore, the transaction does not qualify as a sale. Included in the Balance Sheets as receivables at December 31, 20X2, and December 31, 20X1, are account balances totaling $2,412,000 and $2,867,000, respectively, of uncollected receivables transferred to the financial institution.

> **Note:** For disclosure requirements concerning transfers, sales, and securitizations of receivables, see Chapter 57, "ASC Topic 860: Transfers and Servicing."

Example 14: Factored Accounts Receivable and Factoring Agreement

Accounts receivable comprise the following at December 31, 20X2, and December 31, 20X1:

	20X2	*20X1*
Receivables assigned to factor	$ 6,125,000	$3,655,000
Advances to (from) factor	(2,264,000)	616,000
Amounts due from factor	3,861,000	4,271,000
Unfactored accounts receivable	758,000	869,000
Allowances for returns and allowances	(415,000)	(463,000)
	$ 4,204,000	$4,677,000

Pursuant to a factoring agreement, with recourse against the Company in the event of a loss, the Company's principal bank acts as its factor for the majority of its receivables, which are assigned on a pre-approved basis. At December 31, 20X2, and December 31, 20X1, the factoring charge amounted to 0.25% of the receivables assigned. The Company's obligations to the bank are collateralized by all of the Company's accounts receivable, inventories, and equipment. The advances for factored receivables are made pursuant to a revolving credit and security agreement, which expires on March 31, 20X4. Pursuant to the terms of the agreement, the Company is required to maintain specified levels of working capital and tangible net worth, among other covenants.

Example 15: Accounts Receivable Financing Agreement Includes Issuance of Warrants

In 20X2, the Company entered into an Accounts Receivable Financing Agreement (Financing Agreement) with AMC Bank whereby the Company can finance up to a maximum of $25 million of its eligible accounts receivables with an 80% advance rate. Under the Financing Agreement, the Company is required to repay advances upon the earlier of its receipt of payment on the financed accounts receivables from its customers, or the financed accounts receivable being aged greater than 90 days from date of service. The Financing Agreement has a two-year term, expiring in August 20X4, and bears an annual interest rate of prime rate plus 4.0% (9.25% at December 31, 20X2), with a minimum $15,000 monthly finance charge. The Financing Agreement also contains certain affirmative and negative covenants, and is secured by substantially all of the Company's tangible and intangible assets. As part of the Financing Agreement, in 20X2 the Company issued to AMC Bank warrants to purchase up to 200,000 shares of the Company's common stock with an exercise price of $1.50. The warrants were estimated to have a fair value of $425,000 using the Black-Scholes option-pricing model. The value of the warrants is being amortized into interest expense over the term of the Financing Agreement. At December 31, 20X2, the Company had $17,600,000 outstanding under the Financing Agreement, which represented the maximum borrowings under the Financing Agreement at that time. At December 31, 20X2, the outstanding balance is shown as a current liability under the caption "Accounts receivable financing line" in the Company's balance sheet.

Example 16: Finance Receivables Income Recognition Policy

Interest income on loans is recognized on an accrual basis. Discounts and premiums on loans are amortized to income using the interest method over the remaining period to contractual maturity. The amortization of discounts into income is discontinued on loans that are contractually 90 days past due or when collection of interest appears doubtful.

Accrued interest on loans, including impaired loans, that are contractually 90 days or more past due or when collection of interest appears doubtful is generally reversed and charged against interest income. Income is subsequently recognized only to the extent cash payments are received and the principal balance is expected to be recovered. Such loans are restored to an accrual status only if the loan is brought contractually current and the borrower has demonstrated the ability to make future payments of principal and interest.

Example 17: Finance Receivables Credit Losses Policy

The allowance for credit losses is maintained at an amount management deems adequate to cover inherent losses at the balance sheet date. The Company has implemented and adheres to an internal review system and loss allowance methodology designed to provide for the detection of problem receivables and an adequate allowance to cover credit losses.

Unless an individual loan or borrower relationship warrants separate analysis, the Company generally reviews all loans under $500,000 through a statistical analysis of the expected performance of each loan based on historic trends for similar types of borrowers, loans, collateral and economic circumstances. Those amounts may be adjusted based on an analysis of macro-economic and other trends that are likely to affect the borrower's ability to repay their loan according to their loan terms. Given these evaluations, the amount of the allowance is based upon the summation of general valuation allowances and allocated allowances.

In determining the allowance for credit losses related to borrower relationships of $500,000 or more, the Company evaluates the loans on an individual basis, including an analysis of the borrower's creditworthiness, cash flows and financial status, and the condition and the estimated value of the collateral.

General valuation allowances relate to loans with no well-defined deficiency or weakness and are determined by applying against such receivable balances loss factors for each major loan type that consider past loss experience and loan duration. Allocated allowances relate to loans with well-defined deficiencies or weaknesses and are generally determined by loss factors based on loss statistics or are determined by the excess of the recorded investment in the loan over the fair value of the collateral, where appropriate.

The Company considers a loan to be impaired when, based upon current information and events, it believes it is probable that the Company will be unable to collect all amounts due according to the contractual terms of the loan agreement. In determining impairment, the Company considers large non-homogeneous loans that are on non-accrual, have been restructured or are performing but exhibit, among other characteristics, high loan-to-value ratios. The Company bases the measurement of collateral-dependent impaired loans on the net fair value of the loan's collateral. Non-collateral-dependent loans are valued based on a present value calculation of expected future cash flows, discounted at the loan's effective rate or the loan's observable market price. Cash receipts on impaired loans not performing according to contractual terms are generally used to reduce the carrying value of the loan unless the Company believes it will recover the remaining principal balance of the loan. Impairment losses are included in the allowance for credit losses through a charge to provision for credit losses. Adjustments to impairment losses due to changes in the fair value of collateral of impaired loans are included in provision for credit losses. Upon disposition of an impaired loan, loss of principal, if any, is recorded through a charge-off to the allowance for loan losses.

Example 18: Receivables Used as Collateral

During 20X2, the Company negotiated a new secured $15 million line of credit, of which $3 million is available exclusively for letters of credit. Borrowings under this new credit facility are collateralized by a security interest in the Company's receivables, which had a carrying amount of $23 million at December 31, 20X2. Interest on amounts outstanding under the line of credit is payable at 1% above the prime rate, which was 6.5% at December 31, 20X2. The line of credit matures on April 30, 20X4. The agreement contains certain financial covenants with respect to tangible net worth, liquidity, and other ratios. As of December 31, 20X2, the Company was in compliance with these covenants. Borrowings of $10 million were outstanding under this secured revolving credit facility at December 31, 20X2.

Example 19: Unbilled Accounts Receivable—Contracts

Accounts receivable, net consists of the following:

	20X2	*20X1*
Accounts receivable	$6,723,000	$7,941,000
Unbilled accounts receivable	1,456,000	1,785,000
Allowance for doubtful accounts	(219,000)	(372,000)
	$7,960,000	$9,354,000

In certain of the Company's contracts, contractual billings do not coincide with revenue recognized on the contract. Unbilled accounts receivable represent revenue recorded in excess of amounts billable pursuant to contract provisions and, generally, become billable at contractually specified dates or upon the attainment of milestones. Unbilled amounts are expected to be collected within one year.

Example 20: Unbilled Accounts Receivable—Professional Services

Unbilled accounts receivable result from professional services provided to customers that have not yet been formally invoiced as of the reporting date. Such amounts are generally invoiced within 15 business days of the end of the period in which services are provided.

Nonrefundable Fees and Other Costs

Example 21: Accounting Policy for Nonrefundable Fees, Other Costs, and Interest Income

Loan origination fees and related incremental direct loan origination costs are deferred and amortized to income using the interest method over the contractual life of the loans, adjusted for actual prepayments. Fees received for a commitment to originate or purchase a loan or group of loans are deferred and, if the commitment is exercised, recognized over the life of the loan as an adjustment of yield or, if the commitment expires unexercised, recognized as income upon expiration of the commitment. The amortization of deferred fees and costs is discontinued on loans that are contractually 90 days past due or when collection of interest appears doubtful. Any remaining deferred fees or costs and prepayment fees associated with loans that pay off prior to contractual maturity are included in interest income in the period of payoff.

Interest income on loans is recognized on an accrual basis. Discounts and premiums on loans are amortized to income using the interest method over the remaining period to contractual maturity. The amortization of discounts into income is discontinued on loans that are contractually 90 days past due or when collection of interest appears doubtful.

Accrued interest on loans, including impaired loans, that are contractually 90 days or more past due or when collection of interest appears doubtful is generally reversed and charged against interest income. Income is subsequently recognized only to the extent cash payments are received and the principal balance is expected to be recovered. Such loans are restored to an accrual status only if the loan is brought contractually current and the borrower has demonstrated the ability to make future payments of principal and interest.

Loans and Debt Securities Acquired with Deteriorated Credit Quality

Example 22: Accounting Policy for Acquired Loans and Debt Securities with Deteriorated Credit Quality

The Company acquires loans (including debt securities) individually and in groups or portfolios. For certain acquired loans that have experienced deterioration of credit quality between origination and the Company's acquisition of the loans, the amount paid for a loan reflects the Company's determination that it is probable the Company will be unable to collect all amounts due according to the loan's contractual terms. At acquisition, the Company reviews each loan to determine whether there is evidence of deterioration of credit quality since origination and if it is probable that the Company will be unable to collect all amounts due according to the loan's contractual terms. If both conditions exist, the Company determines whether each such loan is to be accounted for individually or whether such loans will be assembled into pools of loans based on common risk characteristics (e.g., credit score, loan type, and date of origination). The Company considers expected prepayments, and estimates the amount and timing of undiscounted expected principal, interest, and other cash flows (expected at acquisition) for each loan and subsequently aggregated pool of loans. The Company determines the excess of the loan's or pool's scheduled contractual principal and contractual interest payments over all cash flows expected at acquisition as an amount that should not be accreted (nonaccretable difference). The remaining amount—representing the excess of the loan's cash flows expected to be collected over the amount paid—is accreted into interest income over the remaining life of the loan or pool (accretable yield).

Over the life of the loan or pool, the Company continues to estimate cash flows expected to be collected. The Company evaluates at the balance sheet date whether the present value of its loans determined using the effective interest rates has decreased and if so, recognizes a loss. For loans or pools that are not accounted for as debt securities, the present value of any subsequent increase in the loan's or pool's actual cash flows or cash flows expected to be collected is used first to reverse any existing valuation allowance for that loan or pool. For any remaining increases in cash flows expected to be collected, or for loans or pools accounted for as debt securities, the Company adjusts the amount of accretable yield recognized on a prospective basis over the loan's or pool's remaining life.

Example 23: Disclosures for Loans Accounted for as Debt Securities

The Company has acquired loans accounted for as debt securities, for which there was, prior to their being acquired in a transfer, evidence of deterioration of credit quality since origination. It was probable, at acquisition, that all contractually required payments for those loans would not be collected. The outstanding balance (representing amounts owed to the Company at the balance sheet date) and carrying amounts of those loans classified as held-to-maturity securities and available-for-sale securities at December 31, 20X2, and 20X1 are as follows:

(In Thousands)	*December 31, 20X2*	*December 31, 20X1*
Held-to-maturity securities:		
Outstanding balance	$41,000	$42,000
Carrying amount, net	$22,000	$23,000
Available-for-sale securities:		
Outstanding balance	$44,000	$43,000
Carrying amount, net	$25,000	$24,000

(In Thousands)	*Held-to-Maturity Securities*	*Available-for-Sale Securities*
Accretable Yield:		
Balance at December 31, 20X0	$ 11,000	$ 9,000
Additions	1,000	800
Accretion	(2,000)	(1,800)
Disposals	–	–
Balance at December 31, 20X1	10,000	8,000
Additions	1,700	1,000

(In Thousands)	Held-to-Maturity Securities	Available-for-Sale Securities
Accretion	(1,500)	(1,800)
Reclassifications from nonaccretable difference	1,200	700
Disposals	–	–
Balance at December 31, 20X2	$ 11,400	$ 7,900

During the years ended December 31, 20X2, and 20X1, the Company recognized other-than-temporary impairment of $1.5 million and $1 million, respectively. Debt securities acquired each year for which it was probable at acquisition that all contractually required payments would not be collected are as follows:

(In Thousands)	December 31, 20X2	December 31, 20X1
Held-to-maturity securities:		
Contractually required payments receivable	$5,000	$3,400
Cash flows expected to be collected	$4,000	$2,800
Basis in acquired securities	$2,700	$1,700
Available-for-sale securities:		
Contractually required payments receivable	$3,800	$2,600
Cash flows expected to be collected	$3,000	$2,100
Basis in acquired securities	$2,000	$1,300

Certain of the debt securities acquired by the Company are not accounted for using the income recognition model described above because the Company cannot reasonably estimate cash flows expected to be collected. The carrying amounts of such debt securities, all of which are classified as available-for-sale securities, are as follows:

(In Thousands)	December 31, 20X2	December 31, 20X1
Debt securities acquired during the year	$400	$250
Debt securities at the end of the year	$700	$800

Example 24: Disclosures for Loans Not Accounted for as Debt Securities

The Company has loans that were acquired in a transfer for which there was, at acquisition, evidence of deterioration of credit quality since origination and for which it was probable, at acquisition, that all contractually required payments would not be collected. The amounts of those loans at December 31, 20X2, and 20X1 are as follows:

(In Thousands)	*December 31, 20X2*	*December 31, 20X1*
Commercial	$29,000	$28,000
Consumer	8,000	7,000
Outstanding balance	$37,000	$35,000
Carrying amount (net of allowance of $900 and $800)	$25,000	$24,000

(In Thousands)	*Accretable Yield*
Balance at December 31, 20X0	$10,000
Additions	1,000
Accretion	(500)
Reclassifications from nonaccretable difference	–
Disposals	–
Balance at December 31, 20X1	10,500
Additions	1,500
Accretion	(700)
Reclassifications from nonaccretable difference	1,000
Disposals	–
Balance at December 31, 20X2	$12,300

During the years ended December 31, 20X2, and 20X1, the Company increased the allowance for loan losses by a charge to the income statement of $200,000 and $100,000, respectively. No allowances for loan losses were reversed in 20X2 or 20X1.

Loans acquired during each year for which it was probable at acquisition that all contractually required payments would not be collected are as follows:

(In Thousands)	December 31, 20X2	December 31, 20X1
Contractually required payments receivable at acquisition:		
Commercial	$3,300	$3,000
Consumer	1,000	1,100
Subtotal	$4,300	$4,100
Cash flows expected to be collected at acquisition	$3,500	$3,300
Basis in acquired securities loans at acquisition	$2,500	$2,200

Certain of the loans acquired by the Company are not accounted for using the income recognition model described above because the Company cannot reasonably estimate cash flows expected to be collected. The carrying amounts of such loans (which are included in the carrying amount, net of allowance, described above) are as follows:

(In Thousands)	December 31, 20X2	December 31, 20X1
Loans acquired during the year	$300	$250
Loans at the end of the year	$800	$900

Troubled Debt Restructurings by Creditors

Example 25: Troubled Debt Restructuring Program and Recorded Investment in Impaired Loans

In 20X1, the Company initiated a debt restructuring program to provide borrowers who are current with their loan payments a cost effective means to change from an adjustable rate loan to a less costly financing alternative. These loans are considered troubled debt restructurings because the modified interest rates were lower than the interest rates on the original loans and the loans were not re-underwritten to prove the new interest rates were, in fact, market interest rates for borrowers with similar credit quality. Even though the interest rates following the modifications were no less than those offered new borrowers, these loans have been placed on non-accrual status. Interest income is recorded as these borrowers make their loan payments on a cash basis. If these borrowers perform pursuant to the modified terms for six consecutive months, the loans will be placed back on accrual status but they will still be reported as troubled debt restructurings. The specific valuation allowance for these troubled debt restructurings has been calculated as the difference between the recorded investment of the original loan and the present value of the expected cash flows of the modified loan (discounted at the effective interest rate of the original loan based on an expected life). This difference is recorded as a provision for credit losses in current earnings and subsequently amortized over the expected life of the loans or as a reduction of the provision if the loan is prepaid. Included within the 20X2 and 20X1 provision for loan losses was $3 million and $6 million, respectively, related to the creation of a specific allowance associated with the troubled debt restructurings.

The following table presents (a) impaired loans with specific allowances and the amount of such allowances and (b) impaired loans without specific allowances.

(In Thousands)	*Investment Value*	*Specific Allowance*	*Carrying Value*
December 31, 20X2:			
Loans with specific allowances	$40,000	$(5,000)	$35,000
Loans without specific allowances	10,000	–	10,000
Total impaired loans	$50,000	$(5,000)	$45,000
December 31, 20X1:			
Loans with specific allowances	$32,000	$(2,000)	$30,000
Loans without specific allowances	6,000	–	6,000
Total impaired loans	$38,000	$(2,000)	$36,000

The average recorded investment in impaired loans totaled $10 million and $6 million in 20X2 and 20X1, respectively. In 20X2 and 20X1, there was $1 million and $1.2 million, respectively, of interest recognized following impairment on the impaired loan portfolio.

Interest due on non-accrual loans, but excluded from interest income, was approximately $2.5 million and $2 million at December 31, 20X2, and 20X1, respectively.

At December 31, 20X2, the Company had $2 million of commitments to lend additional funds to borrowers whose loans were on non-accrual status.

CHAPTER 18
ASC TOPIC 320: INVESTMENTS—DEBT AND EQUITY SECURITIES

CONTENTS

EXECUTIVE SUMMARY

Debt and Equity Securities

The topic of this chapter applies to both current and noncurrent investments in debt and equity securities. The primary issue in accounting and reporting for debt and equity investments is the appropriate use of fair value. Generally accepted accounting principles (GAAP) require that investments in equity securities that have readily determinable fair values and all investments in debt securities be classified in three categories (held to maturity, trading securities, and available for sale) and be given specific accounting treatments, as follows:

Classification	*Accounting Treatment*
1. *Available for sale*—Debt and equity securities that do not meet the criteria to be classified as held to maturity or trading.	Fair value, with unrealized holding gains and losses reported in other comprehensive income. Nontemporary losses should be charged to earnings.
2. *Held to maturity*—Debt securities that the entity has the positive intent and ability to hold to maturity.	Amortized cost, reduced for nontemporary losses that are charged to earnings. Other unrealized gains or losses should not be recognized.

Classification	Accounting Treatment
3. *Trading securities*—Debt and equity securities bought and held primarily for sale in the near term (e.g., the entity's normal operating cycle).	Fair value, with unrealized holding gains and losses included in earnings.

The following are examples of debt and equity securities:

Debt Securities	Equity Securities
U.S. Treasury securities	Common stock
U.S. government agency securities	Preferred stock
Municipal securities	Warrants
Corporate bonds	Rights
Convertible debt	Call options
Commercial paper	Put options
Collateralized mortgage obligations	
Preferred stock that must be redeemed	
Real estate mortgage investment conduits	
Interest-only and principal-only strips	

Generally, held-to-maturity securities are classified as noncurrent assets until they are within one year of maturity; at that time, they are classified as current assets. Trading securities are classified as current assets. Available-for-sale securities are classified as current or noncurrent, as appropriate.

Accounting Literature

FASB Accounting Standards Codification Topic	Pre-Codification Accounting Literature
320, *Investments—Debt and Equity Securities*	FAS-115, *Accounting for Certain Investments in Debt and Equity Securities*
	FSP FAS 115-1 and FAS 124-1, *The Meaning of Other-Than-Temporary Impairment and Its Application to Certain Investments*

FASB Accounting Standards Codification Topic	*Pre-Codification Accounting Literature*
	FSP FAS 115-2 and FAS 124-2, *Recognition and Presentation of Other-Than-Temporary Impairments*
	EITF 86-40, *Investments in Open-End Mutual Funds That Invest in U.S. Government Securities*
	FASB Implementation Guidance (Q&A), *A Guide to Implementation of Statement 115 on Accounting for Certain Investments in Debt and Equity Securities: Questions and Answers*

DISCLOSURE AND KEY PRESENTATION REQUIREMENTS

Applicable Guidance in ASC Topic 320 After FSP FAS 115-2 and FAS 124-2, *Recognition and Presentation of Other-Than-Temporary Impairments*

Note: The disclosure and key presentation requirements in this section are prescribed by ASC Topic 320, *Investments—Debt and Equity Securities*, based on FSP FAS 115-2 and FAS 124-2, *Recognition and Presentation of Other-Than-Temporary Impairments*, which is effective for interim and annual reporting periods ending after June 15, 2009. Early adoption is permitted for periods ending after March 15, 2009, provided the pending content that links to ASC paragraph 820-10-65-4 (based on FSP FAS 157-4, *Determining Fair Value When the Volume and Level of Activity for the Asset or Liability Have Significantly Decreased and Identifying Transactions That Are Not Orderly*) is also adopted. In addition, if either the pending content in ASC paragraph 820-10-65-4 (based on FSP FAS 157-4) or in ASC paragraph 825-10-65-1 (based on FSP FAS 107-1 and APB 28-1, *Interim Disclosures about Fair Value of Financial Instruments*) is adopted early, the presentation and disclosure requirements in this section must also be adopted early. The presentation and disclosure requirements in this section are not required for earlier periods presented for comparative purposes at initial adoption. In periods after initial adoption, comparative disclosures are required only for periods ending after initial adoption.

Overall

1. Investments in available-for-sale securities and trading securities should be reported separately from similar assets that are subsequently measured using another measurement attribute on the face of the balance sheet by presenting either of the following (ASC 320-10-45-1) (FAS-115, par. 17):

   a. The aggregate of those fair value and non-fair-value amounts in the same line item and parenthetically disclosing the amount of fair value included in the aggregate amount.

   b. Two separate line items displaying the fair value and non-fair-value carrying amounts.

2. Held-to-maturity securities, available-for-sale securities, and trading securities should be reported on a classified balance sheet as either current or noncurrent. (ASC 320-10-45-2) (FAS-115, par. 17) (*Note:* ASC Section 210-10-45, *Balance Sheet–Overall–Other Presentation Matters* [ARB-43, Ch. 3A, *Current Assets and Current Liabilities*], provides further guidance on the required presentation of current and noncurrent assets in the balance sheet.) See Chapter 3, "ASC Topic 210: Balance Sheet."

3. For deferred tax assets that have been recognized relating to net unrealized losses on available-for-sale securities, the following presentation matters should be followed:

   a. If the entity recognizes a valuation allowance at the same time that it establishes the deferred tax asset (or in a later interim period of the same fiscal year in which the deferred tax asset is recognized), the offsetting entry to the valuation allowance should be reported in the component of other comprehensive income classified as unrealized gains and losses on certain investments in debt and equity securities. (ASC 320-10-45-3) (Q&A-115, par. 54)

   b. If the entity initially decided that no valuation allowance was required at the time it established the deferred tax asset but, in a subsequent fiscal year, decides to recognize a valuation allowance, the offsetting entry to the valuation allowance should be included as an item in determining income from continuing operations (i.e., not in other comprehensive income). (ASC 320-10-45-4) (Q&A-115, par. 56)

   c. If, subsequent to the year the deferred tax asset and related valuation allowance were recognized, an entity makes a change in judgment about the level of future years' taxable income such that all or a portion of that valuation allowance is no longer warranted, any reversals in the valuation allowance due to such change should be included as an item in determining income from continuing operations. (ASC 320-10-45-5) (Q&A-115, par. 57)

d. If, subsequent to the year the deferred tax asset and related valuation allowance were recognized, an entity generates taxable income in the current year that can use the benefit of the deferred tax asset, the elimination or reduction of the valuation allowance should be allocated to that taxable income. (ASC 320-10-45-5) (Q&A-115, par. 57)

e. If in the current year the entity recognizes a valuation allowance at the same time that it establishes the deferred tax asset:

(1) The entity should determine the extent to which the valuation allowance is directly related to the unrealized loss and the other previously recognized deductible temporary differences (e.g., an accrual for *other* postemployment benefits). (ASC 320-10-45-6) (Q&A-115, par. 55)

(2) The offsetting entry to the valuation allowance should be reported in the component of other comprehensive income classified as unrealized gains and losses on available-for-sale securities only to the extent the valuation allowance is directly related to the unrealized loss on the available-for-sale securities that arose in the current year. (ASC 320-10-45-6) (Q&A-115, par. 55)

4. Gains and losses that have accumulated before transfers involving trading securities should be classified consistently with realized gains and losses for the category from which the security is being transferred (not the category into which the security is being transferred). (ASC 320-10-45-7) (Q&A-115, par. 44)

5. All or a portion of the unrealized holding gain and loss of an available-for-sale security that is designated as being hedged in a fair value hedge should be recognized in earnings during the period of the hedge, pursuant to ASC paragraphs 815-25-35-1 through 35-4 (FAS-133, par. 22). (ASC 320-10-45-8) (FAS-115, par. 13)

6. Subsequent increases in the fair value of available-for-sale securities should be included in other comprehensive income. (ASC 320-10-45-9) (FAS-115, par. 16)

7. Subsequent decreases in the fair value of available-for-sale securities (if not an other-than-temporary impairment)

should be included in other comprehensive income. (ASC 320-10-45-9) (FAS-115, par. 16)

8. Cash flows from purchases, sales, and maturities of available-for-sale securities and held-to-maturity securities should be classified as cash flows from investing activities and reported gross for each security classification in the statement of cash flows. (ASC 320-10-45-11) (FAS-115, par. 18)

9. Cash flows from purchases, sales, and maturities of trading securities should be classified in the statement of cash flows based on the nature and purpose for which the securities were acquired. (ASC 320-10-45-11) (FAS-115, par. 18)

10. If individual amounts for the three categories of investments (i.e., held-to-maturity, available-for-sale, or trading) are not presented on the face of the balance sheet, they should be disclosed in the notes. (ASC 320-10-45-13) (FAS-115, par. 117)

11. If the entity reports certain investments in debt securities as cash equivalents, the notes should reconcile the reporting classifications used in the balance sheet. (ASC 320-10-45-13) (FAS-115, par. 117)

12. For securities classified as available for sale, the following disclosures should be made for interim and annual periods, by major security type, as of each date for which a balance sheet is presented (ASC 320-10-50-2 through 50-4) (FAS-115, pars. 19 and 20; EITF 86-40) (*Note*: Major security types should be based on the nature and risks of the security. An entity should consider the (shared) activity or business sector, vintage, geographic concentration, credit quality, or economic characteristic in determining whether disclosure for a particular security type is necessary and whether it is necessary to further separate a particular security type into greater detail.):

   a. The amortized cost basis.

   b. The aggregate fair value.

   c. The total other-than-temporary impairment recognized in accumulated other comprehensive income.

   d. Total gains for securities with net gains in accumulated other comprehensive income.

   e. Total losses for securities with net losses in accumulated other comprehensive income.

   f. Information about the contractual maturities of those securities as of the date of the most recent balance sheet presented. (*Note:* Maturity information may be combined in appropriate groupings. Securities that are not due at a single maturity date, such as mortgage-backed securities, may be disclosed separately rather than allocated over several maturity groupings; however, if allocated, the basis for the allocation should also be disclosed.)

13. For securities classified as held to maturity, the following disclosures should be made for interim and annual periods, by major security type, as of each date for which a balance sheet is presented (ASC 320-10-50-5) (FAS-115, par. 19) (*Note*: Major security types should be based on the nature and risks of the security. An entity should consider the (shared) activity or business sector, vintage, geographic concentration, credit quality, or economic characteristic in determining whether disclosure for a particular security type is necessary and whether it is necessary to further separate a particular security type into greater detail.):

   a. The amortized cost basis.

   b. The aggregate fair value.

   c. Gross unrecognized holding gains.

   d. Gross unrecognized holding losses.

   e. Net carrying amount.

   f. The total other-than-temporary impairment recognized in accumulated other comprehensive income.

   g. Gross gains and losses in accumulated other comprehensive income for any derivatives that hedged the forecasted acquisition of the held-to-maturity securities.

   h. Information about the contractual maturities of those securities as of the date of the most recent balance sheet presented. (*Note:* Maturity information may be combined in appropriate groupings. Securities that are not due at a single maturity date, such as mortgage-backed securities, may be disclosed separately rather than allocated over several maturity groupings; however, if allocated, the basis for the allocation should also be disclosed.)

14. The following disclosures should be made for each annual or interim period for which an income statement is presented (ASC 320-10-50-9) (FAS-115, par. 21):

   a. The proceeds from sales of available-for-sale securities and the gross realized gains and gross realized losses on those sales that have been included in earnings.

b. The method used to determine the cost of a security sold or the amount reclassified out of accumulated other comprehensive income into earnings (i.e., specific identification, average cost, or other method used).

c. The gross gains and gross losses included in earnings from transfers of securities from the available-for-sale category into the trading category.

d. The amount of the net unrealized holding gain or loss on available-for-sale securities that has been included in accumulated other comprehensive income for the period.

e. The amount of gains and losses reclassified out of accumulated other comprehensive income into earnings for the period.

f. The portion of trading gains and losses for the period that relates to trading securities still held at the balance sheet date.

15. For any sales of or transfers from securities classified as held-to-maturity, the following disclosures should be made in the notes to the financial statements for each annual or interim period for which an income statement is presented (ASC 320-10-50-10) (FAS-115, par. 22):

a. The net carrying amount of the sold or transferred security.

b. The net gain or loss in accumulated other comprehensive income for any derivative that hedged the forecasted acquisition of the held-to-maturity security.

c. The related realized or unrealized gain or loss.

d. The circumstances leading to the decision to sell or transfer the security. (*Note:* Such sales or transfers should be rare, except for sales and transfers due to the changes in circumstances identified in ASC paragraphs 320-10-25-6(a) through (f) [FAS-115, par. 8].)

Impairment of Securities

1. In periods in which an entity determines that a security's decline in fair value below its amortized cost basis is other than temporary, the entity should present the total other-than-temporary impairment in the income statement with an offset for the amount of the total other-than-temporary impairment that is recognized in other comprehensive income, if any. (ASC 320-10-45-8A) (FSP FAS 115-1 and FAS 124-1, par. 16B)

2. The financial statement in which the components of accumulated other comprehensive income are reported should separately present amounts recognized therein related to held-to-maturity and available-for-sale debt securities for which a portion of an other-than-temporary impairment has been recognized in earnings. (ASC 320-10-45-9A) (FSP FAS 115-1 and FAS 124-1, par. 16C)

3. For all investments in an unrealized loss position for which other-than-temporary impairments have not been recognized in earnings (including investments for which a portion of an other-than-temporary impairment has been recognized in other comprehensive income), the following disclosures should be made in the entity's annual and interim financial statements (ASC 320-10-50-6 through 50-8) (FSP FAS 115-1 and FAS 124-1, par. 17):

    a. As of each date for which a balance sheet is presented, the following quantitative information, in tabular form, should be aggregated by category of investment—each major security type that the entity disclosed in accordance with ASC Subtopic 320-10, (FSP FAS 115-1 and FAS 124-1), and cost-method investments—and segregated by those investments that have been in a continuous unrealized loss position for less than 12 months and those that have been in a continuous unrealized loss position for 12 months or longer:

        (1) The aggregate amount of unrealized losses (i.e., the amount by which amortized cost basis exceeds fair value).

        (2) The aggregate related fair value of investments with unrealized losses.

    b. As of the date of the most recent balance sheet, the following qualitative information, in narrative form, that provides sufficient information to allow the financial statement users to understand the quantitative disclosures and the information that the entity considered (both positive and negative) in reaching the conclusion that the impairments are not other-than-temporary (*Note:* The disclosures required may be aggregated by investment categories, but individually significant unrealized losses generally should not be aggregated.):

        (1) The nature of the investment.

        (2) The cause of the impairment.

        (3) The number of investment positions that are in an unrealized loss position.

        (4) The severity and duration of the impairment.

(5) Other evidence considered by the entity in reaching its conclusions that the investment is not other-than-temporarily impaired, including, for example, performance indicators of the underlying assets in the security (including default rates, delinquency rates and percentage of nonperforming assets), loan to collateral value ratios, third-party guarantees, current levels of subordination, vintage, geographic concentration, industry analyst reports, sector credit ratings, volatility of the security's fair value, and/ or any other information that the entity considers relevant.

4. The following disclosures should be made, by major security type, for annual and interim periods in which an other-than-temporary impairment of a debt security is recognized and only the amount related to a credit loss was recognized in earnings (ASC 320-10-50-8A) (FSP FAS 115-1 and FAS 124-1, par. 18A):

a. The methodology used to measure the amount related to credit loss.

b. The significant inputs used to measure the amount related to credit loss. (Examples of significant inputs include, but are not limited to, performance indicators of the underlying assets in the security (including default rates, delinquency rates, and percentage of nonperforming assets), loan to collateral value ratios, third-party guarantees, current levels of subordination, vintage, geographic concentration, and credit ratings.)

5. A tabular rollforward should be disclosed of the amount related to credit losses recognized in earnings, for each interim and annual reporting period presented, that includes (ASC 320-10-50-8B) (FSP FAS 115-1 and FAS 124-1, par. 18B):

a. The beginning balance of the amount related to credit losses on debt securities held by the entity at the beginning of the period for which a portion of an other-than-temporary impairment was recognized in other comprehensive income.

b. Additions for the amount related to the credit loss for which an other-than-temporary impairment was not previously recognized.

c. Reductions for securities sold during the period (realized).

d. Reductions for securities for which the amount previously recognized in other comprehensive income was recognized in earnings because the entity intends to sell the security or more likely than not will be required to sell the security before recovery of its amortized cost basis.

e.   Additional increases to the amount related to the credit loss for which an other-than-temporary impairment was previously recognized when the investor does not intend to sell the security and it is not more likely than not that the entity will be required to sell the security before recovery of its amortized cost basis.

f.   Reductions for increases in cash flows expected to be collected that are recognized over the remaining life of the security.

g.   The ending balance of the amount related to credit losses on debt securities held by the entity at the end of the period for which a portion of an other-than-temporary impairment was recognized in other comprehensive income.

Applicable Guidance in ASC Topic 320 Before FSP FAS 115-2 and FAS 124-2, *Recognition and Presentation of Other-Than-Temporary Impairments*

Note: The disclosure and key presentation requirements in this section are prescribed by ASC Topic 320, *Investments—Debt and Equity Securities*, prior to the adoption of the guidance based on FSP FAS 115-2 and FAS 124-2, *Recognition and Presentation of Other-Than-Temporary Impairments*, which is effective for interim and annual reporting periods ending after June 15, 2009.

Overall

1.   Investments in available-for-sale securities and trading securities should be reported separately from similar assets that are subsequently measured using another measurement attribute on the face of the balance sheet by presenting either of the following (ASC 320-10-45-1) (FAS-115, par. 17):

a.   The aggregate of those fair value and non-fair-value amounts in the same line item and parenthetically disclosing the amount of fair value included in the aggregate amount.

b.   Two separate line items displaying the fair value and non-fair-value carrying amounts.

2.   Held-to-maturity securities, available-for-sale securities, and trading securities should be reported on a classified balance sheet as either current or noncurrent. (ASC 320-10-45-2)

(FAS-115, par. 17) (*Note:* ASC Section 210-10-45, *Balance Sheet–Overall–Other Presentation Matters*, [ARB-43, Ch. 3A, *Current Assets and Current Liabilities*], provides further guidance on the required presentation of current and noncurrent assets in the balance sheet.)

3. For deferred tax assets that have been recognized relating to net unrealized losses on available-for-sale securities, the following presentation matters should be followed:

   a. If the entity recognizes a valuation allowance at the same time that it establishes the deferred tax asset (or in a later interim period of the same fiscal year in which the deferred tax assert is recognized), the offsetting entry to the valuation allowance should be reported in the component of other comprehensive income classified as unrealized gains and losses on certain investments in debt and equity securities. (ASC 320-10-45-3) (Q&A-115, par. 54)

   b. If the entity initially decided that no valuation allowance was required at the time it established the deferred tax asset but, in a subsequent fiscal year, decides to recognize a valuation allowance, the offsetting entry to the valuation allowance should be included as an item in determining income from continuing operations (i.e., not in other comprehensive income). (ASC 320-10-45-4) (Q&A-115, par. 56)

   c. If, subsequent to the year the deferred tax asset and related valuation allowance were recognized, an entity makes a change in judgment about the level of future years' taxable income such that all or a portion of that valuation allowance is no longer warranted, any reversals in the valuation allowance due to such change should be included as an item in determining income from continuing operations. (ASC 320-10-45-5) (Q&A-115, par. 57)

   d. If, subsequent to the year the deferred tax asset and related valuation allowance were recognized, an entity generates taxable income in the current year that can use the benefit of the deferred tax asset, the elimination or reduction of the valuation allowance should be allocated to that taxable income. (ASC 320-10-45-5) (Q&A-115, par. 57)

   e. If in the current year the entity recognizes a valuation allowance at the same time that it establishes the deferred tax asset:

      (1) The entity should determine the extent to which the valuation allowance is directly related to the unrealized loss and the other previously recognized

deductible temporary differences (e.g., an accrual for other postemployment benefits). (ASC 320-10-45-6) (Q&A-115, par. 55)

   (2) The offsetting entry to the valuation allowance should be reported in the component of other comprehensive income classified as unrealized gains and losses on available-for-sale securities only to the extent the valuation allowance is directly related to the unrealized loss on the available-for-sale securities that arose in the current year. (ASC 320-10-45-6) (Q&A-115, par. 55)

4. Gains and losses that have accumulated before transfers involving trading securities should be classified consistently with realized gains and losses for the category from which the security is being transferred (not the category into which the security is being transferred). (ASC 320-10-45-7) (Q&A-115, par. 44)

5. All or a portion of the unrealized holding gain and loss of an available-for-sale security that is designated as being hedged in a fair value hedge should be recognized in earnings during the period of the hedge, pursuant to ASC paragraphs 815-25-35-1 through 35-4, (FAS-133, par. 22). (ASC 320-10-45-8) (FAS-115, par. 13)

6. Subsequent increases in the fair value of available-for-sale securities should be included in other comprehensive income. (ASC 320-10-45-9) (FAS-115, par. 16)

7. Subsequent decreases in the fair value of available-for-sale securities (if not an other-than-temporary impairment) should be included in other comprehensive income. (ASC 320-10-45-9) (FAS-115, par. 16)

8. Cash flows from purchases, sales, and maturities of available-for-sale securities and held-to-maturity securities should be classified as cash flows from investing activities and reported gross for each security classification in the statement of cash flows. (ASC 320-10-45-11) (FAS-115, par. 18)

9. Cash flows from purchases, sales, and maturities of trading securities should be classified in the statement of cash flows based on the nature and purpose for which the securities were acquired. (ASC 320-10-45-11) (FAS-115, par. 18)

10. If individual amounts for the three categories of investments (i.e., held-to-maturity, available-for-sale, or trading) are not presented on the face of the balance sheet, they

should be disclosed in the notes. (ASC 320-10-45-13) (FAS-115, par. 117)

11. If the entity reports certain investments in debt securities as cash equivalents, the notes should reconcile the reporting classifications used in the balance sheet. (ASC 320-10-45-13) (FAS-115, par. 117)

12. For securities classified as available for sale, the following disclosures should be made, by major security type, as of each date for which a balance sheet is presented (ASC 320-10-50-2 through 50-4) (FAS-115, pars. 19 and 20; EITF 86-40):

    a. The aggregate fair value.

    b. Total gains for securities with net gains in accumulated other comprehensive income.

    c. Total losses for securities with net losses in accumulated other comprehensive income.

    d. Information about the contractual maturities of those securities as of the date of the most recent balance sheet presented. (*Note:* Maturity information may be combined in appropriate groupings. Securities that are not due at a single maturity date, such as mortgage-backed securities, may be disclosed separately rather than allocated over several maturity groupings; however, if allocated, the basis for the allocation should also be disclosed.)

13. For securities classified as held to maturity, the following disclosures should be made, by major security type, as of each date for which a balance sheet is presented (ASC 320-10-50-5) (FAS-115, par. 19):

    a. The aggregate fair value.

    b. Gross unrecognized holding gains.

    c. Gross unrecognized holding losses.

    d. Net carrying amount.

    e. Gross gains and losses in accumulated other comprehensive income for any derivatives that hedged the forecasted acquisition of the held-to-maturity securities.

    f. Information about the contractual maturities of those securities as of the date of the most recent balance sheet presented. (*Note:* Maturity information may be combined in appropriate groupings. Securities that are not due at a single maturity date, such as mortgage-backed securities, may be disclosed separately rather than allocated over several maturity groupings; however, if allocated, the basis for the allocation should also be disclosed.)

14. The following disclosures should be made for each period for which an income statement is presented (ASC 320-10-50-9) (FAS-115, par. 21):

a. The proceeds from sales of available-for-sale securities and the gross realized gains and gross realized losses on those sales that have been included in earnings.

b. The method used to determine the cost of a security sold or the amount reclassified out of accumulated other comprehensive income into earnings (i.e., specific identification, average cost, or other method used).

c. The gross gains and gross losses included in earnings from transfers of securities from the available-for-sale category into the trading category.

d. The amount of the net unrealized holding gain or loss on available-for-sale securities that has been included in accumulated other comprehensive income for the period.

e. The amount of gains and losses reclassified out of accumulated other comprehensive income into earnings for the period.

f. The portion of trading gains and losses for the period that relates to trading securities still held at the balance sheet date.

15. For any sales of or transfers from securities classified as held-to-maturity, the following disclosures should be made in the notes to the financial statements for each period for which an income statement is presented (ASC 320-10-50-10) (FAS-115, par. 22):

a. The net carrying amount of the sold or transferred security.

b. The net gain or loss in accumulated other comprehensive income for any derivative that hedged the forecasted acquisition of the held-to-maturity security.

c. The related realized or unrealized gain or loss.

d. The circumstances leading to the decision to sell or transfer the security. (*Note:* Such sales or transfers should be rare, except for sales and transfers due to the changes in circumstances identified in ASC paragraphs 320-10-25-6(a) through (f) [FAS-115, par. 8].)

Impairment of Securities

1. For all investments in an unrealized loss position for which other-than-temporary impairments have not been recognized, the following disclosures should be made in the entity's annual financial statements (ASC 320-10-50-6 through 50-8) (FSP FAS 115-1 and FAS 124-1, par. 17):

    a. As of each date for which a balance sheet is presented, the following quantitative information, in tabular form, should be aggregated by each category of investment that the entity disclosed in accordance with ASC Subtopic 320-10 (FSP FAS 115-1 and FAS 124-1), and cost-method investments, and segregated by those investments that have been in a continuous unrealized loss position for less than 12 months and those that have been in a continuous unrealized loss position for 12 months or longer:

        (1) The aggregate related fair value of investments with unrealized losses.

        (2) The aggregate amount of unrealized losses (i.e., the amount by which cost exceeds fair value).

    b. As of the date of the most recent balance sheet, additional *qualitative* information, in narrative form, that provides sufficient information to allow the financial statement users to understand the quantitative disclosures and the information that the entity considered (both positive and negative) in reaching the conclusion that the impairments are not other-than-temporary, which could include:

        (1) The nature of the investment.

        (2) The cause of the impairment.

        (3) The number of investment positions that are in an unrealized loss position.

        (4) The severity and duration of the impairment.

        (5) Other evidence considered by the entity in reaching its conclusions that the investment is not other-than-temporarily impaired, including, for example, industry analyst reports, sector credit ratings, volatility of the security's fair value, and/or any other information that the entity considers relevant.

EXAMPLES OF FINANCIAL STATEMENT DISCLOSURES

 The following sample disclosures are available on the accompanying disc.

Example 1: Accounting Policy Note Explains Classification of Marketable Securities as Held to Maturity, Trading, and Available for Sale

The Company determines the appropriate classification of its investments in debt and equity securities at the time of purchase and reevaluates such determinations at each balance sheet date. Debt securities are classified as held to maturity when the Company has the positive intent and ability to hold the securities to maturity. Debt securities for which the Company does not have the intent or ability to hold to maturity are classified as available for sale. Held-to-maturity securities are recorded as either short term or long term on the Balance Sheet, based on contractual maturity date and are stated at amortized cost. Marketable securities that are bought and held principally for the purpose of selling them in the near term are classified as trading securities and are reported at fair value, with unrealized gains and losses recognized in earnings. Debt and marketable equity securities not classified as held to maturity or as trading, are classified as available for sale, and are carried at fair market value, with the unrealized gains and losses, net of tax, included in the determination of comprehensive income and reported in shareholders' equity.

The fair value of substantially all securities is determined by quoted market prices. The estimated fair value of securities for which there are no quoted market prices is based on similar types of securities that are traded in the market.

Example 2: Available-for-Sale Securities Are Classified as Debt and Equity Securities

Available-for-sale securities consist of the following:

		December 31, 20X2		
	Amortized Cost	Gains in Accumulated Other Comprehensive Income	Losses in Accumulated Other Comprehensive Income	Estimated Fair Value
U.S. government securities	$1,412,000	$ -0-	$ (6,000)	$1,406,000
Commercial paper	1,347,000	5,000	(2,000)	1,350,000
Corporate bonds	1,153,000	51,000	(17,000)	1,187,000
Fixed rate notes	100,000	-0-	-0-	100,000
Total debt securities	4,012,000	56,000	(25,000)	4,043,000
Common stock	822,000	100,000	(56,000)	866,000
Preferred stock	140,000	5,000	-0-	145,000
Total equity securities	962,000	105,000	(56,000)	1,011,000
Total available-for-sale securities	$4,974,000	$161,000	$(81,000)	$5,054,000

		December 31, 20X1		
	Amortized Cost	Gains in Accumulated Other Comprehensive Income	Losses in Accumulated Other Comprehensive Income	Estimated Fair Value
U.S. government securities	$1,161,000	$ -0-	$(4,000)	$1,157,000
Commercial paper	1,632,000	9,000	(6,000)	1,635,000

		December 31, 20X1		
	Amortized Cost	*Gains in Accumulated Other Comprehensive Income*	*Losses in Accumulated Other Comprehensive Income*	*Estimated Fair Value*
Corporate bonds	1,788,000	12,000	(73,000)	1,727,000
Fixed rate notes	150,000	-0-	-0-	150,000
Total debt securities	4,731,000	21,000	(83,000)	4,669,000
Common stock	615,000	37,000	(26,000)	626,000
Preferred stock	110,000	4,000	-0-	114,000
Total equity securities	725,000	41,000	(26,000)	740,000
Total available-for-sale securities	$5,456,000	$62,000	$(109,000)	$5,409,000

During the years ended December 31, 20X2, and December 31, 20X1, available-for-sale securities were sold for total proceeds of $823,000 and $617,000, respectively. The gross realized gains on these sales totaled $127,000 and $104,000 in 20X2 and 20X1, respectively. For purpose of determining gross realized gains, the cost of securities sold is based on specific identification. Net unrealized holding gains on available-for-sale securities in the amount of $127,000 and $53,000 for the years ended December 31, 20X2, and December 31, 20X1, respectively, have been included in accumulated other comprehensive income. Total other-than-temporary impairment recognized in accumulated other comprehensive income amounted to $50,000 and $45,000 at December 31, 20X2, and December 31, 20X1, respectively.

Contractual maturities of available-for-sale debt securities at December 31, 20X2, are as follows:

	Estimated Fair Value
Due in one year or less	$2,388,000
Due in 1–2 years	1,161,000
Due in 2–5 years	273,000
Due after 5 years	221,000
Total investments in debt securities	$4,043,000

Actual maturities may differ from contractual maturities because some borrowers have the right to call or prepay obligations with or without call or prepayment penalties.

Example 3: Available-for-Sale Securities Are Classified as Current and Noncurrent Assets

Available-for-sale securities consist of the following:

		December 31, 20X2		
	Amortized Cost	Gains in Accumulated Other Comprehensive Income	Losses in Accumulated Other Comprehensive Income	Estimated Fair Value
Current:				
Auction rate securities	$2,800,000	-0-	-0-	$2,800,000
Municipal bonds and notes	748,000	-0-	(4,000)	744,000
Asset-backed securities	302,000	6,000	(2,000)	306,000
U.S. government obligations	675,000	12,000	(7,000)	680,000
Total current securities	4,525,000	18,000	(13,000)	4,530,000
Noncurrent:				
Auction rate securities	1,300,000	-0-	-0-	1,300,000
Municipal bonds	679,000	8,000	(6,000)	681,000
Corporate bonds	274,000	-0-	(9,000)	265,000
Common stock	413,000	47,000	(26,000)	434,000
Preferred stock	279,000	24,000	(13,000)	290,000
Total noncurrent securities	2,945,000	79,000	(54,000)	2,970,000
Total available-for-sale securities	$7,470,000	$97,000	$(67,000)	$7,500,000

| | *December 31, 20X1* | | | |
	Amortized Cost	*Gains in Accumulated Other Comprehensive Income*	*Losses in Accumulated Other Comprehensive Income*	*Estimated Fair Value*
Current:				
Auction rate securities	$4,300,000	$ -0-	$ -0-	$4,300,000
Municipal bonds and notes	623,000	-0-	(3,000)	620,000
Asset-backed securities	291,000	4,000	(1,000)	294,000
U.S. government obligations	600,000	10,000	(6,000)	604,000
Total current securities	5,814,000	14,000	(10,000)	5,818,000
Noncurrent:				
Auction rate securities	1,450,000	-0-	-0-	1,450,000
Municipal bonds	610,000	7,000	(5,000)	612,000
Corporate bonds	296,000	-0-	(11,000)	285,000
Common stock	471,000	43,000	(29,000)	485,000
Preferred stock	342,000	28,000	(17,000)	353,000
Total noncurrent securities	3,169,000	78,000	(62,000)	3,185,000
Total available-for-sale securities	$8,983,000	$92,000	$(72,000)	$9,003,000

Proceeds from the sales of available-for-sale securities were $511,000 and $307,000 during 20X2 and 20X1, respectively. Gross realized gains on those sales during 20X2 and 20X1 were $107,000 and $95,000, respectively. Gross realized losses on those sales during 20X2 and 20X1 were $53,000 and $46,000, respectively. For purpose of determining gross realized gains and losses, the cost of securities sold is based on average cost. Net unrealized holding gains on available-for-sale securities in the amount of $10,000 and $36,000 for the years ended December 31, 20X2, and December 31, 20X1, respectively, have been included in accumulated other comprehensive income. Total other-than-temporary impairment recognized in accumulated other comprehensive income amounted to $160,000 and $130,000 at December 31, 20X2, and December 31, 20X1, respectively.

Contractual maturities of available-for-sale debt securities at December 31, 20X2, are as follows:

	Estimated Fair Value
Within one year	$4,530,000
After 1-5 years	2,050,000
After 5-10 years	196,000
	$6,776,000

Actual maturities may differ from contractual maturities because some borrowers have the right to call or prepay obligations with or without call or prepayment penalties.

Example 4: Trading Securities

The Company's short-term investments comprise equity and debt securities, all of which are classified as trading securities and are carried at their fair value based on the quoted market prices of the securities at December 31, 20X2, and December 31, 20X1. Net realized and unrealized gains and losses on trading securities are included in net earnings. For purpose of determining realized gains and losses, the cost of securities sold is based on specific identification.

The composition of trading securities, classified as current assets, is as follows at December 31, 20X2, and December 31, 20X1:

	December 31, 20X2		December 31, 20X1	
	Cost	Fair Value	Cost	Fair Value
Treasury bills	$2,796,000	$2,796,000	$2,515,000	$2,515,000
Mutual funds	883,000	765,000	691,000	653,000
Common stock	617,000	501,000	574,000	452,000
Preferred stock	311,000	294,000	282,000	258,000
Total trading securities	$4,607,000	$4,356,000	$4,062,000	$3,878,000

Investment income for the years ended December 31, 20X2, and December 31, 20X1, consists of the following:

	20X2	20X1
Gross realized gains from sale of trading securities	$162,000	$ 129,000
Gross realized losses from sale of trading securities	(71,000)	(46,000)
Dividend and interest income	194,000	123,000
Net unrealized holding losses	(67,000)	(134,000)
Net investment income	$218,000	$ 72,000

Example 5: Held-to-Maturity Securities

At December 31, 20X2, and December 31, 20X1, the Company held investments in marketable securities that were classified as held to maturity and consisted of the following:

	December 31, 20X2			
	Amortized Cost	Unrecognized Holding Gains	Unrecognized Holding Losses	Estimated Fair Value
U.S. government securities	$4,997,000	$ 8,000	$ (3,000)	$5,002,000
States and municipalities	1,170,000	75,000	(10,000)	1,235,000
Corporate bonds	1,219,000	67,000	(11,000)	1,275,000
Total held-to-maturity securities	$7,386,000	$150,000	$(24,000)	$7,512,000

	December 31, 20X1			
	Amortized Cost	Unrecognized Holding Gains	Unrecognized Holding Losses	Estimated Fair Value
U.S. government securities	$3,624,000	$ 9,000	$ (2,000)	$3,631,000
States and municipalities	1,641,000	95,000	(16,000)	1,720,000

	December 31, 20X1			
	Amortized Cost	Unrecognized Holding Gains	Unrecognized Holding Losses	Estimated Fair Value
Corporate bonds	1,023,000	61,000	(13,000)	1,071,000
Total held-to-maturity securities	$6,288,000	$165,000	$(31,000)	$6,422,000

During the years ended December 31, 20X2, and December 31, 20X1, held-to-maturity securities were sold for total proceeds of $917,000 and $733,000, respectively. The gross realized gains on these sales totaled $58,000 and $64,000 in 20X2 and 20X1, respectively. For purpose of determining gross realized gains, the cost of securities sold is based on specific identification.

Contractual maturities of held-to-maturity securities at December 31, 20X2, are as follows:

	Net Carrying Amount
Due in one year or less	$1,380,000
Due in 2-5 years	5,481,000
Due in 6-10 years	525,000
Total investments in held-to-maturity securities	$7,386,000

Actual maturities may differ from contractual maturities because some borrowers have the right to call or prepay obligations with or without call or prepayment penalties.

Example 6: Estimated Fair Value of Held-to-Maturity Securities Approximates Cost

At December 31, 20X2, and December 31, 20X1, the Company had marketable debt securities that were classified as held to maturity and carried at amortized cost. Held-to-maturity securities consisted of the following:

	20X2	20X1
Current:		
U.S. government securities	$1,714,000	$ -0-
Commercial paper	1,975,000	1,810,000
Certificates of deposit	1,315,000	600,000
Corporate notes	2,417,000	1,976,000

	20X2	*20X1*
Total current held-to-maturity securities	7,421,000	4,386,000
Noncurrent:		
U.S. government securities	3,411,000	3,100,000
Corporate notes	3,719,000	2,418,000
Total noncurrent held-to-maturity securities	7,130,000	5,518,000
Total held-to-maturity securities	$14,551,000	$9,904,000

At December 31, 20X2, maturities for noncurrent held-to-maturity securities were between one and two years. At December 31, 20X2, and December 31, 20X1, the estimated fair value of each investment approximated its amortized cost and, therefore, there were no significant unrecognized holding gains or losses.

Example 7: Decline in Market Value Is Considered Other Than Temporary

The Company invests in debt and equity securities of technology companies for business and strategic purposes. Investments in public companies are classified as "available for sale" and are carried at fair value based on quoted market prices. The Company reviews its marketable equity holdings in publicly traded companies on a regular basis to determine if any security has experienced an other-than-temporary decline in fair value. The Company considers the investee company's cash position, earnings and revenue outlook, stock price performance, liquidity and management ownership, among other factors, in its review. If it is determined that an other-than-temporary decline exists in a marketable equity security, the Company writes down the investment to its market value and records the related write-down as an investment loss in its Statement of Operations.

At December 31, 20X2, the Company wrote down to fair market value certain equity security investments. The write-down amounted to $157,000 and was due to a decline in the fair value of the equity security which, in the opinion of management, was considered to be other than temporary. The write-down is included in general and administrative expenses in the accompanying Statement of Operations for 20X2.

Example 8: Transfer of Held-to-Maturity Investments to Available-for-Sale Category

In March 20X2, the Company transferred all of its held-to-maturity investments to the available-for-sale category. Management determined that it no longer had the positive intent to hold its investment in securities classified as held-to-maturity for an indefinite period of time because of management's desire to have more flexibility in managing the investment portfolio. The securities transferred had a total amortized cost of $3,770,000, fair value of $3,862,000 and unrealized gross gains of $218,000 and unrealized gross losses of $126,000 at the time of the transfer. The net unrealized gain of $92,000 was recorded as other comprehensive income at the time of transfer.

Example 9: Pledged Investments

The Company has pledged certain held-to-maturity investments as collateral for payments due under operating leases and for a standby letter of credit related to an operating lease. Total amount of securities pledged at December 31, 20X2, was approximately $736,000, of which $400,000 is classified as a restricted investment. The operating leases expire at various dates through December 31, 20X5. The standby letter of credit expires on March 31, 20X3, but is automatically renewable through the underlying lease expiration date of March 31, 20X5.

Example 10: Impaired Securities—ASC Topic 320 Based on Guidance in FSP FAS 115-1 and FAS 124-1

> **Note:** To facilitate the illustration of narrative disclosures and for simplicity, this example presents only the quantitative information as of the date of the latest balance sheet. However, GAAP requires the quantitative information to be presented as of each date for which a balance sheet is presented.

The following table shows the Company's investments' gross unrealized losses and fair value, aggregated by investment category and length of time that individual securities have been in a continuous unrealized loss position, at December 31, 20X2:

Description of Securities	Less than 12 Months		12 Months or More		Total	
	Fair Value	Unrealized Losses	Fair Value	Unrealized Losses	Fair Value	Unrealized Losses
U.S. Treasury obligations	$1,000,000	$ 15,000	$1,100,000	$ 20,000	$2,100,000	$ 35,000
Federal agency mortgage-backed securities	750,000	18,000	800,000	14,000	1,550,000	32,000
Corporate bonds	1,540,000	60,000	1,300,000	85,000	2,840,000	145,000
Total debt securities	3,290,000	93,000	3,200,000	119,000	6,490,000	212,000
Common stock	860,000	55,000	920,000	150,000	1,780,000	205,000
Total	$4,150,000	$148,000	$4,120,000	$269,000	$8,270,000	$417,000

The Company has determined that the unrealized losses are deemed to be temporary impairments as of December 31, 20X2. The Company believes that the unrealized losses generally are caused by liquidity discounts and increases in the risk premiums required by market participants rather than an adverse change in cash flows or a fundamental weakness in the credit quality of the issuer or underlying assets.

U.S. Treasury Obligations. The unrealized losses on the Company's investments in U.S. Treasury obligations were caused by interest rate increases. The contractual terms of those investments do not permit the issuer to settle the securities at a price less than the amortized cost of the investment. Because the Company has the ability and intent to hold those investments until a recovery of fair value, which may be maturity, the Company does not consider those investments to be other-than-temporarily impaired at December 31, 20X2.

Federal Agency Mortgage-Backed Securities. The unrealized losses on the Company's investment in federal agency mortgage-backed securities were caused by interest rate increases. The Company purchased those investments at a discount relative to their face amount, and the contractual cash flows of those investments are guaranteed by an agency of the U.S. government. Accordingly, it is expected that the securities would not be settled at a price less than the amortized cost of the Company's investment. Because the decline in market value is attributable to changes in interest rates and not credit quality, and because the Company has the ability and intent to hold those investments until a recovery of fair value, which may be maturity, the Company does not consider those investments to be other-than-temporarily impaired at December 31, 20X2.

Corporate Bonds. The Company's unrealized losses on investments in corporate bonds relate to a $1,540,000 investment in ABC Company's Series B Debentures and a $1,300,000 investment in XYZ Company's Series C Debentures. The unrealized losses were primarily caused by (a) a recent decrease in profitability and near-term profit forecasts by industry analysts resulting from intense competitive pricing pressure in the manufacturing industry and (b) a recent sector downgrade by several industry analysts. The contractual terms of those investments do not permit ABC Company and XYZ Company to settle the security at a price less than the amortized cost of the investment. While the credit ratings of ABC Company and XYZ Company have decreased from A to BBB (S&P), the Company currently does not believe it is probable that it will be unable to collect all amounts due according to the contractual terms of the investments. Therefore, it is expected that the debentures would not be settled at a price less than the amortized cost of the investments. Because the Company has the ability and intent to hold these investments until a recovery of fair value, which may be maturity, it does not consider the investment in the debentures of ABC Company and XYZ Company to be other-than-temporarily impaired at December 31, 20X2.

Common Stock. The Company's investments consist primarily of investments in common stock of companies in the consumer tools and appliances industry ($1,100,000 of the total fair value and $155,000 of the total unrealized losses in common stock investments) and the air courier industry ($680,000 of the total fair value and $50,000 of the total unrealized losses in common stock investments). Within the Company's portfolio of common stocks in the consumer tools and appliances industry (all of which are in an unrealized loss position) approximately 35% of the total fair value and 30% of the Company's total unrealized losses are in ABC Company. The remaining fair value and unrealized losses are distributed in four companies. The severity and duration of the impairment correlate with the weak sales experienced recently within the consumer tools and appliance industry. The Company evaluated the near-term prospects of the issuer in relation to the severity and duration of the impairment. Based on that evaluation and the Company's ability and intent to hold those investments for a reasonable period of time sufficient for a forecasted recovery of fair value, the Company does not consider those investments to be other-than-temporarily impaired at December 31, 20X2.

The Company's portfolio of common stocks in the air courier industry consists of investments in 6 companies, 4 of which (or approximately 80% of the total fair value of the investments in the air courier industry) are in an unrealized loss position. The air courier industry and the Company's investees are susceptible to changes in the U.S. economy and the industries of their customers. A substantial number of their principal customers are in the automotive, personal computer, electronics, telecommunications, and related industries, and their businesses have been adversely affected by the slowdown of the U.S. economy, particularly during the first half of 20X2 when the Company's investments became impaired. In addition, the credit ratings of nearly all companies in the portfolio have decreased from A to BBB (S&P or equivalent designation). The severity of the impairments in relation to the carrying amounts of the individual investments is consistent with those market developments. The Company evaluated the near-term prospects of the issuers in relation to the severity and duration of the impairment. Based on that evaluation and the Company's ability and intent to hold those investments for a reasonable period of time sufficient for a forecasted recovery of fair value, the Company does not consider those investments to be other-than-temporarily impaired at December 31, 20X2.

Example 11: Impaired Securities—ASC Topic 320 Based on Guidance in FSP FAS 115-2 and FAS 124-2

> **Note:** To facilitate the illustration of narrative disclosures and for simplicity, this example presents only the quantitative information as of the date of the latest balance sheet. However, GAAP requires the quantitative information to be presented as of each date for which a balance sheet is presented.

The following table shows the Company's investments' gross unrealized losses and fair value, aggregated by investment category and length of time that individual securities have been in a continuous unrealized loss position, at December 31, 20X2:

Description of Securities	Less than 12 Months		12 Months or More		Total	
	Fair Value	Unrealized Losses	Fair Value	Unrealized Losses	Fair Value	Unrealized Losses
U.S. Treasury obligations	$1,000,000	$ 15,000	$1,100,000	$ 20,000	$2,100,000	$ 35,000
Federal agency mortgage-backed securities	750,000	18,000	800,000	14,000	1,550,000	32,000
Corporate bonds	1,540,000	60,000	1,300,000	85,000	2,840,000	145,000
Total debt securities	3,290,000	93,000	3,200,000	119,000	6,490,000	212,000
Common stock	860,000	55,000	920,000	150,000	1,780,000	205,000
Total	$4,150,000	$148,000	$4,120,000	$269,000	$8,270,000	$417,000

The Company has determined that the unrealized losses are deemed to be temporary impairments as of December 31, 20X2. The Company believes that the unrealized losses generally are caused by liquidity discounts and increases in the risk premiums required by market participants rather than an adverse change in cash flows or a fundamental weakness in the credit quality of the issuer or underlying assets.

U.S. Treasury Obligations. The unrealized losses on the Company's investments in U.S. Treasury obligations were caused by interest rate increases. The contractual terms of those investments do not permit the issuer to settle the securities at a price less than the amortized cost of the investment. Because the Company does not intend to sell the investments and it is not more likely than not that the Company will be required to sell the investments before recovery of their amortized cost bases, which may be maturity, the Company does not consider those investments to be other-than-temporarily impaired at December 31, 20X2.

Federal Agency Mortgage-Backed Securities. The unrealized losses on the Company's investment in federal agency mortgage-backed securities were caused by interest rate increases. The Company purchased those investments at a discount relative to their face amount, and the contractual cash flows of those investments are guaranteed by an agency of the U.S. government. Accordingly, it is expected that the securities would not be settled at a price less than the amortized cost bases of the Company's investments. Because the decline in market value is attributable to changes in interest rates and not credit quality, and because the Company does not intend to sell the investments and it is not more likely than not that the Company will be required to sell the investments before recovery of their amortized cost bases, which may be maturity, the Company does not consider those investments to be other-than-temporarily impaired at December 31, 20X2.

Corporate Bonds. The Company's unrealized losses on investments in corporate bonds relate to a $1,540,000 investment in ABC Company's Series B Debentures and a $1,300,000 investment in XYZ Company's Series C Debentures. The unrealized losses were primarily caused by (a) a recent decrease in profitability and near-term profit forecasts by industry analysts resulting from intense competitive pricing pressure in the manufacturing industry and (b) a recent sector downgrade by several industry analysts. The contractual terms of those investments do not permit ABC Company and XYZ Company to settle the security at a price less than the amortized cost basis of the investment. While the credit ratings of ABC Company and XYZ Company have decreased from A to BBB (S&P), the Company currently does not expect ABC

Company and XYZ Company to settle the debentures at a price less than the amortized cost basis of the investments (i.e., the Company expects to recover the entire amortized cost basis of the security). Because the Company does not intend to sell the investment and it is not more likely than not that the Company will be required to sell the investment before recovery of its amortized cost basis, which may be maturity, it does not consider the investment in the debentures of ABC Company and XYZ Company to be other-than-temporarily impaired at December 31, 20X2.

Common Stock. The Company's investments consist primarily of investments in common stock of companies in the consumer tools and appliances industry ($1,100,000 of the total fair value and $155,000 of the total unrealized losses in common stock investments) and the air courier industry ($680,000 of the total fair value and $50,000 of the total unrealized losses in common stock investments). Within the Company's portfolio of common stocks in the consumer tools and appliances industry (all of which are in an unrealized loss position), approximately 35% of the total fair value and 30% of the Company's total unrealized losses are in ABC Company. The remaining fair value and unrealized losses are distributed in four companies. The severity and duration of the impairment correlate with the weak sales experienced recently within the consumer tools and appliance industry. The Company evaluated the near-term prospects of the issuer in relation to the severity and duration of the impairment. Based on that evaluation and the Company's ability and intent to hold those investments for a reasonable period of time sufficient for a forecasted recovery of fair value, the Company does not consider those investments to be other-than-temporarily impaired at December 31, 20X2.

The Company's portfolio of common stocks in the air courier industry consists of investments in six companies, four of which (or approximately 80% of the total fair value of the investments in the air courier industry) are in an unrealized loss position. The air courier industry and the Company's investees are susceptible to changes in the U.S. economy and the industries of their customers. A substantial number of their principal customers are in the automotive, personal computer, electronics, telecommunications, and related industries, and their businesses have been adversely affected by the slowdown of the U.S. economy, particularly during the first half of 20X2 when the Company's investments became impaired. In addition, the credit ratings of nearly all companies in the portfolio have decreased from A to BBB (S&P or equivalent designation). The severity of the impairments in relation to the carrying amounts of the individual investments is consistent with those market developments. The Company evaluated the near-term prospects of the issuers in relation to the severity and duration of the impairment. Based on that evaluation and the Company's ability and intent to hold those investments for a reasonable period of time sufficient for a forecasted recovery of fair value, the Company does not consider those investments to be other-than-temporarily impaired at December 31, 20X2.

Other-Than-Temporary Impairments for Debt Securities

The Company recognizes other-than-temporary impairments (OTTI) for debt securities classified as available for sale in accordance with ASC 320 (based on FSP FAS 115-2 and FAS 124-2). Accordingly, the Company assesses whether it intends to sell or it is more likely than not that it will be required to sell a security before recovery of its amortized cost basis less any current-period credit losses. For debt securities that are considered other-than-temporarily impaired and that the Company does not intend to sell and will not be required to sell prior to recovery of the amortized cost basis, the Company separates the amount of the impairment into the amount that is credit related (credit loss component) and the amount due to all other factors. The credit loss component is recognized in earnings and is the difference between the security's amortized cost basis and the present value of its expected future cash flows discounted at the security's effective yield. The remaining difference between the security's fair value and the present value of future expected cash flows is due to factors that are not credit related and, therefore, is not required to be recognized as losses in the income statement, but is recognized in other comprehensive income. Management believes that the Company will fully collect the carrying value of securities on which it has recorded a non-credit-related impairment in other comprehensive income.

The table below presents a roll-forward of the credit loss component recognized in earnings (referred to as "credit-impaired" debt securities). The credit loss component of the amortized cost represents the difference between the present value of expected future cash flows and the amortized cost basis of the security prior to considering credit losses. The beginning balance represents the credit loss component for debt securities for which OTTI occurred prior to January 1, 20X2. OTTI recognized in earnings in 20X2 for credit-impaired debt securities is presented as additions in two components based upon whether the current period is the first time the debt security was credit-impaired (initial credit impairment) or is not the first time the debt security was credit impaired (subsequent credit impairments). The credit loss component is reduced if the Company sells, intends to sell or believes it will be required to sell previously credit-impaired debt securities. Additionally, the credit loss component is reduced if the Company receives or expects to receive cash flows in excess of what the Company previously expected to receive over the remaining life of the credit-impaired debt security, or if the security matures or is fully written down. Changes in the credit loss component of credit-impaired debt securities were as follows for the year ended December 31, 20X2:

Balance, January 1, 20X2	$ 250,000
Additions:	
Initial credit impairments	180,000
Subsequent credit impairments	50,000
Reductions:	
For securities sold	(25,000)
Due to change in intent to sell or requirement to sell	(10,000)
For increases in expected cash flows	(5,000)
Balance, December 31, 20X2	$ 440,000

Example 12: Auction Rate Securities Classified as Available-for-Sale Investments

At December 31, 20X2, and 20X1, the Company held $2,800,000 and $4,300,000, respectively, of auction rate securities, which are shown as a separately stated current asset in the accompanying financial statements. Also, at December 31, 20X2, and 20X1, the Company held $1,300,000 and $1,450,000, respectively, of auction rate securities related to the Company's standby letters of credit, which collateralize the leases for its Irvine and San Diego offices and are classified as other noncurrent assets. Auction rate securities are variable-rate bonds tied to short-term interest rates with maturities on the face of the securities in excess of 90 days. The Company's investments in these auction rate securities are classified as available-for-sale securities. The securities are recorded at cost, which approximates fair market value because of their variable interest rates, which typically reset every 7 to 35 days. Despite the long-term nature of their stated contractual maturities, the Company has the intent and ability to quickly liquidate these securities; therefore, the Company had no cumulative gross unrealized holding gains or losses, or gross realized gains or losses from these investments. All income generated from these investments was recorded as interest income.

Example 13: Auction Rate Securities Classified as Noncurrent Assets Due to Failed Auctions

The auction rate securities that the Company has invested in are typically re-auctioned every seven to twenty-eight days. However, as a result of liquidity conditions affecting capital markets, particularly in the U.S., specifically for asset-backed securities, every auction for the securities held by the Company over the last several months of 20X2 failed. Due to the failed auctions, the Company has recognized unrealized losses in other comprehensive income of $400,000 ($240,000 net of taxes) for the reduction in fair market value of these securities at December 31, 20X2. The Company believes that the decline in fair market value is indicative of the severe pressure from the sub-prime lending collapse, rather than specific concerns with respect to the issuers of the auction rate securities in which the Company has invested or the securities themselves. The auction rate securities in which the Company has invested consist of debt instruments and perpetual preferred securities. At December 31, 20X2, Moody's Investors Services ratings of these securities ranged from Aa to Aaa, and Standard and Poor's ratings ranged from AA to AAA.

The Company believes that the gross unrealized losses on these securities are temporary in nature and the Company has the intent and, it believes, the ability to hold these securities until they have recovered their cost basis. The Company currently anticipates that the market for these securities will be re-established within 18 to 24 months of December 31, 20X2, but it is possible that a recovery may occur beyond this time period. The Company believes that it has sufficient liquidity to meet its operating cash needs without the sale of these securities. As a result of the factors discussed above, the Company has classified these investments as non-current assets on the consolidated balance sheet at December 31, 20X2.

CHAPTER 19
ASC TOPIC 323: INVESTMENTS—EQUITY METHOD AND JOINT VENTURES

CONTENTS

EXECUTIVE SUMMARY

Note: For cost-method investments, see Chapter 20, "ASC Topic 325: Investments—Other."

Equity Method and Joint Ventures

The equity method of accounting for investments in common stock is appropriate if an investment enables the investor to significantly influence the operating or financial decisions of the investee. Absent evidence to the contrary, an investor is presumed to have the ability to significantly influence an investee if it owns (directly or indirectly) 20% or more of the investee's voting stock. The authoritative literature presumes that significant influence does not exist in an investment of less than 20%. However, this presumption may be overcome by evidence to the contrary. Therefore, significant influence over the operating and financial policies of an investment of less than 20% can occur. The 20% cutoff is intended to be a guideline, subject to individual judgment rather than a rigid rule.

The equity method is not intended as a substitute for consolidated financial statements when the conditions for consolidation are present. Under the equity method, an investment is initially recorded at cost. Thereafter, the carrying amount of the investment is (1) increased for the investor's proportionate share of the investee's earnings or (2) decreased for the investor's proportionate share of the investee's losses or for dividends received from the investee. The effect of this treatment is that net income for the period and stockholders' equity at the end of the period are the same as if the companies had been consolidated.

Accounting Literature

FASB Accounting Standards Codification Topic

Pre-Codification Accounting Literature

323, *Investments—Equity Method and Joint Ventures*

FAS-130, *Reporting Comprehensive Income*

EITF 94-1, *Accounting for Tax Benefits Resulting from Investments in Affordable Housing Projects*

APB-18, *The Equity Method of Accounting for Investments in Common Stock*

DISCLOSURE AND KEY PRESENTATION REQUIREMENTS

1. For investments in common stock accounted for under the equity method of accounting:

   a. The investment should be shown in the balance sheet of an investor as a single amount. (ASC 323-10-45-1) (APB-18, par. 11)

   b. The investor's share of earnings or losses from the investment should be shown in its income statement as a single amount, except for the extraordinary items as noted in item (c) below. (ASC 323-10-45-1) (APB-18, par. 11)

   c. The investor's share of extraordinary items and share of accounting changes reported by the investee should be classified separately in accordance with ASC Subtopic 225-20, *Income Statement—Extraordinary and Unusual Items* (APB-30, *Reporting the Results of Operations—Reporting the Effects of Disposal of a Segment of a Business, and Extraordinary, Unusual, and Infrequently Occurring Events and Transactions*). (ASC 323-10-45-2) (APB-18, par. 19)

   d. The investor should combine its proportionate share of the investee's other comprehensive income amounts with its own other comprehensive income items and display the aggregate of those amounts in an income-statement-type format or in a statement of changes in equity, regardless of how the investee displays other comprehensive income. (ASC 323-10-45-3) (FAS-130, pars. 121 and 122)

2. The following disclosures should be made for investments in common stock accounted for under the equity method of accounting (ASC 323-10-50-2 and 50-3) (APB-18, par. 20) (*Note:* If the investor has more than one investment in common stock, disclosures wholly or partly on a combined basis may be appropriate, considering the significance of an investment to the investor's financial position and results of operations):

   a. The name of each investee and percentage of ownership of common stock.

   b. The accounting policies of the investor with respect to investments in common stock.

   c. The names of any significant investee entities in which the investor holds 20% or more of the voting stock, but the common stock is not accounted for on the equity method, together with the reasons why the equity method is not considered appropriate.

   d. The names of any significant investee corporations in which the investor holds less than 20% of the voting stock and the common stock is accounted for on the equity method, together with the reasons why the equity method is considered appropriate.

   e. The difference, if any, between the amount at which an investment is carried and the amount of underlying equity in net assets and the accounting treatment of the difference.

      Note: The disclosures in items (a)–(e) above may be made parenthetically, in notes to financial statements, or in separate statements or schedules.

   f. For those investments in common stock for which a quoted market price is available, the aggregate value of each identified investment based on the quoted market price. (*Note:* This disclosure is not required for investments in common stock of subsidiaries.)

   g. When investments in common stock of corporate joint ventures or other investments accounted for under the equity method are in the aggregate material, summarized information of assets, liabilities, and results of operations of the investees presented in notes or separate statements, either individually or in groups.

   h. Material effects of possible conversions of outstanding convertible securities, exercise of outstanding options and warrants, and other contingent issuances that could have a significant effect on the investor's share of reported earnings or losses.

3. When a limited partnership investment in a qualified afford-able housing project is accounted for using the effective yield method (ASC 323-740-45-2) (EITF 94-1):

   a. The tax credit allocated, net of the amortization of the investment in the limited partnership, should be recognized in the income statement as a component of income taxes attributable to continuing operations.

   b. Any other tax benefits received should be accounted for in the income statement pursuant to the general requirements of ASC Topic 740, *Income Taxes* (FAS-109, *Accounting for Income Taxes*).

EXAMPLES OF FINANCIAL STATEMENT DISCLOSURES

 The following sample disclosures are available on the accompanying disc. For sample disclosures relating to cost-method investments, see Chapter 20, "ASC Topic 325: Investments—Other."

Example 1: General Accounting Policy Describes the Equity (and Cost) Methods of Accounting

Equity Method. Investee companies that are not consolidated, but over which the Company exercises significant influence, are accounted for under the equity method of accounting. Whether or not the Company exercises significant influence with respect to an Investee depends on an evaluation of several factors including, among others, representation on the Investee company's board of directors and ownership level, which is generally a 20% to 50% interest in the voting securities of the Investee company. Under the equity method of accounting, an Investee company's accounts are not reflected within the Company's Consolidated Balance Sheets and Statements of Operations; however, the Company's share of the earnings or losses of the Investee company is reflected in the caption "Equity loss—share of Investee company losses" in the Consolidated Statements of Operations. The Company's carrying value in an equity method Investee company is reflected in the caption "Ownership interests in Investee companies" in the Company's Consolidated Balance Sheets.

When the Company's carrying value in an equity method Investee company is reduced to zero, no further losses are recorded in the Company's consolidated financial statements unless the Company guaranteed obligations of the Investee company or has committed additional funding. When the Investee company subsequently reports income, the Company will not record its share of such income until it equals the amount of its share of losses not previously recognized.

Cost Method. Investee companies not accounted for under the consolidation or the equity method of accounting are accounted for under the cost method of accounting. Under this method, the Company's share of the earnings or losses of such Investee companies is not included in the Consolidated Balance Sheet or Statement of Operations. However, impairment charges are recognized in the Consolidated Statement of Operations. If circumstances suggest that the value of the Investee company has subsequently recovered, such recovery is not recorded.

When a cost method Investee company initially qualifies for use of the equity method, the Company's carrying value is adjusted for the Company's share of the past results of the Investee's operations. Therefore, prior losses could significantly decrease the Company's carrying value in that Investee company at that time.

Example 2: Disclosure of Summarized Information of Assets, Liabilities, and Results of Operations of Investees Accounted for on the Equity Method

The Company's investments in companies that are accounted for on the equity method of accounting consist of the following: (1) 25% interest in Kalass, Inc., which is engaged in the manufacture and sale of automotive replacement radiators; (2) 30% interest in Safir Industries, a manufacturer of water pumps; and (3) 50% interest in Tetera Co., a manufacturer of rubber bearings. The investments in these companies amounted to $5,542,000 and $4,668,000 at December 31, 20X2, and December 31, 20X1, respectively.

The combined results of operations and financial position of the Company's equity basis investments are summarized below:

	20X2	20X1
Condensed income statement information:		
Net sales	$51,173,000	$49,742,000
Gross margin	$17,321,000	$16,235,000
Net income	$ 2,174,000	$ 1,839,000
Company's equity in net income of affiliates	$ 874,000	$ 716,000
Condensed balance sheet information:		
Current assets	$29,316,000	$31,067,000

	20X2	20X1
Noncurrent assets	20,011,000	17,374,000
Total assets	$49,327,000	$48,441,000
Current liabilities	$26,851,000	$28,992,000
Noncurrent liabilities	12,787,000	11,603,000
Equity	9,689,000	7,846,000
Total liabilities and equity	$49,327,000	$48,441,000

Note: The following tables illustrate the captions used in the Company's Balance Sheets and Income Statements for its equity basis investments described above.

Balance Sheet Presentation

	20X2	20X1
Total current assets	$36,823,000	$37,015,000
Equity in net assets of and advances to affiliates	5,542,000	4,668,000
Property and equipment	11,610,000	10,539,000
Other assets	411,000	402,000
	$54,386,000	$52,624,000

Income Statement Presentation

	20X2	20X1
Income before income taxes	$ 8,941,000	$ 7,916,000
Provision for income taxes	(3,576,000)	(3,287,000)
Income before equity in net income of affiliates	5,365,000	4,629,000
Equity in net income of affiliates	874,000	716,000
Net income	$ 6,239,000	$ 5,345,000

Example 3: Investment Accounted for on the Equity Method Is Reduced to Zero—Investor Is Not Obligated to Provide Additional Financial Support to Investee

The Company has a 40% interest in Shana, Ltd., a manufacturer of medical diagnostic products, which has been accounted for on the equity method since 19X9. The Company's 20X2 operations include a loss of $1,975,000, which represents the Company's share of loss on its investment in Shana, Ltd. The loss resulted largely from Shana, Ltd.'s decision to write-down certain assets, predominantly property and intangibles, in light of current market conditions affecting the medical supplies industry. The loss reduced the Company's investment in Shana, Ltd. to zero and, as a consequence, the Company's future financial results will not be negatively affected by Shana, Ltd.'s ongoing operations. The Company has no obligation to fund future operating losses of Shana, Ltd.

Example 4: Investment Accounted for on the Equity Method Is Reduced to Zero—Investor Is Obligated to Provide Additional Financial Support to Investee

The Company has a 40% interest in Shana, Ltd., a manufacturer of medical diagnostic products, which has been accounted for on the equity method since 19X9. The Company's 20X2 operations include a loss of $1,975,000, which represents the Company's share of loss on its investment in Shana, Ltd. The loss resulted largely from Shana, Ltd.'s decision to write-down certain assets, predominantly property and intangibles, in light of current market conditions affecting the medical supplies industry. The loss reduced the Company's investment in Shana, Ltd. to zero.

Under the terms of an agreement with Shana, Ltd., the Company is obligated to advance additional funds to Shana, Ltd. through July 20X5. As a result, the Company recorded an additional loss of $2,360,000 in 20X2, which represents the estimated amount of such required future advances under the terms of the agreement.

Example 5: Equity Method Used for Less Than 20% Owned Investee because Investor Exercises Significant Influence over Investee's Operating and Financial Activities

The Company has a 15% interest in Fadar, a producer of chemical-based materials, which is accounted for on the equity method because the Company exercises significant influence over Fadar's operating and financial activities. Therefore, the Company's investment in Fadar, which was initially carried at cost, is adjusted annually for the Company's proportionate share of Fadar's earnings or losses.

Example 6: Company Resumes Applying the Equity Method, Which Was Previously Suspended in Prior Years Due to Losses by Investee

The Company has a 30% interest in Fadar, a producer of chemical-based materials. In 20X0, when the Company's share of losses equaled the carrying value of its investment, the Company suspended the use of the equity method, and no additional losses were recognized since the Company was not obligated to provide further financial support for Fadar. The Company's unrecorded share of Fadar's losses for 20X0 and 20X1 totaled $210,000. In 20X2, Fadar reported earnings of $1,200,000, of which the Company's share was $360,000. Accordingly, the Company has included $150,000 in income in 20X2, which represents the excess of the Company's share of Fadar's earnings for 20X2 over the Company's share of prior unrecorded losses.

Example 7: Financial Statements Currently Include on the Equity Basis of Accounting the Accounts of a Previously Consolidated Business

On January 1, 20X2, the Company transferred its medical equipment business segment and contributed certain assets and liabilities, totaling $15 million and $4 million, respectively, to a joint venture named Hope Enterprises (a partnership). The Company's equity interest in the joint venture is 35%. As a result, the 20X1 Income Statement, which included the accounts of the medical equipment business segment on a consolidated basis, has been restated to reflect adjustments of line items for revenue and costs applicable to the medical equipment business segment transferred to the joint venture and to reflect the losses of this business on the equity basis of accounting.

Example 8: Change to Equity Method from Cost Method Due to Increasing Stake in Investee

During 20X2, the Company bought an additional 25% interest in Bodair Co., thereby increasing its holdings to 40%. As a result, the Company changed its method of accounting for this investment from the cost method to the equity method. Under the cost method, the investment is recorded at cost and dividends are treated as income when received. Under the equity method, the Company records its proportionate share of the earnings or losses of Bodair Co. The effect of the change was to increase 20X2 net income by $437,000 ($0.23 per share). The financial statements for 20X1 have been restated for the change, which resulted in an increase of net income for 20X1 of $211,000 ($0.12 per share). Retained earnings as of the beginning of 20X1 has been increased by $589,000 for the effect of retroactive application of the new method.

Example 9: Disclosure of Nature of Transactions between Company and Investee

The Company uses the equity method to account for its 39% investment in Coreson, Inc., a manufacturer of electrical and electronic products and systems. Included in accounts receivable of the Company at December 31, 20X2, and December 31, 20X1, are amounts due from Coreson, Inc. of $298,000 and $357,000, respectively. Included in accounts payable of the Company at December 31, 20X2, and December 31, 20X1, are amounts due to Coreson, Inc. of $481,000 and $517,000, respectively. Transactions with Coreson, Inc. consist of the following:

	20X2	20X1
Sales to Coreson, Inc.	$2,415,000	$2,074,000
Purchases from Coreson, Inc.	$6,712,000	$5,649,000

Example 10: Disclosure of Cumulative Unremitted Earnings and Dividends Received

The Company's investment in and advances to joint venture at December 31, 20X2, and December 31, 20X1, consists of its 25% investment in Keset, Inc., a manufacturer of electronic components. The amount of cumulative unremitted earnings of this joint venture included in the Company's consolidated retained earnings at December 31, 20X2, was $3,892,000. During the years ended December 31, 20X2, and December 31, 20X1, distributions in the amounts of $600,000 and $550,000, respectively, were received from Keset, Inc.

Example 11: Company Has an Obligation to Guarantee Debt of Investee

The Company has an obligation to guarantee a pro rata share of debt incurred by Keeler, a joint venture in which the Company has a 45% interest, up to a maximum of $5,000,000. At December 31, 20X2, the Company has guaranteed the payment of $1,710,000 of the affiliate's indebtedness.

Example 12: Underlying Net Assets Exceed Investment Accounted for on the Equity Method—Excess Relates to Depreciable Assets

The Company's investment in and advances to joint venture at December 31, 20X2, and December 31, 20X1, consists of its 32% investment in Bisara, Co. a manufacturer of medical instruments, which is accounted for on the equity method. At December 31, 20X2, and December 31, 20X1, the Company's share of the underlying net assets of Bisara, Co. exceeded its investment by $1,543,000 and $1,807,000, respectively. The excess, which relates to certain property, plant, and equipment, is being amortized into income over the estimated remaining lives of the assets.

*Example 13: Carrying Value of Investment Accounted for on the
Equity Method Exceeds Underlying Net Assets—Excess Relates to
Depreciable Assets*

The Company accounts for its 29% investment in Kamas, Inc., an
engineering and construction enterprise, under the equity method.
At December 31, 20X2, and December 31, 20X1, the carrying value
of the investment in Kamas, Inc. exceeded the Company's share of
the underlying net assets of Kamas, Inc. by $1,123,000 and
$1,207,000, respectively. The excess, which relates to certain prop-
erty, plant, and equipment, is being amortized against the Company's share of Kamas, Inc.'s net income over the useful lives of the
assets that gave rise to the difference.

*Example 14: Potential Conversion of Outstanding Convertible
Securities and Exercise of Options and Warrants of Investee
May Have a Significant Effect on Investor's Share of Reported
Earnings*

The Company has a 35% interest in Fadar, Inc. a producer of
chemical-based materials, which is accounted for on the equity
method. At December 31, 20X2, and December 31, 20X1, Fadar, Inc.
had outstanding convertible securities, options, and warrants that,
if in the aggregate were converted and exercised, would have
reduced the Company's interest to 26% and, accordingly, would
have reduced the Company's share of earnings in Fadar, Inc. for
20X2 and 20X1 by $195,000 and $167,000, respectively.

*Example 15: Investor's Proportionate Share of Extraordinary Item
Reported by Investee*

The extraordinary item of $320,000 represents the Company's
proportionate share of a gain realized in connection with [*describe*]
by Kametz, Ltd., a manufacturer of electronic parts in which the
Company has a 40% interest that is accounted for on the equity
method. The Company has not provided any income tax related to
its share of the extraordinary gain because it is the Company's
intention to reinvest all undistributed earnings of Kametz, Ltd.
indefinitely.

> **Note:** The following table illustrates the portion of the Income
> Statement reflecting the Company's proportionate share of
> extraordinary item reported by Kametz, Ltd.

Income Statement Presentation

	20X2	20X1
Income before income taxes	$ 8,941,000	$ 7,916,000
Provision for income taxes	(3,576,000)	(3,287,000)
Income before equity in net income of affiliate and extraordinary item	5,365,000	4,629,000
Equity in net income of affiliate, excluding extraordinary gain of $320,000 in 20X2	554,000	716,000
Income before extraordinary item	5,919,000	5,345,000
Extraordinary item—equity in undistributed extraordinary gain of affiliate	320,000	-0-
Net income	$ 6,239,000	$ 5,345,000

CHAPTER 20
ASC TOPIC 325: INVESTMENTS—OTHER

CONTENTS

EXECUTIVE SUMMARY

Note: For equity-method investments, see Chapter 19, "ASC Topic 323: Investments—Equity Method and Joint Ventures."

Cost-Method Investments

Under the cost method, an investor recognizes an investment in the stock of an investee as an asset measured initially at cost. Subsequently, an investor recognizes as income dividends received that are distributed from earnings since the date of acquisition. Dividends received that are distributed from earnings prior to the date of acquisition are recorded as a reduction of the cost of the investment. A cost method investment is reviewed for impairment if factors indicate that a decrease in value of the investment has occurred.

Investments in Insurance Contracts

The cash surrender value of life insurance policies should be carried as an asset and the excess of the premiums paid over the increases in the cash surrender value charged to expense. The cash surrender value of a life insurance policy should be classified as a noncurrent asset, unless the entity plans to surrender the policy within one year of the balance sheet date. Loans against cash surrender values should be shown as current liabilities if due, or intended to be repaid within one year, even though the cash surrender value is shown as a noncurrent asset. If the loan is due after one year, or if the company intends to repay the loan out of the proceeds of the policy, it should be shown as a noncurrent liability (or, less desirably, as an offset against the cash surrender value if the entity has a valid right of setoff).

The owner of a life insurance policy may enter into a life settlement contract with a third-party investor, which does not result in the third-party investor having an insurable interest in the life insurance policy. Under a life settlement contract, the amount of the consideration given by the investor to the owner of the life insurance policy is greater than the cash surrender value of the life insurance policy. The amount of consideration ultimately to be received by the investor is the face value of the policy upon the death of the insured. When accounting for its investment in a life settlement contract, an investor may choose between the investment method or the fair value method. In a classified balance sheet, investments in life settlement contracts that are accounted for under the fair value method should be reported separately from those accounted for under the investment method. In the income statement, investment income under each method of accounting for such contracts should also be separately reported.

Accounting Literature

FASB Accounting Standards Codification Topic	*Pre-Codification Accounting Literature*
325, *Investments—Other*	FSP FAS 115-1 and FAS 124-1, *The Meaning of Other-Than-Temporary Impairment and Its Application to Certain Investments*
	FSP FAS 115-2 and FAS 124-2, *Recognition and Presentation of Other-Than-Temporary Impairments*
	FSP FTB 85-4-1, *Accounting for Life Settlement Contracts by Third-Party Investors*
	EITF 06-5, *Accounting for Purchases of Life Insurance—Determining the Amount That Could Be Realized in Accordance with FASB Technical Bulletin No. 85-4, Accounting for Purchases of Life Insurance*

DISCLOSURE AND KEY PRESENTATION REQUIREMENTS

Cost-Method Investments

Note: The disclosure requirement in item 1 below (which supersedes item 2 below) is prescribed by ASC Topic 325, *Investments—Other,* based on FSP FAS 115-2 and FAS 124-2, *Recognition and Presentation of Other-Than-Temporary Impairments,* which is effective for interim and annual reporting periods ending after June 15, 2009. Early adoption is permitted for periods ending after March 15, 2009, provided the pending content that links to ASC paragraph 820-10-65-4 (based on FSP FAS 157-4, *Determining Fair Value When the Volume and Level of Activity for the Asset or Liability Have Significantly Decreased and Identifying Transactions That Are Not Orderly*) is also adopted. In addition, if either the pending content in ASC paragraph 820-10-65-4 (based on FSP FAS 157-4) or in ASC paragraph 825-10-65-1 (based on FSP FAS 107-1 and APB 28-1, *Interim Disclosures about Fair Value of Financial Instruments*) is adopted early, the disclosure requirement in item 1 below must also be adopted early. This disclosure requirement is not required for earlier periods presented for comparative purposes at initial adoption. In periods after initial adoption, comparative disclosures are required only for periods ending after initial adoption.

1. For cost-method investments, the following disclosures should be made as of each date for which a balance sheet is presented in annual and interim financial statements (ASC 325-20-50-1) (FSP FAS 115-1 and FAS 124-1, par. 18):

   a. The aggregate carrying amount of all cost-method investments.

   b. The aggregate carrying amount of cost-method investments that the investor did not evaluate for impairment.

   c. The fact that the fair value of a cost-method investment is not estimated if there are no identified events or changes in circumstances that may have a significant adverse effect on the fair value of the investment, and either:

      (1) A determination was made in accordance with ASC paragraphs 825-10-50-16 through 50-19 (FAS-107, pars. 14 and 15) that it is not practicable to estimate the fair value of the investment, *or*

      (2) The investor is exempt from estimating annual fair values under ASC Subtopic 825-10, *Financial Instruments–Overall*, (FAS-159, *The Fair Value Option for Financial Assets and Financial Liabilities*), or

      (3) The investor is exempt from estimating interim fair values because it does not meet the definition of a publicly traded company.

2. For cost-method investments, the following disclosures should be made as of each date for which a balance sheet is presented in annual financial statements (ASC 325-20-50-1) (FSP FAS 115-1 and FAS 124-1, par. 18):

   a. The aggregate carrying amount of all cost-method investments.

   b. The aggregate carrying amount of cost-method investments that the investor did not evaluate for impairment.

   c. The fact that the fair value of a cost-method investment is not estimated if there are no identified events or changes in circumstances that may have a significant adverse effect on the fair value of the investment, and either:

      (1) A determination was made in accordance with ASC paragraphs 825-10-50-16 *through* 50-19 (FAS-107, pars. 14 and 15) that it is not practicable to estimate the fair value of the investment, *or*

      (2) The *investor* is exempt from estimating fair value under ASC Subtopic 825-10, *Financial Instruments–Overall* (FAS-159, *The Fair Value Option for Financial Assets and Financial Liabilities*).

Investments in Insurance Contracts

1. The entity should report on the face of the balance sheet its investments in life settlement contracts that are remeasured at fair value separately from those accounted for under the investment method, by either (ASC 325-30-45-1) (FSP FTB 85-4-1):

   a. Displaying separate line items for the fair value method and investment method carrying amounts, *or*

   b. Presenting the aggregate of those fair value method and investment method carrying amounts and parenthetically disclosing the amount of those investments accounted for under the fair value method that are included in the aggregate amount.

2. The entity should classify the amount recognized upon the death of the insured in accordance with ASC paragraph 325-30-35-9 (FSP FTB 85-4-1), in earnings (or other performance indicators for entities that do not report earnings). (ASC 325-30-45-2) (FSP FTB 85-4-1)

3. The entity should report on the face of the income statement the investment income from its investments in life settlement contracts that are remeasured at fair value separately from the investment income from those accounted for under the investment method, by either (ASC 325-30-45-3) (FSP FTB 85-4-1):

   a. Displaying separate line items for the investment income from the investments in life settlement contracts that are accounted for under the fair value method and investment method, *or*

   b. Presenting the aggregate of the investment income in life settlement contracts and parenthetically disclosing the investment income from those investments accounted for under the fair value method that are included in the aggregate amount.

4. For entities applying the fair value method, premiums paid and life insurance proceeds received should be accounted for on the same income statement line item as the changes in fair value are reported. (ASC 325-30-45-4) (FSP FTB 85-4-1)

5. The statement of cash flows should classify cash receipts and cash payments related to life settlement contracts in accordance with ASC Topic 230, *Statement of Cash Flows* (FAS-95, *Statement of Cash Flows*), based on the nature and purpose for which the life settlements were acquired. (ASC 325-30-45-4) (FSP FTB 85-4-1). See Chapter 7, "ASC Topic 230: Statement of Cash Flows."

6. The following disclosures should be made for investments in insurance contracts:

   a. Contractual restrictions on a policyholder's ability to surrender a policy. (ASC 325-30-50-1) (EITF 06-5, par. 11)

   b. The accounting policy for life settlement contracts, including the classification of cash receipts and cash disbursements in the statement of cash flows. (ASC 325-30-50-2) (FSP FTB 85-4-1)

7. For life settlement contracts accounted for under the investment method, the following disclosures should be made (ASC 325-30-50-4 through 50-6) (FSP FTB 85-4-1):

   a. For each of the first five succeeding years from the balance sheet date and thereafter, as well as in the aggregate:

      (1) The number of life settlement contracts.

      (2) The carrying value of the life settlement contracts.

      (3) The face value (death benefits) of the life insurance policies underlying the contracts.

   b. The life insurance premiums anticipated to be paid for each of the five succeeding fiscal years to keep the life settlement contracts in force as of the date of the most recent balance sheet presented.

   c. If the investor becomes aware of new or updated information that causes it to change its expectations on the timing of the realization of proceeds from the investments in life settlement contracts:

      (1) The nature of the information.

      (2) The related effect on the timing of the realization of proceeds from the life settlement contracts.

      (3) Any significant changes to the amounts disclosed in accordance with item (a) above.

8. For life settlement contracts accounted for under the fair value method, the following disclosures should be made (ASC 325-30-50-7 through 50-10) (FSP FTB 85-4-1):

   a. The methods and significant assumptions used to estimate the fair value of investments in life settlement contracts, including any mortality assumptions.

   b. For each of the first five succeeding years from the balance sheet date and thereafter, as well as in the aggregate:

      (1) The number of life settlement contracts.

      (2) The carrying value of the life settlement contracts.

(3) The face value (death benefits) of the life insurance policies underlying the contracts.

c. The reasons for changes in expectation of the timing of the realization of the investments in life settlement contracts, including disclosing significant changes to the amounts disclosed in accordance with item (a) above.

d. For each reporting period presented in the income statement:

(1) The gains or losses recognized during the period on investments sold during the period.

(2) The unrealized gains or losses recognized during the period on investments that are still held at the date of the balance sheet.

EXAMPLES OF FINANCIAL STATEMENT DISCLOSURES

 The following sample disclosures are available on the accompanying disc. For sample disclosures relating to equity-method investments, see Chapter 19, "ASC Topic 323: Investments—Equity Method and Joint Ventures."

Cost-Method Investments

Example 1: General Accounting Policy Describes the Cost Method of Accounting

Investee companies not accounted for under the consolidation or the equity method of accounting are accounted for under the cost method of accounting. Under this method, the Company's share of the earnings or losses of such Investee companies is not included in the Consolidated Balance Sheet or Statement of Operations. However, impairment charges are recognized in the Consolidated Statement of Operations. If circumstances suggest that the value of the Investee company has subsequently recovered, such recovery is not recorded.

Example 2: Cost Method Applied to 20% or More Owned Subsidiary Due to Lack of Significant Influence over Investee's Operating and Financial Activities

At December 31, 20X2, and December 31, 20X1, "Investment in associated company" as shown on the Company's Balance Sheet consists of the cost of an investment in Acker, Inc., in which the Company has a 45% interest. Prior to 20X1, the Company's 45% ownership in this Canadian affiliate was recorded on the equity basis. In 20X1, the Company concluded that it could no longer exert a significant influence over Acker, Inc.'s operating and financial activities; therefore, the Company began accounting for this investment using the cost method effective January 1, 20X1. The carrying value of this investment at December 31, 20X2, and December 31, 20X1, was $725,000, which approximates the Company's pro rata share of Acker, Inc.'s underlying value.

Example 3: Impaired Cost-Method Investments—ASC Topic 325 (Appropriate Based on Guidance in Either (a) FSP FAS 115-1 and FAS 124-1, or (b) FSP FAS 115-2 and FAS 124-2)

> **Note:** To facilitate the illustration of narrative disclosures and for simplicity, this example presents only the quantitative information as of the date of the latest balance sheet. However, GAAP requires the quantitative information to be presented as of each date for which a balance sheet is presented.

The following table shows the Company's cost method investments' gross unrealized losses and fair value, aggregated by length of time that individual securities have been in a continuous unrealized loss position, at December 31, 20X2:

Description of Securities	Less Than 12 Months		12 Months or More		Total	
	Fair Value	Unrealized Losses	Fair Value	Unrealized Losses	Fair Value	Unrealized Losses
Investments in equity securities carried at cost	$200,000	$10,000	$-0-	$-0-	$200,000	$10,000

The aggregate cost of the Company's cost method investments totaled $450,000 at December 31, 20X2. Investments with an aggregate cost of $100,000 were not evaluated for impairment because (a) the Company did not estimate the fair value of those investments in accordance with FASB ASC paragraphs 825-10-50-16 through 50-19, and (b) the Company did not identify any events or changes in circumstances that may have had a significant adverse effect on the fair value of those investments. Of the remaining $350,000 cost of investments, the Company estimated that the fair value exceeded the cost of investments (i.e., the investments were not impaired) with an aggregate cost of $140,000. The remaining $210,000 of cost method investments consists of one investment in a privately owned company in the consumer tools and appliance industry. That investment was evaluated for impairment because of an adverse change in the market condition of companies in the consumer tools and appliance industry. As a result of that evaluation, the Company identified an unrealized loss of $10,000. The severity of the impairment (fair value is approximately 5% less than cost) and the duration of the impairment (less than 3 months) correlate with the weak 20X2 year-end sales experienced within the consumer tools and appliance industry, as reflected by lower customer transactions and lower-than-expected performance in traditional gift categories, such as hardware and power tools. Based on the Company's evaluation of the near-term prospects of the investee and the Company's ability and intent to hold the investment for a reasonable period of time sufficient for a forecasted recovery of fair value, the Company does not consider that investment to be other-than-temporarily impaired at December 31, 20X2.

Investments in Insurance Contracts

Example 4: Company-Owned Life Insurance Policies Are Used as a Funding Source for Postretirement Medical Benefits and Deferred Compensation

Investments in company-owned life insurance policies are made with the intention of utilizing them as a long-term funding source for post-retirement medical benefits and deferred compensation. They are subject to claims by creditors, and the Company can designate them to another purpose at any time. The insurance policies are recorded at their net cash surrender values, as reported by the issuing insurance companies, whose Standard & Poor's credit ratings range from A- to AAA, and totaled $10 million and $8 million at December 31, 20X2, and 20X1, respectively.

Investments in company-owned life insurance consisted of $7 million in traditional whole life policies and $3 million in variable life insurance policies as of December 31, 20X2. In the traditional whole life policies, the investments return a set dividend rate that is periodically adjusted by the insurance companies based on the performance of their long-term investment portfolio. While the amount of the dividend can vary subject to a minimum dividend rate, the cash surrender value of these policies is not exposed to negative returns in that the insurance companies guarantee a minimum dividend rate on these investments. In the variable life policies, the Company is able to allocate the investments across a set of choices provided by the insurance companies. At December 31, 20X2, the investments in the variable life policies were allocated 75% in fixed income securities and 25% in equity securities. The valuation of these investments can fluctuate depending on changes in market interest rates and equity values. The annual net changes in market valuation, normal insurance expenses, and any death benefit gains are reflected in the accompanying income statement. The net effect of these changes in 20X2 and 20X1 resulted in pre-tax income of approximately $750,000 and $600,000, respectively. In 20X2 and 20X1, approximately 35% and 65% of these credits were recorded to "Cost of sales" and "Operating expenses," respectively.

Example 5: Cash Surrender Value of Life Insurance, Net of Policy Loans

The Company has purchased insurance on the lives of certain key executive officers. As beneficiary, the Company receives the cash surrender value if the policy is terminated and, upon death of the insured, receives all benefits payable. Cash value of life insurance is reported in the financial statements net of policy loans. The loans carry interest at a rate of 6.5%, require interest only payments annually, and are collateralized by the cash value of the policies. A summary of "Net cash value of life insurance" as reported in the accompanying Balance Sheets at December 31, 20X2, and December 31, 20X1, is as follows:

	20X2	20X1
Cash surrender value of life insurance	$1,156,000	$1,005,000
Policy loans balances outstanding	(418,000)	(329,000)
Net cash value of life insurance	$ 738,000	$ 676,000

Example 6: Life Settlement Contracts Accounted for under the Investment Method

From time to time, the Company purchases interests in insurance policies to hold for investment purposes. FASB ASC 325-30 states that a purchaser may elect to account for its investments in life settlement contracts using either the investment method or the fair value method. The election is made on an instrument-by instrument basis and is irrevocable. Under the investment method, a purchaser recognizes the initial investment at the purchase price plus all initial direct costs. Continuing costs (policy premiums and direct external costs, if any) to keep the policy in force are capitalized. Under the fair value method, a purchaser recognizes the initial investment at the purchase price. In subsequent periods, the purchaser re-measures the investment at fair value in its entirety at each reporting period and recognizes changes in fair value earnings in the period in which the changes occur.

The Company values its investments in life settlement contracts using the investment method and routinely tests its investment contracts for impairment. There was no impairment recorded for the years ended December 31, 20X2, and 20X1.

The following table describes the Company's life settlement contracts at December 31, 20X2.

Remaining Life Expectancy (in years)	Number of Life Settlement Contracts	Carrying Value	Face Value
0-1	350	$3,050,000	$ 5,000,000
1-2	100	2,000,000	3,000,000
2-3	100	2,500,000	4,500,000
3-4	50	1,050,000	2,500,000
4-5	10	400,000	1,000,000
Thereafter	-	-	-
Total	610	$9,000,000	$16,000,000

Remaining life expectancy for year 0-1 includes all policies that have exceeded their original life expectancy plus those policies that are scheduled to reach their original life expectancy during the next 12 months. Remaining life expectancy is based on original life expectancy estimates and is not an indication of expected maturity. Actual maturity dates in any category may vary significantly (either earlier or later) from the remaining life expectancies reported above.

Premiums to be paid for each of the five succeeding fiscal years to keep the life settlement contracts in force as of December 31, 20X2, are as follows:

Year 1	$ 100,000
Year 2	150,000
Year 3	400,000
Year 4	300,000
Year 5	150,000
Total estimated premiums	$1,100,000

Example 7: Life Settlement Contracts Accounted for under the Fair Value Method

The Company measures the fair value of individual life settlement contracts whenever the carrying value plus the undiscounted future costs that are expected to be incurred to keep the life settlement contract in force exceed the expected proceeds from the contract. In those situations, the fair value is determined on a discounted cash flow basis, incorporating current life expectancy assumptions. The discount rate incorporates current information about market interest rates, the credit exposure to the insurance company that issued the life settlement contract and the Company's estimate of the risk margin an investor in the contracts would require.

At December 31, 20X2, the carrying value of the Company's life settlement contracts was $9 million. These investments are monitored for impairment on a contract-by-contract basis. There was no impairment recorded for the years ended December 31, 20X2, and 20X1.

The following table describes the Company's life settlement contracts at December 31, 20X2:

Remaining Life Expectancy (in years)	Number of Life Settlement Contracts	Carrying Value	Face Value
0-1	350	$3,050,000	$ 5,000,000
1-2	100	2,000,000	3,000,000
2-3	100	2,500,000	4,500,000
3-4	50	1,050,000	2,500,000
4-5	10	400,000	1,000,000
Thereafter	-	-	-
Total	610	$9,000,000	$16,000,000

Remaining life expectancy for year 0-1 includes all policies that have exceeded their original life expectancy plus those policies that are scheduled to reach their original life expectancy during the next 12 months. Remaining life expectancy is based on original life expectancy estimates and is not an indication of expected maturity. Actual maturity dates in any category may vary significantly (either earlier or later) from the remaining life expectancies reported above.

Premiums to be paid for each of the five succeeding fiscal years to keep the life settlement contracts in force as of December 31, 20X2, are as follows:

Year 1	$ 100,000
Year 2	150,000
Year 3	400,000
Year 4	300,000
Year 5	150,000
Total estimated premiums	$1,100,000

CHAPTER 21
ASC TOPIC 330: INVENTORY

CONTENTS

EXECUTIVE SUMMARY

Inventory

Inventory usually is classified as (1) finished goods, (2) work in process, or (3) raw materials. Inventories exclude long-term assets that are subject to depreciation. Inventories are classified as current assets, except when there are excessive quantities that may not reasonably be expected to be used or sold within the normal operating cycle of a business. In this event, the excess inventory is classified as noncurrent.

Generally, inventory should be stated at the *lower of cost or market*. Cost is the sum of the expenditures and charges, direct and indirect, incurred in bringing inventories to their existing condition or location. Cost may be determined by specific identification or by the association of the flow of cost factors, such as first-in, first-out (FIFO); last-in, first-out (LIFO); and average cost.

In the phrase *lower of cost or market*, the term *market* means current replacement cost, whether by purchase or by reproduction, and is limited to the following maximum and minimum amounts:

- *Maximum*—The estimated selling price less any costs of completion and disposal, referred to as net realizable value

- *Minimum*—The net realizable value, less an allowance for normal profit

The write-down of inventory to market usually is reflected in cost of goods sold, unless the amount is unusually material, in which case the loss should be identified separately in the income statement.

Generally, the same principles and methods are used to value inventories for interim financial statements as are used for annual reports. For practical purposes, however, the following exceptions apply:

1. An estimated gross profit frequently is used to determine the cost of goods sold during an interim period. This is acceptable for generally accepted accounting principles (GAAP), as long as periodic physical inventories are taken to adjust the gross profit percentage used.

2. When the LIFO method is used for interim financial statements and a LIFO layer is depleted, in part or in whole, that is expected to be replaced before the end of the fiscal period, the expected cost of replacement for the depleted LIFO inventory can be used in determining cost of goods sold for the interim period.

3. Inventory losses from market declines, other than those expected to be recovered before the end of the fiscal year, are included in the results of operations of the interim period in which the loss occurs. Subsequent gains from market price recovery in later interim periods are included in the results of operation in which the gain occurs, but only to the extent of the previously recognized losses.

4. Standard costs are acceptable in determining inventory valuations for interim financial reporting. In general, the same procedures for standard costs used at the end of the fiscal year should be used for interim financial reporting.

Accounting Literature

FASB Accounting Standards Codification Topic	*Pre-Codification Accounting Literature*
330, *Inventory*	ARB-43, Chapter 4, *Inventory Pricing*
	APB-28, *Interim Financial Reporting*

DISCLOSURE AND KEY PRESENTATION REQUIREMENTS

1. The basis of stating inventories should be consistently applied and disclosed in the financial statements. (ASC 330-10-50-1) (ARB-43, Ch. 4)

2. If a significant change is made in the basis of stating inventories, disclosures should be made of the nature of the change and of its effect, if material, on income. (ASC 330-10-50-1) (ARB-43, Ch. 4)

3. Substantial and unusual losses resulting from the application of lower of cost or market accounting should be disclosed. (ASC 330-10-50-2) (ARB-43, Ch. 4) (*Note:* ASC paragraph 330-10-50-2 (ARB-43, Ch. 4) indicates that it will frequently be desirable to disclose the amount of such losses in the income statement as a charge separately identified from cost of goods sold.)

4. If goods are stated above cost, this fact should be fully disclosed. (ASC 330-10-50-3) (ARB-43, Ch. 4)

5. Where inventories are stated at sales prices, the use of such basis should be fully disclosed. (ASC 330-10-50-4) (ARB-43, Ch. 4)

6. The amounts of net losses on firm purchase commitments accrued under ASC paragraph 330-10-35-17 (ARB-43, Ch. 4),

should be disclosed separately in the income statement. (ASC 330-10-50-5) (ARB-43, Ch. 4)

7. Major categories of inventories (raw materials, work in process, finished goods, and supplies) should be presented, if practicable. (Generally accepted practice)

8. If the LIFO inventory method is used, disclosure should be made of the following (Generally accepted practice):

    a. The difference between the LIFO amount and replacement cost (LIFO reserve).

    b. Amounts from the liquidation of a LIFO layer.

EXAMPLES OF FINANCIAL STATEMENT DISCLOSURES

 The following sample disclosures are available on the accompanying disc.

Example 1: Basis of Valuation and Method of Determining Cost Are Included in Summary of Accounting Policies Note

Inventories are stated at the lower of cost (first-in, first-out) or market (net realizable value).

> **Note:** See Chapter 8, "ASC Topic 235: Notes to Financial Statements," for additional examples of inventory disclosures that are typically included as part of the general note describing the entity's accounting policies.

Example 2: Disclosure of Major Components of Inventory under FIFO

Inventories, consisting of material, material overhead, labor, and manufacturing overhead, are stated at the lower of cost (first-in, first-out) or market and consist of the following at December 31:

	20X2	*20X1*
Raw materials	$ 9,826,000	$ 6,286,000
Work-in-process	3,061,000	1,167,000
Finished goods	6,188,000	8,501,000
	$19,075,000	$15,954,000

Example 3: Disclosure of Major Components of Inventory under LIFO

Inventories consist of the following at December 31:

	20X2	20X1
Finished goods	$ 9,803,000	$ 8,014,000
Work-in-progress	5,047,000	5,386,000
Raw materials	2,003,000	2,042,000
FIFO inventories	16,853,000	15,442,000
Less provision for LIFO method of valuation	(1,230,000)	(1,402,000)
LIFO inventories	$ 15,623,000	$ 14,040,000

Example 4: Inventories Valued on Both Average Cost and LIFO Methods

At December 31, 20X2, and December 31, 20X1, approximately 59% and 53% of total inventories, respectively, were valued on a LIFO basis; the cost of other inventories is principally determined under the average cost method. If all inventories were valued on an average cost basis, total inventories would have been $951,000 and $873,000 higher at December 31, 20X2, and December 31, 20X1, respectively.

Example 5: Reserves for Obsolete Inventories Disclosed

At December 31, 20X2 and December 31, 20X1, the reserve for obsolescence was $1,051,000 and $805,000, respectively. Reserves for obsolescence were increased by $1,782,000 and $1,209,000 for 20X2 and 20X1, respectively. Reserves for obsolescence were reduced, due to inventory written off, by $1,132,000 and $759,000 for 20X2 and 20X1, respectively.

Example 6: Material Losses Resulting from the Write-Down of Inventory to Its Net Realizable Value

Due to changing market conditions in the electronics industry, in 20X2 management conducted a thorough review of the inventory in all of its product lines. As a result, a provision for inventory losses of $4,421,000 was charged against operations in 20X2 to write down inventory to its net realizable value. This was based on the Company's best estimates of product sales prices and customer demand patterns, and its plans to transition its products. It is at least reasonably possible that the estimates used by the Company to determine its provision for inventory losses will be materially different from the actual amounts or results. These differences could result in materially higher than expected inventory provisions, which could have a materially adverse effect on the Company's results of operations and financial condition in the near term.

Example 7: Inventory Held as a Noncurrent Asset

In 20X2, the Company purchased inventory quantities in excess of amounts expected to be utilized in the Company's operating cycle at very favorable terms. At December 31, 20X2, inventory of $780,000 shown on the balance sheet as a noncurrent asset represents that portion of the inventory acquired in excess of amounts expected to be sold in the next twelve months.

Example 8: Inventories Produced in a "Maquiladora" Operation

The Company operates its Mexican manufacturing facilities under the "Maquiladora" program. Pursuant to this program, materials and components owned by the Company are transferred to the Mexican subsidiaries where they are used to produce finished goods. The finished goods are returned to the United States and the Company reimburses the Mexican subsidiaries for their manufacturing costs without any intended significant profit or loss of consequence.

Example 9: Liquidation of LIFO Inventory Quantities

In 20X2 and 20X1, certain inventory quantities were reduced, resulting in liquidations of LIFO inventory quantities carried at lower costs prevailing in prior years. The effect was to increase net income by $676,000 in 20X2 and $493,000 in 20X1.

Example 10: Purchase Contracts

In connection with the EFTX transaction in January 20X1, EFTX and the Company entered into a manufacturing agreement whereby the Company committed to purchase minimum amounts of goods and services used in its normal operations during the first 48 months after the transaction. Future annual minimum purchases remaining under the agreement are $19 million and $22 million for 20X3 and 20X4, respectively. During 20X2 and 20X1, the Company's total purchases under the agreement were $17 million and $13 million, respectively.

Example 11: Firm Price Commitment Manufacturing and Supply Agreement

The Company entered into a firm price commitment manufacturing and supply agreement in connection with the acquisition of the F&D trademarks purchased in 20X2. The agreement was entered into with the seller of the trademarks upon request by the Company to obtain from the seller tools and other manufacturing resources of the seller for the manufacture of products. The manufacturing and supply agreement has created a firm commitment by the Company for a minimum of $4,500,000. A minimum payment of $500,000 on the agreement was due on December 31, 20X2, with three additional payments of $400,000 and five additional payments of $560,000 to follow thereafter, through December 31, 20X6, which is also the date on which the agreement terminates.

Example 12: Commitment to Sell Inventory at a Fixed Price

At December 31, 20X2, the Company has an agreement with a customer to sell a specified minimum number of units of its Eglaze adhesive products over the next thirty months at a fixed price of $10,200,000. The fixed price is equal to approximately 5% above the aggregate selling price at current market prices.

Example 13: Materials Prices Are Linked to the Commodity Markets and Are Subject to Change

The principal raw materials purchased by the Company (fabricated aluminum, plastics, metals, and copper) are subject to changes in market price as these materials are linked to the commodity markets. To the extent that the Company is unable to pass on cost increases to customers, the cost increases could have a significant impact on the results of operations of the Company.

CHAPTER 22
ASC TOPIC 340: OTHER ASSETS AND DEFERRED COSTS

CONTENTS

EXECUTIVE SUMMARY

Capitalized Advertising Costs

In most cases, the costs of advertising should be expensed as incurred or the first time the advertisement occurs. However, there are two exceptions to this general rule:

1. Certain direct-response advertising costs should be capitalized and amortized over the period during which the future benefits or sales are expected to be received.
2. Expenditures for advertising costs that are made subsequent to recognizing revenues related to those costs should be capitalized and charged to expense when the related revenues are recognized.

Insurance Contracts that Do Not Transfer Insurance Risk

Despite its form, an insurance or reinsurance contract may not provide for indemnification of the insured by the insurer against loss or liability. Such contracts may be structured in various ways. There are generally three kinds of risk that may be transferred in a contract that is, in form, an insurance contract:

*   *Underwriting risk*—The uncertainty about the amount of a claim for an insured loss;
*   *Timing risk*—The uncertainty about the timing of payment of a known claim for an insured loss; and
*   *Yield risk*—The uncertainty about the investment return that will be earned on premiums from the date of receipt until the date claims are paid.

Only the first two risks are insurance risks. A contract that transfers only yield risk is a financing transaction, not an insurance transaction.

Accounting Literature

FASB Accounting Standards Codification Topic	*Pre-Codification Accounting Literature*
340, *Other Assets and Deferred Costs*	SOP 93-7, *Reporting on Advertising Costs*

FASB Accounting Standards Codification Topic	*Pre-Codification Accounting Literature*
720, *Other Expenses*	SOP 98-7, *Deposit Accounting: Accounting for Insurance and Reinsurance Contracts That Do Not Transfer Insurance Risk*

DISCLOSURE AND KEY PRESENTATION REQUIREMENTS

Capitalized Advertising Costs

Note: For advertising barter transactions, see Chapter 35, "ASC Topic 605: Revenue Recognition."

1. Qualifying direct-response advertising costs that meet the recognition criteria as capitalized assets of ASC paragraph 340-20-25-4 (SOP 93-7, par. 33), should be reported as assets net of accumulated amortization. (ASC 340-20-45-1) (SOP 93-7, par. 28)

2. The following disclosures should be made in the notes to the financial statements (ASC 340-20-50-1) (SOP 93-7, par. 49):

   a. The accounting policy for reporting advertising costs, indicating whether such costs are expensed as incurred or the first time the advertising takes place.

   b. A description of the direct-response advertising costs reported as assets (if any), the accounting policy for it, and the amortization period.

   c. The total amount charged to advertising expense for each income statement presented, with separate disclosure of amounts, if any, representing a write-down to net realizable value.

   d. The total amount of advertising reported as assets in each balance sheet presented.

Insurance Contracts that Do Not Transfer Insurance Risk

1. For deposit assets and liabilities:

   a. Deposit assets and liabilities should be reported on a gross basis, unless the right of offset exists, as defined in ASC Subtopic 210-20, *Balance Sheet–Offsetting*. (ASC 340-30-45-1) (SOP 98-7, par. 9)

    b. Disclosures should include a description of the contracts accounted for as deposits, and the separate amounts of total deposit assets and total deposit liabilities reported in the balance sheet. (ASC 340-30-50-1) (SOP 98-7, par. 18)

2. For insurance and reinsurance contracts that transfer only significant timing risk and insurance and reinsurance contracts that transfer neither timing risk nor significant underwriting risk, changes in the carrying amount of the deposit should be reported as interest income or interest expense. (ASC 340-30-45-2) (SOP 98-7, par. 11)

3. For insurance and reinsurance contracts that transfer only significant underwriting risk:

    a. Changes in the recorded amount of the deposit (other than the unexpired portion of the coverage provided) should be recorded in an insured's income statement as an offset against the loss recorded by the insured that will be reimbursed under the insurance or reinsurance contract, and in an insured's income statement as an incurred loss. (ASC 340-30-45-3) (SOP 98-7, par. 14)

    b. The reduction in the deposit related to the unexpired portion of the coverage provided should be recorded as an adjustment to incurred losses. (ASC 340-30-45-4) (SOP 98-7, par. 14)

    c. If the insured is an entity other than an insurance entity, the reduction in the deposit related to the unexpired portion of the coverage provided should be recorded as an expense. (ASC 340-30-45-5) (SOP 98-7, par. 14)

    d. The following disclosures should be made regarding the changes in the recorded amount of the deposit (ASC 340-30-50-2) (SOP 98-7, par. 14):

        (1) The present values of initial expected recoveries that will be reimbursed under the insurance or reinsurance contracts that have been recorded as an adjustment to incurred losses.

        (2) Any adjustment of amounts initially recognized for expected recoveries, including separate disclosure of the following individual components of the adjustment: interest accrual, the present value of additional expected recoveries, and the present value of reductions in expected recoveries.

        (3) The amortization expense attributable to the expiration of coverage provided under the contract.

EXAMPLES OF FINANCIAL STATEMENT DISCLOSURES

 The following sample disclosures are available on the accompanying disc.

Capitalized Advertising Costs

Note: For sample disclosures of advertising barter transactions, see Chapter 35, "ASC Topic 605: Revenue Recognition."

Example 1: Advertising Costs Are Expensed as Incurred

Advertising costs are expensed as incurred. Advertising expense totaled $477,000 for 20X2 and $392,000 for 20X1.

Example 2: Advertising Costs Are Expensed the First Time the Advertising Takes Place

Production costs of future media advertising are expensed the first time the advertising takes place. Advertising expense totaled $532,000 for 20X2 and $410,000 for 20X1.

Example 3: Direct-Response Advertising Costs Are Capitalized

Direct-response advertising costs, consisting primarily of catalog book production, printing, and postage costs, are capitalized and amortized over the expected life of the catalog, not to exceed six months. Direct-response advertising costs reported as "Prepaid assets" are $275,000 and $350,000 at December 31, 20X2, and December 31, 20X1, respectively. Total advertising expenses were $1,900,000 and $1,600,000 in 20X2 and 20X1, respectively.

Example 4: Certain Advertising Costs Are Expensed the First Time the Advertising Takes Place, and Direct-Response Advertising Costs Are Capitalized and Written Down to Net Realizable Value

The Company expenses the production costs of advertising the first time the advertising takes place, except for direct-response advertising, which is capitalized and amortized over its expected period of future benefits.

Direct-response advertising consists primarily of magazine advertisements that include order coupons for the Company's products. The capitalized costs of the advertising are amortized over the six-month period following the publication of the magazine in which it appears.

At December 31, 20X2, and December 31, 20X1, capitalized direct-response advertising costs of $570,000 and $612,000, respectively, were included in "Other assets" in the accompanying Balance Sheets. Advertising expense was $5,264,000 in 20X2, including $432,000 for amounts written down to net realizable value related to certain capitalized direct-response advertising costs. Advertising expense was $6,079,000 in 20X1.

Example 5: Advertising Policy on Other Companies' Web Sites Pursuant to Contracts Is Explained

The Company expenses the costs of advertising as incurred. Typically the Company purchases banner advertising on other companies' Web sites pursuant to contracts that have one-to-three year terms and may include the guarantee of (1) a minimum number of impressions, (2) the number of times that an advertisement appears in pages displayed to users of the Web site, or (3) a minimum amount of revenue that will be recognized by the Company from customers directed to the Company's Web site as a direct result of the advertisement. The Company recognizes expense with respect to such advertising ratably over the period in which the advertisement is displayed. In addition, some agreements require additional payments as additional impressions are delivered. Such payments are expensed when the impressions are delivered.

In one case, the Company entered into an agreement for an unspecified number of years. In this case, the Company amortizes as expense the lesser of (1) the number of impressions to date divided by minimum guaranteed impressions or (2) revenue to date divided by minimum guaranteed revenue as a percentage of the total payments.

For the years ended December 31, 20X2, and December 31, 20X1, advertising expense totaled approximately $8,325,000 and $9,890,000, respectively.

Insurance Contracts that Do Not Transfer Insurance Risk

Example 6: Description of Contracts Accounted for as Deposits

The Company may enter into assumed and ceded reinsurance contracts that contain certain loss limiting provisions. These contracts are accounted for using the deposit accounting method in accordance with FASB ASC 340-30, *Deposit Accounting: Accounting for Insurance and Reinsurance Contracts That Do Not Transfer Risk*. Under the deposit method of accounting, revenues and expenses from reinsurance contracts are not recognized as written premium and incurred losses. Instead, the profits or losses from these contracts are recognized net, as other income or expense over the contract or contractual settlement periods. In accordance with FASB ASC 340-30, these contracts are deemed as either transferring only significant timing risk or only significant underwriting risk or transferring neither significant timing nor underwriting risk.

For such contracts, the Company initially records the amount of consideration paid as a deposit asset or received as a deposit liability. Revenue or expense is recognized over the term of the contract, with any deferred amount recorded as a component of assets or liabilities until such time it is earned. The ultimate asset or liability under these contracts is estimated, and the asset or liability initially established, which represents consideration received, is increased or decreased over the term of the contract. The change during the period is recorded in the Company's consolidated statements of operations, with increases and decreases in the ultimate asset or liability shown in other expense, net. As of December 31, 20X2, and 20X1, the Company had reflected in other assets $4 million and $3.5 million, respectively, and in other liabilities $1 million and $800,000, respectively, related to deposit contracts. In cases where cedants retain the consideration on a funds held basis, the Company records those assets in other assets, and records the related investment income on the assets in the Company's consolidated statements of operations as investment income.

CHAPTER 23
ASC TOPIC 350:
INTANGIBLES—GOODWILL AND OTHER

CONTENTS

EXECUTIVE SUMMARY

Intangible assets are assets that lack physical substance. Many kinds of intangible assets may be identified and given reasonably descriptive names such as patents, franchises, trademarks, customer lists and the like. Other types of intangible assets are unidentifiable, such as goodwill.

Goodwill

Goodwill should not be amortized; rather, it should be tested for impairment at a level of reporting referred to as a reporting unit. Assessing goodwill for impairment involves the following steps:

1. Identify potential impairment by comparing the fair value of a reporting unit with its carrying value, including goodwill. If the fair value is less than the recorded amount, impairment exists and the test in step 2 below should be performed. If the fair value is greater than the recorded amount, goodwill is not impaired (and the second step below is not necessary).

2. Measure the amount of the impairment loss by comparing the implied fair value of the reporting unit's goodwill with its carrying amount. The implied fair value of goodwill should be determined in the same way that goodwill is recognized in a business combination; that is, the implied fair value is the excess of the fair value of the reporting unit over the amounts assigned to the reporting unit's assets and liabilities. If the carrying amount of the reporting unit's goodwill is greater than the implied fair value, an impairment loss equal to the difference should be recognized. Subsequent reversals of recognized impairment losses are prohibited.

General Intangibles Other Than Goodwill

Intangible assets that are acquired individually or as part of a group of assets, other than those acquired in a business combination, are initially recorded at their fair value. The cost of a group of assets acquired in a transaction is allocated to the individual assets based on their relative fair values. Goodwill does not arise in such a transaction. Intangible assets that are acquired in a business combination are accounted for in accordance with ASC Topic 805, *Business Combinations*. The costs of intangible assets that are developed internally, as well as the costs of maintaining or restoring intangible assets that have indeterminate lives or that are inherent in a continuing business and related to the entity as a whole, are expensed as incurred.

The accounting for intangible assets, other than goodwill, subsequent to acquisition is based on the asset's useful life. The useful life of the intangible asset is the period over which the asset is expected to contribute directly or indirectly to the entity's future cash flows. An asset for which no legal, regulatory, contractual, competitive, economic, or other factors limit its useful life is considered to have an indefinite useful life.

Accounting Literature

FASB Accounting Standards Codification Topic	*Pre-Codification Accounting Literature*
350, *Intangibles—Goodwill and Other*	FAS-142, *Goodwill and Other Intangible Assets*
	FSP FAS 142-3, *Determination of the Useful Life of Intangible Assets*

DISCLOSURE AND KEY PRESENTATION REQUIREMENTS

Goodwill

1. The aggregate amount of goodwill should be presented as a separate line item in the balance sheet. (ASC 350-20-45-1) (FAS-142, par. 43)

2. The aggregate amount of goodwill impairment losses should be presented as a separate line item in the income statement before the subtotal income from continuing operations (or similar caption), unless a goodwill impairment loss is associated with a discontinued operation. (ASC 350-20-45-2) (FAS-142, par. 43)

3. The amount of any goodwill impairment loss associated with a discontinued operation should be included (on a net-of-tax basis) within the results of discontinued operations. (ASC 350-20-45-3) (FAS-142, par. 43)

   Note: The disclosure requirements in item 4 below are prescribed by ASC Topic 350, *Intangibles–Goodwill and Other*, based on FAS-141R, *Business Combinations*, which is effective for business combinations for which the acquisition date is on or after the beginning of the first annual reporting period beginning on or after December 15, 2008. Early adoption is not permitted. The disclosure requirements in item 5 below should be followed prior to the effective date of the guidance based on FAS-141R.

4. The changes in the carrying amount of goodwill should be disclosed for each period for which a balance sheet is presented, showing separately the following (ASC 350-20-50-1) (FAS-142, par. 45):

   a. The gross amount and accumulated impairment losses at the beginning of the period.

   b. Additional goodwill recognized during the period, except goodwill included in a disposal group that, on acquisition, meets the criteria to be classified as held for sale in accordance with ASC paragraph 360-10-45-9 (FAS-144, par. 30).

   c. Adjustments resulting from the subsequent recognition of deferred tax assets during the period in accordance with ASC paragraphs 805-740-25-2 through 25-4 (FAS-141R, par. 27; FAS-109, par. 30), and 805-740-45-2 (FAS-109, par. 30A).

   d. Goodwill included in a disposal group classified as held for sale in accordance with ASC paragraph 360-10-45-9 (FAS-144, par. 30), and goodwill derecognized during the period without having previously been reported in a disposal group classified as held for sale.

   e. Impairment losses recognized during the period.

   f. Net foreign currency exchange differences arising during the period in accordance with ASC Topic 830, *Foreign Currency Matters* (FAS-52, *Foreign Currency Translation*).

   g. Any other changes in the carrying amounts during the period.

   h. The gross amount and accumulated impairment losses at the end of the period.

   i. For entities that report segment information in accordance ASC Topic 280, *Segment Reporting* (FAS-131, *Disclosures about Segments of an Enterprise and Related*

Information), the above information about goodwill in total and for each reportable segment, and any significant changes in the allocation of goodwill by reportable segment. (*Note*: If any portion of goodwill has not yet been allocated to a reporting unit at the date the financial statements are issued, or are available to be issued as discussed in ASC Section 855-10-25, that unallocated amount and the reasons for not allocating it should be disclosed.)

5. The changes in the carrying amount of goodwill should be disclosed for each period for which a balance sheet is presented, showing separately the following (ASC 350-20-50-1) (FAS-142, par. 45):

   a. The aggregate amount of goodwill acquired.

   b. The aggregate amount of impairment losses recognized.

   c. The amount of goodwill included in the gain or loss on disposal of all or a portion of a reporting unit.

   d. For entities that report segment information in accordance with ASC Topic 280, *Segment Reporting* (FAS-131, *Disclosures about Segments of an Enterprise and Related Information*), the above information about goodwill in total and for each reportable segment, and any significant changes in the allocation of goodwill by reportable segment. (*Note*: If any portion of goodwill has not yet been allocated to a reporting unit at the date the financial statements are issued, or are available to be issued as discussed in ASC Section 855-10-25, that unallocated amount and the reasons for not allocating it should be disclosed.)

6. For each goodwill impairment loss recognized, the following disclosures should be made in the notes to the financial statements that include the period in which the impairment loss is recognized (ASC 350-20-50-2) (FAS-142, par. 47):

   a. A description of the facts and circumstances leading to the impairment.

   b. The amount of the impairment loss and the method of determining the fair value of the associated reporting unit (whether based on quoted market prices, prices of comparable businesses, a present value or other valuation technique, or a combination thereof).

   c. If a recognized impairment loss is an estimate that has not yet been finalized, that fact and the reasons for using an estimate and, in subsequent periods, the nature and amount of any significant adjustments made to the initial estimate of the impairment loss.

General Intangibles Other than Goodwill

1. Intangible assets or classes of intangible assets (other than goodwill), at a minimum, should be aggregated and presented as a separate line item in the balance sheet. (ASC 350-30-45-1) (FAS-142, par. 42) (*Note:* Presentation of individual intangible assets or classes of intangible assets as separate line items is also acceptable.)

2. The amortization expense and impairment losses for intangible assets should be presented in income statement line items within continuing operations. (ASC 350-30-45-2) (FAS-142, par. 42)

3. An impairment loss resulting from applying an impairment test should be excluded from a change in accounting principle. (ASC 350-30-45-3) (FAS-142, par. 42) (*Note:* ASC paragraphs 350-30-35-9 through 35-12 (FAS-142, pars. 14, B61 and B66) and ASC paragraphs 350-30-35-15 through 35-17 (FAS-142, par. 16), require that an intangible asset be tested for impairment when it is determined that the asset should no longer be amortized or should begin to be amortized due to a reassessment of its remaining useful life.)

4. For intangible assets (other than goodwill) acquired either individually or as part of a group of assets (in either an asset acquisition or business combination), the following disclosures should be made in the period of acquisition. (ASC 350-30-50-1) (FAS 142, par. 44) (*Note:* This information should be disclosed separately for each material business combination or in the aggregate for individually immaterial business combinations that are material collectively if the aggregate fair values of intangible assets acquired, other than goodwill, are significant.):

   a. For intangible assets subject to amortization:

      (1) The total amount assigned and the amount assigned to any major intangible asset class.

      (2) The amount of any significant residual value, in total and by major intangible asset class.

      (3) The weighted-average amortization period, in total and by major intangible asset class.

   b. For intangible assets not subject to amortization, the total amount assigned and the amount assigned to any major intangible asset class.

   Note: The disclosure requirement in item (c) below is to be followed until the adoption of the guidance in ASC Topic 805, *Business Combinations*, based on FAS-141R, *Business Combinations*, which is effective for business combinations for which the acquisition date is on or after the beginning of the first annual reporting period beginning on or after December 15, 2008. Thereafter, the disclosure requirement in item (cc) below should be followed. Early adoption is not permitted.

c. The amount of research and development assets acquired and written off in the period and the line item in the income statement in which the amounts written off are aggregated.

cc. The amount of research and development assets acquired in a transaction other than a business combination and written off in the period and the line item in the income statement in which the amounts written off are aggregated.

Note: The disclosure requirement in item (d) below is prescribed by ASC Topic 350, *Intangibles–Goodwill and Other*, based on FSP FAS 142-3, *Determination of the Useful Life of Intangible Assets*, which is effective for fiscal years, and interim periods within those fiscal years, beginning after December 15, 2008, and should be applied prospectively to all intangible assets recognized as of, and subsequent to, the effective date. Early adoption is not permitted.

d. For intangible assets with renewal or extension terms, the weighted-average period before the next renewal or extension (both explicit and implicit), by major intangible asset class.

5. The following disclosures should be made in the financial statements or the notes thereto for each period for which a balance sheet is presented (ASC 350-30-50-2) (FAS-142, par. 45):

a. For intangible assets (other than goodwill) subject to amortization:

(1) The gross carrying amount and accumulated amortization, in total and by major intangible asset class.

(2) The aggregate amortization expense for the period.

(3) The estimated aggregate amortization expense for each of the five succeeding fiscal years.

b. For intangible assets (other than goodwill) not subject to amortization, the total carrying amount and the carrying amount for each major intangible asset class.

Note: The disclosure requirements in items (c) and (d) below are prescribed by ASC Topic 350, *Intangibles—Goodwill and Other*, based on FSP FAS 142-3, *Determination of the Useful Life of Intangible Assets*, which is effective for fiscal years, and interim periods within those fiscal years, beginning after December 15, 2008, and should be applied prospectively to all intangible assets recognized as of, and subsequent to, the effective date. Early adoption is not permitted. (ASC 350-30-65-1) (FSP FAS 142-3)

c. The entity's accounting policy on the treatment of costs incurred to renew or extend the term of a recognized intangible asset.

d. For intangible assets that have been renewed or extended in the period for which a balance sheet is presented:

(1) For entities that capitalize renewal or extension costs, the total amount of costs incurred in the period to renew or extend the term of a recognized intangible asset, by major intangible asset class.

(2) The weighted-average period before the next renewal or extension (both explicit and implicit), by major intangible asset class.

6. For each impairment loss recognized related to an intangible asset (other than goodwill), the following disclosures should be made in the notes to financial statements that include the period in which the impairment loss is recognized (ASC 350-30-50-3) (FAS-142, par. 46):

a. A description of the impaired intangible asset and the facts and circumstances leading to the impairment.

b. The amount of the impairment loss and the method for determining fair value.

c. The caption in the income statement in which the impairment loss is aggregated.

d. If applicable, the segment in which the impaired intangible asset is reported under ASC Topic 280, *Segment Reporting* (FAS-131, *Disclosures about Segments of an Enterprise and Related Information*).

Note: The disclosure requirement in item 7 below is prescribed by ASC Topic 350, *Intangibles–Goodwill and Other*, based on FSP FAS 142-3, *Determination of the Useful Life of Intangible Assets*, which is effective for fiscal years, and interim periods within those fiscal years, beginning after December 15, 2008, and should be applied prospectively to all intangible assets recognized as of, and subsequent to, the effective date. Early adoption is not permitted.

7. For a recognized intangible asset, the entity should disclose information that enables financial statement users to assess the extent to which the expected future cash flows associated

with the asset are affected by the entity's intent and/or ability to renew or extend the arrangement. (ASC 350-30-50-4) (FSP FAS 142-3, par. 13)

EXAMPLES OF FINANCIAL STATEMENT DISCLOSURES

 The following sample disclosures are available on the accompanying disc.

Goodwill

Example 1: Accounting Policy for Impairment of Goodwill

The Company evaluates the carrying value of goodwill during the fourth quarter of each year and between annual evaluations if events occur or circumstances change that would more likely than not reduce the fair value of the reporting unit below its carrying amount. Such circumstances could include, but are not limited to (1) a significant adverse change in legal factors or in business climate, (2) unanticipated competition, or (3) an adverse action or assessment by a regulator. When evaluating whether goodwill is impaired, the Company compares the fair value of the reporting unit to which the goodwill is assigned to the reporting unit's carrying amount, including goodwill. The fair value of the reporting unit is estimated using a combination of the income, or discounted cash flows, approach and the market approach, which utilizes comparable companies' data. If the carrying amount of a reporting unit exceeds its fair value, then the amount of the impairment loss must be measured. The impairment loss would be calculated by comparing the implied fair value of reporting unit goodwill to its carrying amount. In calculating the implied fair value of reporting unit goodwill, the fair value of the reporting unit is allocated to all of the other assets and liabilities of that unit based on their fair values. The excess of the fair value of a reporting unit over the amount assigned to its other assets and liabilities is the implied fair value of goodwill. An impairment loss would be recognized when the carrying amount of goodwill exceeds its implied fair value. The Company's evaluation of goodwill completed during the year resulted in no impairment losses.

Example 2: Disclosure of Gross Carrying Amount of Goodwill and Accumulated Impairment Losses at the Beginning and End of the Period, and Changes in Those Balances during the Period

The changes in the carrying amount of goodwill and accumulated impairment losses for the year ended December 31, 20X2, are as follows:

	Technology Segment	Communications Segment	Total
Balance as of January 1, 20X2			
Goodwill	$1,413,000	$1,104,000	$2,517,000
Accumulated impairment losses	-0-	(200,000)	(200,000)
	1,413,000	904,000	2,317,000
Goodwill acquired during the year	189,000	115,000	304,000
Impairment losses	-0-	(46,000)	(46,000)
Goodwill written off related to sale of business unit	(484,000)	-0-	(484,000)
Balance as of December 31, 20X2			
Goodwill	1,118,000	1,219,000	2,337,000
Accumulated impairment losses	-0-	(246,000)	(246,000)
	$1,118,000	$ 973,000	$2,091,000

The fair value of the communications segment is tested for impairment in the third quarter, after the annual forecasting process. Due to an increase in competition in the California and Arizona cable industry, operating profits and cash flows were lower than expected in the fourth quarter of 20X1 and the first and second quarters of 20X2. Based on that trend, the earnings forecast for the next five years was revised. In September 20X2, a goodwill impairment loss of $46,000 was recognized in the communications reporting unit. The fair value of that reporting unit was estimated using the expected present value of future cash flows.

General Intangibles Other than Goodwill

Example 3: Disclosure of Acquired Intangible Assets in the Periods Subsequent to a Business Combination

> **Note:** This example assumes that the business combination was completed in 20X0 and illustrates the disclosures for acquired intangible assets that are required to be made in the Company's December 31, 20X2, and 20X1, financial statements (the years subsequent to the business combination). For disclosures related to intangible assets acquired in connection

with a business combination, see Chapter 44, "ASC Topic 805: Business Combinations," for sample disclosures.

As of December 31, 20X2, and December 31, 20X1, the Company has the following amounts related to intangible assets:

	December 31, 20X2		December 31, 20X1	
	Gross Carrying Amount	*Accumulated Amortization*	*Gross Carrying Amount*	*Accumulated Amortization*
Amortized intangible assets:				
Trademark	$1,078,000	$ (66,000)	$1,078,000	$ (38,000)
Unpatented technology	475,000	(380,000)	375,000	(220,000)
Other	90,000	(30,000)	90,000	(18,000)
Total	$1,643,000	$(476,000)	$1,543,000	$(276,000)
Unamortized intangible assets:				
Broadcast licenses	$1,400,000		$1,200,000	
Trademark	600,000		450,000	
Total	$2,000,000		$1,650,000	

No significant residual value is estimated for these intangible assets. Aggregate amortization expense for the years ended December 31, 20X2, and December 31, 20X1, totaled $200,000 and $180,000, respectively. The following table represents the total estimated amortization of intangible assets for the five succeeding years:

For the Year Ending December 31	*Estimated Amortization Expense*
20X3	$199,000
20X4	$ 74,000
20X5	$ 74,000
20X6	$ 64,000
20X7	$ 54,000

Example 4: Components of Intangible Assets Disclosed in a Note

Intangible assets consist of the following at December 31:

	20X2	20X1
Patents	$ 450,000	$ 370,000
Trademarks	300,000	210,000
Trade names	415,000	300,000
Copyrights	175,000	175,000
Intellectual property	420,000	225,000
Customer lists	790,000	620,000
Non-compete agreements	600,000	300,000
	3,150,000	2,200,000
Less: accumulated amortization	(1,440,000)	(1,090,000)
Net intangible assets	$ 1,710,000	$ 1,110,000

Amortization of intangible assets amounted to $350,000 for 20X2 and $270,000 for 20X1.

> **Note:** Alternatively, the components of intangible assets may be disclosed on the face of the balance sheet.

Example 5: Accounting Policy for Impairment of Intangible Assets

The Company evaluates the recoverability of identifiable intangible assets whenever events or changes in circumstances indicate that an intangible asset's carrying amount may not be recoverable. Such circumstances could include, but are not limited to (1) a significant decrease in the market value of an asset, (2) a significant adverse change in the extent or manner in which an asset is used, or (3) an accumulation of costs significantly in excess of the amount originally expected for the acquisition of an asset. The Company measures the carrying amount of the asset against the estimated undiscounted future cash flows associated with it. Should the sum of the expected future net cash flows be less than the carrying value of the asset being evaluated, an impairment loss would be recognized. The impairment loss would be calculated as the amount by which the carrying value of the asset exceeds its fair value. The fair value is measured based on quoted market prices, if available. If quoted market prices are not available, the estimate of fair value is based on various valuation techniques, including the discounted value of estimated future cash flows. The evaluation of asset impairment requires the Company to make assumptions about future cash flows over the life of the asset being evaluated. These assumptions require significant judgment and actual results may differ from assumed and estimated amounts. During the year ended December 31, 20X2, the Company recorded an impairment loss of $620,000 related to an intangible asset.

Example 6: Accounting Policy for Patents

Patents are initially measured based on their fair values. Patents are being amortized on a straight-line basis over a period of 10 to 25 years and are stated net of accumulated amortization of $195,000 and $173,000 at December 31, 20X2, and 20X1, respectively. Amortization expense charged to operations was $22,000 for 20X2 and $19,000 for 20X1.

Example 7: Accounting Policy for Trademarks

Trademarks are initially measured based on their fair values. Trademarks are being amortized on a straight-line basis over a period of 5 to 15 years and are stated at cost net of accumulated amortization of $213,000 and $184,000 at December 31, 20X2, and 20X1, respectively. Amortization expense charged to operations was $29,000 for 20X2 and $24,000 for 20X1.

Example 8: Accounting Policy for Organization Costs

Organization costs, including legal fees, are expensed as incurred. Organization costs charged to operations totaled $23,000 and $12,000 for 20X2 and 20X1, respectively.

Example 9: Accounting Policy for Deferred Financing Costs

Costs relating to obtaining the mortgage debt and the Industrial Revenue Bond financing are capitalized and amortized over the term of the related debt using the straight-line method. Accumulated amortization at December 31, 20X2, and 20X1, was $38,000 and $29,000, respectively. Amortization of deferred financing costs charged to operations was $9,000 for 20X2 and $7,000 for 20X1. When a loan is paid in full, any unamortized financing costs are removed from the related accounts and charged to operations.

Example 10: Covenant Not to Compete Agreements

Covenant not to compete (net) of $623,000 and $823,000 at December 31, 20X2, and 20X1, respectively, represents the portion of the purchase price associated with the 20X1 acquisition of Baysol Co. allocated to noncompetition agreements. Under these agreements, the former stockholders of Baysol Co. agreed not to compete with the

Company for a period of five years. The related cost is being amortized on the straight-line method over the terms of the agreements. Accumulated amortization related to the covenant not to compete agreements totaled $377,000 and $177,000 at December 31, 20X2, and 20X1, respectively. Amortization expense charged to operations was $200,000 for 20X2 and $177,000 for 20X1.

Example 11: License Agreement

In 20X2, the Company entered into an agreement to license the rights to certain laboratory equipment developed and manufactured by another company. The purchase price paid for the license was $400,000 in cash which represents its fair value. This amount was recorded as an intangible asset and is being amortized over the period of its estimated benefit period of 10 years. At December 31, 20X2, accumulated amortization was $30,000. Under the terms of the agreement, the Company is also required to pay royalties, as defined, to the licensors semiannually.

Example 12: Patent Acquisition

In 20X0, the Company acquired certain patents pertaining to technology incorporated into certain of the Company's products. The Company paid approximately $1,975,000 for these patents and related expenses upon entering into the agreement. In April 20X2, this agreement was amended such that the Company paid approximately $1,215,000 for additional patent rights and related expenses. The fair value of these patents is being amortized over their expected life of 10 years.

Example 13: Impairment Charge Related to Trademarks

The Company performed, with the assistance of independent valuation experts, an impairment test of the carrying value of the XYZ Trademarks to determine whether any impairment existed. The Company determined that the sum of the expected undiscounted cash flows attributable to the XYZ Trademarks was less than its carrying value and that an impairment write-down was required. Accordingly, the Company calculated the estimated fair value of the intangible asset by summing the present value of the expected cash flows over its life. The impairment was calculated by deducting the present value of the expected cash flows from the carrying value. This assessment resulted in an impairment write-down of $1,050,000, which was included in "Impairment charges" in the accompanying Statement of Operations for the year ended December 31, 20X2.

Example 14: Impairment of Intangible Assets Results in Reduction of Amortization Period

In 20X2, the Company recognized $2,600,000 in impairment losses on certain identified intangible assets that are being amortized (primarily trade names and intellectual property) relating to the Company's electronic components operation. Despite the Company's efforts to improve the operations at this division, several internal and external factors have impacted, and are expected to continue to impact, results of operations. As a result, projected future cash flows from this division were determined to be less than the carrying value of the division's long-lived assets. The revised carrying value of the intangible assets was calculated using discounted estimated future cash flows. Management also determined that the useful life of the trade names and intellectual property should be reduced from 15 to 10 years. The residual balance for these intangible assets, $1,300,000, will be amortized over the remaining 10 years on a straight-line basis.

Example 15: Impairment of Intangible Assets Is Recognized as a Result of Strategic Review of Certain Operations

In 20X2, during the course of the Company's strategic review of its diagnostic chemicals kits operations, the Company recorded a pre-tax charge of $3,200,000 ($1,970,000 after tax) relating to the impairment of certain intangible assets held for use when it was determined that future undiscounted cash flows associated with these assets were insufficient to recover their carrying values. The impaired assets principally represent the company's historic ownership interest in product rights and license agreements. The assets were written down to fair value, which was determined on the basis of future discounted cash flows and confirmed by an independent appraisal.

CHAPTER 24
ASC TOPIC 360: PROPERTY, PLANT, AND EQUIPMENT

CONTENTS

EXECUTIVE SUMMARY

Overall

Fixed assets (also referred to as *property, plant, and equipment; plant assets; capital assets; or tangible long-lived assets*) are used in production, distribution, and services by all enterprises. Examples include land, buildings, furniture, fixtures, machinery, equipment, and vehicles. The nature of the assets employed by a particular enterprise is determined by the nature of its activities.

Fixed assets have two primary characteristics:

1. They are acquired for use in operations and enter into the revenue-generating stream indirectly. They are held primarily for use, not for sale.

2. They have relatively long lives.

Property, plant, and equipment are generally recorded at cost, which includes all normal expenditures of readying an asset for its intended use. However, unnecessary expenditures that do not add to the utility of the asset are charged to expense.

The asset's cost, less any salvage value, is charged to expense (i.e., depreciated) over the asset's estimated useful life in a systematic and rational manner. Commonly used depreciation methods include straight-line, units of production, sum-of-the-years'-digits, and declining balance.

If an entity constructs an asset for the entity's own use, the entity should capitalize the related interest cost incurred as part of the cost of the asset until the asset is substantially complete and ready for its intended use. Once the interest cost is capitalized, it should be depreciated in the same manner as other costs of the underlying asset.

Recognition of impairment of long-lived assets generally is required when events and circumstances indicate that an entity will not be able to recover the carrying amount of those assets. The accounting for impaired assets differs depending on whether the entity intends to dispose of the asset or continue to use it.

Long-Lived Assets Classified as Held and Used

An entity is required to (a) recognize an impairment loss if the carrying amount of a long-lived asset is not recoverable from its expected undiscounted cash flows and (b) measure an impairment loss as the difference between the carrying amount and fair value of the asset.

Once the carrying amount of an impaired asset classified as held and used has been written down to fair value, that value becomes the asset's new cost basis; restoration of a previously recognized impairment loss is prohibited.

An impairment loss recognized for a long-lived asset classified as held and used should be included as a component of income from continuing operations before income taxes.

Long-Lived Assets to Be Disposed of

An entity is required to record a long-lived asset classified as held for sale at the lower of its carrying amount or fair value less cost to sell, and to cease depreciation. A loss should be recognized for any initial or subsequent write-down to fair value less cost to sell. A gain should be recognized for any subsequent increase in fair value less cost to sell, but not in excess of the cumulative loss previously recognized. In order for a long-lived asset to be sold and classified as held for sale, certain specified criteria are required to be met (e.g., the asset should be available for immediate sale in its present condition subject only to usual and customary terms for sales of such assets).

If circumstances arise that would change a plan of sale and an entity, as a result, decides not to sell a long-lived asset previously classified as held for sale, the asset should be reclassified as held and used.

A long-lived asset classified as held for sale should be presented separately in the balance sheet. The assets and liabilities of a disposal group classified as held for sale should be presented separately in the asset and liability sections, respectively, of the balance sheet. Those assets and liabilities should not be offset and presented as a single amount.

Long-lived assets to be disposed of other than by sale (e.g., by abandonment, in an exchange for a similar asset, or in a distribution to owners in a spin-off) should continue to be classified as held and used until they are disposed of, and should be accounted for as discussed above under "Long-Lived Assets Classified as Held and Used." If a long-lived asset is to be abandoned or distributed to owners in a spin-off together with other assets (and liabilities) as a group, and that disposal group is a component of an entity, then the disposal should be accounted for as discontinued operations as discussed in ASC Topic 205, *Presentation of Financial Statements.*

Accounting Literature

FASB Accounting Standards Codification Topic	*Pre-Codification Accounting Literature*
360, *Property, Plant, and Equipment*	FAS-144, *Accounting for the Impairment or Disposal of Long-Lived Assets*
	FSP AUG-AIR-1, *Accounting for Planned Major Maintenance Activities*
	APB-12, *Omnibus Opinion—1967*

DISCLOSURE AND KEY PRESENTATION REQUIREMENTS

Overall

1. An entity should apply the same method of accounting for planned major maintenance activities in annual and interim financial reporting periods. (ASC 360-10-45-1) (FSP AUG-AIR-1, par. 6)

2. The following disclosures should be made in the financial statements or in notes thereto (ASC 360-10-50-1) (APB-12, par. 5):

   a. Depreciation expense for the period.

   b. Balances of major classes of depreciable assets, by nature or function, at the balance sheet date.

   c. Accumulated depreciation, either by major classes of depreciable assets or in total, at the balance sheet date.

   d. A general description of the method or methods used in computing depreciation with respect to major classes of depreciable assets.

Impairment or Disposal of Long-Lived Assets

1. An impairment loss recognized for a long-lived asset (asset group) to be held and used should be included in income from continuing operations before income taxes. (ASC 360-10-45-4) (FAS-144, par. 25)

2. A gain or loss recognized on the sale of a long-lived asset (disposal group) that is not a component of an entity should be included in income from continuing operations before income taxes. (ASC 360-10-45-5) (FAS-144, par. 45)

3. If circumstances arise that previously were considered unlikely and, as a result, an entity decides not to sell a long-lived asset (disposal group) previously classified as held for sale (ASC 360-10-45-6 and 45-7) (FAS-144, par. 39):

   a. The asset (disposal group) should be reclassified as held and used.

   b. Any required adjustment to the carrying amount of the long-lived asset that is reclassified as held and used should be included in income from continuing operations in the period of the subsequent decision not to sell and in the same income statement caption used to report a loss, if any, recognized in accordance with item 2 above.

   c. If a component of an entity is reclassified as held and used, the results of operations of the component previously reported in discontinued operations should be reclassified and included in income from continuing operations for all periods presented.

4. If the criteria for classification as held for sale for a long-lived asset (disposal group) are met after the balance sheet date, but before the financial statements are issued or are available to be issued, the long-lived asset (disposal group) should continue to be classified as held and used in those financial statements, and the following information should be disclosed (ASC 360-10-45-13; 205-20-50-1(a)) (FAS-144, par. 33):

   a. A description of the facts and circumstances leading to the expected disposal.

   b. The expected manner and timing of the disposal.

   c. The carrying amount(s) of the major classes of assets and liabilities included as part of a disposal group, if not separately presented on the face of the balance sheet.

5. Long-lived assets classified as held for sale should be presented separately in the balance sheet. (ASC 360-10-45-14) (FAS-144, par. 46)

6. Long-lived assets to be disposed of other than by sale (e.g., by abandonment, in an exchange measured based on the recorded amount of the nonmonetary asset relinquished, or in a distribution to owners in a spinoff) should be classified as held and used until they are disposed of. (ASC 360-10-45-15) (FAS-144, par. 27)

7. The following disclosures should be made in the notes to financial statements that include the period in which an impairment loss is recognized on long-lived assets classified as held and used (ASC 360-10-50-2) (FAS-144, par. 26):

   a. A description of the impaired long-lived asset (asset group) and the facts and circumstances leading to the impairment.

   b. If not separately presented on the face of the income statement, the amount of the impairment loss and the caption in the income statement (or the statement of activities) that includes that loss.

   c. The method(s) for determining fair value (whether based on a quoted market price, prices for similar assets, or another valuation technique).

   d. If applicable, the segment in which the impaired long-lived asset (asset group) is reported under ASC Topic 280, *Segment Reporting* (FAS-131, *Disclosures about Segments of an Enterprise and Related Information*).

EXAMPLES OF FINANCIAL STATEMENT DISCLOSURES

The following sample disclosures are available on the accompanying disc. For additional information, see:

- Chapter 8, "ASC Topic 235: Notes to Financial Statements," for additional examples of disclosures of property, plant, and equipment that are typically included as part of the entity's general note on significant accounting policies.

- Chapter 9, "ASC Topic 250: Accounting Changes and Error Corrections," for disclosures required in connection with a change in depreciation methods or useful lives.

- Chapter 26, "ASC Topic 410: Asset Retirement and Environmental Obligations," for disclosures required in connection with asset retirement obligations.

- Chapter 52, "ASC Topic 840: Leases," for disclosures required by lessees and lessors of assets held under capitalized leases.

Example 1: Basis for Recording Assets and Depreciation Methods

Property and equipment are recorded at cost. Depreciation is provided over the estimated useful lives of the related assets using the straight-line method for financial statement purposes. The Company uses other depreciation methods (generally, accelerated depreciation methods) for tax purposes where appropriate. Amortization of leasehold improvements is computed using the straight-line method over the shorter of the remaining lease term or the estimated useful lives of the improvements.

Example 2: Different Methods of Depreciation Used for Depreciable Assets

Property, equipment, and special tools are stated at cost, less accumulated depreciation and amortization. Property and equipment placed in service before January 1, 19X6, are depreciated using an accelerated method that results in accumulated depreciation of approximately two-thirds of the asset cost during the first half of the estimated useful life of the asset. Property and equipment placed in service after December 31, 19X5, are depreciated using the straight-line method of depreciation over the estimated useful life of the asset. Special tools are amortized using an accelerated method over periods of time representing the estimated productive life of those tools.

Example 3: Estimated Service Lives of Property and Equipment Disclosed

The estimated service lives of property and equipment are principally as follows:

Buildings and improvements	3–40 years
Machinery and equipment	2–15 years
Computer software	2–5 years
Transportation vehicles	2–6 years

> **Note:** Disclosure of estimated service lives of property and equipment is not required by GAAP. However, in some cases companies disclose the information because it is considered useful.

Example 4: Policy for Repairs and Maintenance, Capitalization, and Disposal of Assets Disclosed

Repairs and maintenance are expensed as incurred. Expenditures that increase the value or productive capacity of assets are capitalized. When property and equipment are retired, sold, or otherwise disposed of, the asset's carrying amount and related accumulated depreciation are removed from the accounts and any gain or loss is included in operations.

> **Note:** Disclosure of policy for repairs and maintenance, capitalization, and disposal of assets is not required by GAAP. However, in some cases companies disclose the information because it is considered useful.

Example 5: Review of Carrying Value of Property and Equipment for Impairment

The Company reviews the carrying value of property, plant, and equipment for impairment whenever events and circumstances indicate that the carrying value of an asset may not be recoverable from the estimated future cash flows expected to result from its use and eventual disposition. In cases where undiscounted expected future cash flows are less than the carrying value, an impairment loss is recognized equal to an amount by which the carrying value exceeds the fair value of assets. The factors considered by management in performing this assessment include current operating results, trends, and prospects, as well as the effects of obsolescence, demand, competition, and other economic factors.

Example 6: Components of Property and Equipment Disclosed in a Note

The following is a summary of property and equipment, at cost less accumulated depreciation, at December 31:

	20X2	20X1
Land	$ 1,500,000	$ 1,500,000
Buildings and improvements	5,250,000	5,250,000
Data processing equipment	1,975,000	1,050,000
Furniture and fixtures	725,000	536,000
Purchased software	612,000	590,000
Internally developed software	388,000	410,000
Transportation equipment	347,000	213,000
Leasehold improvements	290,000	230,000
Construction in progress	200,000	100,000
	11,287,000	9,879,000
Less: accumulated depreciation	(2,804,000)	(2,091,000)
	$ 8,483,000	$ 7,788,000

Depreciation of property and equipment amounted to $713,000 for 20X2 and $671,000 for 20X1.

> **Note:** Alternatively, the components of property and equipment may be disclosed on the face of the balance sheet.

Example 7: Construction in Progress

Construction in progress is stated at cost, which includes the cost of construction and other direct costs attributable to the construction. No provision for depreciation is made on construction in progress until such time as the relevant assets are completed and put into use. Construction in progress at December 31, 20X2, represents machinery under installation.

Example 8: Property and Equipment Include Assets Acquired under Capital Leases

Property, plant, and equipment include gross assets acquired under capital leases of $493,000 and $414,000 at December 31, 20X2, and December 31, 20X1, respectively. Related amortization included in accumulated depreciation was $251,000 and $176,000 at December 31, 20X2, and December 31, 20X1, respectively. Capital leases are included as a component of vehicles and equipment and machinery. Amortization of assets under capital leases is included in depreciation expense.

Example 9: Interest Cost Capitalized

The Company capitalizes interest cost incurred on funds used to construct property, plant, and equipment. The capitalized interest is recorded as part of the asset to which it relates and is amortized over the asset's estimated useful life. Interest cost capitalized was $315,000 and $268,000 in 20X2 and 20X1, respectively.

Example 10: Property Held for Sale

In July 20X2, the Company signed a letter of intent to sell substantially all its plant assets at its manufacturing facility in Cleveland, Ohio. These assets have been classified as "Property held for sale" in the Company's Balance Sheet.

Example 11: Commitment Required under Construction in Progress

The Company is constructing a new facility, which is scheduled to be completed in 20X4. As of December 31, 20X2, the Company incurred and capitalized in "Construction in progress" $1,600,000.

The estimated cost to be incurred in 20X3 and 20X4 to complete construction of the facility is approximately $12 million.

Example 12: Impairment Loss Recognized as a Result of Change in Policy for Replacing Property and Equipment

Effective October 1, 20X2, management approved a revision to the Company's policy of replacing certain transportation equipment and heavy duty machinery and equipment. Under the revised policy, the Company replaces transportation equipment after eight years, and heavy duty machinery and equipment after ten years. The previous policy was to not replace transportation equipment before it was a minimum of ten years old, and heavy duty machinery and equipment before they were a minimum of 12 years old. As a result of this decision, the Company recognized an impairment loss of $4,736,000 in 20X2 for those transportation equipment and heavy duty machinery and equipment scheduled for replacement in the next two years under the new policy. Depreciable lives were also adjusted effective October 1, 20X2, to reflect the new policy.

Example 13: Accounting Policy for Impairment of Fixed Assets and Intangible Assets with Finite Lives

Unlike goodwill and indefinite-lived intangible assets, the accounting rules do not provide for an annual impairment test in determining whether fixed assets (e.g., property, plant, and equipment) and finite-lived intangible assets (e.g., customer lists) are impaired. Instead, they require that a triggering event occur before testing an asset for impairment. Examples of such triggering events include a significant disposal of a portion of such assets, an adverse change in the market involving the business employing the related asset, a significant decrease in the benefits realized from an acquired business, difficulties or delays in integrating the business, and a significant change in the operations of an acquired business.

Once a triggering event has occurred, the impairment test employed is based on whether the intent is to hold the asset for continued use or to hold the asset for sale. If the intent is to hold the asset for continued use, the impairment test involves a comparison of undiscounted cash flows against the carrying value of the asset as an initial test. If the carrying value of such asset exceeds the undiscounted cash flow, the asset would be deemed to be impaired. Impairment would then be measured as the difference between the fair value of the fixed or amortizing intangible asset and the carrying value to determine the amount of the impairment. The Company generally determines fair value by using the discounted cash flow method. If the intent is to hold the asset for sale and certain other criteria are met (i.e., the asset can be disposed of currently, appropriate levels of authority have approved sale, and there is an actively pursuing buyer), the impairment test is a comparison of the asset's carrying value to its fair value less costs to sell. To the extent that the carrying value is greater than the asset's fair value less costs to sell, an impairment loss is recognized for the difference. Assets held for sale are separately presented on the balance sheet and are no longer depreciated.

Example 14: Impairment of Assets Held and Used Recognized as a Result of Strategic Review of Certain Operations

In 20X2, during the course of the Company's strategic review of its diagnostic chemicals kits operations, the Company assessed the recoverability of the carrying value of certain fixed assets, which resulted in impairment losses of $1,400,000. These losses reflect the amounts by which the carrying values of these assets exceed their estimated fair values determined by their estimated future discounted cash flows. The impairment loss is recorded as a component of "Operating expenses" in the Income Statement for 20X2.

Example 15: Impairment of Assets to Be Disposed of by Sale

In 20X2, the Company adopted a plan to dispose of most of its plant assets, machinery and equipment, and furniture and fixtures relating to its manufacturing facility in Boise, Idaho. The Company expects that the final sale and disposal of the assets will be completed in the year 20X3. In connection with the plan of disposal, the Company determined that the carrying values of some of the underlying assets exceeded their fair values. Consequently, the Company recorded an impairment loss of $1,715,000, which represents the excess of the carrying values of the assets over their fair values, less cost to sell. The impairment loss is recorded as a separate line item ("Impairment charge") in the Income Statement for 20X2. The carrying value of the assets that are held for sale is separately presented in the Balance Sheet in the caption "Assets held for sale," and these assets are no longer depreciated.

PART 4—
LIABILITIES

CHAPTER 25
ASC TOPIC 405: LIABILITIES

CONTENTS

EXECUTIVE SUMMARY

Overall

The various types of liabilities, along with the related disclosure requirements, are discussed in numerous chapters throughout this book. For example:

- Exit or disposal activities in Chapter 27, "ASC Topic 420: Exit or Disposal Cost Obligations."
- Debt in Chapter 32, "ASC Topic 470: Debt."

- Dividends payable in Chapter 34, "ASC Topic 505: Equity."
- Income taxes payable in Chapter 43, "ASC Topic 740: Income Taxes."
- Lease obligations in Chapter 52, "ASC Topic 840: Leases."
- Payables to related parties in Chapter 54, "ASC Topic 850: Related Party Disclosures."

See applicable chapters for further guidance.

ASC Topic 405 mainly addresses extinguishments of liabilities and insurance-related assessments.

Extinguishments of Liabilities

For further guidance on extinguishments of liabilities, see Chapter 32, "ASC Topic 470: Debt" and Chapter 57, "ASC Topic 860: Transfers and Servicing."

Insurance-Related Assessments

Insurance entities (as well as noninsurance entities) are subject to a variety of assessments related to insurance activities, including those by state guaranty funds and workers' compensation second-injury funds.

Entities subject to insurance-related assessments should recognize liabilities for those assessments when all of the following conditions are met:

a. An assessment has been imposed, or information available before the financial statements are issued, or are available to be issued, indicates it is probable that an assessment will be imposed;

b. The event obligating an entity to pay an imposed or probable assessment has occurred on or before the date of the financial statements; and

c. The amount of the assessment can be reasonably estimated.

Current practice is generally to allow, but not require, the discounting of liabilities to reflect the time value of money when the aggregate amount of the obligation and the amount and timing of the cash payments are fixed or reliably determinable for a particular liability.

Accounting Literature

FASB Accounting Standards Codification Topic	Pre-Codification Accounting Literature
405, *Liabilities*	SOP 97-3: *Accounting by Insurance and Other Enterprises for Insurance-Related Assessments*

DISCLOSURE AND KEY PRESENTATION REQUIREMENTS

Overall

The various types of liabilities, along with the related disclosure requirements, are discussed in numerous chapters throughout this Manual. See applicable chapters for further guidance.

ASC Topic 405 mainly addresses extinguishments of liabilities and insurance-related assessments.

Extinguishments of Liabilities

For extinguishments of liabilities, see Chapter 32, "ASC Topic 470: Debt" and Chapter 57, "ASC Topic 860: Transfers and Servicing."

Insurance-Related Assessments

1. If amounts pertaining to loss contingencies of insurance-related assessments have been discounted, the following disclosures should be made (ASC 405-30-50-1) (SOP 97-3, par. 27):

   a. The undiscounted amounts of the liability.

   b. Any related asset for premium tax offsets or policy surcharges.

   c. The discount rate used.

2. If amounts pertaining to loss contingencies of insurance-related assessments have not been discounted, the following disclosures should be made (ASC 405-30-50-1) (SOP 97-3, par. 27):

   a. The amounts of the liability.

   b. Any related asset for premium tax offsets or policy surcharges.

   c. The periods over which the assessments are expected to be paid.

    d. The period over which the recorded premium tax offsets or policy surcharges are expected to be realized.

> **Note:** ASC Sections 275-10-50, *Risks and Uncertainties—Overall-Disclosure* (SOP 94-6, *Disclosure of Certain Significant Risks and Uncertainties*) and 450-20-55, *Contingencies—Loss Contingencies-Implementation Guidance and Illustrations* (FAS-5, *Accounting for Contingencies*), provide further guidance on the required disclosures related to loss contingencies. For further guidance, see Chapter 14, "ASC Topic 275: Risks and Uncertainties," and Chapter 30, "ASC Topic 450: Contingencies."

EXAMPLES OF FINANCIAL STATEMENT DISCLOSURES

 The following sample disclosures are available on the accompanying disc.

Overall

Sample disclosures of the various types of liabilities are provided in numerous chapters throughout this Manual. See applicable chapters for further guidance.

ASC Topic 405 mainly addresses extinguishments of liabilities and insurance-related assessments.

Extinguishments of Liabilities

For sample disclosures relating to extinguishments of liabilities, see Chapter 32, "ASC Topic 470: Debt" and Chapter 57, "ASC Topic 860: Transfers and Servicing."

Insurance-Related Assessments

Example 1: Liability for Insurance-Related Assessments Is Discounted

Liabilities for guaranty fund and other insurance-related assessments are accrued when an assessment is probable, when it can be reasonably estimated, and when the event obligating the entity to pay an imposed or probable assessment has occurred. Liabilities for guaranty funds and other insurance-related assessments are discounted at 5% and are included as part of "Other liabilities" on the Balance Sheets. As of December 31, 20X2, the undiscounted and discounted liability balances were $3.5 million and $3.1 million, respectively. As of December 31, 20X1, the undiscounted and discounted liability balances were $2.7 million and $2.2 million, respectively.

As of December 31, 20X2, and 20X1, included in "Other assets" on the Balance Sheets were $400,000 and $300,000, respectively, of related assets for premium tax offsets discounted at 5%. The undiscounted amount of premium tax offsets totaled $500,000 and $380,000 at December 31, 20X2, and 20X1, respectively. This asset is limited to the amount that is able to be offset against premium tax on future premium collections from business written or committed to be written.

Example 2: Liability for Insurance-Related Assessments Is Not Discounted

Liabilities for guaranty fund and other insurance-related assessments are accrued when an assessment is probable, when it can be reasonably estimated, and when the event obligating the entity to pay an imposed or probable assessment has occurred. Liabilities for guaranty funds and other insurance-related assessments are not discounted and are included as part of "Other liabilities" on the Balance Sheets. As of December 31, 20X2, and 20X1, the undiscounted balances were $3.5 million and $2.7 million, respectively. The liability as of December 31, 20X2, is expected to be paid as follows: 20X3—$1.5 million; 20X4—$1.3 million; and 20X5—$700,000.

As of December 31, 20X2, and 20X1, included in "Other assets" on the Balance Sheets were $500,000 and $380,000, respectively, of undiscounted related assets for premium tax offsets. This asset is limited to the amount that is able to be offset against premium tax on future premium collections from business written or committed to be written. As of December 31, 20X2, the recorded asset is expected to be realized as follows: 20X3—$150,000; 20X4—$300,000; and 20X5—$50,000.

CHAPTER 26
ASC TOPIC 410: ASSET RETIREMENT AND ENVIRONMENTAL OBLIGATIONS

CONTENTS

EXECUTIVE SUMMARY

Asset Retirement Obligations

An entity may have a legal obligation for the retirement of a tangible long-lived asset. Such a legal obligation generally is the result of an existing or enacted law, statute, ordinance, or written or oral contract. An entity should recognize the fair value of a liability for an asset retirement obligation in the period in which the retirement obligation is incurred, if a reasonable estimate of fair value can be made. If such an estimate cannot be made in the period the asset retirement obligation is incurred, the liability should be recognized when the fair value can be reasonably estimated.

When a liability is initially recognized for an asset retirement obligation, the entity should capitalize an asset retirement cost by increasing the carrying amount of the related long-lived asset by the same amount as the liability. Such cost should subsequently be charged to expense using a systematic and rational method over the asset's useful life.

After initial measurement, the liability for the asset retirement obligation should be adjusted for changes resulting from (1) the passage of time or (2) revisions to the timing or the amount of the original estimate of undiscounted cash flows. Changes due to the passage of time should first be incorporated into the carrying amount of the liability before adjusting for changes resulting from a revision of either the timing or the amount of estimated cash flows. Changes in the liability due to the passage of time should be measured by applying an interest method of allocation to the liability at the beginning of the period using the credit-adjusted risk-free interest rate that existed when the liability was initially measured. The amount of the change increases the carrying amount of the liability and the expense should be shown as an operating expense in the income statement (called *accretion expense*).

Changes resulting from revisions to the amount and/or timing of the original estimate of undiscounted cash flows should be recognized as an increase or decrease in the carrying amount of the liability and the related asset retirement cost capitalized. Upward revisions should be discounted using the current credit-adjusted risk-free rate. Downward revisions should be discounted using the credit-adjusted risk-free rate that existed when the original liability was recognized. When asset retirement costs change as a result of revisions to estimated cash flows, an entity should adjust the amount of asset retirement cost allocated to expense in the period of change if the change affects that period only, or in the period of change and future periods if the change affects more than one period.

Environmental Obligations

Companies are subject to a wide range of federal, state, and local environmental laws and regulations. The accrual for environmental remediation liabilities should include incremental direct costs of the remediation effort and costs of compensation and benefits for employees to the extent an employee is expected to devote time directly to the remediation effort.

The measurement of the liability should include (a) the entity's allocable share of the liability for a specific site and (b) the entity's share of amounts related to the site that will not be paid by other potentially responsible parties or the government. The measurement of the liability should be based on the following:

1. Enacted laws and existing regulations and policies

2. Remediation technology that is expected to be approved to complete the remediation effort

3. The reporting entity's estimates of what it will cost to perform all elements of the remediation effort when they are expected to be performed

The measurement may be discounted to reflect the time value of money if the aggregate amount of the obligation and the amount and timing of cash payments for the obligation are fixed or reliably determinable.

Accounting Literature

FASB Accounting Standards Codification Topic	*Pre-Codification Accounting Literature*
410, *Asset Retirement and Environmental Obligations*	FAS-5, *Accounting for Contingencies*
	FAS-143, *Accounting for Asset Retirement Obligations*
	EITF 89-13, *Accounting for the Cost of Asbestos Removal*

FASB Accounting Standards Codification Topic	*Pre-Codification Accounting Literature*
	EITF 02-6, *Classification in the Statement of Cash Flows of Payment Made to Settle an Asset Retirement Obligation within the Scope of FASB Statement No. 143*
	SOP 96-1, *Environmental Remediation Liabilities*

DISCLOSURE AND KEY PRESENTATION REQUIREMENTS

Asset Retirement Obligations

1. Accretion expense should be classified as an operating item in the income statement. (ASC 410-20-45-1) (FAS-143, par. 14)

2. Cash payments made to settle an asset retirement obligation should be classified as cash outflow for operating activities in the statement of cash flows. (ASC 410-20-45-2 and 45-3) (EITF 02-6)

3. The following items should be disclosed about an entity's asset retirement obligations (ASC 410-20-50-1) (FAS-143, par. 22):

   a. A general description of the asset retirement obligations and the associated long-lived assets.

   b. The fair value of assets legally restricted for purposes of settling asset retirement obligations.

   c. A reconciliation of the beginning and ending aggregate carrying amount of asset retirement obligations showing separately the changes attributable to the following components, whenever there is a significant change in any of these components during the reporting period:

      (1) Liabilities incurred in the current period.

      (2) Liabilities settled in the current period.

      (3) Accretion expense.

      (4) Revisions in estimated cash flows.

4. If the fair value of an asset retirement obligation cannot be reasonably estimated, that fact and the reasons for it should be disclosed. (ASC 410-20-50-2) (FAS-143, par. 22)

Environmental Obligations

1. If an entity has offset environmental remediation liabilities and related receivables and potential recoveries, and reported the net amount in its financial statements, the entity should have met all the requisite conditions in paragraph 210-20-45-1 (FIN-39, par. 5) for offset. (ASC 410-30-45-2) (SOP 96-1, par. 146) (*Note:* It would be rare, if ever, that an entity would meet all of those conditions.)

2. The related costs and recoveries relating to environmental remediation obligations should be excluded from extraordinary items (because the incurrence of environmental remediation obligations is *not* an event that is unusual in nature). (ASC 410-30-45-3) (SOP 96-1, par. 148)

3. Environmental remediation costs should be charged against operations and reported as a component of operating income in income statements that classify items as operating or nonoperating. (ASC 410-30-45-4) (SOP 96-1, par. 149)

4. Credits arising from recoveries of environmental losses from other parties should be reflected in the same income statement line item as the environmental remediation-related charges. (ASC 410-30-45-4) (SOP 96-1, par. 149)

5. Any earnings on assets that are reflected on the entity's financial statements, and are earmarked for funding its environmental liabilities, should be reported as investment income. (ASC 410-30-45-4) (SOP 96-1, par. 149)

6. Environmental remediation-related expenses and related recoveries attributable to discontinued operations that were accounted for as such, in accordance with ASC Subtopic 205-20, *Presentation of Financial Statements-Discontinued Operations* (APB-30, *Reporting the Results of Operations—Reporting the Effects of Disposal of a Segment of a Business, and Extraordinary, Unusual, and Infrequently Occurring Events and Transactions*), should be classified as discontinued operations. (ASC 410-30-45-5) (SOP 96-1, par. 150)

7. Asbestos treatment costs that are charged to expense should be excluded from extraordinary items. (ASC 410-30-45-6) (EITF 89-13)

8. The following information should be disclosed about recorded accruals for environmental remediation obligations, loss contingencies, and related assets for third-party recoveries (ASC 410-30-50-4 and 50-7) (SOP 96-1, pars. 152 and 161):

   a. Whether the accrual for environmental remediation liabilities is measured on a discounted basis.

    b. If any portion of the accrued obligation is discounted, the undiscounted amount of the obligation, and the discount rate used in the present-value determinations.

9. The following *optional* disclosures are for entities that elect to disclose such items: (ASC 410-30-50-8 through 50-12 and 410-30-50-17) (SOP 96-1, pars. 153, 158, 163, 166, 170 and 172) (*Note*: Entities are *encouraged*, but not required, to disclose this information.):

    a. The event, situation, or set of circumstances that generally triggers recognition of loss contingencies that arise out of the entity's environmental remediation-related obligations (e.g., during or upon completion of the feasibility study).

    b. The entity's policy concerning the timing of recognition of recoveries.

    c. The estimated time frame of disbursements for recorded amounts if expenditures are expected to continue over the long term.

    d. The estimated time frame for realization of recognized probable recoveries, if realization is not expected in the near term.

    e. If an estimate of the probable or reasonably possible loss or range of loss cannot be made, the reasons why it cannot be made.

    f. If information about the reasonably possible loss or the recognized and additional reasonably possible loss for an environmental remediation obligation related to an individual site is relevant to an understanding of the financial position, cash flows, or results of operations of the entity, the following with respect to the site:

        (1) The total amount accrued for the site.

        (2) The nature of any reasonably possible loss contingency or additional loss, and an estimate of the possible loss or the fact that an estimate cannot be made and the reasons why it cannot be made.

        (3) Whether other potentially responsible parties are involved and the entity's estimated share of the obligation.

        (4) The status of regulatory proceedings.

        (5) The estimated time frame for resolution of the contingency.

    g. The estimated time frame for resolution of the uncertainty as to the amount of the loss.

    h. The amount of environmental remediation costs recognized in the income statement in the following detail:

        (1) The amount recognized for environmental remediation loss contingencies in each period.

        (2) The amount of any recovery from third parties that is credited to environmental remediation costs in each period.

        (3) The income statement caption in which environmental remediation costs and credits are included.

    i. The general applicability and impact of environmental laws and regulations upon the entity's business and how the existence of such laws and regulations may give rise to loss contingencies for future environmental remediation.

10. The required disclosures related to loss contingencies should be made in accordance with ASC Subtopic 450-20, *Contingencies–Loss Contingencies* (FAS-5, *Accounting for Contingencies*). (ASC 410-30-50-13 through 50-16) (SOP 96-1, pars. 168 and 171). See Chapter 30, "ASC Topic 450: Contingencies".

EXAMPLES OF FINANCIAL STATEMENT DISCLOSURES

The following sample disclosures are available on the accompanying disc.

Asset Retirement Obligations

Example 1: Reconciliation of Beginning and Ending Carrying Amounts of Asset Retirement Obligations

The Company has recognized asset retirement obligations for the following activities: (1) demolition and remediation activities at manufacturing sites in the United States and Germany, and (2) obligations to remove leasehold improvements at the conclusion of the Company's facility lease.

Asset retirement obligations are recorded in the period in which they are incurred and reasonably estimable, including those obligations for which the timing method of settlement are conditional on a future event that may or may not be within the control of the Company. Retirement of assets may involve efforts such as removal of leasehold improvements, contractually required demolition, and other related activities, depending on the nature and location of the assets. In identifying asset retirement obligations, the Company considers identification of legally enforceable obligations, changes in existing law, estimates of potential settlement dates, and the calculation of an appropriate discount rate to be used in calculating the fair value of the obligations. For those assets where a range of potential settlement dates may be reasonably estimated, obligations are recorded. The Company routinely reviews and reassesses its estimates to determine if an adjustment to the value of the asset retirement obligation is required.

The aggregate carrying amount of asset retirement obligations recognized by the Company was $11,010,000 at December 31, 20X2, and $9,200,000 at December 31, 20X1. The following table shows changes in the aggregate carrying amount of the Company's asset retirement obligations for the year ended December 31, 20X2:

Balance, January 1, 20X2	$ 9,200,000
Additional accruals	2,500,000
Liabilities settled	(1,250,000)
Accretion expense	475,000
Revisions in estimated cash flows	85,000
Balance, December 31, 20X2	$ 11,010,000

Example 2: Fair Value of an Asset Retirement Obligation Cannot Be Reasonably Estimated

Asset retirement obligations generally apply to legal obligations associated with the retirement of a tangible long-lived asset that result from the acquisition, construction or development and the normal operation of a long-lived asset. The Company assesses asset retirement obligations on a periodic basis. If a reasonable estimate of fair value can be made, the fair value of a liability for an asset retirement obligation is recognized in the period in which it is incurred or a change in estimate occurs.

Certain of the Company's production facilities contain asbestos that would have to be removed if such facilities were to be demolished or undergo a major renovation and certain of the Company's production facilities utilize wastewater ponds that would require closure activities should the ponds' use be discontinued. The Company cannot reasonably estimate the fair value of the liability for asbestos removal or wastewater pond closure at its production facilities and, accordingly, has not recorded an asset retirement obligation for these matters.

Environmental Obligations

Example 3: Company Has Been Designated as a Potentially Responsible Party and Accrued Estimated Liability on an Undiscounted Basis

The Company has been designated as a potentially responsible party (PRP) by federal and state agencies with respect to certain sites with which the Company may have had direct or indirect involvement. Such designations are made regardless of the extent of the Company's involvement. These claims are in various stages of administrative or judicial proceedings and include demands for recovery of past governmental costs and for future investigations and remedial actions. In many cases, the dollar amounts of the claims have not been specified and, with respect to a number of the PRP claims, have been asserted against a number of other entities for the same cost recovery or other relief as was asserted against the Company. The Company accrues costs associated with environmental matters, on an undiscounted basis, when they become probable and reasonably estimable. As of December 31, 20X2, and December 31, 20X1, the Company has accrued $1,900,000 and $1,600,000, respectively, which represents its current estimate of the probable cleanup liabilities, including remediation and legal costs. This accrual does not reflect any possible future insurance recoveries but does reflect a reasonable estimate of cost-sharing at multiparty sites.

Although the Company's probable liabilities have been accrued for currently, hazardous substance cleanup expenditures generally are paid over an extended period of time, in some cases possibly more than 30 years. Annual cleanup expenditures during 20X2 and 20X1 were approximately $625,000 and $450,000, respectively.

Example 4: Accrual for Estimated Environmental Remediation Costs Has Been Discounted

The Company is involved in environmental remediation and ongoing compliance at several sites. At December 31, 20X2, the Company estimated, based on engineering studies, total remediation and ongoing monitoring costs to be made in the future to be approximately $6,500,000, including the effects of inflation. Accordingly, the Company recorded a liability of approximately $4,000,000, which represents the net present value of the estimated future costs discounted at 6%. This is management's best estimate of these liabilities, although possible actual costs could range up to 50% higher. The Company has not anticipated any third-party payments in arriving at these estimates.

Example 5: Company Has Not Been Designated as a Potentially Responsible Party but Accrued the Highest Amount in the Range of Potential Loss Because Likelihood of Loss Is Probable

As part of its environmental management program, the Company is involved in various environmental remediation activities. As sites are identified and assessed in this program, the Company determines potential environmental liability. Factors considered in assessing liability include, among others, the following: whether the Company had been designated as a potentially responsible party, the number of other potentially responsible parties designated at the site, the stage of the proceedings, and available environmental technology. As of December 31, 20X2, the Company had identified three sites requiring further investigation. However, the Company has not been designated as a potentially responsible party at any site.

Management has assessed the likelihood that a loss has been incurred at one of its sites as probable and, based on findings included in remediation reports and discussions with legal counsel, estimated the potential loss at December 31, 20X2, to range from $1,500,000 to $2,500,000. As of December 31, 20X2, $2,500,000 had been accrued and is included with "Other accrued liabilities" in the Consolidated Balance Sheets. Although the Company may have a right of contribution or reimbursement under insurance policies, amounts recoverable from other entities with respect to a particular site are not considered until recoveries are deemed probable. No assets for potential recoveries were established as of December 31, 20X2.

Example 6: Company Has Not Been Designated as a Potentially Responsible Party but Accrued the Lowest Amount in the Range of Potential Loss Because Likelihood of Loss Is More Likely Than Remote but Not Probable

The Company assesses reasonably possible environmental liability relating to environmental remediation and ongoing compliance at several sites. Such liability is not probable but is more likely than remote. As of December 31, 20X2, while the Company has not been designated as a potentially responsible party at any site, the amount of environmental liability identified that is reasonably possible is in the range of $2,000,000 to $5,500,000. As of December 31, 20X2, the Company accrued $2,000,000 with respect to potential environmental liability. The Company does not expect to incur liabilities at the higher end of the range, based on the limited information currently available.

Example 7: Environmental Matter May Result in Increased Operating and Capital Costs to the Company

In 20X2, the State of California made a determination that some of the cement materials stored at the Company's Riverside plant are a Type I waste and requested that the Company apply for a formal permit for an on-site landfill. The Company understands that similar notices were sent to other cement manufacturers in the State. The Company is protesting this determination through legal channels and has received a stay to allow it to demonstrate that current management practices pose no threat to the environment. The Company believes that the State's determination ultimately will be reversed or the Company will receive the needed permit or other adequate relief, such as an agreed order requiring certain additional waste management procedures that are less stringent than those generally required for Type I wastes. If the Company is not successful in this regard, however, like other cement producers in the State, the Riverside plant could incur substantially increased operating and capital costs.

Example 8: Accruals for Estimated Future Costs Relate to Divested Operations and Locations No Longer in Operation

The accompanying Consolidated Balance Sheets include accruals for the estimated future costs associated with certain environmental remediation activities related to the past use or disposal of hazardous materials. Substantially all such costs relate to divested operations and to facilities or locations that are no longer in operation. Due to a number of uncertainties, including uncertainty of timing, the scope of remediation, future technology, regulatory changes, and other factors, the ultimate remediation costs may exceed the amounts estimated. However, in the opinion of management, such additional costs are not expected to be material relative to consolidated liquidity, financial position, or future results of operations.

CHAPTER 27
ASC TOPIC 420: EXIT OR DISPOSAL COST OBLIGATIONS

CONTENTS

EXECUTIVE SUMMARY

Exit or Disposal Cost Obligations

A liability for costs associated with exit or disposal activities should be recognized when incurred and measured at its fair value (with limited exceptions). An entity's commitment to an exit or disposal plan, in and of itself, does not create a present obligation that meets the definition of a liability. Examples of costs associated with exit or disposal activities include:

- Contract termination costs (excluding capital leases)
- Costs to consolidate or close facilities
- Costs to relocate employees
- One-time termination benefits provided to terminate employees

Costs associated with an exit or disposal activity that does not involve a discontinued operation should be included in income from continuing operations before taxes in the income statement. If a subtotal "Income from Operations" is presented, it should include the amounts of those costs. Costs associated with an exit or disposal activity involving discontinued operations should be included in the results of discontinued operations.

Accounting Literature

FASB Accounting Standards Codification Topic	Pre-Codification Accounting Literature
420, *Exit or Disposal Cost Obligations*	FAS-146, *Accounting for Costs Associated with Exit or Disposal Activities*

DISCLOSURE AND KEY PRESENTATION REQUIREMENTS

1. The cumulative effect of a change resulting from a revision to either the timing or the amount of estimated cash flows should be reported in the same line item(s) in the income statement used when the related costs were recognized initially in the period of change. (ASC 420-10-45-1) (FAS-146, par. 6)

2. Costs associated with an exit or disposal activity involving a discontinued operation should be included within the results of discontinued operations in accordance with ASC Section 205-20-45, *Presentation of Financial Statements—Discontinued Operations—Other Presentation Matters* (APB-30, *Reporting the Results of Operations—Reporting the Effects of Disposal of a Segment of a Business, and Extraordinary, Unusual, and Infrequently Occurring Events and Transactions*). (ASC 420-10-45-2) (FAS-146, par. B53). See Chapter 2, "ASC Topic 205: Presentation of Financial Statements."

3. Costs associated with an exit or disposal activity that does not involve a discontinued operation should be included in income from continuing operations before income taxes in the income statement. (ASC 420-10-45-3) (FAS-146, par. B53) (*Note:* Separate presentation of exit and disposal costs in the income statement is not prohibited. However, it is prohibited to present exit and disposal costs in the income statement net of income taxes or in any manner that implies they are similar to an extraordinary item. If a subtotal such as income from operations is presented, it should include the amounts of those costs.)

4. Accretion expense should *not* be considered interest cost for purposes of classification in the income statement. (ASC 420-10-45-5) (FAS-146, par. 6)

5. The following disclosures should be made in the period in which an exit or disposal activity is initiated and any subsequent period until the activity is completed (ASC 420-10-50-1) (FAS-146, par. 20):

    a. A description of the exit or disposal activity, including the facts and circumstances leading to the expected activity and the expected completion date.

    b. For each major type of cost associated with the activity (e.g., one-time employee termination benefits, contract termination costs, and other associated costs):

        (1) The total amount expected to be incurred in connection with the activity.

        (2) The amount incurred in the period.

        (3) The cumulative amount incurred to date.

        (4) A reconciliation of the beginning and ending liability balances showing separately the changes during the period attributable to costs incurred and charged to expense, costs paid or otherwise settled, and any adjustments to the liability with an explanation of the reason(s) why.

    c. The line item(s) in the income statement in which the costs in item (b) above are aggregated.

    d. For each reportable segment, as defined in ASC Subtopic 280-10, *Segment Reporting—Overall* (FAS-131, *Disclosures about Segments of an Enterprise and Related Information*):

        (1) The total amount of costs expected to be incurred in connection with the activity.

        (2) The amount incurred in the period.

        (3) The cumulative amount incurred to date, net of any adjustments to the liability with an explanation of the reason(s) why.

    e. If a liability for a cost associated with the activity is not recognized because fair value cannot be reasonably estimated, that fact and the reasons why.

EXAMPLES OF FINANCIAL STATEMENT DISCLOSURES

The following sample disclosures are available on the accompanying disc.

Example 1: Various Costs Associated with Exit or Disposal Activities

As a result of the Company's change in strategy and due to a difficult business environment, in July 20X1 the Company announced plans to restructure its operations to rationalize, integrate and align the resources of the Company. This restructuring program includes workforce reductions, closure of excess facilities, and other charges. The expected completion date is September 20X3.

The restructuring program resulted in costs incurred primarily for (1) workforce reduction of approximately 350 employees across certain business functions and operating units and (2) abandoned or excess facilities relating to lease terminations and non-cancelable lease costs. To determine the lease loss, which is the Company's loss after its cost recovery efforts from subleasing a building, certain estimates were made related to the (1) time period over which the relevant building would remain vacant, (2) sublease terms, and (3) sublease rates, including common area charges. If market rates continue to decrease in these markets or if it takes longer than expected to sublease these facilities, the actual loss could exceed this estimate.

A summary of the restructuring and other costs recognized for the years ended December 31, 20X2, and December 31, 20X1, are as follows:

	Workforce Reduction	Excess Facilities	Other Exit Costs	Total
Amounts expected to be incurred	$2,950,000	$1,875,000	$200,000	$5,025,000
Amounts incurred in: 20X1	$1,950,000	$1,350,000	$ —	$3,300,000
20X2	1,000,000	225,000	200,000	1,425,000
Cumulative amount incurred as of December 31, 20X2	$2,950,000	$1,575,000	$200,000	$4,725,000

The Company expects to incur additional charges of approximately $300,000 during the first half of 20X3, as a result of additional facilities that the Company is planning to vacate as well as other restructuring charges.

At December 31, 20X2, and December 31, 20X1, the accrued liability associated with the restructuring and other related charges consisted of the following:

	Workforce Reduction	Excess Facilities	Other Exit Costs	Total
20X1:				
Charges	$1,950,000	$ 1,350,000	$ -0-	$3,300,000
Payments	(725,000)	(475,000)	-0-	(1,200,000)

	Workforce Reduction	Excess Facilities	Other Exit Costs	Total
Accrued liability at December 31, 20X1	1,225,000	875,000	-0-	$2,100,000
20X2:				
Charges	1,000,000	225,000	200,000	1,425,000
Payments	(870,000)	(630,000)	(200,000)	(1,700,000)
Adjustment	-0-	(50,000)	-0-	(50,000)
Accrued liability at December 31, 20X2	$1,355,000	$ 420,000	$ -0-	$1,775,000

For 20X2, the adjustment of $50,000 to the accrued liability was the result of the Company successfully settling certain contingencies relating to one of its facility leases.

The remaining accrual as of December 31, 20X2, of $1,775,000 consists of $1,600,000 that is expected to be paid during the year ending December 31, 20X3, and $175,000, expected to be paid through various dates by March 31, 20X6.

The restructuring and other related charges are included in the line item "Special charges" in the income statement. The workforce reduction charges relate to the telecommunications business segment. Excess facilities charges and other exit costs relate to the semiconductor segment.

Example 2: One-Time Termination Benefits

In December 20X2, the Company decided to cease operations at one of its manufacturing plants in Victorville, California, primarily because that operation never generated a profit. In connection with this activity, the Company determined that it no longer needs the 100 employees who currently work in that location. The Company notified the employees that they will be terminated in 90 days. Each employee will receive as a termination benefit a cash payment of $5,000, which will be paid at the date an employee ceases rendering service during the 90-day period. The Company recognized a liability of $500,000 in December 20X2, which approximates fair value. The entire amount is outstanding at December 31, 20X2. Because of the short discount period, the liability amount of $500,000 recognized is not materially different from its fair value.

The costs are included in the line item "Termination benefits" in the income statement for the year ended December 31, 20X2, and relate to the Company's telecommunications segment.

Example 3: Abandoned Leased Facilities

In June 20X2, the Company abandoned its administrative office facilities in Laguna Hills and Newport Beach, CA. Although the Company remains obligated under the terms of these leases for the rent and other costs associated with these leases, the Company made the decision to cease using these spaces on June 30, 20X2, and has no foreseeable plans to occupy them in the future. Therefore, the Company recorded a charge to earnings of approximately $575,000 to recognize the costs of exiting the space. The liability is equal to the total amount of rent and other direct costs for the period of time space is expected to remain unoccupied plus the present value of the amount by which the rent paid by the Company to the landlord exceeds any rent paid to the Company by a tenant under a sublease over the remainder of the lease terms, which expire in March 20X8 for Laguna Hills, CA, and April 20X9 for Newport Beach, CA.

CHAPTER 28
ASC TOPIC 430: DEFERRED REVENUE

The disclosure and key presentation requirements for revenue recognition are discussed in detail in ASC Topic 605, *Revenue Recognition*. For further guidance, see Chapter 35, "ASC Topic 605: Revenue Recognition."

CHAPTER 29
ASC TOPIC 440: COMMITMENTS

CONTENTS

EXECUTIVE SUMMARY

Commitments

Commitments typically involve uncompleted transactions or uncertainties that should be disclosed because of their effect on an entity's financial statements. Commitments include long-term contractual obligations with suppliers or customers for future purchases or sales at specified prices and sometimes at specified levels. The terms of commitments should be disclosed and a provision should be made in the financial statements for any material losses expected to be sustained. All of the following situations should be disclosed in the financial statements:

- Obligations to transfer funds in the future for fixed or minimum amounts or quantities of goods or services at fixed or minimum prices (i.e., unconditional purchase obligations).

- Unused letters of credit.

- Long-term leases (see Chapter 52, "ASC Topic 840: Leases").

- Assets pledged as security for loans.

- Pension plans (see Chapter 39, "ASC Topic 715: Compensation—Retirement Benefits").

- The existence of cumulative preferred stock dividends in arrears.

- Commitments, including: (1) a commitment for plant acquisition, and (2) an obligation to reduce debts, maintain working capital, or restrict dividends.

Accounting Literature

FASB Accounting Standards Codification Topic	*Pre-Codification Accounting Literature*
440, *Commitments*	FAS-5, *Accounting for Contingencies*
	FAS-47, *Disclosure of Long-Term Obligations*
	FAS-146, *Accounting for Costs Associated with Exit or Disposal Activities*

DISCLOSURE AND KEY PRESENTATION REQUIREMENTS

1. Disclosures should be made of the following (ASC 440-10-50-1) (FAS-5, par. 19):

    a. Unused letters of credit.

    b. Long-term leases (see Chapter 52, "ASC Topic 840: Leases").

    c. Assets pledged as security for loans.

    d. Pension plans (see Chapter 39, "ASC Topic 715: Compensation—Retirement Benefits").

    e. The existence of cumulative preferred stock dividends in arrears.

    f. Commitments, including the following:

    (1) Commitments for plant acquisition.

      (2)   Obligations to reduce debts.

      (3)   Obligations to maintain working capital.

      (4)   Obligations to restrict dividends.

2.   For unconditional purchase obligations (those meeting the criteria in ASC paragraph 440-10-50-2, [FAS-47, par. 6]) that have *not* been recognized on the entity's balance sheet, the following disclosures should be made (ASC 440-10-50-2, 50-4, and 50-5) (FAS-47, pars. 6–8):

    a.   The nature and term of the obligation.

    b.   The amount of the fixed and determinable portion of the obligation as of the date of the latest balance sheet presented, in the aggregate and, if determinable, for each of the five succeeding fiscal years.

    c.   The nature of any variable components of the obligation.

    d.   The amounts purchased under the obligation (e.g., the "take-or-pay" or "throughput contract") for each period for which an income statement is presented.

    e.   The amount of imputed interest necessary to reduce the unconditional purchase obligation to its present value (this is encouraged but not required).

3.   For unconditional purchase obligations (those meeting the criteria in ASC paragraph 440-10-50-2 [FAS-47, par. 6]) that have been recognized on the entity's balance sheet, the aggregate amount of payments for such unconditional obligations should be disclosed for each of the five years following the date of the latest balance sheet presented. (ASC 440-10-50-2 and 50-6) (FAS-146, pars. 6 and 10)

4.   For an unconditional purchase obligation that also meets the definition of a derivative instrument and is accounted for as a derivative instrument at fair value in the balance sheet, the disclosure requirements of ASC Topic 815 (FAS-133) should be addressed. See Chapter 47, "Topic 815: Derivatives and Hedging."

EXAMPLES OF FINANCIAL STATEMENT DISCLOSURES

The following sample disclosures are available on the accompanying disc. For examples of disclosures of commitments under pension plans, see Chapter 39, "ASC Topic 715: Compensation—Retirement Benefits." For examples of disclosures of lease commitments in connection with lease arrangements, see Chapter 52, "ASC Topic 840, Leases."

General

Example 1: Royalty Commitments

The Company has entered into various license agreements whereby the Company may use certain characters and properties in conjunction with its products. Such license agreements call for royalties to be paid at 5% to 10% of net sales with minimum guarantees and advance payments. Additionally, under one such license, the Company has committed to spend 11% of related net sales, not to exceed $2,000,000, on advertising per year. Royalty expense under these agreements was $1,000,000 in 20X2 and $900,000 in 20X1. Future annual minimum royalty commitments as of December 31, 20X2, are as follows:

20X3	$ 1,200,000
20X4	1,500,000
20X5	1,800,000
20X6	2,500,000
20X7	3,000,000
Thereafter	9,000,000
	$19,000,000

Example 2: Milestone Payment Due upon First Product Approval

The Company is obligated to make a milestone payment to Intexts Corp. of $1,200,000 upon the approval of its first product by the FDA or the governing health authority of any other country. This fee can be offset against future royalty payments. In addition, the Company is obligated to pay royalties on its net sales and a percentage of all revenues received from sublicenses relating to the XTS gene therapy technology. Failure to comply with the terms of the License Agreement with Intexts Corp. may cause its termination, which would have a materially adverse effect on the Company.

Example 3: License Fee Commitments under License Agreement

The Company entered into an agreement to license software to be incorporated into its data conferencing products. Under the agreement, the Company is obligated to pay annual minimum license fees, ranging from $150,000 to $350,000, through the year 20X6 and the Company may cancel the agreement at any time, provided the Company has paid a minimum of $1,000,000 in connection with the agreement. As of December 31, 20X2, the Company had paid $475,000 of the minimum license fees. In February 20X3, the Company re-negotiated the terms of the contract and paid a lump sum figure of $195,000. Under the terms of this new contract, the Company has no further obligation regarding any fees associated with this licensed software.

Example 4: Purchase Contracts

In connection with the EFTX transaction in January 20X1, EFTX and the Company entered into a manufacturing agreement whereby the Company committed to purchase minimum amounts of goods and services used in its normal operations during the first 48 months after the transaction. Future annual minimum purchases remaining under the agreement are $19 million and $22 million for 20X3 and 20X4, respectively. During 20X2 and 20X1, the Company's total purchases under the agreement were $17 million and $13 million, respectively.

Example 5: Firm Price Commitment Manufacturing and Supply Agreement

The Company entered into a firm price commitment manufacturing and supply agreement in connection with the acquisition of the F&D trademarks purchased in 20X2. The agreement was entered into with the seller of the trademarks to obtain from the seller tools and other manufacturing resources of the seller for the manufacture of products, upon request by the Company. The manufacturing and supply agreement has created a firm commitment by the Company for a minimum of $4,500,000. A minimum payment of $500,000 on the agreement was due on December 31, 20X2, with three additional payments of $400,000 and five additional payments of $560,000 to follow thereafter, through December 31, 20X6, which is also the date on which the agreement terminates.

Example 6: Commitment to Reimburse Supplier for Certain Capital Additions in Connection with Production Agreements

The Company has production agreements, which expire in May 20X9, with Elexix, Ltd. to produce certain specialized products for the Company. The agreements require the Company to reimburse Elexix, Ltd. over the terms of the agreements for specified facility additions, not to exceed $2,500,000, required to manufacture the products. Elexix, Ltd. retains title to the facility additions. Furthermore, if the Company terminates the agreements, it is obligated to pay Elexix, Ltd. for the remaining unreimbursed facility additions. The Company recorded expense of $675,000 and $620,000 under the agreements in 20X2 and 20X1, respectively. The remaining unreimbursed facility additions totaled $710,000 at December 31, 20X2.

Example 7: Commitments to Provide Protection Against Price Reductions

The Company has agreements with distributor customers that, under certain conditions, allow for returns of overstocked inventory and provide protection against price reductions initiated by the Company. Allowances for these commitments are included in the Consolidated Balance Sheets as reductions in trade accounts receivable. The Company adjusts sales to distributors through the use of allowance accounts based on historical experience. During 20X2 and 20X1, provisions for these commitments were recorded in the amounts of $3,700,000 and $3,200,000, respectively.

Example 8: Commitment to Sell Inventory at a Fixed Price

At December 31, 20X2, the Company has an agreement with a customer to sell a specified minimum number of units of its Eglaze adhesive products over the next 30 months at a fixed price of $10,200,000. The fixed price is equal to approximately 5% above the aggregate selling price at current market prices.

Example 9: Obligations to Maintain Working Capital and Financial Ratios, Restrict Dividends and Capital Expenditures, and Borrow Money

The Company has a $10 million revolving bank line of credit that expires in August 20X3. Advances under the line of credit bear interest at the bank's prime rate (8.5% at December 31, 20X2) and are secured by inventories and accounts receivable. Under the terms of the line of credit agreement, the Company is required to maintain certain minimum working capital, net worth, profitability levels, and other specific financial ratios. In addition, the agreement prohibits the payment of cash dividends and contains certain restrictions on the Company's ability to borrow money or purchase assets or interests in other entities without the prior written consent of the bank. There were no borrowings under the line of credit at December 31, 20X2.

Example 10: Commitment to Pay Certain Termination Benefits under Employment Agreements

As of December 31, 20X2, the Company had entered into employment agreements with four employees. Under each of the four agreements, in the event employment is terminated (other than voluntarily by the employee or by the Company for cause or upon the death of the employee), the Company is committed to pay certain benefits, including specified monthly severance of not more than $25,000 per month. The benefits are to be paid from the date of termination through May 20X6.

Example 11: Future Commitment for Minimum Salary Levels under Employment Contracts

The Company has employment agreements with its executive officers, the terms of which expire at various times through January 20X3. Such agreements, which have been revised from time to time, provide for minimum salary levels, adjusted annually for cost-of-living changes, as well as for incentive bonuses that are payable if specified management goals are attained. The aggregate commitment for future salaries at December 31, 20X2, excluding bonuses, was approximately $3,500,000.

Example 12: Commitments for Construction and Acquisition of Property and Equipment

At December 31, 20X2, the Company had commitments of approximately $12,000,000 for construction and acquisition of property and equipment, all of which are expected to be incurred in 20X3. Also, in connection with an expansion at the Company's manufacturing facility in Boise, Idaho, capital grants from the State totaling $2,500,000 have been approved, $1,000,000 of which had not been received as of December 31, 20X2, and are contingent upon the Company spending approximately $6,000,000 for plant and equipment in Boise.

Example 13: Commitment to Maintain Liquid Funds to Secure an Obligation

The Company holds $400,000 in short-term U.S. government money market funds to secure a continuing contractual payment obligation of the Company arising from its acquisition of Axis, Ltd. As a result of this agreement, the Company has classified such funds and the interest earned thereon, totaling $416,000 at December 31, 20X2, as "Restricted investments" under noncurrent assets on the accompanying Consolidated Balance Sheets.

Example 14: Commitment to Purchase Capital Stock under Stock Redemption Agreements

The Company has stock redemption agreements with two major stockholders for the purchase of a portion of the common stock from their estates at market value upon death. The Company's commitment under such arrangements, totaling $8,500,000 at December 31, 20X2, is funded by life insurance policies owned by the Company.

Example 15: Commitment to Complete Business Acquisition

In December 20X2, the Company announced that it had entered into a definitive agreement to acquire Akcent, Inc., whose products include remote access networking solutions for the small to medium enterprise market segment. The Company expects that the total cash required to complete the transaction will be approximately $13 million, which will be provided from borrowings on the Company's line of credit.

Example 16: Letters of Credit—Inventory

At December 31, 20X2, and December 31, 20X1, the Company has outstanding irrevocable letters of credit in the amount of $1,800,000 and $700,000, respectively. These letters of credit, which have terms from two months to one year, collateralize the Company's obligations to third parties for the purchase of inventory. The fair value of these letters of credit approximates contract values based on the nature of the fee arrangements with the issuing banks.

Example 17: Letters of Credit—Contracts and Debt Obligations

At December 31, 20X2, standby letters of credit of approximately $2,400,000 have been issued under an agreement, expiring September 30, 20X3. The letters are being maintained as security for performance and advances received on long-term contracts and as security for debt service payments under industrial revenue bond loan agreements. The agreement provides a maximum commitment for letters of credit of $3,500,000 and requires an annual commitment fee of $25,000.

Example 18: Letters of Credit—Self-Insurance Program

The Company has letters of credit of $22,000,000 outstanding at December 31, 20X2. The letters are maintained to back the Company's self-insurance program.

Example 19: Letters of Credit—Operating Lease, the Terms of Which Have Not Been Finalized

At December 31, 20X2, the Company is committed to enter into an operating lease for manufacturing and distribution facilities, the terms of which have not been finalized. In connection with this commitment, during 20X2, the Company issued on its behalf irrevocable standby letters of credit in the amount of $6,500,000. Upon execution of the lease, the letters of credit will be canceled.

Example 20: Bid and Performance Related Bonds

The Company has entered into bid and performance related bonds associated with various contracts. These contracts generally have terms ranging from two to five years. Performance related bonds generally have a term of twelve months. Bid bonds generally have a much shorter term. Potential payments due under these bonds are related to the Company's performance under the applicable contract. The total amount of bid and performance related bonds that were available and undrawn was $5,500,000, excluding restricted cash and cash equivalents of $3,150,000, at December 31, 20X2.

Example 21: Customer Financing

Pursuant to certain financing agreements, the Company is committed to provide future financing in connection with purchases of the Company's products and services. The unfunded commitments were $20,700,000 and $18,600,000 at December 31, 20X2 and December 31, 20X1, respectively. Commitments to extend future financing generally have conditions for funding, fixed expiration or termination dates, and specific interest rates and purposes. The Company attempts to limit its financing credit risk by utilizing an internal credit committee that actively monitors the Company's credit exposure.

Unconditional Purchase Obligations

Example 22: Unconditional Obligation under a Throughput Agreement—Includes Optional Disclosure of Present Value of Required Payments

To secure access to facilities to process high damping rubber compound, the Company has signed a processing agreement with BJ Rubber allowing the Company to submit 150,000 tons for processing annually for 15 years. Under the terms of the agreement, the Company may be required to advance funds against future processing charges if BJ Rubber is unable to meet its financial obligations. The aggregate amount of required payments at December 31, 20X2, is as follows:

20X3	$ 215,000
20X4	200,000
20X5	185,000
20X6	175,000
20X7	150,000

Thereafter	1,260,000
Total	2,185,000
Less: amount representing interest	(1,487,000)
Present value of required payments	$ 698,000

In addition, the Company is required to pay a proportional share of the variable operating expenses of the plant. The Company's total processing charges under the agreement for 20X2 and 20X1 were $289,000 and $266,000, respectively.

Example 23: Unconditional Obligation under Take-or-Pay Agreement—Includes Optional Disclosure of Present Value of Required Payments

To assure a long-term supply, the Company has contracted to purchase 20% of the production of microprocessors of Microteks, Inc. through the year 20X7 and to make minimum annual payments as follows, whether or not it is able to take delivery:

20X3	$ 5,000,000
20X4	5,000,000
20X5	4,500,000
20X6	4,500,000
20X7	4,000,000
Total	23,000,000
Less: amount representing interest	(10,125,000)
Present value of required payments	$12,875,000

In addition, the Company must reimburse Microteks, Inc. for a proportional share of its plant operating expenses. The Company's total purchases under the agreement were $5,769,000 and $5,432,000 in 20X2 and 20X1, respectively.

Example 24: Unconditional Purchase Obligation in Connection with Acquisition—Disclosure of Present Value of Minimum Payments Not Made (Present Value Disclosure Is Optional)

In connection with the EFTX acquisition in January 20X1, EFTX and the Company entered into a manufacturing agreement, whereby the Company committed to purchase minimum amounts of goods and services used in its normal operations during the first 48 months after the transaction. Future annual minimum purchases remaining under the agreement are $19 million and $22 million for 20X3 and 20X4, respectively. During 20X2 and 20X1, the Company's total purchases under the agreement were $17 million and $13 million, respectively.

CHAPTER 30
ASC TOPIC 450: CONTINGENCIES

CONTENTS

EXECUTIVE SUMMARY

Loss Contingencies

An estimated loss from a loss contingency should be accrued by a charge to income if both of the following conditions are met:

1. It is probable that, at the date of the financial statements, an asset has been impaired or a liability incurred.

2. The amount of loss can be reasonably estimated.

Disclosure is required for loss contingencies not meeting both those conditions if a reasonable possibility exists that a loss may have been incurred.

As a general rule, disclosing loss contingencies that have a remote possibility of materializing is not required.

Gain Contingencies

Gains from gain contingencies should *not* be credited to income because to do so might result in the recognition of income before it is realized. Gain contingencies, however, should be adequately disclosed in the notes to the financial statements, and care should be exercised in disclosing gain contingencies to avoid misleading implications as to the recognition of revenue prior to its realization.

Accounting Literature

FASB Accounting Standards Codification Topic	*Pre-Codification Accounting Literature*
450, *Contingencies*	FAS-5, *Accounting for Contingencies*
	SOP 94-6, *Disclosure of Certain Significant Risks and Uncertainties*

DISCLOSURE AND KEY PRESENTATION REQUIREMENTS

Loss Contingencies

1. If loss contingencies have been accrued:

    a. Consideration should be given to disclosing the nature and amount of the accrual for the financial statements not to be misleading. (ASC 450-20-50-1) (FAS-5, par. 9)

    b. The term "reserve" should *not* be used (as that term is limited to an amount of unidentified or unsegregated assets held or retained for a specific purpose). (ASC 450-20-50-1) (FAS-5, par. 9)

    c. If it is at least reasonably possible that the estimated liability will change in the near term due to one or more future confirming events and the effect of the change would be material to the financial statements, the following disclosures should be made (ASC 450-20-50-2; 275-10-50-8 and 50-9) (SOP 94-6, par. 27; FAS-5, pars. 11 and 14):

(1) The nature of the uncertainty.

(2) An indication that it is at least reasonably possible that a change in the estimated liability could occur in the near term.

(3) The factors that cause the estimate to be sensitive to change (this is encouraged but not required).

2. If no accrual is made for a loss contingency (because any of the conditions in ASC paragraph 450-20-25-2 [FAS-5, par. 8] are not met), or if an exposure to loss exists in excess of the amount accrued, the following disclosures should be made if there is at least a reasonable possibility that a loss or an additional loss may have been incurred (ASC 450-20-50-3 through 50-5) (FAS-5, pars. 10 and 59):

a. The nature of the contingency.

b. An estimate of the possible loss or range of loss or a statement that such an estimate cannot be made.

3. Adequate disclosures for unasserted claims or assessments should be made if it is considered probable that a claim will be asserted and there is a reasonable possibility that the outcome will be unfavorable. (ASC 450-20-50-6) (FAS-5, par. 10)

4. For losses arising after the date of an entity's financial statements but before those financial statements are issued or are available to be issued (ASC 450-20-50-9 and 50-10) (FAS-5, par. 11):

a. The following disclosures should be made (when it is necessary to keep the financial statements from being misleading) for unaccrued losses and loss contingencies:

(1) The nature of the loss or loss contingency.

(2) An estimate of the amount or range of loss, or possible loss, or a statement that such an estimate cannot be made.

b. If the amount of an asset impaired or liability incurred can be reasonably estimated, consideration should be given to supplementing the historical financial statements with pro forma financial data giving effect to the loss as if it had occurred at the date of the financial statements. (*Note:* It may be desirable to present pro forma statements, usually a balance sheet only, in columnar form on the face of the historical financial statements.)

Gain Contingencies

1. Contingencies that might result in gains should be adequately disclosed but not reflected in the financial statements since to do so might be to recognize revenue before its realization. (ASC 450-30-50-1) (FAS-5, par. 17) (*Note:* Care should be exercised to avoid misleading implications about the likelihood of realization.)

EXAMPLES OF FINANCIAL STATEMENT DISCLOSURES

 The following sample disclosures are available on the accompanying disc.

Loss Contingencies

Example 1: General Accounting Policy for Contingencies Disclosed as Part of the Accounting Policies Note to the Financial Statements

Certain conditions may exist as of the date the financial statements are issued, which may result in a loss to the Company but which will only be resolved when one or more future events occur or fail to occur. The Company's management and its legal counsel assess such contingent liabilities, and such assessment inherently involves an exercise of judgment. In assessing loss contingencies related to legal proceedings that are pending against the Company or unasserted claims that may result in such proceedings, the Company's legal counsel evaluates the perceived merits of any legal proceedings or unasserted claims as well as the perceived merits of the amount of relief sought or expected to be sought therein.

If the assessment of a contingency indicates that it is probable that a material loss has been incurred and the amount of the liability can be estimated, then the estimated liability would be accrued in the Company's financial statements. If the assessment indicates that a potentially material loss contingency is not probable, but is reasonably possible, or is probable but cannot be estimated, then the nature of the contingent liability, together with an estimate of the range of possible loss if determinable and material, would be disclosed.

Loss contingencies considered remote are generally not disclosed unless they involve guarantees, in which case the nature of the guarantee would be disclosed.

Example 2: No Accrual Is Made for Litigation Because the Likelihood of a Material Adverse Outcome Is Remote

The Company is a defendant in a case that is in the United States District Court in the Northern District of California. The case arose from claims by a former employee that the Company had discriminated against her during her employment at the Company. The suit seeks damages totaling $1,500,000. The Company believes that the claims are without merit and intends to vigorously defend its position. The ultimate outcome of this litigation cannot presently be determined. However, in management's opinion, the likelihood of a material adverse outcome is remote. Accordingly, adjustments, if any, that might result from the resolution of this matter have not been reflected in the financial statements.

Example 3: No Accrual Is Made for Potential Liability Because Management Does Not Believe It Is Probable

A former employee of the Company has filed a workers' compensation claim related to injuries incurred in connection with the September 20X2 fire at the Company's Temecula facility. In the claim, the employee is requesting payment of an additional 50% award of compensation, approximating $450,000, claiming the Company violated a State safety statute in connection with the occurrence of his injury. As of December 31, 20X2, the Company has not recorded a provision for this matter as management intends to vigorously defend these allegations and believes the payment of the penalty is not probable. The Company believes, however, that any liability it may incur would not have a material adverse effect on its financial condition or its results of operations.

Example 4: Accrual Is Made but Exposure Exists in Excess of Amount Accrued

The Company is a defendant in a lawsuit, filed by a former supplier of electronic components alleging breach of contract, which seeks damages totaling $750,000. The Company proposed a settlement in the amount of $500,000, based on the advice of the Company's legal counsel. Consequently, $500,000 was charged to operations in the accompanying 20X2 financial statements. However, if the settlement offer is not accepted by the plaintiff and the case goes to trial, the amount of the ultimate loss to the Company, if any, may equal the entire amount of damages of $750,000 sought by the plaintiff.

Example 5: Unasserted Claim for Penalties Resulting from Contract Delays

In the ordinary course of business, the Company enters into contracts that provide for the assessment by the Company's customers of penalty charges for delays in the required production capability or completion of contracts. At December 31, 20X2, the Company had not achieved the 50% production capacity specified in a major contract, which also provides for penalties of up to $1,500,000. The Company's management believes that failure to meet the contract's production capacity requirement was caused primarily by customer initiated changes and additional customer requirements after the placement of the order and has informed the customer of the delays caused thereby. No claims for penalties have been made by the customer, and although some uncertainty exists as to whether the final delivery date can be achieved, the Company believes it can fulfill all remaining contractual requirements so that ultimately no penalties will have to be paid.

Example 6: Unasserted Claim Relating to Product Defects

In September 20X2, the Company announced that it will conduct an inspection program to eliminate a potential problem with an electrical component supplied to various manufacturers of microwave ovens. The ultimate cost of the repair will not be known until the inspection program is complete, which could have a material effect on the Company's financial condition and results of operations.

Example 7: Contingent Liability Resulting from Government Investigation

The Company is currently the subject of certain U.S. government investigations. If the Company is charged with wrongdoing as a result of any of these investigations, the Company could be suspended from bidding on or receiving awards of new government contracts pending the completion of legal proceedings. If convicted or found liable, the Company could be fined and debarred from new government contracting for a period generally not to exceed three years.

Example 8: Contingent Liability Relating to Businesses Sold

The Company is contingently liable for obligations totaling approximately $4,000,000 under Industrial Revenue Bond Agreements related to manufacturing plants of businesses that were sold. In November 20X2, the Company was notified that an event of default relating to the nonpayment of $300,000 semi-annual interest installment due October 20X2, by the purchaser of the businesses had occurred. The Company has agreed to loan $300,000 to the purchaser to cure the event of default.

Example 9: Contingent Liability Relating to Lease Termination

In September 20X2, the Company notified the developer and landlord of its planned future headquarters in Paramount, California, that the Company intends to terminate the project. The Company had previously entered into a 15-year lease agreement for the new site. Although groundbreaking for the new site has not occurred, the Company anticipates that it will incur lease termination costs. The Company is not able to make a meaningful estimate of the amount or range of loss that could result from an unfavorable resolution of this matter. Consequently, the Company has not provided any accruals for lease termination costs in the financial statements.

Example 10: Contingent Liability Relating to Performance and Payment Bonds Issued by Sureties

The Company is contingently liable to sureties in respect of performance and payment bonds issued by the sureties in connection with certain contracts entered into by the Company in the normal course of business. The Company has agreed to indemnify the sureties for any payments made by them in respect of such bonds.

Example 11: Contingency Resulting from Default under Lease Agreements

The Company leases certain plant machinery and equipment at its manufacturing facility in Boise, Idaho. As a result of the Company's default under its debt obligations, as more fully discussed in Note [X] to the financial statements, the Company is in default under these lease agreements. As a result, the lessors have the right to require the Company to prepay the remaining future lease payments required under the lease agreements. Because the lease payments have been made and are expected to be made in a timely manner, the Company does not expect that the lessors will assert this right under these lease agreements.

Example 12: Lawsuit Settlement Amount Is Recorded at Present Value of Amount to Be Paid

In October 20X2, the Company settled a legal action brought by a group of employees alleging certain discriminatory employment practices by the Company. Under the settlement, the Company has agreed to provide monetary relief in the amount of approximately $2,500,000, to be paid in installments over a five-year period. The present value of the cost of the settlement and estimated additional legal fees totaling $1,900,000, have been included in results of operations for 20X2. The current portion of the liability recorded is approximately $500,000 and the remaining $1,400,000 is classified as a noncurrent liability at December 31, 20X2.

Example 13: Settlement of Claims Is Not Expected to Exceed Company's Insurance Coverage

Through December 31, 20X2, claims valued at approximately $7,000,000 had been filed against the Company relating to product damage associated with the contamination of a formulated agricultural chemical. Management, based on consultation with its legal counsel, believes that the ultimate settlement of claims for this loss will not exceed its insurance coverage, which totals $15,000,000.

Example 14: Company Is without Insurance for Various Risks That Could Adversely Affect the Company's Financial Condition and Operations

Because of the state of the market for insurance in recent years, the Company, and many U.S. corporations, have been unable to obtain insurance for various risks at rates and on terms that they consider reasonable. Consequently, the Company is to a significant degree without insurance for various risks, including those associated with product liability. Although the Company has recorded estimated liabilities for uninsured risks to the extent permitted by generally accepted accounting principles, the absence of various insurance coverages represents a potential exposure for the Company. Therefore, the financial condition and net income of the Company in future periods could be adversely affected if uninsured losses in excess of amounts provided were to be incurred. The portion of liabilities for uninsured losses estimated to be payable after one year is included in "Other noncurrent liabilities" in the accompanying Balance Sheets.

Example 15: Company Involved in Arbitration

The Company had been involved in an arbitration entitled *The Company v. ABC, Ltd.* The case was based on the Company's claims that ABC, Ltd. breached noncompetition provisions and other terms of a distribution agreement between the Company and ABC, Ltd.

In October 20X2, the Company was informed that while it had won the case based on the merits of its claims, any recovery of damages was time barred under the terms of the original agreement between the two parties in the dispute. As a result, the Company was required to pay a portion of ABC, Ltd.'s fees and costs related to the arbitration, in the amount of $800,000. The Company expensed these fees and costs awarded to ABC, Ltd. in 20X2. This payment completes the Company's involvement in the matter.

Example 16: Litigation Settlement Is Subject to a Confidentiality Agreement

In January 20X2, Stuart Construction Co. (Stuart) filed suit against the Company alleging that the Company had failed to provide coated, welded pipe fittings and joints in accordance with contract specifications for a construction project in the Pacific Grove area. In November 20X2, the parties involved agreed to settle the suit. The financial terms of the settlement are subject to a confidentiality agreement; however, the settlement will not have a material effect on the Company's financial condition or results of operations.

Example 17: Company Is Subject to Various Claims and Legal Proceedings in the Ordinary Course of Business That Are Not Considered Material

The Company is subject to various claims and legal proceedings covering a wide range of matters that arise in the ordinary course of its business activities, including product liability claims. Management believes that any liability that may ultimately result from the resolution of these matters will not have a material adverse effect on the financial condition or results of operations of the Company.

Example 18: Contingency Resulting from Audit by the Department of Labor

The Company was audited by the Department of Labor in October 20X1. The Department of Labor determined that numerous employees were improperly classified as exempt and should have been classified as non-exempt. As a result, in the year ended December 31, 20X1, the Company recorded an estimated accrual in the amount of $1,500,000 for the past wages that are due for overtime worked. Based on the overtime questionnaires the Company has received from the applicable employees and a revision to the methodology used to calculate overtime pay approved by the Department of Labor, the Company has revised the estimate for this liability to $825,000, of which $675,000 has been paid through December 31, 20X2. The Company is maintaining the remaining accrual, as further claims are probable until the statute of limitations on these claims expires on November 1, 20X4.

Gain Contingencies

Example 19: Amount of Claim Asserted in Litigation Is Not Specified in the Financial Statement Disclosure

In May 20X2, the Company initiated a legal action against one of its suppliers alleging breach of contract, breach of warranty, and misrepresentation. Management believes, based on the advice of the Company's legal counsel, that the suit could result in a settlement or award by the court in favor of the Company. However, the ultimate outcome of the litigation cannot be determined and no amount has been recognized for possible collection of any claims asserted in the litigation.

Example 20: Amount of Claim Asserted in Litigation Is Specified in the Financial Statement Disclosure

On August 10, 20X2, the Company filed suit against Able & Baker Co., its former management consultant and advisory firm. The complaint charges Able & Baker Co. with professional malpractice, negligent misrepresentation, breach of fiduciary duty, breach of contract, and fraud in connection with its advice and services regarding the Company's sale of Hope Enterprises. The complaint seeks $495,000 in compensatory damages, plus prejudgment interest and punitive damages. Able & Baker Co. has included in its answer to the complaint certain "unasserted counterclaims" for fees and expenses incurred by it. A trial date has not been set yet, and no estimate can be made of the amount of the settlement, if any, that will actually be received.

Example 21: Gain Not Recognized in the Financial Statements until Received

In December 20X2, a federal court jury found that Dobatek, Inc. infringed on some of the Company's patents and awarded the Company $6,000,000 in damages. Dobatek, Inc. will be required to pay interest on the award amount and legal fees. Should Dobatek, Inc. appeal, the jury verdict or the amount of the damage award could be affected; therefore, the Company will not recognize any award amount in the financial statements until it is received.

Example 22: Litigation Settlement Results in Receipt of Award Amount and Gain Recognition

In March 20X2, the Company settled its two year copyright infringement and trade secrets litigation with Britek, Inc. Under the terms of the settlement, Britek, Inc. paid the Company $6,500,000, which was received in full in May 20X2, and the parties have dismissed all pending litigation. The Company recognized a pretax gain, net of related legal fees and other expenses, of $5,300,000 resulting from the settlement, which is included in "Other income" in the 20X2 Consolidated Statement of Operations.

Example 23: Insurance Claim Proceeds Are Recorded as Deferred Gain until Final Settlement

In December 20X1, the Company's Vista manufacturing plant in Detroit was extensively damaged as a result of a fire. A $3,000,000 pretax charge was recorded in 20X1 for expected uninsured costs associated with the incident, including deductibles. In 20X2, the Company received interim payments of $14,500,000 on its insurance claim. The Company is in discussions with its insurers as to additional insurance proceeds that the Company believes it is entitled to. Insurance proceeds received under the Company's property damage claim are being deferred pending final settlement of the claim. The Company expects to record a substantial non-recurring gain in 20X3, representing the difference between the property insurance settlement on the plant and the carrying value of the plant at the time of the explosion. The amount of the gain will be dependent on final construction, clean-up expenditures, and the settlement reached with the Company's insurance carriers. As of December 31, 20X2, $14,500,000 has been recorded as a deferred gain and is included in "Other liabilities" in the accompanying Balance Sheet.

CHAPTER 31
ASC TOPIC 460: GUARANTEES

CONTENTS

EXECUTIVE SUMMARY

Guarantees

The issuance of a guarantee obligates the guarantor in two important ways: (1) the guarantor is obligated to perform over the term of the guarantee in the event that the specified triggering events or conditions occur (the noncontingent aspect) and (2) the guarantor is contingently obligated to make future payments if those triggering events or conditions occur (the contingent aspect). The following are examples of such guarantees:

- Financial guarantees, for example: (1) financial standby letter of credit and (2) guarantee granted to a business or its owners that the revenue of the business for a specified period of time will be at least a specified amount.

- Performance guarantees, for example: (1) performance standby letter of credit, (2) bid bonds, and (3) performance bonds.

- Indemnifications, for example, an indemnification agreement that contingently requires the guarantor to make payments to the indemnified party based on an adverse judgment in a lawsuit.

- Indirect guarantees of the indebtedness of others.

Accounting Literature

FASB Accounting Standards Codification Topic	*Pre-Codification Accounting Literature*
460, *Guarantees* 815, *Derivatives and Hedging*	FAS-5, *Accounting for Contingencies*

FASB Accounting Standards Codification Topic	*Pre-Codification Accounting Literature*
	FIN-45, *Guarantor's Accounting and Disclosure Requirements for Guarantees, Including Indirect Guarantees of Indebtedness of Others*
	FSP FAS 133-1 and FIN 45-4, *Disclosures about Credit Derivatives and Certain Guarantees*
	SOP 01-6, *Accounting by Certain Entities (Including Entities with Trade Receivables) That Lend to or Finance the Activities of Others*

DISCLOSURE AND KEY PRESENTATION REQUIREMENTS

1. An accrual for credit loss on a financial instrument with off-balance-sheet risk (including financial guarantees and financial standby letters of credit) should be recorded separate from a valuation account related to a recognized financial instrument. (ASC 460-10-45-1) (SOP 01-6, par. 8)

2. The following disclosures should be made for certain loss contingencies relating to guarantees made for outside parties even though the possibility of loss may be remote (e.g., guarantees of indebtedness of others, obligations of commercial banks under standby letters of credit, and guarantees to repurchase receivables or other properties that have been sold or assigned) (ASC 460-10-50-2 and 50-3) (FAS-5, par. 12):

    a. The nature of the guarantee.

    b. The amount of the guarantee.

    c. If estimable, the value of any recovery from other outside parties that could be expected to result (e.g., guarantor's right to proceed against an outside party).

3. The following disclosures should be made about each guarantee, or each group of similar guarantees, even if the likelihood of the guarantor's having to make any payments under the guarantee is remote (ASC 460-10-50-4) (FIN-45, par. 13):

    a. The nature of the guarantee.

    b. The approximate term of the guarantee.

c. How the guarantee arose.

d. The events or circumstances that would require the guarantor to perform under the guarantee.

e. The following information about the maximum potential amount of future payments under the guarantee (other than product warranties):

   (1) The maximum potential amount of future payments (undiscounted) that the guarantor could be required to make under the guarantee, which should not be reduced by the effect of any amounts that may possibly be recovered under recourse or collateralization provisions in the guarantee.

   (2) If the terms of the guarantee provide for no limitation to the maximum potential future payments under the guarantee, that fact.

   (3) If the guarantor is unable to develop an estimate of the maximum potential amount of future payments under its guarantee, the reasons why it cannot estimate the maximum potential amount.

f. The current carrying amount of the liability, if any, for the guarantor's obligations under the guarantee, regardless of whether the guarantee is freestanding or embedded in another contract.

g. The nature of any recourse provisions that would enable the guarantor to recover from third parties any of the amounts paid under the guarantee.

h. The nature of any assets held either as collateral or by third parties that, upon the occurrence of any triggering event or condition under the guarantee, the guarantor can obtain and liquidate to recover all or a portion of the amounts paid under the guarantee.

i. If estimable, the approximate extent to which the proceeds from liquidation of assets held either as collateral or by third parties would be expected to cover the maximum potential amount of future payments under the guarantee.

Note: The disclosure requirement in item (j) below is prescribed by ASC Section 460-10-50, *Guarantees—Overall—Disclosure*, based on FSP FAS 133-1 and FIN 45-4, *Disclosures about Credit Derivatives and Certain Guarantees: An Amendment of FASB Statement No. 133 and FASB Interpretation No. 45; and Clarification of the Effective Date of FASB Statement No. 161*), which is effective for reporting periods (annual or interim) ending after November 15, 2008. Early adoption is permitted. (ASC 815-10-65-2) (FSP FAS 133-1 and FIN 45-4, pars. 8 and 9)

j. The current status (i.e., as of the balance sheet date) of the payment/performance risk of the guarantee. (ASC 460-10-50-4; 815-10-65-2) (FIN-45, par. 13a; FSP FAS 133-1 and FIN 45-4, pars. 8 and 9) (*Note*: An entity that uses internal groupings should disclose how those groupings are determined and used for managing risk.)

4. For product warranties and other guarantee contracts, the following disclosures should be made (ASC 460-10-50-8) (FIN-45, par. 14):

a. The information required to be disclosed under item 3 above (except for 3(e) relating to the maximum potential amount of future payments).

b. The guarantor's accounting policy and methodology used in determining its liability for product warranties (including any liability, such as deferred revenue, associated with extended warranties).

c. A tabular reconciliation of the changes in the guarantor's aggregate product warranty liability for the reporting period, showing the following:

(1) The beginning balance of the aggregate product warranty liability.

(2) The aggregate reductions in that liability for payments made (in cash or in kind) under the warranty.

(3) The aggregate changes in the liability for accruals related to product warranties issued during the reporting period.

(4) The aggregate changes in the liability for accruals related to preexisting warranties (including adjustments related to changes in estimates).

(5) The ending balance of the aggregate product warranty liability.

EXAMPLES OF FINANCIAL STATEMENT DISCLOSURES

The following sample disclosures are available on the accompanying disc.

Example 1: Guarantee of Third-Party Indebtedness—No Liability Is Recorded

As of December 31, 20X2, the Company is contingently liable as guarantor with respect to $5,400,000 of indebtedness of Extraped,

Inc., an entity that is owned by the Company's stockholders. The term of the guarantee is through June 30, 20X4. At any time through that date, should Extraped, Inc. be over 90 days delinquent on its debt payments, the Company will be obligated to perform under the guarantee by primarily making the required payments, including late fees and penalties. The maximum potential amount of future payments that the Company is required to make under the guarantee is $3,000,000.

Example 2: Guarantee of Third-Party Indebtedness—Liability Is Recorded

In January 20X2, the Company executed a "Guarantee Agreement" (the Agreement) to guarantee the payment of $500,000 advanced to an affiliate, Steinhart Corp., by Amcor Funding, Inc. The guarantee agreement expires March 31, 20X3. In November 20X2, Steinhart Corp. became insolvent, which triggered an event of default under the terms of the Agreement. At December 31, 20X2, the Company accrued a loss of $500,000 for the full amount of the potential payment that the Company would be required to make under the guarantee. Steinhart Corp. is in the process of liquidating its assets; however, the Company does not expect to recover any of the amounts paid under the guarantee.

Example 3: Guarantee of Indebtedness of Joint Venture Obligates Company to Advance Funds to the Joint Venture if Certain Loan Covenants Are Not Met

The Company holds a 25% ownership interest in Stellark, Inc., which has a $7,000,000 line of credit agreement (Agreement) with First Nations Bank. Under terms of the Agreement, the Company is obligated to advance to Stellark, Inc. a maximum of $2,500,000 if its working capital falls below $500,000 or its current ratio is less than 1. Any funds advanced under this Agreement are available to First Nations Bank. In addition, First Nations Bank may have claims against the Company in an amount not to exceed $2,000,000 of any unsatisfied required advances. The term of the guarantee is through April 30, 20X4. At December 31, 20X2, Stellark, Inc. was in compliance with the terms of the Agreement with First Nations Bank.

Example 4: Assets Held as Collateral in Connection with Guarantee of Future Lease Payments

In March 20X2, the Company sold The Red Shoe, Inc., a chain of 25 stores located throughout Ohio and Michigan. In connection with this sale, the Company has guaranteed that certain lease payments will be made by the purchasers through December 31, 20X5. The maximum amount of future lease payments guaranteed by the

Company totaled $6,800,000 at December 31, 20X2. At December 31, 20X2, the purchasers have set aside $1,000,000 in a trust account for the benefit of the Company, which the Company can obtain to recover any amounts paid under the guarantee. The Company believes that the purchasers will be able to perform under their respective lease agreements and that no payments will be required and no losses incurred under such guarantees.

Example 5: Guaranteed Advance and Royalty Payments in Connection with New Joint Venture

In January 20X2, the Company entered into a joint venture agreement with Sapiex Corp. creating a new limited liability company (LLC) in which the Company holds a 50% ownership interest. On December 1, 20X2, the LLC entered into a license agreement expiring December 31, 20X9, with an option for a five-year automatic extension if the LLC pays the licensor $27,000,000 in royalties during the initial seven-year period of the agreement. The license agreement includes guaranteed minimum royalty payments of $17,000,000 payable over the seven-year initial term and $7,500,000 payable over the five-year renewal period, if applicable. The Company is responsible for funding $8,000,000 of the $17,000,000 guaranteed royalty payments. The guarantee payments include a $3,000,000 advance, paid within 15 days after the agreements were executed, and seven minimum guaranteed installments of $2,000,000, due each January 30, starting in 20X3 and ending 20X9. The Company was responsible for funding $2,000,000 of the initial advance and is responsible for funding $750,000 of the first four and $1,000,000 of the next three of seven yearly installments.

Example 6: Certain Guarantees Are Denominated in Foreign Currencies and May Vary Based on Fluctuations in Foreign Exchange Rates

The Company has unconditionally guaranteed the repayment of certain loans and related interest and fees for an unconsolidated equity investee. The guarantees continue until the loans, including accrued interest and fees, have been paid in full. The maximum amount of the guarantees may vary, but is limited to the sum of the total due and unpaid principal amounts plus related interest and fees. Additionally, the maximum amount of the guarantees, certain of which are denominated in foreign currencies, will vary based on fluctuations in foreign exchange rates. As of December 31, 20X2, the maximum principal amount guaranteed was approximately $9 million.

The Company may recover a portion of its maximum liability upon liquidation of the investee's assets. The proceeds from such liquidation cannot be accurately estimated due to the multitude of factors that would affect the valuation and realization of such proceeds of a liquidation.

Example 7: Company Issued Residual Value Guarantees in Case It Does Not Purchase Leased Property

In connection with various operating leases, the Company issued residual value guarantees, which provide that if the Company does not purchase the leased property from the lessor at the end of the lease term, then the Company is liable to the lessor for an amount equal to the shortage, if any, between the proceeds from the sale of the property and an agreed value. As of December 31, 20X2, the maximum amount of the residual value guarantees was approximately $7.5 million. The Company's management believes that proceeds from the sale of properties under operating leases would exceed the payment obligation and, therefore, no liability to the Company currently exists.

Example 8: Indemnification Guarantee to Landlord and Sublessee under Lease Agreements

The Company leases space in certain buildings, including its corporate headquarters building, under operating leases. The Company has standard indemnification arrangements under those leases that require it to indemnify the landlord against losses, liabilities and claims incurred in connection with the premises covered by the Company leases, its use of the premises, property damage or personal injury, and breach of the lease agreement, as well as occurrences arising from the Company's negligence or willful misconduct. The Company also subleases certain space and agrees to indemnify the sublessee for losses caused by the Company's employees on the premises. The term of these indemnification agreements is generally perpetual from the time of execution of the agreement. The maximum potential amount of future payments the Company could be required to make under these indemnification agreements is unlimited. The Company has never incurred costs to defend lawsuits or settle claims related to these indemnification agreements. As of December 31, 20X2, the Company had not accrued a liability for this guarantee because the likelihood of incurring a payment obligation in connection with this guarantee is remote.

Example 9: Product Warranties

The Company sells the majority of its products to customers along with unconditional repair or replacement warranties for a full year from the date of purchase. The Company determines its estimated liability for warranty claims based on the Company's experience of the amount of claims actually made. It is reasonably possible that the Company's estimate of the accrued product warranty claims will change in the near term. Estimated costs for product warranties are recognized at the time revenue is recognized.

The following is a reconciliation of the changes in the Company's aggregate product warranty liability for the years ended December 31, 20X2, and December 31, 20X1:

	20X2	20X1
Accrued liability at beginning of period	$2,511,000	$1,350,000
Payments made	(1,096,000)	(722,000)
Cost recognized for warranties issued during the period	1,972,000	1,756,000
Changes in estimates for preexisting warranties	(131,000)	127,000
Accrued liability at and of period	$3,256,000	$2,511,000

Example 10: Officers' and Directors' Indemnification Guarantee

The Company's Certificate of Incorporation provides that the Company indemnify its officers and directors for certain events or occurrences that happen by reason of the fact that the officer or director is, was, or has agreed to serve as an officer or director of the Company. The term of the indemnification period is for the officer's or director's lifetime. The maximum potential amount of future payments the Company could be required to make under these indemnification agreements is unlimited; however, the Company has a Director and Officer insurance policy that limits its exposure and enables the Company to recover a portion of any future amounts paid. As of December 31, 20X2, the Company had not accrued a liability for this guarantee, because the likelihood of incurring a payment obligation in connection with this guarantee is remote.

Example 11: Guarantee in Connection with Business Sale Agreements

In connection with agreements for the sale of portions of its business, including certain discontinued operations, the Company has typically retained the liabilities of a business that relate to events occurring prior to its sale, such as tax, environmental, litigation, and employment matters. The Company generally indemnifies the purchaser of a Company's business in the event that a third party asserts a claim against the purchaser that relates to a liability retained by the Company. These types of indemnification guarantees typically extend for a number of years. The Company is unable to estimate the maximum potential liability for these types of indemnification guarantees as the business sale agreements do not specify a maximum amount and the amounts are dependent upon the outcome of future contingent events, the nature and likelihood of which cannot be determined at this time. Historically, the Company has not made any significant indemnification payments under such agreements and no amount has been accrued in the accompanying consolidated financial statements with respect to these indemnification guarantees.

Example 12: Indemnification of Lenders under Credit Facilities

Under its credit facilities, the Company has agreed to indemnify its lenders against costs or losses resulting from changes in laws and regulations, which would increase the lenders' costs, and from any legal action brought against the lenders related to the use of loan proceeds. These indemnifications generally extend for the term of the credit facilities and do not provide for any limit on the maximum potential liability. Historically, the Company has not made any significant indemnification payments under such agreements and no amount has been accrued in the accompanying consolidated financial statements with respect to these indemnification guarantees.

Example 13: Indemnification Guarantee to Customers under Technology License Agreements

The Company licenses technology to certain customers under license agreements that provide for the Company to indemnify the customers against claims of patent and copyright infringement. This indemnity does not apply in the case where the licensed technology has been modified by the customers or combined with other technology, hardware, or data that the Company has not approved. The term of these indemnification agreements is generally perpetual from the time of execution of the agreement. The maximum potential amount of future payments the Company could be required to make under these indemnification agreements is unlimited. The Company has never incurred costs to defend lawsuits or settle claims related to these indemnification agreements. As of December 31, 20X2, the Company had not accrued a liability for this guarantee, because the likelihood of incurring a payment obligation in connection with this guarantee is remote.

Example 14: Indemnification Guarantee to Vendors under Technology License Agreements

The Company licenses technology from third parties under agreements that contain standard indemnification provisions that require the Company to indemnify the third party against losses, liabilities, and claims arising from the Company's unauthorized use or modification of the licensed technology. The term of these indemnification agreements is generally perpetual from the time of execution of the agreement. The maximum potential amount of future payments the Company could be required to make under these indemnification agreements is unlimited. The Company has never incurred costs to defend lawsuits or settle claims related to these indemnification agreements. As of December 31, 20X2, the Company had not accrued a liability for this guarantee, because the likelihood of incurring a payment obligation in connection with this guarantee is remote.

CHAPTER 32
ASC TOPIC 470: DEBT

CONTENTS

EXECUTIVE SUMMARY

Note: For unconditional purchase obligations, see Chapter 29, "ASC Topic 440: Commitments." For financial instruments with characteristics of both liabilities and equity, see Chapter 33, "ASC Topic 480: Distinguishing Liabilities from Equity."

Overall

Debt obligations that, by their terms, are due and payable on demand should be presented as a current liability in the balance sheet. Current liabilities include long-term obligations that are callable because a violation of an objective acceleration clause in a long-term debt agreement may exist at the date of the debtor's balance sheet. Such callable obligations must be classified as a current liability at the debtor's balance sheet date unless one of the following conditions is met:

1. The creditor has waived or subsequently lost the right to demand repayment for more than one year (or operating cycle, if longer) from the balance sheet date.

2. For long-term obligations containing a grace period within which the debtor may cure the violation, it is probable that the violation will be cured within that period, therefore preventing the obligation from being callable.

A short-term obligation can be excluded from current liabilities only if the entity intends to refinance the obligation on a long-term basis and the intent is supported by the ability to refinance in one of the following ways:

1. *Post-balance-sheet-date issuance of a long-term obligation or equity securities.* After the date of an entity's balance sheet, but before that balance sheet is issued or is available to be issued (as discussed in ASC Topic 855, *Subsequent Events*), a long-term obligation or equity securities have been issued for the purpose of refinancing the short-term obligation on a long-term basis.

2. *Financing agreement.* Before the balance sheet is issued or is available to be issued (as discussed in ASC Topic 855, *Subsequent Events*), the entity has entered into a financing agreement that clearly permits the entity to refinance the short-term obligation on a long-term basis on terms that are readily determinable, and certain other requisite conditions are met.

Debt with Conversion and Other Options

The accounting for debt with conversion and other options requires careful consideration of various factors, such as the following:

- Whether the fair value of the common stock into which the debt can be converted exceed the proceeds (i.e., whether a beneficial conversion feature exists).

- Whether the proceeds from the issuance of debt with equity securities or detachable warrants should be allocated between the debt and the other securities.

- If the convertible debt is issued at, or near, par with a put at a multiple of par value, whether the convertible debt contains an embedded derivative (i.e., an embedded conversion option) that should be accounted for separately.

Also, additional specific disclosure requirements apply to debt with conversion and other options. See the "Disclosure and Key Presentation Requirements" section below.

Participating Mortgage Loans

Participating mortgage loans and nonparticipating mortgage loans share all of the following characteristics:

- Debtor-creditor relationships between those who provide initial cash outlays and hold the mortgages, and those who are obligated to make subsequent payments to the mortgage holders;

- Real estate collateral;

- Periodic fixed-rate or floating-rate interest payments; and

- Fixed maturity dates for stated principal amounts.

Also, additional specific disclosure requirements apply to participating mortgage loans. See the "Disclosure and Key Presentation Requirements" section below.

Product Financing Arrangements

A product financing arrangement is a transaction in which an entity sells products to another entity and, in a related transaction, agrees to repurchase the products at a specified price over a specified period. A product financing arrangement should be accounted for as a borrowing rather than as a sale. It should be noted that the accounting for product financing arrangements differs from the accounting for long-term unconditional purchase obligations (See Chapter 29, "ASC Topic 440: Commitments," for unconditional purchase obligations). In a product financing arrangement, the entity is in substance the owner of the product and, therefore, should report the product as an asset and the related obligation as a liability. In contrast, at the time a contract is entered into under an unconditional purchase obligation arrangement, either the product does not yet exist or the product exists in a form unsuitable to the buyer; in other words, the buyer has a right to receive a future product but is not the substantive owner of an existing product.

Modifications and Extinguishments

Debt is considered to be extinguished when the debtor pays the creditor or when the debtor is legally released from being primary obligor. Debt may also be extinguished as a result of a substantial modification of terms or an exchange of instruments. The terms of a debt instrument are substantially modified when *any* of the following three conditions are met:

1. The present value of the cash flows under the modified debt instrument is at least 10% different from the present value of the remaining cash flows under the original debt.

2. A modification or an exchange that affects the terms of an embedded conversion option, from which the change in the fair value of the embedded conversion option (calculated as the difference between the fair value of the embedded conversion option immediately before and after the modification or exchange) is at least 10% of the carrying amount of the original debt instrument immediately prior to the modification or exchange.

3. A modification or exchange of debt instruments that adds a substantive conversion option or eliminates a conversion option that was substantive at the date of the modification or exchange.

Troubled Debt Restructurings by Debtors

A troubled debt restructuring may include: (*a*) a transfer of assets or the issuance of equity securities by the debtor to the creditor in full or partial satisfaction of the debt or (*b*) a modification of the terms of the debt to reduce the near-term payments by reducing the interest rate, future principal payments, or accrued interest.

A modification of the terms of a debt agreement, including a partial settlement, should be treated as a troubled debt restructuring if (*a*) the debtor is experiencing financial difficulties and (*b*) the creditor grants a concession to the debtor for economic or legal reasons related to the debtor's financial difficulties.

Accounting Literature

FASB Accounting Standards Codification Topic	*Pre-Codification Accounting Literature*
470, *Debt*	FAS-6, *Classification of Short-Term Obligations Expected to Be Refinanced*
835, *Interest*	FAS-15, *Accounting by Debtors and Creditors for Troubled Debt Restructurings*

FASB Accounting Standards Codification Topic	*Pre-Codification Accounting Literature*

FAS-47, *Disclosure of Long-Term Obligations*

FAS-78, *Classification of Obligations That Are Callable by the Creditor*

FAS-140, *Accounting for Transfers and Servicing of Financial Assets and Extinguishments of Liabilities*

FAS-145, *Rescission of FASB Statements No. 4, 44, and 64, Amendment of FASB Statement No. 13, and Technical Corrections*

FIN-8, *Classification of a Short-Term Obligation Repaid Prior to Being Replaced by a Long-Term Security*

FTB 79-3, *Subjective Acceleration Clauses in Long-Term Debt Agreements*

EITF 86-5, *Classifying Demand Notes with Repayment Terms*

EITF 86-15, *Increasing-Rate Debt*

EITF 86-30, *Classification of Obligations When a Violation Is Waived by the Creditor*

EITF 95-22, *Balance Sheet Classification of Borrowings Outstanding under Revolving Credit Agreements That Include Both a Subjective Acceleration Clause and a Lockbox Arrangement*

EITF 98-14, *Debtor's Accounting for Changes in Line-of-Credit or Revolving-Debt Arrangements*

APB-14, *Accounting for Convertible Debt and Debt Issued with Stock Purchase Warrants*

FSP APB 14-1, *Accounting for Convertible Debt Instruments That May Be Settled in Cash upon Conversion (Including Partial Cash Settlement)*

FASB Accounting Standards Codification Topic	*Pre-Codification Accounting Literature*
	APB-21, *Interest on Receivables and Payables*
	APB-26, *Early Extinguishment of Debt*
	ARB-43, *Chapter 3A, Current Assets and Current Liabilities*
	SOP 97-1, *Accounting by Participating Mortgage Loan Borrowers*

DISCLOSURE AND KEY PRESENTATION REQUIREMENTS

Overall

1. Significant categories of debt (e.g., notes payable to banks, related-party notes, or capital lease obligations) and the terms, interest rates, maturity rates, and subordinate features should be disclosed. (Generally accepted practice)

2. Long-term loans that include covenants should be classified as noncurrent unless (a) a covenant violation that gives the lender the right to call the debt has occurred at the balance sheet date (or would have occurred absent a loan modification) *and* (b) it is probable that the borrower will not be able to cure the default (comply with the covenant) at measurement dates that are within the next 12 months. (ASC 470-10-45-1) (EITF 86-30)

3. For long-term debt that includes subjective acceleration clauses (ASC 470-10-45-2; 470-10-50-3) (FTB 79-3, par. 3):

   a. Consideration should be given as to whether the debt should be classified as a current liability, depending on the circumstances (e.g., recurring losses, liquidity problems), unless the likelihood of the acceleration of the due date was remote.

   b. Disclosures should be made of the existence of subjective clauses that may accelerate the due date, unless the likelihood of the acceleration of the due date was remote.

4. Borrowings outstanding under a revolving credit agreement that includes both a subjective acceleration clause and a requirement to maintain a lock-box arrangement should be classified as a current liability. (ASC 470-10-45-3 through

45-5; 470-10-45-14) (EITF 95-22; FAS-6, par. 11) (*Note:* However, the obligation may be classified as a noncurrent liability if the entity's intent and ability to refinance on a long-term basis is supported by an agreement to refinance the obligation after the balance sheet date on a long-term basis, based on the provisions in ASC paragraph 470-10-45-14 [FAS-6, par. 11].)

5. Borrowings outstanding under a revolving credit agreement that includes both a subjective acceleration clause and a requirement to maintain a springing lock-box arrangement (i.e., the debtor's cash receipts do not automatically reduce the debt outstanding without another event occurring) should be classified as a long-term liability. (ASC 470-10-45-6) (EITF 95-22)

6. For increasing-rate debt (ASC 470-10-45-7 and 45-8) (EITF 86-15):

   a. The classification of the increasing-rate debt as current or noncurrent should reflect the borrower's anticipated source of repayment (i.e., current assets or a new short-term debt borrowing versus a long term refinancing agreement).

   b. If the debt is paid at par before its estimated maturity, any excess interest accrued should be reflected as an adjustment of interest expense.

7. Debt obligations that, by their terms, are due on demand or will be due on demand within one year (or operating cycle, if longer) from the balance sheet date, even though liquidation may not be expected within that period, should be included in current liabilities. (ASC 470-10-45-9 and 45-10) (EITF 86-5; ARB-43, Ch. 3A, par. 7)

8. Current liabilities should include long-term obligations that are or will be callable by the creditor either because the debtor's violation of a provision of the debt agreement at the balance sheet date makes the obligation callable or because the violation, if not cured within a specified grace period, will make the obligation callable unless one of the following conditions is met (ASC 470-10-45-11 and 45-12; 470-10-50-2) (ARB-43, Ch. 3A, par. 7; FAS-78, par. 16):

   a. The creditor has waived or subsequently lost the right to demand repayment for more than one year (or operating cycle, if longer) from the balance sheet date.

   b. For long-term obligations containing a grace period within which the debtor may cure the violation, it is probable that the violation will be cured within that period, thus preventing the obligation from becoming callable.

Note: If an obligation under this item is classified as a long-term liability, the circumstances should be disclosed.

9. For short-term obligations expected to be refinanced on a long-term basis:

   a. The short-term obligation should be excluded from current liabilities only if the entity intends to refinance the obligation on a long-term basis and the intent to refinance the obligation is supported by an ability to consummate the refinancing (before the balance sheet is issued or is available to be issued) that is demonstrated through either: (a) the issuance of a long-term obligation or equity securities, or (b) the existence of a financing agreement that clearly permits the entity to refinance the short-term obligation on a long-term basis on terms that are readily determinable and meeting certain specific conditions, in accordance with the provisions of ASC paragraphs 470-10-45-14 through 45-21 (FAS-6, pars. 11–14; FIN-8, par. 3). (ASC 470-10-45-12A through 45-21) (FAS-6, pars. 1, 2, 9, and 11–14; FIN-8, par. 3)

   b. If a short-term obligation expected to be refinanced on a long-term basis is excluded from current liabilities, the following disclosures should be made (ASC 470-10-50-4) (FAS-6, par. 15):

      (1) A general description of the financing agreement.

      (2) The terms of any new obligation incurred or expected to be incurred or equity securities issued or expected to be issued as a result of the refinancing.

10. The combined aggregate amount of maturities and sinking fund requirements for all long-term borrowings should be disclosed for each of the five years following the date of the latest balance sheet presented. (ASC 470-10-50-1) (FAS-47, par. 10). See Chapter 34, "ASC Topic 505: Equity," for disclosure guidance that applies to securities, including debt securities.

11. Debt issuance costs should be reported in the balance sheet as deferred charges. (ASC 835-30-45-3) (APB-21, par. 16)

Debt with Conversion and Other Options

Note: The disclosure requirements in this section are prescribed by ASC Subtopic 470-20, *Debt—Debt with Conversion and Other Options,* based on FSP APB 14-1, *Accounting for*

Convertible Debt Instruments That May Be Settled in Cash upon Conversion (Including Partial Cash Settlement), and should be applied retrospectively for all periods presented, except for instruments that were not outstanding during any of the periods that will be presented in the annual financial statements for the period of adoption but were outstanding during an earlier period. For convertible debt instruments that were modified after their original issuance date to provide for cash settlement (including partial cash settlement) upon conversion in a transaction that was not accounted for as an extinguishment, the requirements should be applied retrospectively to the modification date. The disclosure requirements are effective for fiscal years, and interim periods within those fiscal years, beginning after December 15, 2008. Early adoption is not permitted.

1. The following disclosures should be made for convertible debt instruments as of each date for which a balance sheet is presented (ASC 470-20-50-4) (FSP APB 14-1, par. 31):

   a. The carrying amount of the equity component.

   b. The principal amount of the liability component, its unamortized discount, and its net carrying amount.

2. The following disclosures should be made for convertible debt instruments as of the date of the most recent balance sheet presented (ASC 470-20-50-5) (FSP APB 14-1, par. 32):

   a. The remaining period over which any discount on the liability component will be amortized.

   b. The conversion price and the number of shares on which the aggregate consideration to be delivered upon conversion is determined.

   c. The amount by which the instrument's if-converted value exceeds its principal amount, regardless of whether the instrument is currently convertible. (*Note:* This disclosure is required for public entities only.)

   d. Information about derivative transactions (regardless of whether they are accounted for as assets, liabilities, or equity instruments) entered into in connection with the issuance of the convertible debt instruments, including:

      (1) The terms of those derivative transactions.

      (2) How those derivative transactions relate to the convertible debt instruments.

      (3) The number of shares underlying the derivative transactions.

      (4) The reasons for entering into those derivative transactions.

3. The following disclosures should be made for convertible debt instruments for each period for which an income statement is presented (ASC 470-20-50-6) (FSP APB 14-1, par. 33):

   a. The effective interest rate on the liability component for the period.

   b. The amount of interest cost recognized for the period relating to both the contractual interest coupon and amortization of the discount on the liability component.

Participating Mortgage Loans

1. The amortization of the debt discount relating to the participation liability should be included in interest expense. (ASC 470-30-45-1) (SOP 97-1, par. 14)

2. If the participating mortgage loan is extinguished before its due date, the debt extinguishment gain or loss should be reported as required by ASC paragraph 470-50-40-2 (APB-26, par. 20). (ASC 470-30-45-2) (SOP 97-1, par. 16)

3. Gains or losses from extinguishment of debt that meet the criteria for extraordinary items, in accordance with ASC Subtopic 225-20, *Income Statement—Extraordinary and Unusual Items* (APB-30, *Reporting the Results of Operations—Reporting the Effects of Disposal of a Segment of a Business, and Extraordinary, Unusual, and Infrequently Occurring Events and Transactions*), should be classified as extraordinary items. (ASC 470-30-45-3) (SOP 97-1, par. 16)

4. The following disclosures should be made in the borrower's financial statements (ASC 470-30-50-1) (SOP 97-1, par. 17):

   a. The aggregate amount of participating mortgage obligations at the balance sheet date, with separate disclosure of the aggregate participation liabilities and related debt discounts.

   b. Terms of the participations by the lender in either the appreciation in the market value of the mortgaged real estate project or the results of operations of the mortgaged real estate project, or both.

Modifications and Extinguishments

1. Gains or losses from extinguishment of debt that meet the criteria for extraordinary items, in accordance with ASC Subtopic 225-20, *Income Statement—Extraordinary and Unusual Items* (APB-30, *Reporting the Results of Operations—Reporting the Effects of Disposal of a Segment of a Business, and*

Extraordinary, Unusual, and Infrequently Occurring Events and Transactions), should be classified as extraordinary items. (ASC 470-50-45-1) (FAS-145, par. A5)

2. Charges to earnings resulting from application of ASC paragraph 470-50-40-21(c) (EITF 98-14) should *not* been classified as extraordinary items. (ASC 470-50-45-2) (EITF 98-14)

3. If debt was considered to be extinguished by in-substance defeasance under the provisions of FAS-76, *Extinguishment of Debt*, before the effective date of FAS-125, *Accounting for Transfers and Servicing of Financial Assets and Extinguishments of Liabilities*, the following disclosures should be made (ASC 470-50-50-1) (FAS-140, par. 17):

   a. A general description of the transaction.

   b. The amount of debt that is considered extinguished at the end of the period as long as that debt remains outstanding.

Troubled Debt Restructurings by Debtors

1. Consideration should be given to whether all or a portion of the carrying amount of the payable at the time of the restructuring needs to be reclassified in the balance sheet because of changes in the terms (e.g., a change in the amount of the payable due within one year after the date of the debtor's balance sheet). (ASC 470-60-45-1) (FAS-15, par. 16)

2. Consideration should be given to whether a troubled debt restructuring of a short-term obligation after the date of a debtor's balance sheet, but before that balance sheet is issued or is available to be issued, affects the classification of that obligation in accordance with ASC Subtopic 470-10, *Debt—Overall* (FAS-15, *Accounting by Debtors and Creditors for Troubled Debt Restructurings*). (ASC 470-60-45-2) (FAS-15, par. 16)

3. The following disclosures should be made (either in the body of the financial statements or in the accompanying notes) about troubled debt restructurings that have occurred during a period for which financial statements are presented (ASC 470-60-50-1) (FAS-15, par. 25):

   a. For each restructuring, a description of the principal changes in terms, the major features of settlement, or both. (*Note:* Separate restructurings within a fiscal period for the same category of payables, such as accounts payable or subordinated debentures, may be grouped for disclosure purposes.)

   b. Aggregate gain on restructuring of payables.

    c. Aggregate net gain or loss on transfers of assets recognized during the period.

    d. Per-share amount of the aggregate gain on restructuring of payables.

4. The following disclosures should be made in financial statements for periods after a troubled debt restructuring (ASC 470-60-50-2) (FAS-15, par. 26):

    a. The extent to which amounts contingently payable are included in the carrying amount of restructured payables.

    b. Total amounts that are contingently payable on restructured payables and the conditions under which those amounts would become payable or would be forgiven.

EXAMPLES OF FINANCIAL STATEMENT DISCLOSURES

The following sample disclosures are available on the accompanying disc. For examples of disclosures of capital lease obligations, see Chapter 52, "ASC Topic 840: Leases."

Overall

Example 1: Details of Short-Term Debt

Short-term debt consists of the following at December 31, 20X2, and December 31, 20X1:

	20X2	20X1
Demand note payable to bank, secured by machinery and equipment, interest at 10%	$2,137,000	$1,785,000
Demand notes payable to an entity owned by a majority stockholder, unsecured, interest rates ranging from 8% to 11%	971,000	813,000
Demand note payable to a former stockholder, unsecured, interest at 12%	624,000	674,000
Notes payable to officers with initial maturities of 6 to 12 months, unsecured, interest at 9%	237,000	218,000
	$3,969,000	$3,490,000

Example 2: Details of Long-Term Debt

Long-term debt consists of the following at December 31, 20X2, and December 31, 20X1:

	20X2	20X1
Mortgage note payable to bank in monthly installments of $86,000, including interest at 9.25%, due in December 20X9, secured by office building	$ 7,155,000	$ 7,514,000
Industrial Revenue Bonds with varying quarterly principal payments due through December 20X9, including interest at 85% of the current prime rate (8.72% at December 31, 20X2), collateralized by property, plant, and equipment	5,767,000	6,158,000
8% convertible subordinated debentures, due in May 20X8 with annual sinking fund requirements of $280,000, convertible into 833,126 shares of common stock at any time prior to maturity	5,160,000	5,440,000
Note payable to bank in quarterly installments of $47,000, including interest at prime plus 1% (9.25% at December 31, 20X2), due in August 20X7, secured by machinery and equipment	922,000	1,013,000
Note payable to an entity owned by a majority stockholder in semi-annual installments of $75,000, plus interest at 10%, due in April 20X7, unsecured	611,000	701,000
Note payable to supplier in monthly installments of $19,000, non-interest bearing (imputed interest of 12%), due in December 20X4, secured by equipment, less unamortized discount of $51,000 at December 31, 20X2, and $112,000 at December 31, 20X1	398,000	565,000
Other	317,000	492,000
Total debt	20,330,000	21,883,000
Less: current portion	(1,636,000)	(1,519,000)
Long-term debt, less current portion	$ 18,694,000	$ 20,364,000

Future maturities of long-term debt are as follows as of December 31, 20X2:

20X3	$ 1,636,000
20X4	1,758,000
20X5	1,520,000
20X6	1,619,000
20X7	1,748,000
Thereafter	12,049,000
	$20,330,000

Example 3: Long-Term Debt Classified as a Current Liability Due to Covenant Violations

As a result of operating losses, the Company was unable to remain in compliance with the financial covenants arising under substantially all of its long-term note agreements. The creditors have not waived the financial covenant requirements. The Company has been working with the different creditors to restructure the existing debt; however, an agreement satisfactory to the Company has not been reached. A total of $7,856,000 of long-term debt is subject to accelerated maturity and, as such, the creditors may, at their option, give notice to the Company that amounts owed are immediately due and payable. As a result, the full amount of the related long-term debt has been classified as a current liability in the accompanying Balance Sheet at December 31, 20X2. Regardless of the non-compliance with financial covenants, the Company has made every scheduled payment of principal and interest.

Example 4: Short-Term Debt Classified as Long-Term Because Company Has Both Ability and Intent to Refinance the Debt

Commercial paper debt is due within one year, but has been classified as long-term because the Company has the ability through a $25,000,000 credit agreement to convert this obligation into longer term debt. The credit agreement expires in 20X5 and provides for interest on borrowings at prevailing rates. The Company intends to refinance the commercial paper debt by replacing them with long-term debt.

Example 5: Short-Term Debt Classified as Long-Term Because Proceeds of Long-Term Financing Issued Subsequent to Balance Sheet Date Were Used to Retire the Short-Term Debt

On February 13, 20X3, the Company borrowed $1,000,000 from a financial institution at 1% above the prime rate. The loan is secured by inventory and accounts receivable (with a carrying value of $700,000 at December 31, 20X2), is payable in quarterly installments of principal and interest, and matures in December 20X6. The Company has used a portion of the proceeds to pay off the outstanding balance of the 10% short-term notes payable to a finance company, totaling $473,000 at December 31, 20X2. Accordingly, that balance of $473,000 has been classified as long-term debt at December 31, 20X2.

Example 6: Short-Term Debt Classified as Long-Term Because Proceeds from Sale of Stock Subsequent to Balance Sheet Date Are Expected to Be Used to Retire the Short-Term Debt

On January 28, 20X3, the Company sold 300,000 shares of its $.01 par value common stock for $5 per share. Of the total proceeds of $1,500,000, the Company expects to use $695,000 to refinance on a long-term basis the outstanding principal balance of its 11% short-term notes payable to a vendor. Accordingly, the amount of $695,000 has been classified as long-term debt at December 31, 20X2.

Example 7: Bank Waives Noncompliance with Financial Covenants

The Company's credit agreement with the bank contains certain financial covenants that require, among other things, maintenance of minimum amounts and ratios of working capital; minimum amounts of tangible net worth; maximum ratio of indebtedness to tangible net worth; and limits purchases of property, plant and equipment. Certain financial covenants have not been met, and the bank has waived such noncompliance.

Example 8: Borrowings under Revolving Line of Credit and Restrictive Covenants

The Company has available a revolving line of credit with a bank for the lesser of (a) $5,000,000 or (b) the sum of 80% of eligible domestic trade accounts receivable and 55% of eligible inventory, as defined. The line of credit expires in November 20X3, unless extended. Borrowings under the line of credit bear interest (9.25% at December 31, 20X2) at one of the following rates as selected by the Company: LIBOR plus 1% to 2.25%, or the bank's prime rate plus 0.5%. All borrowings are collateralized by substantially all assets of the Company. The outstanding balance on the line of credit was $4,436,000 and $3,879,000 at December 31, 20X2, and December 31, 20X1, respectively. Borrowings under the line of credit are subject to certain financial covenants and restrictions on indebtedness, dividend payments, financial guarantees, business combinations, and other related items. As of December 31, 20X2, the Company is in compliance with all covenants. Retained earnings available for the payment of cash dividends was $657,000 at December 31, 20X2. The carrying amount of receivables that serve as collateral for borrowings totaled $6,300,000 at December 31, 20X2.

Example 9: Credit Facility Classified as a Current Liability as a Result of a Lockbox Arrangement and Subjective Acceleration Clause

The Company's revolving credit facility requires a lockbox arrangement, which provides for all receipts to be swept daily to reduce borrowings outstanding under the credit facility. This arrangement, combined with the existence of a subjective acceleration clause in the revolving credit facility, necessitates the revolving credit facility be classified a current liability on the balance sheet. The acceleration clause allows the Company's lenders to forgo additional advances should they determine there has been a material adverse change in the Company's financial position or prospects reasonably likely to result in a material adverse effect on its business, condition, operations, performance, or properties. Management believes that no such material adverse change has occurred. In addition, at December 31, 20X2, the Company's lenders had not informed the Company that any such event had occurred. The revolving credit facility expires in March 20X7. Management believes that it will continue to borrow on the line of credit to fund its operations over the term of the revolving credit facility.

Example 10: Unused Available Line of Credit

The Company has a demand bank line of credit totaling $6,000,000, including letters of credit, under which the Company may borrow on an unsecured basis at the bank's prime rate. There were no amounts outstanding under this line of credit at December 31, 20X2, and December 31, 20X1. The credit agreement requires compliance with certain financial covenants and expires on April 30, 20X4.

Example 11: Borrowings under Line of Credit May Be Converted into a Term Loan

The line of credit agreement allows the Company to convert the borrowing to a term loan for any outstanding amount upon request prior to the expiration of the agreement.

Example 12: Factoring Agreement

Pursuant to a factoring agreement, the Company's principal bank acts as its factor for the majority of its receivables, which are assigned on a pre-approved basis. At December 31, 20X2, and December 31, 20X1, the factoring charge amounted to 0.25% of the receivables assigned. The Company's obligations to the bank are collateralized by all of the Company's accounts receivable, inventories, and equipment. The advances for factored receivables are made pursuant to a revolving credit and security agreement, which expires on March 31, 20X4. Pursuant to the terms of the agreement, the Company is required to maintain specified levels of working capital and tangible net worth, among other covenants.

The Company draws down working capital advances and opens letters of credit (up to an aggregate maximum of $10 million) against the facility in amounts determined on a formula that is based on factored receivables, inventory, and cost of imported goods under outstanding letters of credit. Interest is charged at the bank's prime lending rate plus 1% per annum (9.25% at December 31, 20X2) on such advances. As of December 31, 20X2, the Company was in compliance with the covenants under its revolving credit facility.

Example 13: Letters of Credit—Inventory

At December 31, 20X2, and December 31, 20X1, the Company has outstanding irrevocable letters of credit in the amount of $1,800,000 and $700,000, respectively. These letters of credit, which have terms from two months to one year, collateralize the Company's obligations to third parties for the purchase of inventory. The fair value of these letters of credit approximates contract values based on the nature of the fee arrangements with the issuing banks.

Example 14: Letters of Credit—Contracts and Debt Obligations

At December 31, 20X2, standby letters of credit of approximately $2,400,000 have been issued under an agreement, expiring September 30, 20X3, which is being maintained as security for performance and advances received on long-term contracts and as security for debt service payments under industrial revenue bond loan agreements. The agreement provides a maximum commitment for letters of credit of $3,500,000 and requires an annual commitment fee of $25,000.

Example 15: Compensating Balance Requirement Is Based on a Percentage of the Available Line of Credit

As part of its line of credit agreement with a bank, the Company is expected to maintain average compensating cash balances, which are based on a percentage of the available credit line. The amount of compensating balances required at December 31, 20X2, was $300,000. The compensating balances are held under agreements that do not legally restrict the use of such funds and, therefore, the funds are not segregated on the face of the Balance Sheet. The compensating cash balances are determined daily by the bank based upon cash balances shown by the bank, adjusted for average uncollected funds and Federal Reserve requirements. During the year ended December 31, 20X2, the Company was in substantial compliance with the compensating balance requirements. Funds on deposit with the bank and considered in the compensating balances are subject to withdrawal; however, the availability of the line of credit is dependent upon the maintenance of sufficient average compensating balances.

Example 16: Compensating Balance Requirement Is a Fixed Amount

As part of its line of credit agreement with a bank, the Company has agreed to maintain average compensating balances of $150,000. The balances are not legally restricted as to withdrawal and serve as part of the Company's normal operating cash.

Debt with Conversion and Other Options

Example 17: Debt Issued with Stock Purchase Warrants—Fair Value of Warrants Recorded as Additional Paid-in Capital

In May 20X2, the Company sold in a private placement to qualified buyers and accredited investors 10,000 Note Units (the Note Offering). Each Note Unit consisted of $1,000 principal amount of 13.5% unsecured Notes (collectively, the Notes) due May 1, 20X9, and one Common Stock Purchase Warrant (collectively the Warrants) to purchase 85 shares of the Company's common stock, par value $ 0.01 per share (the Common Stock), at an exercise price of $3.09 per share, first exercisable after May 20, 20X3. Total funds received of $10,000,000 were allocated $2,000,000 to the Warrants and $8,000,000 to the Notes. The values assigned to both the Notes and the Warrants were allocated based on their relative fair values. The relative fair value of the Warrants of $2,000,000 at the time of issuance, which was determined using the Black-Scholes option-pricing model, was recorded as additional paid-in capital and reduced the carrying value of the Notes. The discount on the Notes is being amortized to interest expense over the term of the Notes. At December 31, 20X2, the unamortized discount on the Notes is approximately $1,825,000.

Interest on the Notes is payable semiannually on May 1 and November 1. The Notes will mature on May 1, 20X9. The Notes are not redeemable at the option of the Company prior to May 1, 20X7.

On or after May 1, 20X7, the Notes are redeemable at the option of the Company, in whole or in part, at an initial redemption price of 106.75% of the aggregate principal amount of the Notes until May 1, 20X8, and at par thereafter, plus accrued and unpaid interest, if any, to the date of redemption.

Example 18: Debt Issued with Stock Purchase Warrants—Fair Value of Warrants Recorded as a Liability

On January 16, 20X2, the Company issued unsecured promissory notes in the aggregate principal amount of $1,000,000 (the Notes) and warrants to purchase the Company's common stock (the Warrants) to Blue Alliance, Inc. The Notes bear interest at a rate of 11%, mature on July 16, 20X3, and are convertible into 542,000 shares of the Company's common stock at a conversion price of $ 1.75 per share. The difference between the conversion price and the fair market value of the common stock on the commitment date (transaction date) resulted in a beneficial conversion feature recorded of $590,000. The associated Warrants are exercisable for 270,000 shares of common stock at an exercise price of $1.75 per share. The Warrants, which expire four years after issuance, were assigned a value of $410,000, estimated using the Black-Scholes valuation model. The following assumptions were used to determine the fair value of the Warrants using the Black-Scholes valuation model: a term of four years, risk-free rate of 3.28%, volatility of 100%, and dividend yield of zero. The discounts on the Notes for the beneficial conversion feature and the Warrants are being amortized to interest expense, using the effective interest method, over the term of the Notes. Total interest expense recognized relating to the beneficial conversion feature and the Warrants discount was $673,000 during the year ended December 31, 20X2.

The holders of the Notes and Warrants have registration rights that require the Company to file a registration statement with the Securities and Exchange Commission to register the resale of the common stock issuable upon conversion of the Notes or the exercise of the Warrants. The ability to register stock is deemed to be outside of the Company's control. Accordingly, the initial fair value of the Warrants of $410,000 was recorded as an accrued warrant liability in the consolidated balance sheet, and is marked to market at the end of each reporting period. At December 31, 20X2, the warrant liability was adjusted to its new fair value of $217,000 as determined by the Company, resulting in a gain of $193,000, which has been reflected in "Interest income and other, net" on the consolidated statement of operations for the year ended December 31, 20X2.

Example 19: Incremental Disclosures for Debt with Conversion and Other Options Prescribed by ASC Subtopic 470-20 Based on Guidance in FSP APB 14-1

> **Note:** This example illustrates the application of the incremental disclosure requirements prescribed by ASC Subtopic 470-20, *Debt—Debt with Conversion and Other Options,* based on FSP APB 14-1, *Accounting for Convertible Debt Instruments That May Be Settled in Cash upon Conversion (Including Partial*

Cash Settlement), which are effective for fiscal years, and interim periods within those fiscal years, beginning after December 15, 2008.

Effective January 1, 2009, the Company adopted FASB ASC 470-20 [formerly provided in FSP APB 14-1, *Accounting for Convertible Debt Instruments That May Be Settled in Cash upon Conversion (Including Partial Cash Settlement)*], which applies to all convertible debt instruments that have a "net settlement feature," which means instruments that by their terms may be settled either wholly or partially in cash upon conversion. Accordingly, the liability and equity components of convertible debt instruments that may be settled wholly or partially in cash upon conversion should be accounted for separately in a manner reflective of their issuer's nonconvertible debt borrowing rate. Previous guidance was provided for accounting for this type of convertible debt instrument entirely as debt. The Company has retrospectively applied this change in accounting for all periods presented. The total effect on prior year retained earnings was a $5 million reduction.

Since the Company's 5% convertible unsecured debentures due 2018 ("5% Debentures") have an option to be settled in cash, they qualify for treatment under this new accounting requirement. The Company's effective borrowing rate for nonconvertible debt at the time of issuance of the 5% Debentures was estimated to be 12%, which resulted in $10 million of the $50 million aggregate principal amount of debentures issued being attributable to equity. As of December 31, 2009, and 2008, there was $2 million and $2.5 million, respectively, of the initial $10 million debt discount, which remained unamortized, and is expected to be amortized through the first put date of the debt in June 2014. As of December 31, 2009, and 2008, the net carrying amount of the remaining debt was $30 million and $32 million, respectively.

The effective interest rate on the debt component for 2009 and 2008 was 7.3% and 7.1%, respectively. In 2009, the Company recognized interest expense of $3.6 million, comprised of $3 million relating to the contractual interest coupon and $600,000 relating to discount amortization. In 2008, the Company recognized interest expense of $3.8 million, comprised of $3.3 million relating to the contractual interest coupon and $500,000 relating to discount amortization.

At date of issuance, the 5% Debentures had an initial conversion rate of approximately 9 shares of common stock per $1,000 principal amount of the 5% Debentures, representing a conversion price of approximately $15 per share of the Company's common stock. As of December 31, 2009, the 5% Debentures had a conversion rate of approximately 8 shares of common stock per $1,000 principal amount of the 5% Debentures, which is equivalent to a conversion price of approximately $13 per share of the Company's common stock.

Holders of the 5% Debentures may convert their 5% Debentures into cash and, if applicable, shares of the Company's common stock prior to their stated maturity only under the following circumstances: (1) the 5% Debentures will be convertible during any calendar quarter after the calendar quarter ending March 31, 2010, if the closing sale price of the Company's common stock for each of 20 or more trading days in a period of 30 consecutive trading days ending on the last trading day of the immediately preceding calendar quarter exceeds 120% of the conversion price in effect on the last trading day of the immediately preceding calendar quarter; (2) the 5% Debentures will be convertible upon the occurrence of a "Fundamental Change," as defined; (3) the 5% Debentures will be convertible if the Company calls the 5% Debentures for redemption; and (4) the 5% Debentures will be convertible at any time from, and including, June 1, 2014.

Participating Mortgage Loans

Example 20: Terms of Loan and Related Contingent Interest Representing Entire Amount of Participation Liability Are Disclosed

In March 20X1, the Company entered into a loan agreement with Norris, Inc. for $5 million. The debt proceeds were used solely to finance the acquisition and development of the XYZ real estate project. The term loan is collateralized by the XYZ project, carries interest at a fixed rate of 9%, and matures on December 15, 20X9. The loan also includes a 15% contingent interest component applied on excess cash flow, as defined in the agreement. In addition, the Company is required to pay profit participation amounts for certain required internal rates of return and price participation amounts based on a percentage of the sales price of each unit in the project. Monthly installments of interest only are payable until the maturity date. Contingent interest is due in quarterly installments. The contingent interest component assigned to the loan agreement with Norris, Inc. has been accounted for in accordance with FASB ASC 470-30, *Participating Mortgage Loans.*

At the inception of the loan in March 20X1, the Company estimated the fair value of the participation liability (contingent component) to be $500,000. At December 31, 20X2, the fair value of the participation liability increased to $800,000, which represents an agreed-upon amount owed to Norris, Inc. For the year ended December 31, 20X2, and 20X1, the Company recognized a participation liability in accordance with FASB ASC 470-30 related to the term loan with Norris, Inc. in an amount equal to the determined fair value. This participation liability is reflected in the liability section of the balance sheet and totaled $800,000 and $500,000 as of December 31, 20X2, and 20X1, respectively.

The unamortized debt discount relating to the participation liability totaled $750,000 and $475,000 at December 31, 20X2, and 20X1, respectively. Amortization of the debt discount of $50,000 and $25,000 relating to the participation liability has been included in interest expense for 20X2 and 20X1, respectively.

Product Financing Arrangements

Example 21: Obligations and Commitments under Product Financing Arrangement

In 20X2, the Company entered into a product financing arrangement with a vendor for the purchase of $13 million of electronic connectors. Accordingly, this inventory and the related short-term debt have been included in the Balance Sheet at December 31, 20X2. The vendor has also made commitments, on the Company's behalf, to purchase additional amounts of the electronic connectors for delivery in 20X3. The average interest rate on the product financing arrangement was 7.3% at December 31, 20X2. Interest expense incurred and paid under this product financing arrangement totaled $186,000 for 20X2. The Company is obligated to pay the vendor under this product financing arrangement upon its receipt of the products.

Modifications and Extinguishments

Example 22: Gain from Early Extinguishment of Debt Does Not Meet the Criteria for Classification as an Extraordinary Item

During the year ended December 31, 20X2, in connection with the settlement of obligations involving Hope Enterprises, the Company recognized a gain of $1,200,000 representing the difference between the fair value of the consideration issued in the settlement transaction and the carrying value of the amounts due Hope Enterprises. The Company evaluated the classification of this gain and determined that the gain does not meet the criteria for classification as an extraordinary item. As a result, the gain has been included as "Gain on early extinguishment of debt" under "Other income (expense)" within income from continuing operations in the accompanying Consolidated Statement of Operations for the year ended December 31, 20X2.

Example 23: Loss from Early Extinguishment of Debt Meets the Criteria for Classification as an Extraordinary Item

In September 20X2, the Company redeemed various outstanding notes and debentures with an aggregate principal value of $2,769,000. The Company paid a premium to the debenture holders, and the transaction resulted in an extraordinary charge. The extraordinary loss of $452,000, net of a tax benefit of $165,000, principally represents the premium paid in connection with the early extinguishment of the debt and unamortized discount. The payments were made out of available cash.

Troubled Debt Restructurings by Debtors

Example 24: Terms of Troubled Debt Modified—Carrying Amount of Troubled Debt Exceeds Future Cash Payments

At December 31, 20X1, the Company had a 12% note payable to its primary bank with an outstanding principal balance of $1,756,000, due in December 20X7. In September 20X2, the Company reached an agreement with the bank to modify the terms of the note, due to cash flow problems experienced by the Company. The bank has agreed to accept a cash payment of $250,000 and installment payments on a note for a total of $900,000 at no interest, due in December 20X7. As a result, the amount of the note to the bank was reduced by $606,000 to reflect the revised terms, and a gain of $352,000 has been included in the Statement of Operations for 20X2.

Example 25: Terms of Troubled Debt Modified—Future Cash Payments Exceed Carrying Value of Troubled Debt

At December 31, 20X1, the Company had an 11% note payable to its primary bank with an outstanding principal balance of $1,500,000, due in December 20X3. In September 20X2, the Company reached an agreement with the bank to modify the terms of the note, due to cash flow problems experienced by the Company. The bank has agreed to extend the due date of the note until December 20X6 and to reduce the interest rate to 9%. The modifications have resulted in an effective interest rate of 8.2% to be applied to the carrying amount of the debt prospectively. Interest expense through the revised maturity date of December 20X6 will be reduced accordingly.

Example 26: Transfer of Assets and Grant of Equity Interest in Full Settlement of Troubled Debt Restructuring—Ordinary Gain Is Recognized on Transfer of Assets and Extraordinary Gain Is Recognized on Restructured Debt

In March 20X2, the Company reached an agreement with its principal vendor to transfer fixed assets and to grant 50,000 shares of the Company's $ 0.01 par value common stock to the vendor in full settlement of a 12% note payable to the vendor due in February 20X4. At the date of transfer, the fair market value of the fixed assets and common stock transferred exceeded their carrying value by $179,000; accordingly, an ordinary gain of $179,000 has been included in the Statement of Operations in 20X2. At the date of transfer, the carrying value of the debt payable to the vendor exceeded the fair market value of the fixed assets and common stock transferred by $611,000; accordingly, an extraordinary gain of $397,000, net of income tax of $214,000, has been included in the Statement of Operations in 20X2.

Example 27: Modified Terms of Troubled Debt Restructuring Include Future Contingent Payments

Due to significant cash flow problems, in April 20X2, the Company modified the terms of its 10% note payable to a principal vendor with an outstanding balance of $1,618,000, due in quarterly installments through May 20X7. The vendor has agreed to (1) accept 2,000,000 shares of the Company's $ 0.01 par value common stock, (2) reduce the required quarterly payments by $35,000 through May 20X7, and (3) receive an additional $50,000 annual payment for each year in which the Company's cash flow from operations exceeds $250,000. As a result of these modifications, the Company recorded a gain of $315,000 in the Statement of Operations in 20X2.

CHAPTER 33
ASC TOPIC 480: DISTINGUISHING LIABILITIES FROM EQUITY

CONTENTS

EXECUTIVE SUMMARY

Distinguishing Liabilities from Equity

PRACTICE ALERT: The requirements in ASC Topic 480 are affected by FSP FAS 150-3, *Effective Date, Disclosures, and Transition for Mandatorily Redeemable Financial Instruments of Certain Nonpublic Entities and Certain Mandatorily Redeemable Noncontrolling Interests under FASB Statement No. 150, Accounting for Certain Financial Instruments with Characteristics of Both Liabilities and Equity* (ASC 480-10-65-1) (FSP FAS 150-3, par. 3), which defers the effective date of such requirements for certain mandatorily redeemable financial instruments and certain mandatorily redeemable noncontrolling interests as follows:

- *Certain mandatorily redeemable financial instruments of nonpublic entities that are not SEC registrants.* The classification, measurement, and disclosure provisions are deferred indefinitely for mandatorily redeemable financial instruments of nonpublic entities, other than those that are mandatorily redeemable on fixed dates and for amounts that either are fixed or are determined by reference to an external index (e.g., interest rate index, currency index). For example, the requirements are deferred indefinitely for shares of nonpublic entities that are required to be redeemed upon the death of the shareholder.

- *Certain mandatorily redeemable noncontrolling interests (commonly known as minority interests) of all entities, public and nonpublic:*

  — For mandatorily redeemable noncontrolling interests that would not have to be classified as liabilities by the subsidiary under the "only upon liquidation" exception, but would be classified as liabilities by the parent in consolidated financial statements, the classification and measurement provisions are deferred indefinitely pending further FASB action.

  — For other mandatorily redeemable noncontrolling interests that were issued before November 5, 2003, the *measurement* provisions are deferred indefinitely pending further FASB action, both for the parent in consolidated financial statements and for the subsidiary that issued the instruments that result in the mandatorily redeemable noncontrolling interest. However, the *classification* provisions are not deferred.

  — During the deferral period, all public entities and nonpublic entities that are SEC registrants are required to follow the *disclosure* requirements in ASC 480-10-50-1 and 50-2 (FAS-150, pars. 26 and 27) (see below), as well as disclosures required by other applicable guidance.

ASC 480 requires that an entity classify a financial instrument that is within its scope as a liability (or an asset in some circumstances) because that financial instrument embodies an obligation of the issuer. The following are examples of an obligation:

- An entity incurs a conditional obligation to transfer assets by issuing (writing) a put option that would, if exercised, require the entity to repurchase its equity shares by physical settlement.

- An entity incurs a conditional obligation to transfer assets by issuing a similar contract that requires or could require a net cash settlement.

- An entity incurs a conditional obligation to issue its equity shares by issuing a similar contract that requires a net share settlement.

Conversely, by issuing shares of stock, an entity generally does not incur an obligation to redeem the shares, and, therefore, that entity does not incur an obligation to transfer assets or issue additional equity shares. However, some issuances of stock (e.g., mandatorily redeemable preferred stock) do impose obligations requiring the issuer to transfer assets or issue its equity shares.

Accounting Literature

FASB Accounting Standards Codification Topic	*Pre-Codification Accounting Literature*
480, *Distinguishing Liabilities from Equity*	FAS-150, *Accounting for Certain Financial Instruments with Characteristics of Both Liabilities and Equity*
	FSP FAS 150-2, *Accounting for Mandatorily Redeemable Shares Requiring Redemption by Payment of an Amount that Differs from the Book Value of Those Shares, under FASB Statement No. 150, "Accounting for Certain Financial Instruments with Characteristics of both Liabilities and Equity"*
	FSP FAS 150-3, *Effective Date, Disclosures, and Transition for Mandatorily Redeemable Financial Instruments of Certain Nonpublic Entities and Certain Mandatorily Redeemable Noncontrolling Interests under FASB Statement No. 150, Accounting for Certain Financial Instruments with Characteristics of Both Liabilities and Equity*

DISCLOSURE AND KEY PRESENTATION REQUIREMENTS

PRACTICE ALERT: The disclosure and key presentation requirements in ASC Topic 480 are affected by FSP FAS 150-3, *Effective Date, Disclosures, and Transition for Mandatorily Redeemable Financial Instruments of Certain Nonpublic Entities and Certain Mandatorily Redeemable Noncontrolling Interests under FASB Statement No. 150, Accounting for Certain Financial Instruments with Characteristics* *of Both Liabilities and Equity* (ASC 480-10-65-1) (FSP FAS 150-3, par. 3), which defers the effective date of such requirements for certain mandatorily redeemable financial instruments and certain mandatorily redeemable noncontrolling interests as follows:

- *Certain mandatorily redeemable financial instruments of nonpublic entities that are not SEC registrants.* The classification, measurement, and disclosure provisions are deferred indefinitely for mandatorily redeemable financial instruments of nonpublic entities, other than those that are mandatorily redeemable on fixed dates and for amounts that either are fixed or are determined by reference to an external index (e.g., interest rate index, currency index). For example, the requirements are deferred indefinitely for shares of nonpublic entities that are required to be redeemed upon the death of the shareholder.

- *Certain mandatorily redeemable noncontrolling interests (commonly known as minority interests) of all entities, public and nonpublic:*

  — For mandatorily redeemable noncontrolling interests that would not have to be classified as liabilities by the subsidiary under the "only upon liquidation" exception, but would be classified as liabilities by the parent in consolidated financial statements, the classification and measurement provisions are deferred indefinitely pending further FASB action.

  — For other mandatorily redeemable noncontrolling interests that were issued before November 5, 2003, the *measurement* provisions are deferred indefinitely pending further FASB action, both for the parent in consolidated financial statements and for the subsidiary that issued the instruments that result in the mandatorily redeemable noncontrolling interest. However, the *classification* provisions are not deferred.

  — During the deferral period, all public entities and nonpublic entities that are SEC registrants are required to follow the *disclosure* requirements in ASC 480-10-50-1 and 50-2 (FAS-150, pars. 26 and 27) (see below), as well as disclosures required by other applicable guidance.

1. Financial instruments that are required to be presented as liabilities (or assets in some circumstances) should *not* be presented between the liabilities section and the equity section of the balance sheet. (ASC 480-10-45-1) (FAS-150, par. 18)

2. For entities that have no equity instruments outstanding but have financial instruments issued in the form of shares (all of which are mandatorily redeemable financial instruments required to be classified as liabilities):

   a. Those instruments should be described as "shares subject to mandatory redemption" in the balance sheet to distinguish those instruments from other liabilities. (ASC 480-10-45-2) (FAS-150, par. 19)

   b. Payments to holders of such instruments and related accruals should be presented separately from payments to and interest due to other creditors in statements of cash flows and income. (ASC 480-10-45-2) (FAS-150, par. 19)

   c. The components of the liability that would otherwise be related to shareholders' interest and other comprehensive income, if any, subject to the redemption feature should be disclosed (e.g., par value and other paid-in amounts of mandatorily redeemable instruments should be disclosed separately from the amount of retained earnings or accumulated deficit). (ASC 480-10-50-4) (FAS-150, par. 28)

3. If all of an entity's shares are subject to mandatory redemption and the entity is not subject to the deferral provisions, as described in the note above (ASC 480-10-45-2A) (FSP FAS 150-2, pars. 1–4):

   a. An excess of the redemption price of the shares over the entity's equity balance should be reported as an excess of liabilities over assets (a deficit), even though the mandatorily redeemable shares are reported as a liability.

   b. If the redemption price of the mandatorily redeemable shares is less than the book value of those shares, the entity should report the excess of that book value over the liability reported for the mandatorily redeemable shares as an excess of assets over liabilities (equity).

4. Mandatorily redeemable shares that are not subject to the deferral provisions, as described in the note above, should be measured at either the present value of the amount to be paid at settlement or the amount of cash that would be paid under the conditions specified in the contract if settlement occurred at the reporting date, recognizing the resulting change in that amount as interest cost (change in redemption amount). (ASC 480-10-45-2B) (FSP FAS 150-2, par. 5)

5. For forward contracts that require physical settlement by repurchase of a fixed number of the issuer's equity shares in exchange for cash, any amounts paid or to be paid to holders

of such contracts in excess of the initial measurement amount should be reflected in interest cost. (ASC 480-10-45-3) (FAS-150, par. 22)

6. For entities that have issued mandatorily redeemable shares of common stock or entered into forward contracts that require physical settlement by repurchase of a fixed number of the issuer's equity shares of common stock in exchange for cash (ASC 480-10-45-4) (FAS-150, par. 25):

   a. The calculation of basic and diluted earnings per share should exclude the common shares that are to be redeemed or repurchased.

   b. Any amounts, including contractual (accumulated) dividends and participation rights in undistributed earnings, attributable to shares that are to be redeemed or repurchased that have not been recognized as interest costs should be deducted in computing income available to common shareholders, consistently with the two-class method.

7. For entities that issue financial instruments with characteristics of both liabilities and equity (recognized under the guidance in ASC Section 480-10-25), the following disclosures should be made (ASC 480-10-50-1) (FAS-150, par. 26):

   a. The nature and terms of the financial instruments.

   b. The rights and obligations embodied in those instruments, including:

      (1) Settlement alternatives, if any, in the contract.

      (2) The entity that controls the settlement alternatives.

8. For all outstanding financial instruments with characteristics of both liabilities and equity (recognized under the guidance in ASC Section 480-10-25), and for each settlement alternative, the following disclosures should be made (ASC 480-10-50-2) (FAS-150, par. 27):

   a. The amount that would be paid, or the number of shares that would be issued and their fair value, determined under the conditions specified in the contract if the settlement were to occur at the reporting date.

   b. How changes in the fair value of the issuer's equity shares would affect those settlement amounts.

   c. The maximum amount that the issuer could be required to pay to redeem the instrument by physical settlement, if applicable.

   d. The maximum number of shares that could be required to be issued, if applicable.

e. That a contract does not limit the amount that the issuer could be required to pay or the number of shares that the issuer could be required to issue, if applicable.

f. For a forward contract or an option indexed to the issuer's equity shares, all of the following:

(1) The forward price or option strike price.

(2) The number of issuer's shares to which the contract is indexed.

(3) The settlement date or dates of the contract, as applicable.

EXAMPLES OF FINANCIAL STATEMENT DISCLOSURES

 The following sample disclosures are available on the accompanying disc.

Example 1: Mandatorily Redeemable Convertible Preferred Stock Reported as a Long-Term Liability

The Company issued 400,000 shares of mandatorily redeemable Series B Convertible Preferred Stock in March 20X1. Each share has a liquidation value of $10 per share. The liquidation value, plus accrued but unpaid dividends, is payable on March 8, 20X9, the mandatory redemption date. The Company has the option to redeem all, but not less than all, of the shares of Series B preferred stock at any time after six years from the date of issuance for a number of shares of the Company's common stock equal to the liquidation value plus accrued and unpaid dividends divided by the current market price of common stock determined in relation to the date of redemption. Under this option, were the redemption to have taken place at December 31, 20X2, each share would have been converted into 1.081 shares of common stock. In addition, each share of preferred stock is convertible, at any time, at the option of the holder into the right to receive shares of the Company's common stock. Initially, each share was convertible into .732 shares of common stock, subject to adjustment in the event of certain dividends and distributions, a merger, consolidation or sale of substantially all of the Company's assets, a liquidation or distribution, and certain other events. Were the conversion to have taken place at December 31, 20X2, each share would have been converted into .732 shares of common stock. Holders of preferred stock are entitled to cumulative annual cash dividends of $1 per share, payable quarterly. In any liquidation of the Company, each share of preferred stock is entitled to a liquidation preference before any distribution may be made on the Company's common stock or any series of capital stock that is junior to the Series B preferred stock. In the event of a change in control of the Company, holders of Series B preferred stock also have specified exchange rights into common stock of the Company or into specified securities or property of another entity participating in the change in control transaction.

At December 31, 20X2, mandatorily redeemable preferred stock, totaling $4,000,000, is reported as a long-term liability in the balance sheet. As of December 31, 20X2, 1,000,000 preferred stock shares are authorized and 400,000 shares are issued and outstanding.

Balance Sheet Presentation

The following presentation illustrates the reporting of the mandatorily redeemable convertible preferred stock as a long-term liability based on this example.

Liabilities:

Accounts payable	$ 2,350,000
Short-term debt	900,000
Accrued expenses	500,000
Total current liabilities	3,750,000
Long-term debt	2,500,000
Mandatorily redeemable convertible preferred stock	4,000,000
Deferred income taxes	725,000
Total liabilities	$10,975,000
Stockholders' equity: (Details omitted)	

Example 2: Initial Public Offering Price of Company's Common Stock Is Used to Determine the Fair Value of the Mandatorily Redeemable Preferred Stock

The Company's series B preferred stock was issued in October 20X0 in conjunction with the Company' acquisition of ABC Co. and related refinancing. Prior to the Company's consummation of the initial public offering in 20X2, there were 50,000 shares of series B preferred stock issued and outstanding. In connection with the issuance of the series B preferred stock, the Company sold each share of series B preferred stock for $1,000, raising approximately $50 million. The series B preferred stock ranked senior to the series A preferred stock and the common stock. The series B preferred stock voted as if converted into common stock. The series B preferred stock was also subject to mandatory redemption of $1,000 per share plus accumulated dividends on August 31, 20X9. In addition to the mandatory redemption, each share of series B preferred stock was entitled to convert into (a) one share of $1,000 redemption value series B1 cumulative redeemable shares, (b) approximately 5 shares of series A preferred stock at December 31, 20X2, and (c) approximately 150 shares of common stock. The series B preferred stock was entitled to a cumulative dividend at an annual rate of 7% of the original issue price per share plus accumulated unpaid dividends, compounded quarterly (which was increased to 9% effective April 20X1 and subsequently reduced to 7% in March 20X2), from the date of issuance. The Company recorded the reduction in the dividend as a $3 million decrease in non-cash interest expense related to redeemable preferred stock in the year ended December 31, 20X2.

The series B preferred stock had been accounted for at fair value under FASB ASC 480 because it had a stated redemption date. In addition, although the series B preferred stock was convertible into other shares, these shares into which the series B was convertible also had the same mandatory redemption date, except for the common shares. However, on the issuance date of the series B preferred stock, the common stock portion of the conversion feature was considered to be a non-substantive feature and, therefore, was disregarded in the mandatorily redeemable determination. The estimated fair value of the series B preferred stock was affected by the fair value of such common stock. Accordingly, the increase or decrease in the fair value of this security has been recorded as either an increase or decrease in interest expense at each reporting period. During the years ended December 31, 20X2, and 20X1, respectively, the Company recorded the related dividend accretion for the change in fair value of the series B preferred stock in the amounts of $7 million and $4 million, respectively, as interest expense. The interest expense recorded by the Company for the dividend accretion for the change in fair value of its series B preferred stock for 20X2 was for the period up to August 15, 20X2, the date on which all shares of series B preferred stock were converted into shares of series A preferred stock, series B1 preferred stock and common stock and on which the Company redeemed all shares of series A preferred stock and series B1 preferred stock, including those issued upon conversion of the series B preferred stock. Given the absence of an active market for the Company's common stock, the Company conducted a contemporaneous valuation analysis to help it estimate the fair value of the Company's common stock that was used to value the conversion option for 20X1. A variety of objective and subjective factors were considered to estimate the fair value of the common stock. Factors considered included contemporaneous valuation analysis using the income and market approaches, the likelihood of achieving and the timing of a liquidity event, such as an initial public offering or sale of the Company, the cash flow and EBITDA-based trading multiples of comparable companies, including the Company's competitors and other similar publicly-traded companies, and the results of operations, market conditions, competitive position and stock performance of these companies. In particular, the Company used the current value method to determine the estimated fair value of its securities by allocating its enterprise value among its different classes of securities. The Company considered such method more applicable than the probability weighted expected return method because of the terms of its redeemable preferred stock.

During 20X2, the Company used the initial public offering price of $8 per share as the fair value of its common stock to determine the fair value of the series B preferred stock and to calculate the non-cash interest expense related to redeemable preferred stock. The series B preferred stock had been recorded on the balance sheet net of unaccreted issuance costs of $600,000 at December 31, 20X1. During 20X2, the Company wrote off all unaccreted issuance costs of $325,000 as all shares of series B preferred stock (including all accrued and unpaid dividends) were converted into shares of series A preferred stock, series B1 preferred stock, and an aggregate of 6 million shares of common stock in connection with the Company's initial public offering.

On October 1, 20X2, the Company used the net proceeds of the initial public offering to redeem all of the outstanding shares of series A preferred stock (including all accrued and unpaid dividends and shares issued upon conversion of the series B preferred stock) and series B1 preferred stock (including shares issued upon conversion of the series B preferred stock).

PART 5—
EQUITY

CHAPTER 34
ASC TOPIC 505: EQUITY

CONTENTS

EXECUTIVE SUMMARY

Note: For financial instruments with characteristics of both liabilities and equity, see Chapter 33, "ASC Topic 480: Distinguishing Liabilities from Equity." For comprehensive income, see Chapter 5, "ASC Topic 220: Comprehensive Income."

Overall

Equity includes the following three broad categories:

1. *Contributed capital*—This represents (a) the amounts paid by common and preferred stockholders when they purchased the company's stock and (b) the amounts arising from subsequent transactions such as treasury stock transactions.

2. *Retained earnings*—This represents the amount of previous income of the company that has not been distributed to owners as dividends or transferred to contributed capital.

3. *Accumulated other comprehensive income*—Examples of other comprehensive income include the following: (a) unrealized gains and losses on certain investments in debt and equity securities, (b) foreign currency translation adjustments, and (c) gains and losses, prior service costs or credits, and transition assets or obligations associated with pension or other postretirement benefits. Components of other comprehensive income are covered in more detail in Chapter 5, "ASC Topic 220: Comprehensive Income," because comprehensive income may be reported in an income statement, in a separate statement of comprehensive income that begins with net income, or in a statement of changes in stockholder's equity.

Generally, the components of stockholders' equity are presented in the following order in the balance sheet:

- Preferred stock
- Common stock
- Additional paid-in capital
- Retained earnings (accumulated deficit)
- Accumulated other comprehensive income (loss)
- Treasury stock

Capital transactions should generally be excluded from the determination of income but should be adequately disclosed in the financial statements.

Capital stock. *Capital stock* represents the legal or stated capital provided by stockholders. Capital stock may consist of common or preferred shares. Common stock usually has (1) the right to vote, (2) the right to share in earnings, (3) a preemptive right to a proportionate share of any additional common stock issued, and (4) the right to share in assets on liquidation. Preferred stock carries certain specified preferences or privileges over common stock. For example, preferred shares may be (1) voting or nonvoting, (2) participating or nonparticipating as to the earnings of the corporation, (3) cumulative or noncumulative as to the payment of dividends, (4) callable for redemption at a specified price, or (5) convertible to common stock.

A corporation's charter contains the types and amounts of stock that it can legally issue, which is called the *authorized capital stock*. When part or all of the authorized capital stock is issued, it is called *issued capital stock*. Because a corporation may own issued capital stock in the form of treasury stock, the amount of issued capital stock in the hands of stockholders is called *outstanding capital stock*.

Additional paid-in capital. Generally, stock is issued with a par value. No-par value stock may or may not have a stated value. *Par* or *stated value* is the amount that is established in the stock account at the time the stock is issued. When stock is issued above or below par value, a premium or discount on the stock is recorded, respectively. A discount reduces paid-in or contributed capital; a premium increases paid-in or contributed capital. A premium on stock is often referred to as "Additional paid-in capital" or "Paid-in capital in excess of par value." Because the issuance of stock at a discount is not legal in many jurisdictions, discounts on stock are not frequently encountered.

Stock subscriptions receivable. A corporation may sell its capital stock by subscriptions. An individual subscriber becomes a stockholder upon subscribing to the capital stock, and, upon full payment of the subscription, a stock certificate evidencing ownership in the corporation is issued. When the subscription method is used to sell capital stock, a subscription receivable account is debited and a capital stock subscribed account is credited. On payment of the subscription, the subscription receivable account is credited and cash or other assets are debited. On the actual issuance of the stock certificates, the capital stock subscribed account is debited and the regular capital stock account is credited.

Stock subscriptions receivable generally should be reported as a deduction from stockholders' equity. They should be shown as an asset only in rare circumstances when the receivables mature in a relatively short period of time and there is substantial evidence of ability and intent to pay.

Appropriation of retained earnings. If a portion of retained earnings is appropriated, the appropriation of retained earnings should be shown within the stockholder's equity section of the balance sheet and be clearly identified as an appropriation of retained earnings.

Costs or losses should not be charged to an appropriation of retained earnings, and no part of the appropriation should be transferred to income.

Cash dividends. A dividend is a pro rata distribution by a corporation, based on shares of a particular class, and usually represents a distribution based on earnings. Cash dividends are the most common type of dividend distribution and are recorded on the books of the corporation as a liability (dividends payable) on the date of declaration.

Stock Dividends and Stock Splits

Stock dividends are distributions of a company's own capital stock to its existing stockholders in lieu of cash. Stock dividends are accounted for by transferring an amount equal to the fair market value of the stock from retained earnings to paid-in capital.

When a stock distribution is generally more than 20% to 25% of the outstanding shares immediately before the distribution, it is considered a stock split. A stock split increases the number of shares of capital stock outstanding, and a reverse stock split decreases the number of shares of capital stock outstanding. In both straight and reverse stock splits, the total dollar amount of stockholders' equity does not change. However, the par or stated value per share of capital stock decreases or increases in proportion with the increase or decrease in the number of shares outstanding.

Treasury Stock

Treasury stock is a company's own capital stock that has been issued and subsequently reacquired. It is ordinarily presented as a reduction in the amount of stockholders' equity. Treasury stock is not considered an asset, because it is widely held that a corporation cannot own part of itself. The status of treasury stock is similar to that of authorized but unissued capital stock. Dividends on a company's own stock are not considered a part of income. Gains and losses on sales of treasury stock should be accounted for as adjustments to capital and not as part of income.

Equity-Based Payments to Non-Employees

An entity may issue equity instruments to non-employees in exchange for the receipt of goods or services. Such transactions may involve a contemporaneous exchange of the equity instruments for goods or services or may involve an exchange that spans several financial reporting periods. This section applies to the following transactions:

- All share-based transactions in which an entity acquires goods or services from a non-employee by issuing equity instruments or by incurring liabilities in amounts based, at least in part, on the price of the entity's shares or that may be settled by issuing equity instruments of the entity.
- Modifications to existing arrangements.

See Chapter 40, "ASC Topic 718: Compensation—Stock Compensation," for transactions in which equity instruments are issued to employees. This section does not apply to:

- Transactions in which equity instruments are issued to employees (see Chapter 40, "ASC Topic 718: Compensation—Stock Compensation").
- Transactions with employee stock ownership plans (see Chapter 40, "ASC Topic 718: Compensation—Stock Compensation").
- Transactions in which equity instruments are issued either to an investor or a lender that provide financing to the issuer, or where equity instruments are issued in a business combination (see Chapter 44, "ASC Topic 805: Business Combinations").

Spinoffs and Reverse Spinoffs

A pro rata distribution to stockholders of the net assets (including shares of a subsidiary or equity investee) of a part of an entity's operations constituting a business is referred to as a spinoff. Spinoffs should be recorded at the carrying amount of the net assets, after reduction for any indicated impairment of value.

Reverse spinoff accounting results in treating the legal spinnee as the accounting spinnor and the legal spinnor as the accounting spinnee. In determining whether reverse spinoff accounting is appropriate, the substance of the spinoff transaction should be considered. If reverse spinoff accounting provides the most accurate depiction of the substance of the transaction, then such accounting should be used.

See Chapter 2, "ASC Topic 205: Presentation of Financial Statements," regarding the presentation of business activities disposed of in a spinoff, including discontinued operations.

Accounting Literature

FASB Accounting Standards Codification Topic	*Pre-Codification Accounting Literature*
505, *Equity*	FAS-5, *Accounting for Contingencies*
	FAS-123R, *Share-Based Payment*
	FAS-129, *Disclosure of Information about Capital Structure*
	FSP FAS 129-1, *Disclosure Requirements under FASB Statement No. 129, Disclosure of Information about Capital Structure, Relating to Contingently Convertible Securities*
	FTB 85-6, *Accounting for a Purchase of Treasury Shares at a Price Significantly in Excess of the Current Market Price of the Shares and the Income Statement Classification of Costs Incurred in Defending against a Takeover Attempt*
	EITF 85-1, *Classifying Notes Received for Capital Stock*
	EITF 98-5, *Accounting for Convertible Securities with Beneficial Conversion Features or Contingently Adjustable Conversion Ratios*
	EITF 00-8, *Accounting by a Grantee for an Equity Instrument to Be Received in Conjunction with Providing Goods or Services*
	EITF 00-18, *Accounting Recognition for Certain Transactions involving Equity Instruments Granted to Other Than Employees*
	EITF 00-27, *Application of Issue No. 98-5 to Certain Convertible Instruments*
	EITF 02-11, *Accounting for Reverse Spinoffs*
	APB-12, *Omnibus Opinion—1967*

FASB Accounting Standards Codification Topic	Pre-Codification Accounting Literature
	ARB-43, *Chapter 1B, Opinion Issued by Predecessor Committee*
	ARB-43, *Chapter 7B, Stock Dividends and Stock Split-ups*

DISCLOSURE AND KEY PRESENTATION REQUIREMENTS

Overall

1. For notes receivable arising from the issuance of equity (ASC 505-10-45-1) (EITF 85-1):

   a. The notes receivable should be presented as a contra-equity account (i.e., offset the notes and stock in the equity section), *or*

   b. If the notes receivable are reported as an asset (very limited circumstances), they should have been collected in cash before issuance of the financial statements or substantial evidence exists of ability and intent to pay within a reasonably short period of time.

2. For appropriations of retained earnings (ASC 505-10-45-3 and 45-4) (FAS-5, par. 15):

   a. They should be shown within the stockholders' equity section of the balance sheet and clearly identified as such.

   b. Costs or losses should *not* be charged to an appropriation of retained earnings.

   c. No part of the appropriation should be transferred to income.

3. The following disclosures should be made for each class of capital stock (generally accepted practice):

   a. Shares authorized, issued, and outstanding.

   b. Par value or stated value.

   c. The number of shares reserved for future issuance and the purpose for such reservation.

4. If both financial position and results of operations are presented, the following disclosures should be made (either in separate statements, or in the basic financial statements or notes thereto) for each period in which both a balance sheet

and an income statement are presented (ASC 505-10-50-2) (APB-12, par. 10):

    a. Retained earnings.

    b. Changes in the other separate accounts comprising stockholders' equity.

    c. Changes in the number of shares of equity securities during at least the most recent annual fiscal period and any subsequent interim period presented.

5. Disclosures should be made of the pertinent rights and privileges of the various securities outstanding, including (ASC 505-10-50-3) (FAS-129, par. 4):

    a. Dividend and liquidation preferences.

    b. Participation rights.

    c. Call prices and dates.

    d. Conversion or exercise prices or rates and pertinent dates.

    e. Sinking-fund requirements.

    f. Unusual voting rights.

    g. Significant terms of contracts to issue additional shares.

6. Disclosures should be made of the number of shares issued upon conversion, exercise, or satisfaction of required conditions during at least the most recent annual fiscal period and any subsequent interim period presented. (ASC 505-10-50-3) (FAS-129, par. 5)

7. The following disclosures should be made for preferred stock or other senior stock that has a preference in involuntary liquidation considerably in excess of the par or stated value of the shares (ASC 505-10-50-4 and 50-5) (FAS-129, pars. 6 and 7):

    a. The liquidation preference of the stock (the relationship between the preference in liquidation and the par or stated value of the shares). (*Note:* That disclosure should be made in the equity section of the balance sheet in the aggregate, either parenthetically or in short, rather than on a per-share basis or through disclosure in the notes.)

    b. The aggregate or per-share amounts at which preferred stock may be called or is subject to redemption through sinking-fund operations or otherwise.

    c. The aggregate and per-share amounts of arrearages in cumulative preferred dividends.

8. For all contingently convertible securities, disclosures should be made of the significant terms of the conversion features,

including (ASC 505-10-50-6 through 50-10) (FSP FAS 129-1, pars. 3–5; EITF 98-5; EITF 00-27) (*Note*: See Chapter 32, "ASC Topic 470: Debt" for incremental disclosure requirements of debt with conversion and other options.):

a.   Events or changes in circumstances that would cause the contingency to be met and any significant features necessary to understand the conversion rights and the timing of those rights (e.g., the periods in which the contingency might be met and the securities may be converted if the contingency is met).

b.   The conversion price and the number of shares into which a security is potentially convertible.

c.   Events or changes in circumstances, if any, that could adjust or change the contingency, conversion price, or number of shares, including significant terms of those changes.

d.   The manner of settlement upon conversion and any alternative settlement methods (e.g., cash, shares, or a combination).

e.   The possible conversion prices and dates, and other significant terms for each convertible instrument.

f.   The terms of the transaction, including the excess of the aggregate fair value of the instruments that the holder would receive at conversion over the proceeds received and the period over which the discount is amortized.

g.   Whether the shares that would be issued upon conversion are included in the calculation of diluted earnings per share and the reasons why or why not.

h.   Information about derivative instruments entered into in connection with the issuance of the contingently convertible securities, including:

   (1)   The terms of the derivative instruments, including terms of settlement).

   (2)   How those instruments relate to the contingently convertible securities.

   (3)   The number of shares underlying the derivative instruments.

   (4)   Any other disclosures required under ASC Topic 815, *Derivatives and Hedging* (FAS-133, *Accounting for Derivative Instruments and Hedging Activities*).

9.   For redeemable securities, disclosures should be made of the amount of redemption requirements (separately by issue or combined) for all issues of capital stock that are redeemable

at fixed or determinable prices on fixed or determinable dates in each of the five years following the date of the latest balance sheet presented. (ASC 505-10-50-11) (FAS-129, par. 8)

Stock Dividends and Stock Splits

1. If a stock dividend is in substance a stock split (as discussed in ASC paragraph 505-20-25-2 [ARB-43, Ch. 7B, par. 11]), the transaction should be described as a stock split effected in the form of a dividend. (ASC 505-20-50-1) (ARB-43, Ch. 7B, par. 11)

Treasury Stock

1. If a corporation's stock is acquired for purposes other than retirement (formal or constructive), or if the ultimate disposition has not yet been decided, the cost of the acquired stock should be shown in one of the following ways (ASC 505-30-45-1) (ARB-43, Ch. 1B, par. 7):

   a. The cost of the acquired stock shown separately as a deduction from the total of capital stock, additional paid-in capital, and retained earnings, *or*

   b. The difference between the cost of the acquired stock and its stated value reflected in capital in a manner appropriate for retired stock (as discussed in ASC paragraphs 505-30-30-7 through 30-10) (ARB-43, Ch. 1B, par. 7).

2. If state laws relating to a corporation's repurchase of its own outstanding common stock restrict the availability of retained earnings for payment of dividends or have other effects of a significant nature, those facts should be disclosed. (ASC 505-30-50-2) (ARB-43, Ch. 1B, par. 11A)

3. If a repurchase of shares is at a price that is significantly in excess of the current market price (ASC 505-30-50-3 and 50-4) (FTB 85-6, par. 3):

   a. Consideration should be given as to whether the entity should allocate the amounts paid to the treasury shares and to other elements of the transaction (as discussed in ASC paragraph 505-30-30-2 [FTB 85-6, par. 1]).

   b. The allocation (if any) of amounts paid to the treasury shares and to other elements of the transaction, and the accounting treatment for such amounts, should be disclosed.

Equity-Based Payments to Non-Employees

1. For assets (other than a note or a receivable) that a grantor has received in return for fully vested, nonforfeitable equity instruments that are issued at the date the grantor and a non-employee grantee enter into an agreement for goods or services (and no specific performance is required by the non-employee grantee in order to retain those equity instruments), such assets should *not* be displayed as contra-equity by the grantor. (ASC 505-50-45-1) (EITF 00-18)

2. For a grantor that acquires goods or services other than employee services in share-based payment transactions, disclosures similar to those required by ASC paragraphs 718-10-50-1 through 50-2 (FAS-123R, pars. 64 and A240) should be provided. (ASC 505-50-50-1) (FAS-123R, par. 65). See Chapter 40, "ASC Topic 718: Compensation—Stock Compensation."

3. For a grantee that provides goods or services other than employee services in share-based payment transactions, the grantee should disclose in accordance with ASC paragraphs 845-10-50-1 and 50-2, (APB-29, par. 28; EITF 00-8), the amount of gross operating revenue recognized as a result of such nonmonetary transactions. (ASC 505-50-50-2) (EITF 00-8). See Chapter 53, "ASC Topic 845: Nonmonetary Transactions."

Spinoffs and Reverse Spinoffs

1. If the accounting spinnee is a component of an entity and meets the conditions for reporting as discontinued operations (as contained in ASC paragraph 205-20-45-1 [FAS-144, par. 42]), the accounting spinnor should report the accounting spinnee as a discontinued operation. (ASC 505-60-45-1) (EITF 02-11)

EXAMPLES OF FINANCIAL STATEMENT DISCLOSURES

The following sample disclosures are available on the accompanying disc.

Overall

Example 1: Details of Stockholders' Equity on the Face of the Balance Sheet

	20X2	20X1
Stockholders' Equity:		
3% cumulative preferred stock; par value $.10; authorized 1,000,000 shares; issued and outstanding 200,000 shares in 20X2 and 100,000 shares in 20X1; aggregate liquidation preference of $2,400,000 in 20X2 and $1,200,000 in 20X1	$ 20,000	$ 10,000
6% convertible preferred stock; par value $.50; authorized 1,000,000 shares; issued and outstanding 400,000 shares in 20X2 and 300,000 shares in 20X1	200,000	150,000
Class A common stock; par value $.01; authorized 100,000,000 shares; issued and outstanding 15,000,000 shares in 20X2 and 13,000,000 shares in 20X1	150,000	130,000
Class B common stock; par value $.01; authorized 50,000,000 shares; issued and outstanding 10,000,000 shares in 20X2 and 20X1	100,000	100,000
Additional paid-in capital	5,475,000	4,692,000
Retained earnings	1,413,000	1,017,000
Accumulated other comprehensive income	80,000	65,000
Less: stock subscriptions receivable	(180,000)	-0-
Less: treasury stock, at cost—150,000 shares in 20X2 and 20X1	(675,000)	(675,000)
Total stockholders' equity	$6,583,000	$5,489,000

Example 2: Statement of Changes in Stockholders' Equity

Note: The following is a comprehensive presentation of changes in components of stockholders' equity shown as a separate statement in the financial statements.

	Preferred Stock		Common Stock		Additional Paid-in Capital	Retained Earnings	Accumulated Other Comprehensive Income	Stock Subscriptions Receivable	Treasury Stock		Total Stockholders Equity
	Shares	Amount	Shares	Amount					Shares	Amount	
Balance at December 31, 20X0	100,000	$10,000	250,000	$2,500	$418,000	$111,000	$56,000	$(8,000)	(4,000)	$(40,000)	$549,500
Net income						316,000					316,000
Foreign currency adjustment							(27,000)				(27,000)
Unrealized gain on marketable securities							34,000				34,000
Cash dividends ($.16 per share)						(58,000)					(58,000)
Exercise of stock options			150,000	1,500	198,500						200,000
Repurchase of preferred stock	(20,000)	(2,000)			(48,000)						(50,000)
Payment received on stock sale								6,000			6,000
Purchase of 10,000 shares									(10,000)	(50,000)	(50,000)
Balance at December 31, 20X1	80,000	8,000	400,000	4,000	568,500	369,000	63,000	(2,000)	(14,000)	(90,000)	920,500
Net income						243,000					243,000
2 for 1 stock split			400,000	4,000	(4,000)						
Conversion of 8% debentures			100,000	1,000	149,000						150,000
Stock issued for acquisition			50,000	500	199,500						200,000
Stock exchanged for services			20,000	200	59,800						60,000
Foreign currency adjustment							(11,000)				(11,000)
Unrealized gain on marketable securities							17,000				17,000
Dividends						(225,000)					(225,000)
Balance at December 31, 20X2	80,000	$8,000	970,000	$9,700	$972,800	$387,000	$69,000	$(2,000)	(14,000)	$(90,000)	$1,354,500

*Example 3: Description of Rights and Privileges of Capital
Stock—Capital Structure Consists of Common Stock*

At December 31, 20X2, the authorized capital of the Company consists of 40,000,000 shares of capital stock comprising 30,000,000 shares of no par common stock and 10,000,000 shares of no par Class A common stock. Both classes of stock have a stated value of $0.001 per share. The Class A Common Stock has certain preferential rights with respect to cash dividends and upon liquidation of the Company. In the case of cash dividends, the holders of the Class A Common Stock will be paid one-half cent per share per quarter in addition to any amount payable per share for each share of Common Stock. In the event of liquidation, holders of the Class A Common Stock are entitled to a preference of $1 per share. After such amount is paid, holders of the Common Stock are entitled to receive $1 per share for each share of Common Stock outstanding. Any remaining amount would be distributed to the holders of the Class A Common Stock and the Common Stock on a pro rata basis.

In general, with respect to the election of directors, the holders of Class A Common Stock, voting as a separate class, are entitled to elect that number of directors, which constitutes 25% of the total membership of the board of directors. Holders of Common Stock, voting as a separate class, are entitled to elect the remaining directors. In all other matters not requiring a class vote, the holders of the Common Stock and the holders of Class A Common Stock vote as a single class provided that holders of Class A Common Stock have one-tenth of a vote for each share held and the holders of the Common Stock have one vote for each share held.

*Example 4: Description of Rights and Privileges of Capital
Stock—Capital Structure Consists of Common and Preferred Stock*

The Company has three classes of capital stock: Preferred Stock, Common Stock, and Class B Common Stock. Holders of Common Stock are entitled to one vote for each share held. Holders of Class B Common Stock generally vote as a single class with holders of Common Stock but are entitled to ten votes for each share held. The Common Stock and Class B Common Stock have equal liquidation and dividend rights except that any regular quarterly dividend declared shall be $0.05 per share less for holders of Class B Common Stock. Class B Common Stock is nontransferable, except under certain conditions, but may be converted into Common Stock on a share-for-share basis at any time.

The preferred stock has an annual dividend rate of 6% and is cumulative. Preferred stockholders are not entitled to voting privileges except on matters involving liquidation, dissolution, or merger of the Company, in which case they are entitled to one vote for each ten shares held.

Example 5: Redeemable Convertible Preferred Stock with a Beneficial Conversion Feature

On June 15, 20X2, the Company issued 250,000 shares of its Series B Preferred Stock, and six-year warrants to purchase 5,528,000 shares of its common stock, in exchange for $9,700,000 in cash, net of issuance costs of $300,000. The Series B Preferred Stock is initially convertible into approximately 4,000,000 shares of the Company's common stock at a conversion price of $2.50 per share. The exercise price for the warrants is $2.95 per share and they were immediately exercisable upon issuance.

The holders of the Series B Preferred Stock and warrants have registration rights that require the Company to file, to have declared effective, and to maintain the effectiveness of a registration statement with the SEC to register the resale of the common stock issuable upon conversion of the Series B Preferred Stock and the common stock issuable upon exercise of the warrants. In the event the Company is unable to cause the registration statement to be declared effective by March 1, 20X3, cash penalties of $7,500 per day are due to the holders during the period commencing on March 1, 20X3, and ending on the date the registration statement is declared effective by the SEC. The ability to register stock is deemed to be outside of the Company's control. Accordingly, the initial fair value of the warrants of $3,100,000 was recorded as an accrued warrant liability in the consolidated balance sheet and is marked to market at the end of each reporting period. At December 31, 20X2, the warrant liability was adjusted to its new fair value of $2,375,000 as determined by the Company, resulting in a gain of $725,000, which has been reflected in "Interest income and other, net" on the consolidated statement of operations.

The initial value attributed to the Series B Preferred Stock of $6,900,000 represents a discount from its initial conversion value of $9,500,000. The Company has determined that the Series B Preferred Stock had a beneficial conversion feature of $2,600,000 as of the date of issuance. The Company recorded this beneficial conversion feature as a deemed dividend upon issuance.

The holders of the Series B Preferred Stock may require the Company to redeem its shares upon certain events, including failure to cause a registration statement to be effective by April 1, 20X3, at a redemption price equal to the greater of 120% of the original purchase price plus any accrued and unpaid dividends or the value of the Series B Preferred Stock on an as-converted-to-common-stock basis. Because the Company has not yet been able to cause a registration statement to be declared effective, the Company determined, as of December 31, 20X2, that it was probable that effectiveness would not be obtained prior to the deadline and that the Series B Preferred Stock should be stated at its redemption value at December 31, 20X2. Accordingly, the Company has recorded a deemed dividend charge of $5,350,000 in order to accrete the Series B Preferred Stock to its $12,250,000 redemption value at December 31, 20X2, which includes $325,000 of dividends accrued through December 31, 20X2.

Example 6: Redemption of Convertible Preferred Stock during the Reporting Period

In December 20X2, the Company redeemed all 200,000 outstanding shares of 5.75% Series A Convertible Preferred Stock (the Preferred Stock). The Preferred Stock was issued to certain former shareholders of Mederatus, Inc. as a portion of the total consideration of the Company's 20X0 acquisition of Mederatus, Inc. The redemption price per share of stock was $10.40 per share, or $2,080,000 in the aggregate, which included a redemption premium of $.40 per share, or $80,000 in the aggregate. The redemption premium of $80,000 is deducted from net earnings to arrive at net earnings applicable to common shareholders in the accompanying Statements of Operations.

Example 7: Conversion of Subordinated Debentures into Common Stock during the Reporting Period

During 20X2, $4,500,000 of the Company's $5,000,000 of 6% Convertible Subordinated Debentures due in 20X7 were converted into 680,000 shares of the Company's common stock at the conversion price of $10.50 per share. As a result of the conversion, $67,000 of costs associated with the issuance of the debentures was charged against additional paid-in capital.

Example 8: Fair Value of Warrants Reclassified from Liabilities to Additional Paid-in Capital upon Elimination of the Net Cash Settlement Provision

In June 20X2, the Company completed a $1,100,000 private placement of its common stock. The Company issued 1,125,000 shares of common stock along with warrants to purchase 410,000 shares of common stock at $1.15 per share, which were valued at $436,000. The Company received approximately $941,000 in net proceeds from this transaction. As the warrants originally included a requirement for net cash settlement if the Company was unable to register the shares to be issued upon exercise of the warrants, these warrants were required to be recorded as a liability until such time as the registration requirements expired. The Company subsequently signed a "Waiver Letter Agreement" with certain warrant holders, which resulted in the warrants being modified to provide for a cashless exercise in the event of a Nonregistration Event, as defined, and the elimination of the net cash settlement provision. In addition, certain penalty provisions were modified to provide that the warrant holders would receive no liquidated damages in the event of a Nonregistration Event. Upon the elimination of the net cash settlement provision, the fair value of the warrants ($311,000) was reclassified from other current liabilities to additional paid-in capital. As of December 31, 20X2, remaining warrants with a fair value of $132,000 are included in other current liabilities in the accompanying consolidated balance sheet.

Example 9: Common Stock Reserved for Future Issuance

At December 31, 20X2, and December 31, 20X1, the Company has reserved 1,389,000 and 1,016,000 shares of its authorized but unissued common stock for possible future issuance in connection with the following:

	20X2	20X1
Exercise and future grants of stock options	660,000	404,000
Exercise of stock warrants	394,000	311,000
Conversion of preferred stock	217,000	183,000
Contingently issuable shares in connection with the XYZ business combination	118,000	118,000
	1,389,000	1,016,000

Example 10: Change from Stated to Par Value

On May 1, 20X2, the Company was reincorporated in Delaware. As a result, each of the Company's classes of stock was changed from a stated value of $0.05 per share to a par value of $0.01 per share, resulting in a decrease in common stock and an increase in additional paid-in capital of $235,000. At the same time, the authorized number of shares of common stock was increased from 10 million to 25 million.

Example 11: Amendment to Certificate of Incorporation

On October 26, 20X2, the Company's stockholders approved an amendment to the Certificate of Incorporation reducing the par value of the common stock from $1 to $.01 per share and increasing the number of authorized shares of common stock from 1 million to 10 million. As a result of the reduction in par value, the "Common stock" account was reduced by $250,000 and the "Additional paid-in capital" account was increased by the same amount in the accompanying Statement of Stockholders' Equity for 20X2.

Example 12: Outstanding Receivables from Sale of Stock Reported as a Reduction of Stockholders' Equity

Notes receivable from stock sales resulting from the exercise of stock options for notes totaled $218,000 and $203,000 at December 31, 20X2, and December 31, 20X1, respectively, and are reported as a reduction of stockholders' equity. The notes are full recourse promissory notes bearing interest at variable rates ranging from 6.25% to 8.50% and are collateralized by the stock issued upon exercise of the stock options. Interest is payable semi-annually and principal is due from 20X3 through 20X6.

Example 13: Cash Dividends

On February 16, 20X2, the board of directors approved an annual cash dividend for 20X2 of $0.03 per share payable on April 15, 20X2, to holders of common stock as of close of business on April 1, 20X2. Cash dividends paid in 20X2 totaled $213,000 and have been charged to retained earnings.

Example 14: Dividends in Arrears Deferred

Payments of annual dividends for 20X2 and 20X1 were deferred by the Company's board of directors on the outstanding preferred stocks because of losses sustained by the Company. As of December 31, 20X2, preferred dividends in arrears amounted to $400,000, or $2 per share, on the 5% Cumulative Preferred Stock.

Example 15: Dividends in Arrears Paid in Amended New Shares of Preferred Stock

Prior to November 20X1, dividends with respect to the Series A Preferred Stock were in arrearage. Effective November 10, 20X1, the Series A Preferred Stock was amended, reclassified, and converted to Amended Series A Preferred Stock. As a consequence of such consent, all dividend arrearages, and accrued and unpaid dividends were paid in additional shares of Amended Series A Preferred Stock.

Stock Dividends and Stock Splits

Example 16: Stock Dividends

On December 1, 20X2, the Company paid a 2% stock dividend to shareholders of record on November 10, 20X2. Based on the number of common shares outstanding on the record date, the Company issued 200,000 new shares. The fair market value of the additional shares issued, aggregating $613,000, was charged to retained earnings, and common stock and additional paid-in capital were increased by $2,000 and $611,000, respectively. All references in the accompanying financial statements to the number of common shares and per-share amounts are based on the increased number of shares giving retroactive effect to the stock dividend.

Example 17: Stock Split during the Reporting Period

On January 30, 20X2, the Company's board of directors declared a two-for-one stock split, effected in the form of a stock dividend, on the shares of the Company's common stock. Each shareholder of record on February 20, 20X2, received an additional share of common stock for each share of common stock then held. The stock was issued March 19, 20X2. The Company retained the current par value of $.01 per share for all shares of common stock. All references in the financial statements to the number of shares outstanding, per-share amounts, and stock option data of the Company's common stock have been restated to reflect the effect of the stock split for all periods presented.

Stockholders' equity reflects the stock split by reclassifying from "Additional paid-in capital" to "Common stock" an amount equal to the par value of the additional shares arising from the split.

Example 18: Stock Split Subsequent to the Balance Sheet Date

On February 18, 20X3, the Company's board of directors authorized a two-for-one split of the common stock effected in the form of a 100% stock dividend to be distributed on or about March 31, 20X3, to holders of record on March 5, 20X3. Accordingly, all references to numbers of common shares and per-share data in the accompanying financial statements have been adjusted to reflect the stock split on a retroactive basis. The par value of the additional shares of common stock issued in connection with the stock split will be credited to "Common stock" and a like amount charged to "Additional paid-in-capital" in 20X3.

Treasury Stock

Example 19: Treasury Stock Purchase

In fiscal 20X1, the board of directors authorized the purchase of up to 1,200,000 shares of the Company's common stock, which may be used to meet the Company's common stock requirements for its stock benefit plans. In fiscal 20X2, the board of directors increased the number of shares of common stock that the Company is authorized to repurchase under this plan by 200,000 shares. During fiscal 20X2 and 20X1, the Company repurchased 473,000 and 518,000 shares, respectively, at an aggregate cost of $4,565,000 and $3,238,000, respectively.

Example 20: Treasury Stock Sale

In October 20X2, the Company sold 125,000 shares of common stock previously held in the treasury for $625,000. The aggregate purchase price of the treasury shares sold exceeded the aggregate sales price by $156,000 and has been charged to "Additional paid-in capital."

Equity-Based Payments to Non-Employees

Example 21: Warrants Issued in Connection with a Financing Agreement

In connection with the Financing Agreement with ABC State Bank, on March 18, 20X2, the Company issued warrants to ABC State Bank for the purchase of 150,000 shares of common stock at an exercise price of $2.25 per share. The fair value of the warrants of $325,000 was determined using the Black-Scholes option-pricing model, using the following assumptions:

Expected volatility	40%
Expected dividends	1.5%
Expected term (in years)	3.5
Risk-free rate	4.5%

The value of the warrants is being amortized into interest expense over the term of the Financing Agreement. The warrants are exercisable at any time on or after November 1, 20X2.

Example 22: Warrants Issued in Connection with a Lease Agreement

In July 20X1, the Company issued a fully vested, nonforfeitable warrant that entitles the holder to purchase 25,000 shares of the Company's common stock at an exercise price of $10.00 per share, in connection with a lease agreement. This warrant is exercisable through July 20X6. The fair value of this warrant, approximately $375,000, is being expensed over the term of the lease. The fair value of this warrant was calculated using the Black-Scholes option-pricing model, including the following assumptions:

Expected volatility	25%
Expected dividends	1%
Expected term (in years)	4
Risk-free rate	3.5%

In addition, in January 20X1, in connection with an equipment lease line, the Company issued a fully vested warrant that entitles the holder to purchase 110,000 shares of the Company's common stock at an exercise price of $1.50 per share. This warrant is exercisable through January 20X8. The fair value of this warrant, approximately $362,000, is being expensed as a cost of financing over the four-year period of the lease line. The fair value of this warrant was calculated using the Black-Scholes option-pricing model, including the following assumptions:

Expected volatility	35%
Expected dividends	1%
Expected term (in years)	3
Risk-free rate	4%

Spinoffs and Reverse Spinoffs

Example 23: Spinoff of a Business Segment

In May 20X2, the Company announced plans to spin off its electronic connectors business to shareholders in a tax-free distribution. In August 20X2, the Company's board of directors approved the spinoff effective December 31, 20X2, to shareholders of record as of December 17, 20X2, through the issuance of shares in a new legal entity, Electors, Inc. Common shares were distributed on a basis of one share of Electors, Inc. for every five shares of the Company's common stock.

The consolidated financial results of the Company have been restated to reflect the divestiture of Electors, Inc. Accordingly, the revenues, costs, and expenses; assets and liabilities; and cash flows of Electors, Inc. have been excluded from their respective captions in the Consolidated Statements of Income, Consolidated Balance Sheets, and Consolidated Statements of Cash Flows. These items have been reported as "Income from discontinued operations, net of income taxes" in the Consolidated Statements of Income; "Net assets of discontinued operations" in the Consolidated Balance Sheets; and "Net cash flows from discontinued operations" and "Net investing and financing activities of discontinued operations" in the Consolidated Statements of Cash Flows.

As of December 31, 20X2, the net assets of the discontinued segment of $4,289,000 have been charged against the Company's retained earnings to reflect the spinoff. During 20X2, the Company recorded a pre-tax charge of $615,000 ($483,000 after taxes) for expenses related to the spinoff.

The following table summarizes financial information for the discontinued operations for all periods presented:

	20X2	20X1
Net sales	$8,300,000	$8,750,000
Income before income taxes	$ 211,000	$ 273,000
Net income	$ 107,000	$ 182,000
Current assets	$2,436,000	$2,543,000
Total assets	$8,161,000	$8,615,000
Current liabilities	$2,597,000	$1,796,000
Total liabilities	$3,872,000	$3,978,000
Net assets of discontinued operations	$4,289,000	$4,637,000

PART 6—
REVENUE

CHAPTER 35
ASC TOPIC 605: REVENUE RECOGNITION

CONTENTS

EXECUTIVE SUMMARY

Products and Services

Revenue from the sale of goods should be recognized when it is both earned and realized or realizable (i.e., the earnings process must be complete or virtually complete and the revenue measurable). Important considerations in product sales are whether title and the significant risks and rewards of ownership have passed to the customer.

Revenue from sales transactions in which the buyer has a right to return the product should be recognized at time of sale only if *all* of the following conditions are met:

1. The price between the seller and the buyer is substantially fixed or determinable.

2. The seller has received full payment, or the buyer is indebted to the seller and the indebtedness is not contingent on the resale of the merchandise.

3. Physical destruction, damage, or theft of the merchandise would not change the buyer's obligation to the seller.

4. The buyer has economic substance and is not a front or conduit existing for the benefit of the seller.

5. No significant obligations exist for the seller to help the buyer resell the merchandise.

6. A reasonable estimate can be made of the amount of future returns.

If all of the above conditions are met, revenue is recognized on sales for which a right of return exists, provided that an appropriate provision is made for costs or losses that may occur in connection with the return of merchandise from the buyer.

Similarly, revenue from providing services should be recognized when it is both earned and realized or realizable (i.e., the earnings process must be complete or virtually complete and the revenue measurable). Providing services typically involves the seller performing an agreed-upon task or tasks for the buyer over an agreed-upon period of time. The services may be provided within a single period or over many periods.

Multiple-Element Arrangements

Sales transactions may involve multiple elements, or deliverables. The elements (or deliverables) may be products or services, or a combination of products and services. In accounting for such multiple-element arrangements, the seller should assess each element to determine if it should be accounted for as a separate element. If an element should be treated separately for revenue recognition purposes, the revenue recognition principles most appropriate for that element should be applied to determine when revenue should be recognized. If an element is not treated separately for revenue recognition purposes, the revenue recognition principles most appropriate for the bundled group of elements should be applied to determine when revenue should be recognized.

Construction-Type and Production-Type Contracts

Revenues from long-term contracts should be recognized under either the percentage-of-completion method or the completed-contract method. The percentage-of-completion method is appropriate in situations in which reliable estimates of the degree of completion are available, in which case a pro rata portion of the income from the contract is recognized in each accounting period covered by the contract. If reliable estimates are not available, the completed-contract method is used, in which income is deferred until the end of the contract period. The percentage-of-completion and the completed-contract methods are not alternatives; an entity should use the appropriate method.

Regardless of the revenue recognition method used, an entity should accrue an anticipated loss on a contract whenever it becomes apparent that the total estimated contract costs (i.e., costs incurred to date, plus estimated costs to complete) will materially exceed the total estimated contract revenue.

Generally, four basic types of contracts are encountered in practice:

1. *Fixed-price or lump-sum contracts.* A fixed-price or lump-sum contract is a contract in which the price is not usually subject to adjustment because of costs incurred by the contractor.

2. *Time-and-material contracts.* Time-and-material contracts are contracts that generally provide for payments to the contractor on the basis of direct labor hours at fixed hourly rates and cost of materials or other specified costs.

3. *Cost-type contracts.* Cost-type contracts provide for reimbursement of allowable or otherwise defined costs incurred plus a fee that represents profit.

4. *Unit-price contracts.* Unit-price contracts are contracts under which the contractor is paid a specified amount for every unit of work performed.

Gains and Losses

The discussion in this chapter relates only to events and transactions in which nonmonetary assets (e.g., property or equipment) are involuntarily converted (e.g., as a result of total or partial destruction, theft, seizure, or condemnation) to monetary assets (e.g., insurance proceeds). To the extent the cost of a nonmonetary asset differs from the amount of monetary assets received, the transaction results in the realization of a gain or loss that should be recognized. Examples of such conversions are total or partial destruction or theft of insured nonmonetary assets and the condemnation of property in eminent domain proceedings.

Other guidance for gains and losses is included in the discussions of the relevant topics in various chapters throughout this Manual.

Principal Agent Considerations

Whether an entity should recognize revenue based on the gross amount billed to a customer or the net amount retained (i.e., the amount billed to a customer less the amount paid to a supplier) depends on the particular facts and circumstances. An entity should consider "gross indicators" and "net indicators" and the relative strength and importance of each indicator in each set of facts and circumstances. For example, a strong indicator of gross reporting is if the entity possesses unmitigated general inventory risk.

Some of the more common issues in the determination of the gross or net presentation include the following:

- Goods or services sold over the Internet.
- Services offered that will be provided by a third-party service provider.
- Shipping and handling costs in connection with products sold.
- The collection of sales and other taxes for the government.

Customer Payments and Incentives

Customer payments and incentives that are subject to the guidance in this chapter relate primarily to the following:

- A vendor's accounting for consideration given by a vendor to a customer (including both a reseller of the vendor's products and an entity that purchases the vendor's products from a reseller) offered by a vendor on either a limited or a continuous basis to a customer, which may take various forms including discounts, coupons, rebates, and free products or services.
- Accounting by a customer (including a reseller) for certain consideration received from a vendor.
- A service provider's accounting for consideration given by the service provider to a manufacturer or reseller of equipment.

Accounting Literature

FASB Accounting Standards Codification Topic

605, *Revenue Recognition*

Pre-Codification Accounting Literature

FAS-5, *Accounting for Contingencies*

FAS-48, *Revenue Recognition When Right of Return Exists*

FIN-30, *Accounting for Involuntary Conversions of Nonmonetary Assets to Monetary Assets*

EITF 99-17, *Accounting for Advertising Barter Transactions*

EITF 99-19, *Reporting Revenue Gross as a Principal versus Net as an Agent*

EITF 00-10, *Accounting for Shipping and Handling Fees and Costs*

EITF 00-21, *Revenue Arrangements with Multiple Deliverables*

EITF 01-9, *Accounting for Consideration Given by a Vendor to a Customer (Including a Reseller of the Vendor's Products)*

EITF 01-14, *Income Statement Characterization of Reimbursements Received for Out-of-Pocket Expenses Incurred*

EITF 02-16, *Accounting by a Customer (Including a Reseller) for Certain Consideration Received from a Vendor*

EITF 06-1, *Accounting for Consideration Given by a Service Provider to a Manufacturer or Reseller of Equipment Necessary for an End-Customer to Receive Service from the Service Provider*

FASB Accounting Standards Codification Topic	*Pre-Codification Accounting Literature*
	EITF 06-3, *How Taxes Collected from Customers and Remitted to Governmental Authorities Should Be Presented in the Income Statement (That Is, Gross versus Net Presentation)*
	ARB-45, *Long-Term Construction-Type Contracts*
	SOP 81-1, *Accounting for Performance of Construction-Type and Certain Production-Type Contracts*

DISCLOSURE AND KEY PRESENTATION REQUIREMENTS

Products and Services

1. For sales made with rights of return (meeting the criteria in ASC paragraph 605-15-25-1) (FAS-48, par. 6), revenue and cost of sales should be reduced to reflect the estimated returns. (ASC 605-15-45-1) (FAS-48, par. 7)

2. The amount of revenue and expense recognized from advertising barter transactions should be disclosed for each income statement period presented. (ASC 605-20-50-1) (EITF 99-17)

3. If an entity engages in advertising barter transactions for which the fair value is not determinable, information regarding the volume and type of advertising surrendered and received (e.g., the number of equivalent pages, the number of minutes, or the overall percentage of advertising volume) should be disclosed for each income statement period presented. (ASC 605-20-50-1) (EITF 99-17)

Multiple-Element Arrangements

> **PRACTICE ALERT:** As this Manual goes to press, the FASB has issued Accounting Standards Update (ASU) No. 2009-13, *Revenue Recognition (Topic 605)—Multiple-Deliverable Revenue Arrangements*, which is effective for revenue arrangements entered into or materially modified in fiscal years beginning on or after June 15, 2010. The disclosure requirements in item 1 below will be superseded by the guidance in ASU No. 2009-13. The disclosure requirements in items 2 through 6 below should

be followed upon adoption of ASU No. 2009-13. Early adoption is permitted. However, if an entity elects early application and the period of adoption is not the first reporting period in the entity's fiscal year, the guidance must be applied through retrospective application from the beginning of the entity's fiscal year.

1. The following disclosures should be made for revenue arrangements with multiple elements (ASC 605-25-50-1) (EITF 00-21):

    a. The accounting policy for recognizing revenue from multiple-deliverable arrangements (e.g., whether deliverables are separable into units of accounting).

    b. The description and nature of such arrangements, including performance, cancellation, termination, or refund-type provisions.

    PRACTICE ALERT: As this Manual goes to press, the FASB has issued Accounting Standards Update (ASU) No. 2009-13, *Revenue Recognition (Topic 605)—Multiple-Deliverable Revenue Arrangements*. The disclosure requirements in items 2 through 6 below are prescribed by ASU No. 2009-13, which supersede the disclosure requirements in item 1 above, and are effective for revenue arrangements entered into or materially modified in fiscal years beginning on or after June 15, 2010. Early adoption is permitted. However, if an entity elects early application and the period of adoption is not the first reporting period in the entity's fiscal year, the guidance must be applied through retrospective application from the beginning of the entity's fiscal year.

2. The following disclosures should be made by similar type of arrangement for revenue arrangements with multiple deliverables (ASC 605-25-50-2):

    a. The nature of the multiple-deliverable arrangements.

    b. The significant deliverables within the arrangements.

    c. The general timing of delivery or performance of service for the deliverables within the arrangements.

    d. The following provisions in the arrangements:

        (1) Performance-type.

        (2) Cancellation-type.

        (3) Termination-type.

        (4) Refund-type.

    e. A discussion of the following variables used to determine selling price (whether vendor-specific objective evidence, third-party evidence, or estimated selling price) for the significant deliverables:

(1) Significant factors.

(2) Inputs.

(3) Assumptions.

(4) Methods.

f. Whether the significant deliverables in the arrangements qualify as separate units of accounting.

g. Why the significant deliverables in the arrangements do not qualify as separate units of accounting, if applicable.

h. The general timing of revenue recognition for significant units of accounting.

i. Separately, the effect of changes in either the selling price or the method or assumptions used to determine selling price for a specific unit of accounting if either one of those changes has a significant effect on the allocation of arrangement consideration.

3. Other qualitative or quantitative disclosures should be provided, as necessary, to understand (ASC 605-25-50-1):

a. An entity's revenue arrangements.

b. How significant judgments made may significantly affect the timing or amount of revenue recognition.

c. How changes in significant judgments made may significantly affect the timing or amount of revenue recognition.

4. If an entity elected early adoption, and the period of adoption is not the first reporting period in the entity's fiscal year, the entity should disclose for all previously reported interim periods in the fiscal year of adoption the following information, at a minimum (ASC 605-25-65-1):

a. Revenue.

b. Income before income taxes.

c. Net income.

d. Earnings per share.

e. The effect of the change for the appropriate captions presented.

5. If the entity adopted on a prospective basis the guidance in this section, the entity should disclose at a minimum the following information by similar types of arrangements in the period of adoption (ASC 605-25-65-1):

a. A description of any change in the units of accounting.

   b. A description of the change in how the entity allocates
       the arrangement consideration to various units of
       accounting.

   c. A description of the changes in the pattern and timing of
       revenue recognition.

   d. If the effect of adoption is material, quantitative informa-
       tion that enables users to understand the effect of the
       change in accounting principle.

   e. Whether the adoption is expected to have a material
       effect on financial statements in periods after the initial
       adoption.

6. If the entity adopted on a retrospective basis the guidance in
    this section, the entity should provide the disclosures
    required by paragraphs 250-10-50-1 through 50-3. (ASC
    605-25-65-1) (See Chapter 9, "ASC Topic 250: Accounting
    Changes and Error Corrections.")

Construction-Type and Production-Type Contracts

1. The note on accounting policies should disclose the meth-
    od(s) of determining earned revenue and the cost of earned
    revenue (e.g., the percentage-of-completion method or the
    completed-contract method), including the policies relating
    to combining and segmenting contracts, if applicable. (ASC
    605-35-50-1) (SOP 81-1, par. 21)

2. When the percentage-of-completion method of accounting is
    used:

    a. The method(s) of measuring the extent of progress
        toward completion (e.g., cost to cost, labor hours) should
        be disclosed. (ASC 605-35-50-2) (SOP 81-1, par. 45)

    b. When an entity departs from use of the percentage-of-
        completion method as its basic accounting policy for a
        single contract or a group of contracts for which reason-
        ably dependable estimates cannot be made (or for which
        inherent hazards make estimates doubtful), such a
        departure from the basic policy should be disclosed.
        (ASC 605-35-50-3) (SOP 81-1, par. 25)

    c. Costs and recognized income not yet billed should be
        shown as current assets, and billings in excess of costs
        and recognized income should be shown as liabilities (in
        most cases current liabilities). (ASC 605-35-45-3) (ARB-
        45, par. 5)

3. When the completed-contract method of accounting is used:

    a. The specific criteria used to determine when a contract is substantially completed should be followed consistently and disclosed in the note on accounting policies. (ASC 605-35-50-4) (SOP 81-1, par. 52)

    b. When an entity departs from use of the completed-contract method as its basic accounting policy for a single contract or a group of contracts, such a departure from the basic policy should be disclosed. (ASC 605-35-50-5) (SOP 81-1, par. 31)

    c. The excess of accumulated costs over related billings should be shown as a current asset, and the excess of accumulated billings over related costs should be shown as liabilities (in most cases current liabilities). (ASC 605-35-45-4) (ARB-45, par. 12) (*Note:* If costs exceed billings on some contracts, and billings exceed costs on others, the contracts should ordinarily be segregated so that the figures on the asset side include only those contracts on which costs exceed billings, and those on the liability side include only those on which billings exceed costs.)

    d. The asset item should be described as costs of uncompleted contracts in excess of related billings (rather than as inventory or work in process), and the liability item should be described as billings on uncompleted contracts in excess of related costs. (ASC 605-35-45-5) (ARB-45, par. 12)

4. For provisions for anticipated losses on contracts (ASC 605-35-45-1 and 45-2) (SOP 81-1, pars. 88 and 89):

    a. The provision for loss should be accounted for in the income statement as an additional contract cost (rather than as a reduction of contract revenue).

    b. Unless the provision for loss is material in amount or unusual or infrequent in nature, the provision should be included in contract cost and not shown separately in the income statement.

    c. If the provision for loss is shown separately in the income statement, it should be shown as a component of the cost included in the computation of gross profit.

    d. The provision for loss should be shown separately as a liability on the balance sheet, if significant (except in circumstances in which related costs are accumulated on the balance sheet, in which case the provisions may be deducted from the related accumulated costs).

    e. In a classified balance sheet, the provision for loss should be shown as a current liability.

5. For contract claims:

   a. If revenue from a claim is recorded, it should be recorded only to the extent that contract costs relating to the claim have been incurred and the recorded amount should be disclosed. (ASC 605-35-50-6) (SOP 81-1, par. 65)

   b. If the entity's practice is to record revenues from claims only when the amounts have been received or awarded, the related amounts should be disclosed. (ASC 605-35-50-7) (SOP 81-1, par. 66)

   c. If the requirements for revenue recognition from claims are not met, and therefore no revenue has been recognized, a contingent asset should be disclosed. (ASC 605-35-50-8; 450-30-50-1) (SOP 81-1, par. 67; FAS-5, par. 17) (*Note:* Care should be exercised to avoid misleading implications about the likelihood of realization.)

6. For revisions of contract estimates:

   a. Appropriate disclosures should be made of the effect of revisions of contract estimates, if the effect is material. (ASC 605-35-50-9; 250-10-50-4) (SOP 81-1, par. 84; FAS-154, par. 22). See Chapter 9, "ASC Topic 250: Accounting Changes and Error Corrections," for disclosure requirements relating to changes in accounting estimates.

   b. Events occurring after the date of the financial statements that are outside the normal exposure and risk aspects of the contract should *not* be considered refinements of the estimating process of the prior year, but rather should be disclosed as subsequent events. (ASC 605-35-50-10) (SOP 81-1, par. 82)

7. Disclosures should be made of extraordinary commitments (outside the ordinary course of business) to complete contracts in process. (ASC 605-35-50-11) (ARB-45, par. 16)

Gains and Losses

1. Gains or losses resulting from involuntary conversions of nonmonetary assets to monetary assets should be classified as extraordinary items or unusual or infrequent items, in accordance with the provisions of ASC Subtopic 225-20, *Income Statement—Extraordinary and Unusual Items* (APB-30, *Reporting the Results of Operations–Reporting the Effects of Disposal of a Segment of a Business, and Extraordinary, Unusual, and Infrequently Occurring Events and Transactions*). (ASC 605-40-45-1) (FIN-30, par. 4)

Principal Agent Considerations

1. In regard to reporting revenue gross as a principal versus net as an agent:

   a. Appropriate considerations should be given to indicators of gross revenue reporting and indicators of net revenue reporting for purposes of determining whether revenue should be reported gross as a principal versus net as an agent. (ASC 605-45-45-1 through 45-18) (EITF 99-19)

   b. For those revenues reported net, any gross transaction volume amounts disclosed on the face of the income statement should *not* be characterized as revenues (a description such as gross billings may be appropriate), nor should they be reported in a column that sums to net income or loss. (ASC 605-45-50-1) (EITF 99-19) (*Note:* This does not apply to the disclosure of taxes collected and remitted to governmental authorities, as discussed below.)

2. For shipping and handling fees and costs:

   a. For entities that determine that shipping and handling fees charged to customers should be reported gross, all amounts billed to a customer in a sale transaction related to shipping and handling should be classified as revenue. (ASC 605-45-45-20) (EITF 00-10)

   b. Shipping and handling costs incurred should *not* be deducted from revenues (i.e., netted against shipping and handling revenues). (ASC 605-45-45-21) (EITF 00-10)

   c. The accounting policy for classifying shipping and handling costs should be disclosed. (ASC 605-45-50-2) (EITF 00-10)

   d. If shipping or handling costs are significant and are *not* included in cost of sales, the amounts of such costs and the line item(s) in which they are included on the income statement should be disclosed. (ASC 605-45-50-2) (EITF 00-10)

3. Reimbursements received for out-of-pocket expenses incurred should be characterized as revenue in the income statement. (ASC 605-45-45-23) (EITF 01-14)

4. For taxes collected from customers and remitted to governmental authorities:

   a. The entity's accounting policy addressing the gross basis (included in revenues and costs) or net basis (excluded from revenues) presentation of these taxes should be disclosed. (ASC 605-45-50-3) (EITF 06-3)

b. For any such taxes that are reported on a gross basis and are significant, the amounts of those taxes included in interim and annual financial statements should be disclosed for each period for which an income statement is presented. (ASC 605-45-50-4) (EITF 06-3) (*Note:* The disclosure of those taxes can be done on an aggregate basis.)

Customer Payments and Incentives

1. In regard to reporting customer payments and incentives:

   a. For a vendor that gives customers a sales incentive or other consideration, the vendor should appropriately address whether that consideration should be characterized in the vendor's income statement as an adjustment of the selling price of the vendor's products or services (i.e., a reduction of revenue) or as a cost incurred by the vendor. (ASC 605-50-45-1 through 45-11) (EITF 01-9)

   b. For a customer that receives cash consideration or sales incentive from a vendor, the customer should appropriately address whether that consideration should be characterized in the customer's income statement as a reduction of cost of sales or as revenue (or other income). (ASC 605-50-45-12 through 45-22) (EITF 02-16; EITF 03-10)

2. The following disclosures should be made by service providers that have programs in which they provide incentives to third-party manufacturers or resellers of equipment necessary for an end-customer to receive service from the service providers (ASC 605-50-50-1) (EITF 06-1):

   a. The nature of the incentive programs.

   b. The amounts recognized in the income statement for those incentive programs and their related classification for each period presented.

EXAMPLES OF FINANCIAL STATEMENT DISCLOSURES

The following sample disclosures are available on the accompanying disc.

Products and Services

Example 1: Revenue Recognition Accounting Policy

The Company recognizes revenue only when all of the following criteria have been met:

- Persuasive evidence of an arrangement exists;
- Delivery has occurred or services have been rendered;
- The fee for the arrangement is fixed or determinable; and
- Collectibility is reasonably assured.

Persuasive Evidence of an Arrangement—The Company documents all terms of an arrangement in a written contract signed by the customer prior to recognizing revenue.

Delivery Has Occurred or Services Have Been Performed—The Company performs all services or delivers all products prior to recognizing revenue. Monthly services are considered to be performed ratably over the term of the arrangement. Professional consulting services are considered to be performed when the services are complete. Equipment is considered delivered upon delivery to a customer's designated location.

The Fee for the Arrangement Is Fixed or Determinable—Prior to recognizing revenue, a customer's fee is either fixed or determinable under the terms of the written contract. Fees for most monthly services, professional consulting services, and equipment sales and rentals are fixed under the terms of the written contract. Fees for certain monthly services, including certain portions of networking, storage, and content distribution and caching services, are variable based on an objectively determinable factor such as usage. Those factors are included in the written contract such that the customer's fee is determinable. The customer's fee is negotiated at the outset of the arrangement and is not subject to refund or adjustment during the initial term of the arrangement.

Collectibility Is Reasonably Assured—The Company determines that collectibility is reasonably assured prior to recognizing revenue. Collectibility is assessed on a customer by customer basis based on criteria outlined by management. New customers are subject to a credit review process, which evaluates the customer's financial position and ultimately its ability to pay. The Company does not enter into arrangements unless collectibility is reasonably assured at the outset. Existing customers are subject to ongoing credit evaluations based on payment history and other factors. If it is determined during the arrangement that collectibility is not reasonably assured, revenue is recognized on a cash basis.

Example 2: Sales Recorded When Products Are Shipped, with Appropriate Provisions for Discounts and Returns

Sales are recorded when products are shipped to customers. Provisions for discounts and rebates to customers, estimated returns and allowances, and other adjustments are provided for in the same period the related sales are recorded. In instances where products are configured to customer requirements, revenue is recorded upon the successful completion of the Company's final test procedures and the customer's acceptance.

Example 3: Revenue from Service Contracts

The Company recognizes revenue on service contracts ratably over applicable contract periods or as services are performed. Amounts billed and collected before the services are performed are included in deferred revenues.

Example 4: Right of Return and Price Protection Exist

Product revenue is generally recognized upon shipment to the customer. The Company grants certain distributors limited rights of return and price protection on unsold products. Product revenue on shipments to distributors that have rights of return and price protection is recognized upon shipment to customers by the distributor.

Example 5: Deferral of Certain Revenue and Gross Margins

Product sales are generally recognized upon shipment of product. However, the Company defers recognition of revenues and gross margin from sales to stocking distributors until such distributors resell the related products to their customers. The Company has deferred recognition of gross margin amounting to $4,000,000 and $3,500,000 as of December 31, 20X2, and December 31, 20X1, respectively.

Example 6: Warranty Contract Revenue

Warranty contract fees are recognized as revenues ratably over the life of the contract and the contract costs are expensed as incurred.

Example 7: Membership Revenue

The Company generally recognizes membership revenue upon the expiration of the membership period, as memberships are generally cancelable for a full refund of the membership fee during the entire membership period, which is generally one year. Revenues generated from certain memberships, which are subject to a pro rata refund, are recognized ratably over the membership period.

Example 8: Royalty Income

Royalty revenue is recognized by the Company upon fulfillment of its contractual obligations and determination of a fixed royalty amount or, in the case of ongoing royalties, upon sale by the licensee of royalty-bearing products, as estimated by the Company.

Example 9: Barter Transactions—Advertising Revenues and Expenses

The Company's barter transactions are recorded at the estimated fair value of the advertisements provided, based on recent historical cash transactions. Barter revenue is recognized when the advertising impressions or other services are delivered to the customer and advertising expense is recorded when the advertising impressions or other services are received from the customer. If the Company receives the advertising impressions or other services from the customer prior to its delivery of the advertising impressions, a liability is recorded; and if the Company delivers the advertising impressions to the customer prior to receiving the advertising impressions or other services, a prepaid expense is recorded on the Consolidated Balance Sheets. For the years ended December 31, 20X2, and December 31, 20X1, the Company recognized approximately $4.2 million and $1.9 million of advertising revenues, respectively, and $3.4 million and $1.5 million of advertising expenses, respectively, from barter transactions. The Company has recognized approximately $1.6 million and $1.1 million in prepaid expenses related to barter transactions as of December 31, 20X2, and December 31, 20X1, respectively.

Example 10: Barter Transactions—Inventory Delivered in Exchange for Future Advertising Credits

In 20X2 and 20X1, the Company entered into barter agreements, whereby it delivered $1,165,000 and $1,059,000, respectively, of its inventory in exchange for future advertising credits and other items. The credits, which expire in November 20X3, are valued at the lower of the Company's cost or market value of the inventory transferred. The Company has recorded barter credits of $115,000 and $236,000 in "Prepaid expenses and other current assets" at December 31, 20X2, and December 31, 20X1, respectively. At December 31, 20X2, and December 31, 20X1, "Other noncurrent assets" include $279,000 and $323,000, respectively, of such credits. Under the terms of the barter agreements, the Company is required to pay cash equal to a negotiated amount of the bartered advertising, or other items, and use the barter credits to pay the balance. These credits are charged to expense as they are used. During the years ended December 31, 20X2, and December 31, 20X1, approximately $1,080,000 and $751,000, respectively, were charged to expense for barter credits used.

The Company assesses the recoverability of barter credits periodically. Factors considered in evaluating the recoverability include management's plans with respect to advertising and other expenditures for which barter credits can be used. Any impairment losses are charged to operations as they are determinable. During the years ended December 31, 20X2, and December 31, 20X1, the Company charged $250,000 and $425,000, respectively, to operations for such impairment losses.

Multiple-Element Arrangements

> **PRACTICE ALERT:** As this Manual goes to press, the FASB has issued Accounting Standards Update (ASU) No. 2009-13, *Revenue Recognition (Topic 605)—Multiple-Deliverable Revenue Arrangements*, which is effective for revenue arrangements entered into or materially modified in fiscal years beginning on or after June 15, 2010. The example below is based on guidance in existence before ASU No. 2009-13. Future editions of this Manual will include updated examples based on the guidance in ASU No. 2009-13.

Example 11: Accounting Policy for Recognizing Revenue in Multiple-Element Arrangements

For those arrangements that include multiple deliverables, the Company first determines whether each service or deliverable meets the separation criteria of FASB ASC Subtopic 605-25, *Multiple-Element Arrangements*. In general, a deliverable (or a group of deliverables) meets the separation criteria if the deliverable has stand-alone value to the customer and if there is objective and reliable evidence of the fair value of the remaining deliverables in the arrangement. Each deliverable that meets the separation criteria is considered a separate "unit of accounting." The Company allocates the total arrangement consideration to each unit of accounting based on the relative fair value of each unit of accounting. The amount of arrangement consideration that is allocated to a delivered unit of accounting is limited to the amount that is not contingent upon the delivery of another unit of accounting.

After the arrangement consideration has been allocated to each unit of accounting, the Company applies the appropriate revenue recognition method for each unit of accounting based on the nature of the arrangement and the services included in each unit of accounting. All deliverables that do not meet the separation criteria of FASB ASC Subtopic 605-25 are combined into one unit of accounting, and the most appropriate revenue recognition method is applied.

In some arrangements, the Company may bill the customer prior to performing services, which would require the Company to record deferred revenue. In other arrangements, the Company may perform services prior to billing the customer, which could require the Company to record unbilled receivables or to defer the costs associated with the services, depending on the terms of the arrangement and the application of the revenue separation criteria of FASB ASC Subtopic 605-25.

Construction-Type and Production-Type Contracts

Example 12: General Accounting Policy for Contracts under the Percentage-of-Completion Method

Sales and cost of sales related to long-term contracts are accounted for under the percentage-of-completion method. Sales under fixed-type contracts are generally recognized upon passage of title to the customer, which usually coincides with physical delivery or customer acceptance as specified in contractual terms. Such sales are recorded at the cost of items delivered or accepted plus a proportion of profit expected to be realized on a contract, based on the ratio of such costs to total estimated costs at completion. Sales, including estimated earned fees, under cost reimbursement-type contracts are recognized as costs are incurred.

Profits expected to be realized on contracts are based on the Company's estimates of total contract sales value and costs at completion. These estimates are reviewed and revised periodically throughout the lives of the contracts with adjustments to profits resulting from such revisions being recorded on a cumulative basis in the period in which the revisions are made. When management believes the cost of completing a contract, excluding general and administrative expenses, will exceed contract-related revenues, the full amount of the anticipated contract loss is recognized.

Revenues recognized in excess of amounts billed are classified as current assets under "Contract work-in-progress." Amounts billed to clients in excess of revenues recognized to date are classified as current liabilities under "Advance billings on contracts."

Example 13: General Accounting Policy for Contracts under the Completed-Contract Method

Revenues from fixed-price contracts are recognized on the completed contract method. This method is used because the typical contract is completed in three months or less, and financial position and results of operations do not vary significantly from those that would result from use of the percentage-of-completion method. A contract is considered complete when all costs except significant items have been incurred and the installation is operating according to specifications or has been accepted by the customer. Revenues from time-and-material contracts are recognized currently as the work is performed.

Contract costs include all direct material and labor costs and those indirect costs related to contract performance, such as indirect labor, supplies, tools, repairs, and depreciation costs. General and administrative costs are charged to expense as incurred. Provisions for estimated losses on uncompleted contracts are made in the period in which such losses are determined.

Costs in excess of amounts billed are classified as current assets under "Costs in excess of billings on uncompleted contracts." Billings in excess of costs are classified as current liabilities under "Billings in excess of costs on uncompleted contracts."

Example 14: Revenue Recognized under Both the Completed-Contract and the Percentage-of-Completion Methods of Accounting

Revenue is recognized on both the completed-contract and the percentage-of-completion methods of accounting. The Company uses the percentage-of-completion method of accounting for all contracts that exceed $1 million in net operating revenues and recognizes such revenue upon incurring costs equal to the lesser of 25% of the contract costs or $500,000. Progress on percentage-of-completion contracts is measured generally by costs incurred to date compared with an estimate of total costs at the project's completion. Provision is made for anticipated losses, if any, on uncompleted contracts.

Example 15: Methods of Measuring Percentage-of-Completion Are Described

Revenues from long-term contracts are recognized on the percentage-of-completion method. Percentage-of-completion is measured principally by the percentage of costs incurred and accrued to date for each contract to the estimated total costs for each contract at completion. Certain of the Company's electrical contracting business units measure percentage-of-completion by the percentage of labor costs incurred to date for each contract to the estimated total labor costs for such contract.

The Company also enters into long-term contracts for the manufacture of products. Sales on production-type contracts are recorded as deliveries are made (units-of-delivery method of percentage-of-completion).

Example 16: Research and Development Contracts with Anticipated Losses

On a selective basis, the Company may enter into a contract to research and develop or manufacture a product with a loss anticipated at the date the contract is signed. These contracts are entered into in anticipation that profits will be obtained from future contracts for the same or similar products. These loss contracts often provide the Company with intellectual property rights that, in effect, establish it as the sole producer of certain products. Such losses are recognized at the date the Company becomes contractually obligated, with revisions made as changes occur in the related estimates to complete.

Example 17: Description of Segmented Contracts

Contracts are segmented between types of services, such as engineering and construction, and, accordingly, gross margin related to each activity is recognized as those separate services are rendered.

Example 18: Concentrations of Credit Risk

The majority of accounts receivable and all contract work-in-progress are from engineering and construction clients in various industries and locations throughout the United States. Most contracts require payments as the projects progress or in certain cases advance payments. The Company generally does not require collateral but in most cases can place liens against the property, plant, or equipment constructed or terminate the contract if a material default occurs. Accounts receivable from customers of the Company's Eastern operations are primarily concentrated in the steel and utility industries. The Company maintains adequate reserves for potential credit losses and such losses have been minimal and within management's estimates.

Example 19: Accounting for Cost Overruns under Fixed-Price Contracts

Under fixed-price contracts, the Company may encounter, and on certain programs from time to time has encountered, cost overruns caused by increased material, labor, or overhead costs; design or production difficulties; and various other factors such as technical and manufacturing complexity, which must be, and in such cases have been, borne by the Company. Adjustments to contract cost estimates are made in the periods in which the facts requiring such revisions become known. When the revised estimate indicates a loss, such loss is provided for currently in its entirety.

Example 20: Details of Contract Receivables Balance

Following are the details of contract receivables at December 31, 20X2, and December 31, 20X1:

	20X2	20X1
Amounts billed:		
Completed contracts	$1,217,000	$1,062,000
Contracts in progress	3,892,000	3,259,000
Retentions	813,000	768,000
	5,922,000	5,089,000
Unbilled	231,000	184,000
	6,153,000	5,273,000
Less: Allowance for doubtful accounts	(197,000)	(239,000)
	$5,956,000	$5,034,000

Of the retentions balance and the unbilled amounts at December 31, 20X2, approximately $613,000 is expected to be collected in the year 20X3, with the balance to be collected in subsequent years as contract deliveries are made and warranty periods expire.

Example 21: Details of Costs and Estimated Earnings on Uncompleted Contracts Reconciled to the Balance Sheets

Costs and estimated earnings on uncompleted contracts and related amounts billed as of December 31, 20X2, and December 31, 20X1, are as follows:

	20X2	20X1
Costs incurred on uncompleted contracts	$ 2,737,507	$ 2,282,127
Estimated earnings	202,211	158,832
	2,939,718	2,440,959
Less: Billings to date	(2,983,243)	(2,479,998)
	$ (43,525)	$ (39,039)

Such amounts are included in the accompanying Balance Sheets at December 31, 20X2, and December 31, 20X1, under the following captions:

	20X2	20X1
Costs and estimated earnings in excess of billings on uncompleted contracts	$ 91,569	$ 73,794
Billings in excess of costs and estimated earnings on uncompleted contracts	(135,094)	(112,833)
	$ (43,525)	$ (39,039)

Example 22: Allowances for Contract Losses Included in Current Liabilities

Other current liabilities at December 31, 20X2, and December 31, 20X1, include allowances for contract losses and other contract allowances aggregating $600,000 and $900,000, respectively.

Example 23: Contract Revenue from Claims Recognized When the Amounts Are Awarded or Resolved

The Company's policy is to recognize contract revenue from claims against customers and others on construction projects only when the amounts are awarded or resolved. Revenues from such claims amounted to $647,000 in 20X2 and $483,000 in 20X1.

Example 24: Contract Revenue from Claims Recognized When Realization Is Probable

The Company's policy is to recognize contract revenue from claims against customers and others on construction projects when realization is probable, the amount could be reasonably estimated, and the claim has reasonable legal basis. Claims involve the use of estimates and it is reasonably possible that revisions to the estimated recoverable amounts of recorded claims may be made in the near-term.

Example 25: Amounts Recognized from Claims and Pending Change Orders Disclosed and Identified in Balance Sheet Captions

Costs and estimated earnings in excess of billings on uncompleted contracts include unbilled revenues for pending change orders of approximately $590,000 and $417,000 at December 31, 20X2, and December 31, 20X1, respectively; and claims of approximately $370,000 and $223,000 at December 31, 20X2, and December 31, 20X1, respectively. In addition, accounts receivable as of December 31, 20X2, and December 31, 20X1, includes claims and contractually billed amounts related to such contracts of approximately $900,000 and $716,000, respectively. Generally, the customer will not pay contractually billed amounts to the Company until final resolution of related claims.

Example 26: Contingent Liability in Respect of Performance and Payment Bonds Issued by Sureties

The Company is contingently liable to sureties in respect of performance and payment bonds issued by the sureties in connection with certain contracts entered into by the Company in the normal course of business. The Company has agreed to indemnify the sureties for any payments made by them in respect of such bonds.

Gains and Losses

Example 27: Extraordinary Loss Related to Involuntary Conversion of a Company's Foreign Plant

In June 20X2, the XYZ government declared its intent to nationalize certain companies, including the Company's manufacturing plant in XYZ. In August 20X2, the Company reached an agreement with the XYZ government, which provides that the XYZ government will purchase the Company's manufacturing plant in XYZ. In December 20X2, the XYZ government's purchase of the Company's manufacturing plant was completed and the Company received an aggregate amount of approximately $150,000. In 20X2, the Company recorded an extraordinary loss of $1 million (including taxes of $300,000), which represents the difference between the carrying amount of the plant and the amounts received from the XYZ government.

Example 28: Extraordinary Gain Related to Insurance Settlement for Earthquake Damage

In September 20X2, the Company's headquarters building in Apple Valley, Florida, was severely damaged by an earthquake. After the settlement with the insurer in December 20X2, the Company retired the building and recognized an extraordinary gain of $624,000, net of income taxes of $310,000, during 20X2.

Principal Agent Considerations

Example 29: Accounting Policy Describes Considerations Given to Indicators of Gross Revenue Reporting and Indicators of Net Revenue Reporting

The Company recognizes revenue from product sales or services rendered when the following four revenue recognition criteria are met:

persuasive evidence of an arrangement exists, delivery has occurred or services have been rendered, the selling price is fixed or determinable, and collectibility is reasonably assured.

The Company evaluates the criteria outlined in FASB ASC Subtopic 605-45, *Principal Agent Considerations*, in determining whether it is appropriate to record the gross amount of product sales and related costs or the net amount earned as commissions. Generally, when the Company is primarily obligated in a transaction, is subject to inventory risk, has latitude in establishing prices and selecting suppliers, or has several but not all of these indicators, revenue is recorded gross. If the Company is not primarily obligated and amounts earned are determined using a fixed percentage, a fixed-payment schedule, or a combination of the two, the Company generally records the net amounts as commissions earned.

Example 30: Shipping and Handling Fees Charged to Customers and Reported as Revenue

Shipping and handling fees billed to customers are classified on the Statement of Operations as "Net sales" and were $2 million and $1.8 million for 20X2 and 20X1, respectively. The associated shipping and handling costs are classified in "Cost of sales" and were $2.3 million and $2.1 million for 20X2 and 20X1, respectively.

Example 31: Shipping and Handling Costs Are Included in Cost of Sales

The Company's shipping and handling costs are included in cost of sales for all periods presented.

> **Note:** If shipping and handling costs are significant and are not included in costs of sales, then disclosure is required of the amount of such costs and the line item in which they are included on the income statement. See the example below for appropriate disclosure when shipping and handling costs are not included in cost of sales.

Example 32: Shipping and Handling Costs Are Included in Selling, General and Administrative Expenses

> **Note:** If shipping and handling costs are significant and are *not* included in costs of sales, then disclosure is required of the amount of such costs and the line item in which they are included on the income statement.

Shipping and handling costs of $785,000 in 20X2 and $692,000 in 20X1 are included in selling, general, and administrative expenses.

Example 33: Taxes Collected from Customers and Remitted to Governmental Authorities—Net Basis

The Company's policy is to present taxes collected from customers and remitted to governmental authorities on a net basis. The Company records the amounts collected as a current liability and relieves such liability upon remittance to the taxing authority without impacting revenues or expenses.

Example 34: Taxes Collected from Customers and Remitted to Governmental Authorities—Gross Basis

The Company reports sales, excise, and value-added taxes on sales transactions on a gross basis in its income statement (included in both revenues and costs). The amounts of those taxes included in revenues and costs totaled $325,000 and $310,000 for the years ended December 31, 20X2, and 20X1, respectively.

Customer Payments and Incentives

Example 35: Vendor's Policy for Providing Sales Incentives to Its Customers

The Company periodically provides incentive offers to its customers to encourage purchases. Such offers include current discount offers (e.g., percentage discounts off current purchases), inducement offers (e.g., offers for future discounts subject to a minimum current purchase), and other similar offers. Current discount offers, when accepted by customers, are treated as a reduction to the purchase price of the related transaction, while inducement offers, when accepted by customers, are treated as a reduction to purchase price based on estimated future redemption rates. Redemption rates are estimated using the Company's historical experience for similar inducement offers. Current discount offers and inducement offers are presented as a net amount in "Net sales."

Example 36: Customer's Policy for Sales Incentives Received from Vendors

The Company accounts for allowances received from merchandise vendors as an adjustment to the prices of the vendor's products. This adjustment is characterized as a reduction of the carrying amount of inventory and, when sold, as cost of sales. The terms of the vendor allowance arrangements are generally one year in length and settle semi-annually. Cost of sales includes allowances from merchandise vendors of $3 million and $2 million in 20X2 and 20X1, respectively.

PART 7—
EXPENSES

CHAPTER 36
ASC TOPIC 705: COST OF SALES AND SERVICES

ASC Topic 705, "Cost of Sales and Services," does not prescribe any specific or incremental disclosure requirements, as the asset liability model used in FASB ASC generally results in the inclusion of those requirements and related guidance in other FASB ASC Topics. For disclosure and key presentation requirements prescribed in other ASC Topics, refer to the applicable chapters in this Manual for further guidance.

CHAPTER 37
ASC TOPIC 710:
COMPENSATION—GENERAL

CONTENTS

EXECUTIVE SUMMARY

Compensated Absences

An entity should accrue a liability for employees' compensation for future absences (e.g., vacations, illnesses, and holidays) if all of the following conditions are met:

1. The company's obligation relating to employees' rights to receive compensation for future absences is attributable to employee's services already rendered.
2. The obligations relate to rights that eventually vest or accumulate.
3. Payment of the compensation is probable.
4. The amount can be reasonably estimated.

If the first three conditions are met but the entity cannot reasonably estimate the amount of the accrual, the reasons for not making the accrual should be disclosed in the notes to the financial statements.

Deferred Compensation—Rabbi Trusts

Rabbi trusts are generally set up to fund compensation for a select group of management or highly paid executives, where amounts earned by an employee are invested in the stock of the employer and placed in the rabbi trust. The deferred compensation obligation of some plans may be settled in cash, shares of the employer's stock, or diversified assets. In other plans, the deferred compensation obligation may be settled only by delivery of the shares of the employer stock.

Other Deferred Compensation Arrangements

Deferred compensation contracts are accounted for individually on an accrual basis. Estimated amounts to be paid under a deferred compensation contract that is not equivalent to a pension plan or a postretirement health or welfare benefit plan are accrued over the period of an employee's active employment from the time the contract is signed to the employee's full eligibility date. If elements of both current and future services are present, only the portion applicable to the current services is accrued.

If individual deferred compensation contracts, as a group, are in substance a retirement plan, they should be accounted for in accordance with GAAP for pension plans, as discussed in ASC Topic 715,

Compensation—Retirement Benefits. Similarly, if individual deferred compensation contracts, as a group, are in substance a postretirement benefit plan other than pensions, they should be accounted for in accordance with GAAP for postretirement benefits, as discussed in ASC Topic 715.

Accounting Literature

FASB Accounting Standards Codification Topic	Pre-Codification Accounting Literature
710, Compensation—General	FAS-43, *Accounting for Compensated Absences*
	EITF 97-14, *Accounting for Deferred Compensation Arrangements Where Amounts Earned Are Held in a Rabbi Trust and Invested*

DISCLOSURE AND KEY PRESENTATION REQUIREMENTS

Compensated Absences

1. For compensated absences (e.g., vacation and sick pay) (ASC 710-10-50-1) (FAS-43, par. 6):

    a. Liabilities should be appropriately accrued and reported for employees' compensation for future absences.

    b. If the entity has not accrued a liability for compensated absences because the amount cannot be reasonably estimated, that fact should be disclosed.

Deferred Compensation—Rabbi Trusts

1. For deferred compensation plans involving rabbi trusts:

    a. The accounts of the rabbi trust should be consolidated with the accounts of the employer in the employer's financial statements. (ASC 710-10-45-1) (EITF 97-14)

    b. If the plan permits diversification and the employee has diversified assets, changes in the fair value of the deferred compensation obligation should *not* be recorded in other comprehensive income (even if changes in the fair value of the assets held by the rabbi trust are recorded in other comprehensive income). (ASC 710-10-45-2) (EITF 97-14)

   c. For earnings per share (EPS) purposes:

     (1) Employer shares held by the rabbi trust should be treated as treasury stock for EPS purposes and excluded from the denominator in the basic and diluted EPS calculations. (ASC 710-10-45-3) (EITF 97-14) (*Note:* However, the obligation under the deferred compensation arrangement should be reflected in the denominator of the EPS computation.)

     (2) If an obligation is required to be settled by delivery of shares of employer stock, those shares should be included in the calculation of basic and diluted EPS. (ASC 710-10-45-4) (EITF 97-14)

     (3) If the obligation may be settled by delivery of cash, shares of employer stock, or diversified assets, those shares should *not* be reflected in basic EPS but should be included in the calculation of diluted EPS. (ASC 710-10-45-4) (EITF 97-14)

Other Deferred Compensation Arrangements

Authoritative literature does not explicitly require any specific disclosures about deferred compensation contracts or arrangements. However, to the extent applicable, disclosures similar to those for pension plans and postretirement benefits are found in practice and are considered informative disclosures. The disclosure and key presentation requirements for pension plans and postretirement benefits other than pensions are discussed under ASC Topic 715. For further guidance, see Chapter 39, "ASC Topic 715: Compensation—Retirement Benefits."

EXAMPLES OF FINANCIAL STATEMENT DISCLOSURES

 The following sample disclosures are available on the accompanying disc.

Compensated Absences

Example 1: Company Has Not Accrued a Liability for Compensated Absences Because the Amount Cannot Be Reasonably Estimated

Employees of the Company are entitled to paid vacation and paid sick days depending on job classification, length of service, and other factors. At December 31, 20X2, and December 31, 20X1, the Company had approximately 1,200 employees. Of this total, approximately 1,000 are hourly employees and 200 are salaried employees. Approximately 98% of the Company's hourly employees and 37% of its salaried employees are represented by a number of labor unions. Each union contract contains different provisions for employee-compensated absences. It is not practicable for the Company to estimate the amount of compensation for future absences; accordingly, no liability for compensated absences has been recorded in the accompanying financial statements. The Company's policy is to recognize the costs of compensated absences when actually paid to employees.

Deferred Compensation—Rabbi Trusts

Example 2: Deferred Compensation Plan Is Funded by Life Insurance Contracts

The Company has a deferred compensation plan that permits employees and independent contractors to defer portions of their compensation, subject to annual deferral limits, and have it credited to one or more investment options in the plan. Deferrals made by employees and independent contractors and earnings thereon are fully accrued and held in a rabbi trust. In addition, the Company may make discretionary contributions to the plan that vest over one to five years. Contributions made by the Company and earnings thereon are accrued over the vesting period and have not been funded to date. Benefits are paid according to elections made by the participants.

The Company made contributions to the plan during 20X2 and 20X1 of $3 million and $2 million, respectively. Changes in the fair value of the vested amounts owed to the participants are adjusted with a corresponding charge (or credit) to compensation and benefits costs. The reduction in the deferred compensation liability recognized in income during 20X2 was $500,000. In 20X1, the deferred compensation liability increased and, therefore, the Company recognized a loss of $100,000.

Included in "Other Liabilities" as of December 31, 20X2, is $2 million reflecting the non-stock liability under this plan. The Company has purchased whole-life insurance contracts on certain employee participants to recover distributions made or to be made under this plan and have recorded the cash surrender value of the policies of $1.5 million in "Other Assets."

Example 3: Deferred Compensation Plan Is Funded by Life Insurance Contracts and Provides Guaranteed Interest Rate

The Company has a deferred compensation plan that permits management and highly compensated employees to defer portions of their compensation and earn a guaranteed interest rate on the deferred amounts. The salaries that have been deferred since the plan's inception have been accrued and the only expense, other than salaries, related to this plan is the interest on the deferred amounts. Interest expense during 20X2 and 20X1 includes $103,000 and $68,000, respectively, related to this plan. The Company has included in "Deferred employee benefits" $1,150,000 and $935,000 at December 31, 20X2, and December 31, 20X1, respectively, to reflect its liability under this plan. The Company has established a rabbi trust to finance obligations under the plan with corporate-owned whole-life insurance contracts on the related employees. The Company has included in "Other assets" $1,200,000 and $967,000 at December 31, 20X2, and December 31, 20X1, respectively, which represents cash surrender value of these policies.

Other Deferred Compensation Arrangements

Example 4: Present Value of Estimated Future Benefit Payments Are Being Accrued over the Service Period

In March 20X2, the Company entered into a deferred compensation agreement with a key executive. The agreement provides for certain postretirement benefits, contingent on certain conditions, beginning in 20X9 and payable over the remaining life of the executive and spouse. The Company accrues the present value of the estimated future benefit payments over the period from the date of the agreement to the retirement date. The Company recognized expense of $141,000 in 20X2 and $102,000 in 20X1 related to this agreement.

Example 5: Deferred Compensation Obligation Is Accrued but Unfunded

The Company has two deferred compensation plans for management and highly compensated associates, whereby participants may defer base compensation and bonuses and earn interest on their deferred amounts. Under one plan, a participant may elect to defer a maximum of 100% of his or her compensation. Under another plan, a participant could elect to defer a minimum of 3% of his or her compensation. These deferred compensation plans are unfunded; therefore, benefits are paid from the general assets of the Company. The total of participant deferrals, which is reflected in long-term liabilities, was $823,000 and $554,000 at December 31, 20X2, and December 31, 20X1, respectively. The participant deferrals earn interest at a rate based on U.S. Government Treasury rates. The interest expense related to this plan was $65,000 in 20X2 and $47,000 in 20X1.

Example 6: Deferred Compensation Balance and Related Expense Previously Recognized Are Reversed

On July 27, 20X2, Mr. White joined the Company as president, chief executive officer, and member of the board of directors. On December 29, 20X2, Mr. White resigned his positions with the Company. In July 20X2, the Company granted 1 million shares of stock options to Mr. White at an exercise price of $1.50 below the stock's per share fair value on the date of grant. This grant resulted in the recording of $1.5 million of deferred compensation, which the Company had begun to recognize over the vesting period of the options. All of Mr. White's options expired unvested upon his resignation. Therefore, the remaining deferred compensation balance, as well as the stock compensation expense recorded during the year, was reversed.

CHAPTER 38
ASC TOPIC 712:
COMPENSATION—NONRETIREMENT
POSTEMPLOYMENT BENEFITS

CONTENTS

EXECUTIVE SUMMARY

Nonretirement Postemployment Benefits

Nonretirement postemployment benefits are benefits provided to former or inactive employees, their beneficiaries, and covered dependents after employment but before retirement. Postemployment benefits may be provided in cash or in kind and may be paid as a result of a disability, layoff, death, or other event. They include, but are not limited to, salary continuation, supplemental unemployment benefits, severance benefits, disability-related benefits (including workers' compensation), job training and counseling, and continuation of benefits such as healthcare benefits and life insurance coverage.

Accounting Literature

FASB Accounting Standards Codification Topic	Pre-Codification Accounting Literature
712, Compensation— Nonretirement Postemployment Benefits	FAS-112, Employers' Accounting for Postemployment Benefits

DISCLOSURE AND KEY PRESENTATION REQUIREMENTS

If the entity has not accrued an obligation for postemployment benefits (e.g., salary continuation, supplemental unemployment benefits, severance benefits, disability related benefits, job training and counseling, and continuation of health and insurance coverage) provided to former or inactive employees, including their beneficiaries and covered dependents, after employment but before retirement, only because the amount cannot be reasonably estimated, that fact should be disclosed. (ASC 712-10-50-2) (FAS-112, par. 7)

EXAMPLES OF FINANCIAL STATEMENT DISCLOSURES

 The following sample disclosures are available on the accompanying disc.

Example 1: Company Discloses Amount of Postemployment Benefits Charged to Operations

> **Note:** Although authoritative literature does not require that the amount of postemployment benefits be disclosed, such disclosure is considered informative.

The Company provides certain postemployment benefits to eligible former or inactive employees and their dependents during the period subsequent to employment but prior to retirement and accrues for the related cost over the service lives of the employees. These benefits include certain disability and healthcare coverage and severance benefits. Postemployment benefit costs charged to operations in 20X2 and 20X1 totaled $97,000 and $73,000, respectively.

Example 2: Company Does Not Disclose Amount of Postemployment Benefits Charged to Operations

> **Note:** Although authoritative literature does not require that the amount of postemployment benefits be disclosed, such disclosure is considered informative.

The Company provides certain postemployment benefits to eligible former or inactive employees and their dependents during the period subsequent to employment but prior to retirement and accrues for the related cost over the service lives of the employees. These benefits include certain disability and healthcare coverage and severance benefits.

Example 3: Company Uses Discounting to Measure the Postemployment Benefit Obligation

> **Note:** The use of discounting in measuring postemployment benefit obligations is permitted but not required.

The Company provides certain benefits to former or inactive employees after employment but before retirement and accrues for the related cost over the service lives of the employees. Those benefits include, among others, disability, severance, and workers' compensation. The assumed discount rate used to measure the postemployment benefit liability was 7% at December 31, 20X2, and 6.5% at December 31, 20X1.

Example 4: Company Is Self-Insured under Its Postemployment Benefit Plans

The Company is self-insured under its employees' short-term and long-term disability plans, which are the primary benefits paid to inactive employees prior to retirement. Following is a summary of the obligation for postemployment benefits included in the Company's balance sheets at December 31, 20X2, and December 31, 20X1:

	20X2	20X1
Included with "Salaries and related liabilities"	$105,000	$102,000
Included with "Other long-term liabilities"	693,000	607,000
	$798,000	$709,000

Example 5: Company Has Not Accrued a Liability for Postemployment Benefits Because the Amount Cannot Be Reasonably Estimated

Generally accepted accounting principles require employers to recognize an obligation for benefits provided to former or inactive employees after employment but before retirement. The Company provides the following postemployment benefits to former and inactive employees: supplemental unemployment benefits, disability-related benefits, and job training and counseling. It is not practicable for the Company to reasonably estimate the amount of its obligation for postemployment benefits; accordingly, no liability for postemployment benefits has been recorded in the accompanying financial statements. The Company's policy is to recognize the costs of such postemployment benefits when actually paid.

CHAPTER 39
ASC TOPIC 715:
COMPENSATION—RETIREMENT
BENEFITS

CONTENTS

EXECUTIVE SUMMARY

A pension plan or postretirement plan may be broadly classified as either a defined benefit plan or a defined contribution plan. A *defined benefit pension plan* is one that contains a pension benefit formula, which generally describes the amount of pension benefit that each employee will receive for services performed during a specified period of employment. In a *defined benefit postretirement plan,* the benefit may be defined in terms of a specified monetary amount (such as a life insurance benefit) or a specified type of benefit (such as all or a percentage of the cost of specified surgical procedures). A *defined contribution pension or postretirement plan* provides an individual account for each participant and specifies how contributions to each individual's account are determined.

A pension or a postretirement plan may be contributory or noncontributory; that is, the employees may be required to contribute to the plan (contributory), or the entire cost of the plan may be borne by the employer (noncontributory). In addition, a pension or postretirement plan may be funded or unfunded; that is, the employees and/or the employer may make cash contributions to the plan trustee (funded), or the employer may make only credit entries on its books reflecting the liability under the plan (unfunded).

Generally accepted accounting principles (GAAP) for employers' accounting for pension or postretirement plans center on the determination of annual expense, referred to as net periodic cost. Net periodic cost has often been viewed as a single amount, but it is actually made up of several components that reflect different aspects of the employer's financial arrangements, as well as the cost of benefits earned by employees.

Defined Benefit Plans

An entity's *net periodic cost* represents the net amount of pension or postretirement cost for a specified period that is charged against income. Under GAAP, the components of net periodic cost are (1) service cost; (2) interest cost on the plan's obligation; (3) actual return on plan assets; (4) amortization of any prior service cost or credit included in accumulated other comprehensive income; (5) recognition of net gain or loss, if any; and (6) amortization of any net transition asset or obligation.

Net periodic cost is estimated in advance at the beginning of a period based on actuarial assumptions, such as the discount rate on the plan's benefit obligation and the expected long-term rate of return on plan assets. At the end of the period, adjustments are made to account for the differences (actuarial gains or losses), if any, between the estimated and actual amounts.

Employers are required to recognize the funded status of a benefit plan as the difference between the fair value of plan assets and the benefit obligations in their balance sheets. For a pension plan, the benefit obligation is the projected benefit obligation; for other postretirement plans, the benefit obligation is the accumulated benefit obligation. The funded status of all overfunded plans are aggregated and recognized as an asset in the employer's balance sheet. Similarly, the funded status of all underfunded plans are aggregated and recognized as a liability in the employer's balance sheet. The aggregate overfunded amount is presented as a noncurrent asset in the employer's balance sheet, whereas the aggregate underfunded amount is presented as a current liability, noncurrent liability, or combination of the two. The current portion is the amount by which the actuarial present value of the benefits included in the benefit obligation payable in the next 12 months or operating cycle, if longer, exceeds the fair value of plan assets.

Defined Contribution Plans

A defined contribution plan provides for individual accounts for each plan participant and contains the terms that specify how contributions are determined for each participant's individual account. Each periodic employer contribution is allocated to each participant's individual account in accordance with the terms of the plan, and benefits are based solely on the amount available in each participant's account at the time of his or her retirement. The amount available in each participant's account at the time of his or her retirement is the total of the amounts contributed by the employer, plus the returns earned on investments of those contributions, plus forfeitures of other participants' benefits that have been allocated to the participant's account, and less any allocated administrative expenses.

Settlements, Curtailments, and Termination Benefits

A *settlement* of a pension or postretirement plan is an irrevocable action that relieves the employer (or the plan) of primary responsibility for an obligation and eliminates significant risks related to the obligation and the assets used to effect the settlement. Examples of transactions that constitute a settlement include (1) making lump-sum cash payments to plan participants in exchange for their rights to receive specified benefits and (2) purchasing nonparticipating annuity or insurance contracts to cover plan benefits.

For a defined benefit pension plan, a *curtailment* is an event that either (1) significantly reduces the expected years of future service of present employees or (2) eliminates for a significant number of employees the accrual of defined benefits for some or all of their future services. For a defined benefit postretirement plan, a *curtailment* is an event that either (1) significantly reduces the expected years of future service of active plan participants or (2) eliminates the accrual of defined benefits for some or all of the future services of a significant number of active plan participants. Examples of curtailments are (1) termination of employees' services earlier than expected, which may or may not involve closing a facility or discontinuing a segment of a business, and (2) termination or suspension of a plan so that employees do not earn additional defined benefits for future services.

Termination benefits are classified as either special or contractual. *Special termination benefits* are those that are offered to employees for a short period in connection with the termination of their employment. *Contractual termination benefits* are those that are required by the terms of an existing plan or agreement and that are provided only on the occurrence of a specified event, such as early retirement or the closing of a facility.

Accounting Literature

FASB Accounting Standards Codification Topic	*Pre-Codification Accounting Literature*
715, *Compensation—Retirement Benefits*	FAS-87, *Employers' Accounting for Pensions*
	FAS-88, *Employers' Accounting for Settlements and Curtailments of Defined Benefit Pension Plans and for Termination Benefits*

FASB Accounting Standards Codification Topic	Pre-Codification Accounting Literature
	FAS-106, *Employers' Accounting for Postretirement Benefits Other Than Pensions*
	FSP FAS 106-2, *Accounting and Disclosure Requirements Related to the Medicare Prescription Drug Improvement and Modernization Act of 2003*
	FAS-132R, *Employers' Disclosures about Pensions and Other Postretirement Benefits (Revised 2003)*
	FSP FAS 132R-1, *Employer's Disclosures about Postretirement Benefit Plan Assets*
	FAS-158, *Employers' Accounting for Defined Benefit Pension and Other Postretirement Plans*
	FASB Implementation Guidance (Q&A), *A Guide to Implementation of Statement 87 on Employers' Accounting for Pensions: Questions and Answers*
	EITF 03-2, *Accounting for the Transfer to the Japanese Government of the Substitutional Portion of Employee Pension Fund Liabilities*

DISCLOSURE AND KEY PRESENTATION REQUIREMENTS

The disclosure requirements for pension plans apply to both public and nonpublic entities. However, with respect to defined benefit pension plans, nonpublic entities are allowed to provide reduced disclosures, if they so elect, regardless of materiality.

In addition, companies that have defined benefit pension plans and other postretirement benefit plans may elect to present the required disclosures for their plans in a parallel format in a single note to the financial statements, since most of the disclosures about defined benefit pension plans and postretirement benefit plans are similar.

> **NOTE:** On December 30, 2008, the FASB issued FSP FAS 132R-1, *Employer's Disclosures about Postretirement Benefit Plan Assets.* This FSP amends FAS-132R, *Employers' Disclosures about Pensions and Other Postretirement Benefits* (ASC 715, *Compensation—Retirement Benefits*), to provide guidance on an employer's disclosures about plan assets of a defined benefit pension or other postretirement plan. This FSP also includes a technical amendment to FAS-132R that requires a nonpublic entity to disclose net periodic benefit cost for each annual period for which an income statement is presented. The disclosures about plan assets required by this FSP, and codified in ASC Topic 715, are effective for fiscal years ending after December 15, 2009. Upon initial application, the new provisions are not required for earlier periods that are presented for comparative purposes. Earlier application of the new provisions is permitted. The technical amendment is effective immediately.

Pension and Postretirement Defined Benefit Plans—Public Entities and Nonpublic Entities That Elect to Voluntarily Provide Additional Disclosures (Annual Periods)

1. The following disclosures should be provided separately for pension plans and other postretirement benefit plans (ASC 715-20-50-1) (FAS-132R, par. 5) (*Note*: Amounts related to the employer's results of operations should be disclosed for each period for which an income statement is presented. Amounts related to the employer's balance sheet should be disclosed as of the date of each balance sheet presented.):

    a. A reconciliation of beginning and ending balances of the benefit obligation showing separately, if applicable, the effects during the period attributable to each of the following (*Note*: For defined benefit pension plans, the benefit obligation is the projected benefit obligation. For defined benefit other postretirement plans, the benefit obligation is the accumulated postretirement benefit obligation.):

        (1) Service cost.

        (2) Interest cost.

        (3) Contributions by plan participants.

        (4) Actuarial gains and losses.

        (5) Foreign currency exchange rate changes.

      (6)   Benefits paid.

      (7)   Plan amendments.

      (8)   Business combinations.

      (9)   Divestitures.

      (10) Curtailments, settlements, and special and contractual termination benefits.

  b. A reconciliation of beginning and ending balances of the fair value of plan assets showing separately, if applicable, the effects during the period attributable to each of the following:

      (1)   Actual return on plan assets.

      (2)   Foreign currency exchange rate changes.

      (3)   Contributions by the employer.

      (4)   Contributions by plan participants.

      (5)   Benefits paid.

      (6)   Business combinations.

      (7)   Divestitures.

      (8)   Settlements.

  c. The funded status of the plans and the amounts recognized in the balance sheet, showing separately the assets and current and noncurrent liabilities recognized. (*Note:* The liability for an underfunded plan should be presented as a current liability, a noncurrent liability, or a combination of both. The current portion (determined on a plan-by-plan basis) is the amount by which the actuarial present value of benefits included in the benefit obligation payable in the next 12 months, or operating cycle, if longer, exceeds the fair value of plan assets. The asset for an overfunded plan should be classified as a noncurrent asset). (ASC 715-20-45-3) (FAS-106, par. 44B; FAS-158, par. B48)

  d. The following information about plan assets (*Note:* This disclosure item is superseded by the disclosure requirement in item (dd) below effective for fiscal years ending after December 15, 2009):

      (1)   The percentage of the fair value of total plan assets held in each major category of plan assets, including at a minimum the following categories: (a) equity securities, (b) debt securities, (c) real estate, and (d) all other assets. (*Note:* Disclosure of additional asset categories and additional information

about specific assets within a category is encouraged if that information is expected to be useful in understanding the risks associated with each asset category and the overall expected long-term rate of return on assets.)

(2) A narrative description of investment policies and strategies, including: (a) target allocation percentages or range of percentages for each major category of plan assets presented on a weighted-average basis as of the measurement date(s) of the latest balance sheet presented, if applicable, and (b) other factors that are pertinent to an understanding of the policies and strategies such as investment goals, risk management practices, permitted and prohibited investments including the use of derivatives, diversification, and the relationship between plan assets and benefit obligations.

(3) A narrative description of the basis used to determine the overall expected long-term rate-of-return-on-assets assumption, such as: (a) the general approach used, (b) the extent to which the overall rate-of-return-on-assets assumption was based on historical returns, (c) the extent to which adjustments were made to those historical returns in order to reflect expectations of future returns, and (d) how those adjustments were determined.

Note: The disclosure requirements in item (dd) below are prescribed by ASC Subtopic 715-20 based on FSP FAS 132R-1, which supersedes the disclosure requirements in item (d) above, effective for fiscal years ending after December 15, 2009. Upon initial application, the provisions of this item are not required for earlier periods that are presented for comparative purposes. Early application of this item is permitted.

dd. The following information about plan assets (ASC 715-20-50-1 and 65-2) (FAS-132R, par. 5; FSP FAS-132R-1, par. 15):

(1) A narrative description of investment policies and strategies, including (a) target allocation percentages or range of percentages considering the major categories of plan assets disclosed pursuant to item (3) below as of the latest balance sheet presented (on a weighted-average basis for employers with more than one plan), and (b) other factors that are pertinent to an understanding of those policies and strategies such as investment goals, risk management

practices, permitted and prohibited investments including the use of derivatives, diversification, and the relationship between plan assets and benefit obligations.

(2) For investment funds disclosed as major categories as described in item (3) below, a description of the significant investment strategies of those funds.

(3) As of each date for which a balance sheet is presented, the fair value of each major category of plan assets. (*Note:* Asset categories should be based on the nature and risks of assets in an employer's plan(s). Examples of major categories include, but are not limited to, the following: (a) cash and cash equivalents; (b) equity securities segregated by industry type, company size, or investment objective; (c) debt securities issued by national, state, and local governments; (d) corporate debt securities; (e) asset-backed securities; (f) structured debt; (g) derivatives on a gross basis segregated by type of underlying risk in the contract, for example, interest rate contracts, foreign exchange contracts, equity contracts, commodity contracts, credit contracts, and other contracts; (h) investment funds segregated by type of fund; and (i) real estate.)

(4) A narrative description of the basis used to determine the overall expected long-term rate-of-return-on-assets assumption, such as: (a) the general approach used, (b) the extent to which the overall rate-of-return-on-assets assumption was based on historical returns, (c) the extent to which adjustments were made to those historical returns in order to reflect expectations of future returns, and (d) how those adjustments were determined. (*Note:* The description should consider the major categories of assets described in item (3) above.)

(5) For each major category of plan assets disclosed pursuant to item (3) above and for each annual period:

(a) The level within the fair value hierarchy in which the fair value measurements in their entirety fall, segregating fair value measurements using quoted prices in active markets for identical assets or liabilities (Level 1), significant other observable inputs (Level 2), and significant unobservable inputs (Level 3).

(b) For fair value measurements of plan assets using significant unobservable inputs (Level 3), a reconciliation of the beginning and ending balances, separately presenting changes during the period attributable to:

(i) Actual return on plan assets, separately identifying the amount related to assets still held at the reporting date, and the amount related to assets sold during the period.

(ii) Purchases, sales and settlements, net.

(iii) Transfers in and (or) out of Level 3, for example, transfers due to changes in the observability of significant inputs.

(c) Information about the valuation technique(s) and inputs used to measure fair value.

(d) A discussion of changes in valuation techniques and inputs, if any, during the period.

e. For defined benefit pension plans, the accumulated benefit obligation.

f. The benefits (as of the date of the latest balance sheet presented) expected to be paid in each of the next five fiscal years and in the aggregate for the five fiscal years thereafter. (*Note:* The expected benefits should be estimated based on the same assumptions used to measure the entity's benefit obligation at the end of the year and should include benefits attributable to estimated future employee service.)

g. The employer's best estimate of contributions expected to be paid to the plan during the next fiscal year beginning after the date of the latest balance sheet presented. (*Note:* Estimated contributions may be presented in the aggregate for contributions required by funding regulations or laws, discretionary contributions, and noncash contributions.)

h. The amount of net benefit cost recognized, showing separately all of the following:

(1) The service cost component.

(2) The interest cost component.

(3) The expected return on plan assets for the period.

(4) The gain or loss component.

(5) The prior service cost or credit component.

      (6)   The transition asset or obligation component.

      (7)   The gain or loss recognized due to settlements or curtailments.

i.   Separately (1) the net gain or loss and net prior service cost or credit recognized in other comprehensive income for the period pursuant to ASC paragraphs 715-30-35-11 and 35-21 and paragraphs 715-60-35-16 and 35-25 (FAS-87, pars. 25 and 29; FAS-106, pars. 52 and 56), and (2) reclassification adjustments of other comprehensive income for the period, as those amounts, including amortization of the net transition asset or obligation, are recognized as components of net periodic benefit cost.

j.   The amounts in accumulated other comprehensive income that have not yet been recognized as components of net periodic benefit cost, showing separately the net gain or loss, net prior service cost or credit, and net transition asset or obligation.

k.   On a weighted-average basis, all of the following assumptions used in the accounting for the plans, specifying in a tabular format, the assumptions used to determine the benefit obligation and the assumptions used to determine net benefit cost:

      (1)   Assumed discount rates.

      (2)   Rates of compensation increase (for pay-related plans).

      (3)   Expected long-term rates of return on plan assets.

l.   The assumed health care cost trend rate(s) for the next year used to measure the expected cost of benefits covered by the plan (gross eligible charges), and a general description of the direction and pattern of change in the assumed trend rates thereafter, together with the ultimate trend rate(s) and when that rate is expected to be achieved. (*Note:* This is applicable to health care postretirement benefit plans only.)

m.   The effect of a one-percentage-point increase and the effect of a one-percentage-point decrease in the assumed health care cost trend rates on (1) the aggregate of the service and interest cost components of net periodic postretirement health care benefit costs and (2) the accumulated postretirement benefit obligation for health care benefits. (*Note*: This is applicable to health care postretirememt benefit plans only. Measuring the sensitivity of the accumulated postretirement benefit obligation and the combined service and interest cost components to a change in the assumed health care cost trend rates requires remeasuring the accumulated postretirement benefit obligation as of the beginning and end of the year. For purposes of this disclosure, all other assumptions should be held constant, and the effects should be measured based on the substantive plan that is the basis for the accounting.)

n. If applicable, the amounts and types of securities of the employer and related parties included in plan assets, the approximate amount of future annual benefits of plan participants covered by insurance contracts, including annuity contracts issued by the employer or related parties, and any significant transactions between the employer or related parties and the plan during the period.

o. If applicable, any alternative method used to amortize prior service amounts or net gains and losses.

p. If applicable, any substantive commitment, such as past practice or a history of regular benefit increases, used as the basis for accounting for the benefit obligation.

q. If applicable, the cost of providing special or contractual termination benefits recognized during the period and a description of the nature of the event.

r. An explanation of any significant change in the benefit obligation or plan assets not otherwise apparent in the preceding disclosures.

s. The amounts in accumulated other comprehensive income expected to be recognized as components of net periodic benefit cost over the fiscal year that follows the most recent balance sheet presented, showing separately the net gain or loss, net prior service cost or credit, and net transition asset or obligation.

t. The amount and timing of any plan assets expected to be returned to the employer during the 12-month period (or operating cycle if longer) that follows the most recent balance sheet presented.

2. The required disclosures should be aggregated for all of an employer's defined benefit pension plans and for all of an employer's other defined benefit postretirement plans unless disaggregating in groups is considered to provide useful information or is otherwise required by items 3 or 4 below. (ASC 715-20-50-2) (FAS-132R, par. 6)

3. If aggregate disclosures are presented, the following additional disclosures should be made (ASC 715-20-50-3) (FAS-132R, par. 6) (*Note*: Disclosures about pension plans with

assets in excess of the accumulated benefit obligation generally may be aggregated with disclosures about pension plans with accumulated benefit obligations in excess of assets. The same aggregation is permitted for other postretirement benefit plans):

    a. The aggregate benefit obligation and aggregate fair value of plan assets for plans with benefit obligations in excess of plan assets as of the measurement date of each balance sheet presented.

    b. The aggregate pension accumulated benefit obligation and aggregate fair value of plan assets for pension plans with accumulated benefit obligations in excess of plan assets.

4. Disclosures about pension plans or other postretirement benefit plans outside the United States should be made separately from those for U.S. plans if the benefit obligations of the plans outside the United States are significant relative to the total benefit obligation and the plans use significantly different assumptions. (ASC 715-20-50-4) (FAS-132R, par. 7)

5. If the expected rate of return on plan assets that is determined as of the beginning of the year changes because of a subsequent interim measurement of both pension or other postretirement plan assets and obligations, disclosures should be made of the beginning and more recently assumed rate, or a properly weighted combination of the two. (ASC 715-20-50-8) (Q&A-87, par. 79)

6. The following transitional disclosures resulting from the transition guidance for FAS-158, *Employers' Accounting for Defined Benefit Pension and Other Postretirement Plans*, should be made (ASC 715-20-65-1) (FAS-158, pars. 15–21 and A11–A31):

    a. In the year that the measurement date provisions of ASC Sections 715-30-35 and 715-60-35 (FAS-158) are initially applied, the separate adjustments of retained earnings and accumulated other comprehensive income from applying the guidance in those ASC Sections.

Pension and Postretirement Defined Benefit Plans—Reduced Disclosure Requirements for Nonpublic Entities (Annual Periods)

1. The following disclosures should be provided separately for pension plans and other postretirement benefit plans (ASC 715-20-50-5) (FAS-132R, par. 8) (*Note*: Amounts related to the employer's results of operations should be disclosed for each

period for which an income statement is presented. Amounts related to the employer's balance sheet should be disclosed as of the date of each balance sheet presented):

a. The benefit obligation, fair value of plan assets, and funded status of the plan.

b. Employer contributions, participant contributions, and benefits paid.

c. The following information about plan assets (*Note:* This disclosure item is superseded by the disclosure requirement in item (cc) below effective for fiscal years ending after December 15, 2009):

    (1) The percentage of the fair value of total plan assets held in each major category of plan assets, including at a minimum the following categories: (a) equity securities, (b) debt securities, (c) real estate, and (d) all other assets. (*Note:* Disclosure of additional asset categories and additional information about specific assets within a category is encouraged if that information is expected to be useful in understanding the risks associated with each asset category and the overall expected long-term rate of return on assets.)

    (2) A narrative description of investment policies and strategies, including: (a) target allocation percentages or range of percentages for each major category of plan assets presented on a weighted-average basis as of the measurement date(s) of the latest balance sheet presented, if applicable, and (b) other factors that are pertinent to an understanding of the policies and strategies such as investment goals, risk management practices, permitted and prohibited investments including the use of derivatives, diversification, and the relationship between plan assets and benefit obligations.

    (3) A narrative description of the basis used to determine the overall expected long-term rate-of-return-on-assets assumption, such as: (a) the general approach used, (b) the extent to which the overall rate-of-return-on-assets assumption was based on historical returns, (c) the extent to which adjustments were made to those historical returns in order to reflect expectations of future returns, and (d) how those adjustments were determined.

Note: The disclosure requirements in item (cc) below are prescribed by ASC Subtopic 715-20 based on FSP FAS 132R-1, which supersedes the disclosure requirements in item (c) above, effective for fiscal years ending after December 15, 2009. Upon initial application, the provisions of this item are not required for earlier periods that are presented for comparative purposes. Early application of this item is permitted.

cc. The following information about plan assets (ASC 715-20-50-1 and 65-2) (FAS-132-R, par. 5; FSP FAS 132R-1, par. 15):

(1) A narrative description of investment policies and strategies, including (a) target allocation percentages or range of percentages considering the major categories of plan assets disclosed pursuant to item (3) below as of the latest balance sheet presented (on a weighted-average basis for employers with more than one plan), and (b) other factors that are pertinent to an understanding of those policies and strategies such as investment goals, risk management practices, permitted and prohibited investments including the use of derivatives, diversification, and the relationship between plan assets and benefit obligations.

(2) For investment funds disclosed as major categories as described in item (3) below, a description of the significant investment strategies of those funds.

(3) As of each date for which a balance sheet is presented, the fair value of each major category of plan assets. (*Note:* Asset categories should be based on the nature and risks of assets in an employer's plan(s). Examples of major categories include, but are not limited to, the following: (a) cash and cash equivalents; (b) equity securities segregated by industry type, company size, or investment objective; (c) debt securities issued by national, state, and local governments; (d) corporate debt securities; (e) asset-backed securities; (f) structured debt; (g) derivatives on a gross basis segregated by type of underlying risk in the contract, for example, interest rate contracts, foreign exchange contracts, equity contracts, commodity contracts, credit contracts, and other contracts; (h) investment funds segregated by type of fund; and (i) real estate.)

(4) A narrative description of the basis used to determine the overall expected long-term rate-of-return-on-assets assumption, such as: (a) the general approach used, (b) the extent to which the overall rate-of-return-on-assets assumption was based on

historical returns, (c) the extent to which adjustments were made to those historical returns in order to reflect expectations of future returns, and (d) how those adjustments were determined. (*Note:* The description should consider the major categories of assets described in item (3) above.)

(5) For each major category of plan assets disclosed pursuant to item (3) above and for each annual period:

(a) The level within the fair value hierarchy in which the fair value measurements in their entirety fall, segregating fair value measurements using quoted prices in active markets for identical assets or liabilities (Level 1), significant other observable inputs (Level 2), and significant unobservable inputs (Level 3).

(b) For fair value measurements of plan assets using significant unobservable inputs (Level 3), a reconciliation of the beginning and ending balances, separately presenting changes during the period attributable to:

(i) Actual return on plan assets, separately identifying the amount related to assets still held at the reporting date, and the amount related to assets sold during the period.

(ii) Purchases, sales and settlements, net.

(iii) Transfers in and (or) out of Level 3, for example, transfers due to changes in the observability of significant inputs.

(c) Information about the valuation technique(s) and inputs used to measure fair value.

(d) A discussion of changes in valuation techniques and inputs, if any, during the period.

d. For defined benefit pension plans, the accumulated benefit obligation.

e. The benefits (as of the date of the latest balance sheet presented) expected to be paid in each of the next five fiscal years and in the aggregate for the five fiscal years thereafter. (*Note:* The expected benefits should be estimated based on the same assumptions used to measure the entity's benefit obligation at the end of the year and should include benefits attributable to estimated future employee service.)

f. The employer's best estimate of contributions expected to be paid to the plan during the next fiscal year beginning after the date of the latest balance sheet presented. (*Note:* Estimated contributions may be presented in the aggregate for contributions required by funding regulations or laws, discretionary contributions, and noncash contributions.)

g. The amounts recognized in the balance sheets, showing separately the postretirement benefit assets and current and noncurrent postretirement benefit liabilities.

h. Separately (1) the net gain or loss and net prior service cost or credit recognized in other comprehensive income for the period pursuant to ASC paragraphs 715-30-35-11 and 35-21 and paragraphs 715-60-35-16 and 35-25 (FAS-87, pars. 25 and 29; FAS-106, pars. 52 and 56), and (2) reclassification adjustments of other comprehensive income for the period, as those amounts, including amortization of the net transition asset or obligation, are recognized as components of net periodic benefit cost.

i. The amounts in accumulated other comprehensive income that have not yet been recognized as components of net periodic benefit cost, showing separately the net gain or loss, net prior service cost or credit, and net transition asset or obligation.

j. On a weighted-average basis, all of the following assumptions used in the accounting for the plans, specifying in a tabular format, the assumptions used to determine the benefit obligation and the assumptions used to determine net benefit cost:

   (1) Assumed discount rates.

   (2) Rates of compensation increase (for pay-related plans).

   (3) Expected long-term rates of return on plan assets.

k. The assumed health care cost trend rate(s) for the next year used to measure the expected cost of benefits covered by the plan (gross eligible charges), and a general description of the direction and pattern of change in the assumed trend rates thereafter, together with the ultimate trend rate(s) and when that rate is expected to be achieved. (*Note:* This is applicable to health care postretirement benefit plans only.)

l. If applicable, the amounts and types of securities of the employer and related parties included in plan assets, the approximate amount of future annual benefits of plan participants covered by insurance contracts, including annuity contracts issued by the employer or related parties, and any significant transactions between the employer or related parties and the plan during the period.

m. The nature and effect of significant nonroutine events, such as amendments, combinations, divestitures, curtailments, and settlements.

n. The amounts in accumulated other comprehensive income expected to be recognized as components of net periodic benefit cost over the fiscal year that follows the most recent balance sheet presented, showing separately the net gain or loss, net prior service cost or credit, and net transition asset or obligation.

o. The amount and timing of any plan assets expected to be returned to the employer during the 12-month period (or operating cycle if longer) that follows the most recent balance sheet presented.

p. The amount of net periodic benefit cost recognized.

2. The required disclosures should be aggregated for all of an employer's defined benefit pension plans and for all of an employer's other defined benefit postretirement plans unless disaggregating in groups is considered to provide useful information or is otherwise required by items 3 or 4 below. (ASC 715-20-50-2) (FAS-132R, par. 6)

3. If aggregate disclosures are presented, the following additional disclosures should be made (ASC 715-20-50-3) (FAS-132R, par. 6) (*Note*: Disclosures about pension plans with assets in excess of the accumulated benefit obligation generally may be aggregated with disclosures about pension plans with accumulated benefit obligations in excess of assets. The same aggregation is permitted for other postretirement benefit plans):

a. The aggregate benefit obligation and aggregate fair value of plan assets for plans with benefit obligations in excess of plan assets as of the measurement date of each balance sheet presented.

b. The aggregate pension accumulated benefit obligation and aggregate fair value of plan assets for pension plans with accumulated benefit obligations in excess of plan assets.

4. Disclosures about pension plans or other postretirement benefit plans outside the United States should be made separately from those for U.S. plans if the benefit obligations of the plans outside the U.S. are significant relative to the total

benefit obligation and the plans use significantly different assumptions. (ASC 715-20-50-4) (FAS-132R, par. 7)

5. If the expected rate of return on plan assets that is determined as of the beginning of the year changes because of a subsequent interim measurement of both pension or other postretirement plan assets and obligations, disclosures should be made of the beginning and more recently assumed rate, or a properly weighted combination of the two. (ASC 715-20-50-8) (Q&A-87, par. 79)

6. The following transitional disclosures resulting from the transition guidance for FAS-158, *Employers' Accounting for Defined Benefit Pension and Other Postretirement Plans*, should be made (ASC 715-20-65-1) (FAS-158, pars. 15–21 and A11–A31):

    a. In the year that the measurement date provisions of ASC Sections 715-30-35 and 715-60-35 (FAS-158) are initially applied, the separate adjustments of retained earnings and accumulated other comprehensive income from applying the guidance in those ASC Sections.

Pension and Postretirement Defined Benefit Plans—Disclosure Requirements for Public Entities (Interim Periods)

1. For each period for which an income statement is presented, disclosures should be made of the amount of net benefit cost recognized, showing separately the following (ASC 715-20-50-6; 270-10-50-1) (FAS-132R, par. 9):

    a. The service cost component.

    b. The interest cost component.

    c. The expected return on plan assets for the period.

    d. The gain or loss component.

    e. The prior service cost or credit component.

    f. The transition asset or obligation component.

    g. The gain or loss recognized due to a settlement or curtailment.

2. Disclosure should be made of the total amount of the employer's contributions paid, and expected to be paid, during the current fiscal year, if significantly different from amounts previously disclosed. (ASC 715-20-50-6; 270-10-50-1) (FAS-132R, par. 9) (*Note:* Estimated contributions may be presented in the aggregate for contributions required by

funding regulations or laws, discretionary contributions, and noncash contributions.)

Pension and Postretirement Defined Benefit Plans—Disclosure Requirements for Nonpublic Entities (Interim Periods)

1. Disclosure should be made of the total amount of the employer's contributions paid, and expected to be paid, during the current fiscal year, if significantly different from amounts previously disclosed. (ASC 715-20-50-7) (FAS-132R, par. 10) (*Note:* Estimated contributions may be presented in the aggregate for contributions required by funding regulations or laws, discretionary contributions, and noncash contributions.)

Disclosures Related to Japanese Governmental Settlement Transactions

1. The following disclosures should be made for the separation of the substitutional portion of the benefit obligation from the corporate portion of the benefit obligation in a Japanese Employee Pension Fund arrangement and the transfer of the substitutional portion and related assets to the Japanese government pursuant to the June 2001 Japanese Welfare Pension Insurance Law amendment (ASC 715-20-50-10) (EITF 03-2):

   a. The difference between the obligation settled and the assets transferred to the government, determined in accordance with the government formula and displayed as a subsidy from the government.

   b. Separate from the government subsidy, the derecognition of previously accrued salary progression at the time of settlement.

Medicare Prescription Drug, Improvement, and Modernization Act

1. The following disclosures should be made in interim and annual financial statements for the first period in which an employer includes the effects of the Medicare subsidy (under the Medicare Prescription Drug, Improvement, and Modernization Act) in measuring the accumulated postretirement benefit obligation and the first period in which an employer includes the effects of the subsidy in measuring net periodic

postretirement benefit cost (ASC 715-60-50-3) (FSP FAS 106-2, par. 21):

   a. The reduction in the accumulated postretirement benefit obligation for the subsidy related to benefits attributed to past service.

   b. The effect of the subsidy on the measurement of net periodic postretirement benefit cost for the current period, including:

     (1) Any amortization of the actuarial gain component in (a) above.

     (2) The reduction in current period service cost due to the subsidy.

     (3) The resulting reduction in interest cost on the accumulated postretirement benefit obligation as a result of the subsidy.

   c. Any other significant change in the benefit obligation or plan assets.

2. For employers that sponsor a postretirement health care benefit plan that provides prescription drug coverage, disclosures should be made of the gross benefit payments (paid and expected), including prescription drug benefits and, separately, the gross amount of the subsidy receipts (received and expected). (ASC 715-60-50-4) (FSP FAS 106-2, par. 22)

3. Until an employer is able to determine whether benefits provided by its plan are actuarially equivalent, the following disclosures should be made in financial statements for interim or annual periods (ASC 715-60-50-6) (FSP FAS 106-2, par. 20):

   a. The existence of the Medicare Prescription Drug, Improvement, and Modernization Act.

   b. That measures of the accumulated postretirement benefit obligation or net periodic postretirement benefit cost do not reflect any amount associated with the subsidy because the employer is unable to conclude whether the benefits provided by the plan are actuarially equivalent to Medicare Part D under the Act.

Defined Contribution Plans

1. The following information about the entity's defined contribution plans should be disclosed separately from the entity's defined benefit plans for all periods presented (ASC 715-70-50-1) (FAS-132R, par. 11):

a. The amount of cost recognized for defined contribution pension plans and for other defined contribution postretirement benefit plans separately from the amount of cost recognized for defined benefit plans.

b. A description of the nature and effect of any significant changes during the period affecting comparability, such as a change in the rate of employer contributions, a business combination, or a divestiture.

Multiemployer Plans

1. The following disclosures should be made regarding multiemployer plans (ASC 715-80-50-1) (FAS-132R, par. 12):

   a. The amount of contributions to multiemployer plans for each annual period for which an income statement is presented. (*Note:* Employers may disclose total contributions to multiemployer plans without disaggregating the amounts attributable to pension plans and other postretirement benefit plans.)

   b. A description of the nature and effect of any changes affecting comparability, such as a change in the rate of employer contributions, a business combination, or a divestiture.

2. The provisions and disclosures of ASC Topic 450, *Contingencies* (FAS-5, *Accounting for Contingencies*), should be applied if it is either probable or reasonably possible that either: (a) an employer would withdraw from the plan under circumstances that would give rise to an obligation, or (b) an employer's contribution to the fund would be increased during the remainder of the contract period to make up a shortfall in the funds necessary to maintain the negotiated level of benefit coverage (a maintenance of benefits clause). (ASC 715-80-50-2) (FAS-132R, par. 13)

EXAMPLES OF FINANCIAL STATEMENT DISCLOSURES

 The following sample disclosures are available on the accompanying disc.

Defined Benefit Plans: Illustrations if ASC Topic 715 Based on FSP FAS 132R-1 Has *Not* Been Adopted

Example 1: Defined Benefit Pension Plans—Public Entities

The Company sponsors two funded defined benefit pension plans for eligible employees who are 21 years of age with one or more years of service and who are not covered by collective bargaining agreements. Benefits paid to retirees are based on age at retirement, years of credited service, and average compensation. The Company's funding policy is to contribute the larger of the amount required to fully fund the plan's current liability or the amount necessary to meet the funding requirements as defined by the Internal Revenue Code.

In addition, the Company sponsors an unfunded Executive Pension Plan. This plan is nonqualified and provides certain key employees defined pension benefits that supplement those provided by the Company's other retirement plans.

Obligations and Funded Status

	20X2	20X1
Change in projected benefit obligation:		
Benefit obligation at beginning of year	$ 27,800,000	$23,200,000
Service cost	1,700,000	1,500,000
Interest cost	1,900,000	2,000,000
Actuarial loss	4,700,000	1,900,000
Divestitures	(100,000)	-0-
Curtailments	(5,800,000)	-0-
Benefits paid	(1,300,000)	(800,000)
Benefit obligation at end of year	$ 28,900,000	$27,800,000
Change in plan assets:		
Fair value of plan assets at beginning of year	$ 22,700,000	$18,300,000
Actual return on plan assets	1,200,000	4,500,000
Employer contributions	1,300,000	700,000
Divestitures	(300,000)	-0-
Benefits paid	(900,000)	(800,000)

	20X2	20X1
Fair value of plan assets at end of year	$ 24,000,000	$ 22,700,000
Funded status at end of the year	$(4,900,000)	$(5,100,000)
Amounts recognized in the balance sheets consist of:		
Noncurrent assets	$ 300,000	$ 300,000
Current liabilities	(1,500,000)	(1,500,000)
Noncurrent liabilities	(3,700,000)	(3,900,000)
	$(4,900,000)	$(5,100,000)

Amounts recognized in accumulated other comprehensive income consist of the following:

	20X2	20X1
Net loss (gain)	$(1,700,000)	$(1,800,000)
Prior service cost (credit)	500,000	1,600,000
	$(1,200,000)	$ (200,000)

Components of net periodic benefit cost and other amounts recognized in other comprehensive income are as follows:

	20X2	20X1
Net Periodic Benefit Cost:		
Service cost	$ 1,700,000	$ 1,500,000
Interest cost on projected benefit obligations	1,900,000	2,000,000
Expected return on plan assets	(1,800,000)	(1,300,000)
Amortization of prior service cost	100,000	200,000
Amortization of actuarial loss	200,000	-0-
Net periodic benefit cost	2,100,000	2,400,000
Other Changes in Plan Assets and Benefit Obligations Recognized in Other Comprehensive Income:		
Net loss (gain)	100,000	300,000
Prior service cost (credit)	(1,000,000)	(800,000)
Amortization of prior service cost	(100,000)	(200,000)

	20X2	20X1
Total recognized in other comprehensive income	(1,000,000)	(700,000)
Total recognized in net periodic benefit cost and other comprehensive income	$ 1,100,000	$1,700,000

The estimated net gain and prior service cost for the defined benefit pension plans that will be amortized from accumulated other comprehensive income into net periodic benefit cost over the next fiscal year are $300,000 and $100,000, respectively.

The following table summarizes the Company-sponsored pension plans that have projected benefit obligations in excess of plan assets and the accumulated benefit obligation of the unfunded Executive Pension Plan in which the accumulated benefit obligation exceeds plan assets:

	20X2	20X1
Projected benefit obligation in excess of plan assets:		
Projected benefit obligation	$3,900,000	$4,200,000
Fair value of plan assets	$2,800,000	$2,600,000
Accumulated benefit obligation in excess of plan assets:		
Accumulated benefit obligation	$1,300,000	$1,100,000
Fair value of plan assets	$ -0-	$ -0-

The accumulated benefit obligation for all defined benefit pension plans was $16,100,000 and $14,700,000 at December 31, 20X2, and December 31, 20X1, respectively.

Assumptions

The following are weighted-average assumptions used to determine benefit obligations at December 31, 20X2, and December 31, 20X1:

	20X2	20X1
Discount rate	6.75%	7.00%
Rate of compensation increase	5.25%	4.75%

The following are weighted-average assumptions used to determine net periodic benefit cost for the years ended December 31, 20X2, and December 31, 20X1:

	20X2	20X1
Discount rate	7.00%	7.25%
Expected long-term return on plan assets	8.00%	7.75%
Rate of compensation increase	5.50%	5.00%

The Company's expected long-term return on plan assets assumption is based on a periodic review and modeling of the plans' asset allocation and liability structure over a long-term period. Expectations of returns for each asset class are the most important of the assumptions used in the review and modeling and are based on comprehensive reviews of historical data and economic/financial market theory. The expected long-term rate of return on assets was selected from within the reasonable range of rates determined by (1) historical real returns, net of inflation, for the asset classes covered by the investment policy and (2) projections of inflation over the long-term period during which benefits are payable to plan participants.

Plan Assets

The Company's pension plan weighted-average asset allocations at December 31, 20X2, and December 31, 20X1, by asset category, are as follows:

	Plan Assets at December 31,	
	20X2	20X1
Asset Category		
Equity securities	55%	52%
Debt securities	28	31
Real estate	10	11
Other	7	6
Total	100%	100%

The Company's target asset allocation as of December 31, 20X2, by asset category, is as follows:

Asset Category	
Equity securities	50–70%
Debt securities	30–50%
Real estate	0–20%
Other	0–20%

The Company's investment policy includes various guidelines and procedures designed to ensure assets are invested in a manner necessary to meet expected future benefits earned by participants. The investment guidelines consider a broad range of economic conditions. Central to the policy are target allocation ranges (shown above) by major asset categories.

The objectives of the target allocations are to maintain investment portfolios that diversify risk through prudent asset allocation parameters, achieve asset returns that meet or exceed the plans' actuarial assumptions, and achieve asset returns that are competitive with like institutions employing similar investment strategies.

The investment policy is periodically reviewed by the Company and a designated third-party fiduciary for investment matters. The policy is established and administered in a manner that is compliant at all times with applicable government regulations.

Equity securities include common stock of Ace Ltd. in the amounts of $1,200,000 (5% of total plan assets) and $1,589,000 (7% of total plan assets) at December 31, 20X2, and December 31, 20X1, respectively.

Cash Flows

The Company expects to contribute $1,500,000 to its pension plan in 20X3.

The following pension benefit payments, which reflect expected future service, as appropriate, are expected to be paid:

20X3	$1,000,000
20X4	1,050,000
20X5	1,175,000
20X6	1,225,000
20X7	1,315,000
Years 20X8–20Y2	7,325,000

Example 2: Defined Benefit Pension Plans—Alternative Reduced Disclosures for a Nonpublic Entity

> **Note:** This example illustrates the alternative reduced disclosures for a nonpublic entity using the same facts in Example 1 above.

The Company sponsors two funded defined benefit pension plans for eligible employees who are 21 years of age with one or more years of service and who are not covered by collective bargaining agreements. Benefits paid to retirees are based on age at retirement, years of credited service, and average compensation. The Company's funding policy is to contribute the larger of the amount required to fully fund the plan's current liability or the amount necessary to meet the funding requirements, as defined by the Internal Revenue Code.

In addition, the Company sponsors an unfunded Executive Pension Plan. This plan is nonqualified and provides certain key employees defined pension benefits that supplement those provided by the Company's other retirement plans.

Obligations and Funded Status

	20X2	20X1
Projected benefit obligation at December 31	$ 28,900,000	$ 27,800,000
Fair value of plan assets at December 31	24,000,000	22,700,000
Funded status at end of year	$(4,900,000)	$(5,100,000)
Amounts recognized in the balance sheets consist of:		
Noncurrent assets	$ 300,000	$ 300,000
Current liabilities	(1,500,000)	(1,500,000)
Noncurrent liabilities	(3,700,000)	(3,900,000)
	$(4,900,000)	$(5,100,000)

Amounts recognized in accumulated other comprehensive income consist of the following:

	20X2	20X1
Net loss (gain)	$(1,700,000)	$(1,800,000)
Prior service cost (credit)	500,000	1,600,000
	$(1,200,000)	$ (200,000)

The following table summarizes the Company-sponsored pension plans that have projected benefit obligations in excess of plan assets and the accumulated benefit obligation of the unfunded Executive Pension Plan in which the accumulated benefit obligation exceeds plan assets:

	20X2	*20X1*
Projected benefit obligation in excess of plan assets:		
Projected benefit obligation	$3,900,000	$4,200,000
Fair value of plan assets	$2,800,000	$2,600,000
Accumulated benefit obligation in excess of plan assets:		
Accumulated benefit obligation	$1,300,000	$1,100,000
Fair value of plan assets	$ -0-	$ -0-

The accumulated benefit obligation for all defined benefit pension plans was $16,100,000 and $14,700,000 at December 31, 20X2, and December 31, 20X1, respectively.

	20X2	*20X1*
Benefit cost	$2,100,000	$2,400,000
Employer contributions	$1,300,000	$ 700,000
Benefits paid	$ 300,000	$ 800,000

Assumptions

The following are weighted-average assumptions used to determine benefit obligations at December 31, 20X2, and December 31, 20X1:

	20X2	*20X1*
Discount rate	6.75%	7.00%
Rate of compensation increase	5.25%	4.75%

The following are weighted-average assumptions used to determine net periodic benefit cost for the years ended December 31, 20X2, and December 31, 20X1:

	20X2	*20X1*
Discount rate	7.00%	7.25%
Expected long-term return on plan assets	8.00%	7.75%
Rate of compensation increase	5.50%	5.00%

The Company's expected long-term return on plan assets assumption is based on a periodic review and modeling of the plans' asset allocation and liability structure over a long-term period. Expectations of returns for each asset class are the most important of the assumptions used in the review and modeling and are based on comprehensive reviews of historical data and economic/financial market theory. The expected long-term rate of return on assets was selected from within the reasonable range of rates determined by (1) historical real returns, net of inflation, for the asset classes covered by the investment policy and (2) projections of inflation over the long-term period during which benefits are payable to plan participants.

Plan Assets

The Company's pension plan weighted-average asset allocations at December 31, 20X2, and December 31, 20X1, by asset category, are as follows:

	Plan Assets at December 31,	
	20X2	*20X1*
Asset Category		
Equity securities	55%	52%
Debt securities	28	31
Real estate	10	11
Other	7	6
Total	100%	100%

The Company's target asset allocation as of December 31, 20X2, by asset category, is as follows:

Asset Category	
Equity securities	50–70%
Debt securities	30–50%
Real estate	0–20%
Other	0–20%

The Company's investment policy includes various guidelines and procedures designed to ensure assets are invested in a manner necessary to meet expected future benefits earned by participants. The investment guidelines consider a broad range of economic conditions. Central to the policy are target allocation ranges (shown above) by major asset categories.

The objectives of the target allocations are to maintain investment portfolios that diversify risk through prudent asset allocation parameters, achieve asset returns that meet or exceed the plans' actuarial assumptions, and achieve asset returns that are competitive with like institutions employing similar investment strategies.

The investment policy is periodically reviewed by the Company and a designated third-party fiduciary for investment matters. The policy is established and administered in a manner that is compliant at all times with applicable government regulations.

Equity securities include common stock of Ace Ltd. in the amounts of $1,200,000 (5% of total plan assets) and $1,589,000 (7% of total plan assets) at December 31, 20X2, and December 31, 20X1, respectively.

Cash Flows

The Company expects to contribute $1,500,000 to its pension plan in 20X3.

The following pension benefit payments, which reflect expected future service, as appropriate, are expected to be paid:

20X3	$1,000,000
20X4	1,050,000
20X5	1,175,000
20X6	1,225,000
20X7	1,315,000
Years 20X8–20Y2	7,325,000

Example 3: Defined Benefit Postretirement Plans—Public Entities

The Company has multiple nonpension postretirement benefit plans. The health care plans are contributory, with participants' contributions adjusted annually; the life insurance plans are noncontributory. The accounting for the health care plans anticipates future cost sharing changes to the written plan that are consistent with the Company's expressed intent to increase retiree contributions each year by 50% of the excess of the expected general inflation rate over 6%. On December 31, 20X2, the Company amended its postretirement health care plans to provide long-term care coverage.

The Company acquired Massari, Ltd. on December 31, 20X2, including its postretirement benefit plans. As a result, the Company's plans were amended to establish parity with the benefits provided by Massari, Ltd.

Obligations and Funded Status

	20X2	20X1
Change in benefit obligation:		
Benefit obligation at beginning of year	$ 738,000	$ 700,000
Service cost	36,000	32,000
Interest cost	65,000	63,000
Plan participants' contributions	20,000	13,000
Amendments	75,000	-0-
Actuarial gain	(24,000)	-0-
Acquisition	600,000	-0-
Benefits paid	(90,000)	(70,000)
Benefit obligation at end of year	$ 1,420,000	$ 738,000
Change in plan assets:		
Fair value of plan assets at beginning of year	$ 206,000	$ 87,000
Actual return on plan assets	(3,000)	24,000
Acquisition	25,000	-0-
Employer contribution	171,000	152,000
Plan participants' contributions	20,000	13,000
Benefits paid	(90,000)	(70,000)
Fair value of plan assets at end of year	$ 329,000	$ 206,000
Funded status at end of year	$(1,091,000)	$(532,000)
Amounts recognized in the balance sheets consist of:		
Noncurrent assets	$ 60,000	$ 70,000
Current liabilities	(350,000)	(400,000)
Noncurrent liabilities	(801,000)	(202,000)
	$(1,091,000)	$(532,000)

Amounts recognized in accumulated other comprehensive income consist of the following:

	20X2	20X1
Net loss (gain)	$ 59,000	$ 60,000
Prior service cost (credit)	585,000	540,000
	$644,000	$600,000

Components of net periodic benefit cost and other amounts recognized in other comprehensive income are as follows:

	20X2	20X1
Net Periodic Benefit Cost:		
Service cost	$ 36,000	$ 32,000
Interest cost	65,000	63,000
Expected return on plan assets	(21,000)	(9,000)
Amortization of prior service cost	30,000	30,000
Recognized net actuarial loss	1,000	1,000
Net periodic benefit cost	111,000	117,000
Other Changes in Plan Assets and Benefit Obligations Recognized in Other Comprehensive Income:		
Net loss (gain)	(1,000)	15,000
Prior service cost (credit)	50,000	60,000
Amortization of prior service cost	(5,000)	(10,000)
Total recognized in other comprehensive income	44,000	65,000
Total recognized in net periodic benefit cost and other comprehensive income	$ 155,000	$ 182,000

The estimated net loss and prior service cost for the defined benefit postretirement plans that will be amortized from accumulated other comprehensive income into net periodic benefit cost over the next fiscal year are $25,000 and $75,000, respectively.

Assumptions

The following are weighted-average assumptions used to determine benefit obligations at December 31, 20X2, and December 31, 20X1:

	20X2	20X1
Discount rate	7.00%	7.25%

The following are weighted-average assumptions used to determine net periodic benefit cost for the years ended December 31, 20X2, and December 31, 20X1:

	20X2	20X1
Discount rate	7.00%	7.25%
Expected long-term return on plan assets	8.25%	8.50%

The Company's expected long-term return on plan assets assumption is based on a periodic review and modeling of the plans' asset allocation and liability structure over a long-term period. Expectations of returns for each asset class are the most important of the assumptions used in the review and modeling and are based on comprehensive reviews of historical data and economic/financial market theory. The expected long-term rate of return on assets was selected from within the reasonable range of rates determined by (1) historical real returns, net of inflation, for the asset classes covered by the investment policy and (2) projections of inflation over the long-term period during which benefits are payable to plan participants.

The following are assumed health care cost trend rates at December 31, 20X2, and December 31, 20X1:

	20X2	20X1
Health care cost trend rate assumed for next year	12%	12.5%
Rate to which the cost trend rate is assumed to decline (the ultimate trend rate)	6%	5%
Year that the rate reaches the ultimate trend rate	20X9	20X9

Assumed health care cost trend rates have a significant effect on the amounts reported for the health care plans. A 1% point change in assumed health care cost trend rates would have the following effects:

	1% Point Increase	1% Point Decrease
Effect on total of service and interest cost components	$122,000	$ (20,000)
Effect on postretirement benefit obligation	$173,000	$(156,000)

Plan Assets

The Company's postretirement benefit plans weighted-average asset allocations at December 31, 20X2, and December 31, 20X1, by asset category, are as follows:

	Plan Assets at December 31,	
	20X2	*20X1*
Asset Category		
Equity securities	57%	54%
Debt securities	26	29
Real estate	12	8
Other	5	9
Total	100%	100%

The Company's target asset allocation as of December 31, 20X2, by asset category, is as follows:

Asset Category	
Equity securities	50–70%
Debt securities	30–50%
Real estate	0–20%
Other	0–20%

The Company's investment policy includes various guidelines and procedures designed to ensure assets are invested in a manner necessary to meet expected future benefits earned by participants. The investment guidelines consider a broad range of economic conditions. Central to the policy are target allocation ranges (shown above) by major asset categories.

The objectives of the target allocations are to maintain investment portfolios that diversify risk through prudent asset allocation parameters, achieve asset returns that meet or exceed the plans' actuarial assumptions, and achieve asset returns that are competitive with like institutions employing similar investment strategies.

The investment policy is periodically reviewed by the Company and a designated third-party fiduciary for investment matters. The policy is established and administered in a manner that complies at all times with applicable government regulations.

Equity securities include common stock of Beas Ltd. in the amounts of $33,000 (10% of total plan assets) and $25,000 (12% of total plan assets) at December 31, 20X2, and December 31, 20X1, respectively.

Cash Flows

The Company expects to contribute $200,000 to its postretirement benefit plans in 20X3.

The following benefit payments, which reflect expected future service, as appropriate, are expected to be paid:

20X3	$125,000
20X4	130,000
20X5	140,000
20X6	150,000
20X7	175,000
Years 20X8–20Y2	860,000

Example 4: Defined Benefit Postretirement Plans—Alternative Reduced Disclosures for a Nonpublic Entity

> **Note:** This example illustrates the alternative reduced disclosures for a nonpublic entity using the same facts in Example 3 above.

The Company has multiple nonpension postretirement benefit plans. The health care plans are contributory, with participants' contributions adjusted annually; the life insurance plans are noncontributory. The accounting for the health care plans anticipates future cost sharing changes to the written plan that are consistent with the Company's expressed intent to increase retiree contributions each year by 50% of the excess of the expected general inflation rate over 6%. On December 31, 20X2, the Company amended its postretirement health care plans to provide long-term care coverage.

The Company acquired Massari, Ltd. on December 31, 20X2, including its postretirement benefit plans. As a result, the Company's plans were amended to establish parity with the benefits provided by Massari, Ltd.

Obligations and Funded Status

	Postretirement Benefits	
	20X2	20X1
Benefit obligation at December 31	$ 1,420,000	$ 738,000
Fair value of plan assets at December 31	329,000	206,000
Funded status at end of year	$(1,091,000)	$(532,000)

	Postretirement Benefits	
	20X2	20X1
Amounts recognized in the balance sheets consist of:		
Noncurrent assets	$ 60,000	$ 70,000
Current liabilities	(350,000)	(400,000)
Noncurrent liabilities	(801,000)	(202,000)
	$(1,091,000)	$(532,000)

Amounts recognized in accumulated other comprehensive income consist of the following:

	20X2	20X1
Net loss (gain)	$ 59,000	$ 60,000
Prior service cost (credit)	585,000	540,000
	$644,000	$600,000

	20X2	20X1
Benefit cost	$111,000	$117,000
Employer contribution	$171,000	$152,000
Plan participants' contributions	$ 20,000	$ 13,000
Benefits paid	$ 90,000	$ 70,000

Assumptions

The following are weighted-average assumptions used to determine benefit obligations at December 31, 20X2, and December 31, 20X1:

	20X2	20X1
Discount rate	7.00%	7.25%

The following are weighted-average assumptions used to determine net periodic benefit cost for the years ended December 31, 20X2, and December 31, 20X1:

	20X2	20X1
Discount rate	7.25%	7.25%
Expected long-term return on plan assets	8.25%	8.50%

The Company's expected long-term return on plan assets assumption is based on a periodic review and modeling of the plans' asset allocation and liability structure over a long-term period. Expectations of returns for each asset class are the most important of the assumptions used in the review and modeling and are based on comprehensive reviews of historical data and economic/financial market theory. The expected long-term rate of return on assets was selected from within the reasonable range of rates determined by (1) historical real returns, net of inflation, for the asset classes covered by the investment policy, and (2) projections of inflation over the long-term period during which benefits are payable to plan participants.

The following are assumed health care cost trend rates at December 31, 20X2, and December 31, 20X1:

	20X2	20X1
Health care cost trend rate assumed for next year	12%	12.5%
Rate to which the cost trend rate is assumed to decline (the ultimate trend rate)	6%	5%
Year that the rate reaches the ultimate trend rate	20X9	20X9

Plan Assets

The Company's postretirement benefit plans weighted-average asset allocations at December 31, 20X2, and December 31, 20X1, by asset category, are as follows:

	Plan Assets at December 31,	
	20X2	20X1
Asset Category		
Equity securities	57%	54%
Debt securities	26	29
Real estate	12	8
Other	5	9
Total	100%	100%

The Company's target asset allocation as of December 31, 20X2, by asset category, is as follows:

Asset Category	
Equity securities	50–70%
Debt securities	30–50%
Real estate	0–20%
Other	0–20%

The Company's investment policy includes various guidelines and procedures designed to ensure assets are invested in a manner necessary to meet expected future benefits earned by participants. The investment guidelines consider a broad range of economic conditions. Central to the policy are target allocation ranges (shown above) by major asset categories.

The objectives of the target allocations are to maintain investment portfolios that diversify risk through prudent asset allocation parameters, achieve asset returns that meet or exceed the plans' actuarial assumptions, and achieve asset returns that are competitive with like institutions employing similar investment strategies.

The investment policy is periodically reviewed by the Company and a designated third-party fiduciary for investment matters. The policy is established and administered in a manner that complies at all times with applicable government regulations.

Equity securities include common stock of Beas Ltd. in the amounts of $33,000 (10% of total plan assets) and $25,000 (12% of total plan assets) at December 31, 20X2, and December 31, 20X1, respectively.

Cash Flows

The Company expects to contribute $200,000 to its postretirement benefit plans in 20X3.

The following benefit payments, which reflect expected future service, as appropriate, are expected to be paid:

20X3	$125,000
20X4	130,000
20X5	140,000
20X6	150,000
20X7	175,000
Years 20X8–20Y2	860,000

Example 5: Disclosures about Defined Benefit Pension Plans and Other Postretirement Benefit Plans Are Presented in a Parallel Format in a Single Note to the Financial Statements

The Company has both funded and unfunded noncontributory defined benefit pension plans that together cover substantially all of its employees. The plans provide defined benefits based on years of service and final average salary.

The Company also has other postretirement benefit plans covering substantially all of its employees. The health care plans are contributory with participants' contributions adjusted annually; the life insurance plans are noncontributory. The accounting for the health care plans anticipates future cost-sharing changes to the written plans that are consistent with the Company's expressed intent to increase retiree contributions each year by 50% of health care cost increases in excess of 6%. The postretirement health care plans include a limit on the Company's share of costs for recent and future retirees.

Obligations and Funded Status

	Pension Benefits		Postretirement Benefits	
	20X2	20X1	20X2	20X1
Change in benefit obligation:				
Benefit obligation at beginning of year	$1,266,000	$1,200,000	$ 738,000	$ 700,000
Service cost	76,000	72,000	36,000	32,000
Interest cost	114,000	108,000	65,000	63,000
Plan participants' contributions	-0-	-0-	20,000	13,000
Amendments	120,000	-0-	75,000	-0-
Actuarial gain	(25,000)	-0-	(24,000)	-0-
Acquisition	900,000	-0-	600,000	-0-
Benefits paid	(125,000)	(114,000)	(90,000)	(70,000)
Benefit obligation at end of year	$2,326,000	$1,266,000	$1,420,000	$ 738,000

	Pension Benefits		Postretirement Benefits	
	20X2	*20X1*	*20X2*	*20X1*
Change in plan assets:				
Fair value of plan assets at beginning of year	$1,068,000	$ 880,000	$ 206,000	$ 87,000
Actual return on plan assets	29,000	188,000	(3,000)	24,000
Acquisition	1,000,000	-0-	25,000	-0-
Employer contribution	75,000	114,000	171,000	152,000
Plan participants' contributions	-0-	-0-	20,000	13,000
Benefits paid	(125,000)	(114,000)	(90,000)	(70,000)
Fair value of plan assets at end of year	$2,047,000	$1,068,000	$ 329,000	$ 206,000
Funded status at end of year	$(279,000)	$(198,000)	$(1,091,000)	$(532,000)
Amounts recognized in the balance sheets consist of:				
Noncurrent assets	$ 64,000	$ -0-	$ -0-	$ 68,000
Current liabilities	(100,000)	(48,000)	(400,000)	(200,000)
Noncurrent liabilities	(243,000)	(150,000)	(691,000)	(400,000)
	$(279,000)	$(198,000)	$(1,091,000)	$(532,000)

Amounts recognized in accumulated other comprehensive income consist of the following:

	Pension Benefits		Postretirement Benefits	
	20X2	*20X1*	*20X2*	*20X1*
Net loss (gain)	$ 83,000	$ 38,000	$ 59,000	$ 60,000
Prior service cost (credit)	260,000	160,000	585,000	540,000
	$343,000	$198,000	$644,000	$600,000

Components of net periodic benefit cost and other amounts recognized in other comprehensive income are as follows:

	Pension Benefits		Postretirement Benefits	
	20X2	*20X1*	*20X2*	*20X1*
Net Periodic Benefit Cost:				
Service cost	$ 76,000	$ 72,000	$ 36,000	$ 32,000
Interest cost	114,000	108,000	65,000	63,000
Expected return on plan assets	(107,000)	(88,000)	(21,000)	(9,000)
Amortization of prior service cost	20,000	20,000	30,000	30,000
Recognized net actuarial loss	8,000	2,000	1,000	1,000
Net periodic benefit cost	111,000	114,000	111,000	117,000
Other Changes in Plan Assets and Benefit Obligations Recognized in Other Comprehensive Income:				
Net loss (gain)	45,000	40,000	(1,000)	(15,000)
Prior service cost (credit)	120,000	70,000	75,000	90,000
Amortization of prior service cost	(20,000)	(20,000)	(30,000)	(30,000)
Total recognized in other comprehensive income	145,000	90,000	44,000	45,000
Total recognized in net periodic benefit cost and other comprehensive income	$ 256,000	$ 204,000	$ 155,000	$ 162,000

The estimated net loss and prior service cost for the defined benefit pension plans that will be amortized from accumulated other comprehensive income into net periodic benefit cost over the next fiscal year are $25,000 and $60,000, respectively. The estimated net loss and prior service cost for the defined benefit postretirement plans that will be amortized from accumulated other comprehensive income into net periodic benefit cost over the next fiscal year are $35,000 and $90,000, respectively.

The accumulated benefit obligation for all defined benefit pension plans was $733,000 and $650,000 at December 31, 20X2, and December 31, 20X1, respectively.

Assumptions

The following are weighted-average assumptions used to determine benefit obligations at December 31, 20X2, and December 31, 20X1:

	Pension Benefits		Postretirement Benefits	
	20X2	20X1	20X2	20X1
Discount rate	6.75%	7.00%	7.00%	7.25%
Rate of compensation increase	5.25%	4.75%	N/A	N/A

The following are weighted-average assumptions used to determine net periodic benefit cost for the years ended December 31, 20X2, and December 31, 20X1:

	Pension Benefits		Postretirement Benefits	
	20X2	20X1	20X2	20X1
Discount rate	7.00%	7.25%	7.25%	7.25%
Expected long-term return on plan assets	8.00%	7.75%	8.25%	8.50%
Rate of compensation increase	5.50%	5.00%	N/A	N/A

The Company's expected long-term return on plan assets assumption is based on a periodic review and modeling of the plans' asset allocation and liability structure over a long-term period. Expectations of returns for each asset class are the most important of the assumptions used in the review and modeling and are based on comprehensive reviews of historical data and economic/financial market theory. The expected long-term rate of return on assets was selected from within the reasonable range of rates determined by (1) historical real returns, net of inflation, for the asset classes covered by the investment policy and (2) projections of inflation over the long-term period during which benefits are payable to plan participants.

The following are assumed health care cost trend rates at December 31, 20X2, and December 31, 20X1:

	20X2	20X1
Health care cost trend rate assumed for next year	12%	12.5%
Rate to which the cost trend rate is assumed to decline (the ultimate trend rate)	6%	5%
Year that the rate reaches the ultimate trend rate	20X9	20X9

Assumed health care cost trend rates have a significant effect on the amounts reported for the health care plans. A 1% point change in assumed health care cost trend rates would have the following effects:

	1% Point Increase	1% Point Decrease
Effect on total of service and interest cost components	$ 22,000	$ (20,000)
Effect on postretirement benefit obligation	$173,000	$(156,000)

Plan Assets

The Company's pension plans' weighted-average asset allocations at December 31, 20X2, and December 31, 20X1, by asset category, are as follows:

	Plan Assets at December 31,	
	20X2	20X1
Asset Category		
Equity securities	55%	52%
Debt securities	28	31
Real estate	10	11
Other	7	6
Total	100%	100%

The Company's pension plans' target asset allocation as of December 31, 20X2, by asset category, is as follows:

Asset Category	
Equity securities	50–70%
Debt securities	30–50%
Real estate	0–20%
Other	0–20%

The Company's investment policy includes various guidelines and procedures designed to ensure assets are invested in a manner necessary to meet expected future benefits earned by participants.

The investment guidelines consider a broad range of economic conditions. Central to the policy are target allocation ranges (shown above) by major asset categories.

The objectives of the target allocations are to maintain investment portfolios that diversify risk through prudent asset allocation parameters, achieve asset returns that meet or exceed the plans' actuarial assumptions, and achieve asset returns that are competitive with like institutions employing similar investment strategies.

The investment policy is periodically reviewed by the Company and a designated third-party fiduciary for investment matters. The policy is established and administered in a manner that is compliant at all times with applicable government regulations.

Equity securities include common stock of Ace Ltd. in the amounts of $102,000 (5% of total plan assets) and $75,000 (7% of total plan assets) at December 31, 20X2, and December 31, 20X1, respectively.

The Company's postretirement benefit plans weighted-average asset allocations at December 31, 20X2, and December 31, 20X1, by asset category, are as follows:

	Plan Assets at December 31,	
	20X2	20X1
Asset Category		
Equity securities	57%	54%
Debt securities	26	29
Real estate	12	8
Other	5	9
Total	100%	100%

The Company's postretirement benefit plans target asset allocation as of December 31, 20X2, by asset category, is as follows:

Asset Category	
Equity securities	40–60%
Debt securities	25–40%
Real estate	0–20%
Other	0–20%

The Company's investment policy includes various guidelines and procedures designed to ensure that assets are invested in a manner necessary to meet expected future benefits earned by participants. The investment guidelines consider a broad range of economic conditions. Central to the policy are target allocation ranges (shown above) by major asset categories.

The objectives of the target allocations are to maintain investment portfolios that diversify risk through prudent asset allocation parameters, achieve asset returns that meet or exceed the plans' actuarial assumptions, and achieve asset returns that are competitive with like institutions employing similar investment strategies.

The investment policy is periodically reviewed by the Company and a designated third-party fiduciary for investment matters. The policy is established and administered in a manner that is compliant at all times with applicable government regulations.

Equity securities include common stock of Beas Ltd. in the amounts of $33,000 (10% of total plan assets) and $25,000 (12% of total plan assets) at December 31, 20X2, and December 31, 20X1, respectively.

Cash Flows

The Company expects to contribute $150,000 to its pension plans and $200,000 to its postretirement benefit plans in 20X3.

The following benefit payments, which reflect expected future service, as appropriate, are expected to be paid:

	Pension Benefits	Postretirement Benefits
20X3	$100,000	$125,000
20X4	105,000	130,000
20X5	118,000	140,000
20X6	125,000	150,000
20X7	135,000	175,000
Years 20X8–20Y2	775,000	860,000

Defined Benefit Plans: Illustrations if ASC Topic 715 Based on FSP FAS 132R-1 Has Been Adopted

Example 6: Defined Benefit Pension Plans—Public Entities

The Company sponsors two funded defined benefit pension plans for eligible employees who are 21 years of age with one or more years of service and who are not covered by collective bargaining agreements. Benefits paid to retirees are based on age at retirement, years of credited service, and average compensation. The Company's funding policy is to contribute the larger of the amount required to fully fund the plan's current liability or the amount necessary to meet the funding requirements, as defined by the Internal Revenue Code.

In addition, the Company sponsors an unfunded Executive Pension Plan. This plan is nonqualified and provides certain key employees defined pension benefits that supplement those provided by the Company's other retirement plans.

Obligations and Funded Status

	20X2	20X1
Change in projected benefit obligation:		
Benefit obligation at beginning of year	$27,800,000	$23,200,000
Service cost	1,700,000	1,500,000
Interest cost	1,900,000	2,000,000
Actuarial loss	4,700,000	1,900,000
Divestitures	(100,000)	-0-
Curtailments	(5,800,000)	-0-
Benefits paid	(1,300,000)	(800,000)
Benefit obligation at end of year	$28,900,000	$27,800,000
Change in plan assets:		
Fair value of plan assets at beginning of year	$22,700,000	$18,300,000
Actual return on plan assets	1,200,000	4,500,000
Employer contributions	1,300,000	700,000
Divestitures	(300,000)	-0-
Benefits paid	(900,000)	(800,000)
Fair value of plan assets at end of year	$24,000,000	$22,700,000
Funded status at end of the year	$(4,900,000)	$(5,100,000)
Amounts recognized in the balance sheets consist of:		
Noncurrent assets	$ 300,000	$ 300,000
Current liabilities	(1,500,000)	(1,500,000)
Noncurrent liabilities	(3,700,000)	(3,900,000)
	$(4,900,000)	$(5,100,000)

Amounts recognized in accumulated other comprehensive income consist of the following:

	20X2	20X1
Net loss (gain)	$(1,700,000)	$(1,800,000)
Prior service cost (credit)	500,000	1,600,000
	$(1,200,000)	$ (200,000)

Components of net periodic benefit cost and other amounts recognized in other comprehensive income are as follows:

	20X2	20X1
Net Periodic Benefit Cost:		
Service cost	$ 1,700,000	$ 1,500,000
Interest cost on projected benefit obligations	1,900,000	2,000,000
Expected return on plan assets	(1,800,000)	(1,300,000)
Amortization of prior service cost	100,000	200,000
Amortization of actuarial loss	200,000	-0-
Net periodic benefit cost	2,100,000	2,400,000
Other Changes in Plan Assets and Benefit Obligations Recognized in Other Comprehensive Income:		
Net loss (gain)	100,000	300,000
Prior service cost (credit)	(1,000,000)	(800,000)
Amortization of prior service cost	(100,000)	(200,000)
Total recognized in other comprehensive income	(1,000,000)	(700,000)
Total recognized in net periodic benefit cost and other comprehensive income	$ 1,100,000	$ 1,700,000

The estimated net gain and prior service cost for the defined benefit pension plans that will be amortized from accumulated other comprehensive income into net periodic benefit cost over the next fiscal year are $300,000 and $100,000, respectively.

The following table summarizes the Company-sponsored pension plans that have projected benefit obligations in excess of plan assets and the accumulated benefit obligation of the unfunded Executive Pension Plan in which the accumulated benefit obligation exceeds plan assets:

	20X2	20X1
Projected benefit obligation in excess of plan assets:		
Projected benefit obligation	$3,900,000	$4,200,000
Fair value of plan assets	$2,800,000	$2,600,000
Accumulated benefit obligation in excess of plan assets:		
Accumulated benefit obligation	$1,300,000	$1,100,000
Fair value of plan assets	$ -0-	$ -0-

The accumulated benefit obligation for all defined benefit pension plans was $16,100,000 and $14,700,000 at December 31, 20X2, and December 31, 20X1, respectively.

Assumptions

The following are weighted-average assumptions used to determine benefit obligations at December 31, 20X2, and December 31, 20X1:

	20X2	20X1
Discount rate	6.75%	7.00%
Rate of compensation increase	5.25%	4.75%

The following are weighted-average assumptions used to determine net periodic benefit cost for the years ended December 31, 20X2, and December 31, 20X1:

	20X2	20X1
Discount rate	7.00%	7.25%
Expected long-term return on plan assets	8.00%	7.75%
Rate of compensation increase	5.50%	5.00%

The Company's expected long-term return on plan assets assumption is based on a periodic review and modeling of the plans' asset allocation and liability structure over a long-term period. Expectations of returns for each asset class are the most important of the assumptions used in the review and modeling and are based on comprehensive reviews of historical data and economic/financial market theory. The expected long-term rate of return on assets was selected from within the reasonable range of rates determined by (1) historical real returns, net of inflation, for the asset classes covered by the investment policy and (2) projections of inflation over the long-term period during which benefits are payable to plan participants.

Plan Assets

The Company's overall investment strategy is to achieve a mix of approximately 75% of investments for long-term growth and 25% for near-term benefit payments with a wide diversification of asset types, fund strategies, and fund managers. The target allocations for plan assets are 65% equity securities, 20% corporate bonds and U.S. Treasury securities, and 15% for all other types of investments. Equity securities primarily include investments in large-cap and mid-cap companies primarily located in the United States. Fixed income securities include corporate bonds of companies from diversified industries, mortgage-backed securities, and U.S. Treasuries. Other types of investments include investments in hedge funds and private equity funds that follow several different strategies.

The fair values of the Company's pension plan assets at December 31, 20X2, by asset category are as follows:

The following are two acceptable alternative methods for disclosing the fair value of major categories of plan assets.

<u>Method 1</u>

		Fair Value Measurements at December 31, 20X2		
Asset Category	*Total*	*Quoted Prices in Active Markets for Identical Assets (Level 1)*	*Significant Observable Inputs (Level 2)*	*Significant Unobservable Inputs (Level 3)*
Cash	$1,750,000	$1,750,000	$	$
Equity securities:				
U.S. large-cap (a)	6,450,000	6,450,000		
U.S. mid-cap growth	1,150,000	1,150,000		
International large-cap value	3,800,000	3,800,000		
Emerging markets growth	900,000	300,000	600,000	
Domestic real estate	1,200,000	250,000	950,000	
Fixed income securities:				
U.S. Treasury securities	2,350,000	2,350,000		
Corporate bonds (b)	2,200,000		2,200,000	
Mortgage-backed securities	550,000		550,000	
Other types of investments:				
Equity long/short hedge funds (c)	600,000			600,000
Event driven hedge funds (d)	500,000			500,000

Fair Value Measurements at December 31, 20X2

Asset Category	Total	Quoted Prices in Active Markets for Identical Assets (Level 1)	Significant Observable Inputs (Level 2)	Significant Unobservable Inputs (Level 3)
Global opportunities hedge funds (e)	400,000			400,000
Multi strategy hedge funds (f)	450,000			450,000
Private equity funds (g)	550,000			550,000
Real estate	1,150,000			1,150,000
Total	$24,000,000	$16,050,000	$4,300,000	$3,650,000

(a) This category comprises low-cost equity index funds not actively managed that track the S&P 500.

(b) This category represents investment grade bonds of U.S. issuers from diverse industries.

(c) This category includes hedge funds that invest both long and short in primarily U.S. common stocks. Management of the hedge funds has the ability to shift investments from value to growth strategies, from small to large capitalization stocks, and from a net long position to a net short position.

(d) This category includes investments in approximately 60% equities and 40% bonds to profit from economic, political, and government-driven events. A majority of the investments are targeted at economic policy decisions.

(e) This category includes approximately 80% investments in non-U.S. common stocks in the health care, energy, information technology, utilities, and telecommunications sectors and approximately 20% investments in diversified currencies.

(f) This category invests in multiple strategies to diversify risks and reduce volatility. It includes investments in approximately 50% U.S. common stocks, 30% global real estate projects, and 20% arbitrage investments.

(g) This category includes several private equity funds that invest primarily in U.S. commercial real estate.

Method 2

		Fair Value Measurements at December 31, 20X2		
Asset Category	*Total*	*Quoted Prices in Active Markets for Identical Assets (Level 1)*	*Significant Observable Inputs (Level 2)*	*Significant Unobservable Inputs (Level 3)*
Cash	$1,750,000	$1,750,000	$	$
Equity securities:				
U.S. companies	4,500,000	4,500,000		
International companies	4,000,000	4,000,000		
Mutual funds (a)	5,000,000	3,450,000	1,550,000	
U.S. Treasury securities	2,350,000	2,350,000		
AA corporate bonds	1,200,000		1,200,000	
A corporate bonds	1,000,000		1,000,000	
Mortgage-backed securities	550,000		550,000	
Equity long/short hedge funds (b)	600,000			600,000
Event driven hedge funds (c)	500,000			500,000
Global opportunities hedge funds (d)	400,000			400,000
Multi strategy hedge funds (e)	450,000			450,000

Asset Category	Total	Fair Value Measurements at December 31, 20X2 Quoted Prices in Active Markets for Identical Assets (Level 1)	Significant Observable Inputs (Level 2)	Significant Unobservable Inputs (Level 3)
Private equity funds (f)	$ 550,000			$ 550,000
Real estate	1,150,000			1,150,000
Total	$24,000,000	$16,050,000	$4,300,000	$3,650,000

(a) Seventy percent of mutual funds invest in common stock of large-cap U.S. companies. Thirty percent of the Company's mutual fund investments focus on emerging markets and domestic real estate common stocks.

(b) This category includes hedge funds that invest both long and short in primarily U.S. common stocks. Management of the hedge funds has the ability to shift investments from value to growth strategies, from small to large capitalization stocks, and from a net long position to a net short position.

(c) This category includes investments in approximately 60% equities and 40% bonds to profit from economic, political, and government-driven events. A majority of the investments are targeted at economic policy decisions.

(d) This category includes approximately 80% investments in non-U.S. common stocks in the health care, energy, information technology, utilities, and telecommunications sectors and approximately 20% investments in diversified currencies.

(e) This category invests in multiple strategies to diversify risks and reduce volatility. It includes investments in approximately 50% U.S. common stocks, 30% global real estate projects, and 20% arbitrage investments.

(f) This category includes several private equity funds that invest primarily in U.S. commercial real estate.

Note: The following information should be disclosed, regardless of the method used for disclosing major categories of plan assets.

Fair Value Measurements Using Significant Unobservable Inputs (Level 3)

	Equity Long/Short Hedge Funds	Event Driven Hedge Funds	Global Opportunities Hedge Funds	Multi Strategy Hedge Funds	Private Equity Funds	Real Estate	Total
Beginning balance at December 31, 20X1	$450,000	$400,000	$ 500,000	$400,000	$425,000	$ 600,000	$2,775,000
Actual return on plan assets:							
Relating to assets still held at the reporting date	(25,000)	50,000	(130,000)	50,000	25,000	50,000	20,000
Relating to assets sold during the period		30,000			50,000		80,000
Purchases, sales, and settlements	150,000	20,000			50,000	500,000	720,000
Transfers in and/or out of Level 3	25,000		30,000				55,000
Ending balance at December 31, 20X2	$ 600,000	$500,000	$ 400,000	$450,000	$550,000	$1,150,000	$3,650,000

The Company's investment policy includes various guidelines and procedures designed to ensure assets are invested in a manner necessary to meet expected future benefits earned by participants. The investment guidelines consider a broad range of economic conditions. Central to the policy are target allocation ranges by major asset categories.

The objectives of the target allocations are to maintain investment portfolios that diversify risk through prudent asset allocation parameters, achieve asset returns that meet or exceed the plans' actuarial assumptions, and achieve asset returns that are competitive with like institutions employing similar investment strategies.

The investment policy is periodically reviewed by the Company and a designated third-party fiduciary for investment matters. The policy is established and administered in a manner that is compliant at all times with applicable government regulations.

<u>Cash Flows</u>

The Company expects to contribute $1,500,000 to its pension plan in 20X3.

The following pension benefit payments, which reflect expected future service, as appropriate, are expected to be paid:

20X3	$1,000,000
20X4	1,050,000
20X5	1,175,000
20X6	1,225,000
20X7	1,315,000
Years 20X8–20Y2	7,325,000

Example 7: Defined Benefit Pension Plans—Alternative Reduced Disclosures for a Nonpublic Entity

> **Note:** This example illustrates the alternative reduced disclosures for a nonpublic entity using the same facts in Example 6 above.

The Company sponsors two funded defined benefit pension plans for eligible employees who are 21 years of age with one or more years of service and who are not covered by collective bargaining agreements. Benefits paid to retirees are based on age at retirement, years of credited service, and average compensation. The Company's funding policy is to contribute the larger of the amount required to fully fund the plan's current liability or the amount necessary to meet the funding requirements, as defined by the Internal Revenue Code.

In addition, the Company sponsors an unfunded Executive Pension Plan. This plan is nonqualified and provides certain key employees defined pension benefits that supplement those provided by the Company's other retirement plans.

Obligations and Funded Status

	20X2	20X1
Projected benefit obligation at December 31	$28,900,000	$27,800,000
Fair value of plan assets at December 31	24,000,000	22,700,000
Funded status at end of year	$(4,900,000)	$(5,100,000)
Amounts recognized in the balance sheets consist of:		
Noncurrent assets	$ 300,000	$ 300,000
Current liabilities	(1,500,000)	(1,500,000)
Noncurrent liabilities	(3,700,000)	(3,900,000)
	$(4,900,000)	$(5,100,000)

Amounts recognized in accumulated other comprehensive income consist of the following:

	20X2	20X1
Net loss (gain)	$(1,700,000)	$(1,800,000)
Prior service cost (credit)	500,000	1,600,000
	$(1,200,000)	$ (200,000)

The following table summarizes the Company-sponsored pension plans that have projected benefit obligations in excess of plan assets and the accumulated benefit obligation of the unfunded Executive Pension Plan in which the accumulated benefit obligation exceeds plan assets:

	20X2	20X1
Projected benefit obligation in excess of plan assets:		
Projected benefit obligation	$3,900,000	$4,200,000
Fair value of plan assets	$2,800,000	$2,600,000
Accumulated benefit obligation in excess of plan assets:		

	20X2	20X1
Accumulated benefit obligation	$1,300,000	$1,100,000
Fair value of plan assets	$ -0-	$ -0-

The accumulated benefit obligation for all defined benefit pension plans was $16,100,000 and $14,700,000 at December 31, 20X2, and December 31, 20X1, respectively.

	20X2	20X1
Benefit cost	$2,100,000	$2,400,000
Employer contributions	$1,300,000	$ 700,000
Benefits paid	$ 300,000	$ 800,000

Assumptions

The following are weighted-average assumptions used to determine benefit obligations at December 31, 20X2, and December 31, 20X1:

	20X2	20X1
Discount rate	6.75%	7.00%
Rate of compensation increase	5.25%	4.75%

The following are weighted-average assumptions used to determine net periodic benefit cost for the years ended December 31, 20X2, and December 31, 20X1:

	20X2	20X1
Discount rate	7.00%	7.25%
Expected long-term return on plan assets	8.00%	7.75%
Rate of compensation increase	5.50%	5.00%

The Company's expected long-term return on plan assets assumption is based on a periodic review and modeling of the plans' asset allocation and liability structure over a long-term period. Expectations of returns for each asset class are the most important of the assumptions used in the review and modeling and are based on comprehensive reviews of historical data and economic/financial market theory. The expected long-term rate of return on assets was selected from within the reasonable range of rates determined by (1) historical real returns, net of inflation, for the asset classes covered by the investment policy and (2) projections of inflation over the long-term period during which benefits are payable to plan participants.

Plan Assets

The Company's overall investment strategy is to achieve a mix of approximately 75% of investments for long-term growth and 25% for near-term benefit payments with a wide diversification of asset types, fund strategies, and fund managers. The target allocations for plan assets are 65% equity securities, 20% corporate bonds and U.S. Treasury securities, and 15% for all other types of investments. Equity securities primarily include investments in large-cap and mid-cap companies primarily located in the United States. Fixed income securities include corporate bonds of companies from diversified industries, mortgage-backed securities, and U.S. Treasuries. Other types of investments include investments in hedge funds and private equity funds that follow several different strategies.

The fair values of the Company's pension plan assets at December 31, 20X2, by asset category are as follows:

The following are two acceptable alternative methods for disclosing the fair value of major categories of plan assets.

Method 1

		Fair Value Measurements at December 31, 20X2		
Asset Category	Total	Quoted Prices in Active Markets for Identical Assets (Level 1)	Significant Observable Inputs (Level 2)	Significant Unobservable Inputs (Level 3)
Cash	$1,750,000	$1,750,000	$	$
Equity securities:				
U.S. large-cap (a)	6,450,000	6,450,000		
U.S. mid-cap growth	1,150,000	1,150,000		
International large-cap value	3,800,000	3,800,000		
Emerging markets growth	900,000	300,000	600,000	
Domestic real estate	1,200,000	250,000	950,000	
Fixed income securities:				
U.S. Treasury securities	2,350,000	2,350,000		
Corporate bonds (b)	2,200,000		2,200,000	
Mortgage-backed securities	550,000		550,000	
Other types of investments:				
Equity long/short hedge funds (c)	600,000			600,000
Event driven hedge funds (d)	500,000			500,000

Fair Value Measurements at December 31, 20X2

Asset Category	Total	Quoted Prices in Active Markets for Identical Assets (Level 1)	Significant Observable Inputs (Level 2)	Significant Unobservable Inputs (Level 3)
Global opportunities hedge funds (e)	400,000			400,000
Multi strategy hedge funds (f)	450,000			450,000
Private equity funds (g)	550,000			550,000
Real estate	1,150,000			1,150,000
Total	$24,000,000	$16,050,000	$4,300,000	$3,650,000

(a) This category comprises low-cost equity index funds not actively managed that track the S&P 500.

(b) This category represents investment grade bonds of U.S. issuers from diverse industries.

(c) This category includes hedge funds that invest both long and short in primarily U.S. common stocks. Management of the hedge funds has the ability to shift investments from value to growth strategies, from small to large capitalization stocks, and from a net long position to a net short position.

(d) This category includes investments in approximately 60% equities and 40% bonds to profit from economic, political, and government-driven events. A majority of the investments are targeted at economic policy decisions.

(e) This category includes approximately 80% investments in non-U.S. common stocks in the health care, energy, information technology, utilities, and telecommunications sectors and approximately 20% investments in diversified currencies.

(f) This category invests in multiple strategies to diversify risks and reduce volatility. It includes investments in approximately 50% U.S. common stocks, 30% global real estate projects, and 20% arbitrage investments.

(g) This category includes several private equity funds that invest primarily in U.S. commercial real estate.

Method 2

Asset Category	Total	Fair Value Measurements at December 31, 20X2		
		Quoted Prices in Active Markets for Identical Assets (Level 1)	Significant Observable Inputs (Level 2)	Significant Unobservable Inputs (Level 3)
Cash	$1,750,000	$1,750,000	$	$
Equity securities:				
U.S. companies	4,500,000	4,500,000		
International companies	4,000,000	4,000,000		
Mutual funds (a)	5,000,000	3,450,000	1,550,000	
U.S. Treasury securities	2,350,000	2,350,000		
AA corporate bonds	1,200,000		1,200,000	
A corporate bonds	1,000,000		1,000,000	
Mortgage-backed securities	550,000		550,000	
Equity long/short hedge funds (b)	600,000			600,000
Event driven hedge funds (c)	500,000			500,000
Global opportunities hedge funds (d)	400,000			400,000

Fair Value Measurements at December 31, 20X2

Asset Category	Total	Quoted Prices in Active Markets for Identical Assets (Level 1)	Significant Observable Inputs (Level 2)	Significant Unobservable Inputs (Level 3)
Multi strategy hedge funds (e)	450,000			450,000
Private equity funds (f)	550,000			550,000
Real estate	1,150,000			1,150,000
Total	$24,000,000	$16,050,000	$4,300,000	$3,650,000

(a) Seventy percent of mutual funds invest in common stock of large-cap U.S. companies. Thirty percent of the Company's mutual fund investments focus on emerging markets and domestic real estate common stocks.

(b) This category includes hedge funds that invest both long and short in primarily U.S. common stocks. Management of the hedge funds has the ability to shift investments from value to growth strategies, from small to large capitalization stocks, and from a net long position to a net short position.

(c) This category includes investments in approximately 60% equities and 40% bonds to profit from economic, political, and government-driven events. A majority of the investments are targeted at economic policy decisions.

(d) This category includes approximately 80% investments in non-U.S. common stocks in the health care, energy, information technology, utilities, and telecommunications sectors and approximately 20% investments in diversified currencies.

(e) This category invests in multiple strategies to diversify risks and reduce volatility. It includes investments in approximately 50% U.S. common stocks, 30% global real estate projects, and 20% arbitrage investments.

(f) This category includes several private equity funds that invest primarily in U.S. commercial real estate.

Note: The following information should be disclosed, regardless of the method used for disclosing major categories of plan assets.

Fair Value Measurements Using Significant Unobservable Inputs (Level 3)

	Equity Long/Short Hedge Funds	Event Driven Hedge Funds	Global Opportunities Hedge Funds	Multi Strategy Hedge Funds	Private Equity Funds	Real Estate	Total
Beginning balance at December 31, 20X1	$450,000	$400,000	$ 500,000	$400,000	$425,000	$ 600,000	$2,775,000
Actual return on plan assets:							
Relating to assets still held at the reporting date	(25,000)	50,000	(130,000)	50,000	25,000	50,000	20,000
Relating to assets sold during the period		30,000			50,000		80,000
Purchases, sales, and settlements	150,000	20,000			50,000	500,000	720,000
Transfers in and/or out of Level 3	25,000		30,000				55,000
Ending balance at December 31, 20X2	$ 600,000	$500,000	$ 400,000	$450,000	$550,000	$1,150,000	$3,650,000

The Company's investment policy includes various guidelines and procedures designed to ensure assets are invested in a manner necessary to meet expected future benefits earned by participants. The investment guidelines consider a broad range of economic conditions. Central to the policy are target allocation ranges by major asset categories.

The objectives of the target allocations are to maintain investment portfolios that diversify risk through prudent asset allocation parameters, achieve asset returns that meet or exceed the plans' actuarial assumptions, and achieve asset returns that are competitive with like institutions employing similar investment strategies.

The investment policy is periodically reviewed by the Company and a designated third-party fiduciary for investment matters. The policy is established and administered in a manner that is compliant at all times with applicable government regulations.

Cash Flows

The Company expects to contribute $1,500,000 to its pension plan in 20X3.

The following pension benefit payments, which reflect expected future service, as appropriate, are expected to be paid:

20X3	$1,000,000
20X4	1,050,000
20X5	1,175,000
20X6	1,225,000
20X7	1,315,000
Years 20X8–20Y2	7,325,000

Example 8: Defined Benefit Postretirement Plans—Public Entities

The Company has multiple nonpension postretirement benefit plans. The health care plans are contributory, with participants' contributions adjusted annually; the life insurance plans are noncontributory. The accounting for the health care plans anticipates future cost sharing changes to the written plan that are consistent with the Company's expressed intent to increase retiree contributions each year by 50% of the excess of the expected general inflation rate over 6%. On December 31, 20X2, the Company amended its postretirement health care plans to provide long-term care coverage.

The Company acquired Massari, Ltd. on December 31, 20X2, including its postretirement benefit plans. As a result, the Company's plans were amended to establish parity with the benefits provided by Massari, Ltd.

Obligations and Funded Status

	20X2	20X1
Change in benefit obligation:		
Benefit obligation at beginning of year	$ 738,000	$ 700,000
Service cost	36,000	32,000
Interest cost	65,000	63,000
Plan participants' contributions	20,000	13,000
Amendments	75,000	-0-
Actuarial gain	(24,000)	-0-
Acquisition	600,000	-0-
Benefits paid	(90,000)	(70,000)
Benefit obligation at end of year	$ 1,420,000	$ 738,000
Change in plan assets:		
Fair value of plan assets at beginning of year	$ 206,000	$ 87,000
Actual return on plan assets	(3,000)	24,000
Acquisition	25,000	-0-
Employer contribution	171,000	152,000
Plan participants' contributions	20,000	13,000
Benefits paid	(90,000)	(70,000)
Fair value of plan assets at end of year	$ 329,000	$ 206,000
Funded status at end of year	$(1,091,000)	$(532,000)
Amounts recognized in the balance sheets consist of:		
Noncurrent assets	$ 60,000	$ 70,000
Current liabilities	(350,000)	(400,000)
Noncurrent liabilities	(801,000)	(202,000)
	$(1,091,000)	$(532,000)

Amounts recognized in accumulated other comprehensive income consist of the following:

	20X2	20X1
Net loss (gain)	$ 59,000	$ 60,000
Prior service cost (credit)	585,000	540,000
	$644,000	$600,000

Components of net periodic benefit cost and other amounts recognized in other comprehensive income are as follows:

	20X2	20X1
Net Periodic Benefit Cost:		
Service cost	$ 36,000	$ 32,000
Interest cost	65,000	63,000
Expected return on plan assets	(21,000)	(9,000)
Amortization of prior service cost	30,000	30,000
Recognized net actuarial loss	1,000	1,000
Net periodic benefit cost	111,000	117,000
Other Changes in Plan Assets and Benefit Obligations Recognized in Other Comprehensive Income:		
Net loss (gain)	(1,000)	15,000
Prior service cost (credit)	50,000	60,000
Amortization of prior service cost	(5,000)	(10,000)
Total recognized in other comprehensive income	44,000	65,000
Total recognized in net periodic benefit cost and other comprehensive income	$ 155,000	$ 182,000

The estimated net loss and prior service cost for the defined benefit postretirement plans that will be amortized from accumulated other comprehensive income into net periodic benefit cost over the next fiscal year are $25,000 and $75,000, respectively.

Assumptions

The following are weighted-average assumptions used to determine benefit obligations at December 31, 20X2, and December 31, 20X1:

	20X2	20X1
Discount rate	7.00%	7.25%

The following are weighted-average assumptions used to determine net periodic benefit cost for the years ended December 31, 20X2, and December 31, 20X1:

	20X2	20X1
Discount rate	7.00%	7.25%
Expected long-term return on plan assets	8.25%	8.50%

The Company's expected long-term return on plan assets assumption is based on a periodic review and modeling of the plans' asset allocation and liability structure over a long-term period. Expectations of returns for each asset class are the most important of the assumptions used in the review and modeling and are based on comprehensive reviews of historical data and economic/financial market theory. The expected long-term rate of return on assets was selected from within the reasonable range of rates determined by (1) historical real returns, net of inflation, for the asset classes covered by the investment policy and (2) projections of inflation over the long-term period during which benefits are payable to plan participants.

The following are assumed health care cost trend rates at December 31, 20X2, and December 31, 20X1:

	20X2	20X1
Health care cost trend rate assumed for next year	12%	12.5%
Rate to which the cost trend rate is assumed to decline (the ultimate trend rate)	6%	5%
Year that the rate reaches the ultimate trend rate	20X9	20X9

Assumed health care cost trend rates have a significant effect on the amounts reported for the health care plans. A 1% point change in assumed health care cost trend rates would have the following effects:

	1% Point Increase	*1% Point Decrease*
Effect on total of service and interest cost components	$122,000	$ (20,000)
Effect on postretirement benefit obligation	$173,000	$(156,000)

Plan Assets

The Company's overall investment strategy is to achieve a mix of approximately 75% of investments for long-term growth and 25% for near-term benefit payments with a wide diversification of asset types, fund strategies, and fund managers. The target allocations for plan assets are 65% equity securities, 20% corporate bonds and U.S. Treasury securities, and 15% for all other types of investments. Equity securities primarily include investments in large-cap and mid-cap companies primarily located in the United States. Fixed income securities include corporate bonds of companies from diversified industries, mortgage-backed securities, and U.S. Treasuries. Other types of investments include investments in hedge funds and private equity funds that follow several different strategies.

The fair values of the Company's postretirement benefit plan assets at December 31, 20X2, by asset category are as follows:

Note: The following are two acceptable alternative methods for disclosing the fair value of major categories of plan assets.

Method 1

| | | Fair Value Measurements at December 31, 20X2 | | |
Asset Category	Total	Quoted Prices in Active Markets for Identical Assets (Level 1)	Significant Observable Inputs (Level 2)	Significant Unobservable Inputs (Level 3)
Cash	$25,000	$25,000	$	$
Equity securities:				
U.S. large-cap (a)	85,000	85,000		
U.S. mid-cap growth	15,000	15,000		
International large-cap value	50,000	50,000		
Emerging markets growth	12,000	4,000	8,000	
Domestic real estate	20,000	7,000	13,000	
Fixed income securities:				
U.S. Treasury securities	30,000	30,000		
Corporate bonds (b)	25,000		25,000	
Mortgage-backed securities	10,000		10,000	
Other types of investments:				
Equity long/short hedge funds (c)	10,000			10,000
Event driven hedge funds (d)	5,000			5,000

Fair Value Measurements at December 31, 20X2

Asset Category	Total	Quoted Prices in Active Markets for Identical Assets (Level 1)	Significant Observable Inputs (Level 2)	Significant Unobservable Inputs (Level 3)
Global opportunities hedge funds (e)	15,000			15,000
Multi strategy hedge funds (f)	6,000			6,000
Private equity funds (g)	12,000			12,000
Real estate	9,000			9,000
Total	$329,000	$216,000	$56,000	$57,000

(a) This category comprises low-cost equity index funds not actively managed that track the S&P 500.

(b) This category represents investment grade bonds of U.S. issuers from diverse industries.

(c) This category includes hedge funds that invest both long and short in primarily U.S. common stocks. Management of the hedge funds has the ability to shift investments from value to growth strategies, from small to large capitalization stocks, and from a net long position to a net short position.

(d) This category includes investments in approximately 60% equities and 40% bonds to profit from economic, political, and government-driven events. A majority of the investments are targeted at economic policy decisions.

(e) This category includes approximately 80% investments in non-U.S. common stocks in the health care, energy, information technology, utilities, and telecommunications sectors and approximately 20% investments in diversified currencies.

(f) This category invests in multiple strategies to diversify risks and reduce volatility. It includes investments in approximately 50% U.S. common stocks, 30% global real estate projects, and 20% arbitrage investments.

(g) This category includes several private equity funds that invest primarily in U.S. commercial real estate.

Method 2

		Fair Value Measurements at December 31, 20X2		
Asset Category	Total	Quoted Prices in Active Markets for Identical Assets (Level 1)	Significant Observable Inputs (Level 2)	Significant Unobservable Inputs (Level 3)
Cash	$25,000	$25,000	$	$
Equity securities:				
U.S. companies	82,000	82,000		
International companies	35,000	35,000		
Mutual funds (a)	65,000	44,000	21,000	
U.S. Treasury securities	30,000	30,000		
AA corporate bonds	13,000		13,000	
A corporate bonds	12,000		12,000	
Mortgage-backed securities	10,000		10,000	
Equity long/short hedge funds (b)	10,000			10,000
Event driven hedge funds (c)	5,000			5,000
Global opportunities hedge funds (d)	15,000			15,000
Multi strategy hedge funds (e)	6,000			6,000

Fair Value Measurements at December 31, 20X2

Asset Category	Total	Quoted Prices in Active Markets for Identical Assets (Level 1)	Significant Observable Inputs (Level 2)	Significant Unobservable Inputs (Level 3)
Private equity funds (f)	12,000			12,000
Real estate	9,000			9,000
Total	$329,000	$216,000	$56,000	$57,000

(a) Seventy percent of mutual funds invest in common stock of large-cap U.S. companies. Thirty percent of the Company's mutual fund investments focus on emerging markets and domestic real estate common stocks.

(b) This category includes hedge funds that invest both long and short in primarily U.S. common stocks. Management of the hedge funds has the ability to shift investments from value to growth strategies, from small to large capitalization stocks, and from a net long position to a net short position.

(c) This category includes investments in approximately 60% equities and 40% bonds to profit from economic, political, and government-driven events. A majority of the investments are targeted at economic policy decisions.

(d) This category includes approximately 80% investments in non-U.S. common stocks in the health care, energy, information technology, utilities, and telecommunications sectors and approximately 20% investments in diversified currencies.

(e) This category invests in multiple strategies to diversify risks and reduce volatility. It includes investments in approximately 50% U.S. common stocks, 30% global real estate projects, and 20% arbitrage investments.

(f) This category includes several private equity funds that invest primarily in U.S. commercial real estate.

Note: The following information should be disclosed regardless of the method used for disclosing major categories of plan assets.

Fair Value Measurements Using Significant Unobservable Inputs (Level 3)

	Equity Long/ Short Hedge Funds	*Event Driven Hedge Funds*	*Global Opportunities Hedge Funds*	*Multi Strategy Hedge Funds*	*Private Equity Funds*	*Real Estate*	*Total*
Beginning balance at December 31, 20X1	$ 6,000	$1,000	$ 30,000	$4,000	$ 3,000	$5,000	$ 49,000
Actual return on plan assets:							
Relating to assets still held at the reporting date	(5,000)	1,000	(25,000)	2,000	4,000	3,000	(20,000)
Relating to assets sold during the period		2,000			2,000		4,000
Purchases, sales, and settlements	4,000	1,000			3,000	1,000	9,000
Transfers in and/or out of Level 3	5,000	—	10,000	—	—	—	15,000
Ending balance at December 31, 20X2	$10,000	$5,000	$ 15,000	$6,000	$12,000	$9,000	$ 57,000

The Company's investment policy includes various guidelines and procedures designed to ensure assets are invested in a manner necessary to meet expected future benefits earned by participants. The investment guidelines consider a broad range of economic conditions. Central to the policy are target allocation ranges (shown above) by major asset categories.

The objectives of the target allocations are to maintain investment portfolios that diversify risk through prudent asset allocation parameters, achieve asset returns that meet or exceed the plans' actuarial assumptions, and achieve asset returns that are competitive with like institutions employing similar investment strategies.

The investment policy is periodically reviewed by the Company and a designated third-party fiduciary for investment matters. The policy is established and administered in a manner that complies at all times with applicable government regulations.

Cash Flows

The Company expects to contribute $200,000 to its postretirement benefit plans in 20X3.

The following benefit payments, which reflect expected future service, as appropriate, are expected to be paid:

20X3	$125,000
20X4	130,000
20X5	140,000
20X6	150,000
20X7	175,000
Years 20X8–20Y2	860,000

Example 9: Defined Benefit Postretirement Plans—Alternative Reduced Disclosures for a Nonpublic Entity

> **Note:** This example illustrates the alternative reduced disclosures for a nonpublic entity using the same facts in Example 8 above.

The Company has multiple nonpension postretirement benefit plans. The health care plans are contributory, with participants' contributions adjusted annually; the life insurance plans are noncontributory. The accounting for the health care plans anticipates future cost sharing changes to the written plan that are consistent with the Company's expressed intent to increase retiree contributions each year by 50% of the excess of the expected general inflation rate over 6%. On December 31, 20X2, the Company amended its postretirement health care plans to provide long-term care coverage.

The Company acquired Massari, Ltd. on December 31, 20X2, including its postretirement benefit plans. As a result, the Company's plans were amended to establish parity with the benefits provided by Massari, Ltd.

Obligations and Funded Status

	Postretirement Benefits	
	20X2	*20X1*
Benefit obligation at December 31	$ 1,420,000	$ 738,000
Fair value of plan assets at December 31	329,000	206,000
Funded status at end of year	$(1,091,000)	$(532,000)
Amounts recognized in the balance sheets consist of:		
Noncurrent assets	$ 60,000	$ 70,000
Current liabilities	(350,000)	(400,000)
Noncurrent liabilities	(801,000)	(202,000)
	$(1,091,000)	$(532,000)

Amounts recognized in accumulated other comprehensive income consist of the following:

	20X2	*20X1*
Net loss (gain)	$ 59,000	$ 60,000
Prior service cost (credit)	585,000	540,000
	$644,000	$600,000

	20X2	*20X1*
Benefit cost	$ 111,000	$ 117,000
Employer contribution	$ 171,000	$ 152,000
Plan participants' contributions	$ 20,000	$ 13,000
Benefits paid	$ 90,000	$ 70,000

Assumptions

The following are weighted-average assumptions used to determine benefit obligations at December 31, 20X2, and December 31, 20X1:

	20X2	20X1
Discount rate	7.00%	7.25%

The following are weighted-average assumptions used to determine net periodic benefit cost for the years ended December 31, 20X2, and December 31, 20X1:

	20X2	20X1
Discount rate	7.25%	7.25%
Expected long-term return on plan assets	8.25%	8.50%

The Company's expected long-term return on plan assets assumption is based on a periodic review and modeling of the plans' asset allocation and liability structure over a long-term period. Expectations of returns for each asset class are the most important of the assumptions used in the review and modeling and are based on comprehensive reviews of historical data and economic/financial market theory. The expected long-term rate of return on assets was selected from within the reasonable range of rates determined by (1) historical real returns, net of inflation, for the asset classes covered by the investment policy, and (2) projections of inflation over the long-term period during which benefits are payable to plan participants.

The following are assumed health care cost trend rates at December 31, 20X2, and December 31, 20X1:

	20X2	20X1
Health care cost trend rate assumed for next year	12%	12.5%
Rate to which the cost trend rate is assumed to decline (the ultimate trend rate)	6%	5%
Year that the rate reaches the ultimate trend rate	20X9	20X9

Plan Assets

The Company's overall investment strategy is to achieve a mix of approximately 75% of investments for long-term growth and 25% for near-term benefit payments with a wide diversification of asset types, fund strategies, and fund managers. The target allocations for plan assets are 65% equity securities, 20% corporate bonds and U.S.

Treasury securities, and 15% for all other types of investments. Equity securities primarily include investments in large-cap and mid-cap companies primarily located in the United States. Fixed income securities include corporate bonds of companies from diversified industries, mortgage-backed securities, and U.S. Treasuries. Other types of investments include investments in hedge funds and private equity funds that follow several different strategies.

The fair values of the Company's postretirement benefit plan assets at December 31, 20X2, by asset category are as follows:

NOTE: The following are two acceptable alternative methods for disclosing the fair value of major categories of plan assets.

Method 1

		Fair Value Measurements at December 31, 20X2		
Asset Category	Total	Quoted Prices in Active Markets for Identical Assets (Level 1)	Significant Observable Inputs (Level 2)	Significant Unobservable Inputs (Level 3)
Cash	$25,000	$25,000	$	$
Equity securities:				
U.S. large-cap (a)	85,000	85,000		
U.S. mid-cap growth	15,000	15,000		
International large-cap value	50,000	50,000		
Emerging markets growth	12,000	4,000	8,000	
Domestic real estate	20,000	7,000	13,000	
Fixed income securities:				
U.S. Treasury securities	30,000	30,000		
Corporate bonds (b)	25,000		25,000	
Mortgage-backed securities	10,000		10,000	
Other types of investments:				
Equity long/short hedge funds (c)	10,000			10,000

Event driven hedge funds (d)	5,000			5,000
Global opportunities hedge funds (e)	15,000			15,000
Multi strategy hedge funds (f)	6,000			6,000
Private equity funds (g)	12,000			12,000
Real estate	9,000			9,000
Total	$329,000	$216,000	$56,000	$57,000

(a) This category comprises low-cost equity index funds not actively managed that track the S&P 500.

(b) This category represents investment grade bonds of U.S. issuers from diverse industries.

(c) This category includes hedge funds that invest both long and short in primarily U.S. common stocks. Management of the hedge funds has the ability to shift investments from value to growth strategies, from small to large capitalization stocks, and from a net long position to a net short position.

(d) This category includes investments in approximately 60% equities and 40% bonds to profit from economic, political, and government-driven events. A majority of the investments are targeted at economic policy decisions.

(e) This category includes approximately 80% investments in non-U.S. common stocks in the health care, energy, information technology, utilities, and telecommunications sectors and approximately 20% investments in diversified currencies.

(f) This category invests in multiple strategies to diversify risks and reduce volatility. It includes investments in approximately 50% U.S. common stocks, 30% global real estate projects, and 20% arbitrage investments.

(g) This category includes several private equity funds that invest primarily in U.S. commercial real estate.

Method 2

| | | Fair Value Measurements at December 31, 20X2 | | |
Asset Category	Total	Quoted Prices in Active Markets for Identical Assets (Level 1)	Significant Observable Inputs (Level 2)	Significant Unobservable Inputs (Level 3)
Cash	$25,000	$25,000	$	$
Equity securities:				
U.S. companies	82,000	82,000		
International companies	35,000	35,000		
Mutual funds (a)	65,000	44,000	21,000	
U.S. Treasury securities	30,000	30,000		
AA corporate bonds	13,000		13,000	
A corporate bonds	12,000		12,000	
Mortgage-backed securities	10,000		10,000	
Equity long/short hedge funds (b)	10,000			10,000
Event driven hedge funds (c)	5,000			5,000
Global opportunities hedge funds (d)	15,000			15,000

Multi strategy hedge funds (e)	6,000			6,000
Private equity funds (f)	12,000			12,000
Real estate	9,000			9,000
Total	$329,000	$216,000	$56,000	$57,000

(a) Seventy percent of mutual funds invest in common stock of large-cap U.S. companies. Thirty percent of the Company's mutual fund investments focus on emerging markets and domestic real estate common stocks.

(b) This category includes hedge funds that invest both long and short in primarily U.S. common stocks. Management of the hedge funds has the ability to shift investments from value to growth strategies, from small to large capitalization stocks, and from a net long position to a net short position.

(c) This category includes investments in approximately 60% equities and 40% bonds to profit from economic, political, and government-driven events. A majority of the investments are targeted at economic policy decisions.

(d) This category includes approximately 80% investments in non-U.S. common stocks in the health care, energy, information technology, utilities, and telecommunications sectors and approximately 20% investments in diversified currencies.

(e) This category invests in multiple strategies to diversify risks and reduce volatility. It includes investments in approximately 50% U.S. common stocks, 30% global real estate projects, and 20% arbitrage investments.

(f) This category includes several private equity funds that invest primarily in U.S. commercial real estate.

Note: The following information should be disclosed regardless of the method used for disclosing major categories of plan assets.

Fair Value Measurements Using Significant Unobservable Inputs (Level 3)

	Equity Long/ Short Hedge Funds	Event Driven Hedge Funds	Global Opportunities Hedge Funds	Multi Strategy Hedge Funds	Private Equity Funds	Real Estate	Total
Beginning balance at December 31, 20X1	$ 6,000	$1,000	$ 30,000	$4,000	$ 3,000	$5,000	$ 49,000
Actual return on plan assets:							
Relating to assets still held at the reporting date	(5,000)	1,000	(25,000)	2,000	4,000	3,000	(20,000)
Relating to assets sold during the period		2,000			2,000		4,000
Purchases, sales, and settlements	4,000	1,000			3,000	1,000	9,000
Transfers in and/or out of Level 3	5,000	—	10,000				15,000
Ending balance at December 31, 20X2	$ 10,000	$5,000	$ 15,000	$6,000	$12,000	$9,000	$ 57,000

The Company's investment policy includes various guidelines and procedures designed to ensure assets are invested in a manner necessary to meet expected future benefits earned by participants. The investment guidelines consider a broad range of economic conditions. Central to the policy are target allocation ranges (shown above) by major asset categories.

The objectives of the target allocations are to maintain investment portfolios that diversify risk through prudent asset allocation parameters, achieve asset returns that meet or exceed the plans' actuarial assumptions, and achieve asset returns that are competitive with like institutions employing similar investment strategies.

The investment policy is periodically reviewed by the Company and a designated third-party fiduciary for investment matters. The policy is established and administered in a manner that complies at all times with applicable government regulations.

Cash Flows

The Company expects to contribute $200,000 to its postretirement benefit plans in 20X3.

The following benefit payments, which reflect expected future service, as appropriate, are expected to be paid:

20X3	$125,000
20X4	130,000
20X5	140,000
20X6	150,000
20X7	175,000
Years 20X8–20Y2	860,000

Example 10: Disclosures about Defined Benefit Pension Plans and Other Postretirement Benefit Plans Are Presented in a Parallel Format in a Single Note to the Financial Statements

The Company has both funded and unfunded noncontributory defined benefit pension plans that together cover substantially all of its employees. The plans provide defined benefits based on years of service and final average salary.

The Company also has other postretirement benefit plans covering substantially all of its employees. The health care plans are contributory with participants' contributions adjusted annually; the life insurance plans are noncontributory. The accounting for the health care plans anticipates future cost-sharing changes to the written plans that are consistent with the Company's expressed intent to increase retiree contributions each year by 50% of health care cost increases in excess of 6%. The postretirement health care plans include a limit on the Company's share of costs for recent and future retirees.

Obligations and Funded Status

	Pension Benefits		Postretirement Benefits	
	20X2	*20X1*	*20X2*	*20X1*
Change in benefit obligation:				
Benefit obligation at beginning of year	$1,266,000	$1,200,000	$ 738,000	$700,000
Service cost	76,000	72,000	36,000	32,000
Interest cost	114,000	108,000	65,000	63,000
Plan participants' contributions	-0-	-0-	20,000	13,000
Amendments	120,000	-0-	75,000	-0-
Actuarial gain	(25,000)	-0-	(24,000)	-0-
Acquisition	900,000	-0-	600,000	-0-
Benefits paid	(125,000)	(114,000)	(90,000)	(70,000)
Benefit obligation at end of year	$2,326,000	$1,266,000	$1,420,000	$738,000

	Pension Benefits		Postretirement Benefits	
	20X2	*20X1*	*20X2*	*20X1*
Change in plan assets:				
Fair value of plan assets at beginning of year	$1,068,000	$ 880,000	$206,000	$ 87,000
Actual return on plan assets	29,000	188,000	(3,000)	24,000
Acquisition	1,000,000	-0-	25,000	-0-
Employer contribution	75,000	114,000	171,000	152,000
Plan participants' contributions	-0-	-0-	20,000	13,000
Benefits paid	(125,000)	(114,000)	(90,000)	(70,000)

	Pension Benefits		Postretirement Benefits	
	20X2	*20X1*	*20X2*	*20X1*
Fair value of plan assets at end of year	$2,047,000	$1,068,000	$ 329,000	$ 206,000
Funded status at end of year	$(279,000)	$(198,000)	$(1,091,000)	$(532,000)
Amounts recognized in the balance sheets consist of:				
Noncurrent assets	$ 64,000	$ -0-	$ -0-	$ 68,000
Current liabilities	(100,000)	(48,000)	(400,000)	(200,000)
Noncurrent liabilities	(243,000)	(150,000)	(691,000)	(400,000)
	$(279,000)	$(198,000)	$(1,091,000)	$(532,000)

Amounts recognized in accumulated other comprehensive income consist of the following:

	Pension Benefits		Postretirement Benefits	
	20X2	*20X1*	*20X2*	*20X1*
Net loss (gain)	$ 83,000	$ 38,000	$ 59,000	$ 60,000
Prior service cost (credit)	260,000	160,000	585,000	540,000
	$343,000	$198,000	$644,000	$600,000

Components of net periodic benefit cost and other amounts recognized in other comprehensive income are as follows:

	Pension Benefits		Postretirement Benefits	
	20X2	*20X1*	*20X2*	*20X1*
Net Periodic Benefit Cost:				
Service cost	$ 76,000	$ 72,000	$ 36,000	$ 32,000
Interest cost	114,000	108,000	65,000	63,000
Expected return on plan assets	(107,000)	(88,000)	(21,000)	(9,000)
Amortization of prior service cost	20,000	20,000	30,000	30,000

	Pension Benefits		Postretirement Benefits	
	20X2	20X1	20X2	20X1
Recognized net actuarial loss	8,000	2,000	1,000	1,000
Net periodic benefit cost	111,000	114,000	111,000	117,000
Other Changes in Plan Assets and Benefit Obligations Recognized in Other Comprehensive Income:				
Net loss (gain)	45,000	40,000	(1,000)	(15,000)
Prior service cost (credit)	120,000	70,000	75,000	90,000
Amortization of prior service cost	(20,000)	(20,000)	(30,000)	(30,000)
Total recognized in other comprehensive income	145,000	90,000	44,000	45,000
Total recognized in net periodic benefit cost and other comprehensive income	$256,000	$204,000	$155,000	$162,000

The estimated net loss and prior service cost for the defined benefit pension plans that will be amortized from accumulated other comprehensive income into net periodic benefit cost over the next fiscal year are $25,000 and $60,000, respectively. The estimated net loss and prior service cost for the defined benefit postretirement plans that will be amortized from accumulated other comprehensive income into net periodic benefit cost over the next fiscal year are $35,000 and $90,000, respectively.

The accumulated benefit obligation for all defined benefit pension plans was $733,000 and $650,000 at December 31, 20X2, and December 31, 20X1, respectively.

Assumptions

The following are weighted-average assumptions used to determine benefit obligations at December 31, 20X2, and December 31, 20X1:

	Pension Benefits		Postretirement Benefits	
	20X2	20X1	20X2	20X1
Discount rate	6.75%	7.00%	7.00%	7.25%

	Pension Benefits		Postretirement Benefits	
	20X2	20X1	20X2	20X1
Rate of compensation increase	5.25%	4.75%	N/A	N/A

The following are weighted-average assumptions used to determine net periodic benefit cost for the years ended December 31, 20X2, and December 31, 20X1:

	Pension Benefits		Postretirement Benefits	
	20X2	20X1	20X2	20X1
Discount rate	7.00%	7.25%	7.25%	7.25%
Expected long-term return on plan assets	8.00%	7.75%	8.25%	8.50%
Rate of compensation increase	5.50%	5.00%	N/A	N/A

The Company's expected long-term return on plan assets assumption is based on a periodic review and modeling of the plans' asset allocation and liability structure over a long-term period. Expectations of returns for each asset class are the most important of the assumptions used in the review and modeling and are based on comprehensive reviews of historical data and economic/ financial market theory. The expected long-term rate of return on assets was selected from within the reasonable range of rates determined by (1) historical real returns, net of inflation, for the asset classes covered by the investment policy and (2) projections of inflation over the long-term period during which benefits are payable to plan participants.

The following are assumed health care cost trend rates at December 31, 20X2, and December 31, 20X1:

	20X2	20X1
Health care cost trend rate assumed for next year	12%	12.5%
Rate to which the cost trend rate is assumed to decline (the ultimate trend rate)	6%	5%
Year that the rate reaches the ultimate trend rate	20X9	20X9

Assumed health care cost trend rates have a significant effect on the amounts reported for the health care plans. A 1% point change in assumed health care cost trend rates would have the following effects:

	1% Point Increase	1% Point Decrease
Effect on total of service and interest cost components	$ 22,000	$ (20,000)
Effect on postretirement benefit obligation	$173,000	$(156,000)

Plan Assets

The Company's overall investment strategy is to achieve a mix of approximately 75% of investments for long-term growth and 25% for near-term benefit payments with a wide diversification of asset types, fund strategies, and fund managers. The target allocations for plan assets are 65% equity securities, 20% corporate bonds and U.S. Treasury securities, and 15% for all other types of investments. Equity securities primarily include investments in large-cap and mid-cap companies primarily located in the United States. Fixed income securities include corporate bonds of companies from diversified industries, mortgage-backed securities, and U.S. Treasuries. Other types of investments include investments in hedge funds and private equity funds that follow several different strategies.

The fair values of the Company's pension and postretirement benefit plan assets at December 31, 20X2, by asset category are as follows:

The following are two acceptable alternative methods for disclosing the fair value of major categories of plan assets.

Method 1

Asset Category	Total	Pension Plan Assets: Fair Value Measurements at December 31, 20X2		
		Quoted Prices in Active Markets for Identical Assets (Level 1)	Significant Observable Inputs (Level 2)	Significant Unobservable Inputs (Level 3)
Cash	$175,000	$175,000	$	$
Equity securities:				
U.S. large-cap (a)	369,000	369,000		
U.S. mid-cap growth	115,000	115,000		
International large-cap value	280,000	280,000		
Emerging markets growth	90,000	60,000	30,000	
Domestic real estate	120,000	100,000	20,000	
Fixed income securities:				
U.S. Treasury securities	135,000	135,000		
Corporate bonds (b)	120,000		120,000	
Mortgage-backed securities	350,000		350,000	
Other types of investments:				
Equity long/short hedge funds (c)	60,000			60,000
Event driven hedge funds (d)	50,000			50,000

Pension Plan Assets:
Fair Value Measurements at December 31, 20X2

Asset Category	Total	Quoted Prices in Active Markets for Identical Assets (Level 1)	Significant Observable Inputs (Level 2)	Significant Unobservable Inputs (Level 3)
Global opportunities hedge funds (e)	40,000			40,000
Multi strategy hedge funds (f)	40,000			40,000
Private equity funds (g)	50,000			50,000
Real estate	53,000			53,000
Total	$2,047,000	$1,234,000	$520,000	$293,000

Postretirement Benefit Plan Assets:
Fair Value Measurements at December 31, 20X2

Asset Category	Total	Quoted Prices in Active Markets for Identical Assets (Level 1)	Significant Observable Inputs (Level 2)	Significant Unobservable Inputs (Level 3)
Cash	$25,000	$25,000		
Equity securities:				
U.S. large-cap (a)	85,000	85,000		
U.S. mid-cap growth	15,000	15,000		

	Total			
International large-cap value	50,000	50,000		
Emerging markets growth	12,000	4,000		8,000
Domestic real estate	20,000	7,000		13,000
Fixed income securities:				
U.S. Treasury securities	30,000	30,000		
Corporate bonds (b)	25,000		25,000	
Mortgage-backed securities	10,000		10,000	
Other types of investments:				
Equity long/short hedge funds (c)	10,000			10,000
Event driven hedge funds (d)	5,000			5,000
Global opportunities hedge funds (e)	15,000			15,000
Multi strategy hedge funds (f)	6,000			6,000
Private equity funds (g)	12,000			12,000
Real estate	$ 9,000			9,000
Total	$329,000	$216,000	$56,000	$57,000

(a) This category comprises low-cost equity index funds not actively managed that track the S&P 500.

(b) This category represents investment grade bonds of U.S. issuers from diverse industries.

(c) This category includes hedge funds that invest both long and short in primarily U.S. common stocks. Management of the hedge funds has the ability to shift investments from value to growth strategies, from small to large capitalization stocks, and from a net long position to a net short position.

(d) This category includes investments in approximately 60% equities and 40% bonds to profit from economic, political, and government-driven events. A majority of the investments are targeted at economic policy decisions.

(e) This category includes approximately 80% investments in non-U.S. common stocks in the health care, energy, information technology, utilities, and telecommunications sectors and approximately 20% investments in diversified currencies.

(f) This category invests in multiple strategies to diversify risks and reduce volatility. It includes investments in approximately 50% U.S. common stocks, 30% global real estate projects, and 20% arbitrage investments.

(g) This category includes several private equity funds that invest primarily in U.S. commercial real estate.

Method 2

Pension Plan Assets:
Fair Value Measurements at December 31, 20X2

Asset Category	Total	Quoted Prices in Active Markets for Identical Assets (Level 1)	Significant Observable Inputs (Level 2)	Significant Unobservable Inputs (Level 3)
Cash	$ 175,000	$ 175,000	$	$
Equity securities:				
U.S. companies	400,000	400,000		
International companies	274,000	274,000		
Mutual funds (a)	300,000	250,000	50,000	
U.S. Treasury securities	135,000	135,000		
AA corporate bonds	70,000		70,000	
A corporate bonds	50,000		50,000	
Mortgage-backed securities	350,000		350,000	
Equity long/short hedge funds (b)	60,000			60,000
Event driven hedge funds (c)	50,000			50,000
Global opportunities hedge funds (d)	40,000			40,000
Multi strategy hedge funds (e)	40,000			40,000
Private equity funds (f)	50,000			50,000
Real estate	53,000			53,000
Total	$2,047,000	$1,234,000	$520,000	$293,000

Postretirement Benefit Plan Assets:
Fair Value Measurements at December 31, 20X2

Asset Category	Total	Quoted Prices in Active Markets for Identical Assets (Level 1)	Significant Observable Inputs (Level 2)	Significant Unobservable Inputs (Level 3)
Cash	$25,000	$25,000	$	$
Equity securities:				
U.S. companies	82,000	82,000		
International companies	35,000	35,000		
Mutual funds (a)	65,000	44,000	21,000	
U.S. Treasury securities	30,000	30,000		
AA corporate bonds	13,000		13,000	
A corporate bonds	12,000		12,000	
Mortgage-backed securities	10,000		10,000	
Equity long/short hedge funds (b)	10,000			10,000
Event driven hedge funds (c)	5,000			5,000
Global opportunities hedge funds (d)	15,000			15,000
Multi strategy hedge funds (e)	6,000			6,000

Private equity funds (f)	12,000			12,000
Real estate	9,000			9,000
Total	$329,000	$216,000	$56,000	$57,000

(a) Seventy percent of mutual funds invest in common stock of large-cap U.S. companies. Thirty percent of the Company's mutual fund investments focus on emerging markets and domestic real estate common stocks.

(b) This category includes hedge funds that invest both long and short in primarily U.S. common stocks. Management of the hedge funds has the ability to shift investments from value to growth strategies, from small to large capitalization stocks, and from a net long position to a net short position.

(c) This category includes investments in approximately 60% equities and 40% bonds to profit from economic, political, and government-driven events. A majority of the investments are targeted at economic policy decisions.

(d) This category includes approximately 80% investments in non-U.S. common stocks in the health care, energy, information technology, utilities, and telecommunications sectors and approximately 20% investments in diversified currencies.

(e) This category invests in multiple strategies to diversify risks and reduce volatility. It includes investments in approximately 50% U.S. common stocks, 30% global real estate projects, and 20% arbitrage investments.

(f) This category includes several private equity funds that invest primarily in U.S. commercial real estate.

The following information should be disclosed, regardless of the method used for disclosing major categories of plan assets.

Pension Plan Assets:
Fair Value Measurements Using Significant Unobservable Inputs (Level 3)

	Equity Long/Short Hedge Funds	Event Driven Hedge Funds	Global Opportunities Hedge Funds	Multi Strategy Hedge Funds	Private Equity Funds	Real Estate	Total
Beginning balance at December 31, 20X1	$ 40,000	$30,000	$ 50,000	$27,000	$22,000	$29,000	$198,000
Actual return on plan assets:							
Relating to assets still held at the reporting date	(10,000)	8,000	(15,000)	13,000	15,000	18,000	29,000
Relating to assets sold during the period		3,000			5,000		8,000
Purchases, sales, and settlements	20,000	9,000			8,000	6,000	43,000
Transfers in and/or out of Level 3	10,000		5,000				15,000
Ending balance at December 31, 20X2	$ 60,000	$50,000	$ 40,000	$40,000	$50,000	$53,000	$293,000

Postretirement Benefit Plan Assets:
Fair Value Measurements Using Significant Unobservable Inputs (Level 3)

	Equity Long/Short Hedge Funds	Event Driven Hedge Funds	Global Opportunities Hedge Funds	Multi Strategy Hedge Funds	Private Equity Funds	Real Estate	Total
Beginning balance at December 31, 20X1	$ 6,000	$1,000	$ 30,000	$4,000	$ 3,000	$5,000	$ 49,000
Actual return on plan assets:							
Relating to assets still held at the reporting date	(5,000)	1,000	(25,000)	2,000	4,000	3,000	(20,000)
Relating to assets sold during the period		2,000			2,000		4,000
Purchases, sales, and settlements	4,000	1,000			3,000	1,000	9,000
Transfers in and/or out of Level 3	5,000		10,000				15,000
Ending balance at December 31, 20X2	$ 10,000	$5,000	$ 15,000	$6,000	$12,000	$9,000	$ 57,000

The Company's investment policy includes various guidelines and procedures designed to ensure assets are invested in a manner necessary to meet expected future benefits earned by participants. The investment guidelines consider a broad range of economic conditions. Central to the policy are target allocation ranges by major asset categories.

The objectives of the target allocations are to maintain investment portfolios that diversify risk through prudent asset allocation parameters, achieve asset returns that meet or exceed the plans' actuarial assumptions, and achieve asset returns that are competitive with like institutions employing similar investment strategies.

The investment policy is periodically reviewed by the Company and a designated third-party fiduciary for investment matters. The policy is established and administered in a manner that is compliant at all times with applicable government regulations.

Cash Flows

The Company expects to contribute $150,000 to its pension plans and $200,000 to its postretirement benefit plans in 20X3.

The following benefit payments, which reflect expected future service, as appropriate, are expected to be paid:

	Pension Benefits	Postretirement Benefits
20X3	$100,000	$125,000
20X4	105,000	130,000
20X5	118,000	140,000
20X6	125,000	150,000
20X7	135,000	175,000
Years 20X8–20Y2	775,000	860,000

Defined Contribution Plans, Interim Period Disclosures, and Other Retirement Benefits Issues

Example 11: Profit Sharing Plan

The Company has a qualified profit sharing plan that covers substantially all full-time employees meeting certain eligibility requirements. The annual contribution is discretionary as determined by the Board of Directors; however, the contributions cannot exceed 15% of compensation for the eligible employees in any one tax year. The Company's contributions to the plan were $325,000 for 20X2 and $215,000 for 20X1.

Example 12: 401(k) Savings Plan

The Company has a 401(k) Plan ("Plan") to provide retirement and incidental benefits for its employees. Employees may contribute from 1% to 15% of their annual compensation to the Plan, limited to a maximum annual amount as set periodically by the Internal Revenue Service. The Company matches employee contributions dollar for dollar up to a maximum of $1,500 per year per person. All matching contributions vest immediately. In addition, the Plan provides for discretionary contributions as determined by the board of directors. Such contributions to the Plan are allocated among eligible participants in the proportion of their salaries to the total salaries of all participants.

Company matching contributions to the Plan totaled $632,000 in 20X2 and $595,000 in 20X1. No discretionary contributions were made in 20X2 or 20X1.

Example 13: Money Purchase Pension Plan

The Company sponsors a trusteed defined contribution money purchase pension plan covering substantially all employees meeting minimum age and service requirements and not covered by collective bargaining agreements. Contributions are based on a percentage of each eligible employee's compensation and are at about 10% of each covered employee's salary. The Company's contributions to the plan totaled $346,000 for 20X2 and $271,000 for 20X1.

Example 14: Incentive Bonus Plan

The Company has an Incentive Bonus Plan ("Bonus Plan") for the benefit of its employees, including executive officers. The total amount of cash bonus awards to be made under the Bonus Plan for any plan year depends primarily on the Company's sales and net income for such year.

For any plan year, the Company's sales and net income must meet or exceed, or in combination with other factors satisfy, levels targeted by the Company in its business plan, as established at the beginning of each fiscal year, for any bonus awards to be made. Aggregate bonus awards to all participants under the Bonus Plan may not exceed 7% of the Company's net income. The board of directors has the authority to determine the total amount of bonus awards, if any, to be made to the eligible employees for any plan year based on its evaluation of the Company's financial condition and results of operations, the Company's business and prospects, and such other criteria as the Board may determine to be relevant or appropriate. The Company expensed $822,000 in 20X2 and $320,000 in 20X1 in conjunction with the Bonus Plan.

Example 15: Combined Disclosures of Defined Contribution Pension Plans and Defined Contribution Postretirement Plans

The Company sponsors several defined contribution pension plans covering substantially all employees. Employees may contribute to these plans and these contributions are matched in varying amounts by the Company. Defined contribution pension expense for the Company was $543,000 for 20X2 and $429,000 for 20X1.

Also, the Company sponsors defined contribution postretirement health care and life insurance benefit plans. Contributions to these plans were $311,000 in 20X2 and $304,000 in 20X1.

Example 16: Union-Sponsored Multiemployer Pension and Postretirement Benefit Plans

The Company participates in various multi-employer union-administered defined benefit pension plans that principally cover production workers. Total contributions to these plans were $472,000 for 20X2 and $461,000 for 20X1.

In addition, the Company participates in various multi-employer, union-administered postretirement benefit plans, which provide for health care and life insurance benefits to both active employees and retirees. Total contributions to these plans were $423,000 for 20X2 and $410,000 for 20X1.

Example 17: Liability Resulting from Withdrawal from Multiemployer Pension Plan Is Recognized in the Financial Statements

Effective October 13, 20X2, the Company decided to withdraw its participation in the Glass Workers Industry Pension Plan. As a result, the Company will be required to contribute its share of the Plan's unfunded benefit obligation. The Company's actuaries have advised that the Company's required contribution at the withdrawal date will be approximately $734,000. As a result, a provision for that amount has been charged against earnings in the 20X2 Statement of Operations.

Example 18: Company Would Not Have a Material Liability If It Withdrew from Multiemployer Pension Plan

The Company's contributions to union-sponsored, defined benefit, multiemployer pension plans were $511,000 in 20X2 and $473,000 in 20X1. These plans are not administered by the Company and contributions are determined in accordance with provisions of negotiated labor contracts. As of December 31, 20X2, the actuarially computed values of vested benefits for these plans were primarily equal to or less than the net assets of the plans. Therefore, the Company would have no material withdrawal liability. However, the

Company has no present intention of withdrawing from any of these plans, nor has the Company been informed that there is any intention to terminate such plans.

Example 19: Curtailment and Special Termination Benefits

In January 20X2, the Company offered a limited program of Retirement Enhancements. The Retirement Enhancements program provided for unreduced retirement benefits to the first 150 employees who retired before December 31, 20X3. In addition, each retiring participant could elect a lump-sum payment of $25,000 or a $400 monthly supplement payable until age 62. As of December 31, 20X2, a total of 125 employees applied for retirement under this program. The Company recorded a charge of $2,936,000 in 20X2 to cover the Retirement Enhancements program.

Example 20: Interim-Period Disclosures—Public Entities

Components of net periodic benefit cost for the Company's pension plan are as follows:

	Three Months Ended September 30		Nine Months Ended September 30	
	20X2	20X1	20X2	20X1
Service cost	$ 1,200,000	$1,100,000	$ 3,700,000	$ 3,400,000
Interest cost	1,400,000	1,156,000	3,900,000	3,250,000
Expected return on plan assets	(1,600,000)	(900,000)	(4,200,000)	(3,900,000)
Amortization of prior service cost	240,000	160,000	525,000	260,000
Amortization of net (gain) loss	70,000	(10,000)	90,000	115,000
Net periodic benefit cost	$ 1,310,000	$1,506,000	$ 4,015,000	$ 3,125,000

Components of net periodic benefit cost for the company's postretirement benefit plan are as follows:

	Three Months Ended September 30		Nine Months Ended September 30	
	20X2	20X1	20X2	20X1
Service cost	$200,000	$170,000	$700,000	$625,000
Interest cost	400,000	350,000	990,000	695,000

	Three Months Ended September 30		Nine Months Ended September 30	
	20X2	20X1	20X2	20X1
Expected return on plan assets	(150,000)	(190,000)	(315,000)	(420,000)
Amortization of prior service cost	(70,000)	(10,000)	(125,000)	(150,000)
Net periodic benefit cost	$ 380,000	$ 320,000	$1,250,000	$ 750,000

The Company previously disclosed in its financial statements for the year ended December 31, 20X1, that it expected to contribute $4,800,000 to its pension plan and $900,000 to its postretirement benefit plan in 20X2. As of September 30, 20X2, contributions of $3,700,000 and $650,000 have been made to the pension plan and postretirement benefit plan, respectively. The Company presently anticipates contributing an additional $1,500,000 to fund its pension plan in 20X2 for a total of $5,200,000. Also, the Company presently anticipates contributing an additional $450,000 to fund its postretirement benefit plan in 20X2 for a total of $1,100,000.

Example 21: Interim-Period Disclosures—Nonpublic Entities

The Company previously disclosed in its financial statements for the year ended December 31, 20X1, that it expected to contribute $4,800,000 to its pension plan and $900,000 to its postretirement benefit plan in 20X2. As of September 30, 20X2, contributions of $3,700,000 and $650,000 have been made to the pension plan and postretirement benefit plan, respectively. The Company presently anticipates contributing an additional $1,500,000 to fund its pension plan in 20X2 for a total of $5,200,000. Also, the Company presently anticipates contributing an additional $450,000 to fund its postretirement benefit plan in 20X2 for a total of $1,100,000.

CHAPTER 40
ASC TOPIC 718:
COMPENSATION—STOCK
COMPENSATION

CONTENTS

EXECUTIVE SUMMARY

Overall

Stock issued to employees may include compensation (compensatory plan) or may not include compensation (noncompensatory plan). A *compensatory plan* is one in which services rendered by employees are compensated for by the issuance of stock. The measurement of compensation expense included in compensatory plans is the primary challenge in accounting for stock issued to employees.

A company is required to recognize the goods acquired or services received in a share-based payment transaction when it obtains the goods or as services are received, with a corresponding increase in equity (generally, paid-in capital) or a liability, depending on whether the instruments granted satisfy the equity or liability classification criteria. With limited exceptions, a share-based payment transaction with *employees* should be measured based on the fair value of the equity instruments issued on the grant date or on the fair value of the liabilities incurred. The fair value of a stock option awarded to an employee generally must be estimated using an option-pricing model (e.g., Black-Scholes) that takes into account, at a minimum, the following six variables:

1. The exercise price of the option

2. The expected term of the option, taking into account both the contractual term of the option and the effects of employees' expected exercise and post-vesting employment termination behavior

3. The current price of the underlying share

4. The expected volatility of the price of the underlying share for the expected term of the option

5. The expected dividends on the underlying share for the expected term of the option

6. The risk-free interest rate(s) for the expected term of the option

It should be noted that the aforementioned requirement applies to nonpublic companies as well; however, if a nonpublic company is unable to estimate the expected volatility of the price of its underlying share, it may measure awards based on a "calculated value," which substitutes the volatility of an appropriate index for the volatility of the company's own share price. [**Note:** The "minimum-value" method is no longer acceptable for nonpublic companies.]

Share-based awards to *nonemployees* should be measured and recognized using the fair-value method, based on the fair value of the equity instruments issued or the fair value of goods or services received, whichever is more reliably measurable.

Employee Stock Ownership Plans

An employee stock ownership plan (ESOP) is a special form of a tax-qualified defined contribution retirement plan. ESOPs invest primarily in the employer's common or convertible preferred stock, and they are allowed to borrow money to purchase the stock There are two kinds of ESOPs: nonleveraged and leveraged.

Key attributes of a *nonleveraged* ESOP include:

- An employer periodically contributing its shares or cash to its nonleveraged ESOP on behalf of employees; and
- The allocation of employer stock obtained by the nonleveraged ESOP to individual participant accounts by the end of the ESOP's fiscal year.

A *leveraged* ESOP borrows money to acquire shares of the employer entity. The ESOP initially holds the shares in a suspense account, which is collateral for the ESOP loan. As the ESOP makes payments on the debt, the shares are released from the suspense account and become available to be allocated to employees' accounts. Released shares must be allocated to individual employee accounts by the end of the ESOP's fiscal year.

Accounting Literature

FASB Accounting Standards Codification Topic	*Pre-Codification Accounting Literature*
718, *Compensation—Stock Compensation*	FAS-123R, *Share-Based Payment*
	EITF 90-4, *Earnings-per-Share Treatment of Tax Benefits for Dividends on Stock Held by an Employee Stock Ownership Plan*
	EITF 06-11, *Accounting for Income Tax Benefits of Dividends on Share-Based Payment Awards*
	SOP 93-6, *Employers' Accounting for Stock Ownership Plans*

DISCLOSURE AND KEY PRESENTATION REQUIREMENTS

Overall

1. For an entity with one or more share-based payment arrangements, the following disclosures should be made (ASC 718-10-50-1 through 50-4) (FAS-123R, pars. 64, A240, A242) (*Note*: This disclosure is not required for interim reporting; see

Chapter 12, "ASC Topic 270: Interim Reporting," for further interim reporting guidance.):

a. A description of the share-based payment arrangement(s), including the general terms of awards under the arrangement(s), such as:

    (1) The requisite service period(s) and any other substantive conditions (including those related to vesting).

    (2) The maximum contractual term of equity (or liability) share options or similar instruments.

    (3) The number of shares authorized for awards of equity share options or other equity instruments.

b. The method the entity uses for measuring compensation cost from share-based payment arrangements with employees.

c. For the most recent year for which an income statement is presented, the following:

    (1) The number and weighted-average exercise prices (or conversion ratios) for each of the following groups of share options (or share units):

        (i) Those outstanding at the beginning of the year.

        (ii) Those outstanding at the end of the year.

        (iii) Those exercisable or convertible at the end of the year.

        (iv) Those granted during the year.

        (v) Those exercised or converted during the year.

        (vi) Those forfeited during the year.

        (vii) Those expired during the year.

    (2) The number and weighted-average grant-date fair value (or calculated value for a nonpublic entity that uses that method, or intrinsic value for awards measured at that value) of equity instruments not specified in (c)(1) above (e.g., nonvested shares), for all of the following groups of equity instruments:

        (i) Those nonvested at the beginning of the year.

        (ii) Those nonvested at the end of the year.

        (iii) Those granted during the year.

        (iv) Those vested during the year.

        (v) Those forfeited during the year.

d. For each year for which an income statement is presented, the following:

   (1) The weighted-average grant-date fair value (or calculated value for a nonpublic entity that uses that method, or intrinsic value for awards measured at that value) of equity options or other equity instruments granted during the year.

   (2) The total intrinsic value of options exercised (or share units converted), share-based liabilities paid, and the total fair value of shares vested during the year.

e. For fully vested share options (or share units) and share options expected to vest at the date of the latest balance sheet, the following:

   (1) For options (or share units) outstanding:

      (i) Number of options (or share units).

      (ii) Weighted-average exercise price (or conversion ratio).

      (iii) Aggregate intrinsic value (except for nonpublic entities).

      (iv) Weighted-average remaining contractual term.

   (2) For options (or share units) currently excisable or convertible:

      (i) Number of options (or share units).

      (ii) Weighted-average exercise price (or conversion ratio).

      (iii) Aggregate intrinsic value (except for nonpublic entities).

      (iv) Weighted-average remaining contractual term.

f. For each year for which an income statement is presented, the following (not required for entities that use the intrinsic value method for awards accounted for under that method):

   (1) A description of the method used during the year to estimate the fair value (or calculated value) of awards under share-based payment arrangements.

   (2) A description of the significant assumptions used during the year to estimate the fair value (or calculated value) of share-based compensation awards, including (if applicable):

      (i) Expected term of share options and similar instruments, including a discussion of the method used to incorporate the contractual term of the instruments and employees' expected exercise and post-vesting employment termination behavior into the fair value (or calculated value) of the instrument.

(ii) Expected volatility of the entity's shares and the method used to estimate expected volatility. (*Note*: An entity that uses a method that employs different volatilities during the contractual term should disclose the range of expected volatilities used and the weighted-average expected volatility. In addition, a non-public entity that uses the calculated value method should disclose: (a) the reasons why it is not practicable for it to estimate the expected volatility of its share price, (b) the appropriate industry sector index that it has selected, (c) the reasons for selecting that particular index, and (d) how it has calculated historical volatility using that index.)

(iii) Expected dividends or, if the method used employs different dividend rates during the contractual term, the range of expected dividends used and the weighted-average expected dividends.

(iv) Risk-free rates or, if the method used employs different risk-free rates, the range of risk-free rates used.

(v) Discount for post-vesting restrictions and the method for estimating it.

g. For an entity that grants equity or liability instruments under multiple share-based payment arrangements with employees, the information specified in items (a) through (f) separately for different types of awards to the extent that the differences in the characteristics of the awards make separate disclosure important to an understanding of the entity's use of share-based compensation. Examples of separate disclosures for different types of awards include:

(1) The weighted-average exercise prices (or conversion ratios) at the end of the year for options (or share units) with a fixed exercise price (or conversion ratio) and those with an indexed exercise price (or conversion ratio).

      (2)   The number of options (or share units) not yet exercisable into those that will become exercisable (or convertible) based solely on fulfilling a service condition and those for which a performance condition must be met for the options (share units) to become exercisable (convertible).

      (3)   Awards that are classified as equity and those classified as liabilities.

h. For each year for which an income statement is presented, the following:

      (1)   Total compensation cost for share-based payment arrangements recognized in income as well as the total related recognized tax benefit.

      (2)   Total compensation cost for share-based payment arrangements capitalized as part of the cost of an asset.

      (3)   A description of significant modifications, including:

          (i)   The terms of the modifications.

          (ii) The number of employees affected.

          (iii) The total incremental compensation cost resulting from the modifications.

i. As of the latest balance sheet date presented, the following:

      (1)   The total compensation cost related to nonvested awards not yet recognized.

      (2)   The weighted-average period over which the total compensation cost related to nonvested awards not yet recognized is expected to be recognized.

j. If not separately disclosed elsewhere, the amount of cash received from exercise of share options and similar instruments granted under share-based payment arrangements and the tax benefit realized from stock options exercised during the annual period.

k. If not separately disclosed elsewhere, the amount of cash used to settle equity instruments granted under share-based payment arrangements.

l. A description of the entity's policy, if any, for issuing shares upon share option exercise (or share unit conversion), including the source of those shares (i.e., new shares or treasury shares).

    m. If as a result of an entity's policy for issuing shares upon share option exercise (or share unit conversion), an entity expects to repurchase shares in the following annual period, an estimate of the amount (or a range, if more appropriate) of shares to be repurchased during that period.

    n. Any other information necessary to understand:

        (1) The nature and terms of share-based payment arrangements that existed during the period and the potential effects of those arrangements on shareholders.

        (2) The effect of compensation cost arising from share-based payment arrangements on the income statement.

        (3) The method of estimating the fair value of the goods or services received, or the fair value of the equity instruments granted (or offered to grant), during the period.

        (4) The cash flow effects resulting from share-based payment arrangements.

    o. Supplemental information that might be useful to investors and creditors (e.g., range of values calculated on the basis of different assumptions and a description of the alternative assumptions), provided that the supplemental information is reasonable and does not lessen the prominence and credibility of the required disclosures described above.

2. See Chapter 11, "ASC Topic 260: Earnings per Share," for earnings per share considerations in connection with equity instruments granted in share-based payment transactions.

Employee Stock Ownership Plans

1. Dividends on preferred stock held by an employee stock ownership plan (ESOP) should be deducted from net income (net of any applicable income tax benefit), when computing both basic and diluted earnings per share (EPS) if that preferred stock is considered outstanding (i.e., if the employee stock ownership plan shares are allocated). (ASC 718-40-45-1) (EITF 90-4)

2. A charge in connection with the issuance of shares or the sale of treasury shares to an ESOP should be reported as unearned ESOP shares (a contra-equity account) and be

presented as a separate item in the balance sheet. (ASC 718-40-45-2) (SOP 93-6, par. 13)

3. For purposes of earnings per share (EPS) for leveraged ESOPs:

   a. ESOP shares that have been committed to be released should be considered outstanding. (ASC 718-40-45-3) (SOP 93-6, par. 28)

   b. ESOP shares that have not been committed to be released should *not* be considered outstanding. (ASC 718-40-45-3) (SOP 93-6, par. 28)

   c. Employers that use dividends on allocated ESOP shares to pay debt service should adjust earnings applicable to common shares in the if-converted computation for the difference (net of income taxes) between the amount of compensation cost reported and the amount of compensation cost that would have been reported if the allocated shares had been converted to common stock at the beginning of the period. (ASC 718-40-45-4) (SOP 93-6, par. 33)

   d. Prior period EPS should *not* be restated for changes in the conversion rates. (ASC 718-40-45-5) (SOP 93-6, par. 34)

   e. For purposes of applying the if-converted EPS method for convertible preferred shares held by an ESOP plan (ASC 718-40-45-6 through 45-8) (SOP 93-6, pars. 31 and 32):

      (1) If the shares have been committed to be released, they should be deemed outstanding in the if-converted EPS computations for diluted EPS if the effect is dilutive.

      (2) If the shares have not been committed to be released, they should be excluded from the if-converted EPS computations for diluted EPS.

      (3) The number of common shares issuable on assumed conversion should be computed based on the greater of (i) the shares issuable at the stated conversion rate, or (ii) the shares issuable if the participants were to withdraw the shares from their accounts.

      (4) The number of common shares issuable on assumed withdrawal should be computed based on the ratio of the average fair value of the convertible stock (or, if greater, its stated minimum value) to the average fair value of the common stock.

  f. For purposes of earnings per share (EPS) for nonleveraged ESOPs (ASC 718-40-45-9) (SOP 93-6, par. 44):

   (1) All shares held by a nonleveraged ESOP should be treated as outstanding in computing the employer's EPS (except the suspense account shares of a pension reversion ESOP, which are not treated as outstanding until they are committed to be released for allocation to participant accounts).

   (2) If a nonleveraged ESOP holds convertible preferred shares, the guidance in item (e) above for leveraged ESOPs should be considered.

 4. The financial statements of an employer sponsoring an ESOP should disclose the following information about the plan, if applicable (ASC 718-40-50-1) (SOP 93-6, par. 53; EITF 90-4):

  a. A description of the plan.

  b. The basis for determining contributions, including the employee groups covered.

  c. The nature and effect of significant matters affecting comparability of information for all periods presented.

  d. For leveraged ESOPs and pension reversion employee stock ownership plans, the basis for releasing shares and how dividends on allocated and unallocated shares are used.

  e. A description of the accounting policies followed for ESOP transactions, including the method of measuring compensation, the classification of dividends on ESOP shares, and the treatment of ESOP shares for EPS computations. (*Note:* If the employer has both old ESOP shares for which it does not adopt the guidance in ASC Subtopic 718-40 (SOP 93-6) and new ESOP shares for which the guidance in ASC Subtopic 718-40 (SOP 93-6) is required, the accounting policies for both blocks of shares should be described.)

  f. The amount of compensation cost recognized during the period.

  g. The number of allocated shares, committed-to-be-released shares, and suspense shares held by the ESOP at the balance sheet date. (*Note:* This disclosure should be made separately for shares accounted for under ASC Subtopic 718-40 (SOP 93-6) and for grandfathered ESOP shares.)

  h. The fair value of unearned ESOP shares at the balance sheet date. (*Note:* Future tax deductions will be allowed only for the ESOP's *cost* of unearned ESOP shares. This disclosure need not be made for old ESOP shares for which the employer does not apply the guidance in ASC Subtopic 718-40 (SOP 93-6).)

i. The existence and nature of any repurchase obligation, including disclosure of the fair value of the shares allocated as of the balance sheet date, which are subject to a repurchase obligation.

j. The amount and treatment in the EPS computation of the tax benefit related to dividends paid to any ESOP, if material.

Income Taxes Related Matters

1. When actual tax deductions for compensation expense taken by an entity on its tax return for share-based payment arrangements differ in amounts and timing from those recorded in the financial statements, the following matters should be addressed (ASC 718-740-45-1 through 45-4) (FAS-123R, pars. 62 and 63):

    a. If a deduction reported on a tax return for an award of equity instruments exceeds the cumulative compensation cost for those instruments recognized for financial reporting, any resulting realized tax benefit that exceeds the previously recognized deferred tax asset for those instruments (i.e., the excess tax benefit) should be recognized as additional paid-in capital. (*Note:* However, an excess of a realized tax benefit for an award over the deferred tax asset for that award should be recognized in the income statement to the extent that the excess stems from a reason other than changes in the fair value of an entity's shares between the measurement date for accounting purposes and a later measurement date for tax purposes.)

    b. The remaining balance, if any, of the write-off of a deferred tax asset related to a tax deficiency not offset against additional paid-in capital should be recognized in the income statement.

2. For employee stock ownership plans (ESOP):

    a. If the cost of shares committed to be released in an ESOP is greater than their fair value, the tax effect of the amount by which the deductible expense exceeds the book expense should be credited to stockholders' equity. (ASC 718-740-45-5) (SOP 93-6, par. 50)

    b. If the cost of shares committed to be released in an ESOP is less than their fair value, the tax effect of the amount by which the book expense exceeds the deductible expense should be charged to stockholders' equity (to the extent of previous credits to stockholders' equity related to cost exceeding fair value of the ESOP shares committed to be released in previous periods). (ASC 718-740-45-6) (SOP 93-6, par. 50)

c. The tax benefit of tax-deductible dividends on allocated ESOP shares should be recorded as a reduction of income tax expense allocated to continuing operations and the tax benefit of tax-deductible dividends on unallocated ESOP shares that are charged to retained earnings should be credited to stockholders' equity. (ASC 718-740-45-7) (SOP 93-6, par. 51)

3. For tax benefits of dividends on share-based payment awards to employees:

a. For any nonvested equity shares, nonvested equity share units, or outstanding equity share options:

(1) Realized income tax benefits from dividends (or dividend equivalents) that are charged to retained earnings and are paid to employees should be recognized as an increase to additional paid-in capital. (ASC 718-740-45-8) (EITF 06-11, par. 4)

(2) The amount recognized in additional paid-in capital should be included in the pool of excess tax benefits available to absorb tax deficiencies on share-based payment awards. (ASC 718-740-45-9) (EITF 06-11, par. 4)

(3) If dividends (or dividend equivalents) paid to employees result in a tax deduction prior to the actual realization of the related tax benefit (e.g., the employer has a net operating loss carryforward), the income tax benefits of those dividends should *not* be recognized until the deduction reduces income taxes payable. (ASC 718-740-45-10) (EITF 06-11, par. 5) (*Note:* The unrealized income tax benefits should be excluded from the pool of excess tax benefits available to absorb potential future tax deficiencies on share-based payment awards.)

b. Dividends (or dividend equivalents) paid to employees on the portion of an award of equity shares or other equity instruments that vests should be charged to retained earnings and, if the related award is not expected to vest, such dividends should be recognized as compensation costs. (ASC 718-740-45-11) (EITF 06-11, par. 6) (*Note:* Such dividends should be reclassified between retained earnings and compensation costs in a subsequent period if the entity changes its forfeiture estimates or actual forfeitures differ from previous estimates.)

c. If an entity's estimate of forfeitures increases (or actual forfeitures exceed the entity's estimates), the tax benefits from dividends that are reclassified from additional paid-in capital to the income statement should be limited to the entity's pool of excess tax benefits available to absorb tax deficiencies on the date of the reclassification. (ASC 718-740-45-12) (EITF 06-11, par. 6)

EXAMPLES OF FINANCIAL STATEMENT DISCLOSURES

 The following sample disclosures are available on the accompanying disc.

Example 1: Multiple Share Option Plans

As of December 31, 20X2, the Company has two share-based compensation plans, which are described in detail below. The compensation cost that has been charged against operations for those plans was $2,940,000 and $2,870,000 for the years ended December 31, 20X2 and 20X1, respectively. The total income tax benefit recognized in the income statement for share-based compensation arrangements was $1,030,000 and $1,010,000 for the years ended December 31, 20X2 and 20X1, respectively. Compensation cost capitalized as part of inventory and fixed assets for 20X2 and 20X1 was $50,000 and $20,000, respectively.

Share Option Plan

The Company's 20X0 Employee Share Option Plan (the Plan), which is shareholder-approved, permits the grant of share options and shares to its employees for up to 8 million shares of common stock. The Company believes that such awards better align the interests of its employees with those of its shareholders. Option awards are generally granted with an exercise price equal to the market price of the Company's stock at the date of grant; those option awards generally vest based on 5 years of continuous service and have 10-year contractual terms. Share awards generally vest over five years. Certain option and share awards provide for accelerated vesting if there is a change in control, as defined in the Plan.

The fair value of each option award is estimated on the date of grant using a lattice-based option valuation model that uses the assumptions noted in the table below. Because lattice-based option valuation models incorporate ranges of assumptions for inputs, those ranges are disclosed. Expected volatilities are based on implied volatilities from traded options on the Company's stock, historical volatility of the Company's stock, and other factors. The Company uses historical data to estimate option exercise and employee termination within the valuation model; separate groups of employees that have similar historical exercise behavior are considered separately for valuation purposes. The expected term of options granted is derived from the output of the option valuation model and represents the period of time that options granted are expected to be outstanding; the range given below results from certain groups of employees exhibiting different behavior. The risk-free rate for periods within the contractual life of the option is based on the U.S. Treasury yield curve in effect at the time of grant.

	20X2	20X1
Expected volatility	25%–40%	24%–38%
Weighted-average volatility	33%	30%
Expected dividends	1.5%	1.5%
Expected term (in years)	5.3–7.8	5.5–8.0
Risk-free rate	6.3%–11.2%	6.0%–10.0%

A summary of option activity under the Plan as of December 31, 20X2, and changes during the year then ended is presented below:

Options	Shares	Weighted-Average Exercise Price	Weighted-Average Remaining Contractual Term	Aggregate Intrinsic Value
Outstanding at January 1, 20X2	4,660,000	$4.2		
Granted	950,000	$6.0		
Exercised	(800,000)	$3.6		
Forfeited or expired	(80,000)	$5.9		
Outstanding at December 31, 20X2	4,730,000	$4.7	6.5	$8,514,000
Exercisable at December 31, 20X2	3,159,000	$4.1	4.0	$7,581,600

The weighted-average grant-date fair value of options granted during the years ended December 31, 20X2 and 20X1, was $1.96 and $1.75, respectively. The total intrinsic value of options exercised during the years ended December 31, 20X2 and 20X1, was $2,520,000 and $2,090,000, respectively.

A summary of the status of the Company's nonvested shares as of December 31, 20X2, and changes during the year ended December 31, 20X2, is presented below:

Nonvested Shares	Shares	Weighted-Average Grant-Date Fair Value
Nonvested at January 1, 20X2	980,000	$4.15
Granted	150,000	$6.35
Vested	(100,000)	$3.57
Forfeited	(40,000)	$5.56
Nonvested at December 31, 20X2	990,000	$4.34

As of December 31, 20X2, there was $2,590,000 of total unrecognized compensation cost related to nonvested share-based compensation arrangements granted under the Plan. That cost is expected to be recognized over a weighted-average period of 4.9 years. The total fair value of shares vested during the years ended December 31, 20X2 and 20X1, was $2,280,000 and $2,100,000, respectively.

During 20X2, the Company extended the contractual life of 200,000 fully vested share options held by 10 employees. As a result of that modification, the Company recognized additional compensation expense of $100,000 for the year ended December 31, 20X2.

Performance Share Option Plan

Under its 20X0 Performance Share Option Plan (the Performance Plan), which is shareholder-approved, each January 1 the Company grants selected executives and other key employees share option awards whose vesting is contingent upon meeting various departmental and company-wide performance goals, including decreasing time to market for new products, revenue growth in excess of an index of competitors' revenue growth, and sales targets for the semiconductor segment. Share options under the Performance Plan are generally granted at-the-money, contingently vest over a period of 1 to 5 years, depending on the nature of the performance goal, and have contractual lives of 7 to 10 years. The number of shares subject to options available for issuance under the Performance Plan cannot exceed five million.

The fair value of each option grant under the Performance Plan was estimated on the date of grant using the same option valuation model used for options granted under the Plan and assumes that performance goals will be achieved. If such goals are not met, no compensation cost is recognized and any recognized compensation cost is reversed. The inputs for expected volatility, expected dividends, and risk-free rate used in estimating those options' fair value are the same as those noted in the table above related to options issued under the Share Option Plan. The expected term for options granted under the Performance Plan in 20X2 and 20X1 is 3.3 to 5.4 years, and 2.4 to 6.5 years, respectively.

A summary of the activity under the Performance Plan as of December 31, 20X2, and changes during the year then ended is presented below:

Performance Options	Shares	Weighted-Average Exercise Price	Weighted-Average Remaining Contractual Term	Aggregate Intrinsic Value
Outstanding at January 1, 20X2	2,533,000	$4.4		
Granted	995,000	$6.0		
Exercised	(100,000)	$3.6		
Forfeited	(604,000)	$5.9		
Outstanding at December 31, 20X2	2,824,000	$4.7	7.1	$5,083,200
Exercisable at December 31, 20X2	936,000	$4.1	5.3	$2,340,000

The weighted-average grant-date fair value of options granted during the years ended December 31, 20X2 and 20X1, was $ 1.73 and $1.60, respectively. The total intrinsic value of options exercised during the years ended December 31, 20X2 and 20X1, was $500,000 and $800,000, respectively. As of December 31, 20X2, there was $1,690,000 of total unrecognized compensation cost related to nonvested share-based compensation arrangements granted under the Performance Plan; that cost is expected to be recognized over a period of 4.0 years.

Cash received from option exercise under all share-based payment arrangements for the years ended December 31, 20X2 and 20X1, was $3,240,000 and $2,890,000, respectively. The actual tax benefit realized for the tax deductions from option exercise of the share-based payment arrangements totaled $1,130,000 and $1,010,000, respectively, for the years ended December 31, 20X2 and 20X1.

The Company has a policy of repurchasing shares on the open market to satisfy share option exercises and expects to repurchase approximately 350,0000 shares during 20X3, based on estimates of option exercises for that period.

Example 2: Nonpublic Entity Uses the Calculated Value Method

> **Note:** With a few exceptions as previously discussed, the disclosure requirements for share based-payments are substantially the same for public and nonpublic entities. However, for nonpublic entities that use the calculated value method, a nonpublic entity should disclose: (a) the reasons it is not practicable to estimate the expected volatility of its share price; (b) the appropriate industry sector index selected; (c) the reasons for selecting the industry sector index; and (d) how historical volatility has been calculated using the industry sector index selected. The following example illustrates these specific disclosure requirements for nonpublic entities that use the calculated value method. For all other applicable disclosure requirements, see Example 1 above.

The Company has elected to use the calculated value method to account for the options it issued in 20X2. A nonpublic entity that is unable to estimate the expected volatility of the price of its underlying share may measure awards based on a "calculated value," which substitutes the volatility of an appropriate index for the volatility of the entity's own share price. Currently, there is no active market for the company's common shares. In addition, management has determined that it is unable to reasonably estimate the fair value of the options on the date of grant because the Company has not issued any new common stock for several years and management has not been able to identify a similar publicly held entity that can be used as a benchmark. Therefore, as a substitute for volatility, the Company used the historical volatility of the Dow Jones Internet Commerce index, which is representative of the company's size and industry. The Company has used the historical closing values of that index to estimate volatility, which was calculated to be 30.2%.

Example 3: Warrants Activity for the Period and Summary of Outstanding Warrants

During the years ended December 31, 20X2, and December 31, 20X1, the board of directors approved the issuance of warrants to purchase an aggregate of 565,000 shares of the Company's common stock. Such warrants are exercisable at prices ranging from $9.50 to

$20.625 per share, vest over periods up to 48 months, and expire at various times through April 20X9.

During the years ended December 31, 20X2, and December 31, 20X1, certain warrant holders exercised warrants to purchase 278,000 and 11,000 shares, respectively, of the Company's common stock for an aggregate of $673,000 and $22,000, respectively.

Included in the issuance of warrants to purchase 565,000 aggregate shares of the Company's common stock is a warrant to purchase 50,000 shares that was issued to a director under the terms of a consulting agreement during fiscal 20X1. Such issuance was accounted for under Financial Accounting Standards Board Statement No. 123 using the Black-Scholes option-pricing model (with the same assumptions as those used for the option), which resulted in the recording of $233,000 and $50,000 in compensation cost during the years ended December 31, 20X2, and December 31, 20X1, respectively.

A summary of warrant activity for 20X2 and 20X1 is as follows:

	Number of Warrants	Weighted-Average Exercise Price	Warrants Exercisable	Weighted-Average Exercise Price
Outstanding, December 31, 20X0	427,000	4.44	409,916	$ 4.13
Granted	350,000	11.95		
Exercised	(11,000)	2.00		
Outstanding, December 31, 20X1	766,000	7.42	493,082	4.91
Granted	215,000	17.31		
Exercised	(278,000)	2.42		
Outstanding, December 31, 20X2	703,000	12.42	482,166	12.20

At December 31, 20X2, the range of warrant prices for shares under warrants and the weighted-average remaining contractual life is as follows:

	Warrants Outstanding			Warrants Exercisable	
Range of Warrant Exercise Price	Number of Warrants	Weighted-Average Exercise Price	Weighted-Average Remaining Contractual Life	Number of Warrants	Weighted-Average Exercise Price
$6.00–9.50	200,000	$ 7.81	5.83	200,000	$ 7.81
11.78-12.81	288,000	11.96	6.01	92,166	12.11
16.88-20.63	215,000	17.31	9.22	190,000	16.88
	703,000			482,166	

Example 4: Leveraged ESOP

The Company sponsors a leveraged employee stock ownership plan (ESOP) that covers all U.S. employees who work twenty or more hours per week. The Company makes annual contributions to the ESOP equal to the ESOP's debt service less dividends received by the ESOP. All dividends received by the ESOP are used to pay debt service. The ESOP shares initially were pledged as collateral for its debt. As the debt is repaid, shares are released from collateral and allocated to active employees, based on the proportion of debt service paid in the year. The debt of the ESOP is recorded as debt and the shares pledged as collateral are reported as unearned ESOP shares in the Balance Sheet. As shares are released from collateral, the Company reports compensation expense equal to the current market price of the shares, and the shares become outstanding for earnings-per-share computations. Dividends on allocated ESOP shares are recorded as a reduction of retained earnings; dividends on unallocated ESOP shares are recorded as a reduction of debt and accrued interest. ESOP compensation expense was $275,000 and $250,000 for 20X2 and 20X1, respectively. The ESOP shares as of December 31, 20X2, and December 31, 20X1, were as follows:

	20X2	20X1
Allocated shares	80,000	40,000
Shares released for allocation	40,000	40,000
Unreleased shares	80,000	120,000
Total ESOP shares	200,000	200,000
Fair value of unreleased shares at December 31	$1,200,000	$1,500,000

Example 5: Leveraged ESOP Used to Fund Employer's Portion of 401(k) Plan

The Company sponsors a 401(k) savings plan under which eligible employees may choose to save up to 6% of salary income on a pre-tax basis, subject to certain IRS limits. The Company matches 50% of employee contributions with Company common stock. The shares for this purpose are provided principally by the Company's employee stock ownership plan (ESOP), supplemented as needed by newly issued shares. The Company makes annual contributions to the ESOP equal to the ESOP's debt service less dividends received by the ESOP. All dividends received by the ESOP are used to pay debt service. The ESOP shares initially were pledged as collateral for its debt. As the debt is repaid, shares are released from collateral and allocated to employees who made 401(k) contributions that year, based on the proportion of debt service paid in the year. The shares pledged as collateral are reported as unearned ESOP shares in the balance sheet. As shares are released from collateral, the Company reports compensation expense equal to the current market price of the shares, and the shares become outstanding for earnings-per-share computations. Dividends on allocated ESOP shares are recorded as a reduction of retained earnings; dividends on unallocated ESOP shares are recorded as a reduction of debt and accrued interest.

Compensation expense for the 401(k) match and the ESOP was $325,000 and $305,000 for 20X2 and 20X1, respectively. The ESOP shares as of December 31, 20X2, and December 31, 20X1 were as follows:

	20X2	*20X1*
Allocated shares	85,000	40,000
Shares released for allocation	50,000	45,000
Unreleased shares	75,000	115,000
Total ESOP shares	210,000	200,000
Fair value of unreleased shares at December 31	$850,000	$1,150,000

CHAPTER 41
ASC TOPIC 720: OTHER EXPENSES

CONTENTS

EXECUTIVE SUMMARY

Insurance Costs

Insurance premiums paid in advance should be charged to expense ratably over the period of the policy. Some insurance policies prescribe a fixed premium rate per "unit of risk" (e.g., payroll hours or inventory levels) and require a deposit (estimated) premium that is later adjusted to reflect the actual units of risk. In these circumstances, the estimated ultimate premium based on the most current information available should be amortized to expense. When the cumulative amortization exceeds the deposit premium, the excess should be recorded as a liability.

Unless the criteria for offsetting are met, an entity should not offset prepaid insurance and receivables for expected recoveries against a recognized incurred but not reported liability of a liability incurred from a past event.

Real and Personal Property Taxes

Real and personal property taxes should be expensed ratably over the fiscal year to which they apply as specified on the tax bill, tax form, or by law. When the assessed valuations or tax rates are not known, estimates should be used for expense recognition. An accrued liability for real and personal property taxes should be included with current liabilities.

Advertising Costs

In most cases, the costs of advertising should be expensed as incurred or the first time the advertisement occurs. However, there are two exceptions to this general rule:

1. Certain direct-response advertising costs should be capitalized and amortized over the period during which the future benefits or sales are expected to be received.

2. Expenditures for advertising costs that are made subsequent to recognizing revenues related to those costs should be capitalized and charged to expense when the related revenues are recognized.

Accounting Literature

FASB Accounting Standards Codification Topic	Pre-Codification Accounting Literature
340, *Other Assets and Deferred Costs* 720, *Other Expenses*	EITF 03-8, *Accounting for Claims-Made Insurance and Retroactive Insurance Contracts by the Insured Entity* ARB-43, Chapter 10A, *Real and Personal Property Taxes* SOP 93-7, *Reporting on Advertising Costs*

DISCLOSURE AND KEY PRESENTATION REQUIREMENTS

Insurance Costs

1. Prepaid insurance and receivables for expected recoveries from insurers should *not* be offset against a recognized incurred but not reported liability or the liability incurred as a result of a past insurable event, unless a right of offset exists under the conditions of paragraph 210-20-45-1, (FIN-39, par. 5). (ASC 720-20-45-1) (EITF 03-8)

2. When an entity changes from occurrence-based insurance to claims-made insurance or elects to significantly reduce or eliminate its insurance coverage, the required disclosures for contingencies should be made if it is at least reasonably possible that a loss has been incurred. (ASC 720-20-50-1) (EITF 03-8). For further guidance, see Chapter 30, "ASC Topic 450: Contingencies."

Real and Personal Property Taxes

1. An accrued liability for real and personal property taxes (whether estimated or definitely known) should be included among the current liabilities. (ASC 720-30-45-1) (ARB-43, Ch. 10A, par. 16)

2. If estimates of accrued liability for real and personal property taxes are subject to a substantial measure of uncertainty, the liability should be described as estimated. (ASC 720-30-45-1) (ARB-43, Ch. 10A, par. 16)

3. The amounts of real and personal property taxes should *not* be combined with taxes on income in the income statement. (ASC 720-30-45-2) (ARB-43, Ch. 10A, par. 18)

Advertising Costs

The following disclosures should be made in the notes to the financial statements for advertising costs (ASC 720-35-50-1) (SOP 93-7, par. 49):

1. The accounting policy for reporting advertising costs, indicating whether such costs are expensed as incurred or the first time the advertising takes place.

2. The total amount charged to advertising expense for each income statement presented.

For capitalized advertising costs, see Chapter 22, "ASC Topic 340: Other Assets and Deferred Costs."

For advertising barter transactions, see Chapter 35, "ASC Topic 605: Revenue Recognition."

EXAMPLES OF FINANCIAL STATEMENT DISCLOSURES

 The following sample disclosures are available on the accompanying disc.

Insurance Costs

Example 1: Insurance Coverage/Self-Insurance

Insurance and claims accruals reflect the estimated cost for bodily injury and property damage, group health, and workers' compensation claims not covered by insurance. The costs for bodily injury and property damage insurance and claims are included in insurance and claims expense in the Statements of Operations. The costs of group health and workers' compensation claims are included in salaries, wages and benefits expense. The insurance and claims accruals are recorded at the estimated ultimate payment amounts. Such insurance and claims accruals are based upon individual case estimates and estimates of incurred-but-not-reported losses using loss development factors based upon past experience. Actual costs related to insurance and claims have not differed materially from estimated accrued amounts for 20X2 and 20X1. An actuary reviews the Company's self-insurance reserves for bodily injury and property damage claims and workers' compensation claims every six months.

The Company is responsible for liability claims up to $250,000, plus administrative expenses, for each occurrence involving bodily injury or property damage since June 1, 20X0. For the policy year beginning December 1, 20X1, the Company increased its self-insured retention and deductible amount to $1 million per occurrence. The Company is also responsible for varying annual aggregate amounts of liability for claims in excess of the self-insured retention/deductible amount.

The Company's primary insurance covers the range of liability under which management expects most claims to occur. If any liability claims are substantially in excess of coverage amounts, such claims are covered under premium-based policies issued by insurance companies to coverage levels that management considers adequate. The Company is also responsible for administrative expenses for each occurrence involving bodily injury or property damage.

The Company assumes responsibility for workers' compensation up to $500,000 per claim. Effective September 1, 20X1, the Company is no longer responsible for the additional $500,000 aggregate for claims between $500,000 and $1,000,000.

Example 2: Receivable Recorded from a Reinsurance Pool

The Company uses a combination of purchased insurance and self-insurance programs to provide for the costs of medical, casualty, liability, vehicular, cargo, and workers' compensation claims. The long-term portion of self-insurance accruals relates primarily to workers' compensation and vehicular claims that are expected to be payable over several years. The Company periodically evaluates the level of insurance coverage and adjusts insurance levels based on risk tolerance and premium expense.

The measurement and classification of self-insured costs requires the consideration of historical cost experience, demographic and severity factors, and judgments about the current and expected levels of cost per claim and retention levels. These methods provide estimates of the undiscounted liability associated with claims incurred as of the balance sheet date, including claims not reported. Changes in these assumptions and factors can materially affect actual costs paid to settle the claims and those amounts may be different than estimates.

The Company participates in a reinsurance pool to reinsure a portion of its workers' compensation and vehicular liabilities. Each participant in the pool cedes claims to the pool and assumes an equivalent amount of claims. Reinsurance does not relieve the Company of its liabilities under the original policy. However, in the opinion of management, potential exposure to the Company for non-payment is minimal. At December 31, 20X2, and 20X1, the Company recorded a liability related to assumed claims of $2 million and $1.5 million, respectively, and had recorded a receivable from the re-insurance pool of $500,000 and $300,000, respectively.

Real and Personal Property Taxes

Example 3: Estimated Accrual for Real and Personal Property Taxes Is Included in Other Current Liabilities

Occupancy costs include fixed rents, real estate and personal property taxes, insurance, and other property costs. Other current liabilities at December 31, 20X2, and 20X1, include an estimated accrued liability for real and personal property taxes of $300,000 and $250,000, respectively.

Advertising Costs

> **Note:** For sample disclosures of advertising barter transactions, see Chapter 35, "ASC Topic 605: Revenue Recognition."

Example 4: Advertising Costs Are Expensed as Incurred

Advertising costs are expensed as incurred. Advertising expense totaled $477,000 for 20X2 and $392,000 for 20X1.

Example 5: Advertising Costs Are Expensed the First Time the Advertising Takes Place

Production costs of future media advertising are expensed the first time the advertising takes place. Advertising expense totaled $532,000 for 20X2 and $410,000 for 20X1.

Example 6: Direct-Response Advertising Costs Are Capitalized

Direct-response advertising costs, consisting primarily of catalog book production, printing, and postage costs, are capitalized and amortized over the expected life of the catalog, not to exceed six months. Direct-response advertising costs reported as "Prepaid assets" are $275,000 and $350,000 at December 31, 20X2, and December 31, 20X1, respectively. Total advertising expenses were $1,900,000 and $1,600,000 in 20X2 and 20X1, respectively.

Example 7: Certain Advertising Costs Are Expensed the First Time the Advertising Takes Place, and Direct-Response Advertising Costs Are Capitalized and Written Down to Net Realizable Value

The Company expenses the production costs of advertising the first time the advertising takes place, except for direct-response advertising, which is capitalized and amortized over its expected period of future benefits.

Direct-response advertising consists primarily of magazine advertisements that include order coupons for the Company's products. The capitalized costs of the advertising are amortized over the six-month period following the publication of the magazine in which it appears.

At December 31, 20X2, and December 31, 20X1, capitalized direct-response advertising costs of $570,000 and $612,000, respectively, were included in "Other assets" in the accompanying balance sheets. Advertising expense was $5,264,000 in 20X2, including $432,000 for amounts written down to net realizable value related to certain capitalized direct-response advertising costs. Advertising expense was $6,079,000 in 20X1.

Example 8: Advertising Policy on Other Companies' Web Sites Pursuant to Contracts Is Explained

The Company expenses the costs of advertising as incurred. Typically the Company purchases banner advertising on other companies' Web sites pursuant to contracts that have one-to-three year terms and may include the guarantee of (1) a minimum number of impressions, (2) the number of times that an advertisement appears in pages displayed to users of the Web site, or (3) a minimum amount of revenue that will be recognized by the Company from customers directed to the Company's Web site as a direct result of the advertisement. The Company recognizes expense with respect to such advertising ratably over the period in which the advertisement is displayed. In addition, some agreements require additional payments as additional impressions are delivered. Such payments are expensed when the impressions are delivered.

In one case, the Company entered into an agreement for an unspecified number of years. In this case, the Company amortizes as expense the lesser of (1) the number of impressions to date divided by minimum guaranteed impressions or (2) revenue to date divided by minimum guaranteed revenue as a percentage of the total payments.

For the years ended December 31, 20X2, and December 31, 20X1, advertising expense totaled approximately $8,325,000 and $9,890,000, respectively.

CHAPTER 42
ASC TOPIC 730: RESEARCH AND DEVELOPMENT

CONTENTS

EXECUTIVE SUMMARY

Research and Development

Generally, research and development costs should be charged to expense when incurred rather than recorded as inventory, component of overhead, or otherwise capitalized. However, intangibles purchased from others and the costs of materials, equipment, and facilities acquired or constructed for research and development activities, and that have alternative future uses, should be capitalized and amortized over their useful lives. Amortization expense related to such capitalized costs should be considered research and development costs.

If an entity enters into an arrangement with other parties that fund its research and development, the accounting and reporting for research and development costs depend on the nature of the obligation that the entity incurs in the arrangement. The nature of the obligation in such arrangements can be classified in one of the following categories:

1.   The obligation is solely to perform contractual research and development services for others.

2.   The obligation represents a liability to repay all of the funds provided by the other parties.

3.   The obligation is partly to perform contractual services and partly a liability to repay some, but not all, of the funds provided by the other parties.

When software for use in research and development activities is purchased or leased, its cost should be charged to expense as incurred unless the software has alternative future uses (in research and development or otherwise). Development of software to be used in research and development activities includes costs incurred by an entity in developing computer software internally for use in its research and development activities, are research and development costs and, therefore, should be charged to expense when incurred. The alternative future use test does not apply to the internal development of computer software to be used in research and development activities (i.e., the alternative future use test applies only to intangibles purchased from others).

Accounting Literature

FASB Accounting Standards Codification Topic	*Pre-Codification Accounting Literature*
730, *Research and Development*	FAS-2, *Accounting for Research and Development Costs*
	FAS-68, *Research and Development Arrangements*
	FAS-86, *Accounting for the Costs of Computer Software to Be Sold, Leased, or Otherwise Marketed*

DISCLOSURE AND KEY PRESENTATION REQUIREMENTS

1. Disclosure should be made of total research and development costs (including those incurred for computer software to be sold, leased, or otherwise marketed) charged to expense in each period for which an income statement is presented. (ASC 730-10-50-1) (FAS-2, par. 13; FAS-86, par. 12)

2. The following disclosures should be made for an entity that accounts for its obligation under a research and development arrangement as a contract to perform research and development for others (ASC 730-20-50-1) (FAS-68, par. 14):

   a. The terms of significant agreements under the research and development arrangement (including royalty arrangements, purchase provisions, license agreements, and commitments to provide additional funding) as of the date of each balance sheet presented.

   b. The amount of compensation earned and costs incurred under such contracts for each period for which an income statement is presented.

3. For an entity that is a party to more than one research and development arrangement, separate disclosures should be made of each arrangement if necessary to understand the effects on the financial statements. (ASC 730-20-50-3) (FAS-68, par. 14) (*Note:* Aggregation of similar arrangements by type may be appropriate, unless separate disclosure is necessary to understand the effects on the financial statements.)

EXAMPLES OF FINANCIAL STATEMENT DISCLOSURES

 The following sample disclosures are available on the accompanying disc.

Example 1: Research and Development Costs Charged to Expense as Incurred

Expenditures for research activities relating to product development and improvement are charged to expense as incurred. Such expenditures amounted to $546,000 in 20X2 and $612,000 in 20X1.

Example 2: Product Development Costs Deferred

The Company defers certain costs related to the preliminary activities associated with the manufacture of its products, which the Company has determined have future economic benefit. These costs are then expensed in the period in which the initial shipment of the related product is made. Management periodically reviews and revises, when necessary, its estimate of the future benefit of these costs and expenses them if it deems there no longer is a future benefit. At December 31, 20X2, and December 31, 20X1, product development costs capitalized totaled $817,000 and $734,000, respectively.

Example 3: Contract to Perform Research and Development Services for Others

The Company has two contracts with Panax, Inc. under which it is obligated to perform certain specific research and development activities. The Company receives royalties under the terms of one of the contracts and licensing fees under the terms of the other contract. Under both contracts, Panax, Inc. can require the Company to purchase their interest in the research and development. Also, under certain circumstances, the Company is obligated to use its own funds if the amount of funds provided by Panax, Inc. is not sufficient to complete the research and development effort.

Compensation earned and costs incurred by the Company under these contracts for the years ended December 31, 20X2, and December 31, 20X1, are as follows:

	20X2	20X1
Royalties and other fees earned	$1,385,000	$1,266,000
Costs incurred charged to operations	$1,102,000	$1,014,000

At December 31, 20X2, and December 31, 20X1, the Company's commitments to provide additional funding under these contracts amounted to $517,000 and $433,000, respectively.

Example 4: Product Development Costs of Computer Software to Be Sold, Leased, or Otherwise Marketed Are Expensed

Software development costs are expensed as incurred until technological feasibility has been established, at which time such costs are capitalized until the product is available for general release to customers. To date, the Company's software has been available for general release concurrent with the establishment of technological feasibility and, accordingly, no development costs have been capitalized.

Software development costs incurred and charged to research and development expense totaled $415,000 and $327,000 for the years ended December 31, 20X2, and December 31, 20X1, respectively.

Example 5: Product Development Costs of Computer Software to Be Sold, Leased, or Otherwise Marketed Are Capitalized

Research and development costs are charged to expense as incurred. However, the costs incurred for the development of computer software that will be sold, leased, or otherwise marketed are capitalized when technological feasibility has been established. These capitalized costs are subject to an ongoing assessment of recoverability based on anticipated future revenues and changes in hardware and software technologies. Costs that are capitalized include direct labor and related overhead.

Amortization of capitalized software development costs begins when the product is available for general release to customers. Amortization is computed as the greater of (1) the ratio of current gross revenues for a product to the total of current and anticipated future gross revenues for the product or (2) the straight-line method over the estimated economic life of the product. Unamortized capitalized software development costs determined to be in excess of net realizable value of the product are expensed immediately.

During the years ended December 31, 20X2, and December 31, 20X1, the Company capitalized product development costs of $4,765,000 and $3,689,000, respectively. During the years ended December 31, 20X2, and December 31, 20X1, amortization of product development costs totaled $357,000 and $346,000, respectively. In addition, in September 20X2, the Company charged $673,000 to operations as a write-down of capitalized computer software costs to their estimated net realizable value.

CHAPTER 43
ASC TOPIC 740: INCOME TAXES

CONTENTS

EXECUTIVE SUMMARY

Income Taxes

The tax consequences of many transactions recognized in the financial statements are included when determining income taxes currently payable in the same accounting period. Sometimes, tax laws differ from the recognition and measurement requirements of financial reporting standards. Differences arise between the tax bases of assets or liabilities and their reported amounts in the financial statements. These differences are called *temporary differences* and they give rise to deferred tax assets and liabilities.

Temporary differences ordinarily reverse when the related asset is recovered or the related liability is settled. A *deferred tax liability* or *deferred tax asset* represents the increase or decrease in taxes payable or refundable in future years as a result of temporary differences and carryforwards at the end of the current year.

The objectives of accounting for income taxes are to recognize:

- The amount of taxes payable or refundable for the current year
- The deferred tax liabilities and assets that result from future tax consequences of events that have been recognized in the enterprise's financial statements or tax returns

To implement these objectives, the following basic principles should be observed at the date of the financial statements:

1. Recognize a *tax liability* or *asset* for the amount of taxes currently payable or refundable.

2. Recognize a *deferred tax liability* or *asset* for the estimated future tax effects of temporary differences or carryforwards.

3. Measure *current* and *deferred tax assets* and *liabilities* based on provisions of enacted tax laws.

4. Reduce the amount of any deferred *tax assets* by a valuation allowance, if necessary, based on available evidence.

The emphasis placed on the balance sheet by the asset/liability method of accounting for income taxes is evident from the focus on the recognition of deferred tax liabilities and assets. The change in these liabilities and assets is combined with the income taxes currently payable or refundable to determine income tax expense.

Accounting Literature

FASB Accounting Standards Codification Topic	*Pre-Codification Accounting Literature*
740, *Income Taxes*	FAS-37, *Balance Sheet Classification of Deferred Income Taxes*
	FAS-109, *Accounting for Income Taxes*

FASB Accounting Standards Codification Topic	*Pre-Codification Accounting Literature*
	FIN-18, *Accounting for Income Taxes in Interim Periods*
	FIN-48, *Accounting for Uncertainty in Income Taxes—An Interpretation of FASB Statement No. 109*
	FSP FIN 48-3, *Effective Date of FASB Interpretation No. 48 for Certain Nonpublic Enterprises*
	EITF 93-13, *Effect of a Retroactive Change in Enacted Tax Rates That Is Included in Income from Continuing Operations*
	EITF 94-10, *Accounting by a Company for the Income Tax Effects of Transactions among or with Its Shareholders under FASB Statement No. 109*
	EITF 98-11, *Accounting for Acquired Temporary Differences in Certain Purchase Transactions That Are Not Accounted for as Business Combinations*
	EITF D-30, *Adjustment Due to Effect of a Change in Tax Laws or Rates*
	EITF D-32, *Intraperiod Tax Allocation of the Tax Effect of Pretax Income from Continuing Operations*
	FASB Staff Implementation Guide (Q&A), *A Guide to Implementation of Statement 109 on Accounting for Income Taxes: Questions and Answers*
	APB-2, *Accounting for the "Investment Credit"*

FASB Accounting Standards Codification Topic	Pre-Codification Accounting Literature
	APB-4, *Accounting for the "Investment Credit" (Amending No. 2)*
	APB-10, *Omnibus Opinion—1966*

DISCLOSURE AND KEY PRESENTATION REQUIREMENTS

Overall

1. The following balance sheet-related presentation and disclosure items should be addressed:

   a. Deferred tax liabilities and assets should be classified separately into current and noncurrent amounts based on the classification of the related asset or liability for financial reporting. (ASC 740-10-45-4 and 45-7) (FAS-37, par. 4; FAS-109, par. 41)

   b. The valuation allowance for a particular tax jurisdiction should be allocated between current and noncurrent deferred tax assets for that tax jurisdiction on a pro rata basis. (ASC 740-10-45-5) (FAS-109, par. 41)

   c. For a particular tax-paying component of an entity and within a particular tax jurisdiction (e.g., federal, state, or local) (ASC 740-10-45-6) (FAS-109, par. 42):

      (1) All current deferred tax liabilities and assets should be offset and presented as a single amount.

      (2) All noncurrent deferred tax liabilities and assets should be offset and presented as a single amount.

      (3) Deferred tax liabilities and assets attributable to different tax-paying components of the entity, or to different tax jurisdictions, should *not* be offset.

   d. A deferred tax liability or asset that is not related to an asset or liability for financial reporting (e.g., contracts accounted for by the percentage-of-completion method for financial reporting and by the completed-contract method for tax purposes), including deferred tax assets related to carryforwards, should be classified according to the expected reversal date of the temporary difference. (ASC 740-10-45-9) (FAS-109, par. 41)

   e. Cash or other assets should *not* be offset against the tax liability or other amounts owing to governmental bodies (except when governments issue securities that are specifically designated as being acceptable for the payment of taxes of those governments). (ASC 740-10-45-13; 210-20-45-6 and 45-7) (APB-10, par. 7)

f. The following components of the net deferred tax liability or asset recognized in the balance sheet should be disclosed (ASC 740-10-50-2) (FAS-109, par. 43):

   (1) The total of all deferred tax liabilities for taxable temporary differences.

   (2) The total of all deferred tax assets for deductible temporary differences, operating loss carryforwards, and tax credit carryforwards.

   (3) The total valuation allowance recognized for deferred tax assets.

g. The net change during the year in the total valuation allowance should be disclosed. (ASC 740-10-50-2) (FAS-109, par. 43)

h. The amounts and expiration dates of operating loss and tax credit carryforwards for tax purposes should be disclosed. (ASC 740-10-50-3) (FAS-109, par. 48)

   Note: The disclosure requirement in item (i) below is prescribed by ASC Topic 740, *Income Taxes*, based on FAS-141R, *Business Combinations*, which is effective for business combinations for which the acquisition date is on or after the beginning of the first annual reporting period beginning on or after December 15, 2008. For business combinations prior to this effective date, the disclosure requirement in item (ii) below is to be followed. (ASC 805-10-65-1) (FAS-141R, pars. 74–76 and A130–A134)

i. Any portion of the valuation allowance for deferred tax assets for which subsequently recognized tax benefits will be credited directly to contributed capital should be disclosed. (ASC 740-10-50-3) (FAS-109, par. 48)

j. Any portion of the valuation allowance for deferred tax assets for which subsequently recognized tax benefits will be allocated to reduce goodwill or other noncurrent intangible assets of an acquired entity or directly to contributed capital should be disclosed. (ASC 740-10-50-3) (FAS-09, par. 48)

k. When a change in an entity's tax status becomes effective after the balance sheet date but before the financial statements are issued or are available to be issued, disclosures should be made of the change in the entity's tax status and the effects of that change, if material. (ASC 740-10-50-4) (Q&A-109, par. 11)

l. The types of significant temporary differences and carry-forwards should be disclosed. (ASC 740 10-50-8) (FAS-109, par. 43) (*Note:* This disclosure is applicable only to nonpublic entities.)

2. The following income statement-related presentation and disclosure items should be addressed:

    a. For changes in tax laws or rates:

        (1) When deferred tax accounts are adjusted for the effect of a change in tax laws or rates, the effect should be included in income from continuing operations for the period that includes the enactment date. (ASC 740-10-45-15) (FAS-109, par. 27)

        (2) When a tax law retroactively changes tax rates, the cumulative tax effect should be included in income from continuing operations. (ASC 740-10-45-16) (EITF 93-13)

        (3) For a change in tax rates on items not included in income from continuing operations that arose during the current fiscal year and prior to the date of enactment, the tax effect of a retroactive change in enacted tax rates on current or deferred tax assets and liabilities related to those items should be included in income from continuing operations in the period of enactment. (ASC 740-10-45-17) (EITF 93-13)

        (4) If an entity were adopting a new accounting standard as of a date prior to the enactment date, the effect of the change in tax laws or rates should be recognized in income from continuing operations for the period that includes the enactment date. (ASC 740-10-45-18) (EITF D-30)

    b. When deferred tax accounts are recognized or derecognized due to a change in tax status, the effect of recognizing or derecognizing the deferred tax liability or asset should be included in income from continuing operations. (ASC 740-10-45-19) (FAS-109, par. 28)

    c. The effect of a change in the beginning-of-the-year balance of a valuation allowance that results from a change in circumstances that causes a change in judgment about the realizability of the related deferred tax asset in future years ordinarily should be included in income from continuing operations. (ASC 740-10-45-20) (FAS-109, par. 26) (*Note*: Limited exceptions apply, mainly related to business combinations, certain equity transactions, and quasi-reorganizations. In addition, the effect of other changes in the balance of a valuation allowance should be allocated among continuing operations and items other than continuing operations.)

d. Changes in valuation allowances due to changed expectations about the realization of deferred tax assets (or a write-off of a preexisting deferred tax asset that can no longer be realized) caused by transactions among or with shareholders should be included in the income statement. (ASC 740-10-45-21) (EITF 94-10)

e. The effect of changes in deferred tax accounts related to assets acquired outside of a business combination should be recognized in continuing operations as part of income tax expense. (ASC 740-10-45-22) (EITF 98-11) (*Note:* A proportionate share of any remaining unamortized deferred credit balance should be recognized as an offset to income tax expense and the deferred credit should *not* be classified as part of deferred tax liabilities or as an offset to deferred tax assets.)

f. The significant components of income tax expense related to continuing operations should be disclosed for each year presented, including the following (ASC 740-10-50-9) (FAS-109, par. 45):

   (1) Current tax expense or benefit.

   (2) Deferred tax expense or benefit (exclusive of items listed below).

   (3) Investment tax credits.

   (4) Government grants (to the extent they have been used to reduce income tax expense).

   (5) The benefits of operating loss carryforwards.

   (6) Tax expense that results from allocating certain tax benefits directly to contributed capital. (*Note:* This disclosure item is prescribed by ASC Topic 805, *Business Combinations*, based on FAS-141R, *Business Combinations*, which is effective for business combinations for which the acquisition date is on or after the beginning of the first annual reporting period beginning on or after December 15, 2008. For business combinations prior to this effective date, an entity should disclose the tax expense that results from allocating certain tax benefits either directly to contributed capital or to reduce goodwill or other noncurrent intangible assets of an acquired entity.) (ASC 805-10-65-1) (FAS-141R, pars. 74–76 and A130–A134)

(7) Adjustments to a deferred tax liability or asset arising from changes in tax laws, tax rates, or the entity's tax status.

(8) Adjustments of the beginning-of-the-year balance of a valuation allowance because of a change in circumstances that causes a change in judgment about the realizability of the related deferred tax asset in future years.

g. The amount of income tax expense or benefit should be properly allocated (intraperiod income tax allocation) to each of the following components of comprehensive income and shareholders' equity and disclosed for each year for which the items are presented (ASC 740-10-50-10; 740-20-45-1 through 45-14; 852-740-45-3) (FAS-109, pars. 26, 35–39, 46, 140, 144, 145; EITF D-32; EITF 94-10):

(1) Continuing operations.

(2) Discontinued operations.

(3) Extraordinary items.

(4) Other comprehensive income.

(5) Items charged or credited directly to shareholders' equity.

h. The nature of significant reconciling items should be disclosed between (a) the reported amount of income tax expense attributable to continuing operations for the year and (b) the amount of income tax expense that would result from applying domestic federal statutory tax rates to pretax income from continuing operations. (ASC 740-10-50-13) (FAS-109, par. 47) (*Note*: A numerical reconciliation, such as the one applicable to public entities, is not required for nonpublic entities.)

3. The method of accounting for investment tax credits (deferral method or flow-through method) and related amount used in the determination of income tax expense should be disclosed. (ASC 740-10-45-27 and 45-28; 740-10-50-20) (APB-2, pars. 14 and 15; APB-4, par. 11)

4. The nature and effect of any other significant matters affecting comparability of information for all periods presented should be disclosed if not otherwise evident from the disclosures discussed in this section. (ASC 740-10-50-14) (FAS-109, par. 47)

5. If the entity is a member of a group that files a consolidated tax return, the following disclosures should be made in its separately issued financial statements (ASC 740-10-50-17) (FAS-109, par. 49):

a. The aggregate amount of current and deferred tax expense for each income statement presented.

b. The amount of any tax-related balances due to or from affiliates as of the date of each balance sheet presented.

c. The principal provisions of the method by which the consolidated amount of current and deferred tax expense is allocated to members of the group and the nature and effect of any changes in that method (and in determining related balances to or from affiliates) during the years for which the disclosures in (a) and (b) above are presented.

Unrecognized Tax Benefits

Note: The requirements in items 1 through 5 below are prescribed by ASC Topic 740, *Income Taxes*, based on FIN-48, *Accounting for Uncertainty in Income Taxes*. For nonpublic enterprises (as defined), these requirements were initially effective for annual financial statements for fiscal years beginning after December 15, 2007 (applied as of the beginning of the enterprise's fiscal year.) Nonpublic enterprises that issued a full set of annual financial statements using the recognition, measurement, and disclosure provisions of FIN-48, prior to February 1, 2008, must continue to apply the guidance based on FIN-48. FASB Staff Position (FSP) FIN 48-3, *Effective Date of FASB Interpretation No. 48 for Certain Nonpublic Enterprises*, which was issued in December 2008, deferred the effective date for nonpublic enterprises (as defined) to annual financial statements for fiscal years beginning after December 15, 2008 (applied as of the beginning of the enterprise's fiscal year). Nonpublic enterprises that elect this deferral should make the disclosures in item 6 below. Nonpublic enterprises that have applied the recognition, measurement, and disclosure provisions based on FIN-48 in a full set of annual financial statements issued before December 30, 2008, are not eligible for the deferral. (ASC 740-10-65-1) (FSP FIN 48-3)

Note: The disclosure requirements in items 3 (a) and (b) below are to be followed until the adoption of the guidance in Accounting Standards Update (ASU) No. 2009-06, *Income Taxes (Topic 740)—Implementation Guidance on Accounting for Uncertainty in Income Taxes and Disclosure Amendments for Nonpublic Entities*, which is effective for interim and annual periods ending after September 15, 2009. ASU 2009-06 eliminates the disclosure requirements in items 3 (a) and (b) below for nonpublic entities. For nonpublic entities that have deferred the application of accounting for uncertainty in income taxes in accordance with paragraph 740-10-65-1(e), as discussed in the note above, the guidance in ASU 2009-06 is effective upon the adoption of those standards.

1. A liability associated with an unrecognized tax benefit should be classified as a current liability (or the amount of a net operating loss carryforward or amount refundable is reduced) to the extent the entity anticipates payment (or receipt) of cash within one year (or the operating cycle, if longer). (ASC 740-10-45-11) (FIN-48, par. 17) (*Note*: The liability for unrecognized tax benefits (or reduction in amounts refundable) should not be combined with deferred tax liabilities or assets.)

2. A liability for an unrecognized tax benefit should *not* be classified as a deferred tax liability unless it arises from a taxable temporary difference. (ASC 740-10-45-12) (FIN-48, par. 18)

3. The following items should be disclosed for each annual reporting period presented (ASC 740-10-50-15) (FIN-48, par. 21):

    a. A tabular reconciliation of the total amounts of unrecognized tax benefits at the beginning and end of the period, which should include at a minimum:

        (1) The gross amounts of the increases and decreases in unrecognized tax benefits as a result of tax positions taken during a prior period.

        (2) The gross amounts of increases and decreases in unrecognized tax benefits as a result of tax positions taken during the current period.

        (3) The amounts of decreases in the unrecognized tax benefits relating to settlements with taxing authorities.

        (4) Reductions to unrecognized tax benefits as a result of a lapse of the applicable statute of limitations.

    b. The total amount of unrecognized tax benefits that, if recognized, would affect the effective tax rate.

    c. The total amounts of interest and penalties recognized in the income statement and the total amounts of interest and penalties recognized in the balance sheet.

    d. For positions for which it is reasonably possible that the total amounts of unrecognized tax benefits will significantly increase or decrease within 12 months of the reporting date:

        (1) The nature of the uncertainty.

        (2) The nature of the event that could occur in the next 12 months that would cause the change.

   (3) An estimate of the range of the reasonably possible change or a statement that an estimate of the range cannot be made.

   e. A description of tax years that remain subject to examination by major tax jurisdictions.

4. For penalties and interest related to underpayment of income taxes:

   a. Penalties should be classified as either income taxes or another expense classification, and interest should be classified as either income taxes or interest expense, based on the accounting policy election of the entity, consistently applied. (ASC 740-10-45-25) (FIN-48, par. 19)

   b. Disclosure should be made of the entity's policy on classification of penalties and interest. (ASC 740-10-50-19) (FIN-48, par. 20)

5. In the initial year of adoption, the cumulative effect of the change on retained earnings as of the date of adoption should be disclosed. (FIN-48, par. 24)

6. For nonpublic entities that have elected to defer the adoption of the guidance based on FIN-48 under FSP FIN 48-3, have the following disclosures been made (ASC 740-10-65-1) (FSP FIN 48-3, par .10):

   a. The fact that the nonpublic entity has elected to defer the application of ASC Topic 740 based on FIN-48.

   b. The nonpublic entity's accounting policy for evaluating uncertain tax positions in each set of financial statements to which the deferral applies.

Additional Required Disclosures for Public Entities

1. The following additional required disclosures should be made by *public* entities (optional for nonpublic entities):

   a. The approximate tax effect of each type of temporary difference and carryforward that gives rise to a significant portion of deferred tax liabilities and assets (before allocation of valuation allowance). (ASC 740-10-50-6) (FAS-109, par. 43)

   b. A reconciliation (using percentages or dollar amounts) of the reported amount of income tax expense attributable to continuing operations for the year to the amount of income tax expense that would result from applying domestic federal statutory tax rates to pretax income from continuing operations. (ASC 740-10-50-12) (FAS-109, par. 47) (*Note:* If alternative tax systems exist, such as the U.S. alternative minimum tax, the regular tax rate should be used.)

c. For a public entity that is not subject to income taxes because its income is taxed directly to its owners, the entity should disclose that fact and the net difference between the tax bases and the reported amounts of the entity's assets and liabilities. (ASC 740-10-50-16) (FAS-109, par. 43)

2. The following items should be disclosed by *public* entities for each annual reporting period presented (ASC 740-10-50-15 and 15A) (FIN-48, par. 21):

a. A tabular reconciliation of the total amounts of unrecognized tax benefits at the beginning and end of the period, which should include at a minimum:

(1) The gross amounts of the increases and decreases in unrecognized tax benefits as a result of tax positions taken during a prior period.

(2) The gross amounts of increases and decreases in unrecognized tax benefits as a result of tax positions taken during the current period.

(3) The amounts of decreases in the unrecognized tax benefits relating to settlements with taxing authorities.

(4) Reductions to unrecognized tax benefits as a result of a lapse of the applicable statute of limitations.

b. The total amount of unrecognized tax benefits that, if recognized, would affect the effective tax rate.

Intraperiod Tax Allocation

1. The amount of income tax expense or benefit should be properly allocated to each of the following components of comprehensive income and shareholders' equity (intraperiod income tax allocation) and disclosed for each year for which the items are presented (ASC 740-10-50-10; 740-20-45-1 through 45-14; 852-740-45-3) (FAS-109, pars. 26, 35–39, 46, 140, 144, 145; EITF D-32; EITF 94-10):

a. Continuing operations.

b. Discontinued operations.

c. Extraordinary items.

d. Other comprehensive income.

e. Items charged or credited directly to shareholders' equity.

Other Considerations or Special Areas

1. The following disclosures should be made whenever a deferred tax liability is not recognized because of the exceptions to comprehensive recognition of deferred taxes related to subsidiaries and corporate joint ventures (ASC 740-30-50-2) (FAS-109, pars. 44 and 145):

   a. A description of the types of temporary differences for which a deferred tax liability has not been recognized and the types of events that would cause those temporary differences to become taxable.

   b. The cumulative amount of each type of temporary difference.

   c. The amount of the unrecognized deferred tax liability for temporary differences related to investments in foreign subsidiaries and foreign corporate joint ventures that are essentially permanent in duration if determination of that liability is practicable, or a statement that determination is not practicable. (*Note:* While ASC paragraph 740-30-25-14 (FAS-109, par. 145) prohibits recognition of a tax benefit for tax deductions or favorable tax rates attributable to future dividends of undistributed earnings for which a deferred tax liability has not been recognized, favorable tax treatment would be reflected in measuring that unrecognized deferred tax liability for disclosure purposes.)

   d. The amount of unrecognized deferred tax liability for temporary differences other than those in item (c) above (i.e., undistributed domestic earnings).

Interim Reporting

1. For interim periods, the tax allocation computation should be made using the estimated fiscal year ordinary income together with unusual items, infrequently occurring items, discontinued operations, and extraordinary items for the year-to-date period, including the following (ASC 740-270-45-1 through 45-8) (FIN-18, pars. 16–20):

   a. Extraordinary items and discontinued operations that will be presented net of related tax effects in the financial statements for the fiscal year should be presented net of related tax effects in interim financial statements.

   b. Unusual or infrequent occurring items that will be separately disclosed in the financial statements for the fiscal year should be separately disclosed as a component of pretax income from continuing operations, and the tax (or benefit) related to such items should be included in the tax (or benefit) related to continuing operations.

2. Disclosures should be made of the reasons for significant variations in the customary relationship between income tax expense and pretax accounting income, if they are not otherwise apparent from the interim period financial statements or from the nature of the entity's business. (ASC 740-270-50-1) (FIN-18, par. 25)

EXAMPLES OF FINANCIAL STATEMENT DISCLOSURES

The following sample disclosures are available on the accompanying disc. For examples of income tax disclosures that are typically described in a note summarizing a company's significant accounting policies, see Chapter 8, "ASC Topic 235: Notes to Financial Statements."

Example 1: Company's Disclosure of the Provision for Income Taxes, Reconciliation of Statutory Rate to Effective Rate, and Significant Components of Deferred Tax Assets and Liabilities

Note: A non-public company may, alternatively, describe in a narrative format the major reconciling items between the statutory tax rate and effective tax rate and the significant components of deferred tax assets and liabilities as shown in Example 2 below.

The federal and state income tax provision (benefit) is summarized as follows:

	Year Ended December 31	
	20X2	*20X1*
Current:		
Federal	$ 250,000	$ (45,000)
State	50,000	5,000
	300,000	(40,000)
Deferred:		
Federal	(80,000)	(125,000)
State	(20,000)	30,000
	(100,000)	(95,000)
Total provision (benefit) for income taxes	$ 200,000	$(135,000)

A reconciliation of the provision (benefit) for income taxes with amounts determined by applying the statutory U.S. federal income tax rate to income before income taxes is as follows:

	Year Ended December 31	
	20X2	20X1
Computed tax at the federal statutory rate of 34%	$ 700,000	$(150,000)
State taxes, net of federal benefit	30,000	20,000
Write-down of asset not deductible	80,000	450,000
Foreign sales corporation benefits	(15,000)	(10,000)
Corporate-owned life insurance	10,000	-0-
Tax exempt interest	(75,000)	(15,000)
Research and development tax credits	(290,000)	-0-
Operating loss carryforwards	(300,000)	(400,000)
Valuation allowance	-0-	(20,000)
Settlement of prior years' audit issues	50,000	-0-
Adjustment of prior years' accruals	15,000	-0-
Other	(5,000)	(10,000)
Provision (benefit) for income taxes	$ 200,000	$(135,000)
Effective income tax rate	10%	(31%)

Deferred income taxes reflect the net tax effects of temporary differences between the carrying amounts of assets and liabilities for financial reporting purposes and the amounts used for income tax purposes. Significant components of the Company's deferred tax assets and liabilities are as follows:

	As of December 31	
	20X2	20X1
Deferred tax assets:		
Inventory capitalization	$450,000	$675,000
Inventory obsolescence	300,000	125,000
LIFO inventory valuation	200,000	150,000
Intercompany profit in inventory	75,000	50,000
Allowance for doubtful accounts	50,000	100,000
Allowance for sales returns	100,000	150,000
Warranty expense	300,000	400,000

	As of December 31	
	20X2	*20X1*
Postretirement benefit obligation	250,000	125,000
Deferred compensation	100,000	50,000
Accrued vacation	125,000	75,000
Deferred revenue	275,000	200,000
Unrealized foreign exchange losses	15,000	10,000
Net operating losses carryforwards	300,000	400,000
Tax credits carryforwards	200,000	100,000
AMT credit	50,000	25,000
Other	5,000	10,000
Total deferred tax assets	2,795,000	2,645,000
Deferred tax liabilities:		
Difference between book and tax depreciation	1,755,000	1,515,000
Unrealized gains on marketable securities	75,000	60,000
Unrealized foreign exchange gains	25,000	40,000
Unremitted earnings of subsidiaries	75,000	50,000
Other	15,000	5,000
Total deferred tax liabilities	1,945,000	1,670,000
Net deferred tax assets before valuation allowance	850,000	975,000
Valuation allowance	(200,000)	(500,000)
Net deferred tax assets	$ 650,000	$ 475,000

Example 2: Company's Disclosure of the Provision for Income Taxes, Major Reconciling Items between the Statutory Tax Rate and Effective Tax Rate, and the Significant Components of Deferred Tax Assets and Liabilities

> **Note:** This example is applicable only to non-public entities. For a sample disclosure that is applicable to a public entity, see Example 1 above.

The federal and state income tax provision (benefit) is summarized as follows:

	Year Ended December 31	
	20X2	20X1
Current:		
Federal	$ 250,000	$ (45,000)
State	50,000	5,000
	300,000	(40,000)
Deferred:		
Federal	(80,000)	(125,000)
State	(20,000)	30,000
	(100,000)	(95,000)
Total provision (benefit) for income taxes	$ 200,000	$(135,000)

The Company's effective income tax rate is lower than what would be expected if the federal statutory rate were applied to income before income taxes primarily because of certain expenses deductible for financial reporting purposes that are not deductible for tax purposes, tax-exempt interest income, research and development tax credits, and operating loss carryforwards.

Deferred income taxes reflect the net tax effects of temporary differences between the carrying amounts of assets and liabilities for financial reporting purposes and the amounts used for income tax purposes. The major temporary differences that give rise to the deferred tax assets and liabilities are as follows: inventory capitalization, LIFO inventory valuation, provision for doubtful accounts, warranty expense, post-retirement benefit obligation, deferred compensation, depreciation, net operating losses carryforwards, and tax credits carryforwards.

Example 3: Disclosure of Net Operating Losses and Tax Credits Carryforwards

At December 31, 20X2, the Company has available unused net operating losses and investment tax credits carryforwards that may be applied against future taxable income and that expire as follows:

Year of Expiration	Net Operating Losses Carryforwards	Investment Tax Credits Carryforwards
20X3	$3,000,000	$1,000,000
20X4	1,000,000	2,000,000
20X5	6,000,000	4,000,000

Year of Expiration	Net Operating Losses Carryforwards	Investment Tax Credits Carryforwards
20X6	4,000,000	3,000,000
20X7	3,000,000	1,000,000
Thereafter up to 20X9	8,000,000	2,000,000
	$25,000,000	$13,000,000

In addition, the Company has available Alternative Minimum Tax credit carryforwards for tax purposes of approximately $1,800,000, which may be used indefinitely to reduce regular federal income taxes.

Example 4: Company Has Substantial Net Operating Loss Carryforwards and a Valuation Allowance Is Recorded

For the years ended December 31, 20X2, and December 31, 20X1, the Company incurred net operating losses and, accordingly, no provision for income taxes has been recorded. In addition, no benefit for income taxes has been recorded due to the uncertainty of the realization of any tax assets. At December 31, 20X2, the Company had approximately $12,500,000 of federal and $8,300,000 of state net operating losses. The net operating loss carryforwards, if not utilized, will begin to expire in 20X9 for federal purposes and in 20X5 for California purposes.

The components of the Company's deferred tax assets/liabilities are as follows:

	As of December 31	
	20X2	20X1
Deferred tax assets:		
Reserves and accruals	$ 613,000	$ 250,000
Credit carryforwards	655,000	367,000
Net operating loss carryforwards	4,700,000	2,645,000
Total deferred tax assets	5,968,000	3,262,000
Deferred tax liabilities:		
Depreciation and amortization	(275,000)	(210,000)
Net deferred tax assets before valuation allowance	5,693,000	3,052,000
Less: Valuation allowance	(5,693,000)	(3,052,000)
Net deferred tax assets	$ -0-	$ -0-

For financial reporting purposes, the Company has incurred a loss in each period since its inception. Based on the available objective evidence, including the Company's history of losses, management believes it is more likely than not that the net deferred tax assets will not be fully realizable. Accordingly, the Company provided for a full valuation allowance against its net deferred tax assets at December 31, 20X2, and December 31, 20X1.

A reconciliation between the amount of income tax benefit determined by applying the applicable U.S. statutory income tax rate to pre-tax loss is as follows:

	Year Ended December 31	
	20X2	*20X1*
Federal statutory rate	$(1,020,000)	$(850,000)
State tax, net of federal impact	(30,000)	(50,000)
Nondeductible stock compensation	370,000	150,000
Tax credit carryforwards generated	(10,000)	(125,000)
Write-off of acquisition related assets	540,000	50,000
Change in valuation allowance on deferred tax assets	150,000	825,000
	$ -0-	$ -0-

Example 5: Company Discloses Its Consideration of Sufficient Positive Evidence to Support Its Conclusion Not to Record a Valuation Allowance

A significant portion of the deferred tax assets recognized relate to net operating loss and credit carryforwards. Because the Company operates in multiple overseas jurisdictions, it considered the need for a valuation allowance on a country-by-country basis, taking into account the effects of local tax law. Where a valuation allowance was not recorded, the Company believes that there was sufficient positive evidence to support its conclusion not to record a valuation allowance. Management believes that the Company will utilize the loss carryforwards in the future because (1) prior to the restructuring charges, the Company had a history of pre-tax income; (2) a significant portion of the loss carryforwards resulted from restructuring costs; (3) management believes that the restructuring of the Company's businesses will reduce their cost structures and that the Company will be profitable and will generate taxable income in the near term; (4) management is aware of viable tax strategies that could be implemented to accelerate taxable income in order to realize a substantial portion of the recorded deferred tax assets; and (5) a significant portion of the net operating losses have an indefinite life or do not expire in the near term. However, there can be no assurance that the Company will generate taxable income or that all of its loss carryforwards will be utilized.

Example 6: Change in Valuation Allowance During the Year Is Described

In 20X2, the valuation allowance increased approximately $1,950,000, composed of increases to allowances due to the uncertainty of realizing research and development tax credits, tax benefits from certain asset impairment write-downs, and net operating loss carryforwards.

Example 7: Reduction in Valuation Allowance Recorded as an Increase in Additional Paid-in Capital in Connection with "Fresh-Start" Accounting

As of December 31, 20X0, the Company had various net deferred tax assets made up primarily of the expected future tax benefit of net operating loss carryforwards, various credit carryforwards, and reserves not yet deductible for tax purposes. A valuation allowance was provided in full against these net deferred tax assets upon the Company's emergence from bankruptcy when "fresh-Start" reporting was adopted.

During 20X2 and 20X1, the Company reduced the valuation allowance related to the remaining net tax assets by $2,800,000 and $1,900,000, respectively. The reduction reflects the Company's expectation that it is more likely than not that it will generate future taxable income to utilize this amount of net deferred tax assets. The benefit from this reduction was recorded as an increase in additional paid-in capital.

Example 8: Tax Benefits Associated with Stock Options Recorded as an Increase to Additional Paid-in Capital

During 20X2 and 20X1, the Company recognized certain tax benefits related to stock option plans in the amount of $1,200,000 and $800,000, respectively. Such benefits were recorded as a reduction of income taxes payable and an increase in additional paid-in capital.

Example 9: Deferred Taxes Not Provided on Undistributed Earnings of Foreign Subsidiaries—Amount of Deferred Tax Liability Not Disclosed

A provision has not been made at December 31, 20X2, for U.S. or additional foreign withholding taxes on approximately $10 million of undistributed earnings of foreign subsidiaries because it is the present intention of management to reinvest the undistributed earnings indefinitely in foreign operations. Generally, such earnings become subject to U.S. tax upon the remittance of dividends and under certain other circumstances. It is not practicable to estimate the amount of deferred tax liability on such undistributed earnings.

Example 10: Deferred Taxes Not Provided on Undistributed Earnings of Foreign Subsidiaries—Amount of Deferred Tax Liability Is Disclosed

The Company has not recorded deferred income taxes applicable to undistributed earnings of foreign subsidiaries that are indefinitely reinvested in foreign operations. Undistributed earnings amounted to approximately $6,000,000 and $5,200,000 at December 31, 20X2, and December 31, 20X1, respectively. If the earnings of such foreign subsidiaries were not definitely reinvested, a deferred tax liability of approximately $1,500,000 and $1,300,000 would have been required at December 31, 20X2, and December 31, 20X1, respectively.

Example 11: Deferred Taxes Recorded on Undistributed Earnings of Foreign Subsidiaries

At December 31, 20X2, the accompanying consolidated Balance Sheet includes a deferred tax liability of $300,000 for the estimated income taxes that will be payable upon the anticipated future repatriation of approximately $1,000,000 of undistributed earnings of foreign subsidiaries in the form of dividends.

Example 12: Subchapter S Status Terminated

Prior to January 1, 20X2, the Company had operated as a C corporation. Effective January 1, 20X2, the stockholders of the Company elected to be taxed under Subchapter S of the Internal Revenue Code. During such period, federal income taxes were the responsibility of the Company's stockholders, as were certain state income taxes. As of the effective date of the election, the Company was responsible for Federal built-in-gain taxes to the extent applicable. Accordingly, the consolidated Statement of Operations for the year ended December 31, 20X2, provides for such taxes. The S corporation election terminated in connection with the consummation of the initial public offering of the Company's common stock on October 10, 20X2.

Example 13: Conversion from an LLC to a C Corporation

From the Company's inception in March 19X7 to February 20X2, the Company was not subject to federal and state income taxes since it was operating as a Limited Liability Company (LLC). On February 2, 20X2, the Company converted from an LLC to a C corporation and, as a result, became subject to corporate federal and state income taxes. The Company's accumulated deficit of $4.3 million at that date was reclassified to additional paid-in capital.

Example 14: Conversion from a C Corporation to an S Corporation

Prior to January 1, 20X2, the Company had operated as a C Corporation. Effective January 1, 20X2, the Company has elected S Corporation status. Earnings and losses after that date will be included in the personal income tax returns of the stockholders and taxed depending on their personal tax strategies. As a result, the Company will not incur any additional income tax obligations, and future financial statements will not include a provision for income taxes. Prior to the change to S Corporation status, income taxes currently payable and deferred income taxes were recorded in the Company's financial statements.

The provision for income taxes consists of the following:

	20X2	20X1
Current	$ –	$ 42,000
Deferred	90,000	(11,000)
	$90,000	$ 31,000

Substantially all of the deferred income tax provision in 20X2 relates to the elimination of the deferred tax asset of $90,000 at the date the election for the change to Subchapter S Status was filed.

Example 15: Conversion from Cash Basis to Accrual Basis for Tax Purposes Results in a Deferred Tax Liability

In the current year, the Company converted from a cash basis to accrual basis for tax purposes in conjunction with its conversion to a C corporation. Due to temporary differences in recognition of revenue and expenses, income for financial reporting purposes exceeded income for income tax purposes. The conversion to the accrual basis along with these temporary differences resulted in the recognition of a net deferred tax liability and a corresponding one-time charge to expense of $3.5 million as of December 31, 20X2.

Example 16: Disclosures about Uncertainty in Income Taxes Prescribed by ASC Topic 740 Based on FIN-48

> **Note:** This example assumes that the reporting entity has adopted the provisions of FIN-48 for the year ended December 31, 2008.

The Company or one of its subsidiaries files income tax returns in the U.S. federal jurisdiction, and various states and foreign jurisdictions. With few exceptions, the Company is no longer subject to U.S. federal, state, and local or non-U.S. income tax examinations by tax authorities for years before 2002. The Internal Revenue Service (IRS) commenced an examination of the Company's U.S. income tax returns for 2003 through 2005 in the first quarter of 2008 that is anticipated to be completed by the end of 2009. As of December 31, 2008, the IRS has proposed certain significant adjustments to the Company's transfer pricing and research credits tax positions. Management is currently evaluating those proposed adjustments to determine if it agrees; but, if accepted, the Company does not anticipate the adjustments would result in a material change to its financial position. However, the Company anticipates that it is reasonably possible that an additional payment in the range of $800,000 to $1,000,000 will be made by the end of 2009.

The Company adopted the provisions of ASC Topic 740, *Income Taxes*, relating to unrecognized tax benefits on January 1, 2008. As a result, the Company recognized approximately a $2,000,000 increase in the liability for unrecognized tax benefits, which was accounted for as a reduction to the January 1, 2008, balance of retained earnings. A reconciliation of the beginning and ending amount of unrecognized tax benefits is as follows:

Balance at January 1, 2008	$3,700,000
Additions based on tax positions related to the current year	100,000
Additions for tax positions of prior years	300,000
Reductions for tax positions of prior years	(600,000)
Settlements	(400,000)
Balance at December 31, 2008	$3,100,000

Included in the balance at December 31, 2008, are $600,000 of tax positions for which the ultimate deductibility is highly certain but for which there is uncertainty about the timing of such deductibility. Because of the impact of deferred tax accounting, other than interest and penalties, the disallowance of the shorter deductibility period would not affect the annual effective tax rate but would accelerate the payment of cash to the taxing authority to an earlier period.

The Company recognizes interest accrued related to unrecognized tax benefits in interest expense and penalties in operating expenses. During the years ended December 31, 2008, 2007, and 2006, the Company recognized approximately $100,000, $110,000, and $120,000 in interest and penalties. The Company had approximately $600,000 and $500,000 for the payment of interest and penalties accrued at December 31, 2008, and 2007, respectively.

Example 17: Disclosures about Uncertainty in Income Taxes Prescribed by ASC Topic 740 Based on Accounting Standards Update No. 2009-06 (Applicable Only to Nonpublic Entities)

> **Note:** The following illustrative disclosures are applicable pursuant to the guidance in Accounting Standards Update (ASU) No. 2009-06, *Income Taxes (Topic 740)—Implementation Guidance on Accounting for Uncertainty in Income Taxes and Disclosure Amendments for Nonpublic Entities*, which is effective for interim and annual periods ending after September 15, 2009. ASU 2009-06 eliminates certain disclosure requirements for nonpublic entities, as previously discussed in this chapter. For nonpublic entities that have deferred the application of accounting for uncertainty in income taxes in accordance with paragraph 740-10-65-1(e), as previously discussed in this chapter, the guidance in ASU 2009-06 is effective upon the adoption of those standards.

The Company or one of its subsidiaries files income tax returns in the U.S. federal jurisdiction, and various states and foreign jurisdictions. With few exceptions, the Company is no longer subject to U.S. federal, state, and local or non-U.S. income tax examinations by tax authorities for years before 2002. The Internal Revenue Service (IRS) commenced an examination of the Company's U.S. income tax returns for 2003 through 2005 in the first quarter of 2009 that is anticipated to be completed by the end of 2010. As of December 31, 2009, the IRS has proposed certain significant adjustments to the Company's transfer pricing and research credits tax positions. Management is currently evaluating those proposed adjustments to determine if it agrees; but, if accepted, the Company does not anticipate the adjustments would result in a material change to its financial position. However, the Company anticipates that it is reasonably possible that an additional payment in the range of $800,000 to $1,000,000 will be made by the end of 2010.

The Company adopted the provisions of ASC Topic 740, *Income Taxes*, relating to unrecognized tax benefits on January 1, 2009. As a result, the Company recognized approximately a $2,000,000 increase in the liability for unrecognized tax benefits, which was accounted for as a reduction to the January 1, 2009, balance of retained earnings.

The Company recognizes interest accrued related to unrecognized tax benefits in interest expense and penalties in operating expenses. During the years ended December 31, 2009 and 2008, the Company recognized approximately $100,000 and $110,000, respectively, in interest and penalties. The Company had approximately

$600,000 and $500,000 for the payment of interest and penalties accrued at December 31, 2009, and 2008, respectively.

Example 18: Election to Defer Application of ASC Topic 740, Income Taxes, Based on FSP FIN 48-3, "Effective Date of FASB Interpretation No. 48 for Certain Nonpublic Enterprises"

In June 2006, the Financial Accounting Standards Board issued FASB Interpretation No. 48 (FIN-48), *Accounting for Uncertainty in Income Taxes—An Interpretation of FASB Statement No. 109.* FIN-48 clarifies the accounting for uncertainty in income taxes recognized in an entity's financial statements in accordance with Statement of Financial Accounting Standards No.109, *Accounting for Income Taxes.* This Interpretation prescribes a recognition threshold and measurement attribute for the financial statement recognition and measurement of a tax position taken or expected to be taken in a tax return. In addition, FIN-48 provides guidance on derecognition, classification, interest and penalties, accounting in interim periods, disclosure, and transition. FASB Staff Position (FSP) FIN 48-3, *Effective Date of FASB Interpretation No. 48 for Certain Nonpublic Enterprises,* which was issued in December 2008, defers the effective date of FIN-48 for nonpublic entities to annual financial statements for fiscal years beginning after December 15, 2008. This guidance was codified into ASC Topic 740, *Income Taxes,* effective July 1, 2009.

The Company has elected to defer the application of this guidance as permitted under generally accepted accounting principles. The Company presently recognizes income tax positions based on management's estimate of whether it is reasonably possible that a liability has been incurred for unrecognized income tax benefits by applying ASC Topic 450, *Contingencies.* The Company will be required to adopt the new requirements in its 2009 annual financial statements. Management is currently assessing the impact of these requirements on its financial statements.

PART 8—
BROAD TRANSACTIONS

CHAPTER 44
ASC TOPIC 805: BUSINESS COMBINATIONS

CONTENTS

EXECUTIVE SUMMARY

ASC Topic 805 Based on Guidance in FAS-141

A *business combination* occurs when an entity (including a new entity formed to complete a business combination) acquires:

1. Net assets that constitute a business (commonly referred to as an *asset acquisition*), or

2. Equity interests of one or more other entities and obtains *control* over that entity or entities (commonly referred to as a *stock acquisition*). Control is generally indicated by ownership by one company, directly or indirectly, of over 50% of the outstanding voting shares of another company.

All business combinations should be accounted for using the purchase method. Under the purchase method of accounting, the purchase price should be allocated to the assets acquired and the liabilities assumed as follows:

1. Assets and liabilities should be recorded at their fair values as of the acquisition date, including intangible assets that meet one of the following criteria:

   a. The intangible assets arise from contractual or other legal rights; those rights do not have to be transferable or separable from the acquired entity or from other rights and obligations

b. The intangible assets can be separated or divided from the acquired entity, and can be sold, transferred, licensed, rented, or exchanged (regardless of whether there is an intent to do so)

2. If the cost of the acquired company exceeds the sum of the amounts assigned to the assets acquired and liabilities assumed, the excess should be recorded as goodwill. An acquired intangible asset that does not meet the criteria in item 1 above should be aggregated and included in the amount recognized as goodwill. Also, the acquiring company should not record as a separate asset any goodwill previously recorded by the acquired company.

3. If the values assigned to the assets acquired and liabilities assumed exceed the cost of the acquired company, the excess (sometimes referred to as negative goodwill) should be allocated as a pro rata reduction of the amounts that otherwise would have been assigned to all of the acquired assets. However, this allocation should exclude the following items:

a. Financial assets other than equity method investments

b. Assets to be disposed of by sale

c. Deferred tax assets

d. Prepaid assets relating to pension or other postretirement benefit plans

e. Any other current assets

If any excess remains after reducing those assets to zero, that remaining excess should be recognized as an extraordinary gain.

ASC Topic 805 Based on Guidance in FAS-141R

In December 2007, the FASB issued Statement of Financial Accounting Standards No. 141 (Revised 2007) (FAS-141R), *Business Combinations* (ASC 805, *Business Combinations*), which replaces FAS-141, *Business Combinations*. The new Statement significantly changes the accounting for business combinations and impact financial statements both on the acquisition date and in subsequent periods. Under the new Statement, an acquiring entity is required to recognize the assets acquired, the liabilities assumed, and any noncontrolling interest in the acquiree, measured at their fair values as of the acquisition date, with limited exceptions.

FAS-141R (ASC 805) applies *prospectively* to business combinations for which the acquisition date is on or after the beginning of the first annual reporting period beginning on or after December 15, 2008 (i.e., January 1, 2009, for entities with calendar year-ends). Earlier adoption *is prohibited.*

The changes in accounting for business combinations under FAS-141R (ASC 805) are extensive and beyond the scope of this Manual. However, the following is a condensed summary of the more significant changes under FAS-141R (ASC 805):

- With limited exceptions, all business combinations (full, partial, or step acquisitions) result in recognizing the identifiable assets and liabilities, as well as the noncontrolling interest in the acquiree, at the full amount of their fair value.

- Equity securities that are issued as part of the purchase price of the acquired entity are measured on the closing date of the transaction.

- Contingent consideration is recognized at fair value at the acquisition date and classified as a liability or as equity. A right to the return of previously transferred consideration is classified as an asset.

- Acquisition costs will be generally expensed as incurred.

- Noncontrolling interests (formerly "minority interests") are valued at fair value at the acquisition date and recognized in the equity section of the balance sheet.

- Assets acquired or liabilities assumed in a business combination that arise from a contingency are recognized at fair value at the acquisition date if the acquisition-date fair value of that asset or liability can be determined during the measurement period (e.g., the acquisition-date fair value of a warranty obligation often can be determined). If the acquisition-date fair value of an asset or a liability arising from a contingency cannot be determined during the measurement period, that asset or a liability is recognized at the acquisition date if both of the following criteria are met: (a) information available before the end of the measurement period indicates that it is probable that an asset existed or that a liability had been incurred at the acquisition date, and (b) the amount of the asset or liability can be reasonably estimated.

- In-process research and development is recorded at fair value as an indefinite-lived intangible asset at the acquisition date.

- Restructuring costs associated with a business combination are generally expensed subsequent to the acquisition date, rather than accrued in the acquisition balance sheet.

- Changes in deferred tax asset valuation allowances and income tax uncertainties after the acquisition date generally will affect income tax expense.

FAS-141R (ASC 805) also includes a substantial number of new disclosure requirements, all of which are addressed in detail later in this chapter.

Accounting Literature

FASB Accounting Standards Codification Topic	*Pre-Codification Accounting Literature*
805, *Business Combinations*	FAS-141, *Business Combinations*
	FAS-141R, *Business Combinations (Effective for fiscal years beginning on or after December 15, 2008)*
	FSP FAS-141R-1, *Accounting for Assets Acquired and Liabilities Assumed in a Business Combination That Arise from Contingencies*
	FAS-109, *Accounting for Income Taxes*
	FIN-4, *Applicability of FASB Statement No. 2 to Business Combinations Accounted for by the Purchase Method*
	FIN-48, *Accounting for Uncertainty in Income Taxes—An Interpretation of FASB Statement No. 109*
	FTB 85-5, *Issues Relating to Accounting for Business Combinations*
	EITF 95-3, *Recognition of Liabilities in Connection with a Purchase Business Combination*
	EITF 04-1, *Accounting For Preexisting Relationships between the Parties to a Business Combination*

DISCLOSURE AND KEY PRESENTATION REQUIREMENTS

Disclosure and Key Presentation Requirements Based on Guidance in FAS-141

> **Note:** The disclosure and key presentation requirements in this section are prescribed by ASC Topic 805, *Business Combinations*, based on FAS-141, *Business Combinations*, which should be followed until the adoption of the revised guidance based on FAS-141R, *Business Combinations*. The requirements of ASC Topic 805 based on FAS-141R (see section below) are effective for business combinations for which the acquisition date is on or after the beginning of the first annual reporting period beginning on or after December 15, 2008. Early adoption is not permitted.

1. The following disclosures should be made in the period in which a material business combination is completed (FAS-141, par. 51):

   a. The name and a brief description of the acquired entity.

   b. The percentage of voting equity interests acquired.

   c. The primary reasons for the acquisition, including a description of the factors that contributed to a purchase price that results in recognition of goodwill.

   d. The period for which the results of operations of the acquired entity are included in the combined entity's income statement.

   e. The cost of the acquired entity and, if applicable, the number of shares of equity interests (e.g., common shares) issued or issuable, the value assigned to those interests, and the basis for determining that value.

   f. A condensed balance sheet disclosing the amount assigned to each major asset and liability caption of the acquired entity at the acquisition date.

   g. Contingent payments, options, or commitments specified in the acquisition agreement and the accounting treatment that will be followed should any such contingency occur.

   h. The amount of purchased research and development assets acquired and written off in the period and the income statement line item in which the amounts written off are aggregated.

   i. If the purchase price allocation has not been finalized, that fact and the reasons therefore.

j. Capital shares reserved for future issuance.

2. If material adjustments are made in the current period to the initial allocation of the purchase price recorded in prior periods, the nature and amount of such adjustments should be disclosed. (FAS-141, par. 51)

3. If the amounts assigned to goodwill or to other intangible assets acquired are significant to the total cost of the acquired entity, the following disclosures should be made (FAS-141, par. 52):

   a. For intangible assets subject to amortization: the amount, residual value, and weighted-average amortization period, in total and by major intangible asset class.

   b. For intangible assets *not* subject to amortization, the total amount assigned and the amount assigned to any major intangible asset class.

   c. The total amount of goodwill and the amount expected to be deductible for tax purposes.

   d. The amount of goodwill by reportable segment, if the combined entity is required to disclose segment information in accordance with ASC 280, *Segment Reporting* (FAS-131, *Disclosures about Segments of an Enterprise and Related Information*).

4. If a series of individually immaterial business combinations that were completed during the period are material in the aggregate, the following disclosures should be made (FAS-141, par. 53):

   a. The number of entities acquired and a brief description of those entities.

   b. The aggregate cost of the acquired entities, the number of equity interests (e.g., common shares) issued or issuable, and the value assigned to those interests.

   c. The aggregate amount of any contingent payments, options, or commitments and the accounting treatment that will be followed should any such contingency occur (if potentially significant to the aggregate cost of the acquired entities).

   d. If the aggregate amount assigned to goodwill or to other intangible assets acquired is significant to the aggregate cost of the acquired entities, the information described in item 3 above should be disclosed.

5. If the combined entity is publicly held (optional for nonpublic companies), the following supplemental information should be disclosed for the period in which a material business combination occurs (or if a series of individually

immaterial business combinations occur that are material in the aggregate) (FAS-141, pars. 54–55):

a. Pro forma results of operations for the current period as though the companies had combined at the beginning of the period, unless the acquisition was at or near the beginning of the period.

b. If comparative statements are presented, pro forma results of operations for the immediately preceding period as though the companies had combined at the beginning of that period.

c. On a pro forma basis, at a minimum: revenue, income before extraordinary items, net income, and earnings per share.

d. The nature and amount of any material, nonrecurring items included in the reported pro forma results of operations.

6. If an extraordinary gain is recognized related to a business combination, the information required by ASC paragraph 225-20-45-11 (APB-30, par. 11), should be disclosed. (FAS-141, par. 56)

7. If a material business combination is completed after the balance sheet date but before the financial statements are issued, the information in items 1 through 3 above should be disclosed, unless not practicable. (FAS-141, par. 57)

8. The following disclosures should be made in the interim financial information of a publicly held entity (optional for nonpublic companies) if a material business combination is completed during the interim period (FAS-141, par. 58):

a. The name and a brief description of the acquired entity.

b. The percentage of voting equity interests acquired.

c. The primary reasons for the acquisition, including a description of the factors that contributed to a purchase price that results in recognition of goodwill.

d. The period for which the results of operations of the acquired entity are included in the combined entity's income statement.

e. The cost of the acquired entity and, if applicable, the number of shares of equity interests (e.g., common shares) issued or issuable, the value assigned to those interests, and the basis for determining that value.

f. Supplemental pro forma information that discloses the results of operations for the current interim period and the current year up to the date of the most recent interim balance sheet presented (and for the corresponding periods in the preceding year) as though the business combination had been completed as of the beginning of the period being reported on. (*Note*: That pro forma information should disclose, at a minimum: revenue, income before extraordinary items, net income, and earnings per share.)

g. The nature and amount of any material, nonrecurring items included in the reported pro forma results of operations.

9. For transfers of net assets or exchanges of shares between entities under common control, the following disclosures should be made (FAS-141, pars. D16-D18):

a. The nature of and effects on earnings per share of nonrecurring intercompany transactions involving long-term assets and liabilities.

b. For the period in which the transfer of assets and liabilities or exchange of equity interests occurred:

(1) The name and brief description of the entity included in the reporting entity as a result of the net asset transfer or exchange of equity interests.

(2) The method of accounting for the transfer of net assets or exchange of equity interests.

10. The following disclosures should be made if a combined entity plans to incur costs from exiting an activity of an acquired entity, involuntarily terminating employees of an acquired entity, or relocating employees of an acquired entity and the activities of the acquired entity that will not be continued are significant to the combined entity's revenues or operating results or the cost recognized from those activities as of the consummation date are material to the combined entity (ASC 420-10-15-3(e); 420-10-50-1; 805-20-55-50 and 55-51) (EITF 95-3, par. 13a-b):

a. For the period in which a purchase business combination occurs:

(1) When the plans to exit an activity or involuntarily terminate or relocate employees of the acquired entity are not final as of the balance sheet date, a description of any unresolved issues, the types of additional liabilities that may result in an adjustment to the purchase price allocation, and how any adjustment will be reported.

(2) A description of the type and amount of liabilities assumed in the purchase price allocation for costs to

exit an activity or involuntarily terminate or relocate employees.

(3) A description of the major actions that make up the plan to exit an activity or involuntarily terminate or relocate employees of an acquired entity.

(4) A description of activities of the acquired entity that will not be continued, including the method of disposition, and the anticipated date of completion and description of employee groups to be terminated or relocated.

b. For all periods presented subsequent to the acquisition date in which a purchase business combination occurred, until a plan to exit an activity or involuntarily terminate or relocate employees of an acquired entity is fully executed:

(1) A description of the type and amount of exit costs, involuntary employee termination costs, and relocation costs paid and charged against the liability.

(2) The amount of any adjustments to the liability account and whether the corresponding entry was an adjustment of the costs of the acquired entity or included in the determination of net income for the period.

11. For business combinations between parties with a preexisting relationship, the following disclosures should be made (EITF 04-1, par. 8):

a. The nature of the preexisting relationship.

b. The settlement amount of the preexisting relationship, if any, and the valuation method used to determine that amount.

c. The amount of any settlement gain or loss recognized and its income statement classification.

Disclosure and Key Presentation Requirements Based on Guidance in FAS-141R

Note: The disclosure and key presentation requirements in this section are prescribed by ASC Topic 805, *Business Combinations*, based on FAS-141R, *Business Combinations*, which is effective for business combinations for which the acquisition date is on or after the beginning of the first annual reporting period beginning on or after December 15, 2008. Early adoption is not permitted.

Overall

1. The acquirer should disclose the following information for each business combination that occurred during the reporting period (ASC 805-10-50-1 and 50-2; 805-20-50-1; 805-30-50-1) (FAS-141R, pars. 67 and 68; FSP FAS-141R-1, par. 14):

    a. The name and a description of the acquiree.

    b. The acquisition date.

    c. The percentage of voting equity interests acquired.

    d. The primary reasons for the business combination and a description of how the acquirer obtained control of the acquiree.

    e. For transactions that are recognized separately from the acquisition of assets and assumptions of liabilities in the business combination:

       (1) A description of each transaction.

       (2) How the acquirer accounted for each transaction.

       (3) The amounts recognized for each transaction and the line item in the financial statements in which each amount is recognized.

       (4) If the transaction is the effective settlement of a pre-existing relationship, the method used to determine the settlement amount.

       (5) The amount of acquisition-related costs.

       (6) The amount recognized as an expense.

       (7) The line item(s) in the income statement in which those expenses are recognized.

       (8) The amount of any issuance costs not recognized as an expense and how they were recognized.

    f. In a business combination achieved in stages:

       (1) The acquisition-date fair value of the equity interest in the acquiree held by the acquirer immediately before the acquisition date.

       (2) The amount of any gain or loss recognized as a result of remeasuring to fair value the equity interest in the acquiree held by the acquirer before the business combination and the line item in the income statement in which that gain or loss is recognized.

    g. For indemnification assets and contingent consideration arrangements:

(1) The amount recognized as of the acquisition date.

(2) A description of the arrangement and the basis for determining the amount of the payment.

(3) An estimate of the range of outcomes (undiscounted) or, if a range cannot be estimated, that fact and the reasons why a range cannot be estimated. (*Note*: If the maximum amount of the payment is unlimited, the acquirer should disclose that fact.)

h. For acquired receivables not subject to the requirements of ASC Subtopic 310-30, *Receivables—Loans and Debt Securities Acquired with Deteriorated Credit Quality* (SOP 03-3, *Accounting for Certain Loans or Debt Securities Acquired in a Transfer*) (*Note*: The disclosure requirements in items (1) through (3) below should be provided by major class of receivables, such as loans, direct finance leases in accordance with ASC Subtopic 840-30, *Leases—Capital Leases* (FAS-13, *Accounting for Leases*), and any other class of receivables):

(1) The fair value of the receivables.

(2) The gross contractual amounts receivable.

(3) The best estimate at the acquisition date of the contractual cash flows not expected to be collected.

i. The amounts recognized as of the acquisition date for each major class of assets acquired and liabilities assumed.

j. For contingencies, the following disclosures should be included in the footnote that describes the business combination (*Note*: An acquirer may aggregate disclosures for assets and liabilities arising from contingencies that are similar in nature):

(1) For assets and liabilities arising from contingencies recognized at the acquisition date: (i) the amounts recognized at the acquisition date and the measurement basis applied, and (ii) the nature of the contingencies.

(2) For contingencies that are not recognized at the acquisition date, the disclosures required by ASC Topic 450 (FAS-5) if the criteria for disclosures therein are met.

k. For each business combination in which the acquirer holds less than 100% of the equity interests in the acquiree at the acquisition date:

(1) The fair value of the noncontrolling interest in the acquiree at the acquisition date.

(2) The valuation technique(s) and significant inputs used to measure the fair value of the noncontrolling interest.

l. A qualitative description of the factors that make up the goodwill recognized, such as expected synergies from combining operations of the acquiree and the acquirer, intangible assets that do not qualify for separate recognition, or other factors.

m. The acquisition-date fair value of the total consideration transferred and the acquisition-date fair value of each major class of consideration, such as:

(1) Cash.

(2) Other tangible or intangible assets, including a business or subsidiary of the acquirer.

(3) Liabilities incurred, for example, a liability for contingent consideration.

(4) Equity interests of the acquirer, including the number of instruments or interests issued or issuable and the method of determining the fair value of those instruments or interests.

n. The total amount of goodwill that is expected to be deductible for tax purposes.

o. If the acquirer is required to disclose segment information in accordance with ASC Subtopic 280-10, *Segment Reporting—Overall* (FAS-131, *Disclosures about Segments of an Enterprise and Related Information*), the amount of goodwill by reportable segment. (*Note:* If the assignment of goodwill to reporting units required by ASC paragraphs 350-20-35-41 through 35-44 (FAS-142, pars. 34 and 35) has not been completed as of the date the financial statements are issued or are available to be issued, the acquirer should disclose that fact.)

p. In a bargain purchase:

(1) The amount of any gain recognized in accordance with ASC paragraph 805-30-25-2 (FAS-141R, par. 36), and the line item in the income statement in which the gain is recognized.

(2) A description of the reasons why the transaction resulted in a gain.

q. If the acquirer is a *public business entity,* as defined:

(1) The amounts of revenue and earnings of the acquiree since the acquisition date included in the

consolidated income statement for the reporting period.

    (2) The revenue and earnings of the combined entity for the current reporting period as though the acquisition date for all business combinations that occurred during the year had been as of the beginning of the annual reporting period (*supplemental pro forma information*).

    (3) If comparative financial statements are presented, the revenue and earnings of the combined entity for the comparable prior reporting period as though the acquisition date for all business combinations that occurred during the current year had occurred as of the beginning of the comparable prior annual reporting period (*supplemental pro forma information*).

  r. For any of the disclosures in item (q) above (applicable only to a *public business entity*) that are impracticable to provide:

    (1) Disclosure of the fact that the information is impracticable to provide.

    (2) An explanation of why disclosure of the information is impracticable to provide.

2. For business combinations with acquisition dates after the reporting date but before the financial statements are issued or are available to be issued, the acquirer should disclose the following (ASC 805-10-50-1, 50-2, and 50-4; 805-20-50-1 and 50-3; 805-30-50-1 and 50-3) (FAS-141R, par. 70):

  a. The information required by item 1 above, if the initial accounting for the business combination is complete at the time the financial statements are issued or are available to be issued.

  b. The following information, if the initial accounting for the business combination is incomplete at the time the financial statements are issued or are available to be issued:

    (1) A description of the disclosures required by item 1 above that could not be made.

    (2) The reason why the disclosures required by item 1 above could not be made.

3. For individually immaterial business combinations occurring during the reporting period that are material collectively, the acquirer should disclose the following information in the aggregate (ASC 805-10-50-1 through 50-3; 805-20-50-1

and 50-2; 805-30-50-1 and 50-2) (FAS-141R, pars. 67-69; FSP FAS-141R-1, par. 14):

a. For transactions that are recognized separately from the acquisition of assets and assumptions of liabilities in the business combination:

  (1) A description of each transaction.

  (2) How the acquirer accounted for each transaction.

  (3) The amounts recognized for each transaction and the line item in the financial statements in which each amount is recognized.

  (4) If the transaction is the effective settlement of a pre-existing relationship, the method used to determine the settlement amount.

  (5) The amount of acquisition-related costs.

  (6) The amount recognized as an expense.

  (7) The line item(s) in the income statement in which those expenses are recognized.

  (8) The amount of any issuance costs not recognized as an expense and how they were recognized.

b. In a business combination achieved in stages:

  (1) The acquisition-date fair value of the equity interest in the acquiree held by the acquirer immediately before the acquisition date.

  (2) The amount of any gain or loss recognized as a result of remeasuring to fair value the equity interest in the acquiree held by the acquirer before the business combination and the line item in the income statement in which that gain or loss is recognized.

c. For indemnification assets and contingent consideration arrangements:

  (1) The amount recognized as of the acquisition date.

  (2) A description of the arrangement and the basis for determining the amount of the payment.

  (3) An estimate of the range of outcomes (undiscounted) or, if a range cannot be estimated, that fact and the reasons why a range cannot be estimated. (*Note*: If the maximum amount of the payment is unlimited, the acquirer should disclose that fact.)

d. For acquired receivables not subject to the requirements of ASC Subtopic 310-30, *Receivables—Loans and Debt Securities Acquired with Deteriorated Credit Quality* (SOP 03-3,

Accounting for Certain Loans or Debt Securities Acquired in a Transfer) (*Note*: The disclosure requirements in items (1) through (3) below should be provided by major class of receivables, such as loans, direct finance leases in accordance with ASC Subtopic 840-30, *Leases—Capital Leases* (FAS-13, *Accounting for Leases*), and any other class of receivables.):

(1) The fair value of the receivables.

(2) The gross contractual amounts receivable.

(3) The best estimate at the acquisition date of the contractual cash flows not expected to be collected.

e. The amounts recognized as of the acquisition date for each major class of assets acquired and liabilities assumed.

f. For contingencies, the following disclosures should be included in the footnote that describes the business combination (*Note*: An acquirer may aggregate disclosures for assets and liabilities arising from contingencies that are similar in nature):

(1) For assets and liabilities arising from contingencies recognized at the acquisition date: (i) the amounts recognized at the acquisition date and the measurement basis applied, and (ii) the nature of the contingencies.

(2) For contingencies that are not recognized at the acquisition date, the disclosures required by ASC Topic 450 (FAS-5) if the criteria for disclosures therein are met.

g. For each business combination in which the acquirer holds less than 100% of the equity interests in the acquiree at the acquisition date:

(1) The fair value of the noncontrolling interest in the acquiree at the acquisition date.

(2) The valuation technique(s) and significant inputs used to measure the fair value of the noncontrolling interest.

h. A qualitative description of the factors that make up the goodwill recognized, such as expected synergies from combining operations of the acquiree and the acquirer, intangible assets that do not qualify for separate recognition, or other factors.

i. The acquisition-date fair value of the total consideration transferred and the acquisition-date fair value of each major class of consideration, such as:

    (1)   Cash.

    (2)   Other tangible or intangible assets, including a business or subsidiary of the acquirer.

    (3)   Liabilities incurred, for example, a liability for contingent consideration.

    (4)   Equity interests of the acquirer, including the number of instruments or interests issued or issuable and the method of determining the fair value of those instruments or interests.

j.   The total amount of goodwill that is expected to be deductible for tax purposes.

k.   If the acquirer is required to disclose segment information in accordance with ASC Subtopic 280-10, *Segment Reporting—Overall* (FAS-131,Disclosures *about Segments of an Enterprise and Related Information*), the amount of goodwill by reportable segment. (*Note:* If the assignment of goodwill to reporting units required by ASC paragraphs 350-20-35-41 through 35-44 (FAS-142, pars. 34 and 35) has not been completed as of the date the financial statements are issued or are available to be issued, the acquirer should disclose that fact.)

l.   In a bargain purchase:

    (1)   The amount of any gain recognized in accordance with ASC paragraph 805-30-25-2 (FAS-141R, par. 36), and the line item in the income statement in which the gain is recognized.

    (2)   A description of the reasons why the transaction resulted in a gain.

m. If the acquirer is a *public business entity,* as defined:

    (1)   The amounts of revenue and earnings of the acquiree since the acquisition date included in the consolidated income statement for the reporting period.

    (2)   The revenue and earnings of the combined entity for the current reporting period as though the acquisition date for all business combinations that occurred during the year had been as of the beginning of the annual reporting period (*supplemental pro forma information*).

    (3)   If comparative financial statements are presented, the revenue and earnings of the combined entity for the comparable prior reporting period as though the acquisition date for all business combinations that occurred during the current year had occurred as of

the beginning of the comparable prior annual reporting period (*supplemental pro forma information*).

n. For any of the disclosures in item (m) above (applicable only to a *public business entity*) that are impracticable to provide:

   (1) Disclosure of the fact that the information is impracticable to provide.

   (2) An explanation of why disclosure of the information is impracticable to provide.

4. For each material business combination, or in the aggregate for individually immaterial business combinations that are material collectively, the acquirer should disclose the following information about the financial effects of adjustments recognized in the current reporting period that relate to business combinations that occurred in the current or previous reporting periods:

   a. If the initial accounting for a business combination is incomplete for particular assets, liabilities, noncontrolling interests, or items of consideration and thus the amounts recognized in the financial statements for the business combination have been determined only provisionally (ASC 805-10-50-5 and 50-6) (FAS-141R, pars. 71 and 72):

      (1) The reasons why the initial accounting is incomplete.

      (2) The assets, liabilities, equity interests, or items of consideration for which the initial accounting is incomplete.

      (3) The nature and amount of any measurement period adjustments recognized during the reporting period in accordance with ASC paragraph 805-10-25-17 (FAS-141R, par. 55).

   b. For each reporting period after the acquisition date until the entity collects, sells, or otherwise loses the right to a contingent consideration asset, or until the entity settles a contingent consideration liability or the liability is cancelled or expires (ASC 805-30-50-4) (FAS-141R, par. 72):

      (1) Any changes in the recognized amounts, including any differences arising upon settlement.

      (2) Any changes in the range of outcomes (undiscounted) and the reasons for those changes.

      (3) The disclosures required by ASC paragraphs 820-10-50-1 through 50-3 (FAS-157, par. 32). See Chapter 48,

"ASC Topic 820: Fair Value Measurements and Disclosures."

   c. A reconciliation of the carrying amount of goodwill at the beginning and end of the reporting period, as required by ASC paragraph 350-20-50-1 (FAS-142, par. 45). (ASC 805-30-50-4) (FAS-141R, par. 72)

5. If the specific disclosures required by ASC Topic 805 (FAS-141R) and other GAAP do not enable users of the financial statements to evaluate: (*a*) the nature and financial effect of a business combination that occurs either during the current reporting period, or after the reporting date but before the financial statements are issued or are available to be issued, or (*b*) the financial effects of adjustments recognized in the current reporting period that relate to business combinations that occurred in the current or previous reporting periods, the acquirer should disclose whatever additional information is necessary to meet those objectives. (ASC 805-10-50-1, 50-5, and 50-7) (FAS-141R, pars. 67, 71, and 73)

Reverse Acquisitions

1. For consolidated financial statements prepared following a reverse acquisition (ASC 805-40-45-1) (FAS-141R, par. A110):

   a. The financial statements should be issued under the name of the legal parent (accounting acquiree) but described in the notes as a continuation of the financial statements of the legal subsidiary (accounting acquirer) with one adjustment to retroactively adjust the accounting acquirer's legal capital to reflect the legal capital of the accounting acquiree.

   b. If comparative information is presented in those consolidated financial statements, it should be retroactively adjusted to reflect the legal capital of the accounting acquiree.

2. Consolidated financial statements prepared following a reverse acquisition should reflect the following items (ASC 805-40-45-2) (FAS-141R, par. A111):

   a. The assets and liabilities of the legal subsidiary (the accounting acquirer) recognized and measured at their precombination carrying amounts.

   b. The assets and liabilities of the legal parent (the accounting acquiree) recognized and measured in accordance with ASC Topic 805 (FAS-141R).

    c. The retained earnings and other equity balances of the legal subsidiary (accounting acquirer) before the business combination.

    d. The amount recognized as issued equity interests in the consolidated financial statements determined by adding the issued equity interest of the legal subsidiary (the accounting acquirer) outstanding immediately before the business combination to the fair value of the legal parent (accounting acquiree) determined in accordance with ASC Topic 805 (FAS-141R). (*Note*: The equity structure, that is, the number and type of equity interests issued, reflects the equity structure of the legal parent, including the equity interests the legal parent issued to effect the combination. Accordingly, the equity structure of the legal subsidiary is restated using the exchange ratio established in the acquisition agreement to reflect the number of shares of the legal parent issued in the reverse acquisition.)

    e. The noncontrolling interest's proportionate share of the legal subsidiary's (accounting acquirer's) precombination carrying amounts of retained earnings and other equity interests.

3. In calculating the weighted-average number of common shares outstanding for purposes of the earnings-per-share (EPS) computation during the period in which the reverse acquisition occurred (ASC 805-40-45-4) (FAS-141R, par. A115):

    a. The number of common shares outstanding from the beginning of that period to the acquisition date should be computed on the basis of the weighted-average number of common shares of the legal acquiree (accounting acquirer) outstanding during the period multiplied by the exchange ratio established in the merger agreement.

    b. The number of common shares outstanding from the acquisition date to the end of that period should be the actual number of common shares of the legal acquirer (the accounting acquiree) outstanding during that period.

4. The basic EPS for each comparative period before the acquisition date presented in the consolidated financial statements following a reverse acquisition should be calculated by dividing (a) the income of the legal acquiree attributable to common shareholders in each of those periods, by (b) the legal acquiree's historical weighted-average number of common shares outstanding multiplied by the exchange ratio

established in the acquisition agreement. (ASC 805-40-45-5) (FAS-141R, par. A116)

Transactions between Entities under Common Control

1. For transfers of net assets or exchanges of equity interests between entities under common control:

   a. The financial statements of the receiving entity should report results of operations for the period in which the transfer occurs as though the transfer of net assets or exchange of equity interests had occurred at the beginning of the period. (ASC 805-50-45-2) (FAS-141R, par. D12) (*Note*: Results of operations for that period will comprise (a) those of the previously separate entities combined from the beginning of the period to the date the transfer is completed and (b) those of the combined operations from that date to the end of the period.)

   b. The receiving entity should present the balance sheet and other financial information as of the beginning of the period as though the assets and liabilities had been transferred at that date. (ASC 805-50-45-4) (FAS-141R, par. D14)

   c. The effects of intercompany transactions on current assets, current liabilities, revenue, and cost of sales for periods presented and on retained earnings at the beginning of the periods presented should be eliminated to the extent possible. (ASC 805-50-45-2) (FAS-141R, par. D12)

   d. Financial statements and financial information presented for prior years should be retrospectively adjusted to furnish comparative information and should indicate clearly that financial data of previously separate entities are combined. (ASC 805-50-45-5) (FAS-141R, par. D13) (*Note*: However, the comparative information in prior years should only be adjusted for periods during which the entities were under common control.)

2. For transfers of net assets or exchanges of equity interests between entities under common control, the following disclosures should be made (ASC 805-50-50-2 through 50-4) (FAS-141R, pars. D12 and D14):

   a. The nature of and effects on earnings per share of nonrecurring intercompany transactions involving long-term assets and liabilities.

   b. For the period in which the transfer of assets and liabilities or exchange of equity interests occurred:

(1)   The name and brief description of the entity included in the reporting entity as a result of the net asset transfer or exchange of equity interests.

(2)   The method of accounting for the transfer of net assets or exchange of equity interests.

c.   Any additional disclosures that are required under ASC Section 850-10-50, Related *Party Disclosures—Overall—Disclosure* (FAS-57, *Related Party Disclosures*). See Chapter 54, "ASC Topic 850: Related Party Disclosures."

Income Tax-Related Matters

1.   For changes in valuation allowances (ASC 805-740-45-2) (FAS-109, par. 30A):

a.   Such changes within the measurement period in valuation allowances for an acquired entity's deferred tax asset that result from new information about facts and circumstances that existed at the acquisition date should be recognized through a corresponding adjustment to goodwill. (*Note*: Once goodwill is reduced to zero, an acquirer should recognize any additional decrease in the valuation allowance as a bargain purchase.)

b.   All other changes in valuation allowances for an acquired entity's deferred tax asset should be reported as a reduction or increase to income tax expense, or a direct adjustment to contributed capital, as required by ASC paragraphs 740-10-45-20 and 45-21 (FAS-109, par. 26; EITF 94-10).

2.   For changes in acquired income tax positions (ASC 805-740-45-4) (FIN-48, par. 12B):

a.   Such changes within the measurement period that result from new information about facts and circumstances that existed at the acquisition date should be recognized through a corresponding adjustment to goodwill. (*Note*: Once goodwill is reduced to zero, an acquirer should recognize the remaining portion of that adjustment as a gain on a bargain purchase.)

b.   All other changes in acquired income tax positions should be reported in accordance with ASC Subtopic 740-10, *Income Taxes—Overall* (FAS-109, *Accounting for Income Taxes*). See Chapter 43, "ASC Topic 740: Income Taxes."

3.   For tax deductions related to replacement awards (ASC 805-740-45-5 and 45-6) (FAS-109, par. A98):

a. If, after the acquisition date, the deduction reported on a tax return for a replacement award classified as equity exceeds the fair-value-based measure of the award, the acquirer should recognize any resulting realized tax benefit that exceeds the previously recognized deferred tax asset for that award related to pre- and postcombination service (i.e., the excess tax benefit) as additional paid-in capital.

b. If, after the acquisition date, the amount deductible on the acquirer's tax return is less than the fair-value-based measure of the award, the write-off of a deferred tax asset related to that deficiency, net of any related valuation allowance, should be (a) offset to the extent of any remaining additional paid-in capital from excess tax benefits from previous share-based payment awards, and (b) any remaining balance, recognized in earnings.

4. Disclosures should be made of changes in an acquirer's valuation allowance for its previously existing deferred tax assets as a result of a business combination. (ASC 805-740-50-1) (FAS-109, par. 45)

EXAMPLES OF FINANCIAL STATEMENT DISCLOSURES

 The following sample disclosures are available on the accompanying disc.

Illustrations Based on Guidance in FAS-141

Example 1: Material Business Combination

In August 20X2, the Company completed the purchase of MBK, Inc., a privately held manufacturer of industrial computer systems and enclosures, by acquiring all of the outstanding capital stock of MBK, Inc. for a total purchase price of $24 million. MBK, Inc.'s results of operations have been included in the consolidated financial statements since the date of acquisition. As a result of the acquisition, the Company is expected to (1) be the leading manufacturer of industrial computer systems and enclosures in Canada and Mexico and (2) reduce costs through economies of scale.

The aggregate purchase price of $24 million consisted of $15 million in cash and common stock valued at $9 million. The value of the 360,000 common shares issued was determined based on the average market price of the Company's common shares over the

2-day period before and after the terms of the acquisition were agreed to and announced.

The following table presents the allocation of the acquisition cost, including professional fees and other related acquisition costs, to the assets acquired and liabilities assumed, based on their fair values:

Cash and cash equivalents	$ 1,000,000
Accounts receivable	4,000,000
Inventories	7,000,000
Other current assets	3,000,000
Property, plant, and equipment	6,000,000
Intangible assets	10,000,000
Goodwill	5,000,000
Total assets acquired	36,000,000
Amounts payable to banks and long-term debt due within one year	(4,000,000)
Other current liabilities	(5,000,000)
Long-term accrued liabilities	(1,000,000)
Long-term debt	(2,000,000)
Total liabilities assumed	(12,000,000)
Net assets acquired	$ 24,000,000

Of the $10 million of acquired intangible assets, $5 million was assigned to registered trademarks that are not subject to amortization and $2 million was assigned to research and development assets that were written off at the date of acquisition. Those write-offs are included in general and administrative expenses. The remaining $3 million of acquired intangible assets have a weighted-average useful life of approximately 4 years. The intangible assets that make up that amount include: computer software of $1.6 million (3-year weighted-average useful life), patents of $900,000 (7-year weighted-average useful life), and other assets of $500,000 (5-year weighted-average useful life).

The $5 million of goodwill was assigned to the technology and communications segments in the amounts of $3 million and $2 million, respectively. Of that total amount, $600,000 is expected to be deductible for tax purposes.

The allocation of the purchase price is based on preliminary data and could change when final valuation of certain intangible assets is obtained.

Example 2: Supplemental Disclosure of Pro Forma Information

> **Note:** The following supplemental disclosure of pro forma information is required only for publicly-held entities (optional for nonpublic entities). If the pro forma effects are not material, the pro forma information presented below should be replaced with the following sentence: "The pro forma effects of the MBK, Inc. acquisition on the Company's consolidated financial statements were not material."

The following (unaudited) pro forma consolidated results of operations have been prepared as if the acquisition of MBK, Inc. had occurred at January 1, 20X1:

	December 31, 20X2	December 31, 20X1
Sales	$79,000,000	$64,000,000
Net income	8,200,000	3,600,000
Net income per share—Basic	1.86	0.82
Net income per share—Diluted	1.58	0.70

The pro forma information is presented for informational purposes only and is not necessarily indicative of the results of operations that actually would have been achieved had the acquisition been consummated as of that time, nor is it intended to be a projection of future results.

Example 3: Exchange of Investment Accounted for on the Equity Method for a Majority Ownership in an Unrelated Entity

On October 15, 20X2, the Company exchanged its 45% interest in Eagle, Co. for 91% of the common stock of Boiler, Co. On that same date, pursuant to a "split-up" of Eagle, Co. structured for tax purposes as a tax-free reorganization under the Internal Revenue Code, Boiler, Co. received 100% of the machining operations of Eagle, Co. The Company has accounted for this transaction under the purchase method of accounting. Accordingly, the carrying value of the Company's equity investment in Eagle, Co., totaling $8,000,000 at October 15, 20X2, was treated as the purchase price for accounting purposes. The assets acquired by Boiler, Co. included substantially all of the real estate and equipment owned by Eagle, Co. in Cleveland, Ohio and used in the machining and boiler assembly operations and certain other assets and liabilities.

Example 4: Amount Initially Assigned to Goodwill Subsequently Revised

In October 20X1, the Company acquired XDEG, Inc., a leading provider of health care information products. The Company issued 3,000,000 shares of common stock and 700,000 common stock options, with a total fair value of $35,000,000, in exchange for all outstanding shares of XDEG, Inc. The Company accounted for the acquisition using the purchase method of accounting for business combinations. The purchase price and costs associated with the acquisition exceeded the preliminary estimated fair value of net assets acquired by $10,200,000, which was preliminarily assigned to goodwill.

During 20X2, the Company completed the valuation of the intangible assets acquired in the XDEG, Inc. transaction. Pursuant to the valuation, the Company expensed $4,400,000 of the excess purchase price representing purchased in-process technology that previously had been assigned to goodwill. In management's judgment, this amount reflects the amount the Company would reasonably expect to pay an unrelated party for each project included in the technology. The value of in-process research and development of $4,400,000 represented approximately 37% of the purchase price and was determined by estimating the costs to develop the purchased technology into commercially viable products, then estimating the resulting net cash flows from each project that was incomplete at the acquisition date, and discounting the resulting net cash flows to their present value. The $4,400,000 charge is included as a component of "Other charges" in the accompanying Consolidated Statements of Operations for the year ended December 31, 20X2. Based on the final valuation, the remaining excess purchase price of $5,800,000 was assigned to existing technologies, trade names, and goodwill.

Example 5: Additional Purchase Price Payments Subsequently Made for Achieving Specified Levels of Profitability

During 20X2, the Company paid $13 million to the former owners of businesses acquired in previous years. These payments resulted from the acquired businesses having achieved specified levels of profitability during designated periods subsequent to the acquisition. These payments were recorded as additional goodwill.

Example 6: Business Combination Pending Government and Shareholder Approval

In November 20X2, the Company signed a definitive agreement to purchase ESY, Inc., a provider of programmable switches. Under the terms of the agreement, between 2,500,000 and 3,000,000 shares of the Company's common stock will be exchanged for all of the out-standing shares and options of ESY, Inc. The agreement is subject to the receipt of certain government approvals and the approval of ESY, Inc.'s shareholders. The transaction is expected to be consummated in the first or second quarter of 20X3. The Company expects to account for the acquisition using the purchase method of accounting for business combinations. The historical operations of ESY, Inc. are not expected to be material to the financial position or results of operations of the Company.

Example 7: Adjustments Made to Previously Determined Values of Assets Acquired in Business Combination

On September 1, 20X1, the Company acquired the stock of Sibik, Ltd. for $27,000,000. Because Sibik, Ltd. was acquired late in 20X1 and was a complex operation, it required a comprehensive review of asset values and liabilities and a significant part of the evaluation had to take into consideration the integration of Sibik, Ltd. The final assessment of asset values, restructuring the manufacturing and marketing organization, and making other necessary changes was not completed until the second quarter of 20X2. The determination of the final fair values resulted in adjustments, made in 20X2, consisting of changes from initially determined values as of September 1, 20X1, as follows:

Increase in goodwill	$ 1,300,000
Increase in property and equipment	2,100,000
Increase in other assets	400,000
Decrease in inventory	(2,800,000)
Decrease in accounts receivable	(1,000,000)

Example 8: Company to Indemnify Prior Owners of Acquired Business for Certain Liabilities

As part of the Company's purchase of certain business operations of Mastol, Inc., the Company agreed to indemnify Mastol, Inc. for certain liabilities that may arise from events that occurred during Mastol's ownership. As this contingency is resolved and if additional consideration is paid, the amount of such payments will be recorded as additional cost of the acquired business and will increase the amount of goodwill recorded for this acquisition.

Example 9: Several Individually Immaterial Business Combinations That Are Material in the Aggregate

In the last quarter of 20X2, the Company acquired the following four entities for a total cost of $6,200,000, which was paid primarily in cash:

- Lillo, Inc., based in Victoria, Canada, a leading provider of telecommunications consulting services.

- Fernex Corp., based in Seattle, Washington, a start-up data networking company.

- Drexxel, Inc., based in San Jose, California, a producer of digital networking technology.

- PBC, Ltd., based in Sydney, Australia, a designer and manufacturer of wireless communications networks.

Goodwill recognized in those transactions amounted to $2,300,000 and that amount is expected to be fully deductible for tax purposes. Goodwill was assigned to the communication and technology segments in the amounts of $1,600,000 and $700,000, respectively.

The Company's Consolidated Financial Statements include the operating results of each business from the date of acquisition. In connection with the acquisition of Fernex Corp., the Company may be required to pay certain additional amounts of up to $1,200,000, payable in common stock and to be accounted for under the purchase method, contingent upon the Company achieving certain agreed-upon technology and other milestones.

Example 10: Research and Development Costs Acquired in a Business Combination Are Capitalized

In October 20X2, the Company purchased the Chickadee division from Seliga & Co., a provider of data networking products and services in the United States, for $9,000,000 in cash. Chickadee's results of operations have been included in the consolidated financial statements since that date. As a result of the acquisition, the Company is expected to (1) be the leading provider of data networking products and services in the United States and (2) reduce costs through economies of scale. Under the terms of the agreement, the Company purchased the Chickadee division, its accounts and notes receivable and tooling equipment, and assumed certain liabilities. The Company also incurred $500,000 of direct, acquisition-related costs, which were capitalized as part of the purchase price.

The purchase price exceeded the fair values of the net assets acquired by $3,200,000. Of this amount, $1,325,000 was assigned to "Purchased in-process research and development," which is being amortized on the straight-line method over the estimated remaining lives of individual projects, ranging from two to five years. The amounts charged to these projects include only costs of materials, equipment, and facilities that the Company deems to have future benefit. The remainder of the excess purchase price, amounting to $1,875,000, was recorded as goodwill and assigned to the technology segment. Of that amount, $300,000 is expected to be deductible for tax purposes.

The following table presents the allocation of the purchase price, including related acquisition costs, to the assets acquired and liabilities assumed based on their fair values at the date of acquisition:

Accounts receivable	$ 2,250,000
Notes receivable	750,000
Tooling equipment	4,900,000
Purchased in-process research and development	1,325,000
Goodwill	1,875,000
Total assets acquired	11,100,000
Accounts payable	(1,000,000)
Accrued liabilities	(600,000)
Total liabilities assumed	(1,600,000)
Net assets acquired	$ 9,500,000

Example 11: Research and Development Costs Acquired in a Business Combination Are Expensed

"Purchased in-process research and development" expense in the 20X2 Statement of Operations represents the value assigned to research and development projects in a purchase business combination of the Chickadee brand from Seliga & Co. These projects were commenced but not yet completed at the date of acquisition; technological feasibility for these projects has not been established, and they have no alternative future use in research and development activities or otherwise. Amounts assigned to purchased in-process research and development meeting these criteria are charged to expense at the date of consummation of the purchase business combination. In 20X2, a charge of $1,325,000 was recorded for purchased in-process research and development costs in conjunction with this business combination, based on preliminary allocations of purchase price.

Example 12: Contingent Future Consideration

In connection with certain acquisitions, the Company has agreed to pay additional consideration in future periods, based upon the attainment by the acquired entity of defined operating objectives. The Company does not accrue contingent consideration obligations prior to the attainment of the objectives. At December 31, 20X2, maximum potential future consideration pursuant to such arrangements, to be resolved over the following six years, is $12 million. Any such payments would result in increases in goodwill.

Illustrations Based on Guidance in FAS-141R

Example 13: Material Business Combination

On June 30, 20X7, the Company acquired 15% of the outstanding common shares of MBK, Inc. (MBK), a provider of data networking products and services in Canada, Mexico, and China. On June 30, 20X9, the Company acquired 60% of the outstanding common shares of MBK. As a result of the acquisition, the Company is expected to be the leading provider of data networking products and services in those markets. It also expects to reduce costs through economies of scale. The goodwill of $2,500,000 arising from the acquisition consists largely of the synergies and economies of scale expected from combining the operations of the Company and MBK. All of the goodwill was assigned to the Company's network segment. None of the goodwill recognized is expected to be deductible for income tax purposes.

The following table summarizes the consideration paid for MBK and the amounts of the assets acquired and liabilities assumed recognized at the acquisition date, as well as the fair value at the acquisition date of the noncontrolling interest in MBK at June 30, 20X9:

Consideration:

Cash	$ 5,000,000
Equity instruments (100,000 common shares of the Company)	4,000,000
Contingent consideration arrangement	1,000,000
Fair value of total consideration transferred	10,000,000
Fair value of the Company's equity interest in MBK held before the business combination	2,000,000
	$12,000,000

Recognized amounts of identifiable assets acquired and liabilities assumed:

Financial assets	$3,500,000

Inventory	1,000,000
Property, plant, and equipment	10,000,000
Identifiable intangible assets	3,300,000
Financial liabilities	(4,000,000)
Liability arising from a contingency	(1,000,000)
Total identifiable net assets	12,800,000
Noncontrolling interest in MBK	(3,300,000)
Goodwill	2,500,000
	$ 12,000,000
Acquisition-related costs (included in selling, general, and administrative expenses in the Company's income statement for the year ended December 31, 20X9)	$ 1,250,000

The fair value of the 100,000 common shares issued as part of the consideration paid for MBK ($4,000,000) was determined on the basis of the closing market price of the Company's common shares on the acquisition date.

The contingent consideration arrangement requires the Company to pay the former owners of MBK 5% of the revenues of XYZ, an unconsolidated equity investment owned by MBK, in excess of $7,500,000 for 20XX, up to a maximum amount of $2,500,000 (undiscounted). The potential undiscounted amount of all future payments that the Company could be required to make under the contingent consideration arrangement is between $0 and $2,500,000. The fair value of the contingent consideration arrangement of $1,000,000 was estimated by applying the income approach. That measure is based on significant inputs that are not observable in the market (i.e., Level 3 inputs). Key assumptions include (1) a discount rate range of 20%–25% and (2) a probability adjusted level of revenues in XYZ between $10,000,000 and $20,000,000. As of December 31, 20X9, the amount recognized for the contingent consideration arrangement, the range of outcomes, and the assumptions used to develop the estimates had not changed.

The fair value of the financial assets acquired includes receivables under capital leases of data networking equipment with a fair value of $2,000,000. The gross amount due under the contracts is $3,100,000, of which $450,000 is expected to be uncollectible.

The fair value of the acquired identifiable intangible assets of $3,300,000 is provisional pending receipt of the final valuations for those assets.

A liability of $1,000,000 has been recognized for expected warranty claims on products sold by MBK during the last three years.

The Company expects that the majority of this expenditure will be incurred in 20XX and that the entire expenditure will be incurred by the end of 20XY. The potential undiscounted amount of all future payments that the Company could be required to make under the warranty arrangements is estimated to be between $500,000 and $1,500,000. As of December 31, 20X9, there has been no change since June 30, 20X9, in the amount recognized for the liability or any change in the range of outcomes or assumptions used to develop the estimates.

The fair value of the noncontrolling interest in MBK, a private company, was estimated by applying the income approach and a market approach. This fair value measurement is based on significant inputs that are not observable in the market and, therefore, represents a Level 3 measurement as defined in FASB ASC Topic 820, *Fair Value Measurements and Disclosures*. Key assumptions include (1) a discount rate range of 20%–25%, (2) a terminal value based on a range of terminal EBITDA multiples between 3 and 5 (or, if appropriate, based on long-term sustainable growth rates ranging between 3% and 6%), (3) financial multiples of companies deemed to be similar to MBK, and (4) adjustments because of the lack of control or lack of marketability that market participants would consider when estimating the fair value of the noncontrolling interest in MBK.

The Company recognized a gain of $500,000 as a result of remeasuring to fair value its 15% equity interest in MBK held before the business combination. The gain is included in other income in the Company's income statement for the year ended December 31, 20X9.

The amounts of MBK's revenue and earnings included in the Company's consolidated income statement for the year ended December 31, 20X9, and the revenue and earnings of the combined entity had the acquisition date been January 1, 20X9, or January 1, 20X8, are:

	Revenue	*Earnings*
Actual from 6/30/20X9– 12/31/20X9	$ 4,090,000	$ 1,710,000
Supplemental pro forma for 1/1/20X9–12/31/20X9	$27,670,000	$12,870,000
Supplemental pro forma for 1/1/20X8–12/31/20X8	$26,985,000	$12,325,000

Example 14: Contingent Future Consideration

In connection with its acquisition of ABC Co., the Company has agreed to pay additional consideration in future periods of 10% of the revenues of ABC Co. in excess of $10,000,000 for 20X3, up to a maximum amount of $3,000,000 (undiscounted). The potential undiscounted amount of all future payments that the Company could be required to make under the contingent consideration arrangement is between $0 and $3,000,000. The fair value of the contingent consideration arrangement of $700,000 was estimated by applying the income approach. That measure is based on significant inputs that are not observable in the market, which FASB ASC Topic 820, *Fair Value Measurements and Disclosures*, refers to as Level 3 inputs. Key assumptions include (1) a discount rate range of 20%–25% and (2) a probability adjusted level of revenues in ABC Co. between $12,000,000 and $25,000,000. As of December 31, 20X2, the amount recognized for the contingent consideration arrangement, the range of outcomes, and the assumptions used to develop the estimates had not changed.

Example 15: Disclosure of Noncontrolling Interest and Valuation Techniques Used to Measure Its Fair Value

The fair value of the noncontrolling interest in ABC Co., a private entity, was estimated by applying the income approach and a market approach. This fair value measurement is based on significant inputs that are not observable in the market and, therefore, represents a Level 3 measurement as defined in FASB ASC Topic 820, *Fair Value Measurements and Disclosures*. Main assumptions include the following:

- A discount rate range of 20%–25%.

- A terminal value based on a range of terminal EBITDA multiples between 3 and 5.

- Financial multiples of companies deemed to be similar to ABC Co.

- Adjustments because of the lack of control or lack of marketability that market participants would consider when estimating the fair value of the noncontrolling interest in ABC Co.

CHAPTER 45
ASC TOPIC 808: COLLABORATIVE ARRANGEMENTS

CONTENTS

EXECUTIVE SUMMARY

Collaborative Arrangements

A collaborative arrangement is a contractual arrangement that involves a joint operating activity involving two (or more) parties that meet both of the following requirements:

1. They are active participants in the activity; and
2. They are exposed to significant risks and rewards dependent on the commercial success of the activity.

The guidance in ASC Topic 808 does not apply to arrangements for which the accounting is specifically addressed within the scope of other authoritative accounting literature.

Accounting Literature

FASB Accounting Standards Codification Topic	*Pre-Codification Accounting Literature*
808, *Collaborative Arrangements*	EITF 07-1, *Accounting for Collaborative Arrangements*

DISCLOSURE AND KEY PRESENTATION REQUIREMENTS

Note: The disclosure requirements in items 1 and 2 below are prescribed by ASC Section 808-10-50, *Collaborative Arrangements—Overall—Disclosure*, based on EITF 07-1, *Accounting for Collaborative Arrangements*, which is effective for fiscal years beginning after December 15, 2008, and interim periods within those fiscal years.

1. In the period in which a collaborative arrangement is entered into, and all annual periods thereafter, a participant to a collaborative arrangement should disclose the following (ASC 808-10-50-1) (EITF 07-1, par. 21) (*Note:* Information related to individually significant collaborative arrangements should be disclosed separately):

   a. Information about the nature and purpose of its collaborative arrangements.

   b. Its rights and obligations under the collaborative arrangements.

   c. The accounting policy for collaborative arrangements.

   d. The income statement classification and amounts attributable to transactions arising from the collaborative arrangement between participants for each period for which an income statement is presented.

2. The following transitional disclosures should be made upon initial application of the guidance in ASC Topic 808, *Collaborative Arrangements* (based on EITF 07-1) (ASC 808-10-65-1):

   a. A description of the prior-period information that has been retrospectively adjusted, if any.

   b. The effect of the change on revenue and operating expenses (or other appropriate captions of changes in the applicable net assets or performance indicator) and on any other affected financial statement line item.

   c. If retrospective application to all prior periods presented is impracticable, the reasons why reclassification was not made, and the effect of the reclassification on the current period. (*Note:* The evaluation of whether transition through retrospective application is practicable should be made on an arrangement by arrangement basis.)

EXAMPLES OF FINANCIAL STATEMENT DISCLOSURES

 The following sample disclosures are available on the accompanying disc.

Example 1: Company Records Cost Recoveries in Research and Development

The Company evaluates whether an arrangement is a collaborative arrangement under FASB ASC Topic 808, *Collaborative Arrangements*, at its inception based on the facts and circumstances specific to the arrangement. The Company also reevaluates whether an arrangement qualifies or continues to qualify as a collaborative arrangement whenever there is a change in either the roles of the participants or the participants' exposure to significant risks and rewards dependent on the ultimate commercial success of the endeavor. For those collaborative arrangements where it is determined that the Company is the principal participant, costs incurred and revenue generated from third parties are recorded on a gross basis in the financial statements.

From time to time, the Company enters into collaborative arrangements for the research and development (R&D), manufacture and/or commercialization of products and product candidates. These collaborations generally provide for non-refundable, upfront license fees, R&D and commercial performance milestone payments, cost sharing, royalty payments and/or profit sharing. The Company's collaboration agreements with third parties are performed on a "best efforts" basis with no guarantee of either technological or commercial success. The following are the Company's existing arrangements:

- *ABC Co. Arrangement.* The Company is in a collaboration and license agreement with ABC Co., which provides them the exclusive rights to develop and commercialize [*description*] in Europe. As part of the agreement, the Company received exclusive worldwide rights to certain ABC Co.'s intellectual property. ABC Co. assumed all development costs in Europe and reimburses the Company for certain worldwide development costs. During the years ended December 31, 20X2, and 20X1, cost recoveries from ABC Co. were $2 million and $1.5 million, respectively, and are included in "Research and development" in the Statement of Operations.

- *XYZ, Inc. Arrangement.* The Company is in a collaboration agreement with XYZ, Inc., which provides them the exclusive rights to develop and commercialize for the Asian market [*description*]. Pursuant to the terms of the agreement, XYZ, Inc. reimburses the Company for certain worldwide development costs. The Company has the right to participate in the promotion of the products in Asia. During the years ended December 31, 20X2, and 20X1, cost recoveries from XYZ, Inc. were $800,000 and $600,000, respectively, and are included in "Research and development" in the Statement of Operations. In addition, during the year ended December 31, 20X2, the Company received an upfront license fee payment of $1 million from XYZ, Inc. This license fee payment is being recognized as revenue over five years. Included in "Other revenues" in the Statement of Operations is $125,000 for the year ended December 31, 20X2, relating to this milestone payment.

Example 2: Company Records a Charge Related to Upfront Licensing and Collaboration Fee

The Company has a collaboration agreement with DEF, Inc. to develop products for [*description*]. The agreement provides the Company with an exclusive license to all of DEF, Inc.'s applicable intellectual property. In October 20X2, at the inception of the agreement, the Company recorded a charge of $500,000 related to the upfront licensing and collaboration fee. The Company will also pay up to $3 million over the next five years in product development costs and regulatory approval milestones. The product development costs will be expensed to "Research and development" as incurred, and the regulatory approval milestones will be recorded as "Other intangible assets" and amortized over the useful life of the product. In addition, DEF, Inc. will receive either a profit-sharing payment of 10% or a royalty of up to 6% of commercial sales. The Company will be responsible for global sales and marketing, which is expected to begin in 20X3, and DEF, Inc. will be responsible for initial manufacturing. The Company recorded $50,000 of product development costs for the year ended December 31, 20X2.

CHAPTER 46
ASC TOPIC 810: CONSOLIDATION

CONTENTS

EXECUTIVE SUMMARY

Overall

PRACTICE ALERT: In December 2007, the FASB issued Statement of Financial Accounting Standards No. 160, *Noncontrolling Interests in Consolidated Financial Statements* (FAS-160) (ASC 810, *Consolidation)*. The new Statement establishes new accounting and reporting standards for the noncontrolling interest in a subsidiary and for the deconsolidation of a subsidiary. Specifically, FAS-160 (ASC 810) requires the recognition of a noncontrolling interest (sometimes called "minority interest") as equity in the consolidated financial statements and separate from the parent's equity. The amount of net income attributable to the noncontrolling interest will be included in consolidated net income on the face of the income statement. FAS-160 (ASC 810) clarifies that changes in a parent's ownership interest in a subsidiary that do not result in deconsolidation are equity transactions if the parent retains its controlling financial interest. In addition, FAS-160 (ASC 810) requires that a parent recognize a gain or loss in net income when a subsidiary is deconsolidated. FAS-160 (ASC 810) also includes expanded disclosure requirements regarding the interests of the parent and its noncontrolling interest.

FAS-160 (ASC 810) does not change extant guidance related to consolidation purpose or consolidation policy or the requirement that a parent consolidate all entities in which it has a controlling financial interest. In addition, FAS-160 (ASC 810) does *not* change the requirements in FASB Interpretation No. 46 (revised December 2003), *Consolidation of Variable Interest Entities* (ASC 810).

The provisions of FAS-160 as codified in ASC 810 are effective for fiscal years, and interim periods within those fiscal years, beginning on or after December 15, 2008 (i.e., January 1, 2009, for entities with calendar year-ends). Earlier adoption is *prohibited*. FAS-160 (ASC 810) applies *prospectively* as of the beginning of the fiscal year in which it is initially adopted, except for the presentation and disclosure requirements. The presentation and disclosure requirements should be applied *retrospectively* for all periods presented.

Before FAS-160 (ASC 810) was issued, limited guidance existed for reporting noncontrolling interests (minority interests). As a result, considerable diversity in practice existed. Noncontrolling interests were reported in the consolidated balance sheet as liabilities, or in the mezzanine section between liabilities and equity. FAS-160 (ASC 810) indicates that noncontrolling interests should be reported as equity in the consolidated financial statements and separate from the parent's equity.

Consolidated financial statements represent the financial position, results of operations, and cash flows of a parent and its subsidiaries as if the group were a single economic enterprise. They are prepared by combining all parent and subsidiary accounts and eliminating intercompany balances and transactions. Consolidated financial statements are presumed to present more meaningful information than separate financial statements and should be used in substantially all cases in which a parent directly or indirectly controls the majority voting interest (more than 50%) of another entity. However, a majority-owned entity should not be consolidated if control does not rest with the majority owner.

Consolidated financial statements usually are justified on the basis that one of the consolidated entities exercises control over the affiliated group. When there is no such control, combined financial statements may be used to accomplish the same results. For example, a group of entities controlled by an individual shareholder should utilize combined financial statements. Combined financial statements are prepared on the same basis as consolidated financial statements except that no entity in the group has a controlling interest in the other.

If a parent's and a subsidiary's fiscal years differ by no more than about three months, it is ordinarily acceptable to consolidate the subsidiary using the subsidiary's financial statements for its fiscal year. However, in those circumstances, intervening events or transactions that materially affect the results of operations or financial position should be disclosed or otherwise recognized.

Variable Interest Entities

PRACTICE ALERT: As this Manual goes to press, the FASB has issued Statement of Financial Accounting Standards No. 167, *Amendments to FASB Interpretation No. 46(R)*, which significantly changes the consolidation rules as they related to variable interest entities (VIEs). FAS-167 specifically changes how a reporting entity determines when an entity that is insufficiently capitalized or is not controlled through voting (or similar rights) should be consolidated. The determination of whether a reporting entity is required to consolidate another entity is based on, among other things, the other entity's purpose and design and the reporting entity's ability to direct the activities of the other entity that most significantly impact the other entity's economic performance. Under FAS-167, it is expected that many off-balance sheet entities previously exempt from consolidation—qualified special-purpose entities (QSPEs)—will be subject to consolidation. Due to the elimination of the QSPE scope exception, the impact of the changes under FAS-167 may be more evident to financial services companies; however, the new guidance will have broad applicability across all industries. In addition, FAS-167 will require a number of new disclosures, including the requirements for a reporting entity to provide additional disclosures about its involvement with VIEs, any significant changes in risk exposure due to that involvement, and how its involvement with a VIE affects the reporting entity's financial statements.

FAS-167 will be effective at the start of a reporting entity's first fiscal year beginning after November 15, 2009 (i.e., 2010 for calendar-year entities). Early application is not permitted.

As this Manual goes to press, the FASB has not yet integrated the provisions of FAS-167 into the Accounting Standards Codification. Readers should be alert to and monitor further developments in this area. The coverage in this chapter is based on ASC Topic 810 before FAS-167. Future editions of this Manual will include expanded coverage of the guidance based on FAS-167 and the appropriate ASC Topics.

PRACTICE ALERT: As this Manual goes to press, the FASB has issued Statement of Financial Accounting Standards No. 166, *Accounting for Transfers of Financial Assets—An Amendment to FASB Statement No. 140*, which enhances information reported to users of financial statements by providing greater transparency about transfers of financial assets and an entity's continuing involvement in transferred financial assets. FAS-166 will require more information about transfers of financial assets, including securitization transactions, and where entities have continuing exposure to the risks related to transferred financial assets. It also eliminates the concept of a "qualifying special-purpose entity" (QSPE), changes the requirements for derecognizing financial assets, and requires additional disclosures. Although the impact of the changes under FAS-166 may be more evident to financial institutions, the new guidance will also apply to nonfinancial entities. For example, the new guidance affects transfers of many types of financial assets, including factoring agreements, sales of trade receivables, mortgage loans, and installment loans.

FAS-166 will be effective at the start of a reporting entity's first fiscal year beginning after November 15, 2009 (i.e., 2010 for calendar-year entities). Early application is not permitted.

As this Manual goes to press, the FASB has not yet integrated the provisions of FAS-166 into the Accounting Standards Codification. Readers should be alert to and monitor further developments in this area. The coverage in this chapter is based on ASC Topic 860 before FAS-166. Future editions of this Manual will include expanded coverage of the guidance based on FAS-166 and the appropriate ASC Topics.

What are variable interests.   Variable interests are the investments or other interests that will absorb portions of a variable interest entity's (VIE) expected losses or receive portions of the VIE's residual returns. Examples of variable interests in a VIE include the following:

- Equity investments that are at risk
- Investments in subordinated beneficial interests
- Investments in subordinated debt instruments
- Guarantees
- Derivative interests
- Service contracts
- Leases with a residual value guarantee
- Written put options

When should a VIE be consolidated.   Generally, there are two steps involved with evaluating whether a VIE should be consolidated: (1) determining whether the entity in question is a variable interest entity and (2) determining who is the primary beneficiary. These questions are addressed below.

Is the entity a variable interest entity. A *variable interest entity* (VIE) is a legal entity (e.g., corporation, partnership, LLP, LLC, trust) that meets any of the following three criteria:

1. *The total equity investment at risk is not sufficient to permit the entity to finance its activities without additional subordinated financial support from other parties.* In other words, the entity's expected losses are greater than the equity investment at risk. There is a rebuttable presumption that an equity investment of less than 10 percent of the entity's total assets is not sufficient to permit an entity to finance its activities without additional subordinated financial support.

2. *As a group, the holders of the equity investment at risk do not have any of the characteristics of a controlling financial interest.* In other words:

   a. As a group, holders of the equity investment at risk cannot directly or indirectly, through voting rights or similar rights, make decisions about the entity's activities that have a significant effect on the success of the entity; or

   b. As a group, holders of the equity investment at risk have no obligation to absorb the expected losses of the entity; or

   c. As a group, holders of the equity investment at risk do not have the rights to receive the expected residual returns of the entity.

3. The equity investors have voting rights that are not proportionate to their economic interests and the activities of the entity involve, or are conducted on behalf of, an investor with a disproportionately small voting interest.

Who is the primary beneficiary. The enterprise that consolidates a VIE is referred to as the *primary beneficiary* of that VIE. A VIE can have only one primary beneficiary. An enterprise is the primary beneficiary of a VIE if the enterprise has variable interests that will (1) absorb a majority of the VIE's expected losses, (2) receive a majority of the VIE's expected residual returns, or (3) both.

If one enterprise will absorb a majority of a VIE's expected losses and another enterprise will receive a majority of that VIE's expected residual returns, the enterprise absorbing a majority of the losses is considered the primary beneficiary and, therefore, should consolidate the VIE.

Measurement of the VIE's assets, liabilities, and noncontrolling interests. With limited exceptions, an enterprise should initially measure the assets, liabilities, and noncontrolling interests of the newly consolidated VIE at their fair values at the date the enterprise first becomes the primary beneficiary. One of the exceptions relates to entities under common control. For VIEs that are under common control with the primary beneficiary, the primary beneficiary should initially measure the assets, liabilities, and noncontrolling interests of the VIE at the amounts at which they are carried in the accounts of the enterprise that controls the VIE.

Accounting Literature

FASB Accounting Standards Codification Topic	*Pre-Codification Accounting Literature*
810, *Consolidation*	FAS-141R, *Business Combinations (Effective for fiscal years beginning on or after December 15, 2008)*
	FAS-160, *Noncontrolling Interests in Consolidated Financial Statements (Effective for fiscal years beginning on or after December 15, 2008)*
	FAS-166, *Accounting for Transfers of Financial Assets—an Amendment to FASB Statement No. 140*
	FAS-167, *Amendments to FASB Interpretation No. 46(R)*
	FIN-46R, *Consolidation of Variable Interest Entities (Revised December 2003)*
	FSP FAS 140-4 and FIN-46R-8, *Disclosures by Public Entities (Enterprises) about Transfers of Financial Assets and Interests in Variable Interest Entities*
	EITF 04-5, *Determining Whether a General Partner, or the General Partners As a Group, Controls a Limited Partnership or Similar Entity When the Limited Partners Have Certain Rights*
	EITF 06-9, *Reporting a Change in (or the Elimination of) a Previously Existing Difference between the Fiscal Year-End of a Parent Company and That of a Consolidated Entity or between the Reporting Period of an Investor and That of an Equity Method Investee*
	ARB-51, *Consolidated Financial Statements*

DISCLOSURE AND KEY PRESENTATION REQUIREMENTS

Overall—ASC Topic 810 Prior to Adoption of Guidance in FAS-160

Note: The disclosure and key presentation requirements in this section are prescribed by ASC Topic 810, *Consolidation,* prior to the adoption of the guidance in FAS-160, *Noncontrolling Interests in Consolidated Financial Statements,* which is effective for fiscal years, and interim periods within those fiscal years, beginning on or after December 15, 2008. Early adoption is not permitted.

1. The following presentation matters should be followed in the preparation of consolidated financial statements:

   a. Intercompany balances and transactions should be eliminated (e.g., open account balances, security holdings, sales and purchases, interest, dividends). (ASC 810-10-45-1) (ARB-51, par. 6)

   b. The consolidated financial statements should exclude gain or loss on transactions among the entities in the consolidated group. (ASC 810-10-45-1) (ARB-51, par. 6)

   c. Any intercompany profit or loss on assets remaining within the consolidated group should be eliminated. (ASC 810-10-45-1) (ARB-51, par. 6)

   d. Consolidated retained earnings should exclude the retained earnings or deficit of a subsidiary at the date of acquisition by the parent. (ASC 810-10-45-2) (ARB-51, par. 9)

   e. When a subsidiary is purchased during the year, the consolidated financial statements should include either (1) the subsidiary in the consolidation as though it had been acquired at the beginning of the year, or (2) the subsidiary's revenue and expenses subsequent to the date of acquisition. (ASC 810-10-45-4) (ARB-51, par. 11)

   f. Shares of the parent that are held by a subsidiary should *not* be treated as outstanding shares in the consolidated balance sheet. (ASC 810-10-45-5) (ARB-51, par. 13)

   g. If income taxes have been paid on intercompany profits on assets remaining within the consolidated group, either (a) those taxes should be deferred, or (b) the intercompany profits to be eliminated in consolidation should be appropriately reduced. (ASC 810-10-45-8) (ARB-51, par. 17)

    h. The retained earnings in the consolidated financial statements should reflect the accumulated earnings of the consolidated group not distributed to the owners of, or capitalized by, the parent. (ASC 810-10-45-9) (ARB-51, par. 18)

  2. If combined financial statements are prepared for a group of related entities (e.g., a group of unconsolidated subsidiaries or commonly controlled entities), intercompany transactions and profits or losses should be eliminated, and minority interests, foreign operations, different fiscal periods, or income taxes should be treated in the same manner as in consolidated financial statements. (ASC 810-10-45-10) (ARB-51, par. 23)

  3. If the consolidated financial statements are prepared using the financial statements of a subsidiary that has a different year-end than the parent (generally the difference is not more than about three months), the effect of intervening events that materially affect the financial position or results of operations should be properly disclosed or otherwise recognized. (ASC 810-10-45-12) (ARB-51, par. 4)

  4. A change to, or the elimination of, a previously existing difference between the parent's reporting period and the reporting period of a consolidated entity (or between the reporting period of an investor and the reporting period of an equity method investee in the parent's or investor's consolidated financial statements) should be reported as a change in accounting principle and properly disclosed in accordance with ASC Topic 250, *Accounting Changes and Error Corrections* (EITF 06-9). (ASC 810-10-45-13; 810-10-50-2) (EITF 06-9). See Chapter 9, "ASC Topic 250: Accounting Changes and Error Corrections."

  5. The consolidation policy that is being followed should be disclosed in the consolidated financial statements. (ASC 810-10-50-1) (ARB-51, par. 5) (*Note:* In most cases, this can be made apparent by the headings or other information in the financial statements, but in other cases a footnote is required.)

Overall—ASC Topic 810 Based on Guidance in FAS-160

Note: The disclosure and key presentation requirements in this section are prescribed by ASC Topic 810, *Consolidation*, based on FAS-160, *Noncontrolling Interests in Consolidated Financial Statements,* and should be applied retrospectively for all periods presented. These requirements are effective for fiscal years, and interim periods within those fiscal years, beginning on or after December 15, 2008. Early adoption is not permitted.

1. The following presentation matters should be followed in the preparation of consolidated financial statements:

    a. Intercompany balances and transactions should be eliminated (e.g., open account balances, security holdings, sales and purchases, interest, dividends). (ASC 810-10-45-1) (ARB-51, par. 6)

    b. The consolidated financial statements should exclude gain or loss on transactions among the entities in the consolidated group. (ASC 810-10-45-1) (ARB-51, par. 6)

    c. Any intercompany profit or loss on assets remaining within the consolidated group should be eliminated. (ASC 810-10-45-1) (ARB-51, par. 6)

    d. Consolidated retained earnings should exclude the retained earnings or deficit of a subsidiary at the date of acquisition by the parent. (ASC 810-10-45-2) (ARB-51, par. 9)

    e. When a subsidiary is initially consolidated during the year, the consolidated financial statements should include the subsidiary's revenues, expenses, gains, and losses only from the date the subsidiary is initially consolidated. (ASC 810-10-45-4) (ARB-51, par. 11)

    f. Shares of the parent that are held by a subsidiary should *not* be treated as outstanding shares in the consolidated balance sheet and, therefore, should be eliminated in the consolidated financial statements and reflected as treasury shares. (ASC 810-10-45-5) (ARB-51, par. 13)

    g. If income taxes have been paid on intercompany profits on assets remaining within the consolidated group, either (a) those taxes should be deferred, or (b) the intercompany profits to be eliminated in consolidation should be appropriately reduced. (ASC 810-10-45-8) (ARB-51, par. 17)

    h. The retained earnings in the consolidated financial statements should reflect the accumulated earnings of the consolidated group, not distributed to the owners of, or capitalized by, the parent. (ASC 810-10-45-9) (ARB-51, par. 18)

2. If combined financial statements are prepared for a group of related entities (e.g., a group of commonly controlled entities), intercompany transactions and profits or losses should be eliminated, and noncontrolling interests, foreign operations, different fiscal periods, or income taxes should be

treated in the same manner as in consolidated financial statements. (ASC 810-10-45-10) (ARB-51, par. 23)

3. If the consolidated financial statements are prepared using the financial statements of a subsidiary that has a different year-end than the parent (generally the difference is not more than about three months), the effect of intervening events that materially affect the financial position or results of operations should be properly disclosed or otherwise recognized. (ASC 810-10-45-12) (ARB-51, par. 4)

4. A change to, or the elimination of, a previously existing difference between the parent's reporting period and the reporting period of a consolidated entity (or between the reporting period of an investor and the reporting period of an equity method investee in the parent's or investor's consolidated financial statements) should be reported as a change in accounting principle and properly disclosed in accordance with ASC Topic 250, *Accounting Changes and Error Corrections* (EITF 06-9). (ASC 810-10-45-13; 810-10-50-2) (EITF 06-9). See Chapter 9, "ASC Topic 250: Accounting Changes and Error Corrections."

5. The noncontrolling interest in a subsidiary should be reported in the consolidated balance sheet within equity, separately from the parent's equity, and that amount should be clearly identified and labeled (e.g., "noncontrolling interest in subsidiaries"). (ASC 810-10-45-15 and 45-16) (ARB-51, pars. 25 and 26) (*Note:* An entity with noncontrolling interests in more than one subsidiary may present those interests in aggregate in the consolidated financial statements.)

6. Revenues, expenses, gains, losses, net income or loss, and other comprehensive income should be reported in the consolidated financial statements at the consolidated amounts (i.e., including the amounts attributable to the owners of the parent and the noncontrolling interest). (ASC 810-10-45-19 and 45-20) (ARB-51, pars. 29 and 30)

7. If losses attributable to the parent and the noncontrolling interest in a subsidiary exceed their interests in the subsidiary's equity, the excess (and any further losses attributable to the parent and the noncontrolling interest) should be attributed to those interests (i.e., the noncontrolling interest should continue to be attributed its share of losses even if that attribution results in a deficit noncontrolling interest balance). (ASC 810-10-45-21) (ARB-51, par. 31)

8. For changes in a parent's ownership interest in a subsidiary while the parent retains its controlling financial interest in the subsidiary (e.g., if the subsidiary issues additional ownership interests, or if the parent sells some of its ownership

interests in its subsidiary) (ASC 810-10-45-22 through 45-24) (ARB-51, pars. 32–34):

a. Such changes should be accounted for as equity transactions (i.e., investments by owners and distributions to owners acting in their capacity as owners) and, therefore, no gain or loss should be recognized in consolidated net income or comprehensive income.

b. The carrying amount of the noncontrolling interest should be adjusted to reflect the change in its ownership interest in the subsidiary.

c. Any difference between the fair value of the consideration received or paid and the amount by which the noncontrolling interest is adjusted should be recognized in equity attributable to the parent.

d. If a change in a parent's ownership interest has occurred in a subsidiary that has accumulated other comprehensive income, the carrying amount of accumulated other comprehensive income should be adjusted to reflect the change in the ownership interest in the subsidiary through a corresponding charge or credit to equity attributable to the parent.

9. The consolidation policy that is being followed should be disclosed in the consolidated financial statements. (ASC 810-10-50-1) (ARB-51, par. 5) (*Note:* In most cases, this can be made apparent by the headings or other information in the financial statements, but in other cases a footnote is required.)

10. For a parent with one or more less-than-wholly-owned subsidiaries, the following disclosures should be made for each reporting period (ASC 810-10-50-1A) (ARB-51, par. 38):

a. Separately, on the face of the consolidated financial statements, the amounts of consolidated net income and consolidated comprehensive income and the related amounts of each attributable to the parent and the noncontrolling interest.

b. Either in the notes or on the face of the consolidated income statement, amounts attributable to the parent for the following, if reported in the consolidated financial statements:

(1) Income from continuing operations.

(2) Discontinued operations.

(3) Extraordinary items.

c. Either in the consolidated statement of changes in equity, if presented, or in the notes to consolidated financial statements, a reconciliation at the beginning and the end of the period of the carrying amount of total equity (net assets), equity (net assets) attributable to the parent, and equity (net assets) attributable to the noncontrolling interest that separately discloses:

(1)   Net income.

(2)   Transactions with owners acting in their capacity as owners, showing separately contributions from and distributions to owners.

(3)   Each component of other comprehensive income.

d.   In the notes to the consolidated financial statements, a separate schedule that shows the effects of any changes in a parent's ownership interest in a subsidiary on the equity attributable to the parent.

11.   If a subsidiary is deconsolidated, the parent should disclose the following (ASC 810-10-50-1B) (ARB-51, par. 39):

a.   The amount of any gain or loss recognized in accordance with ASC paragraph 810-10-45-5 (ARB-51, par. 36).

b.   The portion of any gain or loss related to the remeasurement of any retained investment in the former subsidiary to its fair value.

c.   The caption in the income statement in which the gain or loss is recognized unless separately presented on the face of the income statement.

12.   The following transitional disclosures should be made upon adoption of ASC Topic 810, based on FAS-160 (ASC 810-10-65-1) (FAS-160, par. 6):

a.   If, in the year of adoption, an entity's consolidated net income attributable to the parent would have been significantly different had the previous requirement in ASC paragraph 810-10-45-7 (ARB-51, par. 15) been applied, the entity should disclose pro forma consolidated net income attributable to the parent and pro forma earnings per share as if the previous requirement in ASC paragraph 810-10-45-7) (ARB-51, par. 15) had been applied in the year of adoption.

b.   The presentation and disclosure requirements should be applied retrospectively for all periods presented, as follows:

(1)   The noncontrolling interest should be reclassified to equity.

(2) Consolidated net income should be adjusted to include the net income attributed to the noncontrolling interest.

(3) Consolidated comprehensive income should be adjusted to include the comprehensive income attributed to the noncontrolling interest.

(4) The disclosures in items 10 and 11 above should be provided.

Variable Interest Entities

Note: The disclosure requirements under this caption have been superseded by the guidance in FAS-167, *Amendments to FASB Interpretation No. 46(R)*, which is effective as of the beginning of the first annual reporting period beginning after November 15, 2009, and all interim and annual periods thereafter. Thereafter, the disclosure requirements under the caption "FAS-167, *Amendments to FASB Interpretation No. 46(R)*" below, should be followed. Early adoption is not permitted.

1. If a reporting entity is the primary beneficiary of a variable interest entity (VIE), the following disclosures should be made (unless the primary beneficiary also holds a majority voting interest) (ASC 810-10-50-3) (FIN-46R, par. 23):

   a. The nature, purpose, size, and activities of the VIE.

   b. The carrying amount and classification of consolidated assets that are collateral for the VIE's obligations.

   c. The lack of recourse if creditors (or beneficial interest holders) of a consolidated VIE have no recourse to the general credit of the primary beneficiary.

2. If a reporting entity holds a significant variable interest in a VIE, but is not the primary beneficiary, the following disclosures should be made (ASC 810-10-50-4) (FIN-46R, par. 24):

   a. The nature of its involvement with the VIE and when that involvement began.

   b. The nature, purpose, size, and activities of the VIE.

   c. The reporting entity's maximum exposure to loss as a result of its involvement with the VIE.

3. Disclosures required by ASC Topic 860, *Transfers and Servicing* (FAS-140, *Accounting for Transfers and Servicing of Financial Assets and Extinguishments of Liabilities*), about a VIE should be included in the same note to the financial statements as the information required above. (ASC 810-10-50-5) (FIN-46R, par. 25). See Chapter 57, "ASC Topic 860: Transfers and Servicing."

4. Information about VIEs should be reported in the aggregate for similar entities only if separate reporting would not add material information. (ASC 810-10-50-5) (FIN-46R, par. 25)

5. If a reporting entity with an interest in a VIE, or potential VIE, does not apply the guidance in ASC Topic 810, *Consolidation* (FIN-46R), pertaining to VIEs because of the condition described in ASC paragraph 810-10-15-17(c) (FIN-46R, par. 4) (i.e., a VIE or potential VIE created before December 31, 2003 is unable to obtain the information necessary to apply the applicable guidance), the following information should be disclosed (ASC 810-10-50-6) (FIN-46R, par. 26):

   a. The number of legal entities to which the applicable guidance is not being applied and the reason why the information required to apply this guidance is not available.

   b. The nature, purpose, size (if available), and activities of the legal entities and the nature of the reporting entity's involvement with those legal entities.

   c. The reporting entity's maximum exposure to loss because of its involvement with the legal entities.

   d. The amount of income, expense, purchases, sales, or other measure of activity between the reporting entity and the entities, for all periods presented. (*Note:* However, if it is not practicable to present that information for prior periods that are presented in the first set of financial statements for which this requirement applies, the information for those prior periods is not required.)

   Note: The disclosure requirements in items 6 and 7 below are prescribed by ASC Topic 810, *Consolidation,* based on FIN-46R, *Consolidation of Variable Interest Entities,* as amended by FAS-141R, *Business Combinations.* FAS-141R (ASC Topic 805) is effective for business combinations for which the acquisition date is on or after the beginning of the first annual reporting period beginning on or after December 15, 2008. Early adoption is not permitted.

6. The primary beneficiary of a VIE that is a business should provide the disclosures required by ASC Topic 805, *Business Combinations,* based on FAS-141R. (ASC 810-10-50-3 and 65-1) (FIN-46R, par. 23; FAS-141R, Appendix E, par. E34c). See Chapter 44, "ASC Topic 805: Business Combinations."

7. The primary beneficiary of a VIE that is *not* a business should disclose the amount of gain or loss recognized on the initial consolidation of the VIE. (ASC 810-10-50-3 and 65-1) (FIN-46R, par. 23; FAS-141R, Appendix E, par. E34c)

Note: The disclosure requirements in items 8 through 13 below are prescribed for *public entities* only by ASC Topic 810, *Consolidation*, based on FSP FAS 140-4 and FIN-46R-8, *Disclosures by Public Entities (Enterprises) about Transfers of Financial Assets and Interests in Variable Interest Entities.* These requirements are effective for the first reporting period (interim or annual) ending after December 15, 2008, and apply for each annual and interim reporting period thereafter. Early adoption is permitted. Entities are encouraged to disclose comparative information in periods earlier than the effective date. In periods after initial adoption, comparative disclosures are required only for periods subsequent to the effective date.

Disclosures about VIEs may be reported in the aggregate for similar entities if separate reporting would not provide more useful information to financial statement users. A public entity should disclose how similar entities are aggregated and should distinguish between: (*a*) VIEs that are not consolidated because the reporting entity is not the primary beneficiary but has a significant variable interest or is the sponsor that holds a variable interest; and (*b*) VIEs that are consolidated. In determining whether to aggregate VIEs, the reporting entity should consider quantitative and qualitative information about the different risk and reward characteristics of each VIE and the significance of each VIE to the reporting entity. The disclosures should be presented in a manner that clearly and fully explains to financial statement users the nature and extent of an entity's involvement with VIEs. (ASC 810-10-50-9) (FSP FAS 140-4 and FIN-46R-8, par. C2)

8. For a public entity that is a primary beneficiary in a VIE, that holds a significant variable interest in a VIE but is not the primary beneficiary, or that is a sponsor that holds a variable interest in a VIE, the following disclosures should be made (ASC 810-10-50-12 and 50-13) (FSP FAS 140-4 and FIN-46R-8, par. C4):

   a. The reporting entity's methodology for determining whether it is (or is not) the primary beneficiary of a VIE, including, but not limited to, significant judgments and assumptions made. For example, one way to meet this disclosure would be to provide information about the types of involvements a reporting entity considers significant, supplemented with information about how the significant involvements were considered in determining whether the reporting entity is, or is not, the primary beneficiary.

   b. If the conclusion to consolidate a VIE has changed in the most recent financial statements (e.g., the VIE was previously consolidated and is not currently consolidated):

   (1) The primary factors that caused the change.

    (2) The effect on the reporting entity's financial statements.

  c. Whether the reporting entity has provided financial or other support during the periods presented to the VIE that it was not previously contractually required to provide, including:

    (1) The type of support provided.

    (2) The amount of support provided.

    (3) The primary reasons for providing the support.

    (4) Situations where the reporting entity assisted the VIE in obtaining another type of support.

  d. Qualitative and quantitative information about the reporting entity's involvement (giving consideration to both explicit arrangements and implicit variable interests) with the VIE, including, but not limited to:

    (1) The nature of the VIE.

    (2) The purpose of the VIE.

    (3) The size of the VIE.

    (4) The activities of the VIE.

    (5) How the VIE is financed.

Note: The disclosure requirements in item 9 below are effective prior to the adoption of the guidance in ASC Topic 805, *Business Combinations*, based on FAS 141R, *Business Combinations*, which is effective for business combinations with an acquisition date on or after the beginning of the first annual reporting period beginning on or after December 15, 2008.

9. For a public entity that is the primary beneficiary of a VIE, the following disclosures should be made (ASC 810-10-50-13 and 50-14) (FSP FAS 140-4 and FIN-46R-8, pars. C4 and C5):

  a. For the VIE's assets and liabilities in the balance sheet that are consolidated in the reporting entity's financial statements:

    (1) The carrying amount of the assets and liabilities.

    (2) The classification of the assets and liabilities.

    (3) Qualitative information about the relationship(s) between those assets and associated liabilities. For example, if the VIE's assets can be used only to settle specific obligations of the VIE, the reporting entity should disclose qualitative information about the nature of the restrictions on those assets.

b. The lack of recourse if creditors (or beneficial interest holders) of a consolidated VIE have no recourse to the general credit of the primary beneficiary.

c. The terms of arrangements, giving consideration to both explicit arrangements and implicit variable interests, that could require the reporting entity to provide financial support (e.g., liquidity arrangements and obligations to purchase assets) to the VIE, including events or circumstances that could expose the reporting entity to a loss.

Note: The disclosure requirements in item 10 below are effective after the adoption of the guidance in ASC Topic 805, *Business Combinations*, based on FAS- 141R, *Business Combinations*, which is effective for business combinations with an acquisition date on or after the beginning of the first annual reporting period beginning on or after December 15, 2008.

10. For a public entity that is the primary beneficiary of a VIE, the following disclosures should be made (ASC 810-10-50-13 and 50-14) (FSP FAS 140-4 and FIN-46R-8, pars. C4 and C5):

   a. For the primary beneficiary of a VIE that is a business, the disclosures required by ASC Topic 805 based on FAS 141R. See Chapter 44, "ASC Topic 805: Business Combinations."

   b. For the primary beneficiary of a VIE that is not a business, the amount of gain or loss recognized on the initial consolidation of the VIE.

   c. For the primary beneficiary of a VIE, regardless of whether the VIE is a business:

      (1) For the VIE's assets and liabilities in the balance sheet that are consolidated in the reporting entity's financial statements:

         (i) The carrying amount of the assets and liabilities.

         (ii) The classification of the assets and liabilities.

         (iii) Qualitative information about the relationship(s) between those assets and associated liabilities. For example, if the VIE's assets can be used only to settle specific obligations of the VIE, the reporting entity should disclose qualitative information about the nature of the restrictions on those assets.

      (2) The lack of recourse if creditors (or beneficial interest holders) of a consolidated VIE have no recourse to the general credit of the primary beneficiary.

      (3)   The terms of arrangements, giving consideration to both explicit arrangements and implicit variable interests, that could require the reporting entity to provide financial support (e.g., liquidity arrangements and obligations to purchase assets) to the VIE, including events or circumstances that could expose the reporting entity to a loss.

11.   For a public entity that holds a significant variable interest or is a sponsor that holds a variable interest in a VIE, but is not the VIE's primary beneficiary, the following disclosures should be made (ASC 810-10-50-15) (FSP FAS 140-4 and FIN-46R-8, par. C6):

   a.   For assets and liabilities in the reporting entity's balance sheet that relate to the reporting entity's variable interest in the VIE:

      (1)   The carrying amount of the assets and liabilities.

      (2)   The classification of the assets and liabilities.

   b.   For a reporting entity's exposure to loss as a result of its involvement with the VIE:

      (1)   The reporting entity's maximum exposure to loss.

      (2)   How the maximum exposure to loss is determined.

      (3)   The significant sources of the reporting entity's exposure to loss to the VIE.

      (4)   If applicable, the fact that a reporting entity's maximum exposure to loss as a result of its involvement with the VIE cannot be quantified.

   c.   A tabular comparison of the carrying amount of the liability, as required by (a) (1) above, and the reporting entity's maximum exposure to loss, as required by (b) (1) above.

   d.   Qualitative and quantitative information to allow financial statement users to understand the differences between the two amounts in (c) above. (*Note:* This disclosure should consider, but is not limited to, the terms of arrangements, giving consideration to both explicit arrangements and implicit variable interests, that could require the reporting entity to provide financial support [e.g., liquidity arrangements and obligations to purchase assets] to the VIE, including events or circumstances that could expose the reporting entity to a loss.)

   e.   Information about any of the following (encouraged but not required):

      (1)   Liquidity arrangements.

(2) Guarantees.

(3) Other commitments by third parties that may affect the fair value or risk of the reporting entity's variable interest in the VIE.

12. For a public entity that does not apply the guidance in ASC Subtopic 810-10 (FIN-46R) to one or more VIEs or potential VIEs because of the condition described in ASC paragraph 810-10-15-17(c) (FIN-46R, par. 4(g)), the following disclosures should be made (ASC 810-10-50-16) (FSP FAS 140-4 and FIN-46R-8, par. C8):

   a. The number of legal entities to which that guidance is not being applied and the reason why the information required to apply that guidance is not available.

   b. The nature, purpose, size (if available), and activities of the legal entities.

   c. The nature of the reporting entity's involvement with the legal entities.

   d. The reporting entity's maximum exposure to loss because of its involvement with the legal entities.

   e. For all periods presented, the following amounts between the reporting entity and the legal entities:

      (1) The amount of income.

      (2) The amount of expense.

      (3) The amount of purchases.

      (4) The amount of sales.

      (5) Any other measure of activity between the reporting entity and the legal entities.

13. If the disclosure requirements in items 8 through 12 above are contained in more than one note to the financial statements, cross-references should be made to the other notes that provide the disclosures prescribed for similar entities. (ASC 810-10-50-11) (FSP FAS 140-4 and FIN-46R-8, par. C7)

Note: The disclosure requirements in item 14 below are prescribed for a *public entity* that is either: (*a*) a sponsor that holds a variable interest in a qualifying special-purpose entity (SPE) but was not the transferor (nontransferor entity) of financial assets to the qualifying SPE; or (*b*) a servicer of a qualifying SPE that holds a significant variable interest in the qualifying SPE but was not the transferor (nontransferor) of financial assets to the qualifying SPE. (ASC 810-10-50-17) (FSP FAS 140-4 and FIN-46R-8, par. D1).These disclosure requirements are prescribed by ASC Topic 810, *Consolidation*, based on FSP FAS 140-4 and FIN-46R-8, *Disclosures by Public Entities (Enterprises) about Transfers of Financial Assets and Interests* *in Variable Interest Entities.* These requirements are effective for the first reporting period (interim or annual) ending after December 15, 2008, and apply for each annual and interim reporting period thereafter. Early adoption is permitted. Entities are encouraged to disclose comparative information in periods earlier than the effective date. In periods after initial adoption, comparative disclosures are required only for periods subsequent to the effective date.

Disclosures about SPEs may be reported in the aggregate for similar entities if separate reporting would not provide more useful information to financial statement users. A public entity should disclose how similar entities are aggregated. In determining whether to aggregate qualifying SPEs, the reporting entity should consider quantitative and qualitative information about the different risk and reward characteristics of each qualifying SPE and the importance of each qualifying SPE to the reporting entity. (ASC 810-10-50-18) (FSP FAS 140-4 and FIN-46R-8, par. D2)

14. For a public entity that is either: (*a*) a nontransferor sponsor of a qualifying SPE that holds a variable interest in the qualifying SPE; or (*b*) a nontransferor servicer of a qualifying SPE that holds a significant variable interest in the qualifying SPE, the following disclosures should be made (ASC 810-10-50-19) (FSP FAS 140-4 and FIN-46R-8, par. D3):

    a. The nature of the qualifying SPE.

    b. The purpose of the qualifying SPE.

    c. The size of the qualifying SPE.

    d. The activities of the qualifying SPE.

    e. How the SPE is financed.

    f. For the assets and liabilities recognized in the balance sheet related to the reporting entity's involvement with the qualifying SPE:

        (1) The carrying amount of the assets and liabilities.

        (2) The classification of the assets and liabilities.

    g. The terms of arrangements that could require the reporting entity to provide financial support (le.g., liquidity arrangements and obligations to purchase assets) to the qualifying SPE, including events or circumstances that could expose the reporting entity to loss. (*Note:* This disclosure should consider all available evidence, including, but not limited to: (*1*) explicit written arrangements; (*2*) communications between the sponsor or servicer and the qualifying SPE or its beneficial interest holders; and (*3*) unwritten arrangements that are customary in similar relationships between the sponsor or servicer and the qualifying SPE or its beneficial interest holders.)

h. For a reporting entity's exposure to loss as a result of its involvement with the qualifying SPE:

    (1) The reporting entity's maximum exposure to loss.

    (2) How the maximum exposure to loss is determined.

    (3) The significant sources of the reporting entity's exposure to loss to the qualifying SPE.

    (4) If applicable, the fact that a reporting entity's maximum exposure to loss as a result of its involvement with the qualifying SPE cannot be quantified.

i. Whether the reporting entity has provided financial or other support during the periods presented to the qualifying SPE that it was not previously contractually required to provide, including:

    (1) The type of support provided.

    (2) The amount of support provided.

    (3) The primary reasons for providing the support.

    (4) Situations where the reporting entity assisted the qualifying SPE in obtaining another type of support.

FAS-167, *Amendments to FASB Interpretation No. 46(R)*

Note: The disclosure requirements under the caption "Variable Interest Entities," above, have been superseded by the guidance in FAS-167, *Amendments to FASB Interpretation No. 46(R)*, which is effective as of the beginning of the first annual reporting period beginning after November 15, 2009, and all interim and annual periods thereafter. Thereafter, the disclosure requirements under this caption should be followed. Early adoption is not permitted.

Disclosures about variable interest entities may be reported in the aggregate for similar entities if separate reporting would not provide more useful information to financial statement users. An enterprise should disclose how similar entities are aggregated and should distinguish between: (*a*) variable interest entities that are not consolidated because the enterprise is not the primary beneficiary but has a variable interest; and (*b*) variable interest entities that are consolidated. In determining whether to aggregate variable interest entities, the reporting enterprise should consider quantitative and qualitative information about the different risk and reward characteristics of each variable interest entity and the significance of each variable interest entity to the enterprise. The disclosures should be presented in a manner that clearly explains the nature and extent of an enterprise's involvement with variable interest entities.

If the disclosures are provided in more than one note to the financial statements, the enterprise should provide a cross reference to the other notes to the financial statements that provide the disclosures prescribed in FIN-46R for similar entities.

The principal objectives of the following disclosures are to provide financial statement users with an understanding of: (*a*) the significant judgments and assumptions made by an enterprise in determining whether it must consolidate a variable interest entity and/or disclose information about its involvement in a variable interest entity; (*b*) the nature of restrictions on a consolidated variable interest entity's assets and on the settlement of its liabilities reported by an enterprise in its balance sheet, including the carrying amounts of such assets and liabilities; (*c*) the nature of, and changes in, the risks associated with an enterprise's involvement with the variable interest entity; and (*d*) how an enterprise's involvement with the variable interest entity affects the enterprise's financial position, financial performance, and cash flows. To achieve those objectives, an enterprise may need to supplement these required disclosures.

1. A reporting enterprise should present separately on the face of the balance sheet (FAS-167, Appendix D and FIN-46R par. 22A):

   a. Assets of a consolidated variable interest entity that can be used only to settle obligations of the consolidated variable interest entity.

   b. Liabilities of a consolidated variable interest entity for which creditors (or beneficial interest holders) do not have recourse to the general credit of the primary beneficiary.

2. For an enterprise that is a primary beneficiary of a variable interest entity, or an enterprise that holds a variable interest in a variable interest entity, but is not the entity's primary beneficiary, the following disclosures should be made (FAS-167, Appendix D and FIN-46R par. 22E):

   a. Its methodology for determining whether the enterprise is the primary beneficiary of a variable interest entity, including, but not limited to:

      (1) Significant judgments made.

      (2) Significant assumptions made.

      (*Note:* For example, one way to meet this disclosure requirement would be to provide information about the types of involvements an enterprise considers significant, supplemented with information about how the significant involvements were considered in determining whether the enterprise is the primary beneficiary.)

b. If facts and circumstances change such that the conclusion to consolidate a variable interest entity has changed in the most recent financial statements (e.g., the variable interest entity was previously consolidated and is not currently consolidated):

   (1) The primary factors that caused the change.

   (2) The effect on the enterprise's financial statements.

c. Whether the enterprise has provided financial or other support (explicitly or implicitly) during the periods presented to the variable interest entity that it was not previously contractually required to provide or whether the enterprise intends to provide that support, including:

   (1) The type and amount of support, including situations in which the enterprise assisted the variable interest entity in obtaining another type of support.

   (2) The primary reasons for providing the support.

d. Qualitative and quantitative information about the enterprise's involvement (giving consideration to both explicit arrangements and implicit variable interests) with the variable interest entity, including, but not limited to:

   (1) The nature of the variable interest entity.

   (2) The purpose of the variable interest entity.

   (3) The size of the variable interest entity.

   (4) The activities of the variable interest entity.

   (5) How the variable interest entity is financed.

3. For an enterprise that is the primary beneficiary of a variable interest entity, the following disclosures should be made (FAS-167, Appendix D and FIN-46R par. 23):

   a. If the variable interest entity is a business, the disclosures required by ASC Topic 805, *Business Combinations*, based on FAS-141R.

   b. If the variable interest entity is not a business, the amount of any gain or loss recognized on the initial consolidation of the variable interest entity.

4. For the primary beneficiary of a variable interest entity, the following disclosures should be made (FAS-167, Appendix D and FIN-46R par. 23A):

a. For a variable interest entity's assets and liabilities in the balance sheet that are consolidated in according with FIN-46R:

   (1) Their carrying amounts.

   (2) Their classification.

   (3) Qualitative information about the relationship(s) between those assets and liabilities. (For example, if the variable interest entity's assets can be used only to settle obligations of the variable interest entity, the enterprise should disclose qualitative information about the nature of the restrictions on those assets.)

b. Lack of recourse if creditors (or beneficial interest holders) of a consolidated variable interest entity have no recourse to the general credit of the primary beneficiary.

c. Terms of arrangements, giving consideration to both explicit arrangements and implicit variable interests that could require the enterprise to provide financial support (e.g., liquidity arrangements and obligations to purchase assets) to the variable interest entity, including events or circumstances that could expose the enterprise to a loss.

5. For an enterprise that holds a variable interest in a variable interest entity, but is not the variable interest entity's primary beneficiary, the following disclosures should be made (FAS-167, Appendix D and FIN-46R par. 24):

a. For assets and liabilities in the enterprise's balance sheet that relate to the enterprise's variable interest in the variable interest entity:

   (1) Their carrying amounts.

   (2) Their classification.

b. For the enterprise's exposure to loss as a result of its involvement with the variable interest entity:

   (1) The amount of the enterprise's maximum exposure to loss.

   (2) How the maximum exposure to loss was determined.

   (3) If the enterprise's maximum exposure to loss cannot be quantified, the fact that it cannot be quantified.

   (4) The significant sources of the enterprise's exposure to the variable interest entity.

c. A tabular comparison of the carrying amounts of the assets and liabilities, as required by item a. above and the enterprise's maximum exposure to loss, as required by item b. above, including:

    (1) Qualitative and quantitative information to allow financial statement users to understand the differences between the two amounts.

    (2) A discussion of the terms of arrangements, giving consideration to both explicit arrangements and implicit variable interests, that could require the enterprise to provide financial support (e.g., liquidity arrangements and obligations to purchase assets) to the variable interest entity, including events or circumstances that could expose the enterprise to a loss.

d. Information about the following types of arrangements by third parties that may affect the fair value or risk of the enterprise's variable interest in the variable interest entity (this disclosure is encouraged, but not required):

    (1) Liquidity arrangements.

    (2) Guarantees.

    (3) Other commitments by third parties.

e. If applicable, significant factors considered and judgments made in determining that the power to direct the activities of a variable interest entity that most significantly impact the entity's economic performance is shared in accordance with the guidance in paragraph 14D of FIN-46R.

6. For enterprises that do not apply FIN-46R to one or more variable interest entities or potential variable interest entities under the allowed exclusion in paragraph 4g of FIN-46R (regarding such entities created before December 31, 2003), the following disclosures should be made (FAS-167, Appendix D and FIN-46R par. 26):

a. The number of entities to which FIN-46R is not being applied.

b. The reason that the information required to apply FIN-46R is not available.

c. The nature of the entity(ies).

d. The purpose of the entity(ies).

e. The size (if available) of the entity(ies).

f. The activities of the entity(ies).

g. The nature of the enterprise's involvement with the entity(ies).

    h. The reporting enterprise's maximum exposure to loss because of its involvement with the entity(ies).

    i. The amount of income, expense, purchases, sales, or other measure of activity between the reporting enterprise and the entity(ies) for all periods presented.

    (*Note:* If it is not practicable to present the information for prior periods that are presented in the first set of financial statements for which this requirement applies, the information for those prior periods is not required.)

7. The following transition disclosures should be made in the period of adoption (FAS-167, par. 5):

    a. A description of the transition method(s) applied.

    b. The amount of the consolidated assets or liabilities by the transition method(s) applied in the entity's balance sheet.

    c. The classification of the consolidated assets or liabilities by the transition method(s) applied in the entity's balance sheet.

8. For an enterprise that is required to consolidate an entity as a result of the initial application of FAS-167 and that has elected the fair value option provided in ASC Topic 825, *Financial Instruments*, (FAS-159, *The Fair Value Option for Financial Assets and Financial Liabilities*), for all financial assets and liabilities of that entity, the enterprise should make the following disclosures (FAS-167, par. 6):

    a. Management's reasons for electing the fair value option for a particular entity or group of entities.

    b. If the fair value option is elected for some entities and not others, the reasons for those different elections.

    c. Quantitative information by line item in the balance sheet indicating the related effect on the cumulative effect adjustment to retained earnings of electing the fair value option for an entity.

9. For an enterprise that is required to deconsolidate an entity as a result of the initial application of FAS-167, the amount of any cumulative effect adjustment related to deconsolidation should be disclosed separately from any cumulative effect adjustment related to consolidation of entities. (FAS-167, par.7)

Control of Partnerships and Similar Entities

1. If an entity has consolidated a limited partnership, the entity should appropriately consider financial statement and

disclosure alternatives that may provide additional useful information. (ASC 810-20-45-1) (EITF 04-5) (*Note:* For example, an entity may highlight the effects of consolidating a limited partnership by providing consolidating financial statements or separately classifying the assets and liabilities of the limited partnership(s) on the face of the balance sheet.)

EXAMPLES OF FINANCIAL STATEMENT DISCLOSURES

 The following sample disclosures are available on the accompanying disc.

Consolidation—Illustrations If ASC Topic 810 Based on Guidance in FAS-160 Has *Not* Been Adopted

Example 1: Accounting Policy for Ownership Interests in Investees

The accompanying Consolidated Financial Statements include the accounts of the Company and its majority-owned subsidiary partnerships and corporations, after elimination of all material intercompany accounts, transactions, and profits. Investments in unconsolidated subsidiaries representing ownership of at least 20% but less than 50%, are accounted for under the equity method. Nonmarketable investments in which the Company has less than 20% ownership and in which it does not have the ability to exercise significant influence over the investee are initially recorded at cost and periodically reviewed for impairment.

Example 2: Consolidation Policy Specifically Described

Investee companies in which the Company directly or indirectly owns more than 50% of the outstanding voting securities or those in which the Company has effective control are generally accounted for under the consolidation method of accounting. Under this method, an Investee company's balance sheet and results of operations are reflected within the Company's Consolidated Financial Statements. All significant intercompany accounts and transactions have been eliminated. Minority interests in the net assets and earnings or losses of a consolidated Investee are reflected in the caption "Minority interest" in the Company's Consolidated Balance Sheet and Statement of Operations. Minority interest adjusts the Company's consolidated results of operations to reflect only the Company's share of the earnings or losses of the consolidated Investee company. Upon dilution of control below 50%, the accounting method is adjusted to the equity or cost method of accounting, as appropriate, for subsequent periods.

Example 3: Consolidated Statements Include Subsidiaries with Different Year Ends (Parent Company Has a December Year-End)

The Consolidated Financial Statements include the accounts of the parent company and subsidiaries, after elimination of intercompany accounts and transactions. The accounts of certain subsidiaries are consolidated as of November 30 due to the time needed to consolidate these subsidiaries. No events occurred related to these subsidiaries in December 20X2 and December 20X1 that materially affected the consolidated financial position, results of operations, or cash flows.

Example 4: Change in Reporting Period for Subsidiary from Fiscal Year to Calendar Year—The Parent Company's Reporting Period Is a Calendar Year

Effective January 1, 20X2, the Parent Company changed the reporting period of its majority-owned subsidiary XYZ, Inc. from a fiscal year ending November 30 to a calendar year ending December 31. The results of operations of XYZ, Inc. for the month of December 20X1 (representing the period between the end of its 20X1 fiscal year and the beginning of its new calendar year) amounted to a net income of $350,000. This amount was credited to "Retained earnings" to avoid reporting more than 12 months results of operations in one year. Accordingly, the 20X2 consolidated operations include the results for XYZ, Inc. beginning January 1, 20X2. The cash activity for the one-month stub period is included in "Other cash activities—Stub period, XYZ, Inc." in the Consolidated Statements of Cash Flows.

The following table illustrates the effect on retained earnings as a result of the change in year end of a subsidiary, as reflected in the Consolidated Statement of Stockholders' Equity.

	Common Stock	Additional Paid-in Capital	Retained Earnings	Total
Balances at December 31, 20X0	$500,000	$1,000,000	$2,300,000	$3,800,000
Net income	-0-	-0-	800,000	800,000
Balances at December 31, 20X1	500,000	1,000,000	3,100,000	4,600,000

	Common Stock	Additional Paid-in Capital	Retained Earnings	Total
Net income	-0-	-0-	1,000,000	1,000,000
Dividends	-0-	-0-	(600,000)	(600,000)
Net income for the month ended December 20X1, due to the change in fiscal year-end of a subsidiary	-0-	-0-	350,000	350,000
Balances at December 31, 20X2	$500,000	$1,000,000	$3,850,000	$5,350,000

Example 5: Certain Subsidiaries Are Not Consolidated

The Consolidated Financial Statements include the accounts of the Company and all majority-owned subsidiaries, except for certain insignificant subsidiaries, the investments in which are recorded under the cost method because of restrictions upon the transfer of earnings and other economic uncertainties. All significant intercompany accounts and transactions have been eliminated.

Example 6: Consolidated Financial Statements Include Less Than 50% Owned Entity

The Consolidated Financial Statements include the accounts of the parent company and its subsidiaries, including XYZ Corp. in which the parent company holds a minority interest. At December 31, 20X2, the parent company owned 26% of XYZ Corp.'s capital stock, representing 78% voting control. All significant intercompany accounts and transactions have been eliminated.

Example 7: Change in Ownership in Previously Consolidated Subsidiary Results in Using the Equity Method of Accounting in the Current Period

In 20X0, the Company formed a joint venture with Sycom, Inc. (the Sycom Joint Venture) for the manufacture, distribution, and marketing of leather furniture. The Company originally acquired a 51% interest in the Sycom Joint Venture for $4,000,000 and, accordingly, the joint venture's Financial Statements had been consolidated with the Company's Financial Statements from the acquisition date to

December 31, 20X1. Effective January 1, 20X2, the Company sold a 5% interest in the Sycom Joint Venture for $350,000 reducing its interest to 46%. As a result, in 20X2 the Company's investment in the Sycom Joint Venture is being accounted for using the equity method. The deconsolidation of the Sycom Joint Venture had an insignificant effect on the Company's consolidated total assets and net sales as of and for the year ended December 31, 20X2.

Example 8: Financial Statements Currently Consolidated to Include the Accounts of a Previously Unconsolidated Affiliate

Effective January 1, 20X2, the Company began to consolidate into its Financial Statements the accounts of XYZ Corporation, formerly an unconsolidated affiliate. XYZ Corporation, which primarily manufactures medical equipment, is a venture between the Company and ABC Company of Ohio. The consolidation occurred as a result of revisions of the Stockholders' Agreement between the Company and ABC Company of Ohio. Financial data presented for previous years have not been restated to reflect the consolidation of XYZ Corporation. The consolidation is not material to financial position or results of operations for the periods presented and had no effect on previously reported net income, which included XYZ Corporation on an equity basis.

Example 9: Consolidation of Newly Formed Entity That Has a Minority Interest

In October 20X2, the Company contributed $2,765,000 in assets to a newly created partnership, Hope Enterprises, L.P. (the Partnership), in exchange for a 79% general partner interest in the Partnership. The contributed assets consisted of certain trademarks that are licensed to the Company pursuant to exclusive long-term license agreements, accounts receivable, property and equipment, and cash. In addition, an outside investor contributed $735,000 in cash to the Partnership in exchange for a 21% limited partner interest. For financial reporting purposes, the Partnership's assets and liabilities are consolidated with those of the Company and the outside investor's 21% interest in the Partnership is included in the Company's Financial Statements as minority interest.

Example 10: Presentation of Minority Interest in the Consolidated Financial Statements

Minority interest represents the minority stockholders' proportionate share of the equity of Nostars, Inc. At December 31, 20X2, and December 31, 20X1, the Company owned 22% of Nostars, Inc.'s capital stock, representing 75% voting control. The Company's 75% controlling interest requires that Nostars, Inc.'s operations be included in the Consolidated Financial Statements. The 78% equity interest of Nostars, Inc. that is not owned by the Company is shown as "Minority interest in consolidated subsidiary" in the 20X2 and 20X1 Consolidated Statements of Operations and Consolidated Balance Sheets.

> **Note:** The following table illustrates the presentation of minority interest in the Consolidated Balance Sheets between the liabilities section and the stockholder's equity section ("mezzanine"). However, prior to FAS-160, there were three acceptable alternative presentations of minority interests in the balance sheet: as a liability, as equity, or as a separate "mezzanine" item between liabilities and equity.

	20X2	20X1
Total current liabilities	$15,000,000	$13,000,000
Long-term debt	6,000,000	5,000,000
Deferred income taxes	1,500,000	2,300,000
Minority interest in consolidated subsidiary	1,100,000	1,400,000
Stockholders' equity	7,600,000	6,900,000

The following table illustrates the presentation of minority interest in the Consolidated Statements of Operations as a component of "Other income (expense)."

	20X2	20X1
Net sales	$41,000,000	$37,000,000
Costs and expenses	39,000,000	34,000,000
Operating income	2,000,000	3,000,000
Other income (expense):		
Interest expense	(500,000)	(400,000)
Minority interest in income of subsidiary	(600,000)	(800,000)
Other—Net	200,000	500,000
	(900,000)	(700,000)
Income before income taxes	1,100,000	2,300,000
Income taxes	(450,000)	(900,000)
Net income	$ 650,000	$ 1,400,000

The following table illustrates the presentation of minority interest in the Consolidated Statements of Operations as a separate line item before "Net income."

	20X2	20X1
Net sales	$41,000,000	$37,000,000
Costs and expenses	39,000,000	34,000,000
Operating income	2,000,000	3,000,000
Other income (expense):		
Interest expense	(500,000)	(400,000)
Other—Net	200,000	500,000
	(300,000)	100,000
Income before income taxes and minority interest	1,700,000	3,100,000
Income taxes	(450,000)	(900,000)
Income before minority interest	1,250,000	2,200,000
Minority interest in income of subsidiary	(600,000)	(800,000)
Net income	$ 650,000	$ 1,400,000

Example 11: Parent Company to Spin-Off Previously Consolidated Subsidiary, Resulting in Restatement of Prior Year's Financial Statements

On August 5, 20X2, the Company's Board of Directors approved a plan to spin-off the Company's wholly owned subsidiary, Citrom Specialties, Inc. (Citrom), to the Company's shareholders in the form of a tax-free dividend. The Company has requested and received a ruling from the Internal Revenue Service that this distribution will not be taxable to the Company's shareholders.

The Company's investment in and the results of operations of Citrom are reflected in the Company's Consolidated Financial Statements on the equity method as Citrom is now a temporary investment that the Company anticipates distributing to its shareholders during the year 20X3. Accordingly, the 20X1 Financial Statements have been restated. As a part of the spin-off, approximately $3,000,000 of Citrom's indebtedness to the Company has been contributed as capital. Summary financial information of Citrom consists of the following:

	Year Ended December 31	
	20X2	*20X1*
Net sales	$ 33,000,000	$ 29,000,000
Costs and expenses	35,000,000	30,000,000
Loss before income taxes	(2,000,000)	(1,000,000)
Tax benefit allocated by the parent	250,000	200,000
Net loss	$(1,750,000)	$ (800,000)

	As of December 31	
	20X2	*20X1*
Current assets	$12,000,000	$10,000,000
Fixed assets	2,000,000	1,500,000
Other assets	3,000,000	2,500,000
Total assets	$17,000,000	$14,000,000
Current liabilities	$11,000,000	$ 8,000,000
Long-term liabilities	4,000,000	3,800,000
Shareholders' equity	2,000,000	2,200,000
Total liabilities and shareholders' equity	$17,000,000	$14,000,000

Included in accounts receivable of the Company at December 31, 20X2, and December 31, 20X1, are net amounts due from Citrom of $650,000 and $475,000, respectively. During the years ended December 31, 20X2, and December 31, 20X1, the Company sold medical products and equipment to Citrom totaling $5,500,000 and $4,900,000, respectively.

> **Note:** The following table shows the restatement of the Company's Financial Statements to reflect the spin-off of Citrom.

	Year Ended December 31	
	20X2	*20X1*
Consolidated Statements of Operations		
Net sales	$ 82,000,000	$76,000,000
Costs and expenses	87,000,000	73,000,000
Income (loss) before loss of non-consolidated subsidiary—Citrom	(5,000,000)	3,000,000

	Year Ended December 31	
	20X2	*20X1*
Loss of non-consolidated subsidiary—Citrom	(2,000,000)	(1,000,000)
Income (loss) before income taxes	(7,000,000)	2,000,000
Income taxes benefit (expense)	3,000,000	(800,000)
Net income (loss)	$(4,000,000)	$1,200,000

	As of December 31	
	20X2	*20X1*
Consolidated Balance Sheets		
Total current assets	$45,000,000	$43,000,000
Other assets:		
Investment in non-consolidated subsidiary—Citrom	2,000,000	2,200,000

Example 12: Consolidated Financial Statements Include Nonhomogenous Operations

The Company's Consolidated Financial Statements include the accounts of Max Credit Corp., a wholly owned finance subsidiary. Business operations of this subsidiary consist primarily of financing certain customer obligations resulting from retail sales of home furnishings, accessories, and related other merchandise charged on credit cards. Summarized financial information of Max Credit Corp. is presented below.

	As of December 31	
	20X2	*20X1*
Balance Sheets		
Current assets, primarily accounts receivable	$4,500,000	$4,200,000
Property and equipment	400,000	350,000
Other assets	150,000	100,000
Total assets	$5,050,000	$4,650,000
Short-term debt	$1,000,000	$1,200,000
Accounts payable and accrued liabilities	700,000	650,000

	As of December 31	
	20X2	*20X1*
Long-term debt	550,000	400,000
Stockholders' equity	2,800,000	2,400,000
Total liabilities and stockholders' equity	$5,050,000	$4,650,000

	Year Ended December 31	
	20X2	*20X1*
Income Statements		
Revenues	$6,000,000	$5,000,000
Costs and expenses	5,150,000	4,300,000
Income before income taxes	850,000	700,000
Income taxes	450,000	400,000
Net income	$ 400,000	$ 300,000

Example 13: Financial Statements Include Certain Allocations from Parent for Certain General and Administrative Expenses

The Company is a majority-owned subsidiary of ABC, Inc. The consolidated financial statements include certain allocations from ABC, Inc. for certain general and administrative expenses such as rent, legal services, insurance, and employee benefits. Allocations are based primarily on the Company's headcount located on ABC, Inc.'s premises in relation to total headcount for all ABC, Inc.'s companies located on the premises. Management believes that the method used to allocate the costs and expenses is reasonable; however, such allocated amounts may or may not necessarily be indicative of what actual expenses would have been incurred had the Company operated independently of ABC, Inc. Amounts due to ABC, Inc. totaled approximately $1,613,000 and $1,397, 000 as of December 31, 20X2, and December 31, 20X1, respectively.

The following table summarizes the expenses allocated to the Company by ABC, Inc. for the years ended December 31, 20X2, and December 31, 20X1:

	Year Ended December 31	
	20X2	*20X1*
Rent and facilities	$1,115,000	$1,072,000
Legal services	216,000	191,000

	Year Ended December 31	
	20X2	*20X1*
Insurance	173,000	162,000
Employee benefits	294,000	289,000

Consolidation—Illustrations if ASC Topic 810 Based on Guidance in FAS-160 Has Been Adopted

Example 14: Presentation of the Noncontrolling Interest in the Consolidated Balance Sheet within Equity, but Separately from the Parent's Equity

	20X2	*20X1*
Total current liabilities	$1,500,000	$1,300,000
Long-term debt	2,000,000	5,000,000
Deferred income taxes	500,000	300,000
Equity:		
XYZ Company shareholders' equity:		
Common stock	200,000	200,000
Additional paid-in-capital	42,000	50,000
Retained earnings	194,500	167,000
Accumulated other comprehensive income	22,500	16,000
Total XYZ Company shareholders' equity	459,000	433,000
Noncontrolling interest	26,000	48,000
Total equity	485,000	481,000
Total liabilities and equity	$4,485,000	$7,081,000

Example 15: Presentation of Net Income Attributable to the Parent and the Noncontrolling Interest in the Consolidated Income Statement

	20X2	*20X1*
Revenues	$ 395,000	$ 360,000
Expenses	(330,000)	(305,000)
Income from continuing operations, before tax	65,000	55,000
Income tax expense	(26,000)	(22,000)

	20X2	20X1
Income from continuing operations, net of tax	39,000	33,000
Discontinued operations, net of tax	—	(7,000)
Net income	39,000	26,000
Less: Net income attributable to the noncontrolling interest	(1,500)	(4,000)
Net income attributable to XYZ Company	$ 37,500	$ 22,000
Amounts attributable to XYZ Company common shareholders:		
Income from continuing operations, net of tax	$ 37,500	$ 27,600
Discontinued operations, net of tax	—	(5,600)
Net income	$ 37,500	$ 22,000

Example 16: Presentation of Comprehensive Income Attributable to the Parent and the Noncontrolling Interest on the Face of the Consolidated Statement in Which Comprehensive Income Is Presented

	20X2	20X1
Net income	$ 39,000	$ 26,000
Other comprehensive income, net of tax:		
Unrealized holding gain on available-for-sale securities, net of tax	5,000	15,000
Total other comprehensive income, net of tax	5,000	15,000
Comprehensive income	44,000	41,000
Comprehensive income attributable to the noncontrolling interest	(2,000)	(7,000)
Comprehensive income attributable to XYZ Company	$ 42,000	$ 34,000

Example 17: Presentation in the Consolidated Statement of Changes in Equity of a Reconciliation at the Beginning and End of the Period of the Carrying Amount of Consolidated Equity, Equity Attributable to the Parent, and Equity Attributable to the Noncontrolling Interest

	Total	Comprehensive Income	XYZ Company Shareholders				Non-controlling Interest
			Retained Earnings	Accumulated Other Comprehensive Income	Common Stock	Paid-in Capital	
Beginning balance, 01/01/20X2	$ 481,000	$ -0-	$ 167,000	$16,000	$200,000	$50,000	$ 48,000
Purchase of subsidiary shares from noncontrolling interest	(30,000)					(8,000)	(24,000)
Comprehensive income:							
Net income	39,000	39,000	37,500				1,500
Other comprehensive income, net of tax:							
Unrealized gain on securities	5,000	5,000		4,500			500
Other comprehensive income	5,000	5,000					
Comprehensive income	44,000	$44,000					
Dividends paid on common stock	(10,000)		(10,000)				
Ending balance, 12/31/20X2	$ 485,000		$ 194,500	$22,500	$200,000	$42,000	$ 26,000

Example 18: Notes to the Consolidated Financial Statements Include a Separate Schedule That Shows the Effects of Changes in the Parent Company's Ownership Interest in Its Subsidiary on the Parent's Equity (Schedule Is Only Required If the Parent's Ownership Interest in a Subsidiary Changes in Any Periods Presented in the Consolidated Financial Statements)

	20X2	20X1
Net income attributable to parent company	$ 37,500	$22,000
Transfers (to) from the noncontrolling interest:		
Increase in parent's paid-in-capital for sale of 2,000 subsidiary A common shares	—	10,000
Decrease in parent's paid-in-capital for purchase of 1,000 subsidiary A common shares	(8,000)	—
Net transfers (to) from the noncontrolling interest	(8,000)	10,000
Change from net income attributable to the parent and transfers (to) from the noncontrolling interest	$(29,500)	$32,000

Variable Interest Entities

Example 19: Joint Venture Is a Variable Interest Entity and the Reporting Company Is the Primary Beneficiary

In April 20X1, the Company provided an interest free $12 million loan to an unrelated party as seed capital for a venture (ABC Inc.) organized to participate in providing technical service, and networking technology and equipment to certain organizations in emerging markets. The loan, which is partially secured by an ownership interest in ABC Inc., is payable in eight years and may be called early without penalty. As a result, and the fact that the venture's continuing viability is heavily dependent on the further provision of networking equipment by the Company, the Company has determined that ABC Inc. is a variable interest entity and that the Company is the primary beneficiary. Therefore, ABC Inc. is consolidated into the Company's results as of December 31, 20X2, and December 31, 20X1. ABC Inc. had insignificant revenue during 20X2 and 20X1 and had net losses of $4 million and $3 million for 20X2 and 20X1, respectively. The consolidation of ABC Inc. represented $10 million and $7 million of the total assets of the

Company as of December 31, 20X2, and December 31, 20X1, respectively, and $8 million and $6 million of the total liabilities of the Company as of December 31, 20X2, and December 31, 20X1, respectively. The liabilities of ABC Inc. consolidated by the Company do not represent additional claims on the Company's general assets; rather, they represent claims against the specific assets of ABC Inc. Similarly, the assets of ABC Inc. consolidated by the Company do not represent additional assets available to satisfy claims against the Company's general assets. The creditors of ABC Inc. do not have recourse to the Company, thereby limiting the liability risks associated with the Company's variable interests in ABC Inc.

Example 20: Joint Venture Is a Variable Interest Entity, but the Reporting Company Is Not the Primary Beneficiary

In April 20X1, the Company and ABC Inc. entered into the Max Systems, Inc. (Max) joint venture, which develops medical diagnostic products. As part of the formation of the joint venture, ABC Inc. contributed its existing medical diagnostic center located in Riverside, California to Max, and the Company invested $12 million in exchange for a 49.99% interest in Max and certain supply agreements. Of the total $12 million investment, $10 million was paid to ABC Inc. in April 20X1 and the remaining $2 million was subsequently paid in two installments of $1 million each in December 20X1 and October 20X2.

Max is governed by a Board of Managers, appointed by ABC Inc. and the Company. Since Max's inception, ABC Inc. has, as a result of its majority ownership, appointed the majority of the managers. The number of managers appointed by each party is subject to change as ownership interest changes. Under the Joint Venture Operating Agreement (JV Agreement), the Company may be required to make additional capital contributions to Max, through August 20X4, of up to a maximum amount as defined in the JV Agreement. The Company made additional investments in Max of $1.5 million in 20X1 and $1.8 million in 20X2, which were used for working capital and capital expenditure purposes, and received a return of investment from Max of $2.1 million in 20X2.

This joint venture is a variable interest entity primarily because the holders of the equity interests are protected from the obligation to absorb expected losses that would result from the variability of the cash flows of the joint venture. The Company has determined that it is not the primary beneficiary and, therefore, accounts for its interest in the joint venture using the equity method of accounting.

Example 21: Variable Interest Entity Leases Property to the Reporting Company

The Company consolidates the assets and liabilities of XYZ Realty, an entity from which the Company leases office buildings and a corporate aircraft. XYZ Realty has been determined to be a variable interest entity and the Company has been determined to be its primary beneficiary. Due to the consolidation of XYZ Realty, the Company reflects in its balance sheet: property, plant, and equipment of $15 million and $18 million, other assets of $2 million and $1 million, long-term debt of $15 million and $19 million, and other accrued liabilities of $1.5 million and $1 million, as of December 31, 20X2, and December 31, 20X1, respectively. The liabilities recognized as a result of consolidating XYZ Realty do not represent additional claims on the general assets of the Company. XYZ Realty's creditors have claims only on the specific assets of XYZ Realty.

Example 22: Reporting Company Consolidates Early-Stage Development Variable Interest Entity

In October 20X2, the Company entered into agreements that commit the Company to provide funding to ABC Inc., an early-stage development entity, subject to certain conditions and milestones. The funding is in the form of a $1 million convertible note. In addition, in exchange for providing a limited use license to certain of the Company's intellectual property, the Company received a 40% equity interest in ABC Inc. For accounting purposes, the Company is considered to be the primary beneficiary. Due to the nature of the agreement, the Company determined that since it is essentially providing 100% of the funding, there is no offset for minority interest and, therefore, the Company consolidates 100% of ABC Inc.'s operations until such time as the entity obtains funding from other sources.

Example 23: Reporting Company Deconsolidates Variable Interest Entity and Recognizes a Loss

In 20X2, the Company recognized a loss of $750,000 when it deconsolidated the net assets of ABC Inc., which was previously a consolidated variable interest entity. ABC Inc. continues to develop certain of the Company's product lines; however, the Company is no longer considered to be the primary beneficiary of ABC Inc.'s future profits or losses.

Example 24: Disclosures of Transactions with Special Purpose Entities and Variable Interest Entities under ASC Topic 810 Based on Guidance in FSP FAS 140-4 and FIN 46R-8 (Applicable Only to Public Entities)

Transactions with Special Purpose Entities

The Company enters into various types of on and off-balance sheet transactions with special purpose entities (SPEs) in the normal course of business. SPEs are corporations, trusts or partnerships that are established for a limited purpose. The Company uses SPEs to create sources of financing, liquidity, and regulatory capital capacity for the Company, as well as sources of financing and liquidity, and investment products for the Company's clients. The Company's use of SPEs generally consists of various securitization activities with SPEs, whereby financial assets are transferred to an SPE and repackaged as securities or similar interests that are sold to investors. In connection with the Company's securitization activities, the Company has various forms of ongoing involvement with SPEs, which may include:

- Underwriting securities issued by SPEs and subsequently making markets in those securities.
- Providing liquidity facilities to support short-term obligations of SPEs issued to third-party investors.
- Providing credit enhancement on securities issued by SPEs or market value guarantees of assets held by SPEs through the use of letters of credit, financial guarantees, and credit default swaps.
- Entering into other derivative contracts with SPEs.
- Holding senior or subordinated interests in SPEs.

The SPEs the Company uses are primarily either qualifying SPEs (QSPEs) or variable interest entities (VIEs). A QSPE is a specific type of SPE, which is a passive entity that has significant limitations on the types of assets and derivative instruments it may own and the extent of activities and decision making in which it may engage. For example, a QSPE's activities are generally limited to purchasing assets, passing along the cash flows of those assets to its investors, servicing its assets and, in certain transactions, issuing liabilities. Among other restrictions on a QSPE's activities, a QSPE may not actively manage its assets through discretionary sales or modifications. A QSPE is exempt from consolidation.

A VIE is an entity that has either a total equity investment that is insufficient to permit the entity to finance its activities without additional subordinated financial support or whose equity investors lack the characteristics of a controlling financial interest. A VIE is consolidated by its primary beneficiary, which is the entity that, through its variable interests, absorbs the majority of a VIE's variability. A variable interest is a contractual, ownership, or other interest that changes with the changes in the fair value of the VIE's net assets. The classifications of assets and liabilities in the

Company's consolidated balance sheet associated with transactions with QSPEs and VIEs are as follows at December 31, 20X2:

	Qualified Special Purpose Entities	VIEs That Are Consolidated	VIEs That Are Not Consolidated	Transfers Accounted for as Secured Borrowings	Total
Cash	$ –	$ –	$ 200,000	$ 400,000	$ 600,000
Trading account assets	1,100,000	3,200,000	200,000	300,000	4,800,000
Securities	10,000,000	5,000,000	1,000,000	5,000,000	21,000,000
Mortgages held for sale	500,000	–	–	–	500,000
Loans	–	4,000,000	700,000	1,500,000	6,200,000
Mortgage servicing rights	3,500,000	–	–	–	3,500,000
Other assets	200,000	2,200,000	1,400,000	100,000	3,900,000
Total assets	15,300,000	14,400,000	3,500,000	7,300,000	40,500,000
Short-term borrowings	–	–	600,000	2,000,000	2,600,000
Accrued expenses and other liabilities	600,000	2,000,000	400,000	100,000	3,100,000
Long-term debt	–	–	1,800,000	5,000,000	6,800,000
Minority interests	–	–	200,000	–	200,000
Total liabilities and minority interests	600,000	2,000,000	3,000,000	7,100,000	12,700,000
Net assets	$14,700,000	$12,400,000	$ 500,000	$ 200,000	$27,800,000

The Company uses QSPEs to securitize consumer and commercial real estate loans and other types of financial assets (e.g., auto loans). The Company typically retains the servicing rights from these sales and may continue to hold other beneficial interests in QSPEs. The Company may also provide liquidity to investors in the beneficial interests and credit enhancements in the form of standby letters of credit. Through these securitizations, the Company may be exposed to liability under limited amounts of recourse, as well as standard representations and warranties the Company makes to purchasers and issuers. The amount recorded for this liability is included in other commitments and guarantees in the table below.

The following disclosures regarding the Company's significant continuing involvement with QSPEs and unconsolidated VIEs exclude entities where the Company's only involvement is in the form of investments in trading securities; investments in securities or loans underwritten by third parties; and certain derivatives, such as interest rate swaps or cross currency swaps that have customary terms.

Carrying Values—Asset (Liability) as of December 31, 20X2

	Debt and Equity Interests	Servicing Assets	Derivatives	Other Commitments and Guarantees	Total
Residential mortgage loan securitizations	$ 7,200,000	$3,000,000	$500,000	$(400,000)	$10,300,000
Commercial mortgage loan securitizations	1,500,000	500,000	200,000	(150,000)	2,050,000
Auto loan securitizations	2,000,000	–	100,000	–	2,100,000
Other	300,000	–	(50,000)	–	250,000
Total	$11,000,000	$3,500,000	$750,000	$(550,000)	$14,700,000

Maximum Exposure to Loss as of December 31, 20X2

	Debt and Equity Interests	Servicing Assets	Derivatives	Other Commitments and Guarantees	Total
Residential mortgage loan securitizations	$ 7,200,000	$3,000,000	$2,000,000	$1,500,000	$13,700,000
Commercial mortgage loan securitizations	1,500,000	500,000	200,000	2,300,000	4,500,000
Auto loan securitizations	2,000,000	–	100,000	–	2,100,000
Other	300,000	–	1,000,000	200,000	1,500,000
Total	$11,000,000	$3,500,000	$3,300,000	$4,000,000	$21,800,000

Total QSPEs Assets as of December 31, 20X2

	Total QSPEs Assets
Residential mortgage loan securitizations	$343,000,000
Commercial mortgage loan securitizations	140,000,000
Auto loan securitizations	150,000,000
Other	20,000,000
Total	$653,000,000

In 20X2, the Company recognized net gains of $3,500,000 from sales of financial assets in securitizations and had the following cash flows with its securitization trusts:

	Mortgage Loans	Other Financial Assets
Sales proceeds from securitizations	$150,000,000	$ –
Servicing fees	2,000,000	–
Other interests held	1,000,000	600,000
Purchases of delinquent assets	150,000	–
Net servicing advances	300,000	–

For securitizations completed in 20X2, the following assumptions were used to determine the fair value of mortgage servicing rights and other interests held at the date of securitization.

	Mortgage Servicing Rights	Other Interests Held
Prepayment speed (annual constant prepayment rate)	11.5%	25.6%
Life (in years)	6.2	3.1
Discount rate	8.5%	6.5%
Expected life of loan losses	1.2%	0.7%

Key economic assumptions and the sensitivity of the current fair value to immediate adverse changes in those assumptions at December 31, 20X2, for residential and commercial mortgage servicing rights, and other interests held related to residential mortgage loan securitizations are presented in the following table.

	Mortgage Servicing Rights	Other Interests Held
Fair value of interests held	$4,200,000	$380,000
Expected weighted-average life (in years)	3.7	5.4
Prepayment speed assumption (annual constant prepayment rate)	14.2%	11.6%
Decrease in fair value from:		
10% increase	$ 200,000	$ 25,000
25% increase	$ 500,000	$ 60,000
Discount rate assumption	7.1%	15.3%
Decrease in fair value from:		
100 basis point increase	$ 230,000	$ 25,000
200 basis point increase	$ 440,000	$ 45,000
Credit loss assumption	–	1.1%
Decrease in fair value from:		
10% higher losses	–	$ 15,000
25% higher losses	–	$ 30,000

The sensitivities in the table above are hypothetical and, therefore, caution should be exercised when relying on this data. Changes in fair value based on a 10% variation in assumptions generally cannot be extrapolated because the relationship of the change in the assumption to the change in fair value may not be linear. In addition, in the table above, the effect of a variation in a particular assumption on the fair value of the other interests held is calculated independently without changing any other assumptions. In reality, changes in one factor may result in changes in others (e.g., changes in prepayment speed estimates could result in changes in the discount rates), which might magnify or counteract the sensitivities.

Transactions with Variable Interest Entities

The Company's transactions with VIEs include (a) securitization, (b) investment and financing activities involving collateralized debt obligations (CDOs) backed by asset-backed and commercial real estate securities, (c) collateralized loan obligations (CLOs) backed by corporate loans or bonds, and (d) other types of structured financing. A summary of our involvements with off-balance sheet (unconsolidated) VIEs is as follows:

Carrying Values—Asset (Liability) as of December 31, 20X2

	Debt and Equity Interests	Derivatives	Other Commitments and Guarantees	Total
CDOs	$28,000,000	$2,000,000	$ –	$30,000,000
CLOs	6,000,000	300,000	–	6,300,000
Asset-based lending structures	10,000,000	(500,000)	–	9,500,000
Other	1,500,000	(100,000)	(300,000)	1,100,000
Total	$45,500,000	$1,700,000	$(300,000)	$46,900,000

Maximum Exposure to Loss as of December 31, 20X2

	Debt and Equity Interests	Derivatives	Other Commitments and Guarantees	Total
CDOs	$28,000,000	$6,000,000	$2,300,000	$36,300,000
CLOs	6,000,000	300,000	800,000	7,100,000
Asset-based lending structures	11,000,000	500,000	–	11,500,000
Other	1,800,000	400,000	700,000	2,900,000
Total	$46,800,000	$7,200,000	$3,800,000	$57,800,000

Total VIEs Assets as of December 31, 20X2

	Total VIEs Assets
CDOs	$100,000,000
CLOs	50,000,000
Asset-based lending structures	15,000,000
Other	10,000,000
Total	$175,000,000

Collateralized Debt Obligations and Collateralized Loan Obligations. A CDO or CLO is a securitization where an SPE purchases a pool of assets consisting of asset-backed securities or loans and issues multiple tranches of equity or notes to investors. In some transactions, a portion of the assets are obtained synthetically through the use of derivatives such as credit default swaps or total return swaps.

Generally, CDOs and CLOs are structured on behalf of a third-party asset manager that typically selects and manages the assets for the term of the CDO or CLO. Typically, the asset manager has some discretion to manage the sale of assets of, or derivatives used by, the CDOs and CLOs.

Prior to the securitization, the Company may provide all, or substantially all, of the warehouse financing to the asset manager. The asset manager uses this financing to purchase the assets into a bankruptcy remote SPE during the warehouse period. At the completion of the warehouse period, the assets are sold to the CDO or CLO and the warehouse financing is repaid with the proceeds received from the securitization's investors. The warehousing period is generally less than 12 months in duration. In the event the securitization does not take place, the assets in the warehouse are liquidated. The Company consolidates the warehouse SPEs when it is the primary beneficiary. The Company is the primary beneficiary when it provides substantially all of the financing and, therefore, absorbs the majority of the variability. Sometimes, the Company has loss sharing arrangements, whereby a third-party asset manager agrees to absorb the credit and market risk during the warehousing period or upon liquidation of the collateral in the event a securitization does not take place. In those circumstances, the Company does not consolidate the warehouse SPE because the third-party asset manager absorbs the majority of the variability through the loss sharing arrangement.

In addition to the Company's role as arranger and warehouse financing provider, the Company may have other forms of involvement with these transactions. Such involvements may include underwriter, liquidity provider, derivative counterparty, secondary market maker, or investor. For certain transactions, the Company may also act as the collateral manager or servicer. The Company receives fees in connection with its role as collateral manager or servicer. The Company also earns fees for arranging these transactions and distributing the securities.

The Company assesses whether it is the primary beneficiary of CDOs and CLOs at inception of the transactions based on its expectation of the variability associated with its continuing involvement. Subsequently, the Company monitors its ongoing involvement in these transactions to determine if a more frequent assessment of variability is necessary. Variability in these transactions may be created by credit risk, market risk, interest rate risk, or liquidity risk associated with the CDO's or CLO's assets. An assessment of the variability is performed qualitatively because the Company's continuing involvement is typically senior in priority to the third-party investors in transactions. In most cases, the Company is not the primary beneficiary of these transactions because it does not retain the subordinate interests in these transactions and, accordingly, does not absorb the majority of the variability.

Asset-Based Lending Structures. The Company engages in various forms of structured lending arrangements with VIEs that are collateralized by various asset classes, including auto and other transportation leases, intellectual property, equipment, and general corporate credit. The Company typically provides senior financing, and may act as an interest rate swap or commodity derivative counterparty, when necessary. In most cases, the Company is not the primary beneficiary of these structures because it does not retain a majority of the variability in these transactions.

Other Transactions with VIEs. In April 20X2, the Company reached an agreement to purchase at par auction rate securities that were issued to third-party investors by ABC, Inc. and XYZ Corp., entities that are VIEs (See Note [X] for more information on these VIEs and the details of this agreement). Auction rate securities are debt instruments with long-term maturities, but which reprice more frequently. Certain of these securities were issued by the VIEs. At December 31, 20X2, the Company held in its securities available-for-sale portfolio $15 million of auction rate securities issued by the VIEs that the Company redeemed pursuant to this agreement. At December 31, 20X2, the Company had a liability in its balance sheet of $5 million for additional losses on anticipated future redemptions of auction rate securities issued by the VIEs. Were the Company to redeem all remaining auction rate securities issued by the VIEs that are subject to the agreement, the Company's estimated maximum exposure to loss would be $38 million; however, certain of these securities may be repaid in full by the issuer prior to redemption. The Company does not consolidate the VIEs that issued the auction rate securities because the Company does not expect to absorb the majority of the expected future variability associated with the VIEs' assets.

Summary of Transactions with VIEs. The following is a summary of the Company's transactions with VIEs accounted for as secured borrowings and involvements with consolidated VIEs:

Carrying Values as of December 31, 20X2

	Total Assets	Consolidated Assets	Third-Party Liabilities	Minority Interest
Secured borrowings:				
Auto loan securitizations	$4,500,000	$4,500,000	$3,000,000	$ –
Commercial real estate loans	2,300,000	2,300,000	2,000,000	–
Residential mortgage securitizations	1,500,000	1,000,000	600,000	–
Total secured borrowings	8,300,000	7,800,000	5,600,000	–

	Total Assets	Consolidated Assets	Third-Party Liabilities	Minority Interest
Consolidated VIEs:				
Structured asset finance	7,000,000	3,200,000	2,600,000	200,000
Other	2,100,000	2,100,000	1,500,000	160,000
Total consolidated VIEs	9,100,000	5,300,000	4,100,000	360,000
Total secured borrowings and consolidated VIEs	$17,400,000	$13,100,000	$9,700,000	$360,000

The Company has raised financing through the securitization of certain financial assets in transactions with VIEs accounted for as secured borrowings. The Company also consolidates VIEs where it is the primary beneficiary. In certain transactions, the Company provides contractual support in the form of limited recourse and liquidity to facilitate the remarketing of short-term securities issued to third-party investors. Other than this limited contractual support, the assets of the VIEs are the sole source of repayment of the securities held by third parties.

Combined Financial Statements

Example 25: Combined Financial Statements

The accompanying Combined Financial Statements include the accounts of the following entities, all of which are under common control and ownership:

   Or:

The accompanying Combined Financial Statements include the accounts of the following entities because each entity is owned beneficially by identical shareholders:

Name of Entity	Form of Entity
Amishar, Inc.	Corporation
Sandust, L.P.	Partnership
Basin & Sons	Sole proprietorship

All significant intercompany profits, accounts, and transactions have been eliminated in the combination.

Note: The following table presents the individual components of equity if the combined entities have different ownership forms. This may be presented in the equity section on the face of the balance sheet or in a note to the financial statements.

	As of December 31	
	20X2	*20X1*
Equity		
Stockholders' equity	$1,700,000	$1,500,000
Partners' capital	600,000	700,000
Proprietor's capital	400,000	300,000
Total equity	$2,700,000	$2,500,000

Note: The following table presents the Statement of Changes in Equity accounts if the combined entities have different ownership forms.

| | Amishar, Inc. (Corporation) | | | Sandust, L.P. (Partnership) | Basin & Sons (Proprietorship) |
	Common Stock	Additional Paid-in Capital	Retained Earnings	Partners' Capital	Proprietor's Capital
Balances, December 31, 20X0	$100,000	$400,000	$ 700,000	$ 600,000	$ 300,000
Net income			400,000	300,000	100,000
Cash dividends			(100,000)		
Partner's withdrawals				(200,000)	
Proprietor's withdrawals					(100,000)
Balances, December 31, 20X1	100,000	400,000	1,000,000	700,000	300,000
Net income			400,000	300,000	400,000
Cash dividends			(200,000)		
Partners' withdrawals				(400,000)	
Proprietor's withdrawals					(300,000)
Balances, December 31, 20X2	$100,000	$400,000	$1,200,000	$ 600,000	$ 400,000

CHAPTER 47
ASC TOPIC 815: DERIVATIVES AND HEDGING

CONTENTS

EXECUTIVE SUMMARY

Derivatives and Hedging

A *derivative instrument* is a financial instrument or other contract
with all three of the following characteristics:

1. It has (a) one or more underlyings and (b) one or more
   notional amounts or payment provisions or both. An *underlying* is a specified interest rate, security price, commodity
   price, foreign exchange rate, index of prices or rates, or other
   variable. An underlying may be a price or rate of an asset or
   liability but is not the asset or liability itself. A notional
   amount is a number of currency units, shares, bushels,
   pounds, or other units specified in the contract.

2. It requires no initial net investment or an initial net investment that is smaller than would be required for other types
   of contracts that would be expected to have a similar
   response to changes in market factors.

3. Its terms permit or require net settlement, it can readily be
   settled net by a means outside the contract, or it provides for
   delivery of an asset that puts the recipient in a position not
   substantially different from net settlement.

GAAP require that all derivatives (both assets and liabilities) be
recognized in the balance sheet at fair value. Each derivative instrument is generally classified in one of the following four categories:
(1) no hedge designation, (2) fair value hedge, (3) cash flow hedge,
and (4) hedge of a net investment in a foreign operation.

Accounting Literature

FASB Accounting Standards Codification Topic	*Pre-Codification Accounting Literature*
815, *Derivatives and Hedging*	FAS-129, *Disclosure of Information about Capital Structure*
	FAS-133, *Accounting for Derivative Instruments and Hedging Activities*
	FSP FAS 133-1 and FIN 45-4, *Disclosures about Credit Derivatives and Certain Guarantees*
	FAS-155, *Accounting for Certain Hybrid Financial Instruments*
	FAS-159, *The Fair Value Option for Financial Assets and Financial Liabilities*
	FAS-161, *Disclosures about Derivative Instruments and Hedging Activities*
	FIN-39, *Offsetting of Amounts Related to Certain Contracts*
	EITF 96-11, *Accounting for Forward Contracts and Purchased Options to Acquire Securities Covered by FASB Statement No. 115*
	EITF 00-19, *Accounting for Derivative Financial Instruments Indexed to, and Potentially Settled in, a Company's Own Stock*
	EITF 06-7, *Issuer's Accounting for a Previously Bifurcated Conversion Option in a Convertible Debt Instrument When the Conversion Option No Longer Meets the Bifurcation Criteria in FASB Statement No. 133, Accounting for Derivative Instruments and Hedging Activities*

DISCLOSURE AND KEY PRESENTATION REQUIREMENTS

Note: See Chapter 48, "ASC Topic 820: Fair Value Measurements and Disclosures," for additional disclosures of fair value that are required under ASC Topic 820. See Chapter 49, "ASC Topic 825: Financial Instruments," for additional disclosures when the fair value option is adopted for certain financial assets and financial liabilities.

Note: In March 2008, the FASB issued FAS-161, *Disclosures about Derivative Instruments and Hedging Activities,* which is effective for quarterly interim periods beginning after November 15, 2008, and fiscal years that include those quarterly interim periods. ASC 815 based on FAS-161 changes the disclosure requirements for derivative instruments and hedging activities. Specifically, entities are required to provide enhanced disclosures about (a) how and why an entity uses derivative instruments; (b) how derivative instruments and related hedged items are accounted for under ASC 815; and (c) how derivative instruments and related hedged items affect an entity's financial position, financial performance, and cash flows.

Note: In September 2008, the FASB issued FSP FAS 133-1 and FIN 45-4, *Disclosures about Credit Derivatives and Certain Guarantees,* which is effective for reporting periods (annual or interim) ending after November 15, 2008. Among other matters, ASC 815 based on FSP FAS 133-1 and FIN 45-4 requires (a) disclosures by sellers of credit derivatives, including credit derivatives embedded in a hybrid instrument, and (b) additional disclosures about the current status of the payment/performance risk of a guarantee.

Overall

Note: The disclosure requirements in items 1 through 6 below are to be followed until the adoption of ASC Topic 815, *Derivatives and Hedging,* based on FAS-161, *Disclosures about Derivative Instruments and Hedging Activities,* which is effective for quarterly interim periods beginning after November 15, 2008, and fiscal years that include those quarterly interim periods. Thereafter, the disclosure requirements in items 7 through 15 below are to be followed. Early adoption is permitted.

1. The following disclosures should be made for all derivative instruments (and for nonderivative instruments designated and qualifying as hedging instruments) (ASC 815-10-50-1A and 50-2 through 50-5) (FAS-133, par. 44) (*Note:* Additional

qualitative disclosures about an entity's objectives and strategies for using derivative instruments may be more meaningful if such objectives and strategies are described in the context of an entity's overall risk management profile. If appropriate, an entity is encouraged, but not required, to provide additional qualitative disclosures.):

a. The entity's objectives for holding or issuing the instruments.

b. The context needed to understand the entity's objectives.

c. The entity's strategies for achieving these objectives.

d. The entity's risk management policy for each type of hedge, including a description of the items or transactions for which risks are hedged.

e. For derivative instruments not designated as hedging instruments, the purpose of the derivative activity.

f. The disclosures for items 1(a) through 1(e) above should distinguish between:

   (1) Derivative instruments (and nonderivative instruments) designated as fair value hedging instruments.

   (2) Derivative instruments designated as cash flow hedging instruments.

   (3) Derivative instruments (and nonderivative instruments) designated as hedging instruments for hedges of the foreign currency exposure of a net investment in a foreign operation.

   (4) All other derivatives.

2. For hybrid instruments that are not separated:

   a. For those hybrid financial instruments measured at fair value under the election and under the practicability exception discussed in ASC paragraph 815-15-30-1 (FAS-133, par. 16), the information specified in ASC paragraphs 825-10-50-28 through 50-32 (FAS-159, pars. 18–22) should be disclosed. (ASC 815-15-45-1 and 50-1) (FAS-133, par. 44A; FAS-159, par. C7). See Chapter 49, "ASC Topic 825: Financial Instruments."

   b. Disclosures should be made that will provide information to users of the financial statements that will allow such users to understand the effects on earnings (or other performance indicators for entities that do not report earnings) of changes in the fair value of hybrid financial instruments measured at fair value under the election and under the practicability exception in ASC paragraph

815-15-30-1 (FAS-133, par. 16). (ASC 815-15-50-2) (FAS-133, par. 44B; FAS-155, par. 4e)

3. The following disclosures should be made for the period in which an embedded conversion option previously bifurcated and accounted for as a derivative instrument no longer meets the separation criteria (ASC 815-15-50-3) (EITF 06-7):

   a. A description of the principal changes causing the embedded conversion option to no longer require bifurcation under ASC 815-15 (FAS-133).

   b. The amount of the liability for the conversion option reclassified to stockholders' equity.

4. Disclosure should be made of the accounting policy to offset or not offset fair value amounts recognized for derivative instruments and fair value amounts recognized for the right to reclaim cash collateral (a receivable) or the obligation to return cash collateral (a payable) arising from derivative instrument(s) recognized at fair value executed with the same counterparty under a master netting arrangement. (ASC 815-10-50-7) (FIN-39, par. 10B)

5. The following disclosures should be made of the amounts recognized at the end of each reporting period for the right to reclaim cash collateral or the obligation to return cash collateral (ASC 815-10-50-8) (FIN-39, par. 10B):

   a. If the entity has made an accounting policy decision to offset fair value amounts, separate disclosures of the amounts recognized for the right to reclaim cash collateral or the obligation to return cash collateral that have been offset against net derivative instrument positions.

   b. Separate disclosures of the amounts recognized for the right to reclaim cash collateral or the obligation to return cash collateral under master netting arrangements that have not been offset against net derivative instrument positions.

   c. If the entity has made an accounting policy decision to not offset fair value amounts, separate disclosures of the amounts recognized for the right to reclaim cash collateral or the obligation to return cash collateral under master netting arrangements.

6. The accounting policy for the premium paid (time value) to acquire an option that is classified as held-to-maturity or available-for sale-should be disclosed. (ASC 815-10-50-9) (EITF 96-11)

Note: The disclosure requirements in items 7 through 15 below are prescribed by ASC Topic 815, *Derivatives and Hedging,* based on FAS-161, *Disclosures about Derivative Instruments and Hedging Activities,* which supersede the disclosure requirements in items 1 through 6 above. The disclosure requirements in items 7 through 15 below are effective for quarterly interim periods beginning after November 15, 2008, and fiscal years that include those quarterly interim periods. Early adoption is permitted.

7. The following disclosures should be made for all derivative instruments (and for nonderivative instruments designated and qualifying as hedging instruments) for every annual and interim period for which a balance sheet and income statement are presented (ASC 815-10-50-1A, 50-1B, 50-2, 50-4, and 50-5) (FAS-133, par. 44):

    a. The entity's objectives for holding or issuing the instruments.

    b. The context needed to understand the entity's objectives.

    c. The entity's strategies for achieving these objectives.

    d. For items 7(a) through 7(c) above, information about those instruments in the context of each instrument's primary underlying risk exposure (e.g., interest rate, credit, foreign exchange rate, interest rate and foreign exchange rate, or overall price).

    e. A distinction between those instruments used for risk management purposes and those used for other purposes.

    f. For derivative instruments (and nonderivative instruments) designated as hedging instruments, the disclosures should distinguish between:

        (1) Derivative instruments (and nonderivative instruments) designated as fair value hedging instruments.

        (2) Derivative instruments designated as cash flow hedging instruments.

        (3) Derivative instruments (and nonderivative instruments) designated as hedging instruments of the foreign currency exposure of a net investment in a foreign operation.

    g. For derivative instruments not designated as hedging instruments, the purpose of the derivative activity.

    h. Information that would enable users of an entity's financial statements to understand the volume of its derivative activity. (*Note:* Entities should select the format and the specifics of disclosures relating to their volume of derivative activity that are most relevant and practicable for their individual facts and circumstances.)

i. If additional qualitative disclosures are made about the entity's overall risk exposures relating to interest rate risk, foreign exchange risk, commodity price risk, credit risk, and equity price risk, such qualitative disclosures should include a discussion of those exposures even though the entity does not manage some of those exposures by using derivative instruments. (*Note:* An entity is encouraged, but not required, to provide such additional qualitative disclosures about those risks and how they are managed.)

8. For an entity that holds or issues derivative instruments (and nonderivative instruments designated and qualifying as hedging instruments), the following disclosures should be made for every annual and interim period for which a balance sheet and income statement are presented (ASC 815-10-50-4A through 50-4F) (FAS-133, par. 44C):

a. The line items and fair value amounts of derivative instruments (and nonderivative instruments designated and qualifying as hedging instruments) reported in the balance sheet showing the following (*Note:* Amounts required to be reported for nonderivative instruments that are designated and qualify as hedging instruments should be the carrying value of the nonderivative hedging instrument, including the adjustment for the foreign currency transaction gain or loss on that instrument):

(1) The fair value of derivative instruments (and nonderivative instruments designated and qualifying as hedging instruments) on a gross basis, even when those instruments are subject to master netting arrangements and qualify for net presentation in the balance sheet. (*Note:* Cash collateral payables and receivables associated with those instruments should not be added to or netted against the fair value amounts.)

(2) Fair value amounts presented as separate asset and liability values segregated between derivatives that are designated and qualifying as hedging instruments and those that are not, and by type of derivative contract within those two categories (e.g., interest rate contracts, foreign exchange contracts, equity contracts, commodity contracts, credit contracts, and other contracts).

b. The line items and amount of the gains and losses on derivative instruments (and nonderivative instruments designated and qualifying as hedging instruments) and related hedged items reported either in the income statement or balance sheet (e.g., gains and losses initially recognized in other comprehensive income), with separate presentation of the gains and losses for all of the following by type of contract (e.g., interest rate contracts, foreign exchange contracts, equity contracts, commodity contracts, credit contracts, and other contracts):

   (1) Derivative instruments designated and qualifying as hedging instruments in fair value hedges and related hedged items designated and qualifying in fair value hedges.

   (2) The effective portion of gains and losses on derivative instruments (and nonderivative instruments) designated and qualifying in cash flow hedges and net investment hedges that was recognized in other comprehensive income during the current period.

   (3) The effective portion of gains and losses on derivative instruments (and nonderivative instruments) designated and qualifying in cash flow hedges and net investment hedges recorded in accumulated other comprehensive income during the term of the hedging relationship and reclassified into earnings during the current period.

   (4) The portion of gains and losses on derivative instruments (and nonderivative instruments) designated and qualifying in cash flow hedges and net investment hedges representing: (a) the amount of the hedges' ineffectiveness, and (b) the amount, if any, excluded from the assessment of hedge effectiveness.

   (5) Derivative instruments not designated or qualifying as hedging instruments.

c. The quantitative disclosures required by items 8(a) and 8(b) above should be presented in tabular format, except for the information required for hedged items under item 8(b)(1) above, which can be presented in a tabular or nontabular format. (*Note*: If a proportion of a derivative instrument is designated and qualifying as a hedging instrument and a proportion is not designated and qualifying as a hedging instrument, an entity should allocate the related amounts to the appropriate categories within the disclosure table.)

d. For derivative instruments not designated or qualifying as hedging instruments, if an entity's policy is to include those derivative instruments in its trading activities, and the entity elects to not separately disclose gains and losses as required by item 8b(5) above, the following disclosures should be made:

(1) The gains and losses on trading activities (including both derivative and nonderivative instruments) recognized in the income statement, separately by major types of items (such as fixed income/interest rates, foreign exchange, equity, commodity, and credit).

(2) The line items in the income statement in which trading activities gains and losses are included.

(3) A description of the nature of its trading activities and related risks, and how the entity manages those risks.

(4) A footnote in the required tables referencing the use of alternative disclosures for trading activities.

9. For an entity that holds or issues derivative instruments (or nonderivative instruments designated and qualifying as hedging instruments), the following disclosures should be made for every annual and interim period for which a balance sheet is presented (ASC 815-10-50-4H) (FAS-133, par. 44D) (*Note:* Amounts required to be reported for nonderivative instruments that are designated and qualify as hedging instruments should be the carrying value of the nonderivative hedging instrument, including the adjustment for the foreign currency transaction gain or loss on that instrument):

a. The existence and nature of credit-risk-related contingent features and the circumstances in which the features could be triggered in derivative instruments (or non-derivative instruments designated and qualifying as hedging instruments) that are in a net liability position at the end of the reporting period.

b. The aggregate fair value amounts of derivative instruments (or nonderivative instruments designated and qualifying as hedging instruments) that contain credit-risk-related contingent features that are in a net liability position at the end of the reporting period.

c. The aggregate fair value of assets that are already posted as collateral at the end of the reporting period.

    d. The aggregate fair value of additional assets that would be required to be posted as collateral, if the credit-risk-related contingent features were triggered at the end of the reporting period.

    e. The aggregate fair value of assets needed to settle the instrument immediately, if the credit-risk-related contingent features were triggered at the end of the reporting period.

10. If information on derivative instruments (or nonderivative instruments designated and qualifying as hedging instruments) is disclosed in more than a single footnote, there should be a cross-reference from the derivative instruments (or nonderivative instruments) footnote to other footnotes in which derivative-instrument-related information is disclosed. (ASC 815-10-50-4I) (FAS-133, par. 44E)

11. For hybrid instruments that are not separated:

    a. For those hybrid financial instruments measured at fair value under the election and under the practicability exception discussed in ASC paragraph 815-15-30-1 (FAS-133, par. 16, as amended), the information specified in ASC paragraphs 825-10-50-28 through 50-32 (FAS-159, pars. 18–22) should be disclosed. (ASC 815-15-45-1 and 50-1) (FAS-133, par. 44A; FAS-159, par. C7). See Chapter 49, "ASC Topic 825: Financial Instruments."

    b. Disclosures should be made that will provide information to users of the financial statements that will allow such users to understand the effects on earnings (or other performance indicators for entities that do not report earnings) of changes in the fair value of hybrid financial instruments measured at fair value under the election and under the practicability exception in ASC paragraph 815-15-30-1 (FAS-133, par. 16, as amended). (ASC 815-15-50-2) (FAS-133, par. 44B; FAS-155, par. 4e)

12. The following disclosures should be made for the period in which an embedded conversion option previously bifurcated and accounted for as a derivative instrument no longer meets the separation criteria (ASC 815-15-50-3) (EITF 06-7):

    a. A description of the principal changes causing the embedded conversion option to no longer require bifurcation under ASC 815-15 (FAS-133).

    b. The amount of the liability for the conversion option reclassified to stockholders' equity.

13. Disclosure should be made of the accounting policy to offset or not offset fair value amounts recognized for derivative instruments and fair value amounts recognized for the

right to reclaim cash collateral (a receivable) or the obligation to return cash collateral (a payable) arising from derivative instrument(s) recognized at fair value executed with the same counterparty under a master netting arrangement. (ASC 815-10-50-7) (FIN-39, par. 10B)

14. The following disclosures should be made of the amounts recognized at the end of each reporting period for the right to reclaim cash collateral or the obligation to return cash collateral (ASC 815-10-50-8) (FIN-39, par. 10B):

a. If the entity has made an accounting policy decision to offset fair value amounts, separate disclosures of the amounts recognized for the right to reclaim cash collateral or the obligation to return cash collateral that have been offset against net derivative instrument positions.

b. Separate disclosures of the amounts recognized for the right to reclaim cash collateral or the obligation to return cash collateral under master netting arrangements that have not been offset against net derivative instrument positions.

c. If the entity has made an accounting policy decision to not offset fair value amounts, separate disclosures of the amounts recognized for the right to reclaim cash collateral or the obligation to return cash collateral under master netting arrangements.

15. The accounting policy for the premium paid (time value) to acquire an option that is classified as held-to-maturity or available-for-sale should be disclosed. (ASC 815-10-50-9) (EITF 96-11)

Credit Derivatives

Note: The disclosure requirements in item 1 below are prescribed by ASC Topic 815, *Derivatives and Hedging,* based on FSP FAS 133-1 and FIN 45-4, *Disclosures about Credit Derivatives and Certain Guarantees: An Amendment of FASB Statement No. 133 and FASB Interpretation No. 45; and Clarification of the Effective Date of FASB Statement No. 161,* which is effective for reporting periods (annual or interim) ending after November 15, 2008. Early adoption is permitted.

1. For each period for which a balance sheet is presented, the seller of a credit derivative should disclose the following information for each credit derivative, or each group of similar credit derivatives, even if the likelihood of the seller's having to make any payments under the credit derivative is remote (ASC 815-10-50-4J through 50-4L) (FAS-133, par. 44DD)

(*Note*: For hybrid instruments that have embedded credit derivatives, the seller of the embedded credit derivative should disclose the required information for the entire hybrid instrument, not solely the embedded credit derivatives):

a. The nature of the credit derivative, including:

    (1) The approximate term of the credit derivative.

    (2) The reason(s) for entering into the credit derivative.

    (3) The events or circumstances that would require the seller to perform under the credit derivative.

    (4) The current status (i.e., as of the date of the balance sheet) of the payment/performance risk of the credit derivative, which could be based on either recently issued external credit ratings or current internal groupings used by the seller to manage its risk.

    (5) For an entity that uses internal groupings, how those grouping are determined and used for managing risk.

b. The maximum potential amount of future payments (undiscounted) the seller could be required to make under the credit derivative. (*Note*: The maximum potential amount of future payments should not be reduced by the effect of any amounts that may possibly be recovered under recourse or collateralization provisions in the credit derivative.)

c. The fact that the terms of the credit derivative provide for no limitation to the maximum potential future payments under the contract, if applicable.

d. If the seller is unable to develop an estimate of the maximum potential amount of future payments under the credit derivative, the reasons why it cannot estimate the maximum potential amount.

e. The fair value of the credit derivative as of the date of the balance sheet.

f. The nature of any recourse provisions that would enable the seller to recover from third parties any of the amounts paid under the credit derivative.

g. The nature of any assets held either as collateral or by third parties that, upon the occurrence of any specified triggering event or condition under the credit derivative, the seller can obtain and liquidate to recover all or a portion of the amounts paid under the credit derivative.

h. The approximate extent to which the proceeds from liquidation of those assets held either as collateral or by third parties would be expected to cover the maximum potential amount of future payments under the credit derivative, if estimable. (*Note*: The seller of credit protection should consider the effect of any purchased credit protection with identical underlying(s) in its estimate of potential recoveries.)

Fair Value Hedges

Note: The disclosure requirements in item 1 below are to be followed until the adoption of ASC Topic 815, *Derivatives and Hedging*, based on FAS-161, *Disclosures about Derivative Instruments and Hedging Activities*, which is effective for quarterly interim periods beginning after November 15, 2008, and fiscal years that include those quarterly interim periods. Thereafter, the disclosure requirements in item 2 below are to be followed. Early adoption is permitted.

1. The following disclosures should be made for derivative instruments (and nonderivative instruments that may give rise to foreign currency transaction gains or losses) designated and qualifying as fair value hedging instruments and for the related hedged items, for each reporting period for which a complete set of financial statements is presented (ASC 815-25-50-1) (FAS-133, par. 45):

   a. The net gain or loss recognized in earnings during the reporting period representing: (a) the amount of the hedges' ineffectiveness, (b) the component of the derivative instruments' gain or loss, if any, excluded from the assessment of hedge effectiveness, and (c) a description of where the net gain or loss is reported in the income statement or other statement of financial performance.

   b. The amount of net gain or loss recognized in earnings when a hedged firm commitment no longer qualifies as a fair value hedge.

   Note: The disclosure requirements in item 2 below are prescribed by ASC Topic 815, *Derivatives and Hedging*, based on FAS-161, *Disclosures about Derivative Instruments and Hedging Activities*, which supersede the disclosure requirements in item 1 above. The disclosure requirements in item 2 below are effective for quarterly interim periods beginning after November 15, 2008, and fiscal years that include those quarterly interim periods. Early adoption is permitted.

2. The following disclosures should be made for derivative instruments (and nonderivative instruments that may give rise to foreign currency transaction gains or losses) designated and qualifying as fair value hedging instruments and for the related hedged items, for every annual and interim reporting period for which a balance sheet and an income statement is presented (ASC 815-25-50-1) (FAS-133, par. 45):

   a. The net gain or loss recognized in earnings during the reporting period representing: (*a*) the amount of the hedges' ineffectiveness, and (*b*) the component of the derivative instruments' gain or loss, if any, excluded from the assessment of hedge effectiveness.

   b. The amount of net gain or loss recognized in earnings when a hedged firm commitment no longer qualifies as a fair value hedge.

Cash Flow Hedges

Note: The disclosure requirements in items 1 through 3 below are to be followed until the adoption of ASC Topic 815, *Derivatives and Hedging*, based on FAS-161, *Disclosures about Derivative Instruments and Hedging Activities*, which is effective for quarterly interim periods beginning after November 15, 2008, and fiscal years that include those quarterly interim periods. Thereafter, the disclosure requirements in items 4 through 6 below are to be followed. Early adoption is permitted.

1. The following disclosures should be made for derivative instruments designated and qualifying as cash flow hedging instruments and for the related hedged transactions, for each reporting period for which a complete set of financial statements is presented (ASC 815-30-50-1) (FAS-133, par. 45):

   a. The net gain or loss recognized in earnings during the reporting period representing: (a) the amount of the hedges' ineffectiveness, (b) the component of the derivative instruments' gain or loss, if any, excluded from the assessment of hedge effectiveness, and (c) a description of where the net gain or loss is reported in the income statement or other statement of financial performance.

   b. A description of the transactions or other events that will result in the reclassification into earnings of gains and losses that are reported in accumulated other comprehensive income.

   c. The estimated net amount of the existing gains or losses that are reported in accumulated other comprehensive income at the reporting date that is expected to be reclassified into earnings within the next 12 months.

d. The maximum length of time over which the entity is hedging its exposure to the variability in future cash flows for forecasted transactions excluding those forecasted transactions related to the payment of variable interest on existing financial instruments.

e. The amount of gains and losses reclassified into earnings as a result of the discontinuance of cash flow hedges because it is probable that the original forecasted transactions will not occur by the end of the originally specified time period or within the additional period of time discussed in ASC paragraphs 815-30-40-4 and 40-5 (FAS-133, par. 33).

2. The net gain or loss on derivative instruments designated and qualifying as cash flow hedging instruments that are reported in comprehensive income should be displayed as a separate classification within other comprehensive income. (ASC 815-30-45-1) (FAS-133, par. 46)

3. The following items should be separately disclosed as part of the disclosures of accumulated other comprehensive income (ASC 815-30-50-2) (FAS-133, par. 47):

a. The beginning and ending accumulated derivative instrument gain or loss.

b. The related net change associated with current period hedging transactions.

c. The net amount of any reclassification into earnings.

Note: The disclosure requirements in items 4 through 6 below are prescribed by ASC Topic 815, *Derivatives and Hedging,* based on FAS-161, *Disclosures about Derivative Instruments and Hedging Activities,* which supersede the disclosure requirements in items 1 through 3 above. The disclosure requirements in items 4 through 6 below are effective for quarterly interim periods beginning after November 15, 2008, and fiscal years that include those quarterly interim periods. Early adoption is permitted.

4. The following disclosures should be made for derivative instruments designated and qualifying as cash flow hedging instruments and for the related hedged transactions, for every annual and interim reporting period for which a balance sheet and an income statement is presented (ASC 815-30-50-1) (FAS-133, par. 45):

a. A description of the transactions or other events that will result in the reclassification into earnings of gains and losses that are reported in accumulated other comprehensive income.

b. The estimated net amount of the existing gains or losses that are reported in accumulated other comprehensive income at the reporting date that is expected to be reclassified into earnings within the next 12 months.

c. The maximum length of time over which the entity is hedging its exposure to the variability in future cash flows for forecasted transactions excluding those forecasted transactions related to the payment of variable interest on existing financial instruments.

d. The amount of gains and losses reclassified into earnings as a result of the discontinuance of cash flow hedges because it is probable that the original forecasted transactions will not occur by the end of the originally specified time period or within the additional period of time discussed in ASC paragraphs 815-30-40-4 and 40-5 (FAS-133, par. 33).

5. The net gain or loss on derivative instruments designated and qualifying as cash flow hedging instruments that are reported in comprehensive income should be displayed as a separate classification within other comprehensive income. (ASC 815-30-45-1) (FAS-133, par. 46)

6. The following items should be separately disclosed as part of the disclosures of accumulated other comprehensive income (ASC 815-30-50-2) (FAS-133, par. 47):

a. The beginning and ending accumulated derivative instrument gain or loss.

b. The related net change associated with current period hedging transactions.

c. The net amount of any reclassification into earnings.

Net Investment Hedges

Note: The disclosure requirement in item 1 below is to be followed until the adoption of ASC Topic 815, *Derivatives and Hedging*, based on FAS-161, *Disclosures about Derivative Instruments and Hedging Activities*, which is effective for quarterly interim periods beginning after November 15, 2008, and fiscal years that include those quarterly interim periods. Thereafter, the disclosure requirement in item 1 below is not applicable. Early adoption is permitted.

1. The following disclosure should be made for derivative instruments (and nonderivative instruments that may give

rise to foreign currency transaction gains or losses) designated and qualifying as hedging instruments for hedges of the foreign currency exposure of a net investment in a foreign operation, for each reporting period for which a complete set of financial statements is presented (ASC 815-35-50-1) (FAS-133, par. 45):

a. The net amount of gains or losses included in the cumulative translation adjustment during the reporting period.

Contracts in Entity's Own Equity

1. For freestanding contracts (e.g., forward sales contract, purchase put or call option, written call option) that are indexed to, and potentially settled in, an entity's own stock, the following disclosures should be made (ASC 815-40-50-1 through 50-5) (EITF 00-19):

   a. Changes in the fair value of contracts classified as assets or liabilities as long as the contracts remain classified as assets or liabilities.

   b. If contracts that are classified as assets or liabilities meet the definition of a derivative instrument under the provisions of ASC Subtopic 815-10 (FAS-133), the related disclosures that are required under "Overall," "Fair Value Hedges," "Cash Flow Hedges," and "Net Investment Hedges" above should be made.

   c. If contracts have been reclassified into (or out of) equity during the life of the instrument (in whole or in part), the following disclosures should be made:

      (1) Contract reclassifications (including partial reclassifications).

      (2) The reason for the reclassification.

      (3) The effect on the issuer's financial statements.

      (4) The accounting policy for partial reclassifications.

   d. The pertinent information about the contract, including:

      (1) The forward rate.

      (2) The option strike price.

      (3) The number of issuer's shares to which the contract is indexed.

      (4) The settlement date(s) of the contract.

      (5) The issuer's accounting for the contract (i.e., as an asset, liability, or equity).

e. If the terms of the contract provide settlement alternatives, those settlement alternatives should be disclosed, including who controls the settlement alternatives and the maximum number of shares that could be required to be issued to net share settle a contract, if applicable. (*Note*: ASC paragraph 505-10-50-3 [FAS-129, par. 5] requires additional disclosures for actual issuances and settlements that occurred during the accounting period.) See Chapter 34, "ASC Topic 505: Equity."

f. The fact that a potentially infinite number of shares could be required to be issued to settle the contract, if a contract does not have a fixed or determinable maximum number of shares that may be required to be issued.

g. A contract's current fair value for each settlement alternative (denominated, as relevant, in monetary amounts or quantities of shares) and how changes in the price of the issuer's equity instruments affect those settlement amounts (e.g., the issuer is obligated to issue an additional X shares or pay an additional Y dollars for each $1 decrease in stock price).

h. The disclosures required by ASC paragraph 505-10-50-11 (FAS-129, par. 8) should be made for any equity instrument in the scope of ASC Subtopic 815-40 (EITF 00-19) that is (or would be if the issuer were a public company) classified as temporary equity. (*Note*: This applies to redeemable stock issued by nonpublic entities, regardless of whether the nonpublic entity chooses to classify those securities as temporary equity.) See Chapter 34, "ASC Topic 505: Equity."

EXAMPLES OF FINANCIAL STATEMENT DISCLOSURES

 The following sample disclosures are available on the accompanying disc. For additional information, see the following chapters in this book:

- See Chapter 48, "ASC Topic 820: Fair Value Measurements and Disclosures," for additional disclosures of fair value that are required under ASC Topic 820.

- See Chapter 49, "ASC Topic 825: Financial Instruments," for additional disclosures when the fair value option is adopted for certain financial assets and financial liabilities.

Illustrations If ASC Topic 815 Based on Guidance in FAS-161 Has *Not* Been Adopted

Example 1: Description of Objectives and Strategies for Holding and Issuing Derivatives

The Company holds and issues derivative financial instruments for the purpose of hedging the risks of certain identifiable and anticipated transactions. In general, the types of risks hedged are those relating to the variability of future earnings and cash flows caused by movements in foreign currency exchange rates and changes in commodity prices and interest rates. The Company documents its risk management strategy and hedge effectiveness at the inception of and during the term of each hedge. In hedging the transactions the Company, in the normal course of business, holds and/or issues the following types of derivatives:

Forward rate agreements—The purpose of this instrument is to hedge the fair value of firm purchase or sale commitments denominated in foreign currencies and of the net investments in foreign subsidiaries.

Interest rate swaps—The purpose of this instrument is to hedge the fair value of fixed-rate debt and cash flows of variable-rate financial assets.

Futures contracts—The purpose of this instrument is to hedge the fair value of microchips inventory.

Call and put options—The purpose of this instrument is to hedge the cash flows of forecasted sales or purchases of inventory.

The Company holds and issues such derivatives only for the purpose of hedging such risks, not for speculation. Generally, the Company enters into hedging relationships such that changes in the fair values or cash flows of items and transactions being hedged are expected to be offset by corresponding changes in the values of the derivatives. At December 31, 20X2, hedging relationships exist for short-term investments, bond indebtedness, microchips inventory, firm foreign-currency-denominated purchase commitments, and anticipated purchases and sales of microchips inventory.

Derivatives that have been designated and qualify as fair value hedging instruments are reported at fair value. The gain or loss on the derivative instrument as well as the offsetting gain or loss on the hedged item attributable to the hedged risk are recognized in earnings in the current period.

Derivatives that have been designated and qualify as cash flow hedging instruments are reported at fair value. The gain or loss on the effective portion of the hedge (i.e., change in fair value) is initially reported as a component of other comprehensive income. The remaining gain or loss, if any, is recognized currently in earnings. Amounts in accumulated other comprehensive income are reclassified into net income in the same period in which the hedged forecasted transaction affects earnings.

Example 2: Fair Value Hedging Instruments

The Company enters into interest rate swaps to convert portions of its fixed rate trust-preferred securities to floating rate securities, its fixed rate long term subordinated debt to floating rate debt and to a lesser degree, certain fixed rate loans to variable rate loans. The fixed rate liability instruments are changed to variable rate instruments by entering into "receive fixed/pay variable swaps" and the fixed rate asset instruments are changed to variable rate instruments by entering into "pay fixed/receive variable swaps."

During 20X2 and 20X1, the Company recognized net gains of $84,000 and $67,000, respectively, from derivative instruments designated and qualifying as fair value hedges. All hedges were highly effective; therefore, the gains, which are included in other income, are attributable to the portion of the change in the fair value of the derivative hedging instruments excluded from the assessment of the effectiveness of the hedges.

Also, during 20X2, a previous hedge on a firm future foreign currency commitment no longer qualified as a fair value hedge, because the hedging relationship was no longer deemed to be highly effective. As a result, a loss of $39,000 was recognized in the 20X2 Statement of Operations.

Example 3: Cash Flow Hedging Instruments

The Company uses interest rate swaps to convert floating rate long-term debt to fixed rate debt.

During 20X2 and 20X1, the Company recognized net gains of $72,000 and $59,000, respectively, from cash flow hedges. All hedges were highly effective; therefore, the gains, which are included in other income, are attributable to the portion of the change in the fair value of the derivative hedging instruments excluded from the assessment of the effectiveness of the hedges. Cash flow hedges of forecasted transactions resulted in an aggregate credit balance of $97,000 remaining in accumulated other comprehensive income at December 31, 20X2. The Company expects to transfer approximately $61,000 of that amount to earnings during 20X3 when the forecasted transactions actually occur. All forecasted transactions currently being hedged are expected to occur by 20X4. Also, during 20X2, the Company transferred $41,000 to earnings from accumulated other comprehensive income because a forecasted transaction that was originally expected to occur was cancelled.

Example 4: Hedges of Net Investment in Foreign Operation

The Company uses five-year yen denominated debt to hedge its investment in a Japanese manufacturer of semiconductors. The purpose of this hedge is to protect against adverse movements in exchange rates.

Example 5: Foreign Currency Hedging Activities

The Company manufactures and sells its products in a number of countries throughout the world and, as a result, is exposed to movements in foreign currency exchange rates. The Company's major foreign currency exposures involve the markets in Western and Eastern Europe, Asia, Mexico, and Canada. The primary purpose of the Company's foreign currency hedging activities is to manage the volatility associated with foreign currency purchases of materials and other assets and liabilities created in the normal course of business. The Company primarily utilizes forward exchange contracts and purchased options with maturities of less than 18 months and currency swaps with maturities up to five years.

The Company enters into certain foreign currency derivative instruments that do not meet hedge accounting criteria. These, primarily, are intended to protect against exposure related to intercompany financing transactions and income from international operations. The fair values of these instruments at December 31, 20X2 were recorded as $3,452,000 in assets and $671,000 in liabilities.

In addition, the Company utilizes purchased foreign currency options, forward exchange contracts, and cross currency swaps which qualify as cash flow hedges. These are intended to offset the effect of exchange rate fluctuations on forecasted sales, inventory purchases, intercompany royalties, and intercompany loans denominated in foreign currency. The fair values of these instruments at December 31, 20X2 were recorded as $2,794,000 in assets and $3,125,000 in liabilities. Gains and losses on these instruments are deferred in other comprehensive income (OCI) until the underlying transaction is recognized in earnings. The earnings impact is reported in net sales, cost of products sold, or marketing research and administrative expenses, to match the underlying transaction being hedged. Qualifying cash flow hedges that are currently deferred in OCI will be reclassified into earnings as the underlying transactions are recognized. No currency cash flow hedges were discontinued during the year due to changes in expectations on the original forecasted transactions.

Example 6: Commodity Hedging Activities

Raw materials used by the Company are subject to price volatility caused by weather, supply conditions, political and economic variables, and other unpredictable factors. To manage the volatility related to anticipated inventory purchases, the Company uses futures and options with maturities generally less than one year and swap contracts with maturities up to five years. These market instruments are designated as cash flow hedges. The mark-to-market gain or loss on qualifying commodity hedges is included in other comprehensive income to the extent effective, and reclassified into cost of products sold in the period during which the hedged transaction affects earnings. Qualifying commodity cash flow hedges that are currently deferred in other comprehensive income will be reclassified into earnings as the underlying transactions are recognized. The mark-to-market gains or losses on non-qualifying, excluded, and ineffective portions of hedges are recognized in cost of products sold immediately. No commodity cash flow hedges were discontinued during the year.

Example 7: Description of Derivatives That Have Not Been Designated as Hedges

The Company has the following contracts that have not been designated as hedges:

- Variable rate swap agreement entered into with a major financial institution in which the Company pays a floating rate based on LIBOR and receives a floating rate based on an investment fund index, with payments being calculated on a notional amount. The swap is an overlay to short-term investments and provides diversification benefits. The swap is settled quarterly, marked to market at each reporting date and all unrealized gains and losses are recognized in earnings currently.

- Lumber and other commodity futures designed to manage the Company's consolidated exposure to changes in inventory values due to fluctuations in market prices for selected business units. The Company's commodity futures positions are marked to market at each reporting date and all unrealized gains and losses are recognized in earnings currently. To date, these contract positions have not had a material effect on the Company's financial position, results of operations, or cash flows.

Illustrations If ASC Topic 815 Based on Guidance in FAS-161 Has Been Adopted

> **Note:** The examples in this section illustrate the application of certain disclosure requirements under ASC 815 based on FAS-161, effective for quarterly interim periods beginning after November 15, 2008, and fiscal years that include those quarterly interim periods.

Example 8: Disclosure of Objectives and Strategies for Using Derivative Instruments by Underlying Risk

> **Note:** This example illustrates the disclosure of qualitative information by underlying risks, including volume of activity, and a nontabular presentation of the quantitative information about the hedged items in fair value hedges.

The Company is exposed to certain risks relating to its ongoing business operations. The primary risks managed by using derivative instruments are commodity price risk and interest rate risk. Forward contracts on various commodities are entered into to manage the price risk associated with forecasted purchases of materials used in the Company's manufacturing process. Interest rate swaps are entered into to manage interest rate risk associated with the Company's fixed-rate borrowings.

FASB ASC 815-10 requires companies to recognize all derivative instruments as assets or liabilities at fair value in the statement of financial position. In accordance with FASB ASC 815-10, the Company designates commodity forward contracts as cash flow hedges of forecasted purchases of commodities and interest rate swaps as fair value hedges of fixed-rate borrowings.

Cash flow hedges—For derivative instruments that are designated and qualify as a cash flow hedge, the effective portion of the gain or loss on the derivative is reported as a component of other comprehensive income and reclassified into earnings in the same period or periods during which the hedged transaction affects earnings. Gains and losses on the derivative representing either hedge ineffectiveness or hedge components excluded from the assessment of effectiveness are recognized in current earnings.

As of December 31, 20X2, the Company had the following outstanding commodity forward contracts that were entered into to hedge forecasted purchases:

Commodity	Number of Bushels (000s)
Wheat	10,000
Corn	25,000
Oats	300

Fair value hedges—For derivative instruments that are designated and qualify as a fair value hedge, the gain or loss on the derivative, as well as the offsetting loss or gain on the hedged item attributable to the hedged risk, are recognized in current earnings. The Company includes the gain or loss on the hedged items (i.e., fixed-rate borrowings) in the same line item (interest expense) as the offsetting loss or gain on the related interest rate swaps as follows:

Income Statement Classification	Gain/(Loss) on Swaps	Gain/(Loss) on Borrowings
Interest expense	$(1,050,000)	$600,000

As of December 31, 20X2, the total notional amount of the Company's receive-fixed/pay-variable interest rate swaps was $100 million.

Example 9: Disclosure in Tabular Format of Fair Value Amounts, and Gains and Losses on Derivative Instruments and Related Hedged Items

> **Note:** This example illustrates the tabular disclosure of fair values of derivative instruments in a balance sheet and the effect of derivative instruments on the income statement.

Fair Values of Derivative Instruments

| | Asset Derivatives (in millions of dollars) | | | |
| | December 31, 20X2 | | December 31, 20X1 | |
	Balance Sheet Location	Fair Value	Balance Sheet Location	Fair Value
Asset derivatives designated as hedging instruments under FASB ASC 815-20:				
Interest rate contracts	Other assets	$ 10,000	Other assets	$ 7,000
Foreign exchange contracts	Other assets	15,000	Other assets	8,000
Equity contracts	Other assets	20,000	Other assets	10,000
Commodity contracts	Other assets	25,000	Other assets	12,000
Credit contracts	Other assets	30,000	Other assets	15,000
Other contracts	Other assets	10,000	Other assets	5,000
Total asset derivatives designated as hedging instruments under FASB ASC 815-20		$110,000		$57,000
Asset derivatives not designated as hedging instruments under FASB ASC 815-20:				
Interest rate contracts	Other assets	$ 5,000	Other assets	$ 8,000
Foreign exchange contracts	Other assets	9,000	Other assets	3,000

Asset Derivatives (in millions of dollars)

	December 31, 20X2		December 31, 20X1	
	Balance Sheet Location	*Fair Value*	*Balance Sheet Location*	*Fair Value*
Equity contracts	Other assets	6,000	Other assets	1,000
Commodity contracts	Other assets	4,000	Other assets	7,000
Credit contracts	Other assets	2,000	Other assets	5,000
Other contracts	Other assets	5,000	Other assets	2,000
Total asset derivatives not designated as hedging instruments under FASB ASC 815-20		$ 31,000		$26,000
Total asset derivatives		$141,000		$83,000

Liability Derivatives (in millions of dollars)

	December 31, 20X2		December 31, 20X1	
	Balance Sheet Location	*Fair Value*	*Balance Sheet Location*	*Fair Value*
Liability derivatives designated as hedging instruments under FASB ASC 815-20:				
Interest rate contracts	Other liabilities	$10,000	Other liabilities	$6,000
Foreign exchange contracts	Other liabilities	12,000	Other liabilities	5,000

Liability Derivatives (in millions of dollars)

	December 31, 20X2		December 31, 20X1	
	Balance Sheet Location	*Fair Value*	*Balance Sheet Location*	*Fair Value*
Equity contracts	Other liabilities	5,000	Other liabilities	8,000
Commodity contracts	Other liabilities	20,000	Other liabilities	10,000
Credit contracts	Other liabilities	8,000	Other liabilities	3,000
Other contracts	Other liabilities	5,000	Other liabilities	2,000
Total liability derivatives designated as hedging instruments under FASB ASC 815-20		$60,000		$34,000
Liability derivatives not designated as hedging instruments under FASB ASC 815-20:				
Interest rate contracts	Other liabilities	$ 5,000	Other liabilities	$ 6,000
Foreign exchange contracts	Other liabilities	4,000	Other liabilities	3,000
Equity contracts	Other liabilities	3,000	Other liabilities	2,000
Commodity contracts	Other liabilities	1,000	Other liabilities	4,000
Credit contracts	Other liabilities	2,000	Other liabilities	5,000
Other contracts	Other liabilities	1,000	Other liabilities	2,000

Liability Derivatives (in millions of dollars)

	December 31, 20X2		December 31, 20X1	
	Balance Sheet Location	Fair Value	Balance Sheet Location	Fair Value
Total liability derivatives not designated as hedging instruments under FASB ASC 815-20		$16,000		$22,000
Total liability derivatives		$76,000		$56,000

Effect of Derivative Instruments on the
Income Statement

Derivatives in FASB ASC 815-20 Fair Value Hedging Relationships

Derivatives	Location of Gain or (Loss) Recognized in Income on Derivative	Amount of Gain or (Loss) Recognized in Income on Derivative	
		20X2	20X1
Interest rate contracts	Interest income/ (expense)	$ 400,000	$(600,000)
Foreign exchange contracts	Foreign currency gain/(loss)	(250,000)	300,000
Equity contracts	Other income/ (expense)	100,000	200,000
Commodity contracts	Other income/ (expense)	(300,000)	(150,000)
Credit derivatives	Other income/ (expense)	400,000	(50,000)
Other contracts	Other income/ (expense)	(100,000)	150,000
Total		$ 250,000	$(150,000)

Derivatives in FASB ASC 815-20 Cash Flow Hedging Relationships

Derivatives	Amount of Gain or (Loss) Recognized in Other Comprehensive Income on Derivative (Effective Portion)	
	20X2	20X1
Interest rate contracts	$ 200,000	$ 300,000
Foreign exchange contracts	(100,000)	(150,000)
Equity contracts	(50,000)	400,000
Commodity contracts	400,000	(100,000)
Credit derivatives	(200,000)	200,000
Other contracts	150,000	(100,000)
Total	$ 400,000	$ 550,000

Location of Gain or (Loss) Reclassified from Accumulated Other Comprehensive Income into Income (Effective Portion)	Amount of Gain or (Loss) Reclassified from Accumulated Other Comprehensive Income into Income (Effective Portion)	
	20X2	20X1
Interest income (expense)	$ 50,000	$(100,000)
Sales/Revenue	100,000	200,000
Other income (expense)—interest rate contracts	(25,000)	30,000
Cost of sales	200,000	300,000
Other income (expense)—equity contracts	100,000	50,000
Other income (expense)—foreign exchange contracts	(100,000)	(50,000)
Total	$ 325,000	$ 430,000

Location of Gain or (Loss) Recognized in Income on Derivative (Ineffective Portion and Amount Excluded from Effectiveness Testing)	Amount of Gain or (Loss) Recognized in Income on Derivative (Ineffective Portion and Amount Excluded from Effectiveness Testing)	
	20X2	20X1
Other income (expense)—interest rate contracts	$ 250,000	$(300,000)
Other income (expense)—equity contracts	(50,000)	100,000
Other income (expense)—foreign exchange contracts	200,000	(100,000)
Total	$ 400,000	$(300,000)

Derivatives in FASB ASC 815-20 Net Investment Hedging Relationships

Derivatives	Amount of Gain or (Loss) Recognized in Other Comprehensive Income on Derivative (Effective Portion)	
	20X2	*20X1*
Foreign exchange contracts	$300,000	$(100,000)

Location of Gain or (Loss) Reclassified from Accumulated Other Comprehensive Income Into Income (Effective Portion)	Amount of Gain or (Loss) Reclassified from Accumulated Other Comprehensive Income Into Income (Effective Portion)	
	20X2	*20X1*
Gain or (loss) on sale of subsidiary	$(150,000)	$200,000

Derivatives Not Designated as Hedging Instruments under FASB ASC 815-20

Derivatives	Location of Gain or (Loss) Recognized in Income on Derivative	Amount of Gain or (Loss) Recognized in Income on Derivative	
		20X2	*20X1*
Interest rate contracts	Other income (expense)	$ 200,000	$(300,000)
Foreign exchange contracts	Other income (expense)	100,000	(200,000)
Equity contracts	Other income (expense)	(50,000)	100,000
Commodity contracts	Other income (expense)	60,000	150,000
Credit derivatives	Other income (expense)	(70,000)	(50,000)
Other contracts	Other income (expense)	20,000	(30,000)
Total		$ 260,000	$(330,000)

Example 10: Tabular Disclosure of Nondesignated/Nonqualifying Derivative Instruments That Are Included in an Entity's Trading Activity

> **Note:** This example illustrates one approach for presenting the quantitative information required under FASB ASC 815-10-50-4F (FAS-161, par. 44C(c)) when an entity elects the alternative disclosure for gains and losses on derivative instruments included in its trading activities. Many entities already include the required information about their trading activities in other disclosures within the financial statements. However, an entity that discloses the required information in other disclosures would need to provide a cross-reference from the derivative footnote to other footnotes in which trading derivative-related information is included.

The Effect of Trading Activities on the Statement of Financial Performance for the Years Ended December 31, 20X2, and 20X1

Types of Instrument	Trading Revenue	
	20X2	*20X1*
Fixed income/interest rate	$ 150,000	$ 200,000
Foreign exchange	200,000	400,000
Equity	300,000	500,000
Commodity	100,000	300,000
Credit	250,000	200,000
Other	50,000	100,000
Total	$1,050,000	$1,700,000

Line Item in Statement of Financial Performance	Trading Revenue	
	20X2	*20X1*
Principal/Proprietary transactions	$1,800,000	$2,300,000
Asset management income	500,000	750,000
Other income	100,000	200,000
Total	$2,400,000	$3,250,000

The revenue related to each category includes realized and unrealized gains and losses on both derivative instruments and non-derivative instruments.

Example 11: Disclosure of Contingent Features in Derivative Instruments

> **Note:** This example illustrates the disclosure of credit-risk-related contingent features in derivative instruments as required by paragraph FASB ASC 815-10-50-4H (FAS-161, par. 44D).

Certain of the Company's derivative instruments contain provisions that require the Company's debt to maintain an investment grade credit rating from each of the major credit rating agencies. If the Company's debt were to fall below investment grade, it would be in violation of these provisions, and the counterparties to the derivative instruments could request immediate payment or demand immediate and ongoing full overnight collateralization on derivative instruments in net liability positions. The aggregate fair value of all derivative instruments with credit-risk-related contingent features that are in a liability position on December 31, 20X2, is $30 million for which the Company has posted collateral of $10 million in the normal course of business. If the credit-risk-related contingent features underlying these agreements were triggered on December 31, 20X2, the Company would be required to post an additional $15 million of collateral to its counterparties.

Credit Derivatives—Example Illustrating Application of ASC Topic 815 Based on FSP FAS 133-1 and FIN 45-4

> **Note:** This example illustrates the application of certain disclosure requirements under ASC Topic 815 based on FSP FAS 133-1 and FIN 45-4, effective for reporting periods (annual or interim) ending after November 15, 2008.

Example 12: Seller of Credit Derivative Discloses Nature of Derivative and Potential Exposure

The Company has entered into credit derivative transactions in the ordinary course of its business, with the intention of earning revenue on credit exposure in an unfunded form. In the majority of such transactions, the Company sold credit protection on a designated portfolio of loans or debt securities. Under these arrangements, the Company would incur credit losses only after a shortfall of principal and/or interest, or other credit events, in respect of the protected loans and debt securities, exceeds a specified threshold amount or level of losses.

At December 31, 20X2, all outstanding credit derivative transactions have cash-settled structures in respect of a basket of reference obligations, where the Company's payment obligations may be triggered by payment shortfalls, bankruptcy, and certain other events such as write-downs of the value of underlying assets.

At December 31, 20X2, a total of $25 million (consisting of corporate loans and prime residential mortgages) in net notional exposure of the Company's credit derivative portfolio represented derivatives written for financial institutions. In exchange for a periodic fee, the counterparties receive credit protection with respect to a portfolio of diversified loans they own; therefore, reducing their minimum capital requirements. The credit derivative transactions were structured with early termination rights for counterparties allowing them to terminate these transactions at no cost to the Company at a certain period of time or upon a regulatory event.

The average maturity of the written credit derivative contracts is 4 years. The Company has hedged its exposure by purchasing offsetting derivative contracts of $12 million in net notional amount. The net unhedged position of approximately $13 million represents the maximum exposure to loss on these credit derivative contracts. As of December 31, 20X2, the fair value (which represents the carrying value) of the credit derivative portfolio was $4 million. At December 31, 20X2, the Company has posted $1 million of collateral under these contracts.

The Company does not expect that it will be required to make payments pursuant to the contractual terms of these transactions, given the current performance of the underlying portfolios (less than 1% in losses), the level of subordination, and the expectation that some of the counterparties will terminate these transactions prior to their maturity.

CHAPTER 48
ASC TOPIC 820: FAIR VALUE
MEASUREMENTS AND DISCLOSURES

CONTENTS

EXECUTIVE SUMMARY

Fair Value Measurements and Disclosures

ASC Topic 820 provides guidance for using fair value to measure assets and liabilities and expands disclosures about fair value measurements. ASC Topic 820 establishes a fair value hierarchy that gives the highest priority to quoted prices in active markets (Level 1) and the lowest priority to unobservable data (e.g., the reporting entity's own data) (Level 3) and distinguishes between *observable inputs* and *unobservable inputs*.

The term *inputs* refers to the assumptions that market participants use in pricing the asset or liability. Observable inputs reflect the assumptions market participants would use in pricing the asset or liability based on market data obtained from independent sources. Unobservable inputs reflect an entity's own assumptions about the assumptions market participants would use in pricing the asset or liability. ASC Topic 820 indicates that valuation techniques should maximize the use of observable inputs and minimize the use of unobservable inputs. The fair value hierarchy prioritizes the inputs used in valuation techniques and creates the following three broad levels, with Level 1 being the highest priority:

- *Level 1 inputs*: Level 1 inputs are quoted market prices in active markets for identical assets or liabilities that are accessible at the measurement date (e. g., equity securities traded on the New York Stock Exchange).

- *Level 2 inputs*: Level 2 inputs are from other than quoted market prices included in Level 1 that are observable for the asset or liability, either directly or indirectly (e. g., quoted market prices of similar assets or liabilities in active markets, or quoted market prices for identical or similar assets or liabilities in markets that are not active).

- *Level 3 inputs*: Level 3 inputs are unobservable (e. g., a company's own data) and should be used to measure fair value to the extent that observable inputs are not available.

GAAP also permits, pursuant to the "fair value option," all entities to choose to measure eligible items at fair value at specified election dates. The decision to elect the fair value option is (1) applicable on an instrument-by-instrument basis, with a few exceptions, such as investments otherwise accounted for by the equity method; (2) irrevocable (unless a new election date occurs); and (3) applied only to an entire instrument and not only to specified risks, specific cash flows, or portions of that instrument. For a discussion of the fair value option and related disclosures, see Chapter 49, "ASC Topic 825: Financial Instruments."

Accounting Literature

FASB Accounting Standards Codification Topic	*Pre-Codification Accounting Literature*
820, *Fair Value Measurements and Disclosures*	FAS-157, *Fair Value Measurements*
	FSP FAS 157-2, *Effective Date of FASB Statement No. 157*
	FSP FAS 157-4, *Determining Fair Value When the Volume and Level of Activity for the Asset or Liability Have Significantly Decreased and Identifying Transactions That Are Not Orderly*
	FAS-159, *The Fair Value Option for Financial Assets and Financial Liabilities*
	EITF 08-5, *Issuer's Accounting for Liabilities Measured at Fair Value with a Third-Party Credit Enhancement*

DISCLOSURE AND KEY PRESENTATION REQUIREMENTS

Note: The disclosure and key presentation requirements in items 1 and 2 below are prescribed by ASC Topic 820, *Fair Value Measurements and Disclosures*, based on FAS-157, *Fair Value Measurements*, which is effective for fiscal years beginning after November 15, 2007, and interim periods within those fiscal years, with the following exception. FASB Staff Position (FSP) FAS 157-2, "Effective Date of FASB Statement No. 157," defers the effective date to fiscal years beginning after November 15, 2008, and interim periods within those fiscal years, for all nonfinancial assets and nonfinancial liabilities, except for items that are recognized or disclosed at fair value in the financial statements on a recurring basis (at least annually). An entity that has issued interim or annual financial statements reflecting the application of the measurement and disclosure provisions of ASC Topic 820 (FAS-157) prior to February 12, 2008, must continue to apply all provisions of ASC Topic 820 (FAS-157). Early adoption of ASC Topic 820 (FAS-157) is permitted as long as financial statements for any period (interim or annual) of the fiscal year have not yet been issued. The disclosure requirements of ASC Topic 820 (FAS-157) need not be applied for financial statements for periods presented prior to its initial application.

Entities who have not adopted ASC Topic 820 (FAS-157) should consider the need to make disclosures under other existing pronouncements (e.g., ASC Topic 275, *Risks and Uncertainties* [SOP 94-6, *Disclosure of Certain Significant Risks and Uncertainties*]) in situations where fair value measurements have a significant effect on the financial statements.

The quantitative disclosures in items 1 and 2 below should be presented in a tabular format. (ASC 820-10-50-8) (FAS-157, par. 34). In addition, entities are encouraged, but not required, to (a) combine the fair value information disclosed in accordance with items 1 and 2 below with the fair value information disclosed in accordance with other items in this checklist, and (b) disclose information about other similar measurements (e.g., inventories measured at market value in special circumstances), if practicable. (ASC 820-10-50-9) (FAS-157, par. 35)

1. For assets and liabilities that are measured at fair value on a *recurring basis* subsequent to initial recognition, the following disclosures should be made separately for each major category of assets and liabilities for each annual and interim period (ASC 820-10-50-1 through 50-3; 820-10-50-8) (FAS-157, pars. 32 and 34):

   a. The fair value measurements at the reporting date.

   b. The level within the fair value hierarchy in which the fair value measurements in their entirety fall, segregating fair value measurements using quoted prices in active markets for identical assets or liabilities (Level 1), significant other observable inputs (Level 2), and significant unobservable inputs (Level 3).

   c. For fair value measurements using significant unobservable inputs (Level 3), a reconciliation of the beginning and ending balances, separately presenting changes during the period attributable to the following (*Note:* This reconciliation disclosure may be presented net for derivative assets and liabilities.):

      (1) Total gains or losses for the period (realized and unrealized), segregating those gains or losses included in earnings, and a description of where those gains or losses included in earnings are reported in the income statement.

      (2) Purchases, sales, issuances, and settlements (net).

      (3) Transfers in and (or) out of Level 3 (e.g., transfers due to changes in the observability of significant inputs).

    d. The amount of the total gains or losses for the period in (c) (1) above included in earnings that are attributable to the change in unrealized gains or losses relating to those assets and liabilities still held at the reporting date and a description of where those unrealized gains or losses are reported in the income statement.

    e. The valuation technique(s) used to measure fair value and a discussion of changes in valuation techniques, if any, during the period (*annual periods only*).

2. For assets and liabilities that are measured at fair value on a *nonrecurring basis* in periods subsequent to initial recognition, the following disclosures should be made separately for each major category of assets and liabilities for each annual and interim period (ASC 820-10-50-5 and 50-8) (FAS-157, pars. 33 and 34):

    a. The fair value measurements recorded during the period and the reasons for the measurements.

    b. The level within the fair value hierarchy in which the fair value measurements in their entirety fall, segregating fair value measurements using quoted prices in active markets for identical assets or liabilities (Level 1), significant other observable inputs (Level 2), and significant unobservable inputs (Level 3).

    c. For fair value measurements using significant unobservable inputs (Level 3), a description of the inputs and the information used to develop the inputs.

    d. The valuation technique(s) used to measure fair value and a discussion of changes, if any, in the valuation technique(s) used to measure similar assets and (or) liabilities in prior periods (*annual periods only*).

3. For entities that have not voluntarily applied the provisions of ASC Topic 820, based on FAS-157, in annual or interim financial statements to certain nonfinancial assets and nonfinancial liabilities (in accordance with the delayed adoption date for certain nonfinancial assets and nonfinancial liabilities as described in the note above), the following disclosures should be made (ASC 820-10-50-8A) (FSP FAS 157-2, par. 12):

    a. The fact that the entity has not applied the provisions of ASC Topic 820, based on FAS-157, to such nonfinancial assets and nonfinancial liabilities.

    b. Each major category of assets and liabilities that are recognized or disclosed at fair value for which the entity has not voluntarily applied the provisions of ASC Topic 820, based on FAS-157.

Note: The disclosure requirements in items 4 through 6 below are prescribed by ASC Topic 820, *Fair Value Measurements and Disclosures*, based on FSP FAS 157-4, *Determining Fair Value When the Volume and Level of Activity for the Asset or Liability Have Significantly Decreased and Identifying Transactions That Are Not Orderly*, which is effective for interim and annual reporting periods ending after June 15, 2009. Early adoption is permitted for periods ending after March 15, 2009, provided the pending content that links to ASC paragraph 320-10-65-1 (based on FSP FAS 115-2 and FAS 124-2, *Recognition and Presentation of Other-Than-Temporary Impairments*) is also adopted. In addition, if either the pending content in ASC paragraph 320-10-65-1 (based on FSP FAS 115-2 and FAS 124-2) or in ASC paragraph 825-10-65-1 (based on FSP FAS 107-1 and APB 28-1, *Interim Disclosures about Fair Value of Financial Instruments*) is adopted early, then the requirements in items 4 through 6 below must also be adopted early. The disclosures in items 4 through 6 below are not required for earlier periods presented for comparative purposes at initial adoption. In periods after initial adoption, comparative disclosures are required only for periods ending after initial adoption.

4. For assets and liabilities that are measured at fair value on a recurring basis subsequent to initial recognition, the inputs used to measure fair value and a discussion of changes in inputs, if any, during the period should be disclosed for each major category of assets and liabilities for each period. (ASC 820-10-50-2) (FAS-157, par. 32)

5. For assets and liabilities that are measured at fair value on a nonrecurring basis subsequent to initial recognition, the inputs used to measure fair value and a discussion of changes in inputs, if any, from prior periods should be disclosed for each major category of assets and liabilities for each period. (ASC 820-10-50-5) (FAS-157, par. 33)

6. The following transition disclosures should be made in the period of adoption (ASC 820-10-65-4) (FSP FAS 157-4, par. 22):

    a. A change, if any, in valuation technique and related inputs resulting from the application of the guidance based on FSP FAS 157-4.

    b. A quantification of the total effect of the change in valuation technique and related inputs, if practicable, by major category.

Note: The disclosure requirement in item 7 below is prescribed by ASC Topic 820, *Fair Value Measurements and Disclosures*, based on EITF 08-5, *Issuer's Accounting for Liabilities Measured at Fair Value with a Third-Party Credit Enhancement*, which is effective on a prospective basis in the first reporting period beginning on or after December 15, 2008. Early adoption is permitted.

7. For liabilities issued with an inseparable third-party credit enhancement (e.g., debt that is issued with a contractual third-party guarantee) measured or disclosed at fair value on a recurring basis, the following disclosures should be made (ASC 820-10-50-4A and 65-3) (EITF 08-5):

   a. The existence of a third-party credit enhancement on the entity's issued liability.

   b. The following transitional disclosures in the period of adoption:

      (1) The valuation technique(s) used to measure the fair value of issued liabilities with a third-party credit enhancement.

      (2) A discussion of changes, if any, from the valuation technique(s) used to measure those liabilities in prior periods.

   Note: The disclosure requirements in items 8 and 9 below are prescribed by Accounting Standards Update No. 2009-12, *Fair Value Measurements and Disclosures (Topic 820)— Investments in Certain Entities That Calculate Net Asset Value per Share (or Its Equivalent)*, which is effective for interim and annual periods ending after December 15, 2009. Early adoption is permitted in financial statements for earlier interim and annual periods that have not been issued. If an entity elects to early adopt the measurement amendments, the entity is permitted to defer the adoption of the disclosure provisions until periods ending after December 15, 2009.

8. For investments in certain entities that calculate net asset value per share (or its equivalent, such as member units) and which are measured at fair value on a recurring or nonrecurring basis during the period, the following disclosures should be made separately for each major category of investment for each annual and interim period (ASC 820-10-50-6A):

   (Note: Major category of investment should be determined on the basis of the nature and risks of the investments in a manner consistent with the guidance for major security types in ASC paragraph 320-10-50-1B.)

   a. The fair value of the investments in the major category.

   b. A description of the significant investment strategies of the investee(s) in the major category.

c. The reporting entity's estimate of the period of time over which the underlying assets are expected to be liquidated by the investees, for each major category of investment that includes investments that can never be redeemed with the investees, but the reporting entity receives distributions through the liquidation of the underlying assets of the investees.

d. The amount of the reporting entity's unfunded commitments related to investments in the major category.

e. A general description of the terms and conditions upon which the investor may redeem investments in the major category (e.g., quarterly redemption with 60 days' notice).

f. The circumstances in which an otherwise redeemable investment in the major category (or a portion thereof) might not be redeemable (e.g., investments subject to a lockup or gate).

g. For those otherwise redeemable investments that are restricted from redemption as of the reporting entity's measurement date:

   (1) The reporting entity's estimate of when the restriction from redemption might lapse.

   (2) If the reporting entity cannot estimate when the restriction from redemption might lapse:

      (i) The fact that the entity cannot estimate when the restriction from redemption might lapse.

      (ii) How long the restriction has been in effect.

h. Any other significant restriction on the ability to sell investments in the major category at the measurement date.

i. For an investment(s) that the reporting entity determines that it is probable (as defined in ASC paragraph 820-10-35-62) that it will sell for an amount different from net asset value per share (or its equivalent):

   (1) The total fair value of all such investments.

   (2) The remaining actions required to complete the sale, if any.

j. For a group of investments that would meet the criteria in item i above, but the individual investments to be sold have not been identified (e.g., if a reporting entity decides to sell 20 percent of its investments in private equity funds but the individual investments to be sold have not been identified):

(1) The entity's plans to sell the investments.

(2) The remaining actions required to complete the sale, if any.

9. The entity should disclose the following information in the period of adoption (ASC 820-10-65-6):

a. A change, if any, in valuation technique and related inputs. (*Note:* Revisions resulting from a change in valuation technique or its application should be accounted for as a change in accounting estimate.)

b. The total effect of the change, if practicable.

EXAMPLES OF FINANCIAL STATEMENT DISCLOSURES

Note: For sample disclosures relating to the fair value option, see Chapter 49, "ASC Topic 825: Financial Instruments." For sample disclosures relating to derivatives and hedging, see Chapter 47, "ASC Topic 815: Derivatives and Hedging."

 The following sample disclosures are available on the accompanying disc.

Example 1: Assets and Liabilities Are Measured at Fair Value on a Recurring Basis—Example Is Appropriate If ASC Topic 820 Based on Guidance in FSP FAS 157-4 Has Not Been Adopted

The following are the major categories of assets and liabilities measured at fair value on a recurring basis during the year ended December 31, 20X2, using quoted prices in active markets for identical assets (Level 1); significant other observable inputs (Level 2); and significant unobservable inputs (Level 3).

Description	Level 1: Quoted Prices in Active Markets for Identical Assets	Level 2: Significant Other Observable Inputs	Level 3: Significant Unobservable Inputs	Total at December 31, 20X2
Trading securities	$105,000	$10,000	$ -0-	$115,000
Available-for-sale securities	75,000	-0-	-0-	75,000
Derivatives	25,000	15,000	20,000	60,000

Description	Level 1: Quoted Prices in Active Markets for Identical Assets	Level 2: Significant Other Observable Inputs	Level 3: Significant Unobservable Inputs	Total at December 31, 20X2
Venture capital investments	-0-	-0-	10,000	10,000
Total	$205,000	$25,000	$30,000	$260,000

Note: For liabilities, a similar table should be presented.

The following is a reconciliation of the beginning and ending balances for assets and liabilities measured at fair value on a recurring basis using significant unobservable inputs (Level 3) during the period ended December 31, 20X2:

	Derivatives	Venture Capital Investments	Total
Beginning balance	$14,000	$11,000	$25,000
Total gains or losses (realized/unrealized):			
Included in earnings (or changes in net assets)	11,000	(3,000)	8,000
Included in other comprehensive income	4,000	-0-	4,000
Purchases, issuances, and settlements	(7,000)	2,000	(5,000)
Transfers in and/or out of Level 3	(2,000)	-0-	(2,000)
Ending balance	$20,000	$10,000	$30,000

Note: For liabilities, a similar table should be presented.

	Derivatives	Venture Capital Investments	Total
The amount of total gains or losses for the period included in earnings (or changes in net assets) attributable to the change in unrealized gains or losses relating to assets still held at the reporting date	$7,000	$2,000	$9,000

Gains and losses (realized and unrealized) included in earnings (or changes in net assets) for the period ended December 31, 20X2, are reported in trading revenues and in other revenues as follows:

	Trading Revenues	Other Revenues
Total gains or losses included in earnings (or changes in net assets) for the period ended December 31, 20X2	$11,000	$(3,000)
Change in unrealized gains or losses relating to assets still held at December 31, 20X2	$ 7,000	$ 2,000

> **Note:** In addition, the valuation techniques used to measure fair value and a discussion of any changes in valuation techniques during the period should be disclosed.

Example 2: Assets and Liabilities Are Measured at Fair Value on a Recurring Basis—Example Is Appropriate If ASC Topic 820 Based on Guidance in FSP FAS 157-4 Has Been Adopted

The following are the major categories of assets and liabilities measured at fair value on a recurring basis during the year ended December 31, 20X2, using quoted prices in active markets for identical assets (Level 1); significant other observable inputs (Level 2); and significant unobservable inputs (Level 3).

Description	Level 1: Quoted Prices in Active Markets for Identical Assets	Level 2: Significant Other Observable Inputs	Level 3: Significant Unobservable Inputs	Total at December 31, 20X2
Trading securities: Equity securities-real estate	$105,000	$10,000	$ -0-	$115,000
Available-for-sale securities: Residential mortgage backed securities	-0-	-0-	75,000	75,000
Derivatives	25,000	15,000	20,000	60,000
Venture capital investments	-0-	-0-	10,000	10,000
Total	$130,000	$25,000	$105,000	$260,000

Note: For liabilities, a similar table should be presented.

The following is a reconciliation of the beginning and ending balances for assets and liabilities measured at fair value on a recurring basis using significant unobservable inputs (Level 3) during the period ended December 31, 20X2:

	Residential Mortgage Backed Securities	Derivatives	Venture Capital Investments	Total
Beginning balance	$80,000	$14,000	$ 11,000	$105,000
Total gains or losses (realized/ unrealized):				
Included in earnings (or changes in net assets)	-0-	11,000	(3,000)	8,000

	Residential Mortgage Backed Securities	Derivatives	Venture Capital Investments	Total
Included in other comprehensive income	(5,000)	4,000	-0-	(1,000)
Purchases, issuances, and settlements	-0-	(7,000)	2,000	(5,000)
Transfers in and/ or out of Level 3	-0-	(2,000)	-0-	(2,000)
Ending balance	$75,000	$20,000	$10,000	$105,000

Note: For liabilities, a similar table should be presented.

	Residential Mortgage Backed Securities	Derivatives	Venture Capital Investments	Total
The amount of total gains or losses for the period included in earnings (or changes in net assets) attributable to the change in unrealized gains or losses relating to assets still held at the reporting date	$ -0-	$7,000	$2,000	$9,000

Gains and losses (realized and unrealized) included in earnings (or changes in net assets) for the period ended December 31, 20X2, are reported in trading revenues and in other revenues as follows:

	Trading Revenues	Other Revenues
Total gains or losses included in earnings (or changes in net assets) for the period ended December 31, 20X2	$11,000	$(3,000)
Change in unrealized gains or losses relating to assets still held at December 31, 20X2	$ 7,000	$ 2,000

Note: In addition, the valuation techniques used to measure fair value and a discussion of any changes in valuation techniques during the period should be disclosed.

Note: Further, the inputs used to measure fair value and a discussion of changes in inputs, if any, during the period should be disclosed for each major category of assets and liabilities for each period.

Example 3: Assets and Liabilities Are Measured at Fair Value on a Nonrecurring Basis—Example Is Appropriate If ASC Topic 820 Based on Guidance in FSP FAS 157-4 Has Not Been Adopted

The following are the major categories of assets and liabilities measured at fair value on a nonrecurring basis during the year ended December 31, 20X2, using quoted prices in active markets for identical assets (Level 1); significant other observable inputs (Level 2); and significant unobservable inputs (Level 3):

Description	Level 1: Quoted Prices in Active Markets for Identical Assets	Level 2: Significant Other Observable Inputs	Level 3: Significant Unobservable Inputs	Total at December 31, 20X2	Total Gains (Losses) for the Year Ended December 31, 20X2
Long-lived assets held and used	$ -0-	$ 750,000	$ -0-	$ 750,000	$(250,000)
Goodwill	-0-	-0-	300,000	300,000	(350,000)

Description	Level 1: Quoted Prices in Active Markets for Identical Assets	Level 2: Signifi- cant Other Observable Inputs	Level 3: Significant Unobser- vable Inputs	Total at December 31, 20X2	Total Gains (Losses) for the Year Ended December 31, 20X2
Long-lived assets held for sale	-0-	260,000	-0-	260,000	(150,000)
Total	$ -0-	$1,010,000	$300,000	$1,310,000	$(750,000)

Note: For liabilities, a similar table should be presented.

In accordance with the provisions of the Impairment or Disposal of Long-Lived Assets Subsections of FASB ASC 360-10, long-lived assets held and used with a carrying amount of $1,000,000 were written down to their fair value of $750,000, resulting in an impairment charge of $250,000, which was included in earnings for the period. In addition, long-lived assets held for sale with a carrying amount of $350,000 were written down to their fair value of $260,000, less cost to sell of $60,000 (or $200,000), resulting in a loss of $150,000, which was included in earnings for the period.

In accordance with the provisions of FASB ASC Topic 350, goodwill with a carrying amount of $650,000 was written down to its implied fair value of $300,000, resulting in an impairment charge of $350,000, which was included in earnings for the period.

> **Note:** For fair value measurements using significant unobservable inputs (Level 3), a description of the inputs and the information used to develop them should be disclosed. In addition, the valuation techniques used to measure fair value and a discussion of any changes in the valuation techniques used to measure similar assets or liabilities in prior periods should be disclosed.

Example 4: Assets and Liabilities Are Measured at Fair Value on a Nonrecurring Basis—Example Is Appropriate If ASC Topic 820 Based on Guidance in FSP FAS 157-4 Has Been Adopted

The following are the major categories of assets and liabilities measured at fair value on a nonrecurring basis during the year ended

December 31, 20X2, using quoted prices in active markets for identical assets (Level 1); significant other observable inputs (Level 2); and significant unobservable inputs (Level 3):

Description	Level 1: Quoted Prices in Active Markets for Identical Assets	Level 2: Significant Other Observable Inputs	Level 3: Significant Unobservable Inputs	Total at December 31, 20X2	Total Gains (Losses) for the Year Ended December 31, 20X2
Long-lived assets held and used	$ -0-	$ 750,000	$ -0-	$ 750,000	$(250,000)
Goodwill	-0-	-0-	300,000	300,000	(350,000)
Long-lived assets held for sale	-0-	260,000	-0-	260,000	(150,000)
Total	$ -0-	$1,010,000	$300,000	$1,310,000	$(750,000)

Note: For liabilities, a similar table should be presented.

In accordance with the provisions of the Impairment or Disposal of Long-Lived Assets Subsections of FASB ASC 360-10, long-lived assets held and used with a carrying amount of $1,000,000 were written down to their fair value of $750,000, resulting in an impairment charge of $250,000, which was included in earnings for the period. In addition, long-lived assets held for sale with a carrying amount of $350,000 were written down to their fair value of $260,000, less cost to sell of $60,000 (or $200,000), resulting in a loss of $150,000, which was included in earnings for the period.

In accordance with the provisions of FASB ASC Topic 350, goodwill with a carrying amount of $650,000 was written down to its implied fair value of $300,000, resulting in an impairment charge of $350,000, which was included in earnings for the period.

Note: In addition, the valuation techniques used to measure fair value and a discussion of any changes in the valuation techniques used to measure similar assets or liabilities in prior periods should be disclosed.

Note: Further, the inputs used to measure fair value and a discussion of changes in inputs, if any, from prior periods should be disclosed for each major category of assets and liabilities for each period.

Example 5: Disclosure of Fair Value Measurements of Investments in Certain Entities That Calculate Net Asset Value per Share (or Its Equivalent, Such as Member Units)—Example Is Appropriate If Accounting Standards Update No. 2009-12 Has Been Adopted

Description	Fair Value	Unfunded Commit- ments	Redemption Frequency (If Currently Eligible)	Redemption Notice Period
Equity long/short hedge funds[a]	$ 550,000	$ -	Quarterly	30-60 days
Event driven hedge funds[b]	450,000	-	Quarterly, Annually	30-60 days
Global opportunities hedge funds[c]	350,000	-	Quarterly	30-45 days
Multiple-strategy hedge funds[d]	400,000	-	Quarterly	30-60 days
Real estate funds[e]	470,000	200,000		
Private equity funds— International[f]	430,000	150,000		
Total	$2,650,000	$350,000		

[a] This category includes investments in hedge funds that invest both long and short primarily in U.S. common stocks. Management of the hedge funds has the ability to shift investments from value to growth strategies, from small to large capitalization stocks, and from a net long position to a net short position. The fair values of the investments in this category have been estimated using the net asset value per share of the investments. Investments representing approximately 25 percent of the value of the investments in this category cannot be redeemed because the investments include restrictions that do not allow for redemption in the first 12 to 18 months after acquisition. The remaining restriction period for these investments ranged from three to seven months at December 31, 20X2.

[b] This category includes investments in hedge funds that invest in approximately 60 percent equities and 40 percent bonds to profit from economic, political, and government driven events. A majority of the investments are targeted at economic policy decisions. The fair values of the investments in this category have been estimated using the net asset value per share of the investments.

[c] This category includes investments in hedge funds that hold approximately 80 percent of the funds' investments in non-U.S. common

stocks in the healthcare, energy, information technology, utilities, and telecommunications sectors and approximately 20 percent of the funds' investments in diversified currencies. The fair values of the investments in this category have been estimated using the net asset value per share of the investments. For one investment, valued at $100,000, a gate has been imposed by the hedge fund manager and no redemptions are currently permitted. This redemption restriction has been in place for six months and the time at which the redemption restriction might lapse cannot be estimated.

(d) This category invests in hedge funds that pursue multiple strategies to diversify risks and reduce volatility. The hedge funds' composite portfolio for this category includes investments in approximately 50 percent U.S. common stocks, 30 percent global real estate projects, and 20 percent arbitrage investments. The fair values of the investments in this category have been estimated using the net asset value per share of the investments. Investments representing approximately 15 percent of the value of the investments in this category cannot be redeemed because the investments include restrictions that do not allow for redemption in the first year after acquisition. The remaining restriction period for these investments ranged from four to six months at December 31, 20X2.

(e) This category includes several real estate funds that invest primarily in U.S. commercial real estate. The fair values of the investments in this category have been estimated using the net asset value of the Company's ownership interest in partners' capital. These investments can never be redeemed with the funds. Distributions from each fund will be received as the underlying investments of the funds are liquidated. It is estimated that the underlying assets of the fund will be liquidated over the next 7 to 10 years. Twenty percent of the total investment in this category is planned to be sold. However, the individual investments that will be sold have not yet been determined. Because it is not probable that any individual investment will be sold, the fair value of each individual investment has been estimated using the net asset value of the Company's ownership interest in partners' capital. Once it has been determined which investments will be sold and whether those investments will be sold individually or in a group, the investments will be sold in an action process. The investee fund's management must approve of the buyer before the sale of the investments can be completed.

(f) This category includes several private equity funds that invest primarily in foreign technology companies. These investments can never be redeemed with the funds. Instead, the nature of the investments in this category is that distributions are received through the liquidation of the underlying assets of the fund. If these investments were held, it is estimated that the underlying assets of the fund would be liquidated over 5 to 8 years. However, as of December 31, 20X2, it is probable that all of the investments in this category will be sold at an amount different from the net asset value of the Company's ownership interest in partners' capital. Therefore, the fair values of the investments in this category have been estimated using recent observable transaction information for similar investments and non-binding bids received from potential buyers of the investments. As of December 31, 20X2, a buyer (or buyers) for these investments has not yet been identified. Once a buyer has been identified, the investee fund's management must approve of the buyer before the sale of the investments can be completed.

CHAPTER 49
ASC TOPIC 825: FINANCIAL INSTRUMENTS

CONTENTS

EXECUTIVE SUMMARY

Overall

Various Topics within the FASB Codification (and the applicable Chapters in this book) address financial instrument matters and require disclosures about specific financial instruments, such as receivables, debt and equity securities, debt, contingencies, guarantees, and derivatives. This Chapter addresses the incremental disclosures in ASC Topic 825 about (a) fair value of financial instruments, (b) concentrations of credit risk of all financial instruments, (c) the fair value option for financial assets and financial liabilities, and (d) registration payment arrangements.

Generally accepted accounting principles (GAAP) require all entities to disclose the fair value of their financial instruments and certain information relating to these financial instruments; however, certain disclosures are optional for nonpublic companies that (1) have total assets on the financial statement date of less than $100 million and (2) have no instrument that, in whole or in part, is accounted for as a derivative instrument.

Disclosure of information about significant concentrations of credit risk from an individual counterparty or groups of counterparties for all financial instruments are also required.

Fair Value Option for Financial Assets and Financial Liabilities

The "fair value option" in ASC Topic 825 permits all entities to choose to measure eligible items at fair value at specified election dates. The decision to elect the fair value option is (1) applicable on an instrument-by-instrument basis, with a few exceptions, such as investments otherwise accounted for by the equity method; (2) irrevocable (unless a new election date occurs); and (3) applied only to an entire instrument and not only to specified risks, specific cash flows, or portions of that instrument.

An entity electing to measure eligible financial assets and liabilities at fair value should report unrealized gains and losses in earnings. An entity should report in the balance sheet assets and liabilities measured pursuant to the fair value option separately from similar assets and liabilities measured using another measurement attribute. In the statement of cash flows, an entity should classify cash receipts and cash payments for items measured at fair value according to their nature and purpose.

Registration Payment Arrangements

An entity can issue financial instruments such as equity shares, warrants, or debt instruments that are subject to a registration payment arrangement. These arrangements, which may be issued as a separate agreement or included as a provision of a financial instrument or other agreement, require the issuer to obtain and or maintain a listing on a stock exchange instead of, or in addition to, obtaining and or maintaining an effective registration statement. Failure to meet the requirements of the registration payment arrangement necessitates the issuer transfer consideration to the counterparty.

Accounting Literature

FASB Accounting Standards Codification Topic	Pre-Codification Accounting Literature
825, *Financial Instruments*	FAS-107, *Disclosures about Fair Value of Financial Instruments*

FASB Accounting Standards Codification Topic	*Pre-Codification Accounting Literature*
	FAS-126, *Exemption from Certain Required Disclosures about Financial Instruments for Certain Non-public Entities*
	FAS-157, *Fair Value Measurements*
	FAS-159, *The Fair Value Option for Financial Assets and Financial Liabilities*
	FSP FAS 107-1 and APB 28-1, *Interim Disclosures about Fair Value of Financial Instruments*
	FSP EITF 00-19-2, *Accounting for Registration Payment Arrangements*
	FSP SOP 94-6-1, *Terms of Loan Products That May Give Rise to a Concentration of Credit Risk*

DISCLOSURE AND KEY PRESENTATION REQUIREMENTS

Note: Various Topics within the FASB Codification (and the applicable Chapters in this book) address financial instruments matters and require disclosures about specific financial instruments, such as: receivables; debt and equity securities; debt; contingencies; guarantees; and derivatives. This Chapter addresses the incremental disclosures in ASC Topic 825 about (a) fair value of financial instruments, (b) concentrations of credit risk of all financial instruments, (c) fair value option for financial assets and financial liabilities, and (d) registration payment arrangements.

Overall

Note: The disclosure requirements in item 1 below are to be followed until the adoption of ASC Topic 825, *Financial Instruments,* based on FSP FAS 107-1 and APB 28-1, *Interim Disclosures about Fair Value of Financial Instruments,* which is effective for periods ending after June 15, 2009. Thereafter, the disclosure requirements in item 2 below are to be followed.

Early adoption is permitted for periods ending after March 15, 2009, provided that the guidance based on FSP FAS 157-4, *Determining Fair Value When the Volume and Level of Activity for the Asset or Liability Have Significantly Decreased and Identifying Transactions That Are Not Orderly,* and FSP FAS 115-2 and FAS 124-2, *Recognition and Presentation of Other-Than-Temporary Impairments,* are also adopted. The guidance based on FSP FAS 107-1 and APB 28-1 does not require disclosures for earlier periods presented for comparative purposes at initial adoption. In periods after initial adoption, comparative disclosures are required only for periods ending after initial adoption.

1. The following information about fair value of financial instruments should be disclosed (ASC 825-10-50-3 through 50-16) (FAS-107, pars. 7–14; FAS-126, par. 2):

   Note: These disclosures about the fair value of financial instruments are optional, not required, for an entity that meets *all* of the following criteria as of the most recent year presented: (1) the entity is a nonpublic entity, (2) the entity's total assets are less than $100 million on the date of the financial statements, and (3) the entity has no instrument that, in whole or in part, is accounted for as a derivative instrument, other than commitments related to the origination of mortgage loans to be held for sale during the reporting period.

   Note: If disclosures are not required in the current period, the disclosures for previous years may be omitted if financial statements for those years are presented for comparative purposes. If disclosures are required in the current period, disclosures that have not been reported previously need not be included in financial statements that are presented for comparative purposes.

   a. Fair value of financial instruments for which it is practicable to estimate fair value, either in the body of the financial statements or in the accompanying notes. (For trade receivables and payables, no disclosure is required when the carrying amount approximates fair value). In connection with this item:

      (1) When disclosure is made in the accompanying notes, the fair value should be presented together with the related carrying amount in a form that makes it clear whether the fair value and carrying amount represent assets or liabilities and how the carrying amounts relate to what is reported in the balance sheet.

      (2) Disclosure should be made in a single note or, if disclosed in more than a single note, one of the notes should include a summary table that contains the

fair value and related carrying amounts and cross-references to the locations of the remaining disclosures.

b. The methods and significant assumptions used to estimate the fair value of financial instruments.

c. In disclosing the fair value of a financial instrument, the entity should *not* net that fair value with the fair value of other financial instruments, except to the extent that the offsetting of carrying amounts in the balance sheet is permitted.

d. For financial instruments for which it is concluded that estimating fair value is not practicable, disclosures should be made of: (1) information pertinent to estimating the fair value of the financial instrument or class of financial instruments (such as the carrying amount, effective interest rate, and maturity) and (2) the reasons why it is not practicable to estimate fair value.

Note: The disclosure requirements in item 2 below are prescribed by ASC Topic 825, *Financial Instruments,* based on FSP FAS 107-1 and APB 28-1, *Interim Disclosures about Fair Value of Financial Instruments,* which supersede the disclosure requirements in item 1 above effective for periods ending after June 15, 2009. Early adoption is permitted for periods ending after March 15, 2009, provided that the guidance based on FSP FAS 157-4, *Determining Fair Value When the Volume and Level of Activity for the Asset or Liability Have Significantly Decreased and Identifying Transactions That Are Not Orderly,* and FSP FAS 115-2 and FAS 124-2, *Recognition and Presentation of Other-Than-Temporary Impairments,* are also adopted. The guidance based on FSP FAS 107-1 and APB 28-1 does not require disclosures for earlier periods presented for comparative purposes at initial adoption. In periods after initial adoption, comparative disclosures are required only for periods ending after initial adoption.

2. The following information about fair value of financial instruments should be disclosed (ASC 825-10-50-3 through 50-16) (FAS-107, pars. 7–14; FAS-126, par. 2) (*Note:* For annual reporting periods, the following disclosures apply to all entities. For interim reporting periods, the following disclosures apply only to public entities and are optional for nonpublic entities):

Note: These disclosures about the fair value of financial instruments are optional, not required, for an entity that meets *all* of the following criteria as of the most recent year presented: (1) the entity is a nonpublic entity, (2) the entity's total assets are less than $100 million on the date of the financial statements, and (3) the entity has no instrument that, in whole or in part, is accounted for as a derivative instrument, other than commitments related to the origination of mortgage loans to be held for sale during the reporting period.

Note: If disclosures are not required in the current period, the disclosures for previous years may be omitted if financial statements for those years are presented for comparative purposes. If disclosures are required in the current period, disclosures that have not been reported previously need not be included in financial statements that are presented for comparative purposes.

a. Fair value of financial instruments for which it is practicable to estimate fair value, either in the body of the financial statements or in the accompanying notes. (For trade receivables and payables, no disclosure is required when the carrying amount approximates fair value). In connection with this item:

(1) When disclosure is made in the accompanying notes, the fair value should be presented together with the related carrying amount in a form that makes it clear whether the fair value and carrying amount represent assets or liabilities and how the carrying amounts relate to what is reported in the balance sheet.

(2) Disclosure should be made in a single note or, if disclosed in more than a single note, one of the notes should include a summary table that contains the fair value and related carrying amounts and cross-references to the locations of the remaining disclosures.

b. The methods and significant assumptions used to estimate the fair value of financial instruments.

c. A description of the changes in the method(s) and significant assumptions used to estimate the fair value of financial instruments, if any, during the period.

d. In disclosing the fair value of a financial instrument, the entity should *not* net that fair value with the fair value of other financial instruments, except to the extent that the offsetting of carrying amounts in the balance sheet is permitted.

e. For financial instruments for which it is concluded that estimating fair value is not practicable, disclosures should be made of: (1) information pertinent to estimating the fair value of the financial instrument or class of financial instruments (such as the carrying amount, effective interest rate, and maturity) and (2) the reasons why it is not practicable to estimate fair value.

3. Significant concentrations of credit risk arising from financial instruments (including derivative instruments accounted for under ASC Topic 815 [FAS-133]) should be disclosed, including the following about each significant concentration (ASC 825-10-50-20 and 50-21) (FAS-107, par. 15A) (*Note:* These disclosures do not apply to: (a) employers' and plans' obligations for pension benefits, other postretirement benefits including health care and life insurance benefits, postemployment benefits, employee stock option and stock purchase plans, and other forms of deferred compensation arrangements; (b) insurance contracts, other than financial guarantees and investment contracts; (c) warranty obligations and product warranties; (d) unconditional purchase obligations; and (e) financial instruments of a pension plan):

   a. Information about the activity, region, or economic characteristic that identifies the concentration.

   b. The maximum amount of loss due to credit risk that, based on the gross fair value of the financial instrument, the entity would incur if parties to the financial instruments that make up the concentration failed completely to perform according to the terms of the contracts and the collateral or other security, if any, for the amount due proved to be of no value to the entity.

   c. The entity's policy of requiring collateral or other security to support financial instruments subject to credit risk.

   d. Information about the entity's access to the collateral or other security.

   e. The nature and a brief description of the collateral or other security supporting those financial instruments.

   f. The entity's policy of entering into master netting arrangements to mitigate the credit risk of financial instruments, information about the arrangements for which the entity is a party, and a brief description of the terms of those arrangements, including the extent to which they would reduce the entity's maximum amount of loss due to credit risk.

4. Disclosure is *encouraged*, but not required, of quantitative information about the market risks of financial instruments that is consistent with the way an entity manages or adjusts its market risks (e.g., details of current positions, details of activity during the period, a gap analysis of interest rate repricing or maturity dates, the duration of the financial instruments). (ASC 825-10-50-23) (FAS-107, pars. 15C and 15D)

5. Information on how underwriting procedures are designed to control the credit risk that may arise from future payment increases is *encouraged*, but not required, to be disclosed. (ASC 825-10-55-2) (FSP SOP 94-6-1, par. 8)

Fair Value Option for Financial Assets and Financial Liabilities

Note: The disclosure requirements in items 1 through 7 below are prescribed by ASC Topic 825, *Financial Instruments*, based on FAS-159, *The Fair Value Option for Financial Assets and Financial Liabilities*. The fair value option in ASC Topic 825, based on FAS-159, permits all entities to choose to measure eligible items at fair value at specified election dates. A business entity is required to report unrealized gains and losses on items for which the fair value option has been elected in earnings at each subsequent reporting date. The decision to elect the fair value option is: (*a*) applicable on an instrument-by-instrument basis, with a few exceptions, such as investments otherwise accounted for by the equity method; (*b*) irrevocable (unless a new election date occurs); and (*c*) applied only to an entire instrument and not to only specified risks, specific cash flows, or portions of that instrument.

The disclosures described in items 1 through 7 below are not required for securities classified as trading securities, life settlement contracts measured at fair value, or servicing rights measured at fair value as other disclosure requirements apply to these items. (ASC 825-10-50-25) (FAS-159, par. 17)

1. Assets and liabilities that are measured at fair value under the fair value option should be reported separately from the carrying amounts of similar assets and liabilities measured using another measurement attribute by either (ASC 825-10-45-1 and 45-2) (FAS-159, par. 15):

    a. Presenting the aggregate of fair value and non-fair-value amounts in the same line item in the balance sheet and parenthetically disclosing the amount measured at fair value included in the aggregate amount.

    b. Presenting two separate line items to display the fair value and non-fair-value carrying amounts.

2. For each date for which a balance sheet is presented, the following disclosures should be made (ASC 825-10-50-28) (FAS-159, par. 18):

    a. Management's reasons for electing a fair value option for each eligible item or group of similar eligible items.

b. If the fair value option is elected for some but not all eligible items within a group of similar eligible items:

    (1) A description of those similar items and the reasons for partial election.

    (2) Information to enable users to understand how the group of similar items relates to individual line items on the balance sheet.

c. For each line item in the balance sheet that includes an item or items for which the fair value option has been elected:

    (1) Information to enable users to understand how each line item in the balance sheet relates to major categories of assets and liabilities presented in accordance with the fair value disclosure requirements of ASC Topic 820 (FAS-157). See Chapter 48, "ASC Topic 820: Fair Value Measurements and Disclosures."

    (2) The aggregate carrying amount of items included in each line item in the balance sheet that are not eligible for the fair value option, if any.

d. The difference between the aggregate fair value and the aggregate unpaid principal balance of:

    (1) Loans and long-term receivables (other than securities subject to ASC Topic 320 [FAS-115]) that have contractual principal amounts and for which the fair value option has been elected.

    (2) Long-term debt instruments that have contractual principal amounts and for which the fair value option has been elected.

e. For loans held as assets for which the fair value option has been elected:

    (1) The aggregate fair value of loans that are 90 days or more past due.

    (2) If the entity's policy is to recognize interest income separately from other changes in fair value, the aggregate fair value of loans in nonaccrual status.

    (3) The difference between the aggregate fair value and the aggregate unpaid principal balance for loans that are 90 days or more past due, in nonaccrual status, or both.

f. For investments that would have been accounted for under the equity method if the entity had not chosen to apply the fair value option, the following information:

    (1) The name of each investee and percentage of ownership of common stock.

    (2) The accounting policies of the investor with respect to the investment in common stock.

    (3) When investments in common stock of corporate joint ventures or other investments accounted for under the equity method are in the aggregate material, summarized information of assets, liabilities, and results of operations of the investees should be presented in notes or separate statements, either individually or in groups.

3. For each period for which an income statement is presented, the following disclosures should be made about items for which the fair value option has been elected (ASC 825-10-50-30) (FAS-159, par. 19):

    a. For each line item in the balance sheet, the amounts of gains and losses from fair value changes included in earnings during the period and the line in the income statement in which those gains and losses are reported. (*Note:* An entity is not precluded from meeting this requirement by disclosing amounts of gains and losses that include amounts of gains and losses for other items measured at fair value, such as items required to be measured at fair value.)

    b. A description of how interest and dividends are measured and where they are reported in the income statement.

    c. For loans and other receivables held as assets:

        (1) The estimated amount of gains or losses included in earnings during the period attributable to changes in instrument-specific credit risk.

        (2) How the gains or losses attributable to changes in instrument-specific credit risk were determined.

    d. For liabilities with fair values that have been significantly affected during the reporting period by changes in the instrument-specific credit risk:

        (1) The estimated amount of gains and losses from fair value changes included in earnings that are attributable to changes in the instrument-specific credit risk.

        (2) Qualitative information about the reasons for those changes.

        (3) How the gains and losses attributable to changes in instrument-specific credit risk were determined.

4. For annual periods only, disclosure should be made of the methods and significant assumptions used to estimate the fair value of items for which the fair value option has been elected. (ASC 825-10-50-31) (FAS-159, par. 21)

5. If an entity elects the fair value option at the time (a) the accounting treatment for an investment in another entity changes because the investment becomes subject to the equity method of accounting or the investor ceases to consolidate a subsidiary or variable interest entity but retains an interest, or (b) an event occurs that requires an eligible item to be measured at fair value at the time of the event but does not require fair value measurement at each reporting date after that (excluding the recognition of impairment under lower-of-cost-or-market accounting or other-than-temporary impairment), the following disclosures should be made in the financial statements for the period of the election (ASC 825-10-50-32) (FAS-159, par. 22):

    a. Qualitative information about the nature of the event.

    b. Quantitative information by line item in the balance sheet indicating which line items in the income statement include the effect on earnings of initially electing the fair value option for an item.

6. For items existing at the date of adoption for which the fair value option has been elected, the following disclosures should be made in the annual and first interim financial statements for the year of adoption (FAS-159, par. 27):

    a. A schedule that presents the following by line item in the balance sheet:

        (1) The pretax portion of the cumulative-effect adjustment to retained earnings for items on that line.

        (2) The fair value at the effective date of eligible items for which the fair value option is elected and the carrying amount of those same items immediately before electing the fair value option.

    b. The net effect on the entity's deferred tax assets and liabilities of electing the fair value option.

    c. Management's reasons for electing the fair value option for each existing eligible item or group of similar eligible items.

    d. If the fair value option is elected for some but not all eligible items within a group of similar eligible items:

        (1) A description of those similar items and the reasons for partial election.

(2) Information to enable users to understand how the group of similar items relates to individual line items on the balance sheet.

    e. The amount of valuation allowances that were removed from the balance sheet because they related to items for which the fair value option was elected.

7. For available-for-sale and held-to-maturity securities existing at the date of adoption for which the fair value option has been elected, the following disclosures should be made (FAS-159, par. 28):

    a. The amount of unrealized gains and losses reclassified from accumulated other comprehensive income.

    b. The amount of unrealized gains and losses that was previously unrecognized.

Registration Payment Arrangements

1. The following information should be disclosed about each registration payment arrangement or each group of similar arrangements, even if the likelihood of the issuer having to make any payments under the arrangement is remote (ASC 825-20-50-1 and 50-2) (FSP EITF 00-19-2, par. 12):

    a. The nature of the registration payment arrangement.

    b. The approximate term of the arrangement.

    c. The financial instrument(s) subject to the arrangement.

    d. The events or circumstances that would require the issuer to transfer consideration under the arrangement.

    e. Any settlement alternatives contained in the terms of the registration payment arrangement, including the party that controls the settlement alternatives.

    f. The maximum potential amount of consideration, undiscounted, that the issuer could be required to transfer under the registration payment arrangement, including the maximum number of shares that may be required to be issued.

    g. The fact that the terms of the arrangement provide for no limitation to the maximum potential consideration (including shares) to be transferred, if the terms of the arrangement include such provision.

    h. The current carrying amount of the liability representing the issuer's obligations under the registration payment arrangement and the income statement classification of any gains or losses resulting from changes in the carrying amount of that liability.

EXAMPLES OF FINANCIAL STATEMENT DISCLOSURES

Note: Various Topics within the FASB Codification (and the applicable Chapters in this book) address financial instrument matters and require disclosures about specific financial instruments, such as receivables, debt and equity securities, debt, contingencies, guarantees, and derivatives. Refer to other chapters in this book for those specific disclosure requirements and illustrative disclosures. The examples in this section address the incremental disclosures in ASC Topic 825 about (a) fair value of financial instruments, (b) concentrations of credit risk of all financial instruments, (c) the fair value option for financial assets and financial liabilities, and (d) registration payment arrangements.

 The following sample disclosures are available on the accompanying disc.

Fair Value of Financial Instruments

Note: If ASC Topic 815 based on FSP FAS 107-1 and APB 28-1 is effective, Examples 1 and 2 below should be modified to describe changes, if any, during the period in the methods and significant assumptions used to estimate the fair value of financial instruments.

Example 1: Disclosures about Fair Value of Financial Instruments by a Nonfinancial Entity

The Company uses the following methods and assumptions to estimate the fair value of each class of financial instruments for which it is practicable to estimate such value:

Cash and short-term investments—The carrying amount approximates fair value because of the short maturity of those instruments.

Accounts receivable—The carrying value of accounts receivable approximates fair value due to their short-term nature and historical collectibility.

Long-term investments—The fair values of some investments are estimated based on quoted market prices for those or similar investments. For other investments for which there are no quoted market prices, a reasonable estimate of fair value could not be made without incurring excessive costs. Additional information pertinent to the value of an unquoted investment is provided below.

Accounts payable—The carrying value of accounts payable approximates fair value due to the short-term nature of the obligations.

Long-term debt—The fair value of the Company's industrial bonds is estimated based on the quoted market prices for the same or similar issues or on the current rates offered to the Company for debt of the same remaining maturities. The fair value of the Company's other long-term debt is estimated by discounting the future cash flow using the Company's current borrowing rates for similar types and maturities of debt, except for floating-rate notes for which the carrying amounts were considered a reasonable estimate of fair value.

Foreign currency contracts—The fair value of foreign currency contracts (used for hedging purposes) is estimated by obtaining quotes from brokers.

The estimated fair values of the Company's financial instruments are as follows:

	20X2		20X1	
	Carrying Amount	*Fair Value*	*Carrying Amount*	*Fair Value*
Cash and short-term investments	$1,113,000	$1,113,000	$987,000	$987,000
Accounts receivable	3,218,000	3,218,000	2,946,000	2,946,000
Long-term investments for which it is:				
Practicable to estimate fair value	894,000	894,000	716,000	716,000
Not practicable to estimate fair value	477,000	-0-	412,000	-0-
Accounts payable	(1,171,000)	(1,171,000)	(1,342,000)	(1,342,000)
Long-term debt	(1,561,000)	(1,487,000)	(953,000)	(905,000)
Foreign currency contracts	102,000	102,000	91,000	91,000

It was not practicable to estimate the fair value of an investment representing 14% of the issued common stock of an untraded company; that investment is carried at its original cost of $477,000 and $412,000 at December 31, 20X2, and December 31, 20X1, respectively. Pertinent financial information reported by the untraded company are as follows:

	20X2	20X1
Total assets	$9,818,000	$8,971,000
Stockholders' equity	$5,100,000	$4,539,000
Revenues	$14,676,000	$13,974,000
Net income	$561,000	$398,000

The Company determined the estimated fair value amounts by using available market information and commonly accepted valuation methodologies. However, considerable judgment is required in interpreting market data to develop the estimates of fair value. Accordingly, the estimates presented herein are not necessarily indicative of the amounts that the Company or holders of the instruments could realize in a current market exchange. The use of different assumptions and/or estimation methodologies may have a material effect on the estimated fair values.

Example 2: Disclosures about Fair Value of Financial Instruments by a Financial Entity

The Company uses the following methods and assumptions to estimate the fair value of each class of financial instruments for which it is practicable to estimate such value:

Cash and short-term investments—For those short-term instruments, the carrying amount is a reasonable estimate of fair value.

Investment securities and trading account assets—For securities and derivative instruments held for trading purposes (which include bonds, interest rate futures, options, interest rate swaps, securities sold not owned, caps and floors, foreign currency contracts, and forward contracts) and marketable equity securities held for investment purposes, fair values are based on quoted market prices or dealer quotes. For other securities held as investments, fair value equals quoted market price, if available. If a quoted market price is not available, fair value is estimated using quoted market prices for similar securities.

Loan receivables—For certain homogeneous categories of loans, such as some residential mortgages, credit card receivables, and other consumer loans, fair value is estimated using the quoted market prices for securities backed by similar loans, adjusted for differences in loan characteristics. The fair value of other types of loans is estimated by discounting the future cash flows using the current rates at which similar loans would be made to borrowers with similar credit ratings and for the same remaining maturities.

Deposit liabilities—The fair value of demand deposits, savings accounts, and certain money market deposits is the amount payable on demand at the reporting date. The fair value of fixed-maturity certificates of deposit is estimated using the rates currently offered for deposits of similar remaining maturities.

Long-term debt—Rates currently available to the Company for debt with similar terms and remaining maturities are used to estimate fair value of existing debt.

Commitments to extend credit, standby letters of credit, and financial guarantees written—The fair value of commitments is estimated using the fees currently charged to enter into similar agreements, taking into account remaining terms of the agreements and the present credit-worthiness of the counterparties. For fixed-rate loan commitments, fair value also considers the difference between current levels of interest rates and the committed rates. The fair value of guarantees and letters of credit is based on fees currently charged for similar agreements or on the estimated cost to terminate them or otherwise settle the obligations with the counterparties at the reporting date.

The estimated fair values of the Company's financial instruments are as follows:

	20X2		20X1	
	Carrying Amount	*Fair Value*	*Carrying Amount*	*Fair Value*
Financial assets:				
Cash and short-term investments	$1,230,000	$1,230,000	$1,565,000	$1,565,000
Trading account assets	2,341,000	2,341,000	2,978,000	2,978,000
Investment securities	5,033,000	5,033,000	5,622,000	5,622,000
Loans	10,236,000	-0-	9,253,000	-0-
Less: allowance for loan losses	(632,000)	-0-	(581,000)	-0-
Loans, net of allowance	9,604,000	9,543,000	8,672,000	8,581,000

	20X2		20X1	
	Carrying Amount	Fair Value	Carrying Amount	Fair Value
Financial liabilities:				
Deposits	11,409,000	11,182,000	10,736,000	10,471,000
Securities sold not owned	618,000	618,000	563,000	563,000
Long-term debt	1,762,0000	1,744,000	1,382,000	1,371,000
Unrecognized financial instruments:				
Commitments to extend credit	(5,608,000)	(5,532,000)	(4,923,000)	(4,892,000)
Standby letters of credit	(674,000)	(674,000)	(532,000)	(532,000)
Financial guarantees written	(418,000)	(410,000)	(323,000)	(307,000)

The Company has determined the estimated fair value amounts by using available market information and commonly accepted valuation methodologies. However, considerable judgment is required in interpreting market data to develop the estimates of fair value. Accordingly, the estimates presented herein are not necessarily indicative of the amounts that the Company or holders of the instruments could realize in a current market exchange. The use of different assumptions and/or estimation methodologies may have a material effect on the estimated fair values.

Concentrations of Credit Risk

Example 3: Concentrations of Credit and Market Risk Arising from Derivative Instruments

All of the Company's foreign currency exchange and interest rate derivative instruments involve elements of credit and market risk in excess of the amounts recognized in the consolidated financial statements. The counterparties to the financial instruments consist of a number of major financial institutions. In addition to limiting the amounts of the agreements and contracts it enters into with any one party, the Company monitors its positions with and the credit quality of the counterparties to these financial instruments. The Company does not anticipate nonperformance by any of the counterparties.

*Example 4: Concentration of Credit Risk Virtually Limited and
Collateral Is Not Required*

Financial instruments that potentially subject the Company to
concentrations of credit risk consist primarily of cash and cash
equivalents and accounts receivable. The Company places its cash
and cash equivalents with high quality financial institutions and
limits the amount of credit exposure with any one institution.
Concentrations of credit risk with respect to accounts receivable are
limited because a large number of geographically diverse customers make up the Company's customer base, thus spreading the
trade credit risk. At December 31, 20X2, and December 31, 20X1, no
single group or customer represents greater than 10% of total
accounts receivable. The Company controls credit risk through
credit approvals, credit limits, and monitoring procedures. The
Company performs credit evaluations of its commercial and
industrial customers but generally does not require collateral to
support accounts receivable.

*Example 5: Company Requires Collateral and Has Concentrations in
Accounts Receivable*

The Company sells its products to distributors and original equipment manufacturers throughout the world. The Company performs
ongoing credit evaluations of its customers' financial condition and,
generally, requires collateral, such as letters of credit, whenever
deemed necessary. At December 31, 20X2, three customers, each of
who accounted for more than 10% of the Company's accounts
receivable, accounted for 58% of total accounts receivable in aggregate. At December 31, 20X1, four customers, each of who accounted
for more than 10% of the Company's accounts receivable, accounted
for 52% of total accounts receivable in aggregate.

Example 6: Concentrations in Sales to Few Customers

In 20X2, the two largest customers accounted for 30% and 21% of
sales. In 20X1, the three largest customers accounted for 32%, 19%,
and 18% of sales.

Example 7: Concentrations in Sales to Foreign Customers

During 20X2 and 20X1, approximately 38% and 35%, respectively, of
the Company's net sales were made to foreign customers. An
adverse change in either economic conditions abroad or the Company's relationship with significant foreign distributors could negatively affect the volume of the Company's international sales and the
Company's results of operations.

Example 8: Company Has Accounts Receivable and Contract Concentrations in Specific Industries

The majority of accounts receivable and all contract work in progress are from engineering and construction clients primarily concentrated in the steel and utility industries throughout the United States. The Company generally does not require collateral, but in most cases can place liens against the property, plant, or equipment constructed or terminate the contract if a material default occurs. The Company maintains adequate reserves for potential credit losses and such losses have been minimal and within management's estimates.

Example 9: Cash in Excess of FDIC Insured Limits

The Company maintains its cash in bank deposit accounts which, at times, may exceed federally insured limits. Accounts are guaranteed by the Federal Deposit Insurance Corporation (FDIC) up to certain limits. At December 31, 20X2, and December 31, 20X1, the Company had approximately $1,250,000 and $1,155,000, respectively, in excess of FDIC insured limits. The Company has not experienced any losses in such accounts.

Fair Value Option for Financial Assets and Financial Liabilities

Example 10: Initial Adoption of Fair Value Option under ASC Topic 825 Based on FAS-159

> **Note:** The following schedule provides information about the extent to which the fair value option is elected for existing eligible items at the time of initial adoption in a manner that reconciles to the cumulative-effect adjustment to retained earnings. It also discloses the net effect on the entity's deferred tax assets and liabilities of electing the fair value option and the amount of valuation allowances that were removed from the balance sheet because they related to items for which the fair value option was elected.

Description	Balance Sheet 1/1/ X2 Prior to Adoption of Fair Value Option	Net Gain/ (Loss) Upon Adoption of Fair Value Option	Balance Sheet 1/1/ X2 After Adoption of Fair Value Option
Loans, net	$120,000	$(20,000)	$100,000
Private equity investments	50,000	(10,000)	40,000

Description	Balance Sheet 1/1/ X2 Prior to Adoption of Fair Value Option	Net Gain/ (Loss) Upon Adoption of Fair Value Option	Balance Sheet 1/1/ X2 After Adoption of Fair Value Option
Long-term debt	(70,000)	4,000	(66,000)
Pretax cumulative effect of adoption of the fair value option		(26,000)	
Increase in deferred tax asset		8,000	
Cumulative effect of adoption of the fair value option (charge to retained earnings)		$(18,000)	

The $20,000 net loss for loans that was recorded as part of the cumulative-effect adjustment to retained earnings upon initial adoption of the fair value option includes $3,000, which was removed from the allowance for loan and lease losses.

Management's reasons for electing the fair value option for each existing eligible item or group of similar eligible items are as follows: (*Describe management's reasons*)

> **Note:** If the fair value option is elected for some but not all eligible items within a group of similar eligible items, disclosure should also include (1) a description of those similar items and the reasons for partial election and (2) information to enable users to understand how the group of similar items relates to individual line items on the balance sheet.

Example 11: Fair Value Measurements and Changes in Fair Values Included in Current-Period Earnings (Note Disclosure Integrates Other Required Disclosures)

> **Note:** This example provides information about (1) assets and liabilities measured at fair value on a recurring basis (as required by ASC Topic 820, *Fair Value Measurements and Disclosures*), (2) changes in fair values of assets and liabilities for which the fair value option has been elected in a manner that relates to the balance sheet (as required by ASC Topic 825, *Financial Instruments*), and (3) fair value estimates and corresponding carrying amounts for major categories of assets and liabilities that include items measured at fair value on a recurring basis (in accordance with ASC Topic 825). See Example 12 below for an alternative illustrative disclosure.

Loans are included in loans and lease receivables in the balance sheet. As of December 31, 20X2, approximately $160,000 of lease receivables are included in loans and lease receivables in the balance sheet and are not eligible for the fair value option.

Management's reasons for electing the fair value option for each existing eligible item or group of similar eligible items are as follows: (*Describe management's reasons*)

> **Note:** If the fair value option is elected for some but not all eligible items within a group of similar eligible items, disclosure should also include (1) a description of those similar items and the reasons for partial election and (2) information to enable users to understand how the group of similar items relates to individual line items on the balance sheet.

				Fair Value Measurements at December 31, 20X2, Using		
Description	*Total Carrying Amount in Balance Sheet 12/31/X2*	*Fair Value Estimate 12/31/X2*	*Assets/ Liabilities Measured at Fair Value 12/31/X2*	*Quoted Prices in Active Markets for Identical Assets (Level 1)*	*Significant Other Observable Inputs (Level 2)*	*Significant Unobservable Inputs Level 3)*
Trading securities	$ 115,000	$ 115,000	$ 115,000	$ 105,000	$ 10,000	
Available-for-sale securities	75,000	75,000	75,000	75,000		
Loans, net	400,000	412,000	150,000		100,000	50,000
Derivatives	60,000	60,000	60,000	25,000	15,000	20,000
Private equity investments	125,000	138,000	75,000		25,000	50,000
Long-term debt	(200,000)	(206,000)	(60,000)	(30,000)	(10,000)	(20,000)

Changes in Fair Values for the 12-Month Period Ended December 31, 20X2, for Items Measured at Fair Value Pursuant to Election of the Fair Value Option

Description	*Trading Gains and Losses*	*Other Gains and Losses*	*Interest Income on Loans*	*Interest Expense on Long- Term Debt*	*Total Changes in Fair Values Included in Current-Period Earnings*
Trading securities	$10,000*				$10,000

Changes in Fair Values for the 12-Month Period Ended December 31,
20X2, for Items Measured at Fair Value Pursuant to Election
of the Fair Value Option

Description	Trading Gains and Losses	Other Gains and Losses	Interest Income on Loans	Interest Expense on Long-Term Debt	Total Changes in Fair Values Included in Current-Period Earnings
Available-for-sale securities					
Loans, net		(3,000)	10,000		7,000
Derivatives	5,000*				5,000
Private equity investments	(18,000)				(18,000)
Long-term debt		13,000		(4,000)	9,000

* Disclosure of this amount is neither required nor precluded. This amount is shown here for completeness.

Example 12: Fair Value Measurements and Changes in Fair Values Included in Current-Period Earnings (Note Disclosure Does Not Integrate Other Required Disclosures)

Note: This example provides information about (1) assets and liabilities measured at fair value on a recurring basis (as required by ASC Topic 820, *Fair Value Measurements and Disclosures*) and (2) changes in fair values of assets and liabilities for which the fair value option has been elected in a manner that relates to the balance sheet (as required by ASC Topic 825, *Financial Instruments*). See Example 11 for an alternative illustrative disclosure.

Description	Assets/Liabilities Measured at Fair Value 12/31/X2	Fair Value Measurements at December 31, 20X2, Using		
		Quoted Prices in Active Markets for Identical Assets (Level 1)	Significant Other Observable Inputs (Level 2)	Significant Unobservable Inputs (Level 3)
Trading securities	$115,000	$105,000	$ 10,000	
Available-for-sale securities	75,000	75,000		
Loans	150,000		100,000	50,000
Derivatives	60,000	25,000	15,000	20,000

		Fair Value Measurements at December 31, 20X2, Using		
Description	Assets/ Liabilities Measured at Fair Value 12/31/X2	Quoted Prices in Active Markets for Identical Assets (Level 1)	Significant Other Observable Inputs (Level 2)	Significant Unobservable Inputs (Level 3)
Private equity investments	75,000		25,000	50,000
Long-term debt	(60,000)	(30,000)	(10,000)	(20,000)

	Changes in Fair Values for the 12-Month Period Ended December 31, 20X2, for Items Measured at Fair Value Pursuant to Election of the Fair Value Option			
Description	Other Gains and Losses	Interest Income on Loans	Interest Expense on Long-Term Debt	Total Changes in Fair Values Included in Current-Period Earnings
Trading securities				
Available-for-sale securities				
Loans	$ (3,000)	$10,000		$ 7,000
Derivatives				
Private equity investments	(18,000)			(18,000)
Long-term debt	13,000		(4,000)	9,000

Loans are included in loans and lease receivables in the balance sheet. As of December 31, 20X2, approximately $160,000 of lease receivables are included in loans and lease receivables in the balance sheet and are not eligible for the fair value option.

Management's reasons for electing the fair value option for each existing eligible item or group of similar eligible items are as follows: (*Describe management's reasons*)

> **Note:** If the fair value option is elected for some but not all eligible items within a group of similar eligible items, disclosure should also include (1) a description of those similar items and the reasons for partial election and (2) information to enable users to understand how the group of similar items relates to individual line items on the balance sheet.

Registration Payment Arrangements

Example 13: Payments under Registration Payment Arrangement Issued in Conjunction with Financial Instrument Are Probable and Can Be Reasonably Estimated

On January 16, 20X2, the Company issued unsecured promissory notes in the aggregate principal amount of $1,000,000 (the Notes) and warrants to purchase the Company's common stock (the Warrants) to Blue Alliance, Inc. The Notes bear interest at a rate of 11%, mature on July 16, 20X3, and are convertible into 542,000 shares of the Company's common stock at a conversion price of $1.75 per share. The difference between the conversion price and the fair market value of the common stock on the commitment date (transaction date) resulted in a beneficial conversion feature recorded of $590,000. The associated Warrants are exercisable for 270,000 shares of common stock at an exercise price of $1.75 per share. The Warrants, which expire four years after issuance, were assigned a value of $410,000, estimated using the Black-Scholes valuation model. The following assumptions were used to determine the fair value of the Warrants using the Black-Scholes valuation model: a term of four years, risk-free rate of 3.28%, volatility of 100%, and dividend yield of zero. The values assigned to both the Notes and the Warrants were allocated based on their relative fair values. The discounts on the Notes for the beneficial conversion feature and the Warrants are being amortized to interest expense, using the effective interest method, over the term of the Notes. Total interest expense recognized relating to the beneficial conversion feature and the Warrants discount was $673,000 during the year ended December 31, 20X2.

The holders of the Notes and Warrants have registration rights that require the Company to file a registration statement with the Securities and Exchange Commission (SEC) to register the resale of the common stock issuable upon conversion of the Notes or the exercise of the Warrants. The ability to register stock is deemed to be outside of the Company's control. Accordingly, the initial fair value of the Warrants of $410,000 was recorded as an accrued warrant liability in the consolidated balance sheet and is marked to market at the end of each reporting period. At December 31, 20X2, the warrant liability was adjusted to its new fair value of $217,000 as determined by the Company, resulting in a gain of $193,000, which has been reflected in "Interest income and other, net" on the consolidated statement of operations for the year ended December 31, 20X2.

Under the registration rights agreement, the Company has agreed to use its best efforts (1) to file a registration statement for the resale of the common stock issuable upon conversion of the Notes or the exercise of the Warrants and for the registration statement to be declared effective by the SEC by April 1, 20X3, and (2) to maintain the effectiveness of the registration statement through December 31,

20X5 (the term of the agreement). If the registration statement is not declared effective by the SEC by April 1, 20X3, or its effectiveness is not maintained for the specified period, the Company must pay Blue Alliance, Inc., a lump sum amount of $400,000. At December 31, 20X2, the Company determined that the payment of the entire amount of $400,000 is probable and, therefore, recognized a contingent liability for the same amount in the accompanying financial statements.

CHAPTER 50
ASC TOPIC 830: FOREIGN CURRENCY MATTERS

CONTENTS

EXECUTIVE SUMMARY

Foreign Currency Matters

There are two major areas of foreign operations: (1) translation of
foreign currency financial statements for purposes of consolidation,
combination, or reporting on the equity method and (2) accounting
for and reporting foreign currency transactions.

Before an attempt is made to translate the records of a foreign
operation, the records should be in conformity with generally
accepted accounting principles (GAAP). In addition, if the foreign
statements have any accounts stated in a currency other than their
own, they should be converted into the foreign statement's currency
before translation into U.S. dollars or any other reporting currency.
In summary:

1. Assets, liabilities, and operations of an entity should be
   expressed in the functional currency of the entity. The functional currency of an entity is the currency of the primary
   economic environment in which the entity operates.

2. The current rate of exchange should be used to translate the
   assets and liabilities of a foreign entity from its functional
   currency into the reporting currency. The weighted-average
   exchange rate for the period is used to translate revenue,
   expenses, and gains and losses of a foreign entity from its
   functional currency to the reporting currency. The current rate
   of exchange is used to translate changes in financial position
   other than those items found in the income statement, which
   are translated at the weighted average exchange rate for the
   period.

3. Gain or loss on the translation of foreign currency financial statements is not recognized in current net income but should be reported in other comprehensive income. If remeasurement from the recording currency to the functional currency is necessary prior to translation, however, gain or loss on remeasurement is recognized in current net income.

4. The amounts accumulated in the translation adjustment component of stockholders' equity are realized on the sale or substantially complete liquidation of the investment in the foreign entity.

5. The financial statements of a foreign entity in a country that has had cumulative inflation of approximately 100% or more over a three-year period (highly inflationary) should be remeasured into the functional currency of the reporting entity.

Accounting Literature

FASB Accounting Standards Codification Topic	*Pre-Codification Accounting Literature*
830, *Foreign Currency Matters*	FAS-52, *Foreign Currency Translation*

DISCLOSURE AND KEY PRESENTATION REQUIREMENTS

1. The aggregate transaction gain or loss included in determining net income for the period should be disclosed in the financial statements or notes thereto. (ASC 830-20-45-1 and 50-1) (FAS-52, par. 30)

2. The following disclosures should be made for rate changes that occur after the date of the entity's financial statements (ASC 830-20-50-2; 830-30-50-2) (FAS-52, pars. 32 and 143):

   a. Disclosure for the rate change, including consideration of changes in unsettled transactions from the date of the financial statements to the date the rate changed.

   b. The effects of rate changes on unsettled balances pertaining to foreign currency transactions.

   c. If the effects of rate changes cannot be determined, that fact.

3. An analysis should be provided of the changes in the accumulated amount of translation adjustments (reported in equity as a component of accumulated other comprehensive income), and such analysis should include the following

(ASC 830-30-45-18 and 45-20; 830-30-50-1) (FAS-52, par. 31) (*Note:* This analysis may be provided in a separate financial statement, in notes to the financial statements, or as part of a statement of changes in equity):

a. Beginning and ending amounts of cumulative translation adjustments.

b. The aggregate adjustment for the period resulting from translation adjustments (in accordance with ASC paragraph 830-30-45-12 [FAS-52, par. 13]) and gains and losses from certain hedges and intra-entity balances (in accordance with ASC paragraph 830-20-35-3 [FAS-52, par. 20]).

c. The amount of income taxes for the period allocated to translation adjustments.

d. The amounts transferred from cumulative translation adjustments and included in determining net income for the period as a result of the sale or complete (or substantially complete) liquidation of an investment in a foreign entity.

4. Additional (*optional*) disclosures, such as the following, should be considered to supplement the required disclosures described above (ASC 830-20-50-3) (FAS-52, par. 144):

a. Mathematical effects of translating revenue and expenses at rates that are different from those used in previous financial statements.

b. Economic effects of rate changes (such as effects on selling prices, sales volume, and cost structures).

EXAMPLES OF FINANCIAL STATEMENT DISCLOSURES

 The following sample disclosures are available on the accompanying disc.

Example 1: Foreign Currency Adjustments—Functional Currency Is the Foreign Country's Local Currency

The financial position and results of operations of the Company's foreign subsidiaries are measured using the foreign subsidiary's local currency as the functional currency. Revenues and expenses of such subsidiaries have been translated into U.S. dollars at average exchange rates prevailing during the period. Assets and liabilities have been translated at the rates of exchange on the balance sheet date. The resulting translation gain and loss adjustments are recorded directly as a separate component of shareholders' equity, unless there is a sale or complete liquidation of the underlying foreign investments. Foreign currency translation adjustments resulted in gains of $425,000 and $366,000 in 20X2 and 20X1, respectively.

Transaction gains and losses that arise from exchange rate fluctuations on transactions denominated in a currency other than the functional currency are included in the results of operations as incurred. Foreign currency transaction losses included in operations totaled $57,000 in 20X2 and $46,000 in 20X1.

Example 2: Foreign Currency Adjustments—Functional Currency Is the U.S. Dollar

The Company's functional currency for all operations worldwide is the U.S. dollar. Nonmonetary assets and liabilities are translated at historical rates and monetary assets and liabilities are translated at exchange rates in effect at the end of the year. Income statement accounts are translated at average rates for the year. Gains and losses from translation of foreign currency financial statements into U.S. dollars are included in current results of operations. Gains and losses resulting from foreign currency transactions are also included in current results of operations. Aggregate foreign currency translation and transaction losses included in operations totaled $138,000 in 20X2 and $114,000 in 20X1.

Example 3: Foreign Currency Adjustments—Certain Assets and Liabilities Are Remeasured at Current Exchange Rates While Others Are Remeasured at Historical Rates

The U.S. dollar is the functional currency of the Company's worldwide continuing operations. All foreign currency asset and liability amounts are remeasured into U.S. dollars at end-of-period exchange rates, except for inventories, prepaid expenses and property, plant, and equipment, which are remeasured at historical rates. Foreign currency income and expenses are remeasured at average exchange rates in effect during the year, except for expenses related to balance sheet amounts remeasured at historical exchange rates. Exchange gains and losses arising from remeasurement of foreign currency-denominated monetary assets and liabilities are included in income in the period in which they occur.

Example 4: Foreign Currency Hedging Activities

The Company manufactures and sells its products in a number of countries throughout the world and, as a result, is exposed to movements in foreign currency exchange rates. The Company's major foreign currency exposures involve the markets in Western and Eastern

Europe, Asia, Mexico, and Canada. The primary purpose of the Company's foreign currency hedging activities is to manage the volatility associated with foreign currency purchases of materials and other assets and liabilities created in the normal course of business. The Company primarily utilizes forward exchange contracts and purchased options with maturities of less than 18 months and currency swaps with maturities up to five years.

The Company enters into certain foreign currency derivative instruments that do not meet hedge accounting criteria. These primarily are intended to protect against exposure related to intercompany financing transactions and income from international operations. The fair values of these instruments at December 31, 20X2 were recorded as $3,452,000 in assets and $671,000 in liabilities.

In addition, the Company utilizes purchased foreign currency options, forward exchange contracts, and cross currency swaps which qualify as cash flow hedges. These are intended to offset the effect of exchange rate fluctuations on forecasted sales, inventory purchases, intercompany royalties, and intercompany loans denominated in foreign currency. The fair values of these instruments at December 31, 20X2 were recorded as $2,794,000 in assets and $3,125,000 in liabilities. Gains and losses on these instruments are deferred in other comprehensive income (OCI) until the underlying transaction is recognized in earnings. The earnings impact is reported in net sales, cost of products sold, or marketing research and administrative expenses, to match the underlying transaction being hedged. Qualifying cash flow hedges that are currently deferred in OCI will be reclassified into earnings as the underlying transactions are recognized. No currency cash flow hedges were discontinued during the year due to changes in expectations on the original forecasted transactions.

> **Note:** See Chapter 47, "ASC Topic 815: Derivatives and Hedging," for additional examples.

Example 5: Analysis of the Change in Cumulative Foreign Currency Translation Adjustments

Accumulated other comprehensive income for 20X2 and 20X1 represents foreign currency translation items associated with the Company's European and South American operations. Following is an analysis of the changes in the cumulative foreign currency translation adjustment account for 20X2 and 20X1:

	Accumulated Other Comprehensive Income— Foreign Currency Translation	
	20X2	20X1
Balance at beginning of year	$2,250,000	$1,600,000
Foreign currency translation adjustments	1,317,000	1,100,000
Income tax effect relating to translation adjustments	(540,000)	(450,000)
Amount recognized in operations as a result of the sale of the Company's German subsidiary in 20X2	(625,000)	-0-
Balance at end of year	$2,402,000	$2,250,000

Example 6: Significant Exchange Rate Changes after the Balance Sheet Date

On January 13, 20X3, the Brazilian government allowed the value of its currency, the Real, to float freely against other currencies. Between January 13, 20X3, and March 17, 20X3, the Real's exchange rate to the U.S. dollar has declined as much as 44% from the exchange rate on December 31, 20X2. As nearly all the Company's transactions in Brazil are Real-denominated, translating the results of operations of the Company's Brazilian subsidiary into U.S. dollars at devalued exchange rates will result in a lower contribution to consolidated revenues and operating income. Based on the Real exchange rate to the U.S. dollar on March 17, 20X3, the Company's currency translation of the foreign investment in its Brazilian subsidiary from the Real (functional currency) to the U.S. dollar would result in a devaluation of approximately $6 million. Currency devaluations resulting from translating assets and liabilities from the functional currency to the U.S. dollar are included as a component of other comprehensive income (loss) in stockholders' equity.

Example 7: Company Discloses Nature of Its Operations in Foreign Countries

Substantially all of the Company's products are manufactured in the Dominican Republic, Mexico (under the Maquiladora program), Switzerland, Ireland, and Slovakia. These foreign operations represent captive manufacturing facilities of the Company. The Company's operations are subject to various political, economic, and other risks and uncertainties inherent in the countries in which the Company operates. Among other risks, the Company's operations are subject to the risks of restrictions on transfer of funds; export duties, quotas, and embargoes; domestic and international customs and tariffs; changing taxation policies; foreign exchange restrictions; and political conditions and governmental regulations.

Example 8: Amount of Foreign Earnings Exceeds Amounts Actually Received in the United States

In 20X2 and 20X1, earnings from the Company's French subsidiary totaled $705,000 and $643,000, respectively; dividends received from this subsidiary totaled $500,000 and $400,000 in 20X2 and 20X1, respectively.

Example 9: Company Specifies Percentage of Net Sales Relating to Foreign Operations

Sales to customers outside the United States approximated 35% of net sales in 20X2 and 25% of net sales in 20X1. An adverse change in either economic conditions abroad or the Company's relationship with significant foreign distributors could negatively affect the volume of the Company's international sales and the Company's results of operations.

Example 10: Concentration in Accounts Receivable from Foreign Customers

As of December 31, 20X2, and December 31, 20X1, approximately 38% and 35%, respectively, of the Company's total accounts receivable were due from four foreign customers.

Example 11: Revenues and Long-Lived Assets by Geographic Area

The following table indicates the Company's relative amounts of revenue and the long-lived assets for 20X2 and 20X1 by geographic area:

| | 20X2 | | 20X1 | |
	Revenue	Long-Lived Assets	Revenue	Long-Lived Assets
United States	$50,719,000	$14,395,000	$47,611,000	$13,618,000
Europe:				
Germany	7,592,000	2,530,000	7,058,000	2,367,000
France	6,133,000	1,662,000	5,450,000	1,278,000
Italy	5,562,000	2,129,000	4,923,000	1,854,000
Other	4,397,000	1,012,000	3,820,000	1,299,000

	20X2		20X1	
Total Europe	23,684,000	7,333,000	21,251,000	6,798,000
Other foreign countries	3,789,000	1,126,000	3,214,000	1,011,000
Total	$78,192,000	$22,854,000	$72,076,000	$21,427,000

Example 12: Restrictions on Transfer of Assets of Foreign Operations

The governments and national banking systems of certain countries in which the Company has consolidated foreign affiliates impose various restrictions on the payment of dividends and transfer of funds out of those countries. Additionally, provisions of credit agreements entered into by certain foreign affiliates presently restrict the payment of dividends. The estimated U.S. dollar amount of the foreign net assets included in the Consolidated Balance Sheets that are restricted in some manner as to transfer to the Company was approximately $22 million and $19 million at December 31, 20X2, and December 31, 20X1, respectively.

Example 13: Company's Future Operations Are Dependent on Foreign Operations

The Company's future operations and earnings will depend on the results of the Company's operations in [*foreign country*]. There can be no assurance that the Company will be able to successfully conduct such operations, and a failure to do so would have a material adverse effect on the Company's financial position, results of operations, and cash flows. Also, the success of the Company's operations will be subject to numerous contingencies, some of which are beyond management's control. These contingencies include general and regional economic conditions, prices for the Company's products, competition, and changes in regulation. Since the Company is dependent on international operations, specifically those in [*foreign country*], the Company will be subject to various additional political, economic, and other uncertainties. Among other risks, the Company's operations will be subject to the risks of restrictions on transfer of funds; export duties, quotas, and embargoes; domestic and international customs and tariffs; changing taxation policies; foreign exchange restrictions; and political conditions and governmental regulations.

Example 14: Deferred Taxes Not Provided on Undistributed Earnings of Foreign Subsidiaries—Amount of Deferred Tax Liability Is Not Disclosed

A provision has not been made at December 31, 20X2, for U.S. or additional foreign withholding taxes on approximately $12 million of undistributed earnings of foreign subsidiaries since it is the present intention of management to reinvest the undistributed earnings indefinitely in foreign operations. Generally, such earnings become subject to U.S. tax upon the remittance of dividends and under certain other circumstances. It is not practicable to estimate the amount of deferred tax liability on such undistributed earnings.

Example 15: Deferred Taxes Not Provided on Undistributed Earnings of Foreign Subsidiaries—Amount of Deferred Tax Liability Is Disclosed

The Company has not recorded deferred income taxes applicable to undistributed earnings of foreign subsidiaries that are indefinitely reinvested in foreign operations. Undistributed earnings amounted to approximately $6,000,000 and $5,200,000 at December 31, 20X2, and December 31, 20X1, respectively. If the earnings of such foreign subsidiaries were not definitely reinvested, a deferred tax liability of approximately $1,500,000 and $1,300,000 would have been required at December 31, 20X2, and December 31, 20X1, respectively.

Example 16: Deferred Taxes Recorded on Undistributed Earnings of Foreign Subsidiaries

At December 31, 20X2, the accompanying consolidated Balance Sheet includes a deferred tax liability of $300,000 for the estimated income taxes that will be payable upon the anticipated future repatriation of approximately $1,000,000 of undistributed earnings of foreign subsidiaries in the form of dividends.

CHAPTER 51
ASC TOPIC 835: INTEREST

CONTENTS

EXECUTIVE SUMMARY

Capitalization of Interest Cost

Interest cost should be capitalized as part of the cost of acquiring or constructing certain assets, such as a plant, a warehouse, or a real estate development. To qualify for interest capitalization, assets need a period of time to get them ready for their intended use, which may be either (1) for sale or (2) for use within the business. However, interest cannot be capitalized in the following circumstances:

1. For inventories that are routinely manufactured or otherwise produced in large quantities on a repetitive basis

2. For qualifying assets acquired using gifts or grants that are restricted by the grantor to acquisition of those assets to the extent that funds are available from such gifts or grants

Imputed Interest

When a note is exchanged for property, goods, or services in an arm's-length transaction, it is generally presumed that the interest stated on the note is fair and adequate. If no interest is stated or if the interest stated appears unreasonable, the transaction should be valued at the fair value of the note or property, goods, or services, whichever is more clearly determinable. If such fair value is not readily determinable, the transaction should be valued at the present value of the note, determined by discounting the future cash payments under the note by an appropriate interest rate. The difference between the face amount of the note and its present value represents a discount or premium, which should be amortized over the life of the note using the interest method, or a method that approximates the interest method. The discount or premium amount is not an asset or a liability separable from the note that gives rise to it; therefore, the discount or premium should be reported in the balance sheet as a direct deduction from or addition to the face amount of the note.

Accounting Literature

FASB Accounting Standards Codification Topic	*Pre-Codification Accounting Literature*
230, *Statement of Cash Flows*	FAS-34, *Capitalization of Interest Cost*
835, *Interest*	FAS-95, *Statement of Cash Flows*
	APB-21, *Interest on Receivables and Payables*

DISCLOSURE AND KEY PRESENTATION REQUIREMENTS

1. The following disclosures should be made with respect to interest cost:

   a. For an accounting period in which no interest cost is capitalized, the amount of interest cost incurred and charged to expense during the period. (ASC 835-20-50-1) (FAS-34, par. 21)

b. For an accounting period in which some interest cost is capitalized, the total amount of interest cost incurred during the period and the amount thereof that has been capitalized. (ASC 835-20-50-1) (FAS-34, par. 21)

c. For notes payable or receivable that require the imputation of interest, disclosures should include the following (ASC 835-30-45-1 through 45-3) (APB-21, par. 16):

    (1) A description of the note.

    (2) The effective interest rate.

    (3) The face amount of the note.

    (4) The amount of discount or premium resulting from present value determination. (*Note:* The discount or premium resulting from the determination of present value in cash or noncash transactions is not an asset (i.e., deferred charge) or liability (i.e., deferred credit) separable from the note that gives rise to it. The discount or premium should be reported in the balance sheet as a direct deduction from, or addition to, the face amount of the note.)

    (5) The amortization of the discount or premium to interest.

d. The amount of interest paid (net of amounts capitalized) for each period for which a statement of cash flows is presented. (ASC 230-10-45-25 and 50-2) (FAS-95, par. 29)

2. Debt issuance costs should be reported in the balance sheet as deferred charges. (ASC 835-30-45-3) (APB-21, par. 16)

EXAMPLES OF FINANCIAL STATEMENT DISCLOSURES

 The following sample disclosures are available on the accompanying disc.

Example 1: Interest Cost Capitalized

The Company capitalizes interest cost incurred on funds used to construct property, plant, and equipment. The capitalized interest is recorded as part of the asset to which it relates and is amortized over the asset's estimated useful life. Interest cost capitalized was $315,000 and $268,000 in 20X2 and 20X1, respectively.

> **Note:** The amount of interest cost capitalized may be disclosed as part of the note on property and equipment.

Example 2: Interest Cost Charged to Operations

The Company incurred interest cost of $472,000 in 20X2 and $436,000 in 20X1, all of which were charged to operations.

> **Note:** The amount of interest expense charged to operations may be disclosed on the face of the income statement, or as part of the debt note.

Example 3: Details of Interest Expense, Interest Capitalized, and Interest Paid Provided in a Separate Note

Details of interest cost incurred for the years ended December 31, 20X2, and December 31, 20X1, are as follows:

	20X2	20X1
Interest cost charged to operations	$523,000	$476,000
Interest cost capitalized	91,000	112,000
Total Interest cost incurred	$614,000	$588,000

Interest paid during 20X2 and 20X1, net of capitalized interest, amounted to $511,000 and $458,000, respectively.

Example 4: Interest Cost Incurred in Connection with Product Financing Arrangement

In 20X2, the Company entered into a product financing arrangement with a vendor for the purchase of $13 million of electronic connectors. Accordingly, this inventory and the related short-term debt have been included in the Balance Sheet at December 31, 20X2. The vendor has also made commitments, on the Company's behalf, to purchase additional amounts of the electronic connectors for delivery in 20X3. The average interest rate on the product financing arrangement was 7.3% at December 31, 20X2. Interest expense incurred and paid under this product financing arrangement totaled $193,000 for 20X2.

Example 5: Liability Requires Imputation of Interest

At December 31, 20X2, the Company has included as a liability the present value, computed with an effective annual rate of 10%, of a death benefit related to the termination of an employment contract as a result of the death of the President in 20X2. This termination death benefit will be paid in thirty-six equal monthly installments of $30,000 commencing in April 20X3.

Example 6: Notes Receivable Require Imputation of Interest

In March 20X2, the Company received $50,000 in cash and $2,200,000 in notes in full payment of outstanding trade receivables resulting from the reorganization by a major customer, pursuant to a bankruptcy decree. The notes vary in maturity from six months to five years. They include non-interest bearing notes and notes bearing interest at rates of 4% to 6%. The notes are recorded at the present value of the future cash flows, utilizing an imputed interest of 10%, which equals $2,017,000. Notes receivable are due as follows: $418,000 in 20X3, $536,000 in 20X4, $374,000 in 20X5, $318,000 in 20X6, and $196,000 in 20X7.

CHAPTER 52
ASC TOPIC 840: LEASES

CONTENTS

EXECUTIVE SUMMARY

A lease that transfers substantially all the benefits and risks inherent in the ownership of property should be capitalized. Such a lease is accounted for by the lessee as the acquisition of an asset and the incurrence of a liability. The lessor accounts for such a lease as a sale (sales-type lease) or financing (direct-financing lease). All other leases are referred to as operating leases and should be accounted for as the rental of property.

The following are the broad classifications of leases under generally accepted accounting principles (GAAP):

Lessees	Lessors
Capital lease	Sales-type lease
Operating lease	Direct-financing lease
	Operating lease

Sales-type and direct-financing leases are the lessor's equivalent for a capital lease by a lessee.

Accounting for Leases—Lessees

A lease should be classified as a capital lease by a lessee if the lease meets at least one of the following criteria:

1. By the end of the lease term, ownership of the leased property is transferred to the lessee.

2. The lease contains a bargain purchase option.

3. The lease term is at least 75% of the estimated remaining economic life of the leased property. This criterion is not applicable when the beginning of the lease term falls within the last 25% of the total estimated economic life of the leased property.

4. At the inception of the lease, the present value of the minimum lease payments is at least 90% of the fair value of the leased property. This criterion is not applicable when the beginning of the lease term falls within the last 25% of the total estimated economic life of the leased property.

If none of these criteria are met, the lessee should classify the lease as an operating lease.

In a capital lease, the lessee should record a capital asset and a lease obligation for the same amount. The amount recorded should be the lesser of (1) the fair value of the leased asset at the inception of the lease, or (2) the present value of the minimum lease payments as of the beginning of the lease term. Once capitalized, the leased asset should be depreciated like any owned asset.

Under an operating lease, the lessee generally should charge the lease payments to rent expense on a straight-line basis over the lease term, even if payments are not made on straight-line basis.

Accounting for Leases—Lessors

A *sales-type lease* is a type of capital lease that results in a profit or loss to the lessor and transfers substantially all the benefits and risks inherent in the ownership of the leased property to the lessee. In a sales-type lease, the fair value of the leased property at the inception of the lease differs from its cost or carrying amount, thereby resulting in a profit or loss to the lessor.

A *direct-financing lease* is a type of capital lease that does *not* result in a profit or loss to the lessor but does transfer substantially all the benefits and risks inherent in the ownership of the leased property to the lessee. In a direct-financing lease, the leased property's book value and fair value are the same; therefore, there is no resulting profit or loss.

A lessor should classify a lease as a sales-type or direct-financing lease, whichever is appropriate, if the lease at inception meets at least one of the four criteria discussed above and *both* of the following criteria:

1. Collection of the minimum lease payments is reasonably predictable.

2. No important uncertainties exist for unreimbursable costs yet to be incurred by the lessor. Important uncertainties include extensive warranties and material commitments beyond normal practice. *Executory costs*, such as insurance, maintenance, and taxes, are not considered important uncertainties.

If none of these criteria are met, the lease should be classified as an operating lease by a lessor.

A sales-type lease should be accounted for by a lessor as follows:

1. The lessor should determine the *gross investment in the lease*, which is (a) the minimum lease payments (net of amounts, if any, included therein for executory costs to be paid by the lessor, together with any profit thereon) plus (b) the unguaranteed residual value accruing to the benefit of the lessor.

2. The present value of the gross investment in the lease should be recorded as a receivable in the balance sheet.

3. The difference between the gross investment in the lease (as determined in item 1 above) and its present value (as determined in item 2 above) should be recorded as unearned income and amortized to income over the lease term by the interest method. (The unearned income is included in the balance sheet as a deduction from the related gross investment.)

4. The present value of the minimum lease payments should be recorded as the sales price. The carrying amount of the leased property, plus any initial direct costs and less the present value of the unguaranteed residual value should be charged against income in the same period.

A direct-financing lease should be accounted for by a lessor as follows:

1. The lessor should determine the *gross investment in the lease*, which is (a) the minimum lease payments (net of amounts, if

any, included therein for executory costs to be paid by the lessor, together with any profit thereon) plus (b) the unguaranteed residual value accruing to the benefit of the lessor.

2. The difference between the gross investment in the lease (as determined in item 1 above) and the carrying amount of the leased property should be recorded as unearned income. The unearned income and any initial direct costs should be amortized to income over the lease term by the interest method.

3. The net investment in the lease (i.e., gross investment as determined in item 1 above plus any unamortized initial direct costs less the unearned income) should be recorded as a receivable in the balance sheet.

For operating leases, the lessor should include the cost of the property leased to the lessee in the lessor's balance sheet as property, plant, and equipment and should be depreciated. Material initial direct costs (those directly related to the negotiation and consummation of the lease) are deferred and allocated to income over the lease term. Rental income should be amortized over the lease term on a straight-line basis, unless some other systematic and rational basis is more representative of the time pattern in which income is earned.

Accounting Literature

FASB Accounting Standards Codification Topic	*Pre-Codification Accounting Literature*
840, *Leases*	FAS-13, *Accounting for Leases*
	FAS-98, *Accounting for Leases:*
	• *Sale-Leaseback Transactions Involving Real Estate*
	• *Sales-Type Leases of Real Estate*
	• *Definition of the Lease Term*
	• *Initial Direct Costs of Direct Financing Leases*
	FTB 79-16R, *Effect of a Change in Income Tax Rate on the Accounting for Leveraged Leases*
	EITF 98-9, *Accounting for Contingent Rent*

DISCLOSURE AND KEY PRESENTATION REQUIREMENTS

Lessees

1. The nature and extent of leasing transactions with related parties should be disclosed. (ASC 840-10-50-1) (FAS-13, par. 29)

2. A general description of leasing arrangements should be disclosed including, but not limited to, the following (ASC 840-10-50-2) (FAS-13, par. 16):

   a. The basis on which contingent rental payments are determined.

   b. The existence and terms of renewal or purchase options and escalation clauses.

   c. Restrictions imposed by lease agreements such as those concerning dividends, additional debt, and further leasing.

3. For operating leases:

   a. The following disclosures should be made for operating leases for each period for which an income statement is presented (ASC 840-20-50-1) (FAS-13, par. 16) (*Note:* Rental payments under leases with terms of a month or less that were not renewed need not be included):

      (1) Rental expense.

      (2) Separate amounts for minimum rentals, contingent rentals, and sublease rentals.

   b. The following disclosures should be made for operating leases having initial or remaining noncancelable lease terms in excess of one year (ASC 840-20-50-2) (FAS-13, par. 16):

      (1) Future minimum rental payments required as of the date of the latest balance sheet presented, in the aggregate and for each of the five succeeding fiscal years.

      (2) The total amount of minimum rentals to be received in the future under noncancelable subleases as of the date of the latest balance sheet presented.

   c. Rental costs should be included in the lessee's income from continuing operations. (ASC 840-20-45-1) (FSP FAS 13-1, par. 6)

4. For capital leases, the following disclosures should be made (ASC 840-30-45-1 through 45-3; 840-30-50-1) (FAS-13, pars. 13 and 16; FAS-71, par. 43):

   a. Assets recorded under capital leases and the accumulated amortization thereon as of the date of each balance sheet presented.

   b. The gross amount of assets recorded under capital leases as of the date of each balance sheet presented by major classes according to nature or function. (*Note:* This information may be combined with the comparable information for owned assets.)

   c. Obligations under capitalized leases separately identified in the balance sheet and appropriately classified as current and noncurrent liabilities.

   d. Future minimum lease payments as of the date of the latest balance sheet presented, in the aggregate and for each of the five succeeding fiscal years, with separate deductions from the total for the amount representing executory costs (including any profit thereon), that are included in the minimum lease payments, and for the amount of the imputed interest necessary to reduce the net minimum lease payments to present value.

   e. The total of minimum sublease rentals to be received in the future under noncancelable subleases as of the date of the latest balance sheet presented.

   f. Total contingent rentals actually incurred for each period for which an income statement is presented.

   g. Amortization of capitalized leases separately reported on the income statement or presented in a note to the financial statements. (The amortization may be combined with depreciation expense, but that fact must be disclosed.)

5. For sale-leaseback transactions:

   a. The seller-lessee should include a description of the terms of the sale-leaseback transaction including future commitments, obligations, provisions, or circumstances that require or result in the seller-lessee's continuing involvement. (ASC 840-40-50-1) (FAS-98, par. 17)

   b. If a sale-leaseback transaction is accounted for by the deposit method or as a real estate financing arrangement, the seller-lessee should make the following disclosures (ASC 840-40-50-2) (FAS-98, par. 18):

      (1) The obligation for future minimum lease payments as of the date of the latest balance sheet presented in

the aggregate and for each of the five succeeding fiscal years.

(2) The total of minimum sublease rentals, if any, to be received in the future under noncancelable subleases in the aggregate and for each of the five succeeding fiscal years.

Lessors

1. The nature and extent of leasing transactions with related parties should be disclosed. (ASC 840-10-50-1) (FAS-13, par. 29)

2. A general description of the lessor's leasing arrangements should be disclosed, if leasing (exclusive of leveraged leasing) is a significant part of the lessor's business activities in terms of revenue, net income, or assets. (ASC 840-10-50-4) (FAS-13, par. 23)

3. For lessors that recognize contingent rental income, the following disclosures should be made (ASC 840-10-50-5) (EITF 98-9):

   a. The accounting policy for recognizing contingent rental income.

   b. If contingent rental income is recognized (accrued) prior to the lessee's achievement of the specified target that triggers the contingent rents, the impact on rental income as if the lessor's accounting policy was to defer contingent rental income until the specified target is met.

4. For operating leases:

   a. The leased property should be included with or near property, plant, and equipment in the lessor's balance sheet. (ASC 840-20-45-2) (FAS-13, par. 19)

   b. Accumulated depreciation should be deducted from the investment in the leased property. (ASC 840-20-45-3) (FAS-13, par. 19)

   c. The following disclosures should be made (ASC 840-20-50-4) (FAS-13, par. 23):

      (1) The cost and carrying amount, if different, of property on lease or held for leasing, by major classes of property according to nature or function, and the amount of accumulated depreciation in total as of the date of the latest balance sheet presented.

      (2) Minimum future rentals on noncancelable leases as of the date of the latest balance sheet presented, in the aggregate and for each of the five succeeding fiscal years.

    (3)   Total contingent rentals included in income for each period for which an income statement is presented.

5. For sales-type and direct-financing leases, the following disclosures should be made (ASC 840-30-50-4) (FAS-13, par. 23):

    a. The following components of the net investment in sales-type and direct financing leases as of the date of each balance sheet presented:

        (1)   Future minimum lease payments to be received with separate deductions for: (i) amounts representing executory costs, including any profit thereon, included in the minimum lease payments, and (ii) the accumulated allowance for uncollectible minimum lease payments receivable.

        (2)   The unguaranteed residual values accruing to the benefit of the lessor.

        (3)   Initial direct costs (for direct financing leases only).

        (4)   Unearned income.

    b. Future minimum lease payments to be received for each of the five succeeding fiscal years as of the date of the latest balance sheet presented.

    c. Total contingent rentals included in income for each period for which an income statement is presented.

6. For leveraged leases:

    a. The amount of related deferred taxes should be presented separately from the remainder of the net investment in leveraged leases in the balance sheet. (ASC 840-30-45-5) (FAS-13, par. 47)

    b. Separate presentation should be made (in the income statement or in related notes) of pretax income from the leveraged lease, the tax effect of pretax income, and the amount of investment tax credit recognized as income during the period. (ASC 840-30-45-5) (FAS-13, par. 47)

    c. If leveraged leasing is a significant part of the lessor's business activities in terms of revenue, net income, or assets, the following components of the net investment balance in leveraged leases should be disclosed (ASC 840-30-25-8; 840-30-50-5) (FAS-13, par. 47):

        (1)   Rentals receivable.

        (2)   Investment tax credit receivable.

        (3)   Estimated residual value of the leased assets.

        (4)   Unearned and deferred income.

d. If accounting for the effect on leveraged leases of the change in tax rates results in a significant variation from the customary relationship between income tax expense and pretax accounting income and the reason for that variation is not otherwise apparent, the lessor should disclose the reason for that variation. (ASC 840-30-50-6) (FTB 79-16R, par. 4)

EXAMPLES OF FINANCIAL STATEMENT DISCLOSURES

The following sample disclosures are available on the accompanying disc.

Lessees

Example 1: Operating Leases Include Renewal Options, Increases in Future Minimum Payments, and Payment of Executory Costs

The Company leases many of its operating and office facilities for various terms under long-term, non-cancelable operating lease agreements. The leases expire at various dates through 20X9 and provide for renewal options ranging from three months to six years. In the normal course of business, it is expected that these leases will be renewed or replaced by leases on other properties.

The leases provide for increases in future minimum annual rental payments based on defined increases in the Consumer Price Index, subject to certain minimum increases. Also, the agreements generally require the Company to pay executory costs (real estate taxes, insurance, and repairs). Lease expense totaled $25,500,000 and $24,700,000 during 20X2 and 20X1, respectively.

The following is a schedule by year of future minimum rental payments required under the operating lease agreements:

Year Ending December 31	Amount
20X3	$ 27,000,000
20X4	29,500,000
20X5	31,000,000
20X6	33,500,000
20X7	35,000,000
Thereafter	80,000,000
	$236,000,000

Total minimum lease payments do not include contingent rentals that may be paid under certain leases because of use in excess of specified amounts. Contingent rental payments were not significant in 20X2 or 20X1.

Example 2: Operating Leases Include Sublease Income

The Company leases corporate office and warehouse facilities, machinery and equipment, computers, and furniture under operating lease agreements expiring at various times through 20X9. Substantially all of the leases require the Company to pay maintenance, insurance, property taxes, and percentage rent ranging from 3% to 12%, based on sales volume over certain minimum sales levels. Effective March 20X2, the Company entered into a sublease agreement for its former ware house facility, which expires in September 20X6.

Minimum annual rental commitments under non-cancelable leases are as follows at December 31, 20X2:

Year Ending December 31	Minimum Lease Commitments	Sublease Income	Net Lease Commitments
20X3	$ 5,196,000	$247,000	$ 4,949,000
20X4	4,962,000	247,000	4,715,000
20X5	4,352,000	247,000	4,105,000
20X6	3,511,000	185,000	3,326,000
20X7	3,793,000	-0-	3,793,000
Thereafter	4,430,000	-0-	4,430,000
	$26,244,000	$926,000	$25,318,000

Rental expense, including common area maintenance, was $5,533,000 and $5,391,000, of which $77,000 and $45,000 was paid as percentage rent based on sales volume, for the years ended December 31, 20X2, and December 31, 20X1, respectively.

Example 3: Operating Leases Contain Purchase Option, Contingent Liability, and Restrictive Covenants

The Company has entered into lease agreements relating to certain corporate facilities that would allow the Company to purchase the facilities on or before the end of the lease term in March 20X3 for a specified purchase price. If at the end of the lease term the Company does not purchase the property under lease or arrange a third-party purchase, then the Company would be obligated to the lessor for a guarantee payment equal to a specified percentage of the agreed purchase price for the property. The Company would also be obligated to the lessor for all or some portion of this amount if the price paid by the third party is below 15% of the specified purchase price.

As of December 31, 20X2, the total amount related to the leased facilities for which the Company is contingently liable is $12,000,000. Under the terms of the agreements, the Company is required to maintain restricted investments, as collateral, of approximately $9,500,000 during the remainder of the lease term; this amount is shown as "Restricted long-term deposits" in the Company's Balance Sheet.

The lease agreements also require the Company to comply with certain covenants and to maintain certain financial ratios. As of December 31, 20X2, the Company was in compliance with all ratios and covenants.

Example 4: Operating Leases Contain Rent Abatements and Provisions for Future Rent Increases That Are Amortized on the Straight-Line Method over the Lease Term

The Company has entered into several operating lease agreements, some of which contain provisions for future rent increases, rent free periods, or periods in which rent payments are reduced (abated). The total amount of rental payments due over the lease term is being charged to rent expense on the straight-line method over the term of the lease. The difference between rent expense recorded and the amount paid is credited or charged to "Deferred rent obligation," which is included in "Other current liabilities" in the accompanying Balance Sheet.

Example 5: Rent Expense Includes Contingent Rent and Sublease Rental Income

The following summary shows the composition of total rental expense for all operating leases:

	20X2	20X1
Minimum rents	$5,200,000	$4,750,000
Contingent rents	2,360,000	2,150,000
Less: Sublease rental income	(470,000)	(450,000)
Net rental expense	$7,090,000	$6,450,000

Contingent rents are based on factors other than the passage of time, primarily percentage of revenues in excess of specified amounts.

Example 6: Capital Leases—Future Minimum Lease Payments

The Company leases certain machinery and equipment under agreements that are classified as capital leases. The cost of equipment under capital leases is included in the Balance Sheets as property, plant, and equipment and was $6,943,000 and $6,822,000 at December 31, 20X2, and December 31, 20X1, respectively. Accumulated amortization of the leased equipment at December 31, 20X2, and December 31, 20X1, was approximately $4,720,000 and $4,245,000, respectively. Amortization of assets under capital leases is included in depreciation expense.

The future minimum lease payments required under the capital leases and the present value of the net minimum lease payments as of December 31, 20X2, are as follows:

	Year Ending December 31	Amount
	20X3	$ 1,250,000
	20X4	975,000
	20X5	820,000
	20X6	745,000
	20X7	620,000
	Thereafter	1,527,000
Total minimum lease payments		5,937,000
Less: Amount representing estimated taxes, maintenance, and insurance costs included in total amounts above		(125,000)
Net minimum lease payments		5,812,000
Less: Amount representing interest		(1,855,000)
Present value of net minimum lease payments		3,957,000
Less: Current maturities of capital lease obligations		(823,000)
Long-term capital lease obligations		$ 3,134,000

Example 7: Components of Property under Capital Leases

Assets recorded under capital leases and included in property and equipment in the Company's Balance Sheets consist of the following at December 31, 20X2, and December 31, 20X1:

	20X2	20X1
Distribution and manufacturing facility	$ 3,250,000	$ 3,250,000
Data processing equipment	1,975,000	1,050,000
Furniture and equipment	725,000	536,000
Transportation equipment	347,000	213,000
	6,297,000	5,049,000
Less: Accumulated amortization	(2,514,000)	(2,091,000)
	$ 3,783,000	$ 2,958,000

Example 8: Sale-Leaseback Transaction Accounted for as an Operating Lease Results in Deferred Gain That Is Being Amortized over the Term of the Lease

In March 20X2, the Company sold certain machinery and equipment for $11,525,000. Under the agreement, the Company is leasing back the property from the purchaser over a period of 15 years. The Company is accounting for the leaseback as an operating lease. The gain of $1,630,000 realized in this transaction has been deferred and is being amortized to income in proportion to rent charged over the term of the lease. At December 31, 20X2, the remaining deferred gain of $1,490,000 is shown as "Deferred gain on property sale" in the Company's Balance Sheet.

The lease requires the Company to pay customary operating and repair expenses and to observe certain operating restrictions and covenants, including restrictions on net worth and dividend payments. The lease contains renewal options at lease termination and purchase options at amounts approximating fair market value as of specified dates in the agreement. For the year ended December 31, 20X2, the total rental expense incurred by the Company under this lease was $1,173,000. The minimum lease payments required by the lease are as follows:

Year Ending December 31	Amount
20X3	$ 1,983,000
20X4	1,621,000
20X5	1,372,000
20X6	1,011,000
20X7	963,000
Thereafter	6,523,000
	$13,473,000

Example 9: Sale-Leaseback Transaction Accounted for as an Operating Lease Results in No Gain or Loss

In March 20X2, the Company entered into an agreement with an independent third party to sell and leaseback certain machinery and equipment, which is accounted for as an operating lease. The net carrying value of the machinery and equipment sold was $8,250,000. Because the net carrying value of the machinery and equipment was equal to their sales price, there was no gain or loss recognized on the sale. The lease agreement entered into between the Company and the counterparty was for a minimum lease term of twelve months with three one-year renewal options. For the year ended December 31, 20X2, the total rental expense incurred by the Company under this lease was $1,025,000.

Example 10: Sale-Leaseback Transaction Accounted for as a Financing Arrangement

In April 20X2, the Company completed the refinancing of its headquarters facility under a sale-leaseback arrangement. The facility was sold for $8,230,000, of which $2,300,000 was received in the form of an interest bearing note receivable due in April 20X7, and the remainder $5,930,000 in cash. The cash received was used to pay (1) existing mortgages on the property of $1,425,000, (2) expenses of the transaction of $350,000, and (3) bank debt of $4,155,000. The transaction has been accounted for as a financing arrangement, wherein the property remains on the Company's books and will continue to be depreciated. A financing obligation in the amount of $5,930,000, representing the proceeds, has been recorded under "Financing obligation, sale-leaseback" in the Company's Balance Sheet, and is being reduced based on payments under the lease.

The lease has a term of 12 years for the office and eight years for the warehouse and requires minimum annual rental payments as follows:

Year Ending December 31	Amount
20X3	$1,100,000
20X4	1,128,000
20X5	1,156,000
20X6	1,185,000
20X7	1,215,000
Thereafter	3,216,000
	$9,000,000

The Company has the option to renew the lease at the end of the lease term and the option to purchase the property at the end of the warehouse lease.

Example 11: Contingency Resulting from Default under Lease Agreements

The Company leases certain plant machinery and equipment at its manufacturing facility in Boise, Idaho. As a result of the Company's default under its debt obligations, as more fully discussed in Note [X] to the financial statements, the Company is in default under these lease agreements. As a result, the lessors have the right to require the Company to prepay the remaining future lease payments required under the lease agreements. Because the Company has paid the lease payments and all lease payments are expected to be made in a timely manner, the Company does not expect that the lessors will assert this right under these lease agreements.

Example 12: Lease Termination Results in Contingent Liability

In September 20X2, the Company notified the developer and landlord of its planned future headquarters in Paramount, California, that the Company intends to terminate the project. The Company had previously entered into a 15-year lease agreement for the new site. Although groundbreaking for the new site has not occurred, the Company anticipates that it will incur lease termination costs. The Company is not able to make a meaningful estimate of the amount or range of loss that could result from an unfavorable resolution of this matter. Consequently, the Company has not provided any accruals for lease termination costs in the financial statements.

Example 13: Warrants Issued in Connection with a Lease Agreement

In July 20X1, the Company issued a fully vested, non-forfeitable warrant that entitles the holder to purchase 25,000 shares of the Company's common stock at an exercise price of $10.00 per share, in connection with a lease agreement. This warrant is exercisable through July 20X6. The fair value of this warrant, approximately $375,000, is being expensed over the term of the lease. The fair value of this warrant was calculated using the Black-Scholes option-pricing model. As of June 20X2, this warrant was exercised in full.

In addition, in January 20X1, in connection with an equipment lease line, the Company issued a fully vested warrant that entitles the holder to purchase 110,000 shares of the Company's common stock at an exercise price of $1.50 per share. This warrant is exercisable through January 20X8. The fair value of this warrant, approximately $362,000, is being expensed as a cost of financing over the four-year period of the lease line. The fair value of this warrant was calculated using the Black-Scholes option-pricing model. The warrant was exercised in full during 20X2.

Lessors

Example 14: Operating Leases

Operating leases arise from the leasing of the Company's machinery and equipment to retail customers, primarily in the construction industry in the United States. Initial lease terms generally range from 36 to 84 months. Depreciation expense for assets subject to operating leases is provided primarily on the straight-line method over the term of the lease in amounts necessary to reduce the carrying amount of the asset to its estimated residual value. Estimated and actual residual values are reviewed on a regular basis to determine that depreciation amounts are appropriate. Depreciation expense relating to machinery and equipment held as investments in operating leases was $373,000 for 20X2 and $417,000 for 20X1.

Investments in operating leases are as follows at December 31:

	20X2	20X1
Machinery and equipment, at cost	$4,373,000	$4,770,000
Lease origination costs	63,000	65,000
Accumulated depreciation	(813,000)	(765,000)
Allowance for credit losses	(50,000)	(90,000)
Net investments in operating leases	$3,573,000	$3,980,000

Future minimum rental payments to be received on non-cancelable operating leases are contractually due as follows as of December 31, 20X2:

Year Ending December 31	Amount
20X3	$ 883,000
20X4	645,000
20X5	422,000
20X6	213,000
20X7	105,000
Thereafter	75,000
	$2,343,000

Future minimum rental payments to be received do not include contingent rentals that may be received under certain leases because of use in excess of specified amounts. Contingent rentals were not significant in 20X2 or 20X1.

Example 15: Sales-Type Leases

The components of lease receivables for the net investment in sales-type leases are as follows at December 31:

	20X2	*20X1*
Total minimum lease receivables	$4,100,000	$3,600,000
Less: Allowance for uncollectible Amounts	(125,000)	(100,000)
Net minimum lease payments receivable	3,975,000	3,500,000
Estimated residual values of leased property	230,000	145,000
Less: Unearned interest income	(710,000)	(625,000)
Net investment in sales-type leases	$3,495,000	$3,020,000
Current portion	$1,300,000	$1,050,000
Long-term portion	2,195,000	1,970,000
	$3,495,000	$3,020,000

Future minimum lease receivables due from customers under sales-type leases as of December 31, 20X2, are as follows:

Year Ending December 31	*Amount*
20X3	$ 852,000
20X4	827,000
20X5	793,000
20X6	602,000
20X7	464,000
Thereafter	562,000
	$4,100,000

Future minimum lease receivables do not include contingent rentals that may be received under certain leases because of use in excess of specified amounts. Contingent rentals were not significant in 20X2 or 20X1.

Example 16: Direct-Financing Leases

The components of lease receivables for the net investment in direct financing leases are as follows as of December 31:

	20X2	20X1
Total minimum lease receivables	$ 5,519,000	$ 5,837,000
Less: Allowance for credit losses	(80,000)	(143,000)
Net minimum lease payments receivable	5,439,000	5,694,000
Estimated residual values of leased property	3,720,000	2,923,000
Deferred initial direct costs	125,000	150,000
Less: Unearned income	(2,150,000)	(2,410,000)
Net investment in direct financing leases	$ 7,134,000	$ 6,357,000
Current portion	$ 2,760,000	$ 2,323,000
Long-term portion	4,374,000	4,034,000
	$ 7,134,000	$ 6,357,000

Future minimum lease receivables due from customers under direct-financing leases as of December 31, 20X2, are as follows:

Year Ending December 31	Amount
20X3	$1,906,000
20X4	1,619,000
20X5	949,000
20X6	712,000
20X7	233,000
Thereafter	100,000
	$5,519,000

Unearned income on direct financing leases is recognized in such a manner as to produce a constant periodic rate of return on the net investment in the direct-financing lease.

Future minimum lease receivables do not include contingent rentals that may be received under certain leases because of use in excess of specified amounts. Contingent rentals were not significant in 20X2 or 20X1.

Example 17: Leveraged Leases

Leveraged lease assets acquired by the Company are financed primarily through nonrecourse loans from third-party debt participants. These loans are secured by the lessee's rental obligations and the leased property. Net rents receivable represent gross rents less the principal and interest on the nonrecourse debt obligations. Unguaranteed residual values are principally based on independent appraisals of the values of leased assets remaining at the expiration of the lease. Leveraged lease investments are primarily related to heavy construction and drilling equipment, with original lease terms ranging from 5 to 15 years.

The Company's investment in leveraged leases consists of rentals receivable net of principal and interest on the related nonrecourse debt, estimated residual value of the leased property, and unearned income. The unearned income is recognized as leveraged lease revenue in income from investments over the lease term.

The Company's net investment in leveraged leases comprises the following at December 31, 20X2, and December 31, 20X1:

	20X2	20X1
Net lease receivables	$ 9,819,000	$ 8,761,000
Estimated unguaranteed residual values	10,863,000	9,910,000
Less: Unearned income	(10,150,000)	(9,613,000)
Investment in leveraged leases	$ 10,532,000	$ 9,058,000
Current portion	$ 2,031,000	$ 1,754,000
Long-term portion	8,501,000	7,304,000
	$ 10,532,000	$ 9,058,000

Deferred tax liability arising from leveraged leases totaled approximately $4,125,000 and $3,234,000 at December 31, 20X2, and December 31, 20X1, respectively.

The following is a summary of the components of income from leveraged leases for the years ended December 31, 20X2, and December 31, 20X1:

	20X2	20X1
Pretax leveraged lease income	$237,000	$151,000
Income tax effect	85,000	73,000
Income from leveraged leases	$322,000	$224,000

Leases with Related Parties

Example 18: Company Has a Long-Term Operating Lease with a Related Party

The Company leases its corporate headquarters and warehouse facility from a partnership owned by the two Company shareholders. The lease provides for monthly payments of $32,000, expires in 20X9, and contains a renewal option for an additional seven years. Due to the current economic conditions of the Company, rent was reduced to $32,000 per month from $45,000 per month effective January 1, 20X2. Rent expense incurred and paid to the partnership was $384,000 and $540,000 for 20X2 and 20X1, respectively.

The following is a schedule by year of future minimum rental payments due to the partnership under the operating lease agreement:

Year Ending December 31	Amount
20X3	$ 384,000
20X4	384,000
20X5	416,000
20X6	416,000
20X7	450,000
Thereafter	1,200,000
	$3,250,000

Example 19: Company Has a Month-to-Month Operating Lease with a Related Party

The Company leases its administrative offices on a month-to-month basis from a partnership in which the Company's stockholder is a partner. Total rent paid to the partnership was $123,000 and $117,000 for the years ended December 31, 20X2, and December 31, 20X1, respectively.

Example 20: Company Discloses the Nature and Extent of Several Long-Term Operating Lease Agreements with Affiliated Entities

The Company leases various manufacturing facilities and equipment from companies owned by certain officers and directors of the Company, either directly or indirectly, through affiliates. The leases generally provide that the Company will bear the cost of property taxes and insurance.

Details of the principal operating leases with related parties as of December 31, 20X2, including the effect of renewals and amendments executed subsequent to December 31, 20X2, are as follows:

Name of Related Party/ Description of Lease	*Date of Lease*	*Term*	*Basic Annual Rental Amount*	*Future Minimum Rental Amounts*
Hope Realty Trust:				
Land & building— Chicago	12-13-Y1	15 years	$200,000	$1,000,000
Corporate offices	12-22-Y1	15 years	$100,000	$ 500,000
Machinery & equipment	11-30-Y6	10 years	$125,000	$ 625,000
John Jones Family Trust:				
Land & buildings— Atlanta	6-29-Y6	10 years	$150,000	$ 675,000
Furniture & computers	7-01-Y7	10 years	$100,000	$ 550,000
Mack Realty Trust:				
Land & building— Detroit	6-25-Y6	15 years	$200,000	$1,900,000
Corporate offices	12-28-Y6	10 years	$110,000	$ 550,000
Furniture & equipment	1-1-Y7	10 years	$ 80,000	$ 400,000

Rent incurred and paid to these related parties was $1,069,000 and $1,087,000 for the years ended December 31, 20X2, and December 31, 20X1, respectively.

Future minimum lease payments to these related parties as of December 31, 20X2, are as follows:

Year Ending December 31	*Amount*
20X3	$1,065,000
20X4	1,110,000
20X5	1,150,000
20X6	1,205,000
20X7	1,260,000
Thereafter	685,000
	$6,475,000

CHAPTER 53
ASC TOPIC 845: NONMONETARY TRANSACTIONS

CONTENTS

EXECUTIVE SUMMARY

Nonmonetary Transactions

As a general rule, accounting for nonmonetary transactions (i.e., exchanges and nonreciprocal transfers that involve little or no monetary assets or liabilities) should be based on the fair value of the assets or services involved and any gain or loss should be recognized. However, a nonmonetary exchange should be measured based on the recorded amount of the nonmonetary assets relinquished (after reduction for any impairment of value), and not on the fair values of the exchanged assets, under any of the following circumstances:

- The fair value of the assets received or relinquished is not reasonably determinable.

- The exchange transaction is essentially to facilitate sales to customers other than the parties to the exchange.

- The exchange transaction lacks commercial substance (i.e., the transaction is not expected to result in significant changes in the cash flows of the reporting entity).

An *exchange* is a reciprocal transfer in which each party to the transaction receives and/or gives up assets, liabilities, or services. Exchanges can be either monetary or nonmonetary, or a combination of both. Nonmonetary exchanges usually are for the mutual convenience of two businesses. An example would be an exchange of inventory for trucking services.

A *nonreciprocal transfer* is a transfer of assets or services in one direction, either from an enterprise to its owners or another entity, or from owners or another entity to the enterprise. Examples of non-reciprocal transfers are as follows:

- Distribution of nonmonetary assets, such as marketable equity securities, to stockholders as dividends

- Distribution of nonmonetary assets to stockholders to redeem or acquire outstanding capital stock of the entity

- Distribution of nonmonetary assets, such as capital stock of subsidiaries, to stockholders in corporate liquidations or plans of reorganization that involve disposing of all or a significant segment of the business (such plans are variously referred to as *spin-offs*, *split-ups*, and *split-offs*)

- Distribution of nonmonetary assets to groups of stockholders, pursuant to plans of rescission or other settlements relating to a prior business combination, to redeem or acquire shares of capital stock previously issued in a business combination

- Charitable contributions by an entity

- Contribution of land by a governmental unit for construction of productive facilities by an entity

When a nonmonetary asset is involuntarily converted to a monetary asset, a monetary transaction results, and a gain or loss should be recognized in the period of conversion. The gain or loss is the difference between the carrying amount of the nonmonetary asset and the proceeds from the conversion. Examples of involuntary conversion are the total or partial destruction of property through fire or other catastrophe, theft of property, or condemnation of property by a governmental authority (eminent domain proceedings).

Accounting Literature

FASB Accounting Standards Codification Topic	*Pre-Codification Accounting Literature*
845, *Nonmonetary Transactions*	FIN-30, *Accounting for Involuntary Conversions of Nonmonetary Assets to Monetary Assets*
	EITF 00-8, *Accounting by a Grantee for an Equity Instrument to Be Received in Conjunction with Providing Goods or Services*
	EITF 04-13, *Accounting for Purchases and Sales of Inventory with the Same Counterparty*
	APB-29, *Accounting for Nonmonetary Transactions*

DISCLOSURE AND KEY PRESENTATION REQUIREMENTS

1. The following disclosures should be made for nonmonetary transactions (ASC 845-10-50-1) (APB-29, par. 28):

   a. The nature of the transactions.

   b. The basis of accounting for the assets transferred.

   c. Gains or losses, if any, recognized on transfers.

2. Disclosure should be made in each period's financial statements of the amount of gross operating revenue recognized as a result of nonmonetary transactions. (ASC 845-10-50-2; 505-50-50-2) (EITF 00-8)

3. The amount of revenue and costs (or gains and losses) associated with inventory exchanges recognized at fair value should be disclosed. (ASC 845-10-50-3) (EITF 04-13)

4. Gains and losses resulting from involuntary conversions of nonmonetary assets to monetary assets should be classified as extraordinary items or unusual or infrequent items. (ASC 605-40-45-1) (FIN-30, par. 4)

EXAMPLES OF FINANCIAL STATEMENT DISCLOSURES

 The following sample disclosures are available on the accompanying disc.

Example 1: Barter Transactions—Inventory Delivered in Exchange for Future Advertising Credits

In 20X2 and 20X1, the Company entered into barter agreements whereby it delivered $1,165,000 and $1,059,000, respectively, of its inventory in exchange for future advertising credits and other items. The credits, which expire in November 20X3, are valued at the lower of the Company's cost or market value of the inventory transferred. The Company has recorded barter credits of $115,000 and $236,000 in "Prepaid expenses and other current assets" at December 31, 20X2, and December 31, 20X1, respectively. At December 31, 20X2, and December 31, 20X1, "Other noncurrent assets" include $279,000 and $323,000, respectively, of such credits. Under the terms of the barter agreements, the Company is required to pay cash equal to a negotiated amount of the bartered advertising, or other items, and use the barter credits to pay the balance. These credits are charged to expense as they are used. During the years ended December 31, 20X2, and December 31, 20X1, approximately $1,080,000 and $751,000, respectively, were charged to expense for barter credits used.

The Company assesses the recoverability of barter credits periodically. Factors considered in evaluating the recoverability include management's plans with respect to advertising and other expenditures for which barter credits can be used. Any impairment losses are charged to operations as they are determinable. During the years ended December 31, 20X2, and December 31, 20X1, the Company charged $250,000 and $425,000, respectively, to operations for such impairment losses.

Example 2: Barter Transactions—Advertising Revenues and Expenses

The Company's barter transactions are recorded at the estimated fair value of the advertisements provided, based on recent historical cash transactions. Barter revenue is recognized when the advertising impressions or other services are delivered to the customer and advertising expense is recorded when the advertising impressions or other services are received from the customer. If the Company receives the advertising impressions or other services from the customer prior to its delivery of the advertising impressions, a liability is recorded; and if the Company delivers the advertising impressions to the customer prior to receiving the advertising impressions or other services, a prepaid expense is recorded on the Consolidated Balance Sheets. For the years ended December 31, 20X2, and December 31, 20X1, the Company recognized approximately $4.2

million and $1.9 million of advertising revenues, respectively, and $3.4 million and $1.5 million of advertising expenses, respectively, from barter transactions. The Company has recognized approximately $1.6 million and $1.1 million in prepaid expenses related to barter transactions as of December 31, 20X2 and December 31, 20X1, respectively.

Example 3: Notes Receivable Balance Due from Related Parties Is Paid through Forfeiture of Bonuses

As of December 31, 20X1, the Company had notes receivable due from certain executives and officers amounting to approximately $1,500,000. These notes bear interest at rates ranging from 7.25% to 7.85% and have maturities of six months to five years. In 20X2, $625,000 of the notes receivable balance was paid through forfeiture of management bonuses.

Example 4: Contribution of Subsidiary Stock

During 20X2, the Company's contributions to the Advest Foundation consisted of 55,000 shares of the Company's majority-owned Plantex subsidiary. A pretax gain of $120,000 was recorded on the donations. The shares contributed to the Advest Foundation had a market value of $425,000, which was recorded as a contribution expense in the accompanying 20X2 Income Statement.

Example 5: Distribution of Nonmonetary Assets to Stockholders as Dividends

In 20X2, the Company declared and paid a dividend to its stockholders in the form of shares of common stock of Santorest & Co., whose stock the Company held as an investment. The Company's stockholders received three shares of Santorest & Co. common stock for each share of the Company's stock held. As a result, retained earnings was charged a total of $317,000, which represents the aggregate market value of the shares of Santorest & Co. that were issued as a dividend. In connection with this transaction, the Company recognized a gain of $116,000 in 20X2, which represents the excess of the aggregate market value of the shares of Santorest & Co. issued over the aggregate carrying value of these shares.

Example 6: Spin-Off of a Business Segment

In May 20X2, the Company announced plans to spin off its electronic connectors business to shareholders in a tax-free distribution. In August 20X2, the Company's Board of Directors approved the spin-off effective December 31, 20X2, to shareholders of record as of December 17, 20X2, through the issuance of shares in a new legal entity, Electors, Inc. Common shares were distributed on a basis of one share of Electors, Inc. for every five shares of the Company's common stock.

The consolidated financial results of the Company have been restated to reflect the divestiture of Electors, Inc. Accordingly, the revenues, costs, and expenses; assets and liabilities; and cash flows of Electors, Inc. have been excluded from their respective captions in the Consolidated Statements of Income, Consolidated Balance Sheets, and Consolidated Statements of Cash Flows. These items have been reported as "Income from discontinued operations, net of income taxes" in the Consolidated Statements of Income; "Net assets of discontinued operations" in the Consolidated Balance Sheets; and "Net cash flows from discontinued operations" and "Net investing and financing activities of discontinued operations" in the Consolidated Statements of Cash Flows.

As of December 31, 20X2, the net assets of the discontinued segment of $4,289,000 have been charged against the Company's retained earnings to reflect the spin-off. During 20X2, the Company recorded a pretax charge of $615,000 ($483,000 after taxes) for expenses related to the spin-off.

The following table summarizes financial information for the discontinued operations for all periods presented:

	20X2	20X1
Net sales	$8,300,000	$8,750,000
Income before income taxes	$ 211,000	$ 273,000
Net income	$ 107,000	$ 182,000
Current assets	$2,436,000	$2,543,000
Total assets	$8,161,000	$8,615,000
Current liabilities	$2,597,000	$1,796,000
Total liabilities	$3,872,000	$3,978,000
Net assets of discontinued operations	$4,289,000	$4,637,000

Example 7: Revenues Recognized under Reciprocal Arrangements

On occasion, the Company has purchased goods or services for its operations from organizations at or about the same time that it licensed its software to these organizations. These transactions are recorded at terms the Company considers to be fair value. For these reciprocal arrangements, the Company considers appropriate accounting literature to determine whether the arrangement is a monetary or nonmonetary transaction. Transactions involving the exchange of boot representing 25% or greater of the fair value of the reciprocal arrangement are considered monetary transactions. Monetary transactions and nonmonetary transactions that represent the culmination of an earnings process are recorded at the fair value of the products delivered or products or services received, whichever is more readily determinable, providing the fair values are determinable within reasonable limits. In determining the fair values, the Company considers the recent history of cash sales of the same products or services in similar sized transactions. Revenues from such transactions may be recognized over a period of time as the products or services are received. For nonmonetary reciprocal arrangements that do not represent the culmination of the earnings process, the exchange is recorded based on the carrying value of the products delivered, which is generally zero.

Revenues recognized under reciprocal arrangements were approximately $4,579,000 in 20X2, of which $2,636,000 involved nonmonetary transactions, as defined above. The Company did not recognize any revenues under reciprocal arrangements in 20X1.

CHAPTER 54
ASC TOPIC 850: RELATED PARTY DISCLOSURES

CONTENTS

EXECUTIVE SUMMARY

Related Party Disclosures

In general terms, *related parties* exist when there is a relationship that offers the potential for transactions at less than arm's-length, favorable treatment, or the ability to influence the outcome of events differently from that which might result in the absence of that relationship. A related party may be any of the following:

- *Affiliate*—An affiliate is a party that directly or indirectly controls, is controlled by, or is under common control with another party.

- *Principal owner*—This is generally the owner of record or known beneficial owner of more than 10% of the voting interests of an entity.

- *Management*—Persons having responsibility for achieving objectives of the entity and requisite authority to make decisions that pursue those objectives. This normally includes members of the board of directors, chief executive officer, chief operating officer, president, treasurer, any vice president in charge of a principal business function (e.g., sales, administration, finance), and any other individual who performs similar policymaking functions.

- *Immediate family of management or principal owners*—Generally, this includes spouses, brothers, sisters, parents, children, and spouses of these persons.

- *A parent company and its subsidiaries*—This is typically an entity that "directly or indirectly has a controlling financial interest" in a subsidiary company.

- *Trusts for the benefit of employees*—Trusts for the benefit of employees include pension and profit-sharing trusts that are managed by, or under the trusteeship of, the entity's management.

- *Other parties*—Other parties include any other party that has the ability to significantly influence the management or operating policies of the entity, to the extent that it may be prevented from fully pursuing its own separate interests. The ability to exercise significant influence may be indicated in several ways, such as representation on the board of directors, participation in policy-making processes, material inter-company transactions, interchange of managerial personnel, or technological dependency.

Common related-party transactions include the following:

- Contracts that carry no interest rate or an unrealistic interest rate
- Nonmonetary transactions that involve the exchange of similar assets
- Loan agreements that contain no repayment schedule
- Loans to parties that do not possess the ability to repay
- Services or goods purchased from a party at little or no cost to the entity
- Maintenance of bank balances as compensating balances for the benefit of another
- Intercompany billings based on allocation of common costs
- Leases to an entity from its principal shareholder

Financial statement disclosure of related party transactions is required by GAAP in order for those statements to fairly present financial position, results of operations, and cash flows.

Accounting Literature

FASB Accounting Standards Codification Topic	*Pre-Codification Accounting Literature*
850, *Related Party Disclosures*	FAS-57, *Related Party Disclosures*
	ARB-43, Chapter 1A, *Rules Adopted by Membership*

DISCLOSURE AND KEY PRESENTATION REQUIREMENTS

1. The following disclosures should be made for material related-party transactions (other than compensation arrangements, expense allowances, and other similar items in the ordinary course of business) (ASC 850-10-50-1 and 50-3) (FAS-57, par. 2):

   a. The nature of the relationship of the parties involved.

   b. A description of the transactions, including transactions to which no amounts or nominal amounts were ascribed, for each of the periods for which income statements are presented, and such other information deemed necessary to an understanding of the effects of the transactions on the financial statements.

c. The dollar amounts of transactions for each of the periods for which income statements are presented and the effects of any change in the method of establishing the terms from that used in the preceding period.

d. Amounts due from or to related parties as of the date of each balance sheet presented and, if not otherwise apparent, the terms and manner of settlement.

e. The name of the related party, if necessary to the understanding of the relationship between the parties. (*Note*: In some cases, aggregation of similar transactions by type of related party may be appropriate. Sometimes, the effect of the relationship between the parties may be so pervasive that disclosure of the relationship alone will be sufficient.)

2. Notes or accounts receivable due from officers, employees, or affiliated entities should be shown separately and not included under a general heading, such as notes receivable or accounts receivable. (ASC 850-10-50-2) (ARB-43, Ch. 1A, par. 5)

3. Disclosures concerning related-party transactions should be worded in a manner that does not imply that the transactions were consummated on terms equivalent to those that prevail in arm's-length transactions, unless such representations can be substantiated. (ASC 850-10-50-5) (FAS-57, par. 3)

4. If the reporting entity and one or more other entities are under common ownership or management control and the existence of that control could result in operating results or financial position of the reporting entity significantly different from those that would have resulted if the entities were autonomous, the nature of the control relationship should be disclosed (even though there are no transactions between the entities). (ASC 850-10-50-6) (FAS-57, par. 4)

EXAMPLES OF FINANCIAL STATEMENT DISCLOSURES

The following sample disclosures are available on the accompanying disc.

Example 1: Advances Made to Related Parties for Expansion and Financing Needs

The Company has made advances to PRC Development, an entity owned by the president and certain officers of the Company, primarily to accommodate expansion and other financing needs of this related entity. Such advances bear interest at rates equal to the Company's weighted average cost of borrowing, which for the years ended December 31, 20X2, and December 31, 20X1, was 7.25% and 7.75%, respectively. Interest charged to PRC Development for the years ended December 31, 20X2, and December 31, 20X1, was $379,000 and $493,000, respectively.

Example 2: Company's Corporate Services Agreement with a Related Entity Provides for Payment of a Fee Based on Company's Net Sales

The Company has a corporate services agreement with Odeyssa, Inc., an entity that is controlled by the Company's chairman of the board of directors and president. Under the terms of the agreement, the Company pays a fee to Odeyssa, Inc. for various corporate support staff, administrative services, and research and development services. Such fee equals 2.2% of the Company's net sales, subject to certain adjustments, and totaled $1,975,000 and $1,836,000 in 20X2 and 20X1, respectively.

Example 3: Demand Note Receivable from Stockholder Is Classified as Noncurrent Because Repayment Is Not Anticipated During the Next Year

At December 31, 20X2, and December 31, 20X1, the Company has a note receivable of $295,200 and $268,400, respectively, due from its stockholder that is due upon demand. This note is unsecured and bears interest at 10%. Accrued interest on this note totaled $51,200 and $24,400 as of December 31, 20X2, and December 31, 20X1, respectively, and is included in the note receivable balance. The note receivable has been classified as noncurrent in the accompanying Balance Sheets because repayment is not anticipated during the next year.

Example 4: Notes Receivable Balance Due from Related Parties Is Paid through Forfeiture of Bonuses

As of December 31, 20X1, the Company had notes receivable due from certain executives and officers amounting to approximately $1,500,000. These notes bear interest at rates ranging from 7.25% to 7.85% and have maturities of six months to five years. In 20X2, $625,000 of the notes receivable balance was paid through forfeiture of management bonuses.

Example 5: Company Is Forgiving Loan Balance Due from an Officer

On May 19, 20X0, the Company loaned $500,000 to Dave Jones, a senior vice president of the Company. Mr. Jones executed an unsecured promissory note in favor of the Company that matures on May 18, 20X4. In 20X1, the Company forgave a total of $200,000 of outstanding principal amount and $47,000 in accrued interest. In 20X2, the Company forgave a total of $100,000 of outstanding principal amount and $31,000 in accrued interest. The remaining outstanding balance of the loan as of December 31, 20X2, was $205,000, representing $200,000 in principal and $5,000 in accrued interest, and bears interest at a rate of 7.95%.

Example 6: Loan Payable to Related Company Is Secured and Subordinated to Bank Debt

In November 20X1, Cubes, Ltd., an entity that is partially owned by a minority shareholder of the Company, loaned $1,000,000 to the Company for working capital and equipment financing. The loan is payable in five annual installments of $200,000, plus applicable interest, beginning November 20X2. Interest accrues at the prevailing prime rate plus 1.75% (9% at December 31, 20X2). The loan is secured by inventory, accounts receivable, and machinery and equipment, and is subordinated to the Company's line of credit with the bank. At December 31, 20X2, and December 31, 20X1, the outstanding balance due was $800,000 and $1,000,000, respectively.

Example 7: Loan Covenants Restrict Payment on Shareholder Loan Made to Company

At December 31, 20X2, and December 31, 20X1, the Company's shareholder has advanced $200,000 and $182,000, respectively, to the Company. These loans are represented by three separate demand notes, are unsecured, and carry interest at 10%. Loan covenants and restrictions prohibit the shareholder from receiving any payment on these loans until such time that other loan commitments are satisfied. Accordingly, these shareholder loans are recorded as long-term debt in the accompanying financial statements.

Example 8: Financial Services Agreement with a Related Entity Provides for a Fee at Less Than Prevailing Market Rate

GBG Capital Management (GBG), an entity in which an officer of the Company holds a beneficial interest, performs services for the Company as its agent in connection with negotiations regarding various financial arrangements of the Company. In January 20X1, the Company entered into a Financial Services Agreement for five years with GBG pursuant to which GBG has agreed to render financial advisory and related services to the Company for a fee equal to 90% of the fees that would be charged to the Company by unaffiliated third parties for the same or comparable services. Each year, the Company pays GBG an annual $1,000,000 retainer as an advance against payments due pursuant to this agreement and reimburses GBG for its reasonable out-of-pocket expenses. The Company paid fees to GBG totaling $1,500,000 in 20X2 and $1,300,000 in 20X1 relating to several business acquisitions and dispositions made by the Company.

Example 9: Company's Consulting Agreement with a Shareholder Provides for Future Payment for a Covenant Not to Compete

For the years ended December 31, 20X2, and December 31, 20X1, consulting service fees in the amount of $326,000 and $302,000, respectively, were paid to Dr. Mark Makhoul, a shareholder. Dr. Makhoul provides consulting services to the Company pursuant to a consulting agreement that terminates on December 31, 20X5 (subject to extension for an additional five-year term) and for which he receives annual payments of $300,000. The Company also reimburses Dr. Makhoul for his out-of-pocket expenses in performing such consulting services. In addition, the Company has agreed to pay to Dr. Makhoul $250,000 for a period of 24 months following the termination of his consulting relationship with the Company in exchange for his agreement not to compete with the Company during this period.

Example 10: Company Pays Royalties in Connection with Patents and Licensing Rights Acquired from Related Party

The Company has patents and licensing rights that were acquired from John Teen, the Company's president and major stockholder. As consideration, the Company pays royalties equal to 2.5% of gross sales on all manufactured products covered by the patents and licensing rights. In 20X2 and 20X1, the Company paid royalties of $1,379,000 and $1,243,000, respectively, to Mr. Teen.

Example 11: A Director of the Company Is a Partner in the Law Firm That Acts as Counsel to the Company

A director of the Company is a partner in the law firm that acts as counsel to the Company. The Company paid legal fees and expenses to the law firm in the amount of approximately $375,000 in 20X2 and $210,000 in 20X1.

Example 12: A Director of the Company Is an Owner in an Insurance Agency That Has Written Policies for the Company

A director of the Company has an ownership interest in an insurance agency that has written general liability policies for the Company with premiums totaling $136,000 in 20X2 and $122,000 in 20X1.

Example 13: Company Purchased Land and Buildings from Directors

During 20X2, the Company purchased land and buildings adjoining one of its plants from two Company directors for $1,250,000. The board of directors unanimously approved the purchase, with the two directors involved in the transaction abstaining.

Example 14: Company Sold Building to Chief Executive Officer at a Price That is within the Range of Appraised Values

In 20X2, the Company sold a building to its chief executive officer for $3,750,000 in cash, which was approved by the Company's board of directors. The sales price was in excess of book value, resulting in a gain of $490,000, and was within the range of appraised values. The building had previously been offered for sale to the public for six months.

Example 15: Salary Advance Made to Officer as Part of New Employment Contract

During 20X2, the Company made a $100,000 salary advance to Jane Apostol, an officer, as part of a new employment contract that required her to relocate to Los Angeles, California. According to the terms of the contract, Ms. Apostol is required to repay the loan at $20,000 per year for the next five years, beginning in 20X3.

Example 16: Related Party Supplies Inventory Materials to the Company

The Company has an agreement with Just, Inc., an entity in which a major stockholder of the Company owns a significant interest, which provides for purchases by the Company of electrical equipment, subassemblies, and spare parts. Purchases from Just, Inc. for 20X2 and 20X1 totaled $2,900,000 and $3,750,000, respectively. Accounts payable to Just, Inc. amounted to $1,010,000 and $1,236,000 at December 31, 20X2, and December 31, 20X1, respectively. In addition, in 20X2 the Company made advance payments to Just, Inc. for future inventory purchases in return for lower prices on certain components. Advance payments of $420,000 were included in prepaid expenses at December 31, 20X2.

Example 17: Company Sells a Substantial Portion of Its Products to a Related Entity

The Company sells a substantial portion of its medical instruments products to Horizons, Ltd., an entity in which the Company's vice-president of operations is a majority stockholder. During 20X2 and 20X1, the Company sold approximately $10,400,000 and $8,732,000 of products to Horizons, Ltd. Trade receivables from Horizons, Inc. were $1,923,000 and $1,544,000 at December 31, 20X2, and December 31, 20X1, respectively.

Example 18: Related Parties Reimburse the Company for Allocated Overhead and Administrative Expenses

The Company's managed limited partnerships reimburse the Company for certain allocated overhead and administrative expenses. These expenses generally consist of salaries and related benefits paid to corporate personnel, rent, data processing services, and other corporate facilities costs. The Company provides engineering, marketing, administrative, accounting, information management, legal, and other services to the partnerships. Allocations of personnel costs have been based primarily on actual time spent by Company employees with respect to each partnership managed. Remaining overhead costs are allocated based on the pro rata relationship of the partnership's revenues to the total revenues of all businesses owned or managed by the Company. The Company believes that such allocation methods are reasonable. Amounts charged to managed partnerships and other affiliated companies have directly offset the Company's general and administrative expenses by approximately $5,100,000 and $5,400,000 for the years ended December 31, 20X2, and December 31, 20X1, respectively.

Example 19: Company Has Several Long-Term Operating Lease Agreements with Affiliated Entities

The Company leases various manufacturing facilities and equipment from companies owned by certain officers and directors of the Company, either directly or indirectly, through affiliates. The leases generally provide that the Company will bear the cost of property taxes and insurance.

Details of the principal operating leases with related parties as of December 31, 20X2, including the effect of renewals and amendments executed subsequent to December 31, 20X2, are as follows:

Name of Related Party/ Description of Lease	Date of Lease	Term	Basic Annual Rental Amount	Future Minimum Rental Amounts
Hope Realty Trust:				
Land & building— Chicago	12-13-Y1	15 years	$200,000	$1,000,000
Corporate offices	12-22-Y1	15 years	$100,000	$ 500,000
Machinery & equipment	11-30-Y6	10 years	$125,000	$ 625,000
John Jones Family Trust:				
Land & buildings—Atlanta	6-29-Y6	10 years	$150,000	$ 675,000
Furniture & computers	7-1-Y7	10 years	$100,000	$ 550,000
Kilmer Realty Trust:				
Land & building—Detroit	6-25-Y6	15 years	$200,000	$1,900,000
Corporate offices	12-28-Y6	10 years	$110,000	$ 550,000
Furniture & equipment	1-1-Y7	10 years	$ 80,000	$ 400,000

Rent incurred and paid to these related parties was $1,069,000 and $1,087,000 for the years ended December 31, 20X2, and December 31, 20X1, respectively.

Future minimum lease payments to these related parties as of December 31, 20X2, are as follows:

Year Ending December 31	Amounts
20X3	$1,065,000
20X4	1,110,000
20X5	1,150,000
20X6	1,205,000
20X7	1,260,000
Thereafter	685,000
	$6,475,000

Example 20: Company Has a Month-to-Month Lease with a Related Party

The Company leases its administrative offices on a month-to-month basis from a partnership in which the Company's stockholder is a partner. Total rent paid to the partnership was $123,000 and $117,000 for the years ended December 31, 20X2, and December 31, 20X1, respectively.

Example 21: Companies under Common Control May Experience Change in Operations

The Company's 80% shareholder also controls other entities whose operations are similar to those of the Company. Although there were no transactions between the Company and these entities in 20X2 or 20X1, the 80% shareholder is, nevertheless, in a position to influence the sales volume of the Company for the benefit of the other entities that are under his control.

Example 22: Guarantee of Indebtedness of Related Entity—No Liability Is Recorded

As of December 31, 20X2, the Company is contingently liable as guarantor with respect to $5,400,000 of indebtedness of Extraped, Inc., an entity that is owned by the Company's stockholders. The term of the guarantee is through June 30, 20X4. At any time through that date, should Extraped, Inc. be over 90 days delinquent on its debt payments, the Company will be obligated to perform under the guarantee by primarily making the required payments, including late fees and penalties. The maximum potential amount of future payments that the Company is required to make under the guarantee is $3,000,000.

Example 23: Liability Is Recorded as a Result of Guarantee of Indebtedness of an Affiliate

In January 20X2, the Company executed a "Guarantee Agreement" (the Agreement) to guarantee the payment of $500,000 advanced to an affiliate, Steinhart Corp., by Amcor Funding, Inc. The guarantee agreement expires March 31, 20X3. In November 20X2, Steinhart Corp. became insolvent, which triggered an event of default under the terms of the Agreement. At December 31, 20X2, the Company accrued a loss of $500,000 for the full amount of the potential payment that the Company would be required to make under the guarantee. Steinhart Corp. is in the process of liquidating its assets; however, the Company does not expect to recover any of the amounts paid under the guarantee.

Example 24: Guarantee of Indebtedness of Joint Venture Obligates Company to Advance Funds to the Joint Venture if Certain Loan Covenants Are Not Met

The Company holds a 25% ownership interest in Stellark, Inc., which has a $7,000,000 line of credit agreement (Agreement) with First Nations Bank. Under terms of the Agreement, the Company is obligated to advance to Stellark, Inc. a maximum of $2,500,000 if its working capital falls below $500,000 or its current ratio is less than 1. Any funds advanced under this Agreement are available to First Nations Bank. In addition, First Nations Bank may have claims against the Company in an amount not to exceed $2,000,000 of any unsatisfied required advances. The term of the guarantee is through April 30, 20X4. At December 31, 20X2, Stellark, Inc. was in compliance with the terms of the Agreement with First Nations Bank.

Example 25: Shareholders' Stock Purchase Agreement

The Company and the shareholders have established a Stock Purchase Agreement whereby the Company is obligated to purchase, in the event of the death of any shareholder, all of the decedent's outstanding shares. The repurchase price is determined pursuant to a formula provided in the agreement. The Company has purchased insurance on the lives of the shareholders to help meet its obligation under the Stock Purchase Agreement.

Example 26: Purchase of Deceased Shareholder's Stock at Fair Value

In March 20X2, the death of a shareholder triggered the Buy/Sell provisions of the Stock Purchase Agreement dated January 1, 20X0. The provisions of the Agreement required the Company to purchase the shareholder's stock at fair market value, with a minimum cash payment of 10%.

The fair market value of the stock, as determined by an independent valuation, was $2,675,000. The Company paid $1,000,000 in life insurance policy proceeds against the purchase price. The remaining balance of $1,675,000 was financed at 10%, representing the current corporate borrowing rate, and is payable in 36 equal monthly installments to the shareholder's estate.

Example 27: Sales Commissions Payable to Related Entities

Sales commissions are payable to a company owned by one of the Company's principal stockholders for sales obtained by this related entity. These commissions amounted to approximately $540,000 and $473,000 for the years ended December 31, 20X2, and December 31, 20X1, respectively, of which $145,000 and $132,000 are included in accrued expenses at December 31, 20X2, and December 31, 20X1, respectively.

CHAPTER 55
ASC TOPIC 852: REORGANIZATIONS

CONTENTS

EXECUTIVE SUMMARY

Reorganizations under Chapter 11 of the Bankruptcy Code

The accounting followed by entities reorganizing as going concerns under Chapter 11 of the Bankruptcy Code is similar in many ways to the fresh-start accounting of a quasi-reorganization. However, there are some differences and, therefore, formal reorganizations under Chapter 11 of the Bankruptcy Code should not be confused with quasi-reorganizations. For example, in a quasi-reorganization, a formal plan to restructure liabilities and debt to creditors is not adopted.

An entity should adopt fresh-start accounting upon its emergence from Chapter 11 of the Bankruptcy Code if (1) the reorganization value of the assets of the emerging entity immediately before the date of confirmation by the Court is less than the total of all post-petition liabilities and allowed claims and (2) holders of existing voting shares immediately before confirmation receive less than 50% of the voting shares of the emerging entity.

Quasi-Reorganizations

Under carefully defined circumstances, contributed or paid-in capital generally may be used to restructure a corporation, including the elimination of a deficit in retained earnings. This procedure is called a *quasi-reorganization* or *corporate readjustment*. Such circumstances generally require that the following criteria be met to be eligible to reorganize under quasi-reorganization: (1) the entity must have exhausted all retained earnings; (2) the entire procedure is made known to all persons entitled to vote on matters of general corporate policy, and the appropriate consents to the particular transactions are obtained in advance, in accordance with the applicable law and charter provisions; and (3) the entity must have changed management, lines of business, methods of operations, and such other matters, so that the entity is reasonably expected to have profitable operations based on the restated asset and liability carrying amounts in terms of present conditions. In a quasi-reorganization, a company reduces the carrying amounts of its balance sheet accounts to fair value; the offsetting adjustment should be charged to retained earnings. If the adjustment exceeds the balance in the retained earnings account, any difference should be charged to additional paid-in capital. A new retained earnings account should be established at the effective date of such readjustment, and the effective date generally should be disclosed for a period of ten years.

Accounting Literature

FASB Accounting Standards Codification Topic	*Pre-Codification Accounting Literature*
852, *Reorganizations*	ARB-43, Chapter 7A, *Quasi-Reorganization or Corporate Readjustment*
	SOP 90-7, *Financial Reporting by Entities in Reorganization under the Bankruptcy Code*

FASB Accounting Standards Codification Topic	Pre-Codification Accounting Literature
	PB-11, *Accounting for Preconfirmation Contingencies in Fresh-Start Reporting (nullified upon adoption of guidance related to FAS-141R)*

DISCLOSURE AND KEY PRESENTATION REQUIREMENTS

Reorganizations under Chapter 11 of the Bankruptcy Code

1. The following disclosures should be made by entities in Chapter 11 reorganization proceedings (ASC 852-10-45-13, 45-16, 50-2, 50-3, and 50-5) (SOP 90-7, pars. 23–31, 34):

    a. Claims that are not subject to reasonable estimation.

    b. Principal categories of claims subject to compromise.

    c. The extent to which reported interest expense differs from stated contractual interest.

    d. Reorganization items separately within the operating, investing, and financing categories of the statement of cash flows, preferably using the direct method; and, if the indirect method is used, details of operating cash receipts and payments resulting from the reorganization.

    e. In the earnings per share calculation whether it is probable that the plan will require the issuance of common stock or common stock equivalents, thereby diluting current equity interests.

2. The following disclosures should be made in consolidated financial statements that include one or more entities in reorganization proceedings and one or more entities not in reorganization proceedings (ASC 852-10-50-4) (SOP 90-7, pars. 32–33):

    a. Condensed combined financial statements of the entities in reorganization proceedings.

    b. Intercompany receivables and payables of entities in reorganization proceedings.

3. When entities emerge from Chapter 11 reorganization and adopt fresh-start reporting, the following disclosures should be made in the notes to the initial fresh-start financial statements (ASC 852-10-45-21 and 50-7) (SOP 90-7, par. 39):

    a. Adjustments to the historical amounts of individual assets and liabilities.

b. The amount of debt forgiveness.

c. Significant matters relating to the determination of reorganization value, including:

(1) The method or methods used to determine reorganization value and factors such as discount rates, tax rates, number of years for which cash flows are projected, and method of determining terminal value.

(2) Sensitive assumptions about which there is a reasonable possibility of the occurrence of a variation that would significantly affect the measurement of reorganization value.

(3) Assumptions about anticipated conditions that are expected to be different from current conditions, unless otherwise apparent.

Note: The disclosure requirement in item 4 below is prescribed by ASC Section 852-10-50, *Reorganizations— Overall—Disclosure*, prior to the adoption of the guidance related to FAS-141R, *Business Combinations*, which is effective for business combinations for which the acquisition date is on or after the beginning of the first annual reporting period beginning on or after December 15, 2008. Therefore, the disclosure requirement in item 4 below will no longer be applicable once the guidance related to FAS-141R becomes effective.

4. When entities emerge from Chapter 11 reorganization and adopt fresh-start reporting, the following disclosure should be made by those entities that have recorded an adjustment that resulted from a preconfirmation contingency (ASC 852-10-50-8) (PB-11, pars. 8–9):

a. The adjustment of preconfirmation contingencies that is included in income or loss from continuing operations of the emerged entity.

Quasi-Reorganizations

1. After a quasi-reorganization or corporate readjustment (ASC 852-20-25-4 and 50-2) (ARB-43, Ch. 7A, pars. 6 and 10):

a. The offsetting adjustment should be charged to retained earnings.

b. If the adjustment exceeds the balance in the retained earnings account, the difference should be charged to additional paid-in capital.

c. A new retained earnings account should be established and dated to show that it runs from the effective date of the readjustment. (This dating should be disclosed in the financial statements until such time as the effective date is no longer deemed to possess any special significance, which is generally not more than 10 years.)

2. Assets should be carried forward as of the date of the readjustment at fair amounts. (ASC 852-20-30-2) (ARB-43, Ch. 7A, par. 4)

3. If the fair value of any asset is not readily determinable and a conservative estimate was used (ASC 852-20-30-3 and 35-2) (ARB-43, Ch. 7A, pars. 4–5):

   a. The amount should be described as an estimate.

   b. Any material difference arising through realization, or otherwise, and not attributable to events occurring or circumstances arising after the readjustment date should not be carried to income or retained earnings.

EXAMPLES OF FINANCIAL STATEMENT DISCLOSURES

 The following sample disclosures are available on the accompanying disc.

Reorganizations under Chapter 11 of the Bankruptcy Code

Example 1: Petition for Relief under Chapter 11 of the Bankruptcy Code

On February 13, 20X2, ABC Company (the Debtor) filed petitions for relief under Chapter 11 of the federal bankruptcy laws in the United States Bankruptcy Court for the Western District of Tennessee. Under Chapter 11, certain claims against the Debtor in existence prior to the filing of the petitions for relief under the federal bankruptcy laws are stayed while the Debtor continues business operations as Debtor-in-possession. These claims are reflected in the December 31, 20X2, Balance Sheet as "Liabilities subject to compromise." Additional claims (liabilities subject to compromise) may arise subsequent to the filing date resulting from rejection of executory contracts, including leases, and from the determination by the court (or agreed to by parties in interest) of allowed claims for contingencies and other disputed amounts. Claims secured against the Debtor's assets (secured claims) also are stayed, although the holders of such claims have the right to move the court for relief from the stay. Secured claims are secured primarily by liens on the Debtor's property, plant, and equipment.

The Debtor received approval from the Bankruptcy Court to pay or otherwise honor certain of its prepetition obligations, including employee wages and product warranties. The Debtor has determined that there is insufficient collateral to cover the interest portion of scheduled payments on its prepetition debt obligations. Contractual interest on those obligations amounts to $[amount], which is $[amount] in excess of reported interest expense; therefore, the Debtor has discontinued accruing interest on these obligations.

Example 2: Emergence from Bankruptcy

Upon emergence from its Chapter 11 proceedings in April 20X2, the Company adopted "fresh-start" reporting in accordance with FASB ASC Topic 852, *Reorganizations*, as of March 31, 20X2. The Company's emergence from these proceedings resulted in a new reporting entity with no retained earnings or accumulated deficit as of March 31, 20X2. Accordingly, the Company's financial information shown for periods prior to March 31, 20X2, is not comparable to consolidated financial statements presented on or subsequent to March 31, 20X2.

The Bankruptcy Court confirmed the Company's plan of reorganization. The confirmed plan provided for the following:

Secured Debt—The Company's $[amount] of secured debt (secured by a first mortgage lien on a building located in Nashville, Tennessee) was exchanged for $[amount] in cash and a $[amount] secured note, payable in annual installments of $[amount] commencing on July 1, 20X3, through June 30, 20X6, with interest at 13% per annum, with the balance due on July 1, 20X7.

Priority Tax Claims—Payroll and withholding taxes of $[amount] are payable in equal annual installments commencing on July 1, 20X3, through July 1, 20X8, with interest at 11% per annum.

Senior Debt—The holders of approximately $[amount] of senior subordinated secured notes received the following instruments in exchange for their notes: (a) $[amount] in new senior secured debt, payable in annual installments of $[amount] commencing March 1, 20X3, through March 1, 20X6, with interest at 12% per annum, secured by first liens on certain property, plant, and equipment, with the balance due on March 1, 20X7; (b) $[amount] of subordinated debt with interest at 14% per annum due in equal annual installments commencing on October 1, 20X3, through October 1, 20X9, secured by second liens on certain property, plant, and equipment; and (c) [percent]% of the new issue of outstanding voting common stock of the Company.

Trade and Other Miscellaneous Claims—The holders of approximately $[amount] of trade and other miscellaneous claims received the following for their claims: (a) $[amount] in senior secured debt, payable in annual installments of $[amount] commencing March 1, 20X3, through March 1, 20X6, with interest at 12% per annum, secured by first liens on certain property, plant, and equipment, with the balance due on March 1, 20X7; (b) $[amount] of subordinated debt, payable in equal annual installments commencing October 1, 20X3, through October 1, 20X8, with interest at 14% per annum; and (c) [percent]% of the new issue of outstanding voting common stock of the Company.

Subordinated Debentures—The holders of approximately $[amount] of subordinated unsecured debt received, in exchange for the debentures, [percent]% of the new issue outstanding voting common stock of the Company.

Preferred Stock—The holders of [number] shares of preferred stock received [percent]% of the outstanding voting common stock of the new issue of the Company in exchange for their preferred stock.

Common Stock—The holders of approximately [number] outstanding shares of the Company's existing common stock received, in exchange for their shares, [percent]% of the new outstanding voting common stock of the Company.

Quasi-Reorganizations

Example 3: Quasi-Reorganization Adopted in Connection with Ownership Change and Restructuring of Operations

In recognition of the change in ownership of the Company and the restructuring of operations, the Company believes that future operations are not burdened with the problems of the past. As a result, the Company believed it to be appropriate to adjust the carrying value of assets and liabilities to their fair value as of January 1, 20X2. Following extensive research and consultations with legal counsel and independent accountants, management recommended, and the Company's Board of Directors approved, a quasi-reorganization to be effective as of January 1, 20X2. Accordingly, all assets and liabilities of the Company have been retroactively restated as of January 1, 20X2, to their fair value, determined as follows:

- *Inventories*—market value reduced by selling costs and a reasonable profit allowance
- *Property, plant, and equipment*—recent appraisal values
- *Debt due beyond one year*—principal and interest payments due beyond one year have been discounted at 10%
- *Convertible subordinated debentures*—appraisal from an investment banker
- *Liability for pension plans*—amounts have been discounted at 10%

The following table illustrates the caption used in the Company's stockholders' equity section to show the dating of retained earnings from the effective date of the quasi-reorganization of January 1, 20X2:

	20X2	20X1
Common stock	$ 20,000	$ 700,000
Additional paid-in capital	80,000	900,000
Retained earnings since January 1, 20X2, in connection with quasi-reorganization	373,000	-0-
Accumulated deficit (prior to quasi-reorganization)	-0-	(1,325,000)
Total stockholder's equity	$473,000	$ 275,000

CHAPTER 56
ASC TOPIC 855: SUBSEQUENT EVENTS

CONTENTS

EXECUTIVE SUMMARY

Note: The discussion in this chapter is based on the provisions and requirements prescribed in ASC Topic 855, *Subsequent Events* (FAS-165, *Subsequent Events*), which are effective for interim or annual financial periods ending after June 15, 2009, and should be applied prospectively.

Subsequent Events

Subsequent events are events or transactions that occur after the balance sheet date but before the financial statements are issued (i.e., when they are widely distributed to shareholders and other financial statement users for general use), or are available to be issued (i.e., all approvals necessary for issuance, such as from management and the board of directors, have been obtained). There are two types of subsequent events that require consideration:

1.   Events or transactions that provide additional evidence with respect to conditions that existed at the balance sheet date,

including the estimates inherent in the process of preparing financial statements (Type 1–*Recognized subsequent events*). Examples of such subsequent events include:

- A customer with an outstanding accounts receivable balance as of the balance sheet date and that declares bankruptcy in the subsequent period.

- The subsequent settlement of a litigation at an amount that is different from the amount recorded in the financial statements.

- The subsequent sale of property not being used in operations at a price less than the carrying value in the financial statements.

- The subsequent sale of investments at a price less than the carrying value in the financial statements.

2. Events that provide evidence with respect to conditions that did not exist at the date of the balance sheet but arose subsequent to that date (Type 2–*Nonrecognized subsequent events*). Examples of such subsequent events include:

- Sale of bonds or equity securities.

- Acquisition of a business.

- Loss of plant or inventories as a result of fire or natural disaster occurring after the balance sheet date.

- Loss of receivables resulting from conditions that arose subsequent to the balance sheet date.

- Changes in the fair value of assets or liabilities or foreign exchange rates after the balance sheet date.

- Material commitments to purchase property, plant, and equipment.

- Material commitments under a long-term lease agreement.

Accounting Literature

FASB Accounting Standards Codification Topic	*Pre-Codification Accounting Literature*
855, *Subsequent Events*	FAS-5, *Accounting for Contingencies*
	FAS-165, *Subsequent Events*

DISCLOSURE AND KEY PRESENTATION REQUIREMENTS

Note: The disclosure and key presentation requirements in items 1 through 3 below are prescribed by ASC Topic 855, *Subsequent Events*, based on FAS-165, *Subsequent Events*, and are effective for interim or annual financial periods ending after June 15, 2009, and should be applied prospectively.

1. The entity should disclose the date through which subsequent events have been evaluated and whether that date is the date the financial statements were issued or the date that they were available to be issued. (ASC 855-10-50-1) (FAS-165, par. 12)

2. For nonrecognized subsequent events:

   a. The following disclosures should be made when it is necessary to keep the financial statements from being misleading (ASC 855-10-50-2) (FAS-165, par. 13):

      (1) The nature of the event.

      (2) An estimate of the event's financial effect, or a statement that such an estimate cannot be made.

   b. Consideration should be given to supplementing the historical financial statements with pro forma financial data giving effect to the nonrecognized subsequent event as if it had occurred on the balance sheet date. (ASC 855-10-50-3) (FAS-165, par. 14)

   c. Consideration should be given to presenting pro forma statements (usually a balance sheet only) in columnar form on the face of the historical financial statements. (ASC 855-10-45-1 and 50-3) (FAS-165, par. 14)

3. In the case of reissued financial statements, the entity should disclose the date through which subsequent events have been evaluated in both the originally issued financial statements and the reissued financial statements. (ASC 855-10-50-4) (FAS-165, par. 15)

4. For losses arising after the date of an entity's financial statements but before those financial statements are issued (ASC 450-20-50-9 and 50-10) (FAS-5, par. 11):

   a. The following disclosures should be made (when it is necessary to keep the financial statements from being misleading) for unaccrued losses and loss contingencies:

      (1) The nature of the loss or loss contingency.

(2) An estimate of the amount or range of loss, or possible loss, or a statement that such an estimate cannot be made.

b. If the amount of an asset impaired or liability incurred can be reasonably estimated, consideration should be given to supplementing the historical financial statements with pro forma financial data giving effect to the loss as if it had occurred at the date of the financial statements. (*Note*: It may be desirable to present pro forma statements, usually a balance sheet only, in columnar form on the face of the historical financial statements.)

EXAMPLES OF FINANCIAL STATEMENT DISCLOSURES

The following sample disclosures are available on the accompanying disc.

Accounting Policy

Example 1: Disclosure of Evaluation of Subsequent Events

On [*insert date*], the Company adopted FASB ASC Topic 855, *Subsequent Events*. ASC 855 establishes general standards of accounting for and disclosure of events that occur after the balance sheet date but before financial statements are issued or are available to be issued. Specifically, it sets forth the period after the balance sheet date during which management of a reporting entity should evaluate events or transactions that may occur for potential recognition or disclosure in the financial statements, the circumstances under which an entity should recognize events or transactions occurring after the balance sheet date in its financial statements, and the disclosures that an entity should make about events or transactions that occurred after the balance sheet date. The adoption of ASC 855 had no impact on the Company's financial statements.

In accordance with ASC 855, the Company evaluated subsequent events through March 25, 20X3, the date these financial statements were issued [*or, "the date these financial statements were available to be issued"*]. There were no material subsequent events that required recognition or additional disclosure in these financial statements.

> *Alternatively, an entity may provide reference to the notes for details on specific subsequent events requiring recognition or*

disclosure. For example, the following disclosure may be appropriate:

In accordance with ASC 855, the Company evaluated subsequent events through March 25, 20X3, the date these financial statements were issued [or, *"the date these financial statements were available to be issued"*]. With the exception of those matters discussed in Notes [X] and [Y], there were no material subsequent events that required recognition or additional disclosure in these financial statements. [*The specific subsequent events requiring disclosure would then be provided.*]

Example 2: Disclosure of Evaluation of Subsequent Events in Reissued Financial Statements

The Company evaluated subsequent events through March 25, 20X3, the date these financial statements were originally issued, and through December 10, 20X3, the date these financial statements were reissued. With the exception of those matters discussed in Notes [X] and [Y], there were no material subsequent events that required recognition or additional disclosure in these financial statements. [*The specific subsequent events requiring disclosure would then be provided.*]

Casualty Loss

Example 3: Inventory Destroyed in Fire

In February 20X3, the Company suffered a fire in its main warehouse located in Hillsborough, Virginia. The Company estimates that inventory with a recorded value of approximately $1,200,000 was destroyed. Although the exact amount of the loss is not currently determinable, the Company expects to recover 50% to 75% of the value through insurance proceeds.

Debt/Financing

Example 4: New Financing Arrangement

On January 29, 20X3, the Company entered into a Revolving Loan Agreement (the Loan Agreement) with Ace State Bank. The Loan Agreement provides for borrowings through January 31, 20X8 (the Maturity Date). Borrowings will bear interest at the bank's prime rate. The maximum amount that may be outstanding under the Loan Agreement is $20,000,000 through December 31, 20X4. Thereafter, the maximum amount of borrowings that may be outstanding under the Loan Agreement is reduced by $1,000,000 in calendar 20X5 and by $1,000,000 in each of the following calendar years up to the Maturity Date. Under the terms of the Loan

Agreement, the Company will pay Ace State Bank $200,000 plus an unused commitment fee during the term of the Loan Agreement. The Company will also pay legal, accounting, and other fees and expenses in connection with the Loan Agreement.

Example 5: Issuance of Convertible Subordinated Notes

On January 12, 20X3, the Company executed an agreement with a group of institutional investors whereby the Company issued $12 million in convertible subordinated loan notes. These notes bear an interest rate of 11% per year and mature in 20X5.

Example 6: Maximum Borrowing under Line of Credit

In February and March 20X3, the Company borrowed $800,000 under its line of credit for working capital purposes. As a result, the Company has borrowed the maximum amount available under the credit line. The Company is negotiating with the bank to increase its credit line limit by $2,000,000. However, there can be no assurance that the Company will be successful in increasing its credit line.

Inventory

Example 7: Commitment to Sell Inventory at Fixed Price

On January 15, 20X3, the Company entered into an agreement with a customer to sell a specified minimum number of units of its Eglaze adhesive products over the next thirty months at a fixed price of $10,200,000. The fixed price is equal to approximately 5% above the aggregate selling price at current market prices.

Leases

Example 8: New Operating Lease Agreement

In February 20X3, the Company entered into an operating lease agreement for a manufacturing plant to be constructed in Carson, New Jersey. The total cost of assets to be covered by the lease is limited to $15,000,000. The manufacturing facility is scheduled for completion in June 20X4. Payments under the lease will be determined and will commence upon completion of construction and will continue through the initial lease term of five years. The Company has options to renew the lease for two five-year periods and to purchase the facility at its estimated fair market value at any time during the lease term.

Example 9: Contingent Liability Relating to Lease Termination

In March 20X3, the Company notified the developer and landlord of its planned future headquarters in Paramount, California, that the Company intends to terminate the project. The Company had previously entered into a 15-year lease agreement for the new site. Although groundbreaking for the new site has not occurred, the Company anticipates that it will incur lease termination costs. However, the Company is not able to make a meaningful estimate of the amount or range of loss that could result from an unfavorable resolution of this matter.

License Agreement

Example 10: License Fee Commitments under License Agreement

In February 20X3, the Company entered into an agreement to license software to be incorporated into its data conferencing products. Under the agreement, the Company is obligated to pay annual minimum license fees, ranging from $150,000 to $350,000 through the year 20X6 and the Company may cancel the agreement at any time, provided the Company has paid a minimum of $1,000,000 in connection with the agreement.

Litigation

Example 11: Patent Infringement Lawsuit

On February 13, 20X3, the Company was named as a defendant in a patent infringement suit brought by Pasterine, Ltd., alleging that certain of the Company's products infringe seven patents that Pasterine Ltd. allegedly owns and is seeking a judgment of infringement for each of these asserted patents and other costs. The Company is reviewing the suit and, based on advice from legal counsel, believes that the complaints are without merit. However, no assurance can be given that this matter will be resolved in the Company's favor.

Example 12: Sexual Discrimination Lawsuit

In March 20X3, the Company and two principal officers were named as defendants in a lawsuit brought by a former employee alleging sexual discrimination. Management believes that the lawsuit is without merit and the outcome will not have a material adverse effect on the financial position or results of operations of the Company.

Example 13: Settlement of Threatened Litigation in Connection with Event Occurring after Year-End

In January 20X3, the Company breached its contract with a supplier by failing to buy a minimum amount of certain specified products for the month of January, which the Company was committed to buy under terms of the agreement. The supplier threatened litigation to enforce the terms of the contract. As a result, on March 29, 20X3, the Company agreed to pay $400,000 to the supplier in an out-of-court settlement. The amount will be charged to operations in 20X3.

Property and Equipment

Example 14: Purchase of Assets

On March 4, 20X3, the Company entered into an agreement to purchase a new warehouse and distribution center at a total cost of $4,700,000. The Company opened escrow and made a deposit of $500,000. The purchase price is expected to be financed by the Company's primary bank over five years at an interest rate of 1% above the bank's prime rate.

Example 15: Sale of Assets

On January 23, 20X3, the Company sold one of its warehouse and distribution facility for $4,400,000, with an after tax gain of $890,000. The proceeds were used to repay long-term borrowings.

Example 16: Sale and Leaseback of Facility

Subsequent to December 31, 20X2, the Company entered into a sale and leaseback agreement with regard to its manufacturing facility in Grand Rapids, Michigan. The transaction has been recorded as a sale with the cash proceeds of $11 million used to repay borrowings of $7.5 million and the remainder used for working capital purposes. The Company recorded a gain of $2.5 million on the sale.

Under the terms of the agreement, the Company has committed to lease a portion of the facility for 12 years. The present value of minimum lease payments at inception of the obligation approximates $4 million.

Related Parties

Example 17: Advances Made to Related Parties

In February and March 20X3, the Company made advances totaling $1,200,000 to PRC Development, an entity owned by the president and certain officers of the Company, primarily to accommodate expansion and other financing needs of this related entity. Such advances are unsecured, bear interest at 10%, and are payable in semiannual installments starting April 1, 20X4.

Stockholders' Equity

Example 18: Conversion of Debentures into Common Stock

On March 1, 20X3, the holders of the Company's 10% convertible debentures have elected to convert an aggregate of $4,000,000 principal amount of the debentures into 696,520 shares of the Company's common stock.

Example 19: Sale of Common Stock

On February 11, 20X3, the Company sold 300,000 shares of its common stock at $10 per share. The proceeds will be used for working capital purposes and to pay off long-term debt of approximately $1,300,000.

Example 20: Stock Option Plan

In February 20X3, the Company adopted a Stock Option Plan ("Plan") that provides for the granting of stock options to certain key employees. The Plan reserves 450,000 shares of common stock, including 200,000 shares granted to the president under his employment arrangement. Options under the Plan are to be granted at no less than fair market value of the shares at the date of grant.

Example 21: Stock Split

On March 1, 20X3, the Company's board of directors declared a two-for-one stock split of the common stock effected in the form of a 25% stock dividend, to be distributed on or about April 10, 20X3, to holders of record on March 23, 20X3. Accordingly, all references to number of shares, except shares authorized, and to per share information in the consolidated financial statements have been adjusted to reflect the stock split on a retroactive basis.

Example 22: Amendment to Certificate of Incorporation to Decrease Number of Authorized Shares

Subsequent to December 31, 20X2, the board of directors approved a proposal to amend the Certificate of Incorporation to decrease the number of authorized shares of common stock from 50,000,000 shares to 5,000,000 shares and to effect a one-for-ten reverse split of common stock whereby each ten shares of common stock will be exchanged for one share of common stock. The Amendment will have no effect on the par value of the common stock.

Example 23: Cash Dividend

On January 27, 20X3, the Company declared a cash dividend of $0.07 per share payable on March 3, 20X3, to shareholders of record on February 10, 20X3.

CHAPTER 57
ASC TOPIC 860: TRANSFERS AND SERVICING

CONTENTS

EXECUTIVE SUMMARY

PRACTICE ALERT: As this Manual goes to press, the FASB has issued Statement of Financial Accounting Standards No. 166, *Accounting for Transfers of Financial Assets—An Amendment to FASB Statement No. 140*, which enhances information reported to users of financial statements by providing greater transparency about transfers of financial assets and an entity's continuing involvement in transferred financial assets. FAS-166 will require more information about transfers of financial assets, including securitization transactions, and where entities have continuing exposure to the risks related to transferred financial assets. It also eliminates the concept of a "qualifying special-purpose entity" (QSPE), changes the requirements for derecognizing financial assets, and requires additional disclosures. Although the impact of the changes under FAS-166 may be more evident to financial institutions, the new guidance will also apply to nonfinancial entities. For example, the new guidance affects transfers of many types of financial assets, including factoring agreements, sales of trade receivables, mortgage loans, and installment loans.

FAS-166 will be effective at the start of a reporting entity's first fiscal year beginning after November 15, 2009 (i.e., 2010 for calendar-year entities). Early application is not permitted.

As this Manual goes to press, the FASB has not yet integrated the provisions of FAS-166 into the Accounting Standards Codification. Readers should be alert to and monitor further developments in this area. The coverage in this chapter is based on ASC Topic 860 before FAS-166. Future editions of this Manual will include expanded coverage of the guidance based on FAS-166 and the appropriate ASC Topics.

PRACTICE ALERT: As this Manual goes to press, the FASB has issued Statement of Financial Accounting Standards No. 167, *Amendments to FASB Interpretation No. 46(R)*, which significantly changes the consolidation rules as they related to variable interest entities (VIEs). FAS-167 specifically changes how a reporting entity determines when an entity that is insufficiently capitalized or is not controlled through voting (or similar rights) should be consolidated. The determination of whether a reporting entity is required to consolidate another entity is based on, among other things, the other entity's purpose and design and the reporting entity's ability to direct the activities of the other entity that most significantly impact the other entity's economic performance. Under FAS-167, it is expected that many off-balance sheet entities previously exempt from consolidation—qualified special-purpose entities (QSPEs)—will be subject to consolidation. Due to the elimination of the QSPE scope exception, the impact of the changes under FAS-167 may be more evident to financial services companies; however, the new guidance will have broad applicability across all industries. In addition, FAS-167 will require a number of new disclosures, including the requirements for a reporting entity to provide additional disclosures about its involvement with VIEs, any significant changes in risk exposure due to that involvement, and how its involvement with a VIE affects the reporting entity's financial statements.

FAS-167 will be effective at the start of a reporting entity's first fiscal year beginning after November 15, 2009 (i.e., 2010 for calendar-year entities). Early application is not permitted.

As this Manual goes to press, the FASB has not yet integrated the provisions of FAS-167 into the Accounting Standards Codification. Readers should be alert to and monitor further developments in this area. The coverage in this chapter is based on ASC Topic 810 before FAS-167. Future editions of this Manual will include expanded coverage of the guidance based on FAS-167 and the appropriate ASC Topics.

Sales (Transfers) of Financial Assets

Accounting for transfers of financial assets hinges on the basic notion that each entity involved in the transaction should (a) recognize only assets it controls and liabilities it has incurred, (b) derecognize assets only when control has been surrendered, and (c) derecognize liabilities only when they have been extinguished. Therefore, the guidance presented is a financial-components approach that focuses on control and recognizes that financial assets and liabilities can be divided into a variety of components. The approach analyzes a transfer of a financial asset by examining the component assets (controlled economic benefits) and liabilities (present obligations for probable future sacrifices of economic benefits) that exist after the transfer. Each party to the transfer recognizes the assets and liabilities that it controls after the transfer and no longer recognizes the assets that were surrendered in the transfer.

A transfer of financial assets in which the transferor surrenders control over those financial assets should be accounted for as a sale to the extent that consideration other than beneficial interests in the transferred assets is received in exchange. Transfers of financial assets often occur in which the transferor has some continuing involvement either with the assets transferred or with the transferee.

Transfers of financial assets with continuing involvement raise issues about the circumstances under which the transfers should be considered as sales of all or part of the assets or as secured borrowings and about how transferors and transferees should account for sales and secured borrowings.

Secured Borrowing and Collateral

A transferred financial asset should be considered pledged as collateral to secure an obligation of the transferor (and therefore should not be derecognized) if the transfer of financial assets does not meet the criteria for a sale and the transferor has not surrendered control of the financial asset.

If the transfer of financial assets does not meet the criteria for a sale, both the transferor and the transferee should account for the transfer as a secured borrowing with a pledge of collateral. The accounting for the pledged collateral depends on whether the transferee has the right to sell or repledge the collateral. For example, if the transferee has the right by contract or custom to sell or repledge the collateral, the transferor (debtor) should reclassify that asset and report the asset in its balance sheet separately from unencumbered assets. In addition, if the transferor (debtor) defaults under the terms of the secured contract and is no longer entitled to redeem the pledged asset, the transferor (debtor) should derecognize the pledged asset.

Servicing Assets and Liabilities

Servicing is inherent in all financial assets. Servicing is most often associated with financial assets such as mortgage loans and credit card receivables. Examples of servicing activities include the collection from borrowers of principal, interest, and escrow payments, and the monitoring of delinquencies.

A servicer of financial assets commonly receives benefits of servicing such as revenues from servicing fees, a portion of interest payments, late charges, and other related sources. A servicer is entitled to receive all of those benefits of servicing only if it performs the servicing and incurs the costs of servicing the assets.

Servicing assets are reported separately from servicing liabilities in the balance sheet, with the servicing assets and servicing liabilities further classified by measurement method—the amortization or fair value method. An entity generally may choose between the two prescribed approaches for purposes of carrying out this classification requirement.

Accounting Literature

FASB Accounting Standards Codification Topic	*Pre-Codification Accounting Literature*
860, *Transfers and Servicing*	FAS-140, *Accounting for Transfers and Servicing of Financial Assets and Extinguishments of Liabilities*
	FSP FAS 140-4 and FIN 46R-8, *Disclosures by Public Entities (Enterprises) about Transfers of Financial Assets and Interests in Variable Interest Entities*
	FAS-156, *Accounting for Servicing of Financial Assets*
	FAS-166, *Accounting for Transfers of Financial Assets—an Amendment to FASB Statement No. 140*
	FAS-167, *Amendments to FASB Interpretation No. 46(R)*
	FASB Staff Implementation Guide (Q&A), *A Guide to Implementation of Statement 140 on Accounting for Transfers and Servicing of Financial Assets and Extinguishments of Liabilities: Questions and Answers*
	SOP 01-6, *Accounting by Certain Entities (Including Entities with Trade Receivables) That Lend to or Finance the Activities of Others*

DISCLOSURE AND KEY PRESENTATION REQUIREMENTS

Note: The disclosure and key presentation requirements under the captions: (*a*) Sales (Transfers) of Financial Assets; (*b*) Secured Borrowing and Collateral; and (*c*) Servicing Assets and Liabilities, below, and in ASC Topics 310, 405, 470, 740, and 810, as they pertain to FAS-140, have been superseded by the guidance in FAS-166, *Accounting for Transfers of Financial Assets,* which is effective as of the beginning of the first annual reporting period beginning after November 15, 2009, and all interim and annual periods thereafter. Thereafter, the disclosure requirements under the caption "FAS-166, *Accounting for Transfers of Financial Assets,*" below, should be followed. Early adoption is not permitted.

Disclosures required by FAS-166 may be reported in the aggregate for similar transfers if separate reporting of each transfer would not provide more useful information to financial statement users. A transferor should disclose how similar transfers are aggregated. A transferor should distinguish transfers that are accounted for as sales from transfers that are accounted for as secured borrowings. In determining whether to aggregate the disclosures for multiple transfers, the reporting entity should consider quantitative and qualitative information about the characteristics of the transferred financial assets. For example, consideration should be given, but not limited, to: (*a*) the nature of the transferor's continuing involvement, if any; (*b*) the types of financial assets transferred; (*c*) risks related to the transferred financial assets to which the transferor continues to be exposed after the transfer and the change in the transferor's risk profile as a result of the transfer; and (*d*) the requirements of FSP SOP 94-6-1, *Terms of Loan Products That May Give Rise to a Concentration of Credit Risk.*

The principal objectives of these disclosures is to provide users of the financial statements with an understanding of: (*a*) a transferor's continuing involvement, if any, with transferred financial assets; (*b*) the nature of any restrictions on assets reported by an entity in its balance sheet that relate to a transferred financial asset, including the carrying amounts of those assets: (*c*) how servicing assets and servicing liabilities are reported; and (*d*) for transfers accounted for as sales when a transferor has continuing involvement with the transferred financial assets and for transfers of financial assets accounted for as secured borrowings, how the transfer of financial assets affects a transferor's financial position, financial performance and cash flows. These disclosures are minimum disclosures and should be supplemented as necessary to meet the principal objectives.

Sales (Transfers) of Financial Assets

1. If it is not practicable to estimate the fair value of certain assets obtained or liabilities incurred in transfers of financial assets during the period, disclosure should be made of those items and the reasons why it is not practicable to estimate their fair value. (ASC 860-10-50-1; 860-20-50-9e) (FAS-140, par. 17; FSP FAS 140-4 and FIN-46R-8, par. B11)

2. If the entity has securitized financial assets during any period presented and accounts for that transfer as a sale, the following disclosures should be made for each major asset type (e.g., credit card receivables, automobile loans, mortgage loans) (ASC 860-20-50-3) (FAS-140, par. 17):

    a. The accounting policies for initially measuring the interests that continue to be held by the transferor, if any, and servicing assets and servicing liabilities, if any, including the methodology (whether quoted market price, prices based on sales of similar assets and liabilities, or prices based on valuation techniques) used in determining their fair value.

b. The characteristics of securitizations (a description of the transferor's continuing involvement with the transferred assets, including, but not limited to servicing, recourse, and restrictions on interests that continue to be held by the transferor) and the gain or loss from sale of financial assets in securitizations.

c. The key assumptions used in measuring the fair value of interests that continue to be held by the transferor and servicing assets or servicing liabilities if any at the time of securitization, including at a minimum quantitative information about the following (*Note*: If an entity has made multiple securitizations of the same major asset type during a period, it may disclose the range of assumptions):

(1) Discount rates.

(2) Expected prepayments including the expected weighted-average life of prepayable financial assets.

(3) Anticipated credit losses, if applicable.

d. Cash flows between the securitization special-purpose entity (SPE) and the transferor, unless reported separately elsewhere in the financial statements or notes, including:

(1) Proceeds from new securitizations.

(2) Proceeds from collections reinvested in revolving-period securitizations.

(3) Purchases of delinquent or foreclosed loans.

(4) Servicing fees.

(5) Cash flows received on interests that continue to be held by the transferor.

3. If the entity has interests that continue to be held by the transferor in financial assets that it has securitized or servicing assets or servicing liabilities relating to assets that it has securitized, at the date of the latest balance sheet presented, the following disclosures should be made for each major asset type (e.g., credit card receivables, automobile loans, mortgage loans) (ASC 860-20-50-4) (FAS-140, par. 17):

a. The accounting policies for subsequently measuring those interests, including the methodology (whether quoted market price, prices based on sales of similar assets and liabilities, or prices based on valuation techniques) used in determining their fair value.

b. The key assumptions used in subsequently measuring the fair value of those interests, including at a minimum, quantitative information about the following:

   (1) Discount rates.

   (2) Expected prepayments including the expected weighted-average life of prepayable financial assets.

   (3) Anticipated credit losses, including expected static pool losses, if applicable.

c. A sensitivity analysis or stress test showing the hypothetical effect on the fair value of those interests (including any servicing assets or servicing liabilities) of two or more unfavorable variations from the expected levels for each key assumption that is reported under item (b) above independently from any change in another key assumption, and a description of the objectives, methodology, and limitations of the sensitivity analysis or stress test.

d. For the securitized assets and any other financial assets that it manages together with them (excluding securitized assets that an entity continues to service but with which it has no other continuing involvement):

   (1) The total principal amount outstanding at the end of the period.

   (2) The portion that has been derecognized at the end of the period.

   (3) The portion that continues to be recognized in each category reported in the balance sheet at the end of the period.

   (4) Delinquencies at the end of the period.

   (5) Credit losses, net of recoveries, during the period.

   (6) Average balances during the period. (*Note:* This disclosure item is encouraged, but not required.)

4. For sales of loans and trade receivables, the aggregate amount of gains or losses on the sales (including adjustments to record loans held for sale at the lower of cost or fair value) should be presented separately or disclosed in the notes to the financial statements. (ASC 860-20-50-5) (SOP 01-6, par. 13). See Chapter 17, "ASC Topic 310: Receivables," for disclosure requirements for loans and trade receivables.

Note: The disclosure requirements in items 5 and 6 below are prescribed for *public entities* only by ASC Topic 860, *Transfers* *and Servicing*, based on FSP FAS 140-4 and FIN-46R-8, *Disclosures by Public Entities (Enterprises) about Transfers of Financial Assets and Interests in Variable Interest Entities.* These requirements are effective for the first reporting period (interim or annual) ending after December 15, 2008, and apply for each annual and interim reporting period thereafter. Early adoption is permitted. Entities are encouraged to disclose comparative information in periods earlier than the effective date. In periods after initial adoption, comparative disclosures are required only for periods subsequent to the effective date.

To apply these disclosures, an entity should consider all involvements by the transferor, its consolidated affiliates included in the financial statements being presented, or its agents to be involvements by the transferor. (ASC 860-10-50-7) (FSP FAS 140-4 and FIN-46R-8, pars. B5).

Disclosures may be reported in the aggregate for similar transfers if separate reporting of each transfer would not provide more useful information to financial statement users. In determining whether to aggregate the disclosures for multiple transfers, the reporting entity should consider quantitative and qualitative information about the characteristics of the transferred financial assets. For example, consideration should be given, but not be limited, to the following: (*a*) the nature of the transferor's continuing involvement; (*b*) the types of financial assets transferred; (*c*) risks related to the transferred financial assets to which the transferor continues to be exposed after the transfer and the change in the transferor's risk profile as a result of the transfer; and (*d*) the guidance for risks and uncertainties in ASC paragraph 310-10-50-25 and for concentrations involving loan product terms in ASC paragraphs 825-10-55-1 through 55-2. (ASC 860-10-50-5) (FSP FAS 140-4 and FIN-46R-8, par. B2)

5. For similar transfers that have been aggregated, the disclosures by the transferor should (ASC 860-10-50-5 and 50-6) (FSP FAS 140-4 and FIN-46R-8, pars. B2 and B3):

   a. Indicate how similar transfers are aggregated.

   b. Distinguish between transfers that are accounted for as secured borrowings and transfers that are accounted for as sales.

   c. Distinguish between transfers to qualifying SPEs accounted for as sales and all other transfers accounted for as sales.

6. For securitization or asset-backed financing arrangements accounted for as sales when the transferor has continuing involvement, the following disclosures should be made:

   a. For each income statement presented (ASC 860-20-50-7 and 50-8) (FSP FAS 140-4 and FIN-46R-8, pars. B4 and B11):

(1) Its accounting policies for initially measuring the interests that continue to be held by the transferor, if any, and servicing assets or servicing liabilities, if any.

(2) The characteristics of the transfer, including the following (*Note:* If specific disclosures are required for a particular form of the transferor's continuing involvement by other U.S. generally accepted accounting principles (GAAP) other than that in this item, such information should be cross-referenced with the information in this item in the notes to the financial statements so users can understand the risks retained in the transfer):

(i) A description of the transferor's continuing involvement with the transferred financial assets.

(ii) The gain or loss from the sale of transferred financial assets.

(3) Cash flows between a transferee and the transferor, including:

(i) Proceeds from new transfers.

(ii) Proceeds from collections reinvested in revolving-period transfers.

(iii) Purchases of previously transferred financial assets (or its underlying collateral).

(iv) Servicing fees.

(v) Cash flows received on the interests that continue to be held by the transferor.

b. For each balance sheet presented (ASC 860-20-50-7 and 50-9) (FSP FAS 140-4 and FIN-46R-8, pars. B4 and B11):

(1) Qualitative and quantitative information about the transferor's continuing involvement with transferred financial assets that provides financial statement users with sufficient information to assess the reasons for the continuing involvement and the risks related to the transferred financial assets to which the transferor continues to be exposed after the transfer and the extent that the transferor's risk profile has changed as a result of the transfer (including, but not limited to, credit risk, interest rate risk, and other risks), including the following (*Note:* If specific disclosures are required for a particular form of the transferor's continuing involvement by other U.S. GAAP other than that in this

item, such information should be cross-referenced with the information in this item in the notes to the financial statements so users can understand the risks retained in the transfer):

(i)   For SPEs used to facilitate a transfer of financial assets, if applicable:

    (a)   Their nature.

    (b)   Their purpose.

    (c)   Their size.

    (d)   Their activities.

    (e)   How the SPEs are financed.

(ii)   The total principal amount outstanding.

(iii)   The amount that has been derecognized.

(iv)   The amount that continues to be recognized in the balance sheet.

(v)   The terms of any arrangements that could require the transferor to provide financial support (e.g., liquidity arrangements and obligations to purchase assets) to the transferee or its beneficial interest holders, including a description of any events or circumstances that could expose the transferor to loss. (*Note:* All available evidence should be considered, including, but not limited to, explicit written arrangements, communications between the transferor and the transferee or its beneficial interest holders, and unwritten arrangements customary in similar transfers.)

(vi)   Whether the transferor has provided financial or other support during the periods presented that it was not previously contractually required to provide to the transferee or its beneficial interest holders, including the following when the transferor assisted the transferee or its beneficial interest holders in obtaining support:

    (a)   The type of support.

    (b)   The amount of support.

    (c)   The primary reasons for providing the support.

(vii)   Information about any liquidity arrangements, guarantees, or other commitments by third parties related to the transferred financial assets that may affect the fair value or risk of interest that continues to be held by the transferor. (*Note:* This information is encouraged but not required.)

(2) Its accounting policies for subsequently measuring assets or liabilities that relate to the continuing involvement with the transferred financial assets.

(3) The key inputs and assumptions used in measuring the fair value of assets or liabilities that relate to the transferor's continuing involvement, including at a minimum, quantitative information about the following:

   (i) Discount rates.

   (ii) Expected prepayments including the expected weighted-average life of prepayable financial assets.

   (iii) Anticipated credit losses, including expected static pool losses.

(4) For interests that continue to be held by the transferor in financial assets:

   (i) A sensitivity analysis or stress test showing the hypothetical effect on the fair value of those interests, including any servicing assets or servicing liabilities, of two or more unfavorable variations from the expected levels for each key assumption that is reported under item (3) above, independently from any change in another key assumption.

   (ii) A description of the objectives, methodology, and limitations of the sensitivity analysis or stress test.

(5) Information about the asset quality of transferred financial assets and any other financial assets that it manages together with them separated between the following (*Note:* The information in this item is intended to provide financial statement users with an understanding of the risks inherent in the transferred financial assets, as well as in other financial assets and liabilities that it manages together with transferred financial assets. In determining the information that should be disclosed, an entity should consider other disclosure requirements applicable to the transferred financial asset. For example, information for receivables should

include, but is not limited to: (*a*) delinquencies at the end of the period; and (*b*) credit losses, net of recoveries, during the period.):

 (i) Assets that have been derecognized.

 (ii) Assets that continue to be recognized in the balance sheet.

(6) For assets obtained or liabilities incurred in transfers of financial assets during the period for which it is not practicable to estimate their fair value:

 (i) A description of those items.

 (ii) The reasons why it is not practicable to estimate their fair value.

Secured Borrowing and Collateral

1. If the secured party (transferee) has the right by contract or custom to sell or repledge the collateral, the obligor (transferor) should reclassify and report that asset in its balance sheet separately (e.g., as security pledged to creditors) from other assets not so encumbered. (ASC 860-30-45-1) (FAS-140, par. 15)

2. Liabilities incurred by either the secured party or obligor in securities borrowing or resale transactions should be separately classified in the balance sheet. (ASC 860-30-45-2) (FAS-140, par. 15) (Q&A-140, par. 116)

3. The following disclosures should be made for collateral (ASC 860-30-50-1) (FAS-140, par. 17):

 a. If the entity has entered into repurchase agreements or securities lending transactions, its policy for requiring collateral or other security.

 b. If the entity has pledged any of its assets as collateral that are not reclassified and separately reported in the balance sheet, disclosure should be made of the carrying amount and classification of those assets as of the date of the latest balance sheet presented.

 c. If the entity has accepted collateral that it is permitted by contract or custom to sell or repledge:

  (1) The fair value of the collateral, as of the date of each balance sheet presented.

  (2) The fair value of the portion of that collateral that it has sold or repledged, as of the date of each balance sheet presented.

(3) Information about the sources and uses of that collateral.

4. If an entity sets aside assets solely for the purpose of satisfying scheduled payments of a specific obligation, the nature of restrictions placed on those assets should be disclosed. (ASC 860-30-50-2) (FAS-140, par. 17)

Note: The disclosure requirements in items 5 and 6 below are prescribed for *public entities* only by ASC Topic 860, *Transfers and Servicing,* based on FSP FAS 140-4 and FIN-46R-8, *Disclosures by Public Entities (Enterprises) about Transfers of Financial Assets and Interests in Variable Interest Entities.* These requirements are effective for the first reporting period (interim or annual) ending after December 15, 2008, and apply for each annual and interim reporting period thereafter. Early adoption is permitted. Entities are encouraged to disclose comparative information in periods earlier than the effective date. In periods after initial adoption, comparative disclosures are required only for periods subsequent to the effective date.

5. The following disclosures should be made for collateral (ASC 860-30-50-4) (FSP FAS 140-4 and FIN-46R-8, par. B6):

   a. If the entity has entered into repurchase agreements or securities lending transactions, its policy for requiring collateral or other security.

   b. If the entity has pledged any of its assets as collateral:

      (1) The carrying amount and classification of those assets and associated liabilities as of the date of the latest balance sheet presented.

      (2) Qualitative information about the relationship(s) between those assets and associated liabilities. For example, if assets are restricted solely to satisfy a specific obligation, the carrying amount of those assets and associated liabilities, including a description of the nature of restrictions placed on the assets, should be disclosed.

   c. If the entity has accepted collateral that it is permitted by contract or custom to sell or repledge:

      (1) The fair value of that collateral, as of the date of each balance sheet presented.

      (2) The fair value of the portion of that collateral that it has sold or repledged, as of the date of each balance sheet presented.

      (3) Information about the sources and uses of that collateral.

6. For transfers of financial assets accounted for as secured borrowings, the following disclosures should be made (ASC 860-30-50-5) (FSP FAS 140-4 and FIN-46R-8, par. B12):

   a. The carrying amount and classification of assets and associated liabilities recognized in the transferor's balance sheet at the end of each period presented.

   b. Qualitative information about the relationship(s) between those assets and associated liabilities. For example, if assets are restricted solely to satisfy a specific obligation, the carrying amount of those assets and associated liabilities, including a description of the nature of restrictions placed on the assets, should be disclosed.

Servicing Assets and Liabilities

1. If an entity subsequently measures separately-recognized servicing assets and servicing liabilities using the fair value measurement method and presents the aggregate of: (a) those amounts that are subsequently measured at fair value and (b) those other amounts that are separately recognized and subsequently measured using the amortization method, then disclosure should be made parenthetically on the face of the balance sheet of the amount that is subsequently measured at fair value that is included in the aggregate amount. (ASC 860-50-45-1 and 45-2) (FAS-140, par. 13B)

2. The following disclosures should be made for all servicing assets and servicing liabilities (ASC 860-50-50-2) (FAS-140, par. 17):

   a. Management's basis for determining its classes of servicing assets and servicing liabilities.

   b. A description of the risks inherent in servicing assets and servicing liabilities and, if applicable, the instruments used to mitigate the income statement effect of changes in fair value of the servicing assets and servicing liabilities. (*Note*: Disclosure of quantitative information about the instruments used to manage the risks inherent in servicing assets and liabilities, including the fair value of those instruments at the beginning and end of the period, is encouraged but not required.)

   c. The amount of contractually specified servicing fees, late fees, and ancillary fees earned for each period for which an income statement is presented, including a description of where each amount is reported in the income statement.

3. The following disclosures should be made for servicing assets and servicing liabilities subsequently measured at fair value (ASC 860-50-50-3) (FAS-140, par. 17):

   a. For each class of servicing assets and servicing liabilities, a description of where changes in fair value are reported in the income statement for each period for which results of operations are presented.

   b. For each class of servicing assets and servicing liabilities, the activity in the balance of servicing assets and the activity in the balance of servicing liabilities, including, but not limited to, the following:

      (1) The beginning and ending balances.

      (2) Additions (through purchases of servicing assets, assumptions of servicing obligations, and servicing obligations that result from transfers of financial assets).

      (3) Disposals.

      (4) Changes in fair value during the period resulting from:

         (i) Changes in valuation inputs or assumptions used in the valuation model.

         (ii) Other changes in fair value and a description of those changes.

      (5) Other changes that affect the balance and a description of those changes.

   c. A description of the valuation techniques or other methods used to estimate the fair value of servicing assets and servicing liabilities, which should include the following information if a valuation model is used:

      (1) The methodology.

      (2) The model validation procedures.

      (3) Quantitative and qualitative information about the assumptions used in the valuation model (e.g., discount rates and prepayment speeds).

   d. If instruments are used to mitigate the income statement effect of changes in fair value of the servicing assets and servicing liabilities and quantitative information about the instruments used to manage the risks inherent in those assets and liabilities, including the fair value of those instruments at the beginning and end of the period, is disclosed (see item 2b above):

      (1) A description of the valuation techniques.

    (2) The quantitative and qualitative information about the assumptions used to estimate the fair value of those instruments.

(*Note*: Entities are *encouraged*, but not required, to disclose the information in item d.)

4. The following disclosures should be made for servicing assets and servicing liabilities subsequently measured under the amortization method (ASC 860-50-50-4) (FAS-140, par. 17; Q&A-140, par. 100):

  a. For each class of servicing assets and servicing liabilities, a description of where changes in the carrying amount are reported in the income statement for each period for which results of operations are presented.

  b. For each class of servicing assets and servicing liabilities, the activity in the balance of servicing assets and the activity in the balance of servicing liabilities, including, but not limited to, the following:

    (1) The beginning and ending balances.

    (2) Additions (through purchases of servicing assets, assumption of servicing obligations, and servicing obligations that result from transfers of financial assets).

    (3) Disposals.

    (4) Amortization.

    (5) Application of valuation allowance to adjust carrying value of servicing assets.

    (6) Other-than-temporary impairments.

    (7) Other changes that affect the balance and a description of those changes.

  c. For each class of servicing assets and servicing liabilities, the fair value of recognized servicing assets and servicing liabilities (if estimation of such value is practicable) at the beginning and end of the period.

  d. A description of the valuation techniques or other methods used to estimate fair value of the servicing assets and servicing liabilities, which should include the following information if a valuation model is used:

    (1) The methodology.

    (2) The model validation procedures.

    (3) Quantitative and qualitative information about the assumptions used in the valuation model (e.g., discount rates and prepayment speeds).

   e. If instruments are used to mitigate the income statement effect of changes in fair value of the servicing assets and servicing liabilities and quantitative information about the instruments used to manage the risks inherent in those assets and liabilities, including the fair value of those instruments at the beginning and end of the period, is disclosed (see item 2b above):

     (1) A description of the valuation techniques.

     (2) The quantitative and qualitative information about the assumptions used to estimate the fair value of those instruments.

    (*Note*: Entities are *encouraged*, but not required, to disclose the information in item e.)

   f. The risk characteristics of the underlying financial assets used to stratify recognized servicing assets for purposes of measuring impairment in accordance with ASC paragraph 860-50-35-9 (FAS-140, par. 63).

   g. If the predominant risk characteristics of the underlying financial assets used to stratify recognized servicing assets for purposes of measuring impairment and the resulting stratums change:

     (1) The fact that such change has occurred.

     (2) The reasons for such change.

   h. For each period for which results of operations are presented, the activity by class in any valuation allowance for impairment of recognized servicing assets, including the following:

     (1) Beginning and ending balances.

     (2) Aggregate additions charged to operations.

     (3) Aggregate recoveries credited to operations.

     (4) Aggregate write-downs charged against the allowance.

5. If an entity elects to subsequently measure a class of separately recognized servicing assets and servicing liabilities at fair value in accordance with ASC paragraph 860-50-35-3(d) (FAS-156, par. 11), separate disclosure should be made of the amount of the cumulative-effect adjustment to retained earnings (resulting from the difference between the fair value and the carrying amount, net of any related valuation allowance, of the servicing assets and servicing liabilities that exist at the beginning of the fiscal year in which the entity makes the fair value election). (ASC 860-50-50-5) (FAS-156, par. 11)

Note: The disclosure requirements in items 6 through 8 below are prescribed for *public entities* only by ASC Topic 860, *Transfers and Servicing*, based on FSP FAS 140-4 and FIN-46R-8, *Disclosures by Public Entities (Enterprises) about Transfers of Financial Assets and Interests in Variable Interest Entities.* These requirements are effective for the first reporting period (interim or annual) ending after December 15, 2008, and apply for each annual and interim reporting period thereafter. Early adoption is permitted. Entities are encouraged to disclose comparative information in periods earlier than the effective date. In periods after initial adoption, comparative disclosures are required only for periods subsequent to the effective date.

To apply these disclosures, an entity should consider all involvements by the transferor, its consolidated affiliates included in the financial statements being presented, or its agents to be involvements by the transferor. (ASC 860-10-50-7) (FSP FAS 140-4 and FIN-46 R-8, pars. B5).

Disclosures may be reported in the aggregate for similar transfers if separate reporting of each transfer would not provide more useful information to financial statement users. In determining whether to aggregate the disclosures for multiple transfers, the reporting entity should consider quantitative and qualitative information about the characteristics of the transferred financial assets. For example, consideration should be given, but not be limited, to the following: (*a*) the nature of the transferor's continuing involvement; (*b*) the types of financial assets transferred; (*c*) the risks related to the transferred financial assets to which the transferor continues to be exposed after the transfer and the change in the transferor's risk profile as a result of the transfer; and (*d*) the guidance for risks and uncertainties in ASC paragraph 310-10-50-25 and for concentrations involving loan product terms in ASC paragraphs 825-10-55-1 through 55-2. (ASC 860-10-50-5) (FSP FAS 140-4 and FIN-46R-8, par. B2)

6. For all servicing assets and servicing liabilities, the following disclosures should be made (ASC 860-50-50-7) (FSP FAS 140-4 and FIN-46R-8, par. B8):

   a. Management's basis for determining its classes of servicing assets and servicing liabilities.

   b. A description of the risks inherent in servicing assets and servicing liabilities.

   c. A description of the instruments, if any, used to mitigate the income statement effect of changes in fair value of the servicing assets and servicing liabilities. (Disclosure of quantitative information about the instruments used to manage the risks inherent in servicing assets and servicing liabilities, including the fair value of those instruments at the beginning and end of the period, is encouraged but not required.)

d. The amount of contractually specified servicing fees, late fees, and ancillary fees earned for each period for which results of operations are presented, and a description of where each amount is reported in the income statement.

e. Quantitative and qualitative information about the assumptions used to estimate the fair value (e.g., discount rates, anticipated credit losses, and prepayment speeds). (An entity that provides quantitative information about the instruments used to manage the risks inherent in the servicing assets and servicing liabilities, as encouraged by item (c) above, is also encouraged, but not required, to disclose quantitative and qualitative information about the assumptions used to estimate the fair value of those instruments.)

7. For servicing assets and servicing liabilities subsequently measured at fair value, the following disclosures should be made (ASC 860-50-50-8) (FSP FAS 140-4 and FIN-46R-8, par. B9):

a. For each class of servicing assets and servicing liabilities, the activity in the balance of servicing assets and the activity in the balance of servicing liabilities, including, but not limited to, the following:

(1) The beginning and ending balances.

(2) Additions, through purchases of servicing assets, assumptions of servicing obligations, and servicing obligations that result from transfers of financial assets.

(3) Disposals.

(4) Changes in the fair value during the period resulting from:

(i) Changes in valuation inputs or assumptions used in the valuation model.

(ii) Other changes in fair value, including a description of those changes.

(5) Other changes that affect the balance and a description of those changes.

b. A description of where changes in fair value are reported in the income statement for each period for which results of operations are presented.

8. For servicing assets and servicing liabilities subsequently amortized in proportion to and over the period of estimated net servicing income or loss and assessed for impairment or increased obligation, the following disclosures should

be made (ASC 860-50-50-9) (FSP FAS 140-4 and FIN-46R-8, par. B10):

a. For each class of servicing assets and servicing liabilities, the activity in the balance of servicing assets and the activity in the balance of servicing liabilities, including, but not limited to, the following:

   (1) The beginning and ending balances.

   (2) Additions, through purchases of servicing assets, assumptions of servicing obligations, and servicing obligations that result from transfers of financial assets.

   (3) Disposals.

   (4) Amortization.

   (5) Application of valuation allowance to adjust carrying value of servicing assets.

   (6) Other-than-temporary impairments.

   (7) Other changes that affect the balance and a description of those changes.

b. A description of where changes in the carrying amount are reported in the income statement for each period for which results of operations are presented.

c. For each class of servicing assets and servicing liabilities, the fair value of recognized servicing assets and servicing liabilities at the beginning and end of the period if it is practicable to estimate the value.

d. The risk characteristics of the underlying financial assets used to stratify recognized servicing assets for purposes of measuring impairment in accordance with ASC paragraph 860-50-35-9 (FAS-140, par. 63).

e. For each period for which results of operations are presented, the activity by class in any valuation allowance for impairment of recognized servicing assets, including:

   (1) Beginning and ending balances.

   (2) Aggregate additions charged to operations.

   (3) Aggregate recoveries credited to operations.

   (4) Aggregate write-downs charged against the allowance.

FAS-166, *Accounting for Transfers of Financial Assets*

Note: The disclosure and key presentation requirements under the captions: (*a*) Sales (Transfers) of Financial Assets; (*b*) Secured Borrowing and Collateral; and (*c*) Servicing Assets and Liabilities, above, and in ASC Topics 310, 405, 470, 740, and 810, as they pertain to FAS-140, have been superseded by the guidance in FAS-166, *Accounting for Transfers of Financial Assets,* which is effective as of the beginning of the first annual reporting period beginning after November 15, 2009, and all interim and annual periods thereafter. Thereafter, the disclosure requirements under this caption should be followed. Early adoption is not permitted.

1. The following disclosures should be made for collateral (FAS-166, Appendix D and FAS-140, par. 17):

    a. If the entity has entered into repurchase agreements or securities lending transactions, its policy for requiring collateral or other security.

    b. If the entity has pledged any of its assets as collateral that are not reclassified and separately reported in the balance sheet, the following disclosures should be made:

        (1) The carrying amounts and classifications of both those assets and associated liabilities as of the date of the latest balance sheet presented.

        (2) Qualitative information about the relationship(s) between those assets and associated liabilities.

        (*Note:* For example, if assets are restricted solely to satisfy a specific obligation, the carrying amounts of those assets and associated liabilities, including a description of the nature of restrictions placed on the assets, should be disclosed.)

    c. If the entity has accepted collateral that it is permitted by contract or custom to sell or repledge, the following disclosures should be made:

        (1) The fair value of the collateral, as of the date of each balance sheet presented.

        (2) The fair value of the portion of that collateral that it has sold or repledged, as of the date of each balance sheet presented.

        (3) Information about the sources and uses of that collateral.

2. If debt was considered to be extinguished by in-substance defeasance, disclosures should include a general description of the transaction and the amount of debt that is considered

extinguished at the end of each period that debt remains outstanding. (FAS-166, Appendix D and FAS-140, par. 17)

3. The following disclosures should be made for all servicing assets and servicing liabilities (FAS-166, Appendix D and FAS-140, par. 17):

   a. Management's basis for determining its classes of servicing assets and servicing liabilities.

   b. A description of the risks inherent in servicing assets and servicing liabilities and, if applicable, the instruments used to mitigate the income statement effect of changes in fair value of the servicing assets and servicing liabilities. (*Note*: Disclosure of quantitative information about the instruments used to manage the risks inherent in servicing assets and liabilities, including the fair value of those instruments at the beginning and end of the period, is encouraged but not required.)

   c. The amount of contractually specified servicing fees, late fees, and ancillary fees earned for each period for which an income statement is presented, including a description of where each amount is reported in the income statement.

   d. Quantitative and qualitative information about the assumptions used to estimate the fair value (e.g., discount rates, anticipated credit losses, and prepayment speeds). (*Note:* An entity that provides quantitative information about the instruments used to manage the risks inherent in the servicing assets and servicing liabilities also is encouraged, but not required, to disclose quantitative and qualitative information about the assumptions used to estimate the fair value of those instruments.)

4. The following disclosures should be made for servicing assets and servicing liabilities subsequently measured at fair value (FAS-166, Appendix D and FAS-140, par. 17):

   a. For each class of servicing assets and servicing liabilities, a description of where changes in fair value are reported in the income statement for each period for which results of operations are presented.

   b. For each class of servicing assets and servicing liabilities, the activity in the balance of servicing assets and the activity in the balance of servicing liabilities, including, but not limited to, the following:

      (1) The beginning and ending balances.

      (2) Additions (through purchases of servicing assets, assumptions of servicing obligations, and recognition of servicing obligations that result from transfers of financial assets).

      (3) Disposals.

      (4) Changes in fair value during the period resulting from:

         (i) Changes in valuation inputs or assumptions used in the valuation model.

         (ii) Other changes in fair value and a description of those changes.

      (5) Other changes that affect the balance and a description of those changes.

5. The following disclosures should be made for servicing assets and servicing liabilities subsequently measured under the amortization method (FAS-166, Appendix D and FAS-140, par. 17):

    a. For each class of servicing assets and servicing liabilities, a description of where changes in the carrying amount are reported in the income statement for each period for which results of operations are presented.

    b. For each class of servicing assets and servicing liabilities, the activity in the balance of servicing assets and the activity in the balance of servicing liabilities, including, but not limited to, the following:

      (1) The beginning and ending balances.

      (2) Additions (through purchases of servicing assets, assumptions of servicing obligations, and recognition of servicing obligations that result from transfers of financial assets).

      (3) Disposals.

      (4) Amortization.

      (5) Application of valuation allowance to adjust carrying value of servicing assets.

      (6) Other-than-temporary impairments.

      (7) Other changes that affect the balance and a description of those changes.

    c. For each class of servicing assets and servicing liabilities, the fair value of recognized servicing assets and servicing liabilities at the beginning and end of the period.

    d. The risk characteristics of the underlying financial assets used to stratify recognized servicing assets for purposes of measuring impairment in accordance with paragraph 63 of FAS-140.

e. For each period for which results of operations are presented, the activity by class in any valuation allowance for impairment of recognized servicing assets, including the following:

(1) Beginning and ending balances.

(2) Aggregate additions charged to operations.

(3) Aggregate recoveries credited to operations.

(4) Aggregate write-downs charged against the allowance.

6. For securitizations, asset-backed financing arrangements, and similar transfers accounted for as sales when the transferor has continuing involvement (as defined) with the transferred financial assets, the following disclosures should be made (FAS-166, Appendix D and FAS-140, par. 17):

a. For each period for which an income statement is presented:

(1) The characteristics of the transfer (including a description of the transferor's continuing involvement with the transferred financial assets, the nature and initial fair value of the assets obtained as proceeds and the liabilities incurred in the transfer) and the gain or loss from sale of transferred financial assets.

(2) For initial fair value measurements of assets obtained and liabilities incurred in the transfer, the following information:

(i) The level within the fair value hierarchy in which the fair value measurements in their entirety fall, segregating fair value measurements using quoted prices in active markets for identical assets or liabilities (Level 1), significant other observable inputs (Level 2), and significant unobservable inputs (Level 3).

(ii) The key inputs and assumptions used in measuring the fair value of assets obtained and liabilities incurred as a result of the sale that relate to the transferor's continuing involvement including, at a minimum, but not limited to, and if applicable, quantitative information about the following (*Note*: If an entity has aggregated multiple transfers during a period, it may disclose the range of assumptions.):

(a)   Discount rates.

(b)   Expected prepayments including the expected weighted-average life of prepayable financial assets.

(c)   Anticipated credit losses, including expected static pool losses.

(iii) The valuation technique(s) used to measure fair value.

(3)   Cash flows between a transferor and a transferee, including:

(i)   Proceeds from new transfers.

(ii) Proceeds from collections reinvested in revolving-period transfers.

(iii) Purchases of previously transferred financial assets.

(iv) Servicing fees.

(v)   Cash flows received from a transferor's beneficial interests.

b. For each period for which a balance sheet is presented (regardless of when the transfer occurred):

(1)   Qualitative and quantitative information about the transferor's continuing involvement with transferred financial assets that provides financial statement users with sufficient information to assess the reasons for the continuing involvement and the risks related to the transferred financial assets to which the transferor continues to be exposed after the transfer and the extent that the transferor's risk profile has changed as a result of the transfer (including, but not limited to, credit risk, interest rate risk, and other risks), including:

(i)   The total principal amount outstanding, the amount that has been derecognized, and the amount that continues to be recognized in the balance sheet.

(ii) The terms of any arrangements that could require the transferor to provide financial support (e.g., liquidity arrangements and obligations to purchase assets) to the transferee or its beneficial interest holders, including a description of any events or circumstances that could expose the transferor to loss and the amount of the maximum exposure to loss.

    (iii) Whether the transferor has provided financial or other support during the periods presented that it was not previously contractually required to provide to the transferee or its beneficial interest holders, including when the transferor assisted the transferee or its beneficial interest holders in obtaining support, including:

        (a) The type and amount of support.

        (b) The primary reasons for providing support.

    (iv) Information about any liquidity arrangements, guarantees, and/or other commitments provided by third parties related to the transferred financial assets that may affect the transferor's exposure to loss or risk of the related transferor's interest. (*Note:* This disclosure is encouraged, but not required.)

(2) The entity's accounting policies for subsequently measuring assets or liabilities that relate to the continuing involvement with the transferred financial assets.

(3) The key inputs and assumptions used in measuring the fair value of assets or liabilities that relate to the transferor's continuing involvement, including at a minimum, but not limited to, and if applicable, quantitative information about the following (*Note:* If an entity has aggregated multiple transfers during a period, it may disclose the range of assumptions.):

    (i) Discount rates.

    (ii) Expected prepayments including the expected weighted-average life of prepayable financial assets.

    (iii) Anticipated credit losses, including expected static pool losses.

(4) For the transferor's interests in the transferred financial assets, a sensitivity analysis or stress test showing the hypothetical effect on the fair value of those interests (including any servicing assets or servicing liabilities) of two or more unfavorable variations from the expected levels for each key assumption that is reported under item (3) above independently from any change in another key assumption, and a description of the objectives, methodology, and limitations of the sensitivity analysis or stress test.

(5) Information about the asset quality of transferred financial assets and any other assets that it manages together with them. This information should be separated between assets that have been derecognized and assets that continue to be recognized in the balance sheet. This information is intended to provide financial statement users with an understanding of the risks inherent in the transferred financial assets as well as in other assets and liabilities that it manages together with transferred financial assets. For example, information for receivables should include, but is not limited to:

   (i) Delinquencies at the end of the period.

   (ii) Credit losses, net of recoveries, during the period.

7. For transfers of financial assets accounted for as secured borrowings, the following disclosures should be made for each period for which a balance sheet is presented (FAS-166, Appendix D and FAS-140, par. 17):

   a. The carrying amounts and classifications of both assets and associated liabilities recognized in the transferor's balance sheet.

   b. Qualitative information about the relationship(s) between those assets and associated liabilities recognized in the transferor's balance sheet. (*Note:* For example, if assets are restricted solely to satisfy a specific obligation, the carrying amounts of those assets and associated liabilities, including a description of the nature of restrictions placed on the assets.)

EXAMPLES OF FINANCIAL STATEMENT DISCLOSURES

The following sample disclosures are available on the accompanying disc.

Example 1: Summary of Significant Accounting Policies—Receivable Sales

When the Company sells receivables in securitizations of automobile loans, credit card loans, and residential mortgage loans, it may hold interest-only strips, one or more subordinated tranches, and in some cases a cash reserve account, all of which are interests that continue to be held by the transferor in the securitized receivables. In addition, the Company may obtain servicing assets or assume servicing liabilities that are initially measured at fair value. Gain or loss on sale of the receivables depends, in part, on both (1) the previous carrying amount of the financial assets involved in the transfer, allocated between the assets sold and the interests that continue to be held by the transferor based on their relative fair value at the date of transfer and (2) the proceeds received. To obtain fair values, quoted market prices are used, if available. However, quotes generally are not available for interests that continue to be held by the transferor, thus the Company estimates fair value based on the present value of future expected cash flows estimated using management's best estimates of the key assumptions—credit losses, prepayment speeds, forward yield curves, and discount rates commensurate with the risks involved.

Example 2: Detailed Disclosures by Major Asset Type about the Characteristics of Securitizations, Related Gains or Losses, Key Assumptions, and Certain Cash Flows

Credit Card Securitizations. The Company enters into securitization transactions, which allow for the sale of credit card receivables to unrelated entities, to finance the consumer revolving credit receivables generated by the Company's finance operation. For transfers of receivables that qualify as sales, the Company recognizes gains or losses as a component of the Company's finance operation. In these securitizations, the Company retains servicing rights and subordinated interests.

At December 31, 20X2, the total principal amount of loans managed was $54 million. Of the total loans, the principal amount of loans securitized was $52 million, and the principal amount of loans held for sale was $2 million. The aggregate amount of loans that were 31 days or more delinquent was $3 million at December 31, 20X2. The principal amount of losses net of recoveries amounted to $1 million and $1.5 million for the years ended December 31, 20X2 and December 31, 20X1, respectively.

The Company receives annual servicing compensation approximating 2% of the outstanding principal loan balance of the receivables and retains the rights to future cash flows arising after the investors in the securitization trusts have received the return for which they contracted. The investors and the securitization trusts have no recourse to the Company's other assets for failure of debtors to pay when due. The Company's retained interests are subordinate to investors' interests. Their value is subject to credit, prepayment, and interest rate risks on the transferred financial assets. The servicing fees specified in the credit card securitization agreements adequately compensate the finance operation for servicing the securitized assets; accordingly, no servicing asset or liability has been recorded.

The Company recognized pretax gains of $3.3 million and $2.6 million on the securitization of credit card loans for the years ended December 31, 20X2, and December 31, 20X1, respectively.

The table below summarizes certain cash flows received from and paid to securitization trusts:

	20X2	20X1
Proceeds from new securitizations	$4,100,000	$3,500,000
Proceeds from collections reinvested in previous credit card securitizations	$9,400,000	$8,300,000
Servicing fees received	$1,250,000	$1,210,000
Other cash flows received on retained interests*	$1,050,000	$1,000,000
Purchases of delinquent or foreclosed assets	$(135,000)	$ (95,000)
Servicing advances	$(295,000)	$(263,000)
Repayment of servicing advances	$ 260,000	$ 225,000

* This amount represents cash flows received from retained interests by the transferor other than servicing fees, including cash flows from interest-only strips and cash above the minimum required level in cash collateral accounts.

In determining the fair value of retained interests, the Company estimates future cash flows using management's best estimates of key assumptions such as finance charge income, default rates, payment rates, forward yield curves, and discount rates. The Company employs a risk-based pricing strategy that increases the stated annual percentage rate for accounts that have a higher predicted risk of default. Accounts with a lower risk profile may qualify for promotional financing.

Rights recorded for future finance income from serviced assets that exceed the contractually specified servicing fees are carried at fair value, amounted to $2.7 million and $2.1 million at December 31, 20X2, and December 31, 20X1, respectively, and are included in net accounts receivable.

Key economic assumptions used in measuring the retained interests at the date of securitization resulting from securitizations completed during the year were as follows:

	20X2	20X1
Prepayment speed	14.0%	13.1%
Weighted-average life (in years)	.5	.4
Expected credit losses	6.2%	5.6%
Discount rate	11.0%	12.2%

The fair value of retained interests at December 31, 20X2, was $6.5 million, with a weighted-average life of 5 months. The following table shows the key economic assumptions used in measuring the fair value of retained interests at December 31, 20X2, and a sensitivity analysis showing the hypothetical effect on the fair value of those interests when there are unfavorable variations from the assumptions used:

	Assumptions Used (Annual)	Impact on Fair Value of 10% Adverse Change	Impact on Fair Value of 20% Adverse Change
Prepayment speed	15.0%	$200,000	$1,375,000
Expected credit losses	6.1%	$550,000	$1,125,000
Discount rate	14.0%	$160,000	$1,170,000

These sensitivities are hypothetical and should be used with caution. In this table, the effect of a variation in a particular assumption on the fair value of the retained interest is calculated without changing any other assumption; in reality, changes in one factor may result in changes in another, which might magnify or counteract the sensitivities.

Automobile Loan Securitizations. The Company also has asset securitization programs, operated through special purpose subsidiaries on behalf of the Automart Group, to finance the consumer installment credit receivables generated by Automart's automobile loan finance operation. For transfers of receivables that qualify as sales, the Company recognizes gains or losses as a component of Automart's finance operation. In these securitizations, the Company retains servicing rights and subordinated interests.

At December 31, 20X2, the total principal amount of loans managed was $30 million. Of the total loans, the principal amount of loans securitized was $29 million, and the principal amount of loans held for sale or investment was $1 million. The principal amount of loans that were delinquent 31 days or more was $400,000 at December 31, 20X2. The principal amount of losses net of recoveries amounted to $175,000 and $120,000 for the years ended December 31, 20X2, and December 31, 20X1, respectively.

The Company receives annual servicing fees approximating 1% of the outstanding principal balance of the securitized automobile loans and retains the rights to future cash flows arising after the investors in the securitization trusts have received the return for which they contracted. The investors and the securitization trusts have no recourse to the Company's other assets for failure of debtors to pay when due. The Company's retained interests are subordinate to investors' interests. Their value is subject to credit, prepayment, and interest rate risks on the transferred financial assets. The servicing fees specified in the automobile loan securitization agreements adequately compensate the finance operation for servicing the accounts; accordingly, no servicing asset or liability has been recorded.

The Company recognized pretax gains of $1.1 million and $1.3 million on the securitization of automobile loans for the years ended December 31, 20X2, and December 31, 20X1, respectively.

The table below summarizes certain cash flows received from and paid to securitization trusts:

	20X2	20X1
Proceeds from new securitizations	$3,800,000	$3,200,000
Proceeds from collections reinvested in previous automobile loan securitizations	$2,600,000	$2,100,000
Servicing fees received	$ 75,000	$ 660,000
Other cash flows received on retained interests[*]	$ 350,000	$ 300,000
Purchases of delinquent or foreclosed assets	$(121,000)	$ (82,000)
Servicing advances	$(274,000)	$(241,000)
Repayment of servicing advances	$ 241,000	$ 208,000

[*] This amount represents cash flows received from retained interests by the transferor other than servicing fees, including cash flows from interest-only strips and cash above the minimum required level in cash collateral accounts.

In determining the fair value of retained interests, the Company estimates future cash flows using management's best estimates of key assumptions such as finance charge income, default rates, prepayment rates, and discount rates. The Company employs a risk-based pricing strategy that increases the stated annual percentage rate for accounts that have a higher predicted risk of default. Accounts with a lower risk profile may qualify for promotional financing.

Rights recorded for future finance income from serviced assets that exceed the contractually specified servicing fees are carried at fair value, amounted to $1.4 million and $1.2 million at December 31, 20X2, and December 31, 20X1, respectively, and are included in net accounts receivable.

Key economic assumptions used in measuring the retained interests at the date of securitization resulting from securitizations completed during the year were as follows:

	20X2	20X1
Prepayment speed	1.0%	1.0%
Weighted-average life (in years)	1.8	1.7
Expected credit losses	3.2%	3.4%
Discount rate	12.0%	13.0%

The fair value of retained interests at December 31, 20X2, was $2.5 million, with a weighted-average life of 1.7 years. The following table shows the key economic assumptions used in measuring the fair value of retained interests at December 31, 20X2, and a sensitivity analysis showing the hypothetical effect on the fair value of those interests when there are unfavorable variations from the assumptions used:

	Assumptions Used (Annual)	Impact on Fair Value of 10% Adverse Change	Impact on Fair Value of 20% Adverse Change
Prepayment speed	1.3%	$85,000	$195,000
Expected credit losses	3.0%	$50,000	$100,000
Discount rate	14.0%	$35,000	$165,000

These sensitivities are hypothetical and should be used with caution. In this table, the effect of a variation in a particular assumption on the fair value of the retained interest is calculated without changing any other assumption; in reality, changes in one factor may result in changes in another, which might magnify or counteract the sensitivities.

Expected credit losses for static pools are as follows:

	Automobile Loans Securitized in	
Actual and Projected Credit Losses (%) as of:	*20X2*	*20X1*
December 31, 20X2	5.1	5.0
December 31, 20X1	4.5	

Example 3: Transfer of Accounts Receivable Does Not Qualify as a Sale

The Company has an asset securitization program with a large financial institution to sell, with recourse, certain eligible trade receivables up to a maximum of $12 million. As receivables transferred to the financial institution are collected, the Company may transfer additional receivables up to the predetermined facility limit. Gross receivables transferred to the financial institution amounted to $9,760,000 and $10,397,000 in 20X2 and 20X1, respectively. The Company has the right, and is obligated, to repurchase transferred receivables under the program and, therefore, the transaction does not qualify as a sale. Included in the Balance Sheets as receivables at December 31, 20X2, and December 31, 20X1, are account balances totaling $2,412,000 and $2,867,000, respectively, of uncollected receivables transferred to the financial institution.

Example 4: Transfer of Accounts Receivable Qualifies as a Sale

During 20X2, the Company sold certain receivables ("Receivables") as part of its plan to reduce debt. The net book value of Receivables sold was $12.8 million for which the Company received approximately $13.2 million in cash proceeds. In 20X1, the Company sold similar assets with a net book value of $7.6 million for cash proceeds of $7.9 million. These transactions were accounted for as sales and as a result the related Receivables have been excluded from the accompanying Consolidated Balance Sheets. The agreements underlying the sale of Receivables contain provisions that indicate the Company is responsible for up to 15% of end-user customer payment defaults on sold Receivables. Accordingly, the Company provides reserves for the probable and reasonably estimable portion of these liabilities. Additionally, the Company typically services the sold Receivables whereby it continues collecting payments from the end user customer on the behalf of the purchaser of the Receivables. The Company estimates the fair value of this service arrangement as a percentage of the sold Receivables and amortizes this amount to income over the estimated life of the service period. At December 31, 20X2, and December 31, 20X1, there was $123,000 and $109,000, respectively, of deferred service fees included in accrued liabilities on the Consolidated Balance Sheets. For the years ended December

31, 20X2, and December 31, 20X1, there was $32,000 and $27,000, respectively, of deferred service fees amortized to income.

Example 5: Factored Accounts Receivable and Factoring Agreement

Accounts receivable comprise the following at December 31, 20X2, and December 31, 20X1:

	20X2	20X1
Receivables assigned to factor	$ 6,125,000	$3,655,000
Advances to (from) factor	(2,264,000)	616,000
Amounts due from factor	3,861,000	4,271,000
Unfactored accounts receivable	758,000	869,000
Allowances for returns and allowances	(415,000)	(463,000)
	$ 4,204,000	$4,677,000

Pursuant to a factoring agreement, with recourse against the Company in the event of a loss, the Company's principal bank acts as its factor for the majority of its receivables, which are assigned on a preapproved basis. At December 31, 20X2, and December 31, 20X1, the factoring charge amounted to 0.25% of the receivables assigned.

The Company's obligations to the bank are collateralized by all of the Company's accounts receivable, inventories, and equipment. The advances for factored receivables are made pursuant to a revolving credit and security agreement, which expires on March 31, 20X4. Pursuant to the terms of the agreement, the Company is required to maintain specified levels of working capital and tangible net worth, among other covenants.

Example 6: Mortgage Servicing Rights

Upon sale or securitization of servicing retained mortgages, the Company capitalizes mortgage servicing rights. The Company determines fair value based on the present value of estimated net future cash flows related to servicing income. In estimating net future cash flows from servicing income, the Company first determines net future servicing income, which is future servicing revenue less future servicing expense over the expected life of the servicing arrangement. Servicing revenue includes contractual servicing fees and other ancillary fees, and prepayment and late fees. Servicing expenses consist of direct servicing costs and allocated indirect expenses relating to the servicing operations. Servicing expenses also include an estimate for the interest cost to carry advances to the securitization trusts, which approximates 20 basis points of the mortgage loans in the securitization trusts. The Company uses a

15% discount rate to calculate the present value of net future cash flows relating to servicing income. The servicing rights are amortized in proportion to and over the period of estimated net future servicing fee income. The Company periodically reviews capitalized servicing rights for valuation impairment. The Company's periodic valuation of its servicing rights considers the amount of advances which have been made and that are expected to be made, an estimate of the cost to carry such advances, and the estimated period of time over which the advances will be outstanding. At December 31, 20X2, and December 31, 20X1, there were no valuation allowances on mortgage servicing rights.

The activity in mortgage servicing rights (net) during the years ended December 31, 20X2, and December 31, 20X1, is summarized as follows:

	20X2	20X1
Mortgage servicing rights, net, at beginning of year	$ 4,050,000	$ 6,100,000
Mortgage servicing rights activity during the year:		
Originated	1,200,000	1,500,000
Amortized	(1,900,000)	(2,550,000)
Charged-off	-0-	(1,000,000)
Mortgage servicing rights, net, at end of year	$ 3,350,000	$ 4,050,000

The mortgage servicing rights are amortized over the estimated lives of the loans to which they relate. During the year ended December 31, 20X1, the Company reduced the carrying value of its mortgage servicing rights by $1,000,000, reflecting management's estimate of the effects of increased costs associated with the Company's increased early intervention efforts in servicing delinquencies in the servicing portfolio.

Example 7: Collateral and Pledged Assets

The Company's policy is to take possession of securities purchased under agreements to resell. The market value of securities to be repurchased and resold is monitored, and additional collateral is obtained where appropriate to protect against credit exposure.

Collateral. At December 31, 20X2, the approximate market value of collateral received by the Company that may be sold or repledged by the Company was $7.2 million. This collateral was received in connection with resale agreements and derivative transactions. At

December 31, 20X2, $3.1 million of the collateral received by the Company had been sold or repledged in connection with repurchase agreements, securities sold not yet purchased, and derivative transactions.

Pledged Assets. At December 31, 20X2, certain investment securities and other assets with a carrying value of $9.7 million were pledged as collateral, of which $8.2 million may not be sold or repledged by the secured parties, for borrowings to secure public and trust deposits, and for other purposes.

Example 8: Tabular Disclosure of Changes in Servicing Assets and Servicing Liabilities Subsequently Measured Using the Fair Value Measurement Method

	Class 1		Class 2	
	Servicing Asset	Servicing Liability	Servicing Asset	Servicing Liability
Fair value at January 1, 20X2	$1,800,000	$1,500,000	$1,750,000	$1,300,000
Additions:				
Purchases of servicing assets	400,000	N/A	300,000	N/A
Assumption of servicing obligations	325,000	470,000	720,000	540,000
Servicing obligations that result from transfers of financial assets	210,000	315,000	460,000	525,000
Subtractions:				
Disposals	(150,000)	(260,000)	(190,000)	(350,000)
Changes in fair value:				
Due to change in valuation inputs or assumptions used in the valuation model	230,000	(175,000)	(165,000)	280,000
Other changes in fair value	145,000	(60,000)	75,000	100,000

	Class 1		Class 2	
	Servicing Asset	Servicing Liability	Servicing Asset	Servicing Liability
Other changes that affect the balance	90,000	(50,000)	80,000	65,000
Fair value at December 31, 20X2	$3,050,000	$1,740,000	$3,030,000	$2,460,000

Example 9: Tabular Disclosure of Changes in Servicing Assets and Servicing Liabilities Subsequently Measured Using the Amortization Method

	Class 3		Class 4	
	Servicing Asset	Servicing Liability	Servicing Asset	Servicing Liability
Carrying amount at January 1, 20X2	$1,200,000	$1,400,000	$1,310,000	$1,070,000
Additions:				
Purchases of servicing assets	350,000	N/A	200,000	N/A
Assumption of servicing obligations	125,000	170,000	320,000	230,000
Servicing obligations that result from transfers of financial assets	185,000	265,000	390,000	415,000
Subtractions:				
Disposals	(150,000)	(260,000)	(190,000)	(500,000)
Amortization	(60,000)	(80,000)	(90,000)	(70,000)
Application of valuation allowance to adjust carrying values of servicing assets	(80,000)	N/A	(40,000)	N/A
Other-than-temporary impairments	(110,000)	(100,000)	(105,000)	(165,000)

	Class 3		Class 4	
	Servicing Asset	*Servicing Liability*	*Servicing Asset*	*Servicing Liability*
Carrying amount before valuation allowance	1,460,000	1,395,000	1,795,000	980,000
Other changes that affect the balance	125,000	(75,000)	80,000	95,000
Valuation allowance for servicing assets:				
Beginning balance	170,000	N/A	400,000	N/A
Provisions/ recoveries	60,000	N/A	(50,000)	N/A
Application of valuation allowance to adjust carrying values of servicing assets	80,000	N/A	(40,000)	N/A
Other-than-temporary impairments	(50,000)	N/A	(80,000)	N/A
Sales and disposals	(100,000)	N/A	(120,000)	N/A
Ending balance	160,000	N/A	110,000	N/A
Carrying amount at December 31, 20X2	$1,425,000	$1,320,000	$1,765,000	$1,075,000

Fair Value Disclosures:

Fair value at January 1, 20X2	$1,300,000	$1,350,000	$1,400,000	$1,000,000
Fair value at December 31, 20X2	$1,350,000	$1,300,000	$1,600,000	$1,025,000

Example 10: Disclosures of Transactions with Special Purpose Entities and Variable Interest Entities under ASC Topic 860 Based on Guidance in FSP FAS 140-4 and FIN 46R-8 (Applicable Only to Public Entities)

Transactions with Special Purpose Entities

The Company enters into various types of on and off-balance sheet transactions with special purpose entities (SPEs) in the normal course of business. SPEs are corporations, trusts, or partnerships that are established for a limited purpose. The Company uses SPEs to create sources of financing, liquidity, and regulatory capital capacity for the Company, as well as sources of financing and liquidity, and investment products for the Company's clients. The Company's use of SPEs generally consists of various securitization activities with SPEs, whereby financial assets are transferred to an SPE and repackaged as securities or similar interests that are sold to investors. In connection with the Company's securitization activities, the Company has various forms of ongoing involvement with SPEs, which may include the following:

- Underwriting securities issued by SPEs and subsequently making markets in those securities.

- Providing liquidity facilities to support short-term obligations of SPEs issued to third-party investors.

- Providing credit enhancement on securities issued by SPEs or market value guarantees of assets held by SPEs through the use of letters of credit, financial guarantees, and credit default swaps.

- Entering into other derivative contracts with SPEs.

- Holding senior or subordinated interests in SPEs.

The SPEs the Company uses are primarily either qualifying SPEs (QSPEs) or variable interest entities (VIEs). A QSPE is a specific type of SPE, which is a passive entity that has significant limitations on the types of assets and derivative instruments it may own and the extent of activities and decision making in which it may engage. For example, a QSPE's activities are generally limited to purchasing assets, passing along the cash flows of those assets to its investors, servicing its assets and, in certain transactions, issuing liabilities. Among other restrictions on a QSPE's activities, a QSPE may not actively manage its assets through discretionary sales or modifications. A QSPE is exempt from consolidation.

A VIE is an entity that has either a total equity investment that is insufficient to permit the entity to finance its activities without additional subordinated financial support or whose equity investors lack the characteristics of a controlling financial interest. A VIE is consolidated by its primary beneficiary, which is the entity that, through its variable interests, absorbs the majority of a VIE's variability. A variable interest is a contractual, ownership, or other interest that changes with changes in the fair value of the VIE's net assets. The classifications of assets and liabilities in the Company's consolidated balance sheet associated with transactions involving QSPEs and VIEs are as follows at December 31, 20X2:

	Qualified Special Purpose Entities	VIEs That Are Consolidated	VIEs That Are Not Consolidated	Transfers Accounted for as Secured Borrowings	Total
Cash	$ –	$ –	$ 200,000	$ 400,000	$ 600,000
Trading account assets	1,100,000	3,200,000	200,000	300,000	4,800,000
Securities	10,000,000	5,000,000	1,000,000	5,000,000	21,000,000
Mortgages held for sale	500,000	–	–	–	500,000
Loans	–	4,000,000	700,000	1,500,000	6,200,000
Mortgage servicing rights	3,500,000	–	–	–	3,500,000
Other assets	200,000	2,200,000	1,400,000	100,000	3,900,000
Total assets	15,300,000	14,400,000	3,500,000	7,300,000	40,500,000
Short-term borrowings	–	–	600,000	2,000,000	2,600,000
Accrued expenses and other liabilities	600,000	2,000,000	400,000	100,000	3,100,000
Long-term debt	–	–	1,800,000	5,000,000	6,800,000
Minority interests	–	–	200,000	–	200,000
Total liabilities and minority interests	600,000	2,000,000	3,000,000	7,100,000	12,700,000
Net assets	$14,700,000	$12,400,000	$ 500,000	$ 200,000	$27,800,000

The Company uses QSPEs to securitize consumer and commercial real estate loans and other types of financial assets (e.g., auto loans). The Company typically retains the servicing rights from these sales and may continue to hold other beneficial interests in QSPEs. The Company may also provide liquidity to investors in the beneficial interests and credit enhancements in the form of standby letters of credit. Through these securitizations, the Company may be exposed to liability under limited amounts of recourse, as well as standard representations and warranties the Company makes to purchasers and issuers. The amount recorded for this liability is included in other commitments and guarantees in the table below.

The following disclosures regarding the Company's significant continuing involvement with QSPEs and unconsolidated VIEs exclude entities where the Company's only involvement is in the form of investments in trading securities; investments in securities or loans underwritten by third parties; and certain derivatives such as interest rate swaps or cross currency swaps that have customary terms.

Carrying Values—Asset (Liability) as of December 31, 20X2

	Debt and Equity Interests	Servicing Assets	Derivatives	Other Commitments and Guarantees	Total
Residential mortgage loan securitizations	$ 7,200,000	$3,000,000	$ 500,000	$(400,000)	$10,300,000
Commercial mortgage loan securitizations	1,500,000	500,000	200,000	(150,000)	2,050,000
Auto loan securitizations	2,000,000	–	100,000	–	2,100,000
Other	300,000	–	(50,000)	–	250,00
Total	$11,000,000	$3,500,000	$ 750,000	$(550,000)	$14,700,000

Maximum Exposure to Loss as of December 31, 20X2

	Debt and Equity Interests	Servicing Assets	Derivatives	Other Commitments and Guarantees	Total
Residential mortgage loan securitization	$ 7,200,000	$3,000,000	$2,000,000	$1,500,000	$13,700,000
Commercial mortgage loan securitizations	1,500,000	500,000	200,000	2,300,000	4,500,000
Auto loan securitizations	2,000,000	–	100,000	–	2,100,000
Other	300,000	–	1,000,000	200,000	1,500,000
Total	$11,000,000	$3,500,000	$3,300,000	$4,000,000	$21,800,000

Total QSPEs Assets as of December 31, 20X2

	Total QSPEs Assets
Residential mortgage loan securitizations	$343,000,000
Commercial mortgage loan securitizations	140,000,000
Auto loan securitizations	150,000,000
Other	20,000,000
Total	$653,000,000

In 20X2, the Company recognized net gains of $3,500,000 from sales of financial assets in securitizations and had the following cash flows with its securitization trusts:

	Mortgage Loans	Other Financial Assets
Sales proceeds from securitizations	$150,000,000	$ –
Servicing fees	2,000,000	–
Other interests held	1,000,000	600,000
Purchases of delinquent assets	150,000	–
Net servicing advances	300,000	–

For securitizations completed in 20X2, the following assumptions were used to determine the fair value of mortgage servicing rights and other interests held at the date of securitization.

	Mortgage Servicing Rights	Other Interests Held
Prepayment speed (annual constant prepayment rate)	11.5%	25.6%
Life (in years)	6.2	3.1
Discount rate	8.5%	6.5%
Expected life of loan losses	1.2%	0.7%

Key economic assumptions and the sensitivity of the current fair value to immediate adverse changes in those assumptions at December 31, 20X2, for residential and commercial mortgage servicing rights, and other interests held related to residential mortgage loan securitizations are presented in the following table.

	Mortgage Servicing Rights	Other Interests Held
Fair value of interests held	$4,200,000	$380,000
Expected weighted-average life (in years)	3.7	5.4
Prepayment speed assumption (annual constant prepayment rate)	14.2%	11.6%
Decrease in fair value from:		

	Mortgage Servicing Rights	*Other Interests Held*
10% increase	$200,000	$25,000
25% increase	$500,000	$60,000
Discount rate assumption	7.1%	15.3%
Decrease in fair value from:		
100 basis point increase	$230,000	$25,000
200 basis point increase	$440,000	$45,000
Credit loss assumption	–	1.1%
Decrease in fair value from:		
10% higher losses	–	$15,000
25% higher losses	–	$30,000

The sensitivities in the table above are hypothetical and, therefore, caution should be exercised when relying on this data. Changes in fair value based on a 10% variation in assumptions generally cannot be extrapolated because the relationship of the change in the assumption to the change in fair value may not be linear. In addition, in the table above, the effect of a variation in a particular assumption on the fair value of the other interests held is calculated independently without changing any other assumptions. In reality, changes in one factor may result in changes in others (e.g., changes in prepayment speed estimates could result in changes in the discount rates), which might magnify or counteract the sensitivities.

Transactions with Variable Interest Entities

The Company's transactions with VIEs include (a) securitization, (b) investment and financing activities involving collateralized debt obligations (CDOs) backed by asset-backed and commercial real estate securities, (c) collateralized loan obligations (CLOs) backed by corporate loans or bonds, and (d) other types of structured financing. A summary of our involvements with off-balance sheet (unconsolidated) VIEs is as follows:

Carrying Values—Asset (Liability) as of December 31, 20X2

	Debt and Equity Interests	*Derivatives*	*Other Commitments and Guarantees*	*Total*
CDOs	$28,000,000	$2,000,000	$–	$30,000,000

	Debt and Equity Interests	Derivatives	Other Commitments and Guarantees	Total
CLOs	6,000,000	300,000	–	6,300,000
Asset-based lending structures	10,000,000	(500,000)	–	9,500,000
Other	1,500,000	(100,000)	(300,000)	1,100,000
Total	$45,500,000	$1,700,000	$(300,000)	$46,900,000

Maximum Exposure to Loss as of December 31, 20X2

	Debt and Equity Interests	Derivatives	Other Commitments and Guarantees	Total
CDOs	$28,000,000	$6,000,000	$2,300,000	$36,300,000
CLOs	6,000,000	300,000	800,000	7,100,000
Asset-based lending structures	11,000,000	500,000	–	11,500,000
Other	1,800,000	400,000	700,000	2,900,000
Total	$46,800,000	$7,200,000	$3,800,000	$57,800,000

Total VIEs Assets as of December 31, 20X2

	Total VIEs Assets
CDOs	$100,000,000
CLOs	50,000,000
Asset-based lending structures	15,000,000
Other	10,000,000
Total	$175,000,000

Collateralized Debt Obligations and Collateralized Loan Obligations. A CDO or CLO is a securitization where an SPE purchases a pool of assets consisting of asset-backed securities or loans and issues multiple tranches of equity or notes to investors. In some transactions, a portion of the assets are obtained synthetically through the use of derivatives such as credit default swaps or total return swaps. Generally, CDOs and CLOs are structured on behalf of a third-party asset manager that typically selects and manages the assets for the term of the CDO or CLO. Typically, the asset manager has some discretion to manage the sale of assets of, or derivatives used by, the CDOs and CLOs.

Prior to the securitization, the Company may provide all, or substantially all, of the warehouse financing to the asset manager. The asset manager uses this financing to purchase the assets into a bankruptcy remote SPE during the warehouse period. At the completion of the warehouse period, the assets are sold to the CDO or CLO and the warehouse financing is repaid with the proceeds received from the securitization's investors. The warehousing period is generally less than 12 months in duration. In the event the securitization does not take place, the assets in the warehouse are liquidated. The Company consolidates the warehouse SPEs when it is the primary beneficiary. The Company is the primary beneficiary when it provides substantially all of the financing and, therefore, absorbs the majority of the variability. Sometimes, the Company has loss sharing arrangements, whereby a third-party asset manager agrees to absorb the credit and market risk during the warehousing period or upon liquidation of the collateral in the event a securitization does not take place. In those circumstances, the Company does not consolidate the warehouse SPE because the third-party asset manager absorbs the majority of the variability through the loss sharing arrangement.

In addition to the Company's role as arranger and warehouse financing provider, the Company may have other forms of involvement with these transactions. Such involvements may include underwriter, liquidity provider, derivative counterparty, secondary market maker, or investor. For certain transactions, the Company may also act as the collateral manager or servicer. The Company receives fees in connection with its role as collateral manager or servicer. The Company also earns fees for arranging these transactions and distributing the securities.

The Company assesses whether it is the primary beneficiary of CDOs and CLOs at inception of the transactions based on its expectation of the variability associated with its continuing involvement. Subsequently, the Company monitors its ongoing involvement in these transactions to determine if a more frequent assessment of variability is necessary. Variability in these transactions may be created by credit risk, market risk, interest rate risk, or liquidity risk associated with the CDO's or CLO's assets. An assessment of the variability is performed qualitatively because the Company's continuing involvement is typically senior in priority to the third-party investors in transactions. In most cases, the Company is not the primary beneficiary of these transactions because the Company does not retain the subordinate interests in these transactions and, accordingly, does not absorb the majority of the variability.

Asset-Based Lending Structures. The Company engages in various forms of structured lending arrangements with VIEs that are collateralized by various asset classes, including auto and other transportation leases, intellectual property, equipment, and general corporate credit. The Company typically provides senior financing, and may act as an interest rate swap or commodity derivative counterparty, when necessary. In most cases, the Company is not the primary beneficiary of these structures because the Company does not retain a majority of the variability in these transactions.

Other Transactions with VIEs. In April 20X2, the Company reached an agreement to purchase at par auction rate securities that were issued to third- party investors by ABC, Inc. and XYZ Corp., entities that are VIEs (See Note [X] for more information on these VIEs and the details of this agreement). Auction rate securities are debt instruments with long-term maturities, but which reprice more frequently. Certain of these securities were issued by the VIEs. At December 31, 20X2, the Company held in its securities available-for-sale portfolio $15 million of auction rate securities issued by the VIEs that the Company redeemed pursuant to this agreement. At December 31, 20X2, the Company had a liability in its balance sheet of $5 million for additional losses on anticipated future redemptions of auction rate securities issued by the VIEs. Were the Company to redeem all remaining auction rate securities issued by the VIEs that are subject to the agreement, the Company's estimated maximum exposure to loss would be $38 million; however, certain of these securities may be repaid in full by the issuer prior to redemption. The Company does not consolidate the VIEs that issued the auction rate securities because the Company does not expect to absorb the majority of the expected future variability associated with the VIEs' assets.

Summary of Transactions with VIEs. The following is a summary of the Company's transactions with VIEs accounted for as secured borrowings and involvements with consolidated VIEs:

Carrying Values as of December 31, 20X2

	Total Assets	Consolidated Assets	Third-Party Liabilities	Minority Interest
Secured borrowings:				
Auto loan securitizations	$4,500,000	$4,500,000	$3,000,000	$ —
Commercial real estate loans	2,300,000	2,300,000	2,000,000	—
Residential mortgage securitizations	1,500,000	1,000,000	600,000	—
Total secured borrowings	8,300,000	7,800,000	5,600,000	—

	Total Assets	Consolidated Assets	Third-Party Liabilities	Minority Interest
Consolidated VIEs:				
Structured asset finance	7,000,000	3,200,000	2,600,000	200,000
Other	2,100,000	2,100,000	1,500,000	160,000
Total consolidated VIEs	9,100,000	5,300,000	4,100,000	360,000
Total secured borrowings and consolidated VIEs	$17,400,000	$13,100,000	$9,700,000	$360,000

The Company has raised financing through the securitization of certain financial assets in transactions with VIEs accounted for as secured borrowings. The Company also consolidates VIEs where it is the primary beneficiary. In certain transactions, the Company provides contractual support in the form of limited recourse and liquidity to facilitate the remarketing of short-term securities issued to third-party investors. Other than this limited contractual support, the assets of the VIEs are the sole source of repayment of the securities held by third parties.

Example 11: Disclosures of Servicing Assets and Liabilities under ASC Topic 860 Based on Guidance in FSP FAS 140-4 and FIN 46R-8 (Applicable Only to Public Entities)

The Company recognizes the rights to service mortgage loans for others, or mortgage servicing rights (MSRs), as assets whether the Company purchases the MSRs or the MSRs result from an asset transfer. The Company determines the fair value of servicing rights at the date of transfer using the present value of estimated future net servicing income, using assumptions that market participants use in their estimates of values. The Company uses quoted market prices when available to determine the value of other interests held. Gain or loss on sale of loans depends on (1) proceeds received and (2) the previous carrying amount of the financial assets transferred and any interests the Company continues to hold (such as interest-only strips) based on relative fair value at the date of transfer. To determine the fair value of MSRs, the Company uses a valuation model that calculates the present value of estimated future net servicing income. The Company uses assumptions in the valuation model that market participants use in estimating future net servicing income, including estimates of prepayment speeds, discount rate, default rates, cost to service, escrow account earnings, contractual servicing fee income, ancillary income, and late fees.

The Company has elected to initially measure and carry its MSRs related to residential mortgage loans (residential MSRs) using the fair value method. Under the fair value method, these residential MSRs are carried in the balance sheet at fair value and the changes in fair value, primarily due to changes in valuation inputs and assumptions and to the collection/realization of expected cash flows, are reported in noninterest income in the period in which the change occurs.

Amortized MSRs, which include commercial MSRs, are carried at the lower of cost or market value. These MSRs are amortized in proportion to, and over the period of, estimated net servicing income. The amortization of MSRs is analyzed monthly and is adjusted to reflect changes in prepayment speeds, as well as other factors.

The following are changes in residential MSRs measured using the fair value method:

	December 31, 20X2	December 31, 20X1
Fair value, beginning of year	$33,100,000	$34,000,000
Purchases	600,000	1,500,000
Acquired	1,400,000	–
Servicing from securitizations or asset transfers	6,200,000	7,000,000
Sales	(450,000)	(3,200,000)
Net additions	7,750,000	5,300,000
Changes in fair value:		
Due to changes in valuation model inputs or assumptions[a]	(5,700,000)	(1,200,000)
Other changes in fair value[b]	(3,100,000)	(5,000,000)
Total changes in fair value	(8,800,000)	(6,200,000)
Fair value, end of year	$32,050,000	$33,100,000

[a] Principally reflects changes in discount rates and prepayment speed assumptions, mostly due to changes in interest rates.

[b] Represents changes due to collection/realization of expected cash flows over time.

The following are the changes in amortized MSRs:

	December 31, 20X2	December 31, 20X1
Balance, beginning of year	$1,250,000	$1,000,000
Purchases	100,000	400,000
Acquired	2,000,000	–
Servicing from securitizations or asset transfers[c]	50,000	150,000
Amortization	(250,000)	(300,000)
Balance, end of year	$3,150,000	$1,250,000
Fair value of amortized MSRs:		
Beginning of year	$1,600,000	$1,300,000
End of year	$3,500,000	$1,600,000

[c] Based on December 31, 20X2, assumptions, the weighted-average amortization period for MSRs added during the year was approximately 6.5 years.

The following are the components of the Company's managed servicing portfolio:

	December 31, 20X2	December 31, 20X1
Loans serviced for others	$190,000,000	$140,000,000
Owned loans serviced	25,000,000	10,000,000
Total owned servicing	215,000,000	150,000,000
Subservicing	3,500,000	3,000,000
Total managed servicing portfolio	$218,500,000	$153,000,000
Ratio of MSRs to related loans serviced for others	0.92%	1.35%

The components of mortgage banking noninterest income were as follows:

	December 31, 20X2	December 31, 20X1
Servicing income, net:		
Servicing fees[d]	$ 6,500,000	$ 7,200,000
Changes in fair value of residential MSRs:		
Due to changes in valuation model inputs or assumptions[e]	(5,700,000)	(1,200,000)
Other changes in fair value[f]	(3,100,000)	(5,000,000)
Total changes in fair value of residential MSRs	(8,800,000)	(6,200,000)
Amortization	(250,000)	(300,000)
Net derivative gains (losses) from economic hedges[g]	5,600,000	2,100,000
Total servicing income, net	3,050,000	2,800,000
Net gains on mortgage loan origination/sales activities	1,600,000	1,900,000
All other	250,000	400,000
Total mortgage banking noninterest income	$ 4,900,000	$ 5,100,000
Market-related valuation changes to MSRs, net of economic hedge results (e) + (g)	$ (100,000)	$ 900,000

[d] Includes contractually specified servicing fees, late charges, and other ancillary revenues.

[e] Principally reflects changes in discount rates and prepayment speed assumptions, mostly due to changes in interest rates.

[f] Represents changes due to collection/realization of expected cash flows over time.

[g] Represents results from free-standing derivatives (economic hedges) used to hedge the risk of changes in fair value of MSRs. See Note [X]—Free-Standing Derivatives for further discussion.

PART 9—
OTHER

CHAPTER 58
ASC TOPIC 915: DEVELOPMENT STAGE ENTITIES

CONTENTS

EXECUTIVE SUMMARY

Development Stage Entities

A *development stage entity* is one in which principal operations have not commenced or principal operations have generated an insignificant amount of revenue. A development stage entity issues the same basic financial statements as any other entity, and such statements should be prepared in conformity with generally accepted accounting principles (GAAP). Accordingly, determining whether a particular cost should be charged to expense when incurred or should be capitalized or deferred should be based on the same accounting standards regardless of whether the entity incurring the cost is already operating or is in the development stage.

The financial statements of an entity that is in the development stage should be identified as those of a development stage enterprise. In addition, the statements should include certain disclosures, including cumulative amounts of revenues, expenses, and cash flows from the entity's inception.

Accounting Literature

FASB Accounting Standards Codification Topic	*Pre-Codification Accounting Literature*
915, *Development Stage Entities*	FAS-7, *Accounting and Reporting by Development Stage Enterprises*

DISCLOSURE AND KEY PRESENTATION REQUIREMENTS

1. The financial statements issued by a development stage entity should include the following:

   a. A balance sheet, including any cumulative net losses reported with a descriptive caption, such as "deficit accumulated during the development stage," in the stockholders' equity section. (ASC 915-210-45-1) (FAS-7, par. 11)

   b. A statement of stockholders' equity showing from the entity's inception (ASC 915-215-45-1 and 45-2) (FAS-7, par. 11) (*Note:* Separate issuances of equity securities within the same fiscal year for the same type of consideration and for the same amount per equity unit may be combined in the statement of stockholders' equity):

      (1) For each issuance, the date and number of shares of stock, warrants, rights, or other equity securities issued for cash and for other consideration.

      (2) For each issuance, the dollar amounts (per share or other equity unit and in total) assigned to the consideration received for shares of stock, warrants, rights, or other equity securities. (*Note:* Dollar amounts should be assigned to any noncash consideration received.)

      (3) For each issuance involving noncash consideration, the nature of the noncash consideration and the basis for assigning amounts.

    c. An income statement showing amounts of revenues and expenses for each period covered by the income statement and, in addition, cumulative amounts from the entity's inception. (ASC 915-225-45-1) (FAS-7, par. 11) (*Note:* For a dormant entity that is reactivated to undertake development stage activities, the disclosure of cumulative amounts should be from inception of the development stage.)

    d. A statement of cash flows showing the cash inflows and cash outflows for each period for which an income statement is presented and, in addition, cumulative amounts from the entity's inception. (ASC 915-230-45-1) (FAS-7, par. 11)

2. The financial statements should be identified as those of a development stage entity. (ASC 915-205-45-4) (FAS-7, par. 12)

3. The notes should include a description of the nature of the development stage activities in which the entity is engaged. (ASC 915-235-50-1) (FAS-7, par. 12)

4. If this is the first year in which the entity is no longer considered to be in the development stage, there should be a disclosure that in prior years the entity had been in the development stage. (ASC 915-235-50-2) (FAS-7, par. 12)

5. If the entity is no longer a development stage entity and financial statements from the years of the development stage are presented on a comparative basis, the cumulative amounts and other additional disclosures related to a development stage entity, as described in items 1 through 4 above, should be omitted from presentation. (ASC 915-205-45-5) (FAS-7, par. 13)

EXAMPLES OF FINANCIAL STATEMENT DISCLOSURES

The following sample disclosures are available on the accompanying disc.

Note: Examples 1 to 6 below assume that the entity was formed on July 1, 20X0, and that financial statements for the years ended December 31, 20X2, and December 31, 20X1, are presented. Note that the Statements of Operations, Statements of Stockholders' Equity, and Statements of Cash Flows must be from inception even though Comparative Financial Statements for 20X2 and 20X1 are presented. Details of other note disclosures (e.g., property and equipment, stock options, income taxes) are omitted because they are similar to other businesses.

Example 1: Balance Sheets of a Development Stage Enterprise

Prostech Corp.
(A Development Stage Enterprise)
Balance Sheets
December 31, 20X2, and December 31, 20X1

	December 31	
	20X2	*20X1*
Assets		
Current assets:		
Cash and equivalents	$ 74,353	$ 250,255
Total current assets	74,353	250,255
Property and equipment, net	2,111	2,439
Other assets	1,065	-0-
Total assets	$ 77,529	$ 252,694
Liabilities and Stockholders' Equity		
Current liabilities:		
Accounts payable and accrued liabilities	$ 68,824	$ 15,460
Total current liabilities	68,824	15,460
Stockholders' equity:		
Preferred Stock—$0.01 par value, 5,000,000 shares authorized, none issued at December 31, 20X2, and December 31, 20X1	-0-	-0-
Common Stock—$.001 par value, 40,000,000 shares authorized, 7,537,319 issued at December 31, 20X2, and 5,979,528 at December 31, 20X1	7,538	5,980
Additional paid-in capital	751,584	675,252
Note receivable for common stock issued	(7,242)	-0-
Deficit accumulated during development stage	(743,175)	(443,998)
Total stockholders' equity	8,705	237,234
Total liabilities and stockholders' equity	$ 77,529	$ 252,694

Example 2: Statements of Operations of a Development Stage Enterprise

Prostech Corp.
(A Development Stage Enterprise)
Statements of Operations
For the Years Ended December 31, 20X2, and December 31, 20X1,
and the Period from July 1, 20X0, (Inception) to December 31, 20X2

	For the Years Ended December 31		July 1, 20X0, (Inception) to December 31,
	20X2	20X1	20X2
Revenue	$ 193,500	$ -0-	$ 243,500
Costs and expenses:			
Cost of sales	-0-	-0-	-0-
Research and development	345,592	283,922	669,514
Selling, general, and administrative	151,315	174,472	345,787
Total costs and expenses	496,907	458,394	1,015,301
Loss from operations	(303,407)	(458,394)	(771,801)
Interest income	4,230	14,396	28,626
Net loss	$(299,177)	$(443,998)	$(743,175)

Example 3: Statements of Stockholders Equity of a Development Stage Enterprise

Prostech Corp. (A Development Stage Enterprise)
Statements of Stockholders Equity for the Period from July 1, 20X0, (Inception) to December 31, 20X2

	Common Stock		Additional Paid-in Capital	Note Receivable for Common Stock Issued	Deficit Accumulated during Development Stage	Total
	Number of Shares	Amount				
Issuance of Common Stock on July 1, 20X0 for cash at $.12 per share	5,616,528	$5,617	$657,465	$ -0-	$ -0-	$ 663,082
Net loss July 1, 20X0 to December 31, 20X0	-0-	-0-	-0-	-0-	-0-	-0-
Balance at December 31, 20X0	5,616,528	5,617	657,465	-0-	-0-	663,082
Distribution of Common Stock for services at $.05 per share	363,000	363	17,787	-0-	-0-	18,150
Net loss for 20X1	-0-	-0-	-0-	-0-	(443,998)	(443,998)
Balance at December 31, 20X1	5,979,528	5,980	675,252	-0-	(443,998)	237,234
Issuance of Common Stock for cash upon exercise of options at $.05 per share	1,410,000	1,410	69,090	-0-	-0-	70,500
Issuance of Common Stock for cash and note receivable at $.05 per share	147,791	148	7,242	(7,242)	-0-	148
Net loss for 20X2	-0-	-0-	-0-	(299,177)	(299,177)	(299,177)
Balance at December 31, 20X2	7,537,319	$7,538	$751,584	$(7,242)	$(743,175)	$ 8,705

Example 4: Statements of Cash Flows of a Development Stage Enterprise

Prostech Corp.
(A Development Stage Enterprise)
Statements of Cash Flows
For the Years Ended December 31, 20X2, and
December 31, 20X1, and the Period from July 1, 20X0,
(Inception) to December 31, 20X2

	For the Years Ended December 31		July 1, 20X0, (Inception) to December 31,
	20X2	20X1	20X2
Cash Flows from Operating Activities			
Net loss	$(299,177)	$(443,998)	$(743,175)
Adjustments to reconcile net loss to net cash used in operating activities:			
Depreciation	828	300	1,128
Non-cash distribution of common stock	-0-	18,150	18,150
Increase in accounts payable and accrued liabilities	53,364	15,460	68,824
Other, net	(1,065)	-0-	(1,065)
Net Cash Used in Operating Activities	(246,050)	(410,088)	(656,138)
Cash Flows from Investing Activities			
Purchase of property and equipment	(500)	(2,739)	(3,239)
Net Cash Used in Investing Activities	(500)	(2,739)	(3,239)
Cash Flows from Financing Activities			
Proceeds from issuance of common stock upon exercise of options	70,500	-0-	70,500
Proceeds from sale of common stock	148	-0-	663,230

	For the Years Ended December 31		July 1, 20X0, (Inception) to December 31,
	20X2	20X1	20X2
Net Cash Provided by Financing Activities	70,648	-0-	733,730
Net Increase (Decrease) in Cash and Equivalents	(175,902)	(412,827)	74,353
Cash and Equivalents, Beginning of Period	250,255	663,082	-0-
Cash and Equivalents, End of Period	$ 74,353	$ 250,255	$ 74,353

Example 5: Description of Development Stage Operations

Prostech Corp. (Company) was incorporated on July 1, 20X0, in Delaware. Shares of Common Stock of the Company totaling 5,616,528 shares were sold for a total cash consideration of $663,082.

The Company is a development stage entity and is primarily engaged in the development of pharmaceuticals to treat urological disorders. The initial focus of the Company's research and development efforts will be the generation of products for the treatment and diagnosis of prostate cancer. The production and marketing of the Company's products and its ongoing research and development activities will be subject to extensive regulation by numerous governmental authorities in the United States. Prior to marketing in the United States, any drug developed by the Company must undergo rigorous preclinical (animal) and clinical (human) testing and an extensive regulatory approval process implemented by the Food and Drug Administration (FDA) under the Food, Drug and Cosmetic Act. The Company has limited experience in conducting and managing the preclinical and clinical testing necessary to obtain regulatory approval. There can be no assurance that the Company will not encounter problems in clinical trials that will cause the Company or the FDA to delay or suspend clinical trials.

The Company's success will depend in part on its ability to obtain patents and product license rights, maintain trade secrets, and operate without infringing on the proprietary rights of others, both in the United States and other countries. There can be no assurance that patents issued to or licensed by the Company will not be challenged, invalidated, or circumvented, or that the rights granted thereunder will provide proprietary protection or competitive advantages to the Company.

For the year ended December 31, 20X2, revenues of $193,500 were from a research agreement. The Company has no significant operating history and, from July 1, 20X0, (inception) to December 31, 20X2, has generated a net loss of $743,175. The accompanying financial statements for the year ended December 31, 20X2, have been prepared assuming the Company will continue as a going concern. During the year 20X3, management intends to raise additional debt and/or equity financing to fund future operations and to provide additional working capital. However, there is no assurance that such financing will be consummated or obtained in sufficient amounts necessary to meet the Company's needs.

The accompanying financial statements do not include any adjustments to reflect the possible future effects on the recoverability and classification of assets or the amounts and classifications of liabilities that may result from the possible inability of the Company to continue as a going concern.

Example 6: Disclosure That Company Was in the Development Stage in Prior Years

> **Note:** Example 6 below assumes that the Company is considered an operating company in the year 20X3 and that 20X2 was the last year that the Company was in the development stage.

Prostech Corp. (Company) was incorporated on July 1, 20X0, in Delaware and was in the development stage through December 31, 20X2. The year 20X3 is the first year during which the Company is considered an operating company and is no longer in the development stage.

CHAPTER 59
GOING CONCERN

CONTENTS

EXECUTIVE SUMMARY

Going Concern

PRACTICE ALERT: As this Manual goes to press, the FASB has outstanding a proposed accounting standard, *Going Concern,* to require that the entity itself assess its ability to continue as a going concern. Specifically, this proposed statement would provide guidance on the preparation of financial statements as a going concern and on management's responsibility to evaluate a reporting entity's ability to continue as a going concern. It also would require certain disclosures when either financial statement is not prepared on a going concern basis or when there is substantial doubt as to an entity's ability to continue as a going concern. Similar guidance currently resides in the auditing literature in AU Section 341, *The Auditor's Consideration of an Entity's Ability to Continue as a Going Concern*, of the AICPA Codification of Statements on Auditing Standards. However, the FASB has decided that this guidance also belongs in the accounting literature because it is management's responsibility to assess the ongoing viability of the reporting entity. Practitioners should be alert to further developments in this area.

Information that raises uncertainty about an entity's ability to continue as a going concern generally relates to the entity's ability to meet its maturing obligations without selling operating assets, undergoing debt restructuring, or revising operations based on outside pressures or similar strategies. If there is substantial doubt about an entity's ability to continue as going concern for a period of time not to exceed one year beyond the date of the financial statements, adequate disclosures should be made in the financial statements. If the substantial doubt about the entity's ability to continue as a going concern is alleviated, disclosures should be made of the conditions and events that initially caused the substantial doubt, their possible effects, and mitigating factors (e.g., management's plans).

Accounting Literature

The disclosure requirements in this chapter are based on those prescribed in Statement on Auditing Standards (SAS) No. 59 (AU Section 341), *The Auditor's Consideration of an Entity's Ability to Continue as a Going Concern.*

DISCLOSURE AND KEY PRESENTATION REQUIREMENTS

The disclosure requirements in this chapter are based on those prescribed in Statement on Auditing Standards (SAS) No. 59 (AU Section 341), *The Auditor's Consideration of an Entity's Ability to Continue as a Going Concern.*

1. If, after considering management's plans, a conclusion is reached that there is substantial doubt about the entity's ability to continue as a going concern for a period of time not to exceed one year beyond the balance sheet date, the financial statements should include the following disclosures (AU 341.10):

    a. Pertinent conditions and events giving rise to the assessment of substantial doubt about the entity's ability to continue as a going concern for a period of time not to exceed one year beyond the balance sheet date

b. The possible effects of such conditions and events

c. Management's evaluation of the significance of those conditions and events and any mitigating factors

d. Possible discontinuance of operations

e. Management's plans (including relevant prospective financial information)

f. Information about the recoverability or classification of recorded asset amounts or the amounts or classification of liabilities

2. When substantial doubt about the entity's ability to continue as a going concern for a period of time not to exceed one year from the balance sheet date is alleviated, the financial statements should include the following disclosures (AU 341.11):

a. The principal conditions and events that initially caused the auditor to believe there was substantial doubt

b. The possible effects of such conditions and events, and any mitigating factors, including management's plans

EXAMPLES OF FINANCIAL STATEMENT DISCLOSURES

 The following sample disclosures are available on the accompanying disc.

Example 1: Going-Concern Issues Arising from Recurring Losses and Cash Flow Problems

As shown in the accompanying financial statements, the Company has incurred recurring losses from operations, and as of December 31, 20X2, the Company's current liabilities exceeded its current assets by $800,000 and its total liabilities exceeded its total assets by $1,900,000. These factors raise substantial doubt about the Company's ability to continue as a going concern. Management has instituted a cost reduction program that included a reduction in labor and fringe costs. In addition, the Company has redesigned certain product lines, increased sales prices on certain items, obtained more favorable material costs, and has instituted more efficient management techniques. Management believes these factors will contribute toward achieving profitability. The accompanying financial statements do not include any adjustments that might be necessary if the Company is unable to continue as a going concern.

Example 2: Going-Concern Issues Arising from Default of Certain Loan Agreements

The Company incurred a loss of approximately $3,200,000 in 20X2 and continued to experience certain decreases in working capital. As a result, the Company is in technical default of certain covenants contained in its credit and loan agreement with its primary lender. In addition, this default has triggered events of default under certain other obligations of the Company, including a $2,000,000 interim capital financing notes and certain promissory notes secured by real estate and equipment. The holders of the interim capital financing notes and promissory notes may, at their option, give notice to the Company that amounts are immediately due and payable. As a result, $10,500,000 of the Company's total long-term debt has been classified as a current liability in the accompanying Balance Sheet at December 31, 20X2.

The Company's default of the loan agreements described above raise substantial doubt about the Company's ability to continue as a going concern. The Company is currently working with all of its lenders to obtain necessary waivers under the terms of the various agreements and is negotiating with its primary lender to stabilize its lender relationships by establishing certain internal operating and management plans. The Company also retained the services of an outside consulting firm to institute and implement all required programs to accomplish management's objectives. The Company is also evaluating the disposal of certain assets, raising new capital for future operations, and selectively increasing certain product prices. However, there can be no assurance that the Company will be successful in achieving its objectives.

The accompanying financial statements have been prepared assuming that the Company will continue as a going concern; however, the above conditions raise substantial doubt about the Company's ability to do so. The financial statements do not include any adjustments to reflect the possible future effects on the recoverability and classification of assets or the amounts and classifications of liabilities that may result should the Company be unable to continue as a going concern.

Example 3: Company Has Sufficient Funds to Meet Its Needs over the Next Year but Is Uncertain about Whether It Can Accomplish Its Business Objectives over the Following Years

The Company has sustained recurring losses and negative cash flows from operations. Over the past year, the Company's growth has been funded through a combination of private equity, bank debt, and lease financing. As of December 31, 20X2, the Company had approximately $200,000 of unrestricted cash. On January 12, 20X3, the Company executed an agreement with a group of private investors whereby the Company issued $10,000,000 in convertible subordinated loan notes. The Company believes that, as a result of this, it currently has sufficient cash and financing commitments to meet its funding requirements over the next year. However, the Company has experienced and continues to experience negative operating margins and negative cash flows from operations, as well as an ongoing requirement for substantial additional capital investment. The Company expects that it will need to raise substantial additional capital to accomplish its business plan over the next several years. In addition, the Company may wish to selectively pursue possible acquisitions of businesses, technologies, content, or products complementary to those of the Company in the future in order to expand its presence in the marketplace and achieve operating efficiencies. The Company expects to seek to obtain additional funding through a bank credit facility or private equity. There can be no assurance as to the availability or terms upon which such financing and capital might be available.

Example 4: Liquidity Disclosure—Company Discusses Liquidity Issues but Believes Actions It Has Taken Will Enable It to Continue as a Going Concern over the Next Year

At December 31, 20X2, the Company had cash and cash equivalents of $36,300,000, a working capital deficit of $15,693,000 and an accumulated deficit of $67,847,000. Additionally, the Company has incurred losses since its inception as infrastructure costs were incurred in advance of obtaining customers. Subsequent to year end, the Company ceased making payments due under certain operating lease agreements as part of an effort to restructure payment terms.

Management has taken several actions to ensure that the Company will continue as a going concern through December 31, 20X3, including the closing of two data centers, headcount reductions, and reductions in discretionary expenditures. Further, as discussed in Note [X], the Company has entered into an agreement in which it will (1) receive approximately $50 million in additional cash; (2) convert amounts due to ABC, Inc. into equity; and (3) restructure lease payments subsequent to year end. Management believes that these actions will enable the Company to continue as a going concern through December 31, 20X3.

Example 5: Company's Successful Operations Are Dependent on Those of Its Parent

The Company has historically relied on its parent to meet its cash flow requirements. The parent company has cash available in the amount of approximately $83,000 as of December 31, 20X2, and a working capital deficit of $80 million. The Senior Secured Notes in the amount of $65 million have been reclassified because the Company's parent does not currently have sufficient funds to make the next interest payment (in the approximate amount of $6 million) due in May 20X3. Failure by the parent to make such payment could allow the holders of the Notes to declare all amounts outstanding immediately due and payable. The Company and its parent will need additional funds to meet the development and exploratory obligations until sufficient cash flows are generated from anticipated production to sustain operations and to fund future development and exploration obligations.

The parent plans to generate the additional cash needed through the sale or financing of its domestic assets held for sale and the completion of additional equity, debt, or joint venture transactions. There is no assurance, however, that the parent will be able to sell or finance its assets held for sale or to complete other transactions in the future at commercially reasonable terms, if at all, or that the Company will be able to meet its future contractual obligations.

Accounting Resources on the Web

The following World Wide Web addresses are just a few of the resources on the Internet that are available to practitioners. Because of the evolving nature of the Internet, some addresses may change. In such a case, refer to one of the many Internet search engines, such as Yahoo (http://www.yahoo.com).

Accounting Research Manager
http://www.accountingresearchmanager.com

AICPA http://www.aicpa.org/

American Accounting Association
http://www.accounting.rutgers.com

CCH Integrated Solutions
http://cchgroup.com/books/default

FASAB http://www.fasab.gov

FASB http://www.fasb.org

Federal Tax Law http://www.taxsites.com/federal.html

Fedworld http://www.fedworld.gov

GASB http://www.gasb.org

Government Accountability Office http://www.gao.gov

House of Representatives http://www.house.gov

International Accounting Standards Board
http://www.iasb.org.uk

IRS Digital Daily http://www.irs.ustreas.gov/prod.cover.html

Learning Center http://cch.learningcenter.com

Library of Congress http://www.loc.gov

Office of Management and Budget http://www.gpo.gov

ProSystem fx Engagement http://www.epacesoftware.com

Public Company Accounting Oversight Board
http://www.pcaobus.org

Securities and Exchange Commission http://www.sec.gov

Thomas Legislative Research http://thomaslocal.gov

Cross-Reference

CROSS-REFERENCE FROM FASB ACCOUNTING STANDARDS CODIFICATION TOPIC TO PRE-CODIFICATION ACCOUNTING LITERATURE

This locator provides instant cross-reference between a FASB Accounting Standards Codification Topic and the corresponding pre-codification accounting literature, as they relate to financial statement disclosures. FASB Accounting Standards Codification Topics are listed chronologically on the left in the same order in which they appear in this *Special Edition: GAAP Financial Statement Disclosures Manual*. Original pre-codification pronouncements are listed on the right.

FASB ACCOUNTING STANDARDS CODIFICATION TOPIC	PRE-CODIFICATION ACCOUNTING LITERATURE
105, *Generally Accepted Accounting Principles*	FAS-168, *The "FASB Accounting Standards Codification™" and the Hierarchy of Generally Accepted Accounting Principles*
205, *Presentation of Financial Statements*	FAS-144, *Accounting for the Impairment or Disposal of Long-Lived Assets*
	EITF 87-24, *Allocation of Interest to Discontinued Operations*
	EITF 03-13, *Applying the Conditions in Paragraph 42 of FASB Statement No. 144 in Determining Whether to Report Discontinued Operations*
	ARB-43, Chapter 2A, *Comparative Financial Statements*
210, *Balance Sheet*	FAS-6, *Classification of Short-Term Obligations Expected to Be Refinanced*
	FIN-39, *Offsetting of Amounts Related to Certain Contracts*
	APB-10, *Omnibus Opinion—1966*
	ARB-43, Chapter 3A, *Current Assets and Current Liabilities*
215, *Statement of Shareholder Equity*	See ASC 505, *Equity*
220, *Comprehensive Income*	FAS-130, *Reporting Comprehensive Income*
	FAS-133, *Accounting for Derivative Instruments and Hedging Activities*

	SOP 01-6, *Accounting by Certain Entities (Including Entities with Trade Receivables) That Lend to or Finance the Activities of Others*
	SOP 03-3, *Accounting for Certain Loans or Debt Securities Acquired in a Transfer*
	Practice Bulletin 1, *Purpose and Scope of AcSEC Practice Bulletins and Procedures for Their Issuance*
320, *Investments—Debt and Equity Securities*	FAS-115, *Accounting for Certain Investments in Debt and Equity Securities*
	FSP FAS 115-1 and FAS 124-1, *The Meaning of Other-Than-Temporary Impairment and Its Application to Certain Investments*
	FSP FAS 115-2 and FAS 124-2, *Recognition and Presentation of Other-Than-Temporary Impairments*
	EITF 86-40, *Investments in Open-End Mutual Funds That Invest in U.S. Government Securities*
	FASB Implementation Guidance (Q&A), *A Guide to Implementation of Statement 115 on Accounting for Certain Investments in Debt and Equity Securities: Questions and Answers*
323, *Investments—Equity Method and Joint Ventures*	FAS-130, *Reporting Comprehensive Income*
	EITF 94-1, *Accounting for Tax Benefits Resulting from Investments in Affordable Housing Projects*
	APB-18, *The Equity Method of Accounting for Investments in Common Stock*
325, *Investments—Other*	FSP FAS 115-1 and FAS 124-1, *The Meaning of Other-Than-Temporary Impairment and Its Application to Certain Investments*
	FSP FAS 115-2 and FAS 124-2, *Recognition and Presentation of Other-Than-Temporary Impairments*
	FSP FTB 85-4-1, *Accounting for Life Settlement Contracts by Third-Party Investors*
	EITF 06-5, *Accounting for Purchases of Life Insurance—Determining the Amount That Could Be Realized in Accordance with FASB Technical Bulletin No. 85-4, Accounting for Purchases of Life Insurance*
330, *Inventory*	ARB-43, Chapter 4, *Inventory Pricing*
	APB-28, *Interim Financial Reporting*

340, *Other Assets and Deferred Costs*	SOP 93-7, *Reporting on Advertising Costs*
	SOP 98-7, *Deposit Accounting: Accounting for Insurance and Reinsurance Contracts That Do Not Transfer Insurance Risk*
350, *Intangibles—Goodwill and Other*	FAS-142, *Goodwill and Other Intangible Assets*
	FSP FAS 142-3, *Determination of the Useful Life of Intangible Assets*
360, *Property, Plant, and Equipment*	FAS-144, *Accounting for the Impairment or Disposal of Long-Lived Assets*
	FSP AUG-AIR-1, *Accounting for Planned Major Maintenance Activities*
	APB-12, *Omnibus Opinion—1967*
405, *Liabilities*	SOP 97-3: *Accounting by Insurance and Other Enterprises for Insurance-Related Assessments*
410, *Asset Retirement and Environmental Obligations*	FAS-5, *Accounting for Contingencies*
	FAS-143, *Accounting for Asset Retirement Obligations*
	EITF 89-13, *Accounting for the Cost of Asbestos Removal*
	EITF 02-6, *Classification in the Statement of Cash Flows of Payment Made to Settle an Asset Retirement Obligation within the Scope of FASB Statement No. 143*
	SOP 96-1, *Environmental Remediation Liabilities*
420, *Exit or Disposal Cost Obligations*	FAS-146, *Accounting for Costs Associated with Exit or Disposal Activities*
430, *Deferred Revenue*	See ASC 605, *Revenue Recognition*
440, *Commitments*	FAS-5, *Accounting for Contingencies*
	FAS-47, *Disclosure of Long-Term Obligations*
	FAS-146, *Accounting for Costs Associated with Exit or Disposal Activities*
450, *Contingencies*	FAS-5, *Accounting for Contingencies*
	SOP 94-6, *Disclosure of Certain Significant Risks and Uncertainties*
460, *Guarantees*	FAS-5, *Accounting for Contingencies*
	FIN-45, *Guarantor's Accounting and Disclosure Requirements for Guarantees, Including Indirect Guarantees of Indebtedness of Others*

FSP FAS 133-1 and FIN 45-4, *Disclosures about Credit Derivatives and Certain Guarantees*

SOP 01-6, *Accounting by Certain Entities (Including Entities with Trade Receivables) That Lend to or Finance the Activities of Others*

470, *Debt*

FAS-6, *Classification of Short-Term Obligations Expected to Be Refinanced*

FAS-15, *Accounting by Debtors and Creditors for Troubled Debt Restructurings*

FAS-47, *Disclosure of Long-Term Obligations*

FAS-78, *Classification of Obligations That Are Callable by the Creditor*

FAS-140, *Accounting for Transfers and Servicing of Financial Assets and Extinguishments of Liabilities*

FAS-145, *Rescission of FASB Statements No. 4, 44, and 64, Amendment of FASB Statement No. 13, and Technical Corrections*

FIN-8, *Classification of a Short-Term Obligation Repaid Prior to Being Replaced by a Long-Term Security*

FTB 79-3, *Subjective Acceleration Clauses in Long-Term Debt Agreements*

EITF 86-5, *Classifying Demand Notes with Repayment Terms*

EITF 86-15, *Increasing-Rate Debt*

EITF 86-30, *Classification of Obligations When a Violation Is Waived by the Creditor*

EITF 95-22, *Balance Sheet Classification of Borrowings Outstanding under Revolving Credit Agreements That Include Both a Subjective Acceleration Clause and a Lockbox Arrangement*

EITF 98-14, *Debtor's Accounting for Changes in Line-of-Credit or Revolving-Debt Arrangements*

APB-14, *Accounting for Convertible Debt and Debt Issued with Stock Purchase Warrants*

FSP APB 14-1, *Accounting for Convertible Debt Instruments That May Be Settled in Cash upon Conversion (Including Partial Cash Settlement)*

APB-21, *Interest on Receivables and Payables*

APB-26, *Early Extinguishment of Debt*

ARB-43, Chapter 3A, *Current Assets and Current Liabilities*

SOP 97-1, *Accounting by Participating Mortgage Loan Borrowers*

480, *Distinguishing Liabilities from Equity*

FAS-150, *Accounting for Certain Financial Instruments with Characteristics of Both Liabilities and Equity*

FSP FAS 150-2, *Accounting for Mandatorily Redeemable Shares Requiring Redemption by Payment of an Amount that Differs from the Book Value of Those Shares, under FASB Statement No. 150, "Accounting for Certain Financial Instruments with Characteristics of both Liabilities and Equity"*

FSP FAS 150-3, *Effective Date, Disclosures, and Transition for Mandatorily Redeemable Financial Instruments of Certain Nonpublic Entities and Certain Mandatorily Redeemable Noncontrolling Interests under FASB Statement No. 150, Accounting for Certain Financial Instruments with Characteristics of Both Liabilities and Equity*

505, *Equity*

FAS-5, *Accounting for Contingencies*

FAS-123R, *Share-Based Payment*

FAS-129, *Disclosure of Information about Capital Structure*

FSP FAS 129-1, *Disclosure Requirements under FASB Statement No. 129, Disclosure of Information about Capital Structure, Relating to Contingently Convertible Securities*

FTB 85-6, *Accounting for a Purchase of Treasury Shares at a Price Significantly in Excess of the Current Market Price of the Shares and the Income Statement Classification of Costs Incurred in Defending against a Takeover Attempt*

EITF 85-1, *Classifying Notes Received for Capital Stock*

EITF 98-5, *Accounting for Convertible Securities with Beneficial Conversion Features or Contingently Adjustable Conversion Ratios*

EITF 00-8, *Accounting by a Grantee for an Equity Instrument to Be Received in Conjunction with Providing Goods or Services*

EITF 00-18, *Accounting Recognition for Certain Transactions involving Equity Instruments Granted to Other Than Employees*

EITF 00-27, *Application of Issue No. 98-5 to Certain Convertible Instruments*

EITF 02-11, *Accounting for Reverse Spinoffs*

APB-12, *Omnibus Opinion—1967*

	ARB-43, *Chapter 1B, Opinion Issued by Predecessor Committee*
	ARB-43, *Chapter 7B, Stock Dividends and Stock Split-ups*
605, *Revenue Recognition*	FAS-5, *Accounting for Contingencies*
	FAS-48, *Revenue Recognition When Right of Return Exists*
	FIN-30, *Accounting for Involuntary Conversions of Nonmonetary Assets to Monetary Assets*
	EITF 99-17, *Accounting for Advertising Barter Transactions*
	EITF 99-19, *Reporting Revenue Gross as a Principal versus Net as an Agent*
	EITF 00-10, *Accounting for Shipping and Handling Fees and Costs*
	EITF 00-21, *Revenue Arrangements with Multiple Deliverables*
	EITF 01-9, *Accounting for Consideration Given by a Vendor to a Customer (Including a Reseller of the Vendor's Products)*
	EITF 01-14, *Income Statement Characterization of Reimbursements Received for Out-of-Pocket Expenses Incurred*
	EITF 02-16, *Accounting by a Customer (Including a Reseller) for Certain Consideration Received from a Vendor*
	EITF 06-1, *Accounting for Consideration Given by a Service Provider to a Manufacturer or Reseller of Equipment Necessary for an End-Customer to Receive Service from the Service Provider*
	EITF 06-3, *How Taxes Collected from Customers and Remitted to Governmental Authorities Should Be Presented in the Income Statement (That Is, Gross versus Net Presentation)*
	ARB-45, *Long-Term Construction-Type Contracts*
	SOP 81-1, *Accounting for Performance of Construction-Type and Certain Production-Type Contracts*
705, *Cost of Sales and Services*	N/A
710, *Compensation—General*	FAS-43, *Accounting for Compensated Absences*
	EITF 97-14, *Accounting for Deferred Compensation Arrangements Where Amounts Earned Are Held in a Rabbi Trust and Invested*

Index

CD-ROM Instructions

SYSTEM REQUIREMENTS

- IBM PC or compatible computer with CD-ROM drive
- Windows 95 or higher
- Microsoft Word 7.0 for Windows™ or compatible word processor
- 10 MB available on hard drive

The CD-ROM provided with the *Special Edition: GAAP Financial Statement Disclosures Manual* contains electronic versions of the over 750 separate sample disclosures presented in the book. Disclosures are available as separate pages within files for each chapter. The CD-ROM also includes the complete financial statement disclosures checklist, covering all types of disclosures, including items for special financial statement topics, the balance sheet, the income statement, and the statement of cash flows. Questions addressed in the checklist are keyed to specific references to the relevant topics of the *FASB Accounting Standards Codification*™ as well as references to pre-Codification FASB literature.

Subject to the conditions in the license agreement and the limited warranty, which are reproduced at the end of this book, you may duplicate the files on this disc, modify them as necessary, and create your own customized versions. Using the disc in any way indicates that you accept the terms of the license agreement.

USING THE CD-ROM

The data disc is intended for use with your word processing software. Each document is provided in Rich Text Format. These files can be read by all compatible word processors, including Microsoft Word for Windows and WordPerfect 7 or above. Check your owner's manual for information on the conversion of documents as required.

USING THE DOCUMENTS

The list of the Disc Contents is avaiable on your disc in a file called _contents.rtf. You can open this file and view it on your screen and use it to link the documents you're interested in, or print a hard copy to use for reference.

(1)   Open the file _contents.rtf in your word processor.

(2)   Locate the file you wish to access, and click on the hyper-linked file name. Your word processor will then open the file.

(3)   You may copy files from the CD-ROM to your hard disk. To edit files you have copied, remember to clear the read-only attribute from the file. To do this, select the name of the file in My Computer, right-click the filename, then choose Properties, and clear the Read-only checkbox.

SOFTWARE SUPPORT

If you experience any difficulties installing or running the electronic files and cannot resolve the problem using the information pre-sented here, call technical support at 800-835-0105 or visit the Web site at http://support.cch.com.

a Wolters Kluwer business

SOFTWARE LICENSE AGREEMENT FOR ELECTRONIC FILES TO ACCOMPANY SPECIAL EDITION: GAAP FINANCIAL STATEMENT DISCLOSURES MANUAL (THE "BOOK")

READ THE TERMS AND CONDITIONS OF THIS LICENSE AGREEMENT CAREFULLY BEFORE INSTALLING THE SOFTWARE (THE "PROGRAM") TO ACCOMPANY THE SPECIAL EDITION: GAAP FINANCIAL STATEMENT DISCLOSURES MANUAL (THE "BOOK"). THE PROGRAM IS COPYRIGHTED AND LICENSED (NOT SOLD). BY INSTALLING THE PROGRAM, YOU ARE ACCEPTING AND AGREEING TO THE TERMS OF THIS LICENSE AGREEMENT. IF YOU ARE NOT WILLING TO BE BOUND BY THE TERMS OF THIS LICENSE AGREEMENT, YOU SHOULD PROMPTLY RETURN THE PACKAGE IN RE-SELLABLE CONDITION AND YOU WILL RECEIVE A REFUND OF YOUR MONEY. THIS LICENSE AGREEMENT REPRESENTS THE ENTIRE AGREEMENT CONCERNING THE PROGRAM BETWEEN YOU AND CCH (REFERRED TO AS "LICENSOR"), AND IT SUPERSEDES ANY PRIOR PROPOSAL, REPRESENTATION, OR UNDERSTANDING BETWEEN THE PARTIES.

1. License Grant. Licensor hereby grants to you, and you accept, a nonexclusive license to use the Program CD-ROM and the computer programs contained therein in machine-readable, object code form only (collectively referred to as the "Software"), and the accompanying User Documentation, only as authorized in this License Agreement. The Software may be used only on a single computer owned, leased, or otherwise controlled by you; or in the event of the inoperability of that computer, on a backup computer selected by you. Neither concurrent use on two or more computers nor use in a local area network or other network is permitted without separate authorization and the possible payment of other license fees. You agree that you will not assign, sublease, transfer, pledge, lease, rent, or share your rights under the License Agreement. You agree that you may not reverse engineer, decompile, disassemble, or otherwise adapt, modify, or translate the Software.

Upon loading the Software into your computer, you may retain the Program CD-ROM for backup purposes. In addition, you may make one copy of the Software on a set of diskettes (or other storage medium) for the purpose of backup in the event the Program Diskettes are damaged or destroyed. You may make one copy of any additional User Documentation (such as the README.TXT file or the "About the Computer Disc" section of the Book) for backup purposes. Any such copies of the Software or the User Documentation shall include Licensor's copyright and other proprietary notices. Except as authorized under this paragraph, no copies of the program or any portions thereof may be made by you or any person under your authority or control.

2. Licensor's Rights. You acknowledge and agree that the Software and the User Documentation are proprietary products of Licensor protected under U.S. copyright law. You further acknowledge and agree that all right, title, and interest in and to the Program, including associated intellectual property rights, are and shall remain with Licensor. This License Agreement does not convey to you an interest in or to the Program, including associated intellectual property rights, which are and shall remain with Licensor. This License Agreement does not convey to you an interest in or to the Program, but only a limited right of use revocable in accordance with the terms of the License Agreement.

3. License Fees. The license fees paid by you are paid in consideration of the licenses granted under this License Agreement.

4. Term. This License Agreement is effective upon your installing this software and shall continue until terminated. You may terminate this License Agreement at any time by returning the Program and all copies thereof and extracts therefrom to Licensor. Licensor may terminate this License Agreement upon the breach by you of any term hereof. Upon such termination by Licensor, you agree to return to Licensor the Program and all copies and portions thereof.

5. Limited Warranty. Licensor warrants, for our benefit alone, for a period of 90 days from the date of commencement of this License Agreement (referred to as the "Warranty Period") that the Program CD-ROM in which the Software is contained is free from defects in material and workmanship. If during the Warranty Period, a defect appears in the Program diskettes, you may return the Program to Licensor for either replacement or, at Licensor's option, refund of amounts paid by you under this License Agreement. You agree that the foregoing constitutes your sole and exclusive remedy for breach by Licensor of any warranties made under this Agreement. EXCEPT FOR THE WARRANTIES SET FORTH ABOVE, THE PROGRAM, AND THE SOFTWARE CONTAINED THEREIN, ARE LICENSED "AS IS", AND LICENSOR DISCLAIMS ANY AND ALL OTHER WARRANTIES, WHETHER EXPRESS OR IMPLIED, INCLUDING, WITHOUT LIMITATION, ANY IMPLIED WARRANTIES OF MERCHANTABILITY OR FITNESS FOR A PARTICULAR PURPOSE.

6. Limitation of Liability. Licensor's cumulative liability to you or any other party for any loss or damages resulting from any claims, demands, or actions arising out of or relating to this Agreement shall not exceed the license fee paid to Licensor for the use of the Program. IN NO EVENT SHALL LICENSOR BE LIABLE FOR ANY INDIRECT, INCIDENTAL, CONSEQUENTIAL, SPECIAL, OR EXEMPLARY DAMAGES (INCLUDING, BUT NOT LIMITED TO, LOSS OF DATA, BUSINESS INTERRUPTION, OR LOST PROFITS) EVEN IF LICENSOR HAS BEEN ADVISED OF THE POSSIBILITY OF SUCH DAMAGES.

7. Miscellaneous. This License Agreement shall be construed and governed in accordance with the laws of the State of Delaware. Should any term of this License Agreement be declared void or unenforceable by any court of competent jurisdiction, such declaration shall have no effect on the remaining terms hereof. The failure of either party to enforce any rights granted hereunder or to take action against the other party in the event of any breach hereunder shall not be deemed a waiver by that party as to subsequent enforcement of rights or subsequent actions in the event of future breaches.